A HISTORY OF THE
LOS ANGELES LABOR MOVEMENT
1911–1941

PUBLICATIONS OF THE
INSTITUTE OF INDUSTRIAL RELATIONS
UNIVERSITY OF CALIFORNIA

A HISTORY OF
THE LOS ANGELES LABOR
MOVEMENT, 1911–1941

By LOUIS B. PERRY
AND RICHARD S. PERRY

UNIVERSITY OF CALIFORNIA PRESS
BERKELEY AND LOS ANGELES
1963

UNIVERSITY OF CALIFORNIA PRESS
BERKELEY AND LOS ANGELES
CALIFORNIA

❖

CAMBRIDGE UNIVERSITY PRESS
LONDON, ENGLAND

d

PRINTED IN THE UNITED STATES OF AMERICA

FOREWORD

MUCH OF LABOR HISTORY is made at the local level. Thus, if we are to understand American labor's past, we must reconstruct its story community by community. To this end, the Institute of Industrial Relations has sponsored a research project on the history of the labor movement in Los Angeles from its inception in 1859 to the entry of the United States into World War II in 1941.

The first part of this undertaking was published in 1955 with Grace Heilman Stimson's distinguished study, *Rise of the Labor Movement in Los Angeles.* The second now follows with the estimable volume by Louis B. and Richard S. Perry, *A History of the Los Angeles Labor Movement, 1911–1941.* Together they present a comprehensive, panoramic, and often dramatic history of labor in a major American city.

Louis B. Perry is the president of Whitman College; Richard S. Perry is professor of business and economics at San Fernando Valley State College.

The Institute expresses its appreciation to the following members of the reading committee who reviewed the manuscript: John W. Caughey, Paul Bullock, and Irving Bernstein, all of the University of California, Los Angeles.

The viewpoint expressed is that of the authors and may not necessarily be that of the Institute of Industrial Relations or of the University of California.

BENJAMIN AARON, *Director*
Institute of Industrial Relations
University of California, Los Angeles

PREFACE

A HISTORY of any part of the labor movement must of necessity be the story of people. The term "movement" connotes events associated with the thoughts and the subsequent actions of a group united by a common philosophy, aim, or ambition. The term "labor" provides the economic setting with respect to the people doing the thinking and the acting under the banner of the unifying agent.

Much has been published on the labor movement of this country from the national point of view, but only in relatively recent years have studies been done on a regional basis. Enough has been written on local movements, however, to keep the present volume from being considered a pathfinder in this respect. Its uniqueness must be found in its treatment of a regional labor movement that in itself possessed distinctive characteristics in comparison with other areas or, indeed, with the nation as a whole.

The labor movement in Los Angeles is unique, but not for reasons of its own choosing. Although the casual observer visiting the city today would not see much current evidence of differences in methods of organization, leadership, union composition, or basic philosophy as compared with labor in any other metropolitan area, the background of the movement is sufficiently different to warrant its separate study. Even though the road to organization for all or any part of labor in this country has never been easy, it was particularly fraught with difficulties in the City of the Angels. With the possible exception of San Francisco during the 1920's, it is doubtful if the labor movement has ever faced antiunion employer groups so powerful and well organized as those in Los Angeles. Although the open shop or American Plan was popular over much of the country in the period between World War I and the Great Depression, it was virtually a law in Los Angeles for nearly half a century. Beginning with the printers' strike of 1890, the open shop continued as the dominant "system" of labor relations until World War II. In the forefront of the open-shop forces was the Los Angeles *Times,* first under the leadership of General Harrison Gray Otis and later under his son-in-law, Harry Chandler. Issuing the call to battle in the 1890 strike, the *Times* never laid down its weapons, though they were dulled by the economic growth following the declaration of war in Europe in 1939, which changed the character of industry in Los Angeles.

A part of this story already has been told by Grace Heilman Stimson in her excellent volume.[1] Beginning with the earliest stirrings of organized labor in Los Angeles in the middle of the last century, she carries her story through the metal trades strike of 1910, the bombing of the *Times,* and its aftermath, the trial of the McNamara brothers. Few events in the history of organized labor in the United States stirred the nation as did the holocaust of October 1, 1910, when twenty-one employees of the *Times* lost their lives in this regional battle of capital and labor.

It is doubtful if the time sequence of the current study will bring forth any event as striking as this one; yet, from labor's viewpoint, the years 1911 to 1941 were more important than the earlier period. Beginning with the sterile years following the McNamaras' confession, the bribery trials of their lawyer, Clarence Darrow, and the subsequent strengthening of antilabor feeling in Los Angeles, the story in this volume closes with the feverish final attempts to maintain the open shop in the late 1930's. Organized employers under the leadership of the Merchants' and Manufacturers' Association fought a last-ditch battle with their backs to the wall—a wall composed of the national legislation of the New Deal era which gave organized labor the right to bargain collectively, and bearing the handwriting of the changing industrial composition of the greater Los Angeles area. No longer was the city's economy based on "each citizen taking in his neighbor's washing." Instead, it was becoming a diversified industrial complex. The local consumer-oriented and service-type industries, along with agriculture, became less dominant. National firms that were accustomed to dealing with unions were infiltrating the area. Many locally-owned concerns were becoming too large to continue the paternalism of the open shop. World War II was about to sound the death knell of the Los Angeles characterized by the All-Year Club, General Otis, and the Southern Pacific. A modern metropolis was about to be born and with it a strong regional labor movement. The year 1940 was the first one to see Los Angeles labor in a position "to exert a significant influence, by reason of its own strength, on the community's economic and political affairs." [2]

The story of these thirty years from 1911 through 1940 has been confined primarily to the city of Los Angeles. This has not been easy to do, but was necessary for the purpose at hand. The difficulties were increased by the fact that many unions with their headquarters in the city and affiliated with the Los Angeles Central Labor Council had jurisdictions going beyond the city's borders. In spite of this problem, an effort has been made to limit the study principally to union activities within the Los Angeles urban area. The main exceptions to this rule have been the longshoring and seafaring unions at San Pedro and the railroad brotherhoods. Even here their activities, though often part of a national or regional program, have been considered basically with respect to their impact on Los Angeles proper or its harbor.

A word should be said about the limitations of the study with respect to the extractive industries. Until relatively recent years Los Angeles County was primarily agricultural. Even today the average citizen is not aware of the high value of agricultural commodities produced in the county each year. For purposes of this study, however, a line had to be drawn which excluded, for the most part, any organized labor activities relating to agriculture, fishing, or other extractive industries. It is for this reason that the antiunion efforts of such employer groups as the Associated Farmers are not discussed, except as they relate to internal city affairs. Regardless of the domicile of some of the leading spirits of this group, their open-shop interests affected primarily rural areas. Likewise, even though the Los Angeles Central Labor Council occasionally gave help to migrant laborers in the fields of the county, such activities were distinctly off its beaten path. Further, during the early 1920's Japanese, and to some extent Filipino, exclusion was an important political issue on which local labor took an official stand not unlike that taken a number of decades earlier with respect to the Chinese coolie question. But the issue was mainly one of agricultural labor, not urban workers, and thus was deemed not worthy of lengthy discussion.

An illustration may help to clarify the treatment of urban as against rural labor in Los Angeles and environs. In the 1930's many efforts were made to organize a number of the larger dairies serving the city. Many of these were outside Los Angeles, and the workers concerned were milkers. In other instances, the organizing activity involved not only the milkers but also the drivers who trucked the milk into the city for delivery. If only the milkers were having organizing difficulties, the dispute was considered outside the jurisdiction of the study; but the entrance of the drivers on the scene involved the teamsters' union and the city's labor movement. Under such circumstances, the subject assumed a complexion requiring more extensive treatment. It also brought in the Associated Farmers as a group of agricultural employers having some relationship to the open-shop Merchants' and Manufacturers' Association, the Los Angeles Chamber of Commerce, and possibly other employer groups as well. The same comments pertain to the oil workers. Although a few of their unions had headquarters in the city, little activity directly affecting them occurred within the city limits. Thus they became only incidental parts of the flow of events relating to Los Angeles labor proper, entering the picture only when they were drawn, briefly, into the main stream of the city's labor movement.

In common with all historical studies, the present one has had to face a dual problem. One aspect of it has been the usual difficulty of tying together chronological and topical sequences, but the other and more important aspect has been to frame a story of the continuous development of a labor movement. Perhaps that development may be likened to a mud pot at Yellowstone National Park. The whole mass is stirring, moving, with outbreaks of bubbles here and there at irregular intervals, sometimes at increased tempo, sometimes at a greatly reduced rate. Certain groups of bubbles seem to evidence periods of climax leading to a conclusion of activity; yet, after a short time, they begin to appear again. Our problem has been to get at the origins of the changes in the bubbles of activity of organized labor in Los Angeles, and to establish trends and relationships. Close study has shown that the trend over much of the period 1911–1941 was a painfully slow yet steady increase in strength of the local labor movement; but only historical perspective capped by the organizing successes of the 1930's brought this conclusion.

Even in a labor movement as weak as that of Los Angeles through much of this period, there were still many day-to-day activities which were important to the participants but which cannot be reported in detail unless of significance to the major trend of the time. Each day saw negotiations with different employers by various unions, or policy meetings of union officials, or elections of new labor leaders, or a strike, or a myriad other successful and unsuccessful activities. But only certain parts of this activity have a bearing on the main story, and these must be carefully selected, sifted, and placed in proper perspective. The forest must be found and not be sacrificed to the trees.

One problem that plagues a study of the organized labor movement covering any part of the years before World War II is the inadequacy of membership statistics. In a situation like that of Los Angeles before 1940, the difficulties of finding reliable figures are especially great. The statistics of union membership are based on the collection of dues and per capita taxes. These are affected by such factors as fluctuations in employment and unemployment, the desirability of presenting a strong front to a belligerent employer, the size of the payment due to an

international from a local, and other related circumstances. The open-
shop war in Los Angeles compounded the task of obtaining representative membership figures. The local labor movement quite naturally wanted to appear stronger than it really was, in the aggregate
as well as with respect to the size of its locals. Membership figures,
therefore, frequently tended to be well padded. Strike statistics often
showed as much as a tenfold variation between those on strike, according to the employer concerned, and those out "on the bricks," as
reported by the union. As a consequence the reliability of membership figures and similar data cannot be guaranteed, and even the ap-
proximations may be quite incorrect in some instances. The problems
with respect to statistics on union strength, as enumerated by Leo
Wolman in his well-known study, are illustrated quite aptly in the
Los Angeles experience.[3]

At the risk of mentioning the obvious, it should be pointed out
that the subject at hand is one in which it is easy to permit personal
prejudices to ride virtually unchecked. Although every effort has been
made to eliminate such prejudices, critics will undoubtedly ascribe
some bias to the authors of the book. This risk will have to be taken.
Tempers frequently run high in discussions centering on the labor
movement; the issues involved are often black or white depending on
whether one is employer or worker. The grays may develop eventually
around the collective bargaining table, but in much of early labor
history in Los Angeles, final compromises were frequently missing.
Although time erases the worst of the vindictive memories in the
minds of participants in labor disputes, a story such as this one cannot be built exclusively on interviews with aging leaders from both
sides; rather, it must be based on printed evidence that often is highly
inflamed and partisan. In dealing with this material, however, we
have attempted to maintain an objective point of view.

Those seeking bibliographical material for further study of some
aspect of organized labor in Los Angeles may be helped or disappointed by what they find here. Needless to say, the bibliography
is not complete. The minutes of many individual union meetings
were not surveyed. Every page of every Los Angeles newspaper published in the years 1911–1940 was not scanned. Hundreds of leaflets
undoubtedly issued by employers and unions, which may be in someone's private but unknown collection, were not checked. At the same
time no apologies are offered for the bibliography that has been used.
Every effort has been made to seek all sides of issues. The main news-

papers of both capital and labor were thoroughly inspected. Where particular events attracted undue public attention, additional current sources were checked. The minutes of the Los Angeles Central Labor Council, as well as those of the CIO Industrial Union Council, were read item by item. Local activities were placed in their regional, state, and national settings by bibliographical effort as appropriate. Finally, certain of the old-timers, now fast disappearing, who lived through the days from 1911 to 1941 either as members of the open-shop forces or as leaders of the local labor movement, were asked to reach back into memory's closet for those anecdotes of personal experience which would be available through no other source.

A study like this would not be possible except for the assistance and the encouragement of a large number of able and interested persons. The initial idea for research on the development of the labor movement in Los Angeles came from Dr. Gordon S. Watkins, friend, adviser, and former provost of the University of California at Riverside. Through Dr. Watkins, the John Randolph Haynes and Dora Haynes Foundation of Los Angeles gave liberal assistance in the form of two summer grants to further the research of one of the authors. The Institute of Industrial Relations gave generously of its funds to aid the other author and, in addition, furnished the secretarial assistance, the editorial know-how, and the guidance to carry the manuscript to its final form for publication. Particular gratitude is expressed to Dr. Irving Bernstein for his confidence in the authors, his ability to produce small sums of money at strategic times to cover various incidental expenses, and his gentle but persuasive prodding. Anne Cook of the Institute was instrumental in making the manuscript appear to be the product of authors much more professional than those who were actually doing the writing.

The detailed and painstaking gathering of the materials necessary to complete a study like this was done by a group of loyal students, both graduate and undergraduate. Again, the Institute of Industrial Relations made possible the hiring of Peter King and Lee Auchampaugh, whose background as graduate students in history made them invaluable, not only because of their knowledge of research techniques, but also in the suggestions they were able to make to the authors. The Claremont Graduate School Committee on Research and Publications expressed its faith in the study by awarding a series of grants to one of the authors, which made possible the hiring of several able undergraduates from Pomona College to assist in digging out details.

Louise Thomas and David Young were particularly prominent in this work and revealed themselves to have ability beyond that normally expected of undergraduates.

No writing is done without sacrifice. Economists are prone to express this in terms of the opportunity cost factor: the real cost of a given use of time and resources is the loss incurred by sacrificing the alternative uses of equivalent time and resources. It is hard to state what we might have done with all the time spent on this study, but certainly some of it would have been devoted to a few more fishing trips and more hours at the beach or at home with our respective families. To them we want to express our thanks for bearing with us.

LOUIS B. PERRY
RICHARD S. PERRY

CONTENTS

TABLES

[xvi]

I. THE PAST SHAPES THE FUTURE

THE LOS ANGELES labor movement faced the second decade of the twentieth century in an environment shaped by factors stemming from the national economy. It was definitely the era of the successful entrepreneur. Beginning with the years after the panic of 1893, he became the hero as well as the leader of the hour. Under his urging American business surged forward to successive new heights, interrupted only temporarily by setbacks in 1907–1908, 1913–1914, and 1920–1922. Although the muckrakers sought to dim his halo, it took the depression following the stock market crash of 1929 to diminish his influence and his status.

As a businessman responsible for the rapid growth of the economy from 1897 to 1929, the entrepreneur combined the abundance of capital, the plentiful supply of cheap labor from immigrant sources as well as from native population growth, and the rapid advance of technology to produce a rising gross national product and an advancing standard of living.[1] New construction began to change the Victorian faces of the nation's cities into their modern forms. New products such as the automobile and, later, the radio and the moving picture realigned the employment pattern. The advantages of large-scale production became more obvious, as evidenced by the growth of plants and firms. More emphasis was placed on the techniques of scientific management and less on time-worn rules of thumb.

From the viewpoint of the wage earner, however, the rising standard of living had its drawbacks. As a factor of production, he was a cost to the businessman. The trend toward the centralization of operating control and policy, as well as of financial responsibility, in the hands of executives far from the point of production, a characteristic of economic development which was becoming more pronounced with each passing decade, meant increasing impersonality in employment relations. Many executives were inclined to make decisions largely on the basis of cost sheets, reports from immediate subordinates, and business trends, without regard to the human factor. Efficiency was measured by ability to turn out profits and dividends. Labor power as an element of cost was treated just as were the other components of a manufacturing operation, impartially and with an eye to its most efficient utilization. Organizations of wage earners, if not under the control of business executives, were frequently considered as frustrating to the aim of maximum resource use by hampering decision making and thus interfering with management prerogatives.

[1]

But if organizations of wage earners were anathema to many business leaders, aggregations of firms were not. The early years of the century were characterized by the formation of large corporations, as well as by the further growth of many that had been started before 1890. Evidence soon began to accumulate, however, that large size was not justified by alleged economies of operation. Disclosures of graft and of what editorial writers called "predatory greed" began to be made.[2] Few basic industries seemed to be exempt, with the most glaring examples appearing in meat packing, oil, steel, and tobacco. The federal government soon found that a reform in American capitalism was necessary; President Theodore Roosevelt initiated action that was consummated in the passage of the Clayton and Federal Trade Commission acts in 1914 under a new administration. Reform was in the air in the years just before World War I.

But reform was not confined to building fences around the expansion plans of American business executives. It was also found in such areas as income distribution, banking, and foreign trade. Reports that some 2 per cent of the population owned 60 per cent of the wealth lent encouragement to the passage of an income tax amendment to the Constitution in 1913 in order to reduce the regressiveness of the tax structure. The Pujo Money Trust Investigation Committee of the House of Representatives revealed the great concentration of money and credit which had developed through interlocking directorates, stockownership, and consolidations of banks, investment houses, and insurance firms. The resultant centering of control over money and credit in the hands of a few persons helped to bring about the establishment of the Federal Reserve System in 1913 as a countervailing power. International trade was encouraged by passage of the Underwood Tariff early in the first Wilson administration, which lowered duties almost to the level prevailing under the Walker Tariff fifteen years before the Civil War.[3]

The beginning of World War I in 1914 did not diminish the trend toward reform. The economy of the United States, which had been undergoing a recession since 1913, began to reap the benefits of being a major neutral nation. Less emphasis was placed on regulating the American entrepreneur in big business, as the reform effort shifted to the international scene. The Adamson Act of 1916, which provided a basic eight-hour day for the nation's railroads, represented the last piece of major domestic reform legislation until the depression of the 1930's. Reform interest, instead, centered on the European conflict and soon became idealistic in seeking to "make the world safe for democracy." Only when the country found itself involved in the worst depression in its history did reform return to the national scene, after "Black Thursday," October 24, 1929.

1. THE CALIFORNIA BOOM

The period following the panic of 1893 was one of rapid growth not only for the nation but also for California. Although rapid expansion was not unfamiliar to the state as a whole, it was a more recent experience for southern California. Improved transportation, resulting from the extension of rail lines to the southern counties in the 1870's and 1880's, had initiated a phase of growth that was to continue into the indefinite future and was particularly evident before and after World War I. The economy of the state, moreover, did more than simply expand with that of the nation. It tended to grow even faster, as indicated by per capita income figures—and this despite a rapidly rising population. The Los Angeles *Times,* in its annual Midwinter Edition of January 1, 1913, boasted that California was the richest place in the world, with a per capita wealth of $2,335 and an estimated population of 2,700,000. New wealth was assertedly being created at the rate of a billion dollars a year, and twenty-seven of the state's fifty-eight counties were entirely free of debt. In the period 1900–1920 the population of California increased from 1,485,053 to 3,426,861, or approximately 131 per cent. In almost the same period, 1899–1919, the number of wage earners in manufacturing rose from 77,224 to 243,692, or 216 per cent. Although in relation to population this increase seems very substantial, the nonmanufacturing character of the state during these years is indicated by the comparatively small total figure for wage earners. Even so, rapidity of growth is evident in the fact that for each person in the state in 1900 there were 2.31 individuals in 1920, and for each wage earner in manufacturing in 1899 there were 3.16 in 1919.[4]

So rapidly did the state grow that native-born Californians were almost curiosities. California, particularly its southern half, became the mecca for the snowbound Easterner and especially his Midwestern cousin. Where else in the nation could one pick oranges and at the same time look at snow-capped peaks as things of beauty rather than as omens of bad weather? Where else could one throw snowballs, yet on the same day bask at the seashore, as claimed by the advertisements of southern California booster organizations? Each winter saw an inmigration of temporary residents from colder climes. Special excursion rates offered by the railroads brought in a winter tourist influx which began in October and lasted until the following March. Not all these tourists, however, were paying passengers. Some rode in "side-door pull-mans" and resided in "hobo jungles" up and down the state during the winter.

For the first three decades of the century the annual influx of tourists was a marked event, particularly in Los Angeles. The paying tourists were a source of support for business; indeed they often meant the difference between a good year and a bad year. The nonpaying arrivals were received in the railroad yards by a welcoming committee of the local police force and were either sent on their way or placed in work camps; those escaping the police clutches set up housekeeping in tin-can shacks and packing boxes.

But tourists did not enter the state only for the winter. Many of them decided to become permanent residents. Fathers in outside employment who were used to being laid off in cold weather were enticed by the prospect of reasonably steady work all the year. Mothers, tired of putting boots, leggings, and heavy coats on small children only to have to take them off again a few minutes later, were intrigued by the healthful value of a warm sun along with less work in caring for offspring. Lured by the climate, the outdoor living, the direct appeals of chambers of commerce and booster organizations, as well as by expositions like those held in San Francisco and San Diego in 1915, tourists found an area that seemed to hold much for the future.

The completion of the Panama Canal in 1913 was also a boon to world trade development for the Pacific Coast. Los Angeles had completed its harbor breakwater in 1912, just in time to capitalize on the improved water route.[5] In 1913 the southern city finished the Owens River aqueduct, which gave it a reasonably ample source of water for further industrial and agricultural development. Moreover, the absence of a restrictive usury law attracted capital for the use of the small farmer or the businessman as well as the consumer.

Much of the state's growth after 1893 occurred in the eleven counties south of that transverse mountain range, the Tehachapi, which separates the state geographically as well as, to some degree, culturally, economically, and socially. In 1900 these southern counties had about 350,000 residents, or less than a third of the total in the northern area. By 1920 they counted 1,400,000, or almost three-fourths of the number living in the north. In the same period Los Angeles became the largest city in California, thus overshadowing San Francisco, heretofore the major metropolis of the state. By 1920 the city of Los Angeles had more persons within its corporate limits than had resided in the entire county in 1910. A total of 319,198 residents were officially credited to it in the earlier year, and 504,131 were found in the county. Ten years later, the city had 576,673 residents, and the county, a total of 936,455.[6]

The increasingly important economic role filled by Los Angeles, in contrast with San Francisco, could be seen in the comparative rate of increase in bank clearings in the first twelve years of the century. While bank clearings in San Francisco city and county rose from about $1 billion in 1900 to $2.6 billion in 1912, those of the city of Los Angeles increased from $123 million to $1.25 billion in the same period. Thus, whereas the increase for twelve years was 2.6:1 for the northern city, it was better than 10:1 for Los Angeles. The next thirteen years were to see an additional sevenfold increase in bank clearings in Los Angeles.[7]

Why was this growth occurring? To a large degree it was attributable to the expansion in the entire state, which had been evident over many decades. Los Angeles, however, had an even milder climate than much of California, and could be expected to benefit from this fact. In addition, lack of adequate transportation connections by rail with the East had probably retarded its earlier growth in contrast with San Francisco; thus it had a later but more aggressive start in attracting citizens from other parts of the country. But were there other factors? General Harrison Gray Otis, publisher-owner of the Los Angeles *Times* and for nearly three decades after 1890 the avowed leader in the fight to maintain the open shop in Los Angeles, thought that there were. Writing in 1910 before the explosion that destroyed the *Times* building on October 1 of that year, he stated his conviction that industrial freedom—that is, the lack of effective labor organization—was responsible for the city's growth and greatness and that future rewards would be even more substantial:

We have not yet, it may be, entirely thrown off industrial thralldom—but we are steadily approaching that magnificent goal for which brave and free men should everywhere contend, until the entire country is free in this respect, with the right firmly established for every citizen to freely pursue, under the law, any honest avocation or employment of his choice, and to be protected in that right from disturbance, menace and maltreatment by the whole power of the law.[8]

Regardless of the specific sources of the expansion, the Los Angeles of 1910–1913 was booming. The rate of growth initiated in the 1890's continued to accelerate, and, by 1940, was to take the city through the stages of economic development experienced by New York City over a period of 150 years. Even in 1911 Los Angeles residents were feeling the pains of traffic congestion. Projects suggested to ease the pains included a monorail from San Fernando Valley to the harbor and a double-track subway from the Plaza to Twelfth Street for the use of the Pacific Electric Railway and the Los Angeles Railway.[9] Little did the proponents of these plans realize that there was no foreseeable end to the problem, and that ideas such as the monorail would continue as dreams for another half century. As the editor of the real estate and development section of the *Times* wrote in September, 1911: ". . . Los Angeles is entering upon a period of prosperity and progress unprecedented in the history of this or any other city in the United States. . . . Realty brokers, bankers, capitalists and businessmen generally, alert ever to such indications, are certain of it." [10]

A short time later, early in 1913, it was predicted that the Los Angeles of 1938 would have a population of 2,500,000, a diversified industrial complex rather than excessive dependence on tourists, transportation problems completely solved by the monorail as well as raised highways and pedestrian walks, and bank clearings of more than $15 billion. Although the prediction was to prove overenthusiastic, it was in keeping with the temper of the times. After all, a city issuing a building permit every ten minutes of every working day and building a new home or apartment house every seventeen minutes of every working day could be expected to view the future as unlimited, especially when it had just finished granting more building permits for the year than any other city in America.[11]

2. POSITION OF THE WORKINGMAN

But where was labor in the midst of this progress? Had the little fellow carrying a lunch bucket and putting in a ten-hour day become the forgotten man? Certainly General Otis, the Merchants' and Manufacturers' Association, and the advocates of the open shop were not ignoring him. They wanted to make sure that he was not tempted to join labor organizations that might introduce the "walking delegate" or business agent into the field of industrial relations. But were they interested in him beyond this point? And how was he faring in these years at the beginning of the second decade of the new century? Certainly he faced increasing expenses, for the cost of living rose steadily during the period 1910–1914 over the United States as a whole. By 1914, despite a recession, it was about a sixth higher than it had been during 1906–1909 for the average American workingman. If he was employed in manufacturing or building construction, his wages rose approximately as much as the cost of living. If he was employed in transportation, in public utilities, or in bituminous coal mining, his wage increases lagged and equaled about two-thirds of the rise in the cost of living.

Mutually counteracting forces operated on wages in general in the period from 1900 to 1914. Rapidly expanding industrialization and easy profit margins permitted the possibility of higher money wages, but the large inflow of immigrants tended to put a brake on the achievement of actual increases. Employment remained generally good from 1910 to 1913, but then fell off when a recession hit the country. By 1914 unemployment in the nation had approximately tripled, with at least a million workers laid off and many others placed on short workweeks.[12]

Los Angeles did not escape the rise in the cost of living. Although one of the arguments used by open-shop proponents was that the low cost of living in the city made labor organization unnecessary, Los Angeles was not really unique in this regard. Figures printed in the *Times,* champion of industrial freedom through the open shop and booster of the low-living-cost concept, did not entirely support its publisher's thesis that living expenses possibly were lower than in any other city in the nation. Table 1 shows that in 1911 Chicago, Detroit, Baltimore, Cleveland, Milwaukee, Minneapolis, and New Orleans were approximately on a par with Los Angeles in regard to rent and food, the two major items in a workingman's budget. The figures were compiled by the *Times* and were accompanied by a long list of specific prices for items ranging from fish to flats.

It was fortunate for organized labor in Los Angeles that the bombing of the *Times* building on October 1, 1910, came at a time when employment conditions were reasonably good.[13] Had employers not been faced with the need for skilled employees, the bombing and its aftermath, the confessions of the McNamara brothers on December 1, 1911, might have caused more serious layoffs of known union men and a stronger disinclination to rehire those who had participated in the extensive metal trades strike that began on June 1, 1910, and was not officially concluded until February, 1912. Although some of the former metal trades strikers complained of discrimination against them in job placement, the condition of the Los Angeles economy was such that the employment level was satisfactory until the latter part of 1913.[14] The city was still primarily a regional trading center with consequent emphasis on service and distributive industries, but its rapid growth was also giving importance to the construction trades. Early in January, 1913, a *Times* editorial declared: "The Job Is Chasing the Man." Pointing out that the classified section of Sunday, December 29, 1912, had listed openings for 435 males and 672 females, whereas only 107

TABLE 1

INDEX OF RENT AND FOOD CHARGES IN SELECTED CITIES
OF THE UNITED STATES, 1911
(New York City = 100)

City	Rent	Food
New York	100	100
Chicago	70	94
Philadelphia	79	96
Baltimore	54	97
Boston	82	105
Cincinnati	93	92
Cleveland	64	99
Detroit	57	91
Milwaukee	66	93
Minneapolis	77	95
New Orleans	72	100
Newark	78	106
Pittsburgh	94	102
St. Louis	101	97
San Francisco	80	98
Los Angeles	78	90

SOURCE: Los Angeles *Times*, Sept. 24, 1911; Jan. 1, 1912. Identical figures were published for both dates.

males and 116 females had advertised for positions, it stated: "There was never a time in the industrial history of this country when labor of all kinds was better paid, better housed, better clothed, better treated or in more active and constant demand in these United States than it is today."[15]

But the reckoning was soon to come. Before the year was out an increasing number of men walked the streets looking for work, as the recession that developed in the United States just before World War I began to have its repercussions in Los Angeles. Building permits, valued at $21,684,100 in 1910 and reaching $31,641,921 in 1913, fell to $17,361,925 in 1914.[16] If the job had been chasing the man early in 1913, it was running the other way by late summer. The *Citizen*, organ of the Los Angeles Central Labor Council, estimated unemployment at 15,000 by August. By December, E. W. Scripps's *Record*, which was not inclined to cover up any fact that would support labor and embarrass the *Times* and the Merchants' and Manufacturers' Association, estimated that 20,000 men and 10,000 women were actively seeking work. Councilman Fred C. Wheeler, socialist and labor leader, advocated placing the unemployed at work in the city parks. The Central Labor Council, in a resolution supporting a mass meeting of the unemployed at Blanchard Hall, stated that 35,000 were out of work. It asked the City Council to authorize an expenditure of at least $5 million for immediate public improvements, with the funds to be obtained by a special bond election or any other method that seemed feasible. The *Times*, however, not wanting to embarrass the city it had boosted so long, differed with the above figures and published a letter to the mayor from an organization called the Good Fellows' Committee which, in effect, denied the truth of reports that 30,000 to 40,000 people were out of work. Rather, it declared, only about 3,000 heads of families were in desperate straits without employment, while 2,000 unattached "floaters" who would not work were circulating in the city as part of the winter hobo contingent. Another 1,000 family heads were said to be desperate for cash but still in possession of resources, such as paid-up homes.[17]

Reports from various unions to the Central Labor Council indicated that unemployment was serious. Those that seemed to be the worst hit, with the approximate percentage of the membership out of work, were:

Carpenters No. 1763	50%
Iron Workers No. 51	50
Millmen No. 884	45
Waiters No. 17	40
Painters No. 267	30
Bakers No. 37	25
Cooks No. 27	25
Electrical Workers No. 61	25
Web Pressmen No. 18	20
Barbers No. 295	15

Machinists Local No. 311 reported that 1,200 of that craft had been laid off by the Southern Pacific shops, and that the men in several other large firms were working only half time. Only Stereotypers Local No. 58 reported no unemployment, and Tailors Local No. 81 indicated that it had been little affected as yet.[18]

Although the downturn associated with the unemployment was nationwide, certain indigenous factors aggravated the situation in Los Angeles. The rapid in-migration quickly became a problem, especially as many of the tourists were penniless. The *Times*, particularly in its annual Midwinter Edition, had for years been encouraging visitors to come to California. On January 1, 1913, it listed twenty reasons why persons should come to the state and, in particular, to southern California. These ran the gamut from the enjoyment of healthier, longer lives to the availability of reasonably priced, detached, single dwellings for workers who were free agents and interested in avoiding union interference. It even pointed out that the area was a mecca for vegetarians and that there were plenty of tropical and semitropical plants with which to adorn one's home! With the advent of depression, however, these enticements to come to the Golden State were the target of much criticism. Under the headline "What's the Matter with Los Angeles?" the *Record* pointed out in the fall of 1913 that thousands were jobless and others were barely eking out a living wage. It censured the railroads for distributing folders throughout the East with glowing descriptions of opportunities in the City of the Angels, in an effort to build up rail revenues.[19] It criticized the president of the Los Angeles Chamber of Commerce for saying that the solution to the unemployment problem was to advertise for more factories. In the opinion of the *Record,* such advertising would undoubtedly be based on the usual argument of the availability of a large supply of cheap labor which probably would be increased by the opening of the Panama Canal. This, it believed, would lend further encouragement to the open-shop policy which allegedly kept wages low, thus increasing the misery of the workingman.

That in-migration was continuing in the face of an increase in the jobless in the fall of 1913 seemed evident. The Los Angeles Central Labor Council stated that its constituent locals reported many workers entering Los Angeles from the East. It subsequently drafted and sent to all state and local labor organizations in the United States a circular letter warning the unemployed not to come to the city.[20] Individual local unions did likewise through their international organizations, but with little success. That curious California institution, the home-seekers' excursion train, sponsored by the railroads and aided by the advertising of Los Angeles booster organizations in the states east of the Rockies, continued to bring in more residents along with the tourists. Estimates of the total number of persons entering the city by this means between October, 1913, and March, 1914, ranged from 30,000 to 40,000. Most of those who came to stay were not people of means seeking to retire and live the rest of their lives in a warm climate, but were persons with little money who hoped to find employment.

The chief of police pointed out that overadvertising was bringing in more people than could get jobs, and that this was increasing the

crime rate.[21] Labor leaders believed that the advertising was a deliberate attempt to provide three men for every job, and thus keep wages
low and unions weak. Although the blame was placed on the open-
shop forces in general, the specific responsibility was laid on the
Merchants' and Manufacturers' Association, a charge denied by its
executive secretary, F. J. Zeehandelaar. He pointed out, to the contrary,
that it was not the province of the association to distribute literature
of an advertising nature. The hundreds of letters it received each year
from individuals asking about employment were always turned over
to the appropriate trade associations for reply. Zeehandelaar further
stated that if work opportunities were poor, travel to Los Angeles by
those seeking employment was actually discouraged. Nevertheless, in
testimony before the United States Commission on Industrial Relations, C. F. (Curly) Grow, prominent local labor leader and organizer
for the metal trades, expressed his belief that from 20 to 25 per cent
of the unemployment in the winter of 1913–14 was caused by the
open-shop procedure of encouraging the in-migration of an excessively
large labor supply. He had difficulty, however, in answering the next
question of the commission: In that event, how did he explain the fact
that San Francisco, a union town, had experienced relatively more unemployment than Los Angeles during that winter?[22] Whatever the
effect of the advertising in the East, the City Council eventually found
it necessary to warn labor to stay away from the city during the
depression.

A period of unemployment such as struck the city in 1913–1914
always revived local criticisms by organized labor and its supporters of
the immigration policy of the federal government, as well as that of
regional employers. Particular wrath was vented against the railroads
and their use of Mexican labor. Workers from below the border were
brought in for railroad construction projects. When these were completed, the Mexicans, having become accustomed to the country, did
not want to return and tended to migrate to the towns. Not knowing
the language and yet finding the living better than below the border,
they were difficult to organize. Unskilled for the most part, they were
the first to feel the impact of unemployment and constituted the
heaviest burden on the relief rolls of charitable organizations. Their
ranks were augmented each winter by other Mexicans working in
agriculture who went to the cities and towns when the winter rains
began; this forced them into temporary unemployment even when
general business conditions were good.[23]

The ghosts of the Chinese exclusion fights of earlier decades also plagued the city during these years, continuing through the early 1920's. The recession and its consequent unemployment caused a temporary stepping up of anti-Asiatic feeling, but the *Times* did not share in it. To General Otis, the Orientals, as a prime source of agricultural labor, were instrumental in maintaining a free flow of produce into the city. Although he did not sanction a peonage system discovered to be operating in connection with the smuggling of Chinese labor from Mexico, he did insist on the need for both Japanese and Chinese laborers in the fields of the state. The Central Labor Council took an entirely different position. Noting that the same interests in favor of the Asians in 1913 had supported them two decades earlier, the *Citizen* asked whether or not labor wanted to continue to have the "Yellow serpent in California's Paradise." Believing that a new danger existed in the possible immigration of European labor via the Panama Canal, it further questioned if local residents wanted to have their fruit handled by "the filthy fingers of the filthy Chinese." The *Record* supported the *Citizen* by asking Los Angeles employers to fire all Chinese and Japanese in order to give jobs to local citizens. As most Orientals saved a large share of their incomes, they would suffer little from such discharge and would always make out somehow. The paper also argued that Orientals eventually sent most of their money back home, whereas local citizens spent funds with local merchants. The issue was of sufficient importance to result in a proposed resolution for complete exclusion of Asians at the 1914 convention of the American Federation of Labor.[24]

Regardless of the causes of unemployment in the city, or the arguments over its extent, action had to be taken to alleviate the worst of the distress. On the national level the problem led to the establishment, for the first time, of public employment offices in several cities, including New York and Los Angeles. The Second National Conference on Unemployment, held in December, 1914, declared for a concept later known in the 1930's as a "shelf of public works" to provide employment during the slack seasons and lean years of private industry. Locally, the most constructive move was the establishment of the free Municipal Employment Bureau, which began operations at the end of December, 1913. Initially swamped by the jobless, it gradually built up a reputation for effective job placement, reporting after a year of operation that it had filled a total of 28,860 positions. The California Industrial Relations Commission complimented it by stating that it was the only successful free municipal employment bureau in the United States at the time. Although the bureau was accused of sending men out on jobs where a strike was in progress without sufficient notification of the situation, this criticism was overcome soon after its establishment by a requirement that men sent out as possible strike-breakers must be fully apprised of the existence of a strike.[25]

The Municipal Employment Bureau was not the only means used to aid the jobless. Before its establishment the City Council had voted the sum of $1,500 per month for three months to assist in relief work, but this was only a drop in the bucket. As the $5 million originally asked by the Central Labor Council seemed excessive, a compromise proposition was passed for provision of work in the city parks and on municipal public works projects. Subsequently, the Municipal Charities Commission offered park work by the day with free carfare, but there were few takers. Most of the men seeking employment wanted legitimate jobs, not relief, and as a consequence registered instead with the Municipal Employment Bureau. The *Times,* however, chose to interpret the lack of success of the Charities Commission as a sign that the majority of the unemployed were not really willing to "exchange honest labor for wages" with which to meet the necessities of life. The fact that these men would get but one or two dollars a day in contrast with better wages on a regular job was not acknowledged by the paper. Early in 1914 the City Council appropriated an additional $3,500 to plant trees along the city's streets and set up a lot-cleaning bureau to clear weeds from vacant lots. Plans also were announced for a work camp in Griffith Park which would pay single men a dollar a day and married men two dollars. This effort, however, brought the council under the fire of organized labor, which accused it of seeking to hire men for public work at minimal wages, thus taking advantage of their lack of employment. Furthermore, two dollars per day for eight hours was declared to be the floor under the state minimum wage law with respect to municipal employment, so that the one-dollar wage did not become effective.[26]

The Municipal Charities Commission established the work camps, however, and coöperated with the Municipal Employment Bureau in job placement. The latter made four groupings of those needing employment, based on family status, citizenship, and relief record. Heads of families were placed, where possible, on jobs within the city limits at two dollars a day for eight hours. Unmarried American citizens were given three meals and lodging for four hours of useful work each day in one of the two work camps in Griffith Park. Aliens, chiefly Mexicans, were given third priority, followed by those who habitually lived on public charity or were in the hobo category. Most of the latter, when found, were turned over to the police. The employment provided for those in the first two categories was largely pick and shovel work. The camps for single men were actually operated only from January 5 to March 30, 1914, by which time the emergency was declared largely over. At no time was the number of residents in the camps in excess of 108, and every effort was made to find permanent work through the Municipal Employment Bureau for both married and unmarried men who were not aliens or permanent loafers.[27]

The Central Labor Council did its bit to care for the unemployed by feeding as many union men as possible in the Rathskeller of the Labor Temple. In the period from January through April, 1914, when unemployment was at its worst, free meals were dispensed to nearly 200 men each day. Some of the jobless sought to alleviate their conditions by a little organizing of their own. Under the leadership of "General" Morris Rose, a group of the less prosperous winter tourists who arrived via freight trains established what he chose to call an army, numbering about 400 men, with headquarters under the North Main Street bridge over the Los Angeles River. Rose, a printer by trade, claimed that his sole interest was to find jobs for his men. Seeking to hold a meeting of his army and others in the Plaza, he was arrested along with twenty-seven of his pickets who had been left to guard the camp in the river bed. After establishing that his intentions were peaceful, he and his men were released and permitted to camp in the river without molestation. The police hoped that he would leave the area to join a similar group in Sacramento, but instead Rose set up an employment office in the river bed and said he was ready to furnish from one to a thousand men of various skills on short notice at $2.50 for an eight-hour day, rather than the higher union scale. As a result, he was accused of being paid by open-shop supporters to stir up trouble among union members, but this he denied.[28]

Whatever his origin, "General" Rose added a humorous note to the seriousness of the unemployment situation. Flourishing a large roll of bank notes, he sought blankets and food for his followers only to be accused by them later of using the money to get drunk. When they threatened to mob him, he acceded to the appointment of a new treasurer. He secured identification buttons for his army on which were printed the words "Army Unemployed—Los Angeles." The police finally tired of his operations and told him to move the army by the end of March or be kicked out of town. Rose retaliated by threatening to seize the industrial community of Vernon, register all his men as voters, call an election, and take over the government. He would then raise taxes so high in Vernon that property would be confiscated and his men thus be provided with homes. As if this were not enough, he also threatened to move his army and set up camp in the fashionable residential districts of Los Angeles.

Rose was undoubtedly an effective organizer but his powers were limited, for his army began to melt away with warmer weather. A newspaper which had been published for a short time was abandoned, and various groups of the river-bed dwellers began to move north. Rose himself refused to join the socialists, who made a bid for his services, and would not let his men sleep in the hall of the Young People's Socialist League, but required them to remain in the river bed. On March 30, however, he was deposed and a "Captain" Kelly took command on the orders of a "Major" Buck of Sacramento, who was declared to be the real leader of the unemployed armies of San Diego, Sacramento, and Los Angeles. Shortly thereafter the police, disturbed by the publicity received by the army and the nuisance it created, arrested ninety-two of its members for violating a city ordinance against sleeping in the river bed. The army completely disbanded after this action. Its disappearance relieved, but did not eliminate, the unemployment problem. The winter of 1914–15 saw the usual increase in the ranks of the jobless, as the seasonal penniless tourists returned. This problem continued to plague the city for two more winters before it was alleviated by the prosperity born of World War I.[29]

3. The Open-Shop Philosophy

Except that employment was reasonably good for a few years after the destruction of the *Times* building in 1910, organized labor found the Los Angeles environment distinctly unfriendly in the half decade before World War I. Faced with a rising cost of living and, after 1913, with what seemed to be a permanent unemployment problem, the organized worker in Los Angeles had little for which to be thankful except less cold and more sunshine than he would have had in a more northerly part of the nation. The organizing campaign of 1910–1911 had betokened the possibility of victory for the unions in breaking the hold of the open shop, firmly established in the preceding two decades. Not even the *Times* bombing had really been considered a threat to the campaign, for the city's labor leaders did not believe that it could possibly have been done by union men. The confession of the Mc-Namara brothers in December, 1911, destroyed the vision of a union-ized Los Angeles and led to the "immediate and perhaps inevitable result . . . [of] a trying period of readjustment, of declining membership, of waning vitality." [30] The organizing campaign was abandoned; the possibility of victory for organized labor and the socialists in the mayoralty election of December, 1911, was completely eliminated; and Los Angeles was destined to be marked with the open-shop label for the next thirty years.

The strength of the open shop in contrast with that of the unions was revealed when the United States Commission on Industrial Relations held hearings in the city in September, 1914, under the chairmanship of an eminent Midwestern lawyer, Frank P. Walsh. The commission was empowered to seek a remedy for industrial unrest, which it initially believed was caused by the migratory character of labor, particularly on the Pacific Coast. Noting that there had never been an adequate industrial survey of labor over the nation nor any effort, based on certain knowledge, to eliminate the periodic labor tie-ups in the industrial system, Mr. Walsh stated: "If we achieve nothing else, we will at least supply a mass of data susceptible of use, we believe, in solving some of the problems presented—illogically, it would seem—by a democracy of great material resources which is confronted today by food and unemployment problems, as well as the slow disintegration of its industrial system." [31] As the commission considered itself as an advisory body to Congress in connection with the possible framing of laws dealing with industrial relations, it believed its hearings in Los Angeles were of paramount importance for obtaining information on the open shop in operation. After spending seven days listening to testimony in the city, and additional periods in other open-shop areas such as Paterson, New Jersey, Lead, South Dakota, and parts of Colorado, it stated in its final report that "under the best possible conditions, and granting the most excellent motives on the part of employers, freedom does not exist either politically, industrially, or socially, and that the fiber of manhood will inevitably be destroyed by the continuance of the existing situation. . . ." Los Angeles, in particular,

was sharply criticized for the labor conditions which had developed during its "open shop" regime. . . . It is significant that the only claim ordinarily made for the conditions in such . . . localities is that "they are as good as are secured by the union." As a matter of fact, there are few establishments which make this boast, and in the majority the conditions were found to be far below any acceptable standards. [32]

The commission concluded that the real causes of industrial unrest in the United States were the unjust distribution of wealth and income; unemployment and the denial of opportunity to earn a living;

the denial of justice in the creation, adjudication, and administration of law; and the failure to give labor the right and the opportunity to form effective labor organizations. The last cause was particularly pertinent in Los Angeles.[33] The commission foreshadowed the National Industrial Recovery Act of 1933 with its famous Section 7(a) when it recommended that individuals be given the right to form associations for the advancement of their collective interest without fear of discharge.

Upon the termination of the commission, but before the publication of its findings, the *Times* editorialized:

> The representatives of the labor unions on the Federal Commission on Industrial Relations knew as much about industrial relations as a salted mackerel knows about the Constitution of the United States. They considered that they performed their duties, or at least earned their salaries, when they fell on their faces before the cockney anarchist Sam Gompers and licked the dust from his august feet. . . .
>
> Some of the reports of the Federal Commission on Industrial Relations will live in political literature as rare specimens of envy, malice and intellectual imbecility. The life of the commission came to an end by limitation last Monday with the filing of its foolish reports. Let honest men thank God that it is dead and hope that we "ne'er may look up its life again." [34]

The fact that the commission was supposedly an objective body composed of representatives of labor, management, and the public was of no concern to the *Times* and General Otis.

What elicited these comments from the *Times* before publication of the commission's findings? In all likelihood it was the testimony by representatives of organized labor in Los Angeles which disturbed General Otis and the supporters of the open shop, giving them premonitions concerning the eventual printed conclusions and recommendations of the commission. Local labor leaders took the opportunity afforded by the hearings to say that the so-called "open shop" was really an antiunion shop. They characterized industrial relations in Los Angeles as completely unilateral, with the average workingman at the mercy of employers who believed that the essence of successful bargaining was to allow a single workman to present his grievance to his boss, man to man. Frederick Palmer had portrayed the open shop in 1911 as an example of coöperation of banker, employer, and newspaper for selfish aims, under the leadership of the Merchants' and Manufacturers' Association:

> Otis has taught it strictly military principles. His Adjutant General is the secretary of the Association, Felix J. Zeehandelaar. A soft-spoken, suave man is "Zee," there in his office all day looking after tactical detail. Back of "Zee,"

always alert, is Otis with his daily newspaper ready to beat any laggard into line. . . . Few business men would choose to run athwart the hidden forces of the "M. and M." and the open attacks of Otis and the *Times*.[35]

Three years later, at the time of the commission hearings, the evidence of the continued existence of the open shop seemed indisputable. The *Times* itself would not recognize a union card, and the large employers in Los Angeles followed its example; in many industries a central labor bureau kept a record on each employee which could be used as a black list.[36]

Yet labor's accusation that the open shop was an antiunion shop was not airtight. A number of open-shop supporters insisted that it was just what its name implied, with no discrimination against a man because of his union membership. Fred L. Baker, a top business leader and owner of the Baker Iron Works, one of the major open-shop industrial plants of Los Angeles, stated that the Merchants' and Manufacturers' Association, to the best of his knowledge, always advocated the open shop only in the strict definition of the term. Baker also testified that he belonged to the Founders' and Employers' Association, which maintained an employment bureau in the city for molders, and that his company kept a list of its working molders with the bureau. If work slackened at the Baker plant, the foreman notified the bureau secretary who would then seek to place laid-off men elsewhere. It was Baker's contention that the list was not used for any other purpose, to his knowledge, and was never sent outside the city.[37]

The supporters of the open shop had very positive reasons for their position, which centered as much on management prerogatives as on actual labor cost factors. Frequent attempts were made to justify it to the residents of the city. For example, Secretary Zeehandelaar of the M and M pointed out in 1914 that the deposits in savings banks in Los Angeles, totaling $105,229,867, were held by 257,769 depositors, of whom 80 per cent were laboring men or members of their families. An allegedly persistent search on his part had shown no other city in the nation with a similar record.[38]

The claims of organized labor that union men were more efficient than nonunion employees were often blasted by open-shop advocates, with particular reference to San Francisco, which was known during the years before 1921 as a union town. As the leadership of and the impulse for the metal trades strike of 1910 had come from the northern city, Los Angeles employers were anxious to disprove any thesis that northern organized labor was superior to the largely unorganized force in the southern city. San Francisco employers, on the other hand, seemed to believe that if hours and wages were the same in all trades in both cities, the competition would be about equal.[39]

The testimony of a number of employers before the Commission on Industrial Relations dealt specifically with the relative efficiency of union and nonunion labor. Thomas Haverty, a plumbing and heating contractor in Los Angeles for twenty-two years, stated that he had hired both union and nonunion men and had failed to perceive any significant difference between them. If there was any difference, he believed that it might be in favor of the latter in quality but not in quantity of work performed. Haverty paid the union scale for all work done. His experience in employing San Francisco journeymen had led him to believe that his own plumbers were slightly better; plumbers from the north were lazier and were not used to doing as much work per day as were those in Los Angeles. Similar statements were made by John F. Craig of the Craig Shipbuilding Company of Long Beach, who made the further point that men working under the open shop were likely to show more interest in their work, which gave him more output per hour of work even though he paid union wages. Craig did not object to unions per se but rather to the means they used to force their demands on employers. He agreed with General Otis' testimony that, although unionism had shortened hours and improved working conditions, these gains had been more than offset by losses through strikes and lockouts, so that both employers and employees were worse off than under the open shop. Otis had utilized figures from his own composing room to show that in his firm, where labor stoppages did not occur, wages and hours were better than under union conditions. He claimed that his linotype operators earned from $5.50 to $7.50 per night of seven hours under the piecework system, whereas similar operators working under the union scale on a fixed-time basis received $5.50 for eight hours.[40]

Another argument frequently advanced in favor of the open shop was that it contributed to homeownership and consequently to good citizenship on the part of wage earners. E. Avery McCarthy, manager of a construction firm, told the commission that of the 1,233 homes built by his firm between 1904 and 1914, 90 per cent were owned and occupied by wage earners. McCarthy further estimated that 10 per cent of the city's wage earners owned their homes completely free of encumbrances.[41] Los Angeles, he said, prided itself on being a city of detached homes without the tenement problems of the older cities of the East. Labor leaders, on the contrary, thought of homeownership as a device to make workers slaves to their jobs. A worker whose home was not paid for was likely to bend to the will of his employer in order not to lose his job and possibly the equity in his residence through inability to make payments. A worker who owned his home free and clear was relatively immobile and consequently unlikely to move in order to take advantage of better employment opportunities elsewhere. Open-shop supporters spoke of the independence of spirit and the true American citizenship evidenced by homeownership; unionists considered homeownership as actually detrimental to such independence, preventing the worker from protesting the conditions under which he labored and the wages he worked for. Figures produced for the commission in 1914 demonstrated that the average workingman's home in the city was worth about $2,000, including the lot. Such a home was usually a four- or five-room, fully plastered house complete with bath on a standard lot of 40 by 150 feet. The rooms were about 10 or 11 by 12 feet. Monthly payments were $18, $20, or $22, depending on how rapidly the occupant wanted to pay off his debt. The down payment required was usually about $200, or 10 per cent. Interest charges on the unpaid balance were frequently as high as 1 per cent per month.[42]

The opponents of organized labor in Los Angeles claimed that the open shop provided a high standard of living for workers. Mrs. Frances N. Noel of the Women's Trade Union League, however, refuted this assertion, stating that the open-shop policy had "established a high standard of living for a few on top, and maintained . . . a standard of constant insecurity for the men in the middle . . . the smaller business man, and an entirely insecure existence for the people in the third stratum of life." A similar sentiment was voiced by Curly Grow in answer to statements of General Otis and Secretary Zeehandelaar that Los Angeles was among the most prosperous cities in the nation and possibly the world. Grow asserted that

the prosperous condition in this city is not enjoyed by those who toil, but . . . we have men in this city and combinations of men who are very, very prosperous; who have tremendous wealth; who dominate all the civic and social life, and industrial life—own everything, running just like you might say a spider's legs; that they extend out into all avenues in every section of this city . . . they are very prosperous, and if labor was only half so prosperous as these gentlemen I think we would be very well satisfied.[43]

Whatever the arguments for or against the open shop, neither side could prove its case conclusively. Labor leaders could cite specific cases of black-listing as well as discrimination against union men in hiring, and similar indications of antiunion activities, but they could not produce irrefutable evidence of the superiority of organized workers over unorganized men or of the existence of a widespread antiunion shop. Management, on the other hand, could not demonstrate that the unorganized worker was more efficient or that the open shop was responsible for the prosperity of the city. Zeehandelaar, in representing open-shop employers at the commission hearings, did his best to show that the workers in the City of the Angels were better off than elsewhere, but under cross-examination he had to admit that much of the prosperity could stem from economic rather than industrial factors.[44] On one basic issue, however, there was no question: the city's top businessmen, under the leadership of the Merchants' and Manufacturers' Association and the *Times,* did not want to deal with representatives of national and international unions in collective bargaining. To the city's labor leaders, this attitude meant that unions had an uphill fight for recognition, whether the management position was evidenced in the operation of an impartial open shop or of an antiunion shop in a particular firm.

Thus the battle lines drawn up in 1890 in the printers' strike against the newspapers of the city remained in existence better than two decades later. On the one side were the *Times* and the Merchants' and Manufacturers' Association with its membership of nearly 750 firms, or about 80 to 85 per cent of the larger establishments in the city. Although the M and M, founded in 1896, was not organized to fight unions, it assumed this role a year later in a strike against Los Angeles breweries. Its original constitution did not even mention labor or the open shop. The association managed fiestas, sought to persuade people to buy Los Angeles goods, opposed state-wide prohibition, and performed other services of a community character.[45] But its main claim to fame in the years just before World War I lay in its staunch stand against collective bargaining involving outside union representatives, a position it was to maintain steadfastly for nearly three more decades. On the other side was organized labor, represented mainly by the Los Angeles Central Labor Council with its ninety-one affiliated organizations, whose total membership was about 15,000 in 1911.[46] Weakened by the confessions of the McNamara brothers and the failure of the metal trades strike, organized labor was still the underdog in the battle but was not yet willing to fly the white flag of surrender. Though small and relatively quiescent for much of the subsequent two decades, the labor movement of the city remained alive, continued the struggle against the open shop, and laid the foundations for its growth in the late 1930's and early 1940's.

II. LABOR SMOLDERS, 1911–1914

1. The Fight for Survival in the Metal and Building Trades

ALTHOUGH ORGANIZED LABOR in Los Angeles was relatively quiet after the McNamara confessions of December, 1911, there was not a complete absence of activity. The organizing campaign of 1910–1911, however, was halted by the startling acknowledgments of responsibility for the *Times* disaster of October 1, 1910, and Los Angeles labor thus saw its heretofore unmatched effort to break the back of the open shop brought to an end by the ill-advised actions of men from outside the local movement. Because of the adverse public opinion after the confessions, the subsequent loss of the mayoralty election by Job Harriman and the Socialist Party, and the coming trial of the McNamaras' defense attorney, Clarence Darrow, on bribery charges, it seemed best to end the metal trades strike which had been initiated in June, 1910. Accordingly, in late February, 1912, V. J. O'Leary of the boiler-makers, George Gunrey of the molders, and E. H. Misner of the machinists, representing the metal trades, met with William B. Hoswell, secretary of the Founders' and Employers' Association. The original demands of the metal craftsmen had centered on union recognition and the eight-hour day. Through a verbal agreement reached at this meeting, however, the unions called off the strike on the promise of the employers to rehire the men without discrimination as employment opportunities arose.[1] Fortunately, this was before employment was affected by the 1913 downturn in business activity. Though no formal agreement was negotiated, the more important groups involved in the strike—molders, boilermakers, machinists, blacksmiths, and patternmakers—received wage increases averaging 5 cents an hour. The first four groups accepted a nine-hour day, and the patternmakers, taking advantage of a relative shortage of men in their trade, secured an eight-hour day.

The strike settlement could not be interpreted as a victory over the open shop despite these concessions. A telling blow had been struck by the McNamaras against the unions of the city, which far offset any subsequent short-term gains. The bombing, in effect, was responsible for defeating the 1910–1911 organizational campaign and strike. Nevertheless, the unions had managed to swing a segment of public opinion against the Merchants' and Manufacturers' Association, so that there was less need for secrecy about the activities of organized labor, particularly in regard to the times and places of union meetings.[2]

A feeble attempt to rally the member locals of the Los Angeles Central Labor Council through a "Get Together Conference" was made early in 1912, and an eight-point program of action was drawn up. The effort died, however, for lack of interest. The apathy and general discouragement of the period were also evidenced in the membership figures of the Central Labor Council. At the time of the strike settlement, the central body had ninety-three affiliated unions and a total membership of 11,290. Five months later, with the same number of affiliates, its membership had declined to 10,737. During the final six months of 1912, the loss of membership and interest continued. The number of constituent locals fell to eighty-eight by January, 1913, whereas unaffiliated unions rose from fifteen in July, 1912, to twenty by the end of the year. Although individual membership figures were not given by Secretary L. W. Butler of the council in his semiannual report of January, 1913, it is quite certain that total membership in the city's labor movement was no higher, if not absolutely lower, than it had been the preceding July.[3]

The repercussions of the termination of the strike were felt for several years by the unions involved. The Metal Trades Council was forced to reorganize in the spring of 1912. Although the settlement had promised the reëmployment of strikers without discrimination, union members complained of some difficulties in securing jobs in struck plants despite the relatively high level of employment. Two years later J. W. Buzzell, secretary and business agent for the Metal Trades Council and a patternmaker by trade, testified before the United States Commission on Industrial Relations that conditions in the metal trades were still bad. The union scale was practically nonexistent and only the machinists had one or two union shops; none existed in the other metal trades. On the basis of figures gathered from his fellow unionists, Buzzell listed the hourly rates paid in the summer of 1914:

	Current rate	Union rate requested
Molders and coremakers	27½–37½¢	50¢
Patternmakers	40 –50	50
Boilermakers	32½–45	50
Blacksmiths	25 –50	50
Machinists	25 –40	50

The nine-hour day prevailed, with straight time for overtime and a wage scale about 25 per cent below the union level. Buzzell further claimed that wages and conditions were the worst on the coast.[4]

Fred Baker of the open-shop Baker Iron Works and Secretary Hoswell of the Founders' and Employers' Association disagreed with the labor spokesman. Payroll data from the Baker Iron Works for August, 1914, however, indicated that the wage rates were as follows:

	Current rate
Molders	40 –44½¢
Coremakers	30
Patternmakers	42½
Boilermakers	45
Blacksmiths	30
Machinists	37½

Thus wages paid in his own shop disproved Baker's claim that Buzzell's figures were wrong.[5] Hoswell, who had records of the scales prevailing in all member shops of his organization, testified that the wages reported for molders were not 27½ to 37½ cents but ranged from 37½ to 50 cents per hour. Of the men employed by the members of the association, 127 received as much as 40 to 50 cents an hour, and 75 were paid 44½ to 50 cents.[6]

Buzzell, not to be downed so easily, cited a specific example of poor wages and working conditions affecting machinists. At the Chalmers auto garage, although wages were 40 cents an hour, working time was irregular, running from nine to sixteen hours a day. The men often had to wait as long as an hour or two for jobs to come in without receiving pay. The Chalmers shop allegedly had a card system which provided a set time for each job; if the job was not done in the assigned period, no compensation was received for the extra time spent in completing it. Employees were occasionally charged for work spoiled. Straight time was paid for all overtime, and those refusing to work beyond nine hours were laid off or discharged. Buzzell claimed that similar conditions existed at the Cadillac, Packard, and Pierce-Arrow shops. He also compared the situation in Los Angeles with that in San Francisco, where patternmakers received a minimum of $5 for an eight-hour day as compared with the 40 to 50 cents an hour in the southern city for nine hours or more.[7]

Los Angeles labor leaders further accused metal trades employers of black-listing union members through their association's employment bureau. Replying to this charge, Hoswell told the commission that any man could obtain a card for a position from his office, even though he had quit his job in another shop. The association did not permit one shop to hire men away from another, but the impression that a man could not work where he pleased was erroneous.[8] Although Baker claimed ignorance of a black list, J. E. Timmons, president of the Central Labor Council, demonstrated the effect of the association's hiring procedure by pointing out that the ironworkers were only about 25 per cent organized. He testified that men working for the Baker Iron Works, the Llewellyn Iron Works, and the Union Iron Works had been fired the day after they attended union meetings. Thus, workers who wanted to join a union feared that to do so would cost them their livelihood.[9]

There seems little doubt that the Founders' and Employers' Association had the necessary records to operate a black list in the metal trades, and that they controlled employment in most of the local metal shops. Hoswell's job was to keep troublemakers from employment in open shops, and his office mechanism was admirably structured to accomplish this purpose. On the other hand, Baker's attitude was characteristic of the viewpoint of employers; he simply wanted to run his business in his own way because his money was at stake. He gave preference to nonunion men because they were not subject to strike calls which interrupted operations. Baker himself admitted that he could not see any difference in efficiency between union and nonunion employees, and he had no objection to their organizing so long as they did not bother him, use violent methods, or seek pay for services not performed. When asked by members of the commission if he had any objection to the use of the boycott by unions, he stated that he did not, as he used it himself. He expressed his willingness to meet with committees of his own employees but, having operated an open shop since 1886, he would continue to throw into the wastebasket any overtures received from unions. Baker's cure for industrial unrest was a permanent industrial commission with broad plenary powers to deal with labor affairs. He also favored a state minimum wage law, which represented a more enlightened viewpoint than might have been expected from one of labor's adversaries in the open-shop war.[10]

The defeat of the metal trades unions in the strike of 1910–1912 did not completely discourage them from further efforts to organize in the next few years. Machinists Local No. 311 won a new contract with the breweries in 1913, providing for wage increases ranging from $1 to $4 a week. Boycotts were continued against the Stevens Ice Machine Company and the Los Angeles Creamery, though with only minimal results. By the spring of 1915 the Los Angeles molders had a relatively strong union. The patternmakers were possibly the first to recover from the strike, probably again because of the highly skilled nature of their trade as well as an active demand for their work. Although only about 50 per cent organized by 1914, they were fast regaining strength under the energetic leadership of their business agent. Iron Workers Local No. 51 had been almost destroyed by the long struggle. Those members who had struck had great difficulty in finding jobs, and early in 1912 a number went to San Diego to help in the free-speech fight conducted there by the Industrial Workers of the World. A year later, however, the pile drivers among the ironworkers began to show signs of life; they acquired enough new members to initiate an organizing attempt on several pier jobs in the Santa Monica Bay area. But the effort failed and the work was completed by nonunion men.[11]

The blacksmiths partly recovered from the effects of the metal trades strike as a result of the successful organizing efforts of the horseshoers. Although the general blacksmiths reported discrimination in reëmployment as late as the spring of 1914, the horseshoers, not yet affected by the advent of the automobile, were 90 per cent organized by August, 1912, and 98 per cent of the members were at work. They claimed to have a nine-hour day with Saturday off—conditions better than those enjoyed by that craft in any other city in the United States or Canada. Horseshoers Local No. 124 coöperated with Steam and Operating Engineers Local No. 72 in seeking to have the Merchant Independent Ice Company discharge a nonunion engineer, but without success. Similar difficulties were experienced by the engineers at the Stevens Ice Company, the Union Ice Company, and the National Ice Company. The last two firms employed union engineers in northern California but refused to do so in the south. A resolution presented at the 1914 convention of the California State Federation of Labor requested that these firms be placed on the state-wide unfair list.[12]

The boilermakers and the machinists' helpers were possibly the most severely affected by the metal trades strike. Both crafts were extensively employed in railroad shops and were hit doubly hard when, in September, 1911, a strike was called against the Harriman lines running into the city—the Southern Pacific and the San Pedro, Los Angeles, and Salt Lake railroads. The two strikes so decimated the membership of these unions that they gave up their charters.[13]

The sheet metal workers, like the boilermakers and the machinists' helpers, were caught in a web of trouble that stemmed from other causes as well as the strike of 1910–1912. In the early 1900's wood as a construction material began to be replaced in some uses by metal. The sheet metal workers of the country initially claimed jurisdiction over the installation of metal construction materials, but soon found themselves in conflict with the United Brotherhood of Carpenters and Joiners, which was jealously guarding its shrinking area of activity. The issue centered on the installation of metal trim, which had been introduced in 1906 as a building material, and resulted in a dispute that was to continue for many years. As there were fewer sheet metal workers than carpenters, and as they occupied a less strategic position in the construction industry, employers tended to support the carpenters in the interunion battle. The carpenters maintained that any work once done by them should remain under their jurisdiction regardless of changes in the type of material used. Although the struggle was temporarily compromised in May, 1926, at the urging and with the help of the American Federation of Labor, the interim warfare was trying to all concerned. Sheet Metal Workers Local No. 108 in Los Angeles thus found itself fighting not only the open shop but also the carpenters when the national jurisdictional dispute spread to southern California. In the years immediately before World War I, strikes to organize shops or jobs often resulted in carpenters taking the places of sheet metal workers. Hence Local No. 108 made very little progress in improving its weakened status of early 1912.[14]

Groups other than the metal trades were hurt by the surge in strength of the open shop which followed the end of the long strike. Building trades unions showed only an occasional spark of life, even though these years of rapid economic growth in Los Angeles were marked by considerable expansion in the construction field. New towns in the suburbs, such as Van Nuys in San Fernando Valley, were being laid out. New plants were being established and old ones enlarged, with the result that value added by manufacture within the city rose from $29,673,666 in 1909 to $44,517,197 in 1914. Although building permits declined in the recession beginning in the latter part of 1913, they had increased to $31,641,921 in that year from $21,684,100 in 1910. Part of the present-day downtown sky line appeared in these years, with construction of the Van Nuys, Hollingsworth, Los Angeles Investment Company, Los Angeles Athletic Club, Brockman, Gates Hotel, Black, and Title Guarantee buildings. Twenty-two major downtown structures were erected in 1912 alone. In the fall of 1911 the *Times* expressed its belief that the city was growing faster than any other large city on the American continent, and was erecting more buildings and putting more money into construction than any other city of like size in the United States.[15]

The unprecedented construction activity did not have its counterpart in the growth of organized labor in the building trades, though in 1913 visiting officers of the Building Trades Department of the American Federation of Labor found conditions more satisfactory than reports had led them to expect. In the first six months of that year the Los Angeles Building Trades Council reported a gain of 2,425 members among its affiliated unions, the organization of five new unions, and the formation of additional councils in nearby cities; and it stated its intent to establish at least one union in every building craft in the city. The gain in membership did not come easily, however; failures in organizing efforts tended to outweigh successes. The building trades had to fight open-shop contractors every step of the way, some of whom tried to undermine the unions by requiring their employees to subscribe to stock in their corporations through payroll deduction plans. It was hoped that ownership of a share in the company would preclude any desire to join a union.[16]

The arrest of the McNamara brothers and of Ortie McManigal, leaders in the *Times* bombing, had put the quietus on a general building trades strike that had been called on May 1, 1911, along with a walkout sponsored at the same time by the District Council of Carpenters. Excluding the carpenters, only about 300 men walked out, 200 of whom returned in a few days. The others were easily replaced.[17] A year later another attempt was made by the Building Trades Council to unionize construction jobs in the city. The leaders were Anton Johannsen of San Francisco, organizer for the State Building Trades Council and at that time under indictment for illegal transportation of dynamite into Los Angeles via interstate carrier; A. J. Mooney, secretary of the Los Angeles Building Trades Council; and J. W. Bibby, local organizer. After preliminary meetings in the early spring of 1912, union officials appointed a group called the Committee of 15 to lay plans for the new offensive. In a referendum vote, 71 per cent of the members of the unions in the Building Trades Council, who constituted about 20 per cent of all building craftsmen in the city, favored a strike for the closed shop, to begin on June 13. Hours and wages were not issues in the dispute.

Between 1,500 and 2,000 men were affected by the strike, but only about 300 or 400 actually walked out; the work stoppage was limited to construction jobs employing both nonunion and union men. De-

spite claims that more than 300 jobs were struck and that many contractors signed with the union, the response to the strike call was
apathetic, probably because of the lack of specific grievances, the fear
of losing good jobs, and the failure of the crafts to support one another. The plumbers and the marble setters, the most enthusiastic
participants in the strike, caused some delay in the installation of
plumbing and the setting and finishing of marble. But replacements
for them, as well as for other strikers, were soon found. As strike benefits were not forthcoming, and the international unions failed to give
the necessary support, the strike was called off on June 27, after about
two weeks. Nevertheless, the unions claimed that every craft gained
in numbers and in strength and that 143 construction jobs were unionized; but statements by the employers to the contrary demonstrated
that the open shop still held sway.[18]

For the rest of 1912 and well into 1913, the Building Trades Council
was plagued by internal strife. Most of the difficulty stemmed from
the willingness of the plasterers to work with nonunion men and the
refusal of the cement workers to join the Building Trades Council, although they were affiliated with the Central Labor Council. When
Cement Workers Local No. 3 asked the Central Labor Council for
working cards, it was told to join the Building Trades Council, as the
central organization did not issue work permits. The local's refusal to
do so resulted in a three-cornered conflict which was not resolved until
complaints from Los Angeles leaders led the cement workers' international to revoke the local's charter and thus force its ouster from the
Central Labor Council. The plasterers' trouble arose when they consented to work an eight-hour day for $5 beside nonunion men who
were paid the same wage. Complaints against their action became so
strong that the plasterers left the Building Trades Council before the
latter could unseat them. A report to their international, along with
the complaint concerning the cement workers, brought a delegation
to the city from the AFL Building Trades Department in the interests
of labor unity. Meanwhile the State Building Trades Council held its
annual convention in Los Angeles in an effort to arouse enthusiasm
and organizational loyalty among the various crafts. Although not
uniformly successful, the effort did result in a membership gain of
nearly 2,500 men in the Building Trades Council's affiliated unions
in the first half of 1913.[19]

Individual construction trades unions continued their efforts to
make gains. The District Council of Carpenters, coöperating with the
Building Trades Council in the strike called on May 1, 1911, de-

manded wages of $4 a day. Although none of the contractors would make a commitment in writing, a number replied verbally that they would pay the increase, and others agreed to do so if contractors in general would accede to the request. When the local builders' association, however, refused to discuss the matter, the District Council called out its men.

The strike lasted eleven weeks. Of a total of 5,000 union carpenters in the District Council, approximately 1,100 registered as strikers. Of these, only 356 were receiving strike benefits the second week, the others having returned to work at the $4 wage requested. As the remaining strikers were gradually absorbed at the new rate, the dispute was discontinued after the eleventh week. The total cost to the international union was $10,640; this did not include money paid out by the general strike committee in Los Angeles, which averaged $3 per week per man on strike. Total benefits paid to each striker were $7 a week. Despite the cost, the effort was deemed a victory for the carpenters, although they did not obtain a union shop. It demonstrated that, for this craft, union membership could provide some benefits. Nevertheless, the carpenters suffered heavy membership losses in 1912, but the trend was reversed under the impetus of the building boom. By May, 1913, their key local, No. 158, was the largest union in the city.[20]

Testimony before the Commission on Industrial Relations by employers and labor leaders in 1914 revealed that the carpenters were far from having a union shop. H. W. Bryson, manager of the F. O. Engstrum Company, one of the largest general contractors in the city, stated that his firm did not recognize unions and, in fact, did not employ union men if this could be avoided. To the best of his knowledge, no general contractor in Los Angeles recognized the unions. His own employees, many of whom had been with him from twelve to fourteen years, worked an eight-hour day, except for the woodworking men employed in the planing mill, who put in nine hours. Wages were based on competition and on the rates required to get the craftsmen needed.

Similar testimony by P. J. McDonald and R. H. Arnold, both owners of planing mills, established that the carpenters had made little progress in unionizing such plants. Most of the employers belonged to the Southern California Mill Owners' Association, operated on a nine-hour day six days a week, and paid shop wages varying from $2.25 to $5 a day. Locals No. 882 and 884 of the millmen had sought to obtain the union shop despite the opposition of association employers. A few such agreements had been signed, but the drop in construction in

1914 wreaked havoc on the unions, with five mills cutting wages by 50 to 75 cents a day and many millmen leaving the city because of lack of work.

C. R. Gore, business agent for the District Council of Carpenters, admitted to the commission that carpenters were far from having job control in Los Angeles. Union members, who received $4 for the eight-hour day, frequently worked on the same project with nonunion men, who might be paid as little as $2.25 a day. Union carpenters were paid time and a half for overtime, but the unorganized often worked up to eleven hours at straight time. Gore explained this discrepancy in wages in terms of quantity of work. The union man "had to deliver the goods" to be worth the premium over unorganized workers.[21]

The bricklayers represented one of the better-organized building crafts in the city in 1910–1914. Local manifestations of the national jurisdictional struggles with the International Association of Marble Workers seemed to be very minor. In 1913 the Los Angeles bricklayers were instrumental in starting a local of stonemasons, with an initial roster of eighteen members. On the whole, however, though participating in the general activities of the Building Trades Council, they felt no need for organizational campaigns. Testimony at the commission hearings left little doubt that skilled bricklayers were in demand, at least until the building slump in 1914. Zeehandelaar of the M and M credited the Los Angeles bricklayers with 100 per cent organization in 1914, although he stated that they did not have the closed shop. Estimates of impartial persons such as Professor Ira B. Cross of the University of California were below this figure, and a union business agent guessed at 87 per cent. Whatever the extent of organization, good union bricklayers were needed in the city and were often given preference over less efficient nonunion men.[22]

The granite cutters also were able to stand up to the open shop, largely through job control in quarries and the financial backing of their international in paying strike benefits. In May, 1913, two stone yards on East First Street sought to maintain open shops. The Granite Cutters Union immediately put pressure on the quarries, and the two firms found their supplies cut off. A subsequent state-wide strike of the granite cutters in 1915 gained a wage increase from $5 to $5.60 per day.[23]

Other building trades locals made somewhat less progress in their organizing activities. The marble setters maintained their union and tried to secure recognition through several strikes, though without complete success. A new union of floor layers, Local No. 1612, was formed in May, 1913, with twenty-six members, but it faced an uncertain future in the depression of the following year. Although the painters and paper hangers and the roofers kept their locals alive and active, they participated only in minor strikes in the years 1910–1914. For at least part of this time the painters and paper hangers did not belong to the Central Labor Council, and thus failed to support the latter's effort to hold the city's labor movement together. The lathers grew in strength during 1912, but a struggle ensued the following year between Local No. 42 and a group of so-called "independents." Differences were patched up in October, 1913, and a new local was established. The addition of the independents to the parent body increased the membership by about 200 men.[24]

Plumbers Local No. 78 declared for the union shop early in January, 1912, and participated in the strike sponsored by the Building Trades Council the following June. About half of the city's journeymen plumbers belonged to the union, and usually refused to work on the same job with nonunion men. The building boom in Los Angeles had attracted a large number of men from other areas, many of whom had set up shops of their own. Edward Beirne, business agent for Local No. 78 and president of the Building Trades Council in 1914 as well as a former president of the union, estimated that the number of plumbing shops in the city rose from about 60 in 1904 to 200 ten years later. Competition for jobs was keen among the journeymen, and this limited the job control exercised by the union. Wages were generally lower than in San Francisco, even on union jobs. The scale in the northern city in 1914 was $6 for eight hours, whereas it was about $4.50 in Los Angeles. Nonunion plumbers in the south often worked for as little as $2.50 to $3, though most of the competent men were in Local No. 78 and drew the higher wage. Thomas Haverty, pioneer plumbing contractor, differed with Beirne over the quality of work done by union as against nonunion journeymen, but both agreed that working conditions were essentially the same in all firms regardless of the degree of organization, except that hours tended to be longer where the union shop did not prevail. Though occasionally there was discrimination against a union plumber, black-listing was virtually unknown to the trade. The average plumbing shop was small, the proprietor had often been a member of the union himself, and relations between him and his men were congenial. Employers did not complain about work restriction on the part of the union men and seemed quite free of pressure from open-shop supporters to abstain from signing union contracts.[25]

At this time three locals of the International Brotherhood of Electrical Workers—Nos. 61, 82, and 370—were functioning in the city. Only Local No. 61, consisting mainly of linemen, participated in aggressive organizing activity in these years. In December, 1912, the linemen employed by the Pacific Telephone and Telegraph Company in southern California decided to demand a reduction in hours from nine to eight, a wage increase of 50 cents a day, and Saturday afternoons off without pay. The main issue was the wage increase which, if granted, would bring their pay to $4.25 a day. After the union had taken a strike vote, the company countered with an offer of a 25-cent raise. This was accepted by the linemen, particularly because the increase would also be given to six other crafts employed in telephone installation and maintenance: rackmen, powermen, batterymen, test-board men, repeater men, and cable splicers' helpers.[26]

A factional dispute originating among the linemen of the San Francisco area in 1909 stirred up discord in Los Angeles, as well as throughout the state, which was injurious to the organized labor movement as a whole. In both cities there were dual unions which claimed allegiance to different internationals. In Los Angeles the linemen were divided into Reid-Murphy Local No. 61, associated with the independent International Brotherhood of Electrical Workers of Springfield, Illinois, and McNulty Local No. 61, affiliated with the International Brotherhood of Electrical Workers, AFL. Both locals were composed of good union men, many of whom were top craftsmen. In March, 1913, at the request of the Building Trades Council, acting on instructions from the Executive Council of the AFL, the Los Angeles Central Labor Council unseated the independent Reid-Murphy local and placed the McNulty group in good standing. The loss of the sixty men of the Reid-Murphy faction resulted in the passage of a resolution, introduced by the patternmakers at an April meeting of the Labor Council, that at the next AFL convention Los Angeles delegates should press for the inclusion or the exclusion of both groups until they settled their differences.[27]

In May the Light and Power Council of California, with which the electrical workers' unions of the state were affiliated, called a strike against the Pacific Gas and Electric Company for an increase in wages and a day off each week. The strike was confined largely to the Bay area, and most of the strikers belonged to Reid-Murphy Local No. 151 of San Francisco. The McNulty faction, affiliated with the council as San Francisco Local No. 6, sought to break the strike by forming a new union which recruited its members from Local No. 6. The new organization succeeded in its strikebreaking attempt and signed a three-year contract with the utility, leaving the Reid-Murphy men out in the cold. The 1913 AFL convention in Seattle, notified of the trouble, sent President Samuel Gompers and other members of the Executive Council to San Francisco to settle the interunion dispute. On November 28, 1913, the AFL officials met with the leaders of the Reid-Murphy and McNulty factions, and together they worked out an agreement providing for admission of all linemen into locals of the International Brotherhood of Electrical Workers, AFL, without prejudice, by February, 1914. Actually it was not until October, 1914, that the headquarters of the Reid-Murphy group closed its books and transferred its assets to the AFL international, after a court order had established the IBEW, AFL, as the legal custodian of all funds held by the independent Reid-Murphy unions.[28]

Organized linemen in Los Angeles had watched the northern dispute with more than a little interest. The defeat of the Reid-Murphy local strengthened the McNulty group in Los Angeles. The Reid-Murphy faction, separated from the main body of the local labor movement, began to disintegrate. A few of its members, disgruntled with the established organizations, joined the Industrial Workers of the World. The rest made overtures to McNulty Local No. 61, which had disapproved of the strikebreaking action of its northern brethren, and by March 27, 1914, the two Los Angeles groups had amalgamated into one union. This action gave Local No. 61 a membership of nearly 600 linemen and the strength of a united front six months before the dispute was ended at the international level.[29]

2. Other Unions and the Open Shop

Although the Merchants' and Manufacturers' Association constantly sought to quench the flames of organizational activity, and the *Times* used the two bribery trials of Clarence Darrow in 1912–1913 as anti-union publicity weapons, unions continued to survive in other fields as well as in those directly associated with the expanding construction and allied industries of the city. As local manufacturers were not able to compete with more centrally located firms for major markets in the Midwest and East until World War II, production emphasis outside the building and metal trades before 1940 tended to be placed on serving the final consumption needs of a rapidly increasing population in southern California. Thus nondurable goods manufacturing and the various service trades were important in Los Angeles, and outweighed the durable goods sector in value of output throughout the first four decades of the century. Unions were active in many of these fields ranging from the amusement trades to the trucking industry.

The strongest unions in the amusement trades were Projectionists Local No. 150 and Musicians Local No. 47. The latter had not supported the McNamara brothers because C. L. Bagley, its president, had been convinced that they were guilty and that their case was hopeless long before the confessions of December, 1911. In October of that year the musicians set a new pay scale providing a 16 per cent increase for members playing in the theaters of the city. All except seven of the theaters agreed to the new scale. One of the holdouts was the Regal, which had been on the unfair list of the Central Labor Council since 1909. Stage Employees Local No. 33, the musicians, the projectionists, the Allied Printing Trades Council, and the White Rats Actors Union had been waging an active campaign against the Regal for more than two years, but had failed to win an agreement from the management. The other obdurate theaters were the two Clune houses and the Empress, Pantages, College, and Hyman organizations. Three of these capitulated to the musicians in January, 1912, signing a three-year agreement with a wage increase of $1 a week. The union thus failed to realize its original demand for a $2 increase, and was unable to organize the other four struck theaters. Early the following year Local No. 47 incurred the wrath of the *Times* when its members refused to play in the Shrine Band a few minutes before it was to march in the Shrine circus parade, a charitable fund-raising effort.[30]

Moving Picture Projectionists Local No. 150 was opposed by some of the same theaters that fought the wage demands of the musicians. The major houses belonged to the Theater Managers' Association, bent on maintaining the open shop. Early in 1913 the projectionists tried to organize the Manhattan, Bell, Wonderland, Shell, Banner, National, Novelty, Electric, and North Broadway houses, but won agreements from only three of them. In December, 1913, it was reported that the Lyceum and Garrick houses were running a school for projectionists and, along with the Century, were hiring only nonunion labor. Although the union had little success in organizing the major theaters, it increased its membership in 1914 and maintained reasonable job control over other moving picture houses in the city.[31]

The brewery trades were strong after the settlement of their yearlong strike against the breweries of the city in April, 1911. The brewery workers, the bottlers, and the beer drivers were represented by unions affiliated with the International Brewery Workers Union, and steam engineers, coopers, machinists, and stationary firemen employed in the industry were also organized. Despite active opposition from the Merchants' and Manufacturers' Association and the breweries, the strike begun on May 19, 1910, resulted in continuation of a closed shop in open-shop Los Angeles. Old contracts were renewed, with the drivers obtaining a wage increase of $2 a week and the bottlers a $1 raise.[32] As workingmen were believed to be the major consumers of beer, employers involved in its manufacture, distribution, and sale were especially vulnerable to the threat of a boycott.

Outside the brewery trades, the clothing unions were the only ones to make any headway with the closed or union shop in the period 1911–1914. The three most active unions were Ladies' Tailors No. 52 of the International Ladies' Garment Workers Union, Journeymen Tailors No. 81, and Garment Workers No. 125 of the United Garment Workers of America. A hatters' union, Local No. 22 of the United Hatters of North America, was relatively small and the one strike it conducted, in 1914, was of minor significance. The Amalgamated Clothing Workers did not organize a local in the Los Angeles area until 1920.

Ladies' Tailors No. 52 was fortunate in having able leaders. On August 4, 1911, it struck against Krystal & Company, but the dispute lasted only two weeks. In November, contrary to the advice of the international, the union initiated a general strike against all firms manufacturing women's garments, and reported that sixteen small firms signed contracts within two weeks; the larger concerns, however, formed an association and set up a black list against the local. After about six weeks the union called off the strike, but because of slack conditions in the trade, in addition to the black list, only about 10 per cent of the strikers returned to their old jobs. Moreover, the union was financially unable to continue the dispute without international support. Although this was apparently a victory for the open shop, a unity of spirit that developed during the dispute contributed to a subsequent successful organizing drive which added about sixty new members to the union by February, 1912, and brought victory in five strikes in the following two and a half years. By October, 1914, Ladies' Tailors No. 52 had contracts with Hackel and Gutterman, Hackel and Company, Skoss and Fried, Michaelson and Director, and M. Saks and Company. Much of this progress was due to able leadership in the local, assisted by AFL organizer Charles Feider. The major gains of the union included the eight-hour day, no Sunday work, the elimination of piecework, and an equal sharing by all employees in the inevitable unemployment in slack periods. Such fruitful activity was in sharp contrast with the weak organizing efforts of many Los Angeles unions in these years.[33]

Tailors Local No. 81 engaged in a strike against Charles Levy and Son in July, 1911, over the issue of union recognition. After two months the firm signed a bill of prices and the union claimed a great victory, for Levy and Son was one of the larger manufacturing establishments in men's clothing in the city. A year later the Journeymen Tailors Union of America sponsored a nationwide organizational drive in such cities as Los Angeles, San Francisco, Oakland, Milwaukee, Trenton, and Birmingham. Local No. 81 coöperated by striking five firms—Popkin and Nestor, Haber and Company, McGregor and Company, Brauer Tailoring Company, and Foreman and Clark, the last in conjunction with the retail clerks. The dispute was finally settled to the local's satisfaction in November, 1914. The union gained better working conditions as well as a net membership increase of about forty tailors. The conflict was marked by bitterness on both sides, particularly because several of the shop proprietors were former union members who opposed the local after becoming entrepreneurs.[34]

Local No. 125 of the United Garment Workers was slower than its sister unions in coming to life after the *Times* bombing, but it had an advantage in being concentrated in the manufacture of work clothing. In 1911 the local had about 450 members, all of whom were employed. Its strength and strategic position encouraged it to initiate an organizing campaign which culminated in a strike against the P. A. Newmark Shirt Company on March 1, 1913, when the firm refused to sign a new agreement granting a raise for the performance of certain steps in the manufacturing process. The strikers sought to establish an effective boycott of work shirts, Newmark's principal product. The campaign was conducted throughout the country by correspondence as well as by calls on the main buyers of the firm's output. Sales were gradually whittled down until only 89 of the original 300 employees remained at work. After sixteen months Newmark agreed to terms providing for a union shop, preferential employment for strikers, and the payment of back dues by any members of the union who had continued to work during the strike. Similar success was achieved with the Brownstein-Louis Company and with Cohn-Goldwater, both also engaged in the manufacture of work clothing and thus vulnerable to an effective boycott.

At the hearings of the Commission on Industrial Relations in 1914, the United Garment Workers and the Journeymen Tailors were singled out as exceptions to the effectiveness of the open-shop campaign. The desirability of having the union label on work clothing had given Local No. 125 union-shop contracts with the major manufacturers. Even Zeehandelaar testified that he believed all overall as well as other garment factories were closed shops. Although in fact the firms were union rather than closed shops, and not all the manufacturers were in this category, Zeehandelaar's statement was in effect an admission of failure to achieve a complete open shop in the manufacture of clothing, especially of work clothing.[35]

The Brownstein-Louis agreement negotiated by the United Garment Workers was typical of those granted by manufacturers of work clothing in 1913–1914 in Los Angeles. It provided for the union shop by requiring new employees to join the union within thirty days. The workweek was forty-eight hours, with time and a half beyond this period for salaried employees and piece and a half for all workers on piece rates. Double time or double piece was paid for all work done on Sundays or holidays. Legal holidays were declared to be New Year's Day, Christmas, Admission Day, Thanksgiving Day, Washington's Birthday, Memorial Day, Labor Day, the Fourth of July, and all Sundays. The union label was to be sewed in all garments, and a grievance procedure was to be set up. Journeymen cutters were to receive a wage of not less than $22.50 per week for the one-year term of the contract. This agreement was quite typical of the trade, but it was atypical for the industrial community at large.[36]

In contrast with the clothing workers, the culinary trades, except for the bartenders, fought an almost constant battle against the open shop. Their members worked long hours at low wages in a myriad of small establishments, including, in 1914, 224 cafés, restaurants, and cash houses, 18 hotels, 6 clubs, and 38 cafeterias and dairy lunchrooms. Except for the few unionized establishments, working conditions were almost uniformly poor. Waitresses frequently had to use the same dressing rooms as waiters. The eight-hour law for women was often violated, with girls working six to eight hours beyond the normal forty-eight-hour week. Shifts were broken so that waitresses sometimes had to spend thirteen hours a day, from 6 A.M. to 7 P.M., in the area of the establishment in order to work seven or eight hours, and many of them worked seven days a week on such broken shifts. Many housewives worked part time in peak periods as "pin-money" employees. Nonunion wages were as low as $3 to $7 for a week of fifty-six to fifty-eight hours. Part-time girls were paid from 35 to 50 cents for three hours, plus their lunch. If they worked five hours a day, they were given two meals and from $3.50 to $5 a week. Union wages for waitresses who were steadily employed were $8 for a forty-eight-hour week. Regular part-time girls received 60 cents and lunch for two and a half hours or less. Those working five hours a day on steady jobs received two meals and $6 per week of six days. Union houses were permitted to break a shift only once, whereas nonunion establishments often had two gaps in a daily stint.

Waiters were not much better off except in wages, though they had to depend on tips in order to exist. Hours were such that little family life was possible for a steadily employed man. Regular waiters in first-class cafés and cash houses, working ten to twelve hours a day, received from $8 to $10 for a seven-day week. Wages in second-class cafés were $7 to $12 a week, and in clubs and hotels, from $35 to $60 per month. Part-time waiters usually received two meals and from $5 to $7 each week. As a rule, waiters, unlike waitresses, had to pay for their own food unless they were working short hours. Uniforms were furnished by the employees except at clubs, and waiters had to pay the bus boys wherever they were used. Kitchen help with steady employment worked ten to twelve hours out of a period of fifteen hours on the premises of the employer. Chefs were paid $20 to $40 a week; second cooks, $10 to $25; third cooks, $10 to $20; and kitchen helpers, $7 to $10. Most of them worked a seven-day week.[37]

Despite the long hours, some culinary employees had time for union activity, especially in the more important hotels and restaurants. Cooks and Waiters Local No. 27 was the strongest organization after the bartenders. It reported 250 members in 1911, not including 25 cooks' helpers who were organized in a separate union, but it was forced to dispute for jurisdiction with an independent Cooks' Association and an employer-sponsored Angelus Cooks' Club. In addition, the employment of Orientals at even lower wages than those cited above hampered organizing efforts. Life for the cooks' and waiters' union was largely a series of small skirmishes with widely dispersed employers, some of whom operated on a narrow margin but had ready access to a plentiful, cheap labor supply to replace workers walking out for better conditions and wages. Although culinary employees tended to be transient and labor turnover was high, the costs involved were at least partly offset by the difficulties in unionizing such workers and by the relatively low wages.[38]

The bartenders were an exception to the rule of bare survival among the culinary trades. Their union had 476 members in November, 1911; an increase to 643 by April, 1913, after an aggressive organizing campaign, made it the third largest union in the city. The major problem was not one of membership but of opposing a rising clamor in favor of prohibition. The fear of consequent unemployment doubtless contributed to the union's growth. Further, in return for the bartenders' support in local-option elections, employers refrained from opposing union activities. (This attitude was also an element in the success of other unions in organizing the breweries of the city.) The efforts of the bartenders to protect their jobs from the feared effects of prohibition resulted in one of the few instances of pre–World War I coöperation between unions and employers in the "white spot of the open-shop cities of America." Mutual survival was a strong enough issue to force concessions from both camps. The bartenders were instrumental in 1914 in pushing a resolution opposing national prohibition through the Central Labor Council. They also fought efforts to place Japanese in saloons as cooks and waiters instead of white personnel, who were potential if not actual members of the cooks' and waiters' union. The two unions coöperated in this struggle because the Japanese, as aliens, would not be able to vote "wet" on any local-option issue or state or national prohibition proposal. But the effort was not uniformly successful; it was estimated that no less than 700 Japanese were employed in the saloons of the city in the latter part of 1914.[39]

The printing trades unions had been labor's standard-bearers in the original conflict ushering in the open-shop era in Los Angeles—the 1890 strike of Typographical Union No. 174 against the *Times* and three other daily newspapers. During the next two decades the struggle between the printers and the *Times* was to be of paramount importance to the city's labor movement, as Mrs. Stimson points out:

> The most significant single event in the history of industrial relations in Los Angeles, before 1910, was the strike of the Typographical Union against the four daily newspapers in August, 1890. It quickly resolved itself into the almost endless controversy between the *Times* and the printers which was to dominate the local labor scene for years to come.[40]

But the printing trades unions did not continue to dominate the local scene after 1910. The rapid growth of Los Angeles brought other unions and other disputes to the fore. Local No. 174, the leading union in the local printing trades, became disinclined, as a matter of policy, to precipitate an open break with an employer. Further, the newspapers of Los Angeles, with the exception of the *Times*, were largely under union control. It was the less organized book and job printing industry that provided most of the conflicts with the open shop.

The struggle against the *Times*, however, continued to smolder beneath the surface, though it did not burst into flame in 1911–1914. Testimony before the Commission on Industrial Relations in 1914 revealed the intensity of feeling between the printing unions and the *Times,* as well as the open-shop firms in the book and job industry, particularly in regard to wages. General Otis stated that the average weekly wages of twelve linotype operators in his composing room ranged up to $46.15. Charles Scott, organizer for the International Typographical Union and a former president of Local No. 174, pointed out that only four of the twelve were paid the union scale of $32 for six seven-and-a-half-hour days. Scott claimed further that the *Times* paid a daily scale ranging from $3.98 to $5.63, as compared with $5.33 on union newspapers. Otis, however, favored the piece-rate system and paid twenty-seven of his operators on this basis. Five of them received 13 cents per 1,000 ems, and the other twenty-two were paid 11.5 cents, which, he claimed, amounted to an average weekly wage of $35.10 for six seven-hour days. Scott in turn argued that to earn that amount a man working seven hours a day at 11.5 cents per 1,000 ems would have to set 9,000 or 10,000 ems an hour, almost a physical impossibility.

Whatever the true situation, there was no doubt that the *Times* intended to remain an open shop and to resist all organized labor in Los Angeles. This was evident in General Otis' statement that he had employed linotypers from the independent Printers' Protective Fraternity during the strike of 1890, importing them from Kansas City, and that men of this organization were still in his employ. In his view the fraternity was "a body of organized labor of the better sort, which has no affiliation with either the international or the local typographical union. Members of this reasonable and dependable organization have been chiefly employed by us, together with other non-union workmen. . . ." [41] The opinions of leaders of the Typographical Union concerning the strikebreaking fraternity were frequently unprintable.

Although unsuccessful in establishing a union shop at the *Times,* the printers of Local No. 174 did have agreements with the other five daily papers in Los Angeles. The minimum wage of $32 for a six-day week of seven and a half hours daily applied to morning newspapers; evening papers paid an official union scale of $29. The 1914 agreement between the local and the Los Angeles Newspaper Publishers' Association provided for the employment only of members of Local No. 174 in composing rooms, wages of not less than $5.335 per day, time and a half for overtime, a full day's employment for members beginning work on any one day, and a seven-and-a-half-hour day. The membership of the local at this time was 550, with steady growth anticipated during the remainder of the year because of the projected meeting of the 1915 convention of the international in Los Angeles.[42]

The situation in book and job printing was much less favorable to the unions. An active open-shop employers' association, the Printers' Trade Alliance, existed for the specific purpose of dealing with industrial relations. In 1914 Irwin H. Rice, president of George Rice and Sons, a printing house that had been operating in Los Angeles for thirty-six years, testified before the commission that the leading firms in book and job printing were open shop. A large number of their employees were hired through a labor service bureau which, though ostensibly not discriminating against union members, was in a position to maintain a black list. All employees of members of the Printers' Trade Alliance had the right to appeal grievances directly to the heads of the firms, over the authority of foremen, but the privilege was seldom used. In a poll of thirteen of the leading job shops in the city, employing 267 men, Rice had discovered that eight of them had at one time operated as union shops, that seven of these had become open shops because of union rules, and that in one firm the change had been the choice of the foreman. Of the eight, five reported increased output after becoming open shops, one could see no change, and two did not report. Ten of the thirteen shops claimed no discrimination against union men, and all but four were aware that some union members were employed.

Rice correctly defined an open shop as one where union and non-union men worked side by side; in his own plant he tried to maintain a balance between the two groups. His main grievance against unions seemed to be that they did not keep their agreements, and he therefore advocated forcing them to incorporate. Under questioning, however, he admitted that he did not know of any instances where unions had broken agreements, and finally stated that he was not opposed to unionism as such but only to certain aspects of it. It was his belief that unions had improved working conditions, but he wanted to encourage responsibility on their part by making the local union itself, rather than its individual members, liable for damages for unlawful invasion of the rights of others.[43]

H. W. Dennett of Local No. 174 was sharply critical of conditions in book and job printing in Los Angeles:

No city in America is more thoroughly demoralized in the printing industry than Los Angeles. This condition must be accounted for by the number of non-union men and the M. and M. Association. Non-union conditions make it impossible for the employers to maintain a uniform wage. Wages range anywhere from $1.50 up to union scale, but in the majority of cases it is $14 to $18. There are three or four shops, especially those receiving the favor of the M. and M. Association, that are prosperous. We have suffered on account of conditions, but not so much as the employers.[44]

Dennett estimated that the book and job business was about 65 per cent organized, but, less this be thought reasonably good, he pointed out that there were so many small printing plants that it was impossible for employers to hold the line on prices. It was his belief that Los Angeles had more such shops than the combined total in all other cities in the United States. This obvious exaggeration nevertheless indicated the strength of feeling on the subject. Even the larger plants were hurt by the competition of "sidewalk" printers. The former used commercial printing as a filler between big jobs, but small printers, who bid for this type of work, reduced the amount of filler available and consequently caused irregular employment in large shops and extensive price cutting. To demonstrate the open-shop character of the Printers' Trade Alliance, Dennett exhibited the following printed item, dated August 19, 1914:

The undersigned employing printers of Los Angeles call your attention to the fact that the campaign literature and printing matter distributed by you as a candidate for public office carried the union label, indicating that you believe in the principles of the closed shop, which if in full effect would deprive the independent American workingman of the right to earn an honest living.

We desire to bring this fact to your notice, in order that you may know that such principles are not in accord with those of most right-thinking American citizens.

We feel that if the idea of the closed shop is in accord with your political ideas, you are not a safe candidate for a public position.

Office of the secretary,
303 East Fourth Street,
Los Angeles

The address was that of George Rice and Sons, headed by Irwin H. Rice.[45]

Other printing trades unions were Press Feeders No. 37, Photoengravers No. 32, Pressmen No. 78, Bookbinders No. 63, Stereotypers No. 58, and Web Pressmen No. 18. In addition, a local of lithographers was formed in 1914. Except for minor strikes and lockouts, as well as some unemployment incident to the business downturn in late 1913, all these small organizations maintained themselves without significant change during these years.

The bakers were one of the more active union groups in the years following the bombing of the *Times*. They were divided into cracker, Jewish, and general bakers. The last were by far the most important and were organized into Local No. 37, one of the oldest unions in the city. The cracker bakers initiated their union on February 22, 1911, and were immediately locked out by the Bishop Candy and Cracker Company. Local No. 37 and the cracker bakers carried on a boycott against this company until a lack of funds dropped the matter into the lap of the Central Labor Council. Committees of striking girls canvassed the proprietors of some 1,200 stores in the Los Angeles area for their coöperation in the boycott, but there was little tangible result. Although Bishop allegedly lost business, the employment of its locked-out bakers by other firms, coupled with the marriages of a number of the female strikers, eventually caused the dissolution of the strike committee and failure successfully to combat the lockout.

Bakers Union No. 37, though assisting in the boycott, was more vitally concerned with matters directly affecting it, particularly a strong employer front which was soon to be bolstered by the entrance of chain baking firms into Los Angeles. Its principal grievance in 1911 was that some of its members worked as long as fifteen hours a day. By means of a strike threat, the bakers induced all the large baking firms except Meeks-Barnes and Walker to agree to a nine-hour day. A boycott instituted against these two firms was unsuccessful. Meeks-Barnes and Walker eventually sold out to a national chain in 1914. The bakers feared these national organizations, known to them as "bread trusts," because of their financial resources as well as their invulnerability to the "divide and conquer" organizing technique which could be used against small, competitive shops. Before the year was out, there were three national baking firms with branches in Los Angeles, all of which were operated as open shops.[46]

Meanwhile, the bakers of Local No. 37 continued their drive to improve working conditions, wages, and hours in small shops. Although they had been partly successful in winning the nine-hour day in 1911, there were still the problems of overtime, Sunday work, hourly rates, and rest periods. Three years later, in June, 1914, C. D. Shields, secretary of the local, claimed improvements in all these areas in many shops, though a few large bakeries operated by members of the "bread trust" were not coöperating. Gains included the achievement of an eight-to-ten-hour day, a six-day week, thirty minutes for lunch and rest after five hours of work, and weekly wages of $21 for bakers, $24 for foremen, and $18 for bench and machine hands. A few months later, at the 1914 convention of the California State Federation of Labor, it was reported that fifty bakeries in Los Angeles had signed contracts granting substantially the above provisions.

Although all the bakers suffered from some unemployment in late 1913 and early 1914, Jewish Bakers No. 63 chose to strike that spring for more money as well as pay for religious holidays. At the same time efforts were made to organize the French bakers. Sixty men walked out under the leadership of Marcel Wille, organizer for the international, and skirmishes involving police and pickets occurred at several shops, including the Franco-American Bakery at Castelar and College streets. But the struck shops were so small and widely scattered that the master baker–employers were able to hire enough help to continue operations. The issues were compromised, however, and the strike was settled after a few days with all employees returning to work.[47]

Among the service trades, Barbers Local No. 295, originally organized in 1901, was fortunate in having C. M. Feider, an able international organizer, working in its behalf. Not only did he assist the barbers, but he also found time to aid the organizing efforts of other unions, and was rewarded in the fall of 1914 by being elected a vicepresident of the barbers' international. Although the *Times* claimed that Local No. 295 was weak, this statement was belied by reports indicating a membership of 400 in June, 1914, a guaranteed wage of $15 a week in all union shops, a ten-and-a-half-hour day, and a six-day week. In contrast with the barbers, the butchers had relatively little strength. Despite the help of M. R. Grunhof, an international organizer, they made little headway in 1913 against the open-shop packing houses and meat retailers.

A combination of the open shop and Oriental competition hampered the organization of laundry workers in 1911–1914. The Orientals operated small shops with an average of four employees, who were not averse to working long hours for low wages. The resultant pressure on white firms made it difficult to maintain wage structures that provided a reasonable standard of living for their employees. In addition, most of the latter were women who were willing to work for less because they were merely supplementing the income of a family breadwinner or were single and only temporarily employed while looking for the right marriage prospect. Women who depended on laundry work to support themselves and dependents were hard pressed to make ends meet. The Excelsior Laundry paid the following typical wages to female workers:

Number of girls	Weekly wage
10	$ 7.00
6	7.50
35	8.00
14	9.00
2	10.00
5	11.00
12	12.00
1	13.00
1	14.00
1	15.00
1	18.00
1	21.00

The ten girls earning $7 were employed on the shaking table; they were mostly of foreign extraction and lived with their families. All the women worked an eight-hour day and a six-day week. The situation among female laundry workers in San Francisco was much better than in Los Angeles, allegedly as a result of unionization. Although performing similar types of work, women employees in the north received higher wages; only 34 per cent were paid less than $9 a week, as compared with 65 per cent in the southern city. A union of laundry workers existed in Los Angeles, but it was opposed by a strong employers' organization, the Southern California Laundry Association.[48]

Retail clerks, especially women working in five-and-dime and department stores, were also poorly paid. Wages tended to be pin money for married women or the interim income of young girls, most of whom were unskilled. The retail clerks' union was reorganized in May, 1912, but barely maintained itself during the subsequent several years, even with the help of two international organizers. The testimony of Mrs. Katherine P. Edson, a member of the State Industrial Welfare Commission, before the Commission on Industrial Relations in 1914 gave a reasonably objective picture of working conditions for women employed as retail clerks. She stated that the five-and-ten-cent stores were the worst offenders in the payment of low wages to women, especially to young girls. The latter, often hired at a tender age, were paid as little as $4 to $4.50 a week. Maximum wages up to 1914 had been $6 regardless of age or experience. Mrs. Edson noted, however, that public opinion had been strong enough to effect some improvement, so that as of September, 1914, the minimum wage was $5, the maximum $10, and most of the women were at least eighteen years of age.

Mrs. Edson, in all fairness to employers, pointed out that wages and working conditions in Los Angeles department stores were better than in most cities over the nation and almost as good as those in unionized San Francisco. Child labor had almost been eliminated, and public opinion had forced through wage increases which had raised the minimum from $4 to $6 a week, though a few stores still paid $4.50 or $5. Most department and dry goods stores paid at least $25 a month to their women employees; cash girls and cashiers, who were gradually being replaced by machines, received the lowest wages. Saleswomen with experience usually were paid a minimum of $8 a week. Most of these stores had lunchrooms and cafeterias as well as places where women clerks could rest. Special commendation was given to the Boston Store, Coulter's, Blackstone, Hamburger, Bullock's, the Broadway Department Store, the Fifth Street Store, and a number of women's specialty houses.[49]

Arthur Letts, proprietor of the Broadway Department Store, president of the National Retail Dry Goods Association, and member of the Merchants' and Manufacturers' Association, voiced a typical paternalistic open-shop viewpoint when he testified on working conditions for women clerks in his store. Employee welfare had been a prime interest of his for eighteen years. Not only was his store equipped with safety features, such as a fire department and elevators, but it also had modern ventilation, showers, lockers, toilets, and a hospital for employees. No one under sixteen was hired, and the absolute minimum wage was $6 a week for a basic eight-hour day. All those eighteen or above received at least $8. Workers starting at $8 were raised to at least $9 within one year; those living away from home were paid at least $10; and women with children were paid $12. A vacation of one week with pay was granted to all employees who had been with the firm a year or more. Despite Letts's concern for his employees' welfare, he was clearly a strong supporter of the open shop, as evidenced by his testimony regarding his grievance procedure:

> For eighteen years I have been trying to get an entirely satisfactory system and I believe that I now have such a system. In order to remove any barriers, I have asked the employees to elect their own committee with which I would cooperate at all times in the adjustment of all grievances. The employees have an association of their own and they publish a magazine once a month.
>
> I might state that I don't think that there is any need for a clerks' union in any store where the employer is in close touch with his employees and where there is a hearty spirit of cooperation.

In Letts's opinion, the open-shop policy had made it possible for the working people of Los Angeles to find employment regardless of their previous experience and to enjoy a high standard of living.[50]

The paternalistic attitude of employers like Letts made it difficult for the retail clerks' union to organize their employees, especially in large stores. Other reasons for the lack of organizing success included the tendency for young girls to work only temporarily while looking forward to marriage, and for married women to regard their wages as pin money or as a means of helping their husbands pay for a home or hedge against unemployment; the usual white-collar antipathy toward unions; and the prevalence of small firms in retail trade. This formidable combination of factors made the clerks' union an insecure element in the local labor movement for the following three decades.

The teamsters, like the retail clerks, were weak during the years immediately preceding World War I. Formed in 1900, the union had become in the subsequent seven years one of the strongest labor organizations in the city, enjoying harmonious relations with the major employers who were combined in a Draymen's Association. In 1907, however, the Merchants' and Manufacturers' Association persuaded the employers not to renew their contracts with the union. After a ten-day strike the union was defeated and all but wiped out. Discrimination against teamsters who had participated in the strike reduced the union membership from 500 to 35. The union slowly began to rebuild, but did not again assume much importance in the local picture until the late 1930's. The disputes that arose between 1907 and World War I were minor and had no long-run significance. The open shop reigned supreme in the trucking industry.[51]

Two lockouts involving the teamsters occurred in the period 1911–1914, one at the Los Angeles Transfer Company, and the other at the Citizens' Independent Ice Company. The latter dispute was the more important, beginning in May, 1914, and lasting for several months. Two years earlier the teamsters had complained that other unions were not supporting their policy of asking drivers involved in the joint activities of several crafts to produce union cards. In addition, they had asked their international to send an organizer to southern California. The possibility that Michael Casey, president of the teamsters' union in San Francisco, might be sent caused the *Times* to assail him bitterly even before his selection was confirmed. The reason for the tirade was that Casey's union had recently participated in a strike marked by considerable violence. According to the *Times*, nonunion teamsters in the Bay city had been "clubbed, and even murdered. One of the favorite methods of disabling the strike-breakers was to surround a wagon, haul the driver from his seat and break his arm with an iron bar. Casey is the reported originator of this method. . . ." Whether or not Casey gave new life to the Los Angeles teamsters, they did win the support of other unions in the Citizens' Independent Ice Company dispute. It ended in August with the entire plant unionized, including engineers, firemen, machinists, drivers, and helpers. A two-year contract was signed, and shifts were reduced from twelve to eight hours a day. Such a victory for the teamsters was unusual. Testimony before the Commission on Industrial Relations in September showed that the trucking industry in Los Angeles was only about 10 per cent organized. Wages were as low as $9 for a six-day week, whereas before 1907 the minimum scale had been $2.25 a day.[52]

Other trades besides the teamsters lacked strength during these years. Locals of cigar makers, furniture workers, upholsterers, expressmen, and flour and cereal workers maintained a marginal existence. The leather workers, exhausted by their long strike initiated in 1910 against Brydon Brothers and Los Angeles Saddlery, were in a poor financial condition. The trunk and case workers were more fortunate. In 1911 they signed up all the local firms employing their members, and enjoyed relative peace for the next two years. In November, 1913, however, the Berman Trunk Company defied the union and refused to sign an agreement. The boycott threatened by the union was welcomed by Berman, who claimed the free advertising would help his business.[53]

3. 1914—A BLEAK FUTURE?

To some degree the attitude expressed by the Berman Trunk Company revealed the ineffectiveness of organized labor in Los Angeles at the time of the outbreak of war in Europe. The *Times* was at least partly right when it stated in January, 1915: "Hard times have hit the Central Labor Council and trade unionism in this city is at its dying gasp." [54] The newspaper claimed that the Labor Council was heavily in debt, that its officers were trying to avoid being served by creditors, and that its secretary and assistant secretary had not been paid their salaries for two weeks. It pointed out that the Union Labor Temple Association was having trouble selling its stock in order to pay off its mortgage, and was forced to rent its auditorium for boxing bouts because neither the poolroom nor the barber shop was even paying expenses. The labor movement was not really "dying," but there is little doubt that it entered the war years in an enfeebled condition.

The troubles of the Union Labor Temple Association were evidence of general apathy and discouragement. The Labor Temple had been completed in 1910, after seven years of fund-raising and construction activity. It could not have been finished at a more inopportune time than in the year of the bombing of the *Times,* but enough unions were interested in its future to keep up the payments on the mortgage. By 1913 only $95,000 remained to be paid, while the valuation placed on the building was about $350,000. The real problem, however, was that $14,000 had to be raised each year to meet interest payments as well as payments on the principal. Beginning in August, 1913, members of the local labor movement were asked to subscribe to shares of stock, the proceeds to be applied against the debt. Ten months later the campaign was stalled on dead center, overshadowed by internal conflicts within the Central Labor Council and between it and the Building Trades Council. Complaints appeared in the *Citizen* that union men were not patronizing the barber shop, the dance floor, or the bar, and that at least 10,000 members of local unions had purchased no Labor Temple stock, even at the low price of $1.50 a share.[55]

Apathy and disorder were also evident in the unsuccessful organizing campaign of 1913–1914 and the disagreement between the Central Labor Council and the Building Trades Council over a proposed power bond issue. Work on the organizing campaign was initiated in October, 1913, at the Fresno convention of the California State Federation of Labor. Secretary Paul Scharrenberg of the state organization agreed to circularize all member unions for funds to organize Los Angeles. Secretary L. W. Butler of the Central Labor Council, placed in charge of the campaign, set up a committee to conduct the drive. Los Angeles unions were asked to supply the names of nonunion craftsmen to whom literature could be sent concerning the advantages of union membership. At this time at least forty eligible trades had no representation in the Central Labor Council, and twenty-four unions in other crafts were weak and in need of new blood.

The actual campaign got under way on January 1, 1914. In March Butler announced that 25,000 nonunion men had received preliminary literature on the need for their affiliation with the unions, and the *Citizen* called the drive the most comprehensive ever attempted in the city—but it failed. The blame could be placed on various factors: lack of financial support from international unions; the adverse publicity resulting from the second bribery trial of Clarence Darrow; the revelations in Indianapolis regarding the use of dynamite by unionists, which were generously publicized by the *Times*; or the activities of open-shop advocates in the city. Whatever the cause, the result was clear.

Vice-President Frank Belcher of District No. 2 (Los Angeles), in his report at the State Federation of Labor convention in November, 1914, pronounced the benediction for the organizing campaign when he said that "despite the huge sums of money sent into the city the general conditions remain practically unchanged. . . . The gains in membership, such as there has [sic] been, does not in any way compare with the great increase in population." [56]

Whenever success does not attend the activities of a group, it is easy for the membership to find relief in mutual criticism and disagreement. Whether or not this underlay the trouble between the Central Labor Council and the Building Trades Council in 1914, there was no doubt that bitter feeling existed and that it contributed to the continuing stagnation of the local labor movement and aided the open-shop forces in their efforts to quell Los Angeles unions. The immediate cause of the rift was a proposed $6,500,000 city power bond issue which was favored by the Central Labor Council. With the nation in the throes of a prewar depression, the bonds were seen as a source of employment for many union men. A secondary factor in the dispute was the claim of the building trades that the *Citizen* did not give proper publicity to all organized labor and, in particular, to unions in the construction field.

To emphasize their dissatisfaction, a number of the building trades unions withdrew from the Central Labor Council, thus decreasing the council's revenue from the per capita tax. In addition, they started a new labor paper, the *Union Labor Bulletin,* edited by A. J. Mooney, secretary of the Building Trades Council. As expected, the paper opposed the power bonds. The Merchants' and Manufacturers' Association and the Los Angeles Realty Board also opposed the bonds; thus the building trades unions found themselves with strange bedfellows. Charges and countercharges were hurled between the two labor groups through the pages of the *Citizen* and the *Bulletin.* The Building Trades Council accused the Central Labor Council of selling out to the public power "octopus." The latter, in turn, charged that the building trades unions were playing into the hands of the *Times,* General Otis, and the M and M, and were controverting the AFL policy of favoring municipal ownership. When three officers of the Central Labor Council—George A. Wright, president; George W. McDonald, conductor; and F. C. Marsh, member of the executive board—permitted their names to be used on antibond literature, their positions were promptly declared vacated. J. E. Timmons, a housesmith by trade and former manager of the Union Labor Temple Association as well as former secretary of the Building Trades Council, was immediately elected the new president.[57]

Although the rift in labor's ranks was healed after a few months and the *Union Labor Bulletin* ceased publication, the dissension was one more factor contributing to the weakness of the local labor movement as it entered the war period. Nearly five years had elapsed since the bombing of the *Times,* but Los Angeles unions had still not recovered from its impact. Although some progress had been made by a few locals, labor was only smoldering—every effort to kindle a strong flame of organizational activity stirred but a momentary spark of interest. As will be seen in chapter iv, the open-shop principle of industrial relations continued to be paramount in the Los Angeles area as the eyes of the nation turned toward the conflagration in Europe. Meanwhile, an examination will be made of the open-shop influence within another segment of the Los Angeles economy—the rail lines of the area.

III. THE OPEN RAILS

THE YEARS immediately following the bombing of the *Times* were marked by a long strike on the Western and Midwestern railroads controlled by E. H. Harriman. Two of these lines, the Southern Pacific and the San Pedro, Los Angeles, and Salt Lake, entered Los Angeles and, with the Atchison, Topeka, and Santa Fe, constituted the rail connections between Los Angeles and the rest of the nation. Indirectly, the long arm of Harriman control also extended into the interior of the city, and linked it with its environs. The Pacific Electric Railway, providing interurban service in the Los Angeles area, was a child of the Southern Pacific, which controlled its operations. The Los Angeles Railway, possessor of the street railway franchise within the city, was owned by Henry E. Huntington, long-time power in the Southern Pacific as well as pillar of strength in local open-shop circles.

Neither the Pacific Electric nor the Los Angeles Railway was unionized, despite various attempts in the past to organize their operating and maintenance employees. Unions were functioning, however, on the interstate railroads, although the operating employees were the only workers able consistently to oppose management with some success on basic issues of hours and wages. The rail unions in Los Angeles seldom took part in the activities of the Central Labor Council because they had no direct connection with local employers. But there were differences among the rail unions in their degree of participation in local affairs. The operating brotherhoods tended to be more aloof, concerned mainly with national and state labor problems affecting their jobs. The nonoperating unions, particularly those in shop crafts, were jurisdictionally confined to a smaller area and hence were more interested in local labor activities. The strike on the Harriman system from 1911 to 1915, which extended over the entire Western United States as well as the Mississippi Valley, directly involved these shop employees and was of prime concern to Los Angeles residents because of the initial tie-up of traffic and the subsequent loss of jobs. Los Angeles shopmen thus found open-shop employers arrayed against them, with the *Times* acting as both mouthpiece and whip.

1. THE HARRIMAN STRIKE, 1911–1915

The railroad shop crafts did not recover from the disastrous effects of the 1894 Pullman strike and the depression of the 'nineties until 1900, but by then they were again ready for united action. This time the foe was the piecework system instituted in 1902 by the Union Pacific, a Harriman line. The machinists, the boilermakers, and the black-smiths struck together, and the dispute quickly spread to the Southern Pacific because of its alleged role in supplying rolling stock to the Union Pacific. In June, 1903, Harriman abolished the piecework, granted the reinstated strikers a 10 per cent increase in pay, and established a nine-hour day, but he retained nonunionists hired during the dispute. Three years later, in September, 1906, the boilermakers in the Southern Pacific shops in Los Angeles successfully struck to support their helpers' demand for higher wages. Soon thereafter all machinists employed on the railroad's Pacific Coast lines were granted a wage increase. The next summer, after a strike of two months, the Pacific Division of the Southern Pacific compromised a dispute with the boilermakers which had arisen because their helpers disliked a shop foreman in Los Angeles.[1]

The machinists, who were organized into railroad system groups, established four regional organizations covering the entire nation. The first formal system federation of the various shop crafts was organized on the Southern Railroad in 1908. The different shop crafts continued to present separate lists of demands to management, but the requests were the same and the resulting signed agreements all contained a similar thirty-day termination clause. In 1910 the machinists, the boilermakers, and the blacksmiths won a joint victory against the Missouri Pacific which led to a system federation on that road. Among the large number of such federations subsequently formed was the System Federation of the Harriman Lines, founded on June 5, 1911, in Salt Lake City. In keeping with this trend, the AFL convention of 1908 authorized the establishment of a Railway Employees' Department, which initially confined itself, however, to educational and legislative activities instead of giving direct aid to the system federations. The ineffectiveness of the Railway Employees' Department, coupled with the opposition of the railroads to the system federations, led the latter to establish a Federation of Federations of Railway Employees at Chicago on April 15, 1912. Dual unionism was not an issue because the same shop craft internationals were in both the AFL and the new system group. In fact, at its next meeting the AFL department ratified the legislation passed by the 1912 Chicago convention of the Federation of Federations, and the two groups coalesced.[2]

The growth of system federations and the 1911–1915 dispute on the Harriman lines were manifestations of a general unrest among railroad men over the nation, largely attributed to inadequate wage adjustments in the face of a steadily rising cost of living and to layoffs of shopmen in the years after the panic of 1907. The rail managements, in turn, were subjected to increasing pressure from the Interstate Commerce Commission in the regulation of rail rates, especially after the passage of the Mann-Elkins Act of 1910. Rail rates could not be raised so indiscriminately as in previous years. When the ICC denied rate increases, the roads tended to turn down worker requests for higher wages and, in fact, sought to cut costs by layoffs of men, particularly because traffic requirements became lower early in 1911. In March of that year the Southern Pacific put its general shop force on a five-day week with an eight-hour day, reducing wages accordingly. Further contraction in August, 1911, resulted in actual layoffs and an estimated net decrease of 25 per cent in shop forces. In Los Angeles, for example, approximately 400 men were released, allegedly because of a lower volume of business, though the unions claimed that the railroad's purpose was to intimidate the shop unions which, in the meantime, had joined the Harriman system federation. It should be noted, however, that by late 1911 more than 80,000 men had been laid off by the railroads of the nation. There was little doubt that a crisis was shaping up on a number of roads, including the Harriman lines.[3]

On July 1, 1911, representatives of the shop unions served a thirty-day notice of their desire for a new contract on the managements of the roads in the Harriman system. Copies of the proposed contract were sent out by the unions on July 19, as was the custom, thus giving both sides an opportunity to study the proposals before a joint meeting. The demands submitted by all the shop crafts (blacksmiths, machinists, boilermakers, carmen, sheet metal workers) were identical and included the following:

1. Recognition of the System Federation of the Harriman Lines as collective bargaining agent.

2. All employees to be paid by the hour, with the abolition of monthly bonuses or premium systems of compensation.

3. A flat wage increase of 7 cents an hour and a bonus payment of one hour's wage each week for all shop employees.

4. Overtime to be paid at time and a half, with double time after midnight.

5. An eight-hour day and a six-day week, with night men to be allowed nine hours' pay for eight hours' work.

6. All present and future shop employees not members of a union in the federation to be required to join one within thirty days.

7. Competency of employees entering service to be determined within thirty days after employment.

8. Physical examinations and personal records of employees to be eliminated.

9. Men not to be required to work on engines outside shops in bad weather; no work to be done on engines undergoing repairs until cleaned; roundhouses to be piped within ninety days to carry away steam blown out of engines.

10. Workmen not to be discharged or suspended without the previous consent of a shop employees' committee.

11. Employees in outlying districts to be given leaves of absence and transportation when requested ten days in advance.

12. Free transportation for employees, dependent members of their families, and union representatives.

13. Employees to be given leaves of absence for ninety days as a substitute for dismissals in slack periods.

14. Promotion of the senior man in a given shop to the position of foreman on the occurrence of a vacancy.

15. Equal membership on the board of directors of the hospital association.

16. Apprentices to be limited to one for every four mechanics, with foremen responsible for the release of those not showing aptitude for their crafts.

Three days later, on July 22, the managements advised the shop unions that they would not meet with them as a body but only as individual craft organizations, as heretofore. H. J. Small, superintendent of motive power for the Pacific System of the Southern Pacific, then sent a letter to all shop employees under his jurisdiction pointing out that they had been given wage increases averaging 12.5 per cent and, in some instances, 30 per cent in the preceding five years. He further said that the wage and hour demands would increase shop expenses in the Pacific System by about $2,796,000 a year, when the Southern Pacific already had a relatively higher shop labor cost than any other railroad in the nation. Although rejecting the demands, Small said he would discuss the issues with representatives of the individual shop crafts.[4]

Union officials noted that, despite Small's alleged willingness to meet with them, the Southern Pacific was building high board fences around a number of its main yards, including Los Angeles, and was hiring men for guard duty. They therefore decided to appeal to the top officials of the Harriman system in the East in an effort to avert a strike. In Chicago, on August 24, Julius Kruttschnitt, vice-president and general manager of maintenance and operations, met J. W. Kline, president of the International Brotherhood of Blacksmiths and Helpers, representing all the shop crafts. Kruttschnitt told Kline that he could not meet with any system federation committee on the issues but would be glad to talk with the international officials of the individual unions. Accordingly, Kline corresponded with the general officers of the machinists, the boilermakers, the carmen, and the sheet metal workers and arranged a conference with Kruttschnitt and officials of the Southern Pacific in San Francisco on September 1, the Harriman system providing free transportation. The conference lasted more than two hours, but the only tangible result was Kruttschnitt's agreement to meet with the separate crafts regarding the demands. He declared, however, that he would risk a strike on the Harriman system rather than negotiate with the system federation.[5]

The time was fast approaching for a showdown. The shop unions had already notified Southern Pacific officials that existing agreements on wages and hours would be canceled in thirty days. Strike votes had already been taken among shop employees on all the roads of the Harriman system, including the Southern Pacific. Although the balloting indicated that the men were strongly in favor of a strike if demands were not met, shopmen in Los Angeles were reported as being for peace. But the Southern Pacific was preparing for war: high fences or stockades around the yards continued to be built; boxcars and cabooses were being fitted out with bunks for possible use by guards and strikebreakers; arc lights were being installed at shop terminals to facilitate night observation. E. E. Calvin, vice-president and general manager of the Southern Pacific, said that his management could not understand why the unions insisted on the federation, but that his line did not intend to meet the wage and hour demands anyway. Kline, speaking for all the shop crafts, insisted that a strike could be avoided only if management recognized the system federation on all the Harriman lines; then the unions would be willing to compromise on the other issues. He pointed out that fifty-two other railroad companies were dealing with system federations without disastrous results.

Kline also raised the question of abolition of the personal record system kept by the Union Pacific and the Southern Pacific, contending that it amounted to a black list. Southern Pacific officials replied that it was necessary in order to administer the pension system voluntarily established by their road. Regardless of the truth of this matter, men continued to be laid off by the Southern Pacific at Los Angeles and other points in the weeks preceding the strike. Such layoffs were supposed to affect first younger men and men without families, and then older men and family heads, but union leaders claimed that this established procedure was not being followed; instead, layoffs were being used as a union-fighting device. Hugh L. Dickson, general counsel of the Brotherhood of Locomotive Firemen and Enginemen, disputed this charge in a statement made at San Bernardino, California, on August 27, in which he expressed his belief that the four organizations of men in train service would not strike, and that the layoffs were legitimate and were dictated entirely by the national decline in railroad business.[6]

The odds on the outcome of a possible strike seemed to favor the railroads. The layoffs created a reservoir of men, some of whom would undoubtedly accept employment in the event of a strike. The decline in operations in 1911 had made it possible to get along with fewer shopmen in the roundhouses. The preparations made by the lines to continue operating during a strike tended to strengthen their position. There was also the possibility that other lines not affected by the dispute would do some shop work for the struck roads. At San Bernardino, for example, the Santa Fe could thus assist the San Pedro, Los Angeles, and Salt Lake line. The *Times* illustrated the odds by a cartoon showing a shopman on the railroad tracks holding a club in the face of a train that was bearing down on him.

That the union leaders realized the difficulties facing them may be seen from the fact that the strike was deferred at least twice. The first deferment set the strike call for September 8; a second postponement pushed it ahead to September 30. In the interim period union officials continued to seek a way to prevent a walkout without retreating from their insistence on recognition of the system federation. They held meetings in both San Francisco and Los Angeles in an effort to assess the situation and to feel the pulse of the rank and file. A minor setback occurred on September 10 when the executive council of the machinists refused to sanction any strike called on the Illinois Central, which, though not a part of the Harriman system, was connected with it at Chicago through the Chicago and Northwestern. On September 26, however, the annual convention of the International Association of Machinists, held at Davenport, Iowa, reversed this stand and voted to support a walkout. This made possible the issuance of a final joint ultimatum to Kruttschnitt, calling a strike for September 30 if he continued to refuse to meet with the unions as a federation.

But Kruttschnitt had already made up his mind. Earlier in the month he had publicly stated that he would not negotiate with the federation and that a strike would fail, as the railroads had men standing by to fill any gaps in the ranks of shopmen. On the eve of the walkout, it was estimated that 35,000 men would be thrown out of work on the Harriman lines alone, and that the Illinois Central would also be affected by a strike to be called simultaneously. E. E. Calvin of the Southern Pacific expressed sympathy for the older men who might join the strike, for they would lose their seniority status and pensions and would have trouble finding other jobs. But the die had been cast, and at 10 A.M. on Saturday, September 30, 1911, the strike was on.[7]

The walkout affected the Illinois Central system from Chicago to New Orleans as well as the Harriman lines to the west. Although the former was not in the Harriman system, the Union Pacific, a component of the latter, owned a large block of its stock. The Harriman system included railroads extending throughout the Pacific Coast and the Southwestern states, reaching east as far as Omaha in the Midwest and New Orleans in the South. A successful strike on both the Harriman and Illinois Central lines could thus strangle the economy of a large part of the United States. In California the main subsidiary lines affected by the walkout were the Southern Pacific; the San Pedro, Los Angeles, and Salt Lake; the Union Pacific; the Central Pacific; the Arizona and Eastern; and the Oregon and California Railroad. The first two lines entered Los Angeles, but the city was also served by the Santa Fe, which was not involved in the dispute and provided a means of contact between southern California and Chicago. The fundamental issue of a system federation was the same for all the lines, though the Illinois Central had several more crafts involved besides the five basic shop groups. These included the steamfitters, the painters, the railway clerks, and several federal labor unions. The clerks went out in advance of the other unions on August 25. A total of more than 40,000 men struck at shops as widely separated as Seattle and Water Valley, Mississippi.[8]

The immediate impact on Los Angeles was the walkout of 1,300 shopmen, including members of Locals No. 115 and 410 of the Brotherhood of Railway Carmen and Locals No. 92 and 529 of the International Brotherhood of Boilermakers and Helpers, as well as workmen affiliated with several other unions. Standard strike benefits were $7 a week for all crafts except the machinists, who were paid $6 a week if single and $8 if married. A mass meeting of all the strikers held at the Labor Temple on the first day of the walkout was attended by an

overflow crowd variously estimated at 1,200 to 2,000 persons, not all
of whom were on strike. Addresses were given by local union leaders
as well as by Job Harriman, candidate for mayor on the socialist ticket.
The *Times* claimed that many of the strikers present were unwilling
participants who were induced to walk out and attend the meeting on
the basis of statements that the men at other shops on the Harriman
system were standing firm on the strike. "When the shopmen learn that
they have been duped to the extent that there are many places where
the strike order had far from unanimous support it may involve the
leaders on a charge of misrepresentation." [9]

The *Times* was partly right; not all the shopmen struck throughout
the system or in Los Angeles, but this did not indicate a lack of support.
Approximately 1,000 of the 1,400 employed at the Los Angeles shops
of the Southern Pacific walked out, and the entire shop force of 300
struck at the nearby yards of the San Pedro, Los Angeles, and Salt
Lake.[10] Although this suggested a high degree of acceptance of the
strike, the *Times,* true to its open-shop tradition, was not ready to
admit that this was so:

As the men left the shops they walked as one walks at a funeral. It was not a
pleasant prospect leaving a remunerative job and agreeable surroundings for
the uncertain future that follows in the wake of a strike. Some are near the
age when the liberal pension policy of the Harriman system would retire
them with an income for the rest of their days; others were thinking of the
rule recently adopted to the effect that inexperienced railroad men over 35
years old will not be taken into the service, and no one over 45 years of age is
eligible for employment.[11]

This statement, and others like it, were calculated to show that the
walkout was a failure from the beginning. On October 2 the *Times*
quoted Calvin of the Southern Pacific as saying that 60 per cent of the
shopmen in his jurisdiction had refused to strike, and that strike
leaders had concentrated their efforts on Los Angeles, selecting it as
the chief battleground. "It is reported in labor-union circles that they
are actually paying some of the men, whom it was hard to drag out,
full wages to remain in idleness and keep away from the shops." [12]

The *Record,* sympathetic to the union cause, reported that 400 of
the strikers in Los Angeles were nonunion men, thus making it difficult
for the roads to recruit strikebreakers. At first little attempt was made
to find replacements, for allegedly the equipment was in excellent
shape and would need little maintenance. The trains were running
on time and, except for pickets, there was little evidence of a dispute.
Strikers picketed the local yards but did not attempt to molest trains

or workers. After a few days, however, both the Southern Pacific and the Salt Lake issued ultimatums to their striking employees to return to work by October 6 or forfeit their seniority and other privileges; nevertheless, nearly all the strikers stayed out. The railroads thereupon set about obtaining replacements to rebuild their shop forces both locally and elsewhere on their lines, though they released statements that their rolling stock was in good condition and that no engine failures had occurred. The unions, on the other hand, claimed just the opposite, ascribing such failures to inadequate and unskilled maintenance crews. Similar charges and countercharges marked the remainder of the year, but the evidence suggests that the strike interfered very little with the operation of trains in and out of Los Angeles.[13]

Little violence developed in Los Angeles in the course of the dispute. In fact, in 1911–1912 only 118 arrests of strikers or their sympathizers were recorded throughout the whole Southern Pacific system. What violence did occur in Los Angeles was minor in character and came only after the strike had been under way for several weeks. The city at this time was occupied with the McNamara trial and the forthcoming mayoralty election, in which Job Harriman was a candidate on the socialist ticket with the support of a large segment of organized labor. Local strike violence would not have been expedient, but it was almost inevitable that sooner or later the city's antipicketing law would be violated. Unfortunately for labor, the first violations took place on November 16, before the municipal election, and involved E. H. Misner, president of the Central Labor Council. Misner and three other men were accused of calling a guard a "scab" and of attempting to lead a mob in attacking him.

Instances of name calling on streetcars, around railroad yards, and on public streets began to be reported as the strike wore on and a settlement was not forthcoming. The managements of the roads refused to meet with the strikers' representatives so long as recognition of the system federation was an issue, and the longer the strike continued, the more successful they were in recruiting strikebreakers. In spite of the fact that there were two large Harriman shops in Los Angeles, a strong open-shop city where excitement was running high over the McNamara trials and the coming election, only one case of actual assault was reported: a sixty-nine-year-old shopworker was beaten on November 4 as he left the yards of the Southern Pacific for his home. There was some doubt that this could be attributed to union thugs, as the *Times* implied, because men nearing retirement age had been permitted by the strikers to remain on their jobs even though such action would normally be called strikebreaking. In this instance, the shopman involved had been with the Southern Pacific for thirty years and was eligible for a pension.[14]

There was violence, however, in areas other than Los Angeles. When the dispute began the Illinois Central obtained a sweeping federal injunction prohibiting strike activity of any kind in the state of Mississippi, but this did not stop strikers from attacking a train carrying "scabs" at McComb; ten strikebreakers were killed and several cars were burned. Other disturbances broke out at Water Valley and New Orleans, and further injunctions were secured in Kentucky and Illinois.

On the Harriman lines, violence occurred at several widely scattered points in the final months of 1911. At Portland, Oregon, a pitched battle took place between thirty nonunion employees of the car shops and pickets camped just outside the stockade entrance. Earlier, air hoses had been cut on fourteen freight cars. Attempts of unionists to persuade strikebreakers to leave their jobs at the Mission Bay shops of the Southern Pacific in San Francisco ended in fist fights between the strikers and the guards. Trouble also developed at Oakland as a result of picket-line provocations. Two unmanned engines were started at Taft, California, and turned loose in the yard but were soon stopped when they struck ore cars on the main line. At nearby Bakersfield, pickets and strikebreakers started brawling in the street, causing the death of an innocent bystander. Beatings were reported at Fresno, California, and Tucson, Arizona. In Houston, Texas, when a train bearing strikebreakers was attacked, one man was killed and another seriously injured. A bomb exploded under a Southern Pacific passenger train in El Paso, but no loss of life was reported. Union leaders claimed that some deaths, which had no relationship to conflict between strikers and strikebreakers, were caused by inadequate maintenance of locomotive boilers. The annual reports of chief inspectors of locomotive boilers to the Interstate Commerce Commission, covering fifteen major railroads in the United States for the period from July 1, 1911, to July 1, 1912, showed forty-three deaths from boiler explosions, thirty-two of them on the Southern Pacific.[15] The latter figure seems too high to have been a mere coincidence.

Although the parties to the dispute did not meet for further discussion of the issues after the strike began on September 30, several efforts were made by or through outsiders to work out a compromise. On October 9, at Reno, Nevada, the local federation of shop employees, claiming that a boiler explosion two days earlier had partly destroyed a roundhouse and seriously injured a worker, asked the federal and state governments to inspect all rolling stock sent out by the Sparks shops of the Southern Pacific. On the same day, at Jackson, Mississippi, President C. H. Markham of the Illinois Central conferred with Governor Noll, but refused to accede to the latter's request to arbitrate the issues. A month later the governors of the states served by both the Illinois Central and the Union Pacific made a joint effort to mediate the dispute, but the railroad managements refused their offer. The employers found themselves increasingly able to run their shops satisfactorily with nonunionists and believed that time was on their side, as the strike was obviously becoming an endurance contest. That the general officers of the unions recognized this was apparent from their appeals to the federal government in December to condemn defective equipment they alleged was being turned out at the shops of all the struck roads.

In Los Angeles the Salt Lake shops illustrated how the railroads had prepared to wait indefinitely for the unions to concede defeat. Manned by 350 nonunion workers, many of whom had been brought in from other cities, these shops were entirely surrounded by a stockade guarded by armed men, hired mainly through detective agencies. The employees worked, ate, and slept in the yards, which, in effect, constituted a completely equipped community. Ample meals were served in a comfortable mess hall under the direction of a steward and a chef, by waiters from the dining-car service. Work clothes were procured at a clothing department, and laundry was taken care of by the railroad. A barber was on duty in a fully appointed shop, and shower baths and other facilities were available. Sleeping quarters were set up in three ventilated, electrically lighted bunkhouses, each served by a janitor who kept the beds in order and maintained a reading room. Doctors from the medical department of the railroad visited the stockade each day. Similar conditions prevailed at other shops of the railroad.[16]

Early in the strike there were periodic rumors in Los Angeles that the dispute would soon be settled. The Harriman lines had been placed on the unfair lists of both the Los Angeles Central Labor Council and the AFL, and constant reference to the walkout was made at the meetings of the local central body. On October 5 strike leaders predicted a settlement in thirty days, claiming that the roads were crippled; President Misner of the Central Labor Council stated that the air brakes on all trains would begin to give out before the end of the month. Two weeks later the morale of the strikers was bolstered by the ill-founded rumor that 1,000 members of Los Angeles lodges of the brotherhoods of conductors, trainmen, engineers, firemen, and telegraphers would strike on November 2, but this was quickly denied by an official of the conductors. The operating unions remained on the job throughout the dispute.[17]

At the end of October the *Times* suggested that the strikers throw in the towel, stating that the shopmen

have gained nothing, and would have gained nothing if the railroad company had succumbed to the demands of the labor leaders and subjected its business to their domination. . . . The strike was ordered not to benefit labor, but to afford larger opportunities for graft and blackmail to the labor leaders.

. . . against their foolish strike The Times warned the shop workers. It besought them not to listen to the leaders who misled them to their undoing. The Times is the friend of workingmen.[18]

But the strikers were not ready to quit. Their families were getting along with strike benefits, and they still looked for a compromise settlement. As the year ended, another rumor predicted that the strike would be over in about a month, but it again proved to be a false hope. The new year saw the beginning of financial hardship for the men. Contributions were sent to Los Angeles strikers from northern California, and a benefit was staged in their behalf in the Labor Temple on May 23, 1912. Men began to seek employment elsewhere or lived off the hope that published statements of leaking locomotive boilers being repaired in Los Angeles with sawdust, bran, manure, and cement were really true.[19]

In June, in an attempt to rally waning support for the strike among other unions in the state, the Los Angeles Central Labor Council passed this resolution:

RESOLVED; That the Federation of Federations of railroad workers request the Central labor [sic] Council of Los Angeles, Cal., to appoint a Committee of Five to act with a like committee from the County General Committee of the Socialist party to arrange a series of Mass Protest Meetings in the large industrial centers of the state in support of striking shopmen on the Harriman and Illinois Central Lines. . . .[20]

The resolution was never effectively implemented—and the strike went on. Early in 1913 Los Angeles labor circles were still expecting victory, but the railroads had long since begun to ignore the dispute. Strikebreakers and nonunionists had acquired the needed skills to keep the rolling stock in repair, and the public hardly seemed aware that a dispute was in progress. Eventually the unions had to recognize the inevitable; on October 31, 1914, the Railway Employees' Department of the AFL discontinued all strike benefits, and eight months later, on June 28, 1915, declared the strike at an end, nearly four years after it began. The announcement received almost no newspaper publicity.

The situation in Los Angeles in the middle of 1914 illustrated the impact of the strike on the participants and their dependents. Although no children were taken from school by families continuing to live in the city, some twenty youngsters were forced into child labor. Two hundred families were broken up and left the city. Many strikers had to sell their homes, and a large number of foreclosures were reported, though not verified. There were no recorded cases of bankruptcy, but approximately twenty-five of garnishment. Loyalty to the walkout thus required sacrifice and suffering.[21]

The basic issue of the strike was recognition of the system federation on the Harriman lines. Before the dispute occurred, Julius Kruttschnitt, conceding that unionism had come to stay, said that he would treat with the shop crafts as individual unions. At the same time M. F. Ryan, international president of the Brotherhood of Railway Carmen, was quoted in the *Times* as saying:

> The concession we ask is nothing but a plain business proposition such as a majority of the big railroad systems have already agreed to. The idea is to save the unions and railroads of the Harriman system money, time and trouble under a plan whereby all five unions in treating with the railroads may be represented by one committee. Heretofore the Harriman system has shown a disposition to play one union against the other.[22]

Kruttschnitt was afraid of the power of a united union organization, however, and risked a strike to retard its development.

The strike failed for a number of reasons. The 1911 slowdown in rail business, with subsequent layoffs all over the nation, contributed to the formation of a skilled labor pool which contained men willing to return to work even when their fellow unionists were walking the picket lines. Moreover, strikebreakers not previously connected with the shop crafts were recruited for positions in roundhouses. Employment agencies were active in cities such as Los Angeles, Chicago, New York, Philadelphia, Baltimore, Bethlehem, Buffalo, and Pittsburgh. Among these were the Frank E. Hannan Company, the Waddell-Mahon Corporation, and the Pinkerton National Detective Agency. Men were furnished at a commission cost of $5 per head plus transportation and subsistence from the point of hiring to the job. The recruiting railroad also paid the expense of rent, advertising, telephone, and other incidentals pertinent to the employment program.

Men were not hired indiscriminately, but were usually examined physically as well as with reference to their level of skill. Usually they were informed that they were taking the places of strikers, though an

exception occurred in Los Angeles. In 1914 the Municipal Employment Bureau, assisted by the employment officers of some of the
fraternal orders in the area, procured an average of three mechanics
a day for the roads. But the bureau had not told some of the men,
especially a group sent to the Salt Lake shops in Las Vegas, Nevada,
that they were replacing strikers. Councilman Fred C. Wheeler, socialist
and former president of the Central Labor Council, blasted this
practice. The resulting scandal caused the Municipal Employment
Bureau to make certain that a potential worker knew that a dispute
was in progress before accepting a position in a struck plant.[23]

An alleged reason for the failure of the strike was the reluctance of
many shopmen fully to support the walkout. The *Times* claimed that
this was true in Los Angeles, and there were indications that it had
occurred elsewhere. Complaints were made, for example, that the vote
taken among roundhouse workers in Bakersfield, Tucson, and Las
Vegas was not on the strike question, but rather on whether or not to
give leaders authority to deal with management concerning recognition
of the federation. The workers allegedly were given to understand that
a good bluff would win the day and that a strike would not be necessary. The fact that the ballot results were not announced in Los
Angeles gave rise to the conjecture that the shopmen were not even
in favor of a bluff.

On his return from a trip to Chicago early in the dispute, John J.
Byrne, assistant passenger traffic manager for the Santa Fe in Los
Angeles, stated that the strike had been called against the better judgment of top union leaders. Supposedly they had done their best to
prevent the walkout, but had lost the ball to younger subsidiary
officials who were eager for a trial of strength. Realizing that falling
earnings and declining employment, together with the possibility of
lower tariff rates, would not predispose the railroads to raise wages,
the leaders emphasized recognition of the federation as the main issue.[24]
Some lack of support from the ranks even on this question was indicated by W. L. Park, vice-president of the machinists' local at Paducah,
Kentucky, on the Illinois Central system. In a telegram sent to President James O'Connell of the International Association of Machinists
early in October, 1911, Park claimed the strike ballot had been illegal.

It was claimed . . . that it was not a strike vote, that it was only to show the
company the strength of the movement. The matter of becoming members of
the so-called federation was not put to us for a vote. This ballot was not taken
at a machinists' meeting. Machinists were not allowed to discuss the question.
Men who were not members of our organization were allowed in the meeting

and they were the only ones allowed to talk on the subject. They did not ascertain whether the men who voted were members of our organization, if so, let them produce the ballot. We have positive proof that some men voted who were not eligible to vote.[25]

Although the strike failed to win recognition of the system federation, it may be argued that it was only a little premature and that it had been called at the wrong time. The unions were temporarily weakened but the railroads did not take advantage of that fact to impose lower wages or poorer working conditions on the shopmen. On a few lines, such as the Union Pacific, a virtual open shop existed for a number of years after the strike. The Railway Employees' Department, however, took an optimistic view in its report to the 1915 AFL convention:

The Department was instrumental in securing and having secured valuable data in connection with the cause and effect of the Harriman and Illinois Central Strike, inaugurated September 30, 1911, and presented same at the hearings before the Commission on Industrial Relations, which consumed four days in taking evidence. We feel assured that through the report of the Commission to Congress, the public will learn the truth and the position of the men will be vindicated, and it is our hope and belief that their report will result in the enactment of legislation that will make for industrial peace, and that will make secure the rights of the wage-earner.[26]

Out of their experience in this and other disputes, railroad workers began to forge a more militant philosophy which became increasingly evident in World War I and subsequent years. Government operation of the railroads during the war enabled the shopworkers to secure national agreements similar to those that had long been in force for the operating brotherhoods.[27]

2. The Engineers' Dispute and Its Aftermath, 1913-1917

Although the operating brotherhoods did not take an active part in the shopmen's strike against the Harriman and Illinois Central systems, they were far from quiescent in their own behalf. Like the shopmen, their members were increasingly restive in the face of alleged injustices centering mainly on their need for higher wages to meet the rising cost of living after the panic of 1907. At this time the basic law designed to handle grievances between railroads and their train-service or operating employees was the Erdman Act of 1898. Under it the commissioner of labor and the chairman of the Interstate Commerce Commission mediated disputes, though voluntary arbitration by a board of three persons was an alternative procedure. Because of growing labor dissatisfaction and antagonism after the panic of 1907, Congress amended the 1898 law by the Newlands Act of 1913, which established a permanent board of arbitration with power to take the initiative in disputes between the railroads and their operating employees. It also provided for temporary boards of arbitration of either three or six persons who, by majority vote, could make an award of the permanent board binding and to whom all unsettled questions arising from the award had to be referred.[28]

The operating brotherhoods were far from satisfied with arbitration procedures under the federal law. In 1913 their discontent resulted in a major move by engineers, firemen, and hostlers of ninety-eight railroads west of Chicago, nearly every line west of Ft. William, Ontario, and the Illinois Central, to press for increased and standardized wages and improved working conditions. The men pointed out that their last wage increase had been a 10 per cent boost in 1910, yet their job responsibilities had become heavier and the cost of living had continued to rise. They further alleged that, despite increasing profits, the railroads had not shown proper regard for the welfare of their employees. Some 55,000 men were behind the move, operating the rolling stock on 140,000 miles of track. All three of the railroads entering Los Angeles—Southern Pacific, Santa Fe, and Salt Lake—would be affected if the threatened dispute materialized.

Negotiations proceeded for three months, until October, but the managements would not submit to the demands for wage increases, claiming that they would amount to a 50 per cent rise in labor costs, or a total of $33 million. The main issue was the request for an eight-hour day to replace the current ten-hour day. The companies contended that reduction of the workday would necessitate shortening all railroad divisions and relocating yards and shops, and that the cost would be prohibitive. To management, therefore, the wage demands were really hidden demands for overtime. On October 12 both sides agreed to arbitration, though the engineers had previously refused to consider such action. They claimed that the rail managements had emasculated earlier arbitration decisions, as they were not court orders, either by ignoring them completely or by interpreting them to suit themselves. The negotiating committee for the unions, however, believing that adverse public relations might result from their unwillingness to use arbitration, agreed to try it once again. The obvious failure of the Harriman system shopmen's strike and the existence of a recession at this time may also have influenced their decision.[29]

The agreement to submit the dispute to arbitration did not deter train-service employees from striking on the Southern Pacific lines between El Paso and New Orleans. Engineers, firemen, trainmen, and conductors went out for five days in November, 1913, over wage demands and grievances including alleged breach of contract and the company's refusal to treat with a joint committee of the brotherhoods. Although the strike did not spread to California, the resulting traffic tie-up backed up shipments all the way to San Francisco. Passenger service from that city to New Orleans through Los Angeles was reduced to one train a day each way, and freight traffic delays caused serious uneasiness in the sugar-beet and rice industries. Federal arbitration ended the strike, however, and the men returned to work without prejudice.[30]

The arbitration decisions both in this case and in the engineers' dispute with the Western railroads pleased neither side and failed to end the unrest. By 1915 labor leaders were calling for congressional investigation of the arbitration procedure as well as for repeal of the Newlands Act. As living costs continued to rise, the train-service brotherhoods, conscious of their power, became more vocal in demanding the eight-hour day with time and a half for overtime. The war in Europe had stimulated industrial activity in the United States, and rail traffic had rapidly increased in volume. The financial reports of the carriers began to look very favorable, as operating costs did not start to rise until the latter part of 1916. In September, 1916, for example, the Southern Pacific reported gross earnings of $152,694,228.19 for a twelve-month period, more than $22 million above those of the preceding year.[31]

The "Big Four" brotherhoods of locomotive engineers, firemen, conductors, and trainmen, well aware of the rising profit margins of the carriers, sought further wage adjustments as well as the eight-hour day. When negotiations between the brotherhoods and management committees throughout the early months of 1916 proved fruitless, the companies offered to submit the differences to arbitration, but the union leaders had lost confidence in this method of settling disputes and threatened to strike. Fears were voiced in some parts of the country, including Los Angeles, concerning the effects of a strike on areas that depended heavily on the railroads for key food items. President Wilson thereupon invited both parties to a conference in Washington, at which he proposed that the eight-hour day be adopted with pro rata pay for overtime. He offered to appoint a commission to study the results of the change and to make suggestions for such financial relief for the carriers as might be necessary to overcome the added costs. When the management representatives rejected the President's suggestions, the unions promptly called a nationwide strike for September 4. The President then took the problem to the Congress on August 29, asking for an eight-hour law. Congress responded on September 2 by passing the Adamson Act, which, among other things, established the eight-hour day on American railroads as of January 1, 1917. This effectively canceled the strike.[32]

The railroad managements, however, were not ready to accept what they considered a highhanded action to force them into a wage settlement. Declaring the law unconstitutional, the Burlington, Santa Fe, and Union Pacific railroads filed suits in various federal district courts against application of the law. Defendants in Los Angeles included Albert Schoonover, United States district attorney for the Southern District of California, and seven local officials of the operating brotherhoods. As the court cases dragged on, the Big Four again threatened to strike 250,000 miles of rail lines on March 15, 1917, if their demands were not met and the Adamson Act was not enforced. Officials of the Southern Pacific met in San Francisco to organize a freight embargo should the dispute erupt and the trains cease to roll. The brotherhoods postponed their strike until March 19. On the morning before it was to take effect the railroads decided to yield, and that same afternoon the United States Supreme Court declared the Adamson Act constitutional.

Thus for a time the nation was spared a railroad walkout. In Los Angeles, there was rejoicing that the city would not be shut off from the rest of the country, but there was no evidence that open-shop adherents supported the rail managements' decision.[33] As one observer said, "Never had such a sweeping labor victory been achieved at virtually no cost in wages lost or loss of public good will." [34] Shortly thereafter the United States entered the war, and on January 1, 1918, the federal government took over operation of the rail lines. The unrest among steam railroad workers, however, was only temporarily stayed.

3. Los Angeles Railway and Pacific Electric Railway, 1914–1919

Like their brethren on the interstate railroads, the train-service employees of the interurban Pacific Electric Railway and intracity Los Angeles Railway wanted to improve their wages and working conditions in the prewar and war years. Unlike their brethren, they did not have the force of union organization behind their efforts. Both the local railways were completely dominated by the open-shop philosophy, and it was the firm intention of their managements to keep them that way. Early attempts had been made to organize the platform employees of both electric lines. The low wages of 18 to 22.5 cents an hour paid to crews on the cars of a predecessor corporation, the Los Angeles Cable Railway, precipitated a dispute in December, 1889, when the carmen formed an organization to protest to the management. The railway officials posted notices threatening a lockout unless the men abandoned the union. After three months of uncertainty, the carmen yielded and all employees except those the management chose to call agitators remained with the company.

Thirteen years later, in February, 1903, organizers from the Amalgamated Association of Street and Electric Railway Employees began working among motormen and conductors on the Pacific Electric and Los Angeles railways. Little came of the organizing effort; as soon as the managements learned of it, sixty-eight men who had allegedly joined the union were discharged. Two months later Lemuel D. Biddle, an active organizer and leader in the city's labor movement, led 500 Mexican track laborers of the Pacific Electric in a strike for a wage increase. At first the company granted the demand, unaware that an organizer not in its employ was behind the move. When it discovered that fact, however, it canceled the raise and brought in laborers to replace those who had walked out. Later the same month six motormen and four conductors on the Los Angeles Railway pulled a "quickie" strike at Fifth and Spring streets at the evening rush hour. The motormen carried the handles of their controllers and air brakes with them, causing a delay in moving the cars. They also tried to get other crews to leave their posts, but police officers soon arrived and restored order. The sole demand was recognition of the union. A few more men struck later in the evening, but by the next morning all cars were moving normally and the strike was over. Thirteen men lost their jobs as a result of their participation in this unsuccessful walkout.[35]

Working hours and wages seem to have been a frequent source of irritation to the platform men employed by the Los Angeles Railway. Although the odds were much against a successful labor organization, the nucleus of a union developed in 1911 in the form of Carmen's Local No. 410, an affiliate of the Central Labor Council. Several attempts to reduce the long hours were made on a state-wide basis in the form of legislative bills making a ten-hour day mandatory on local and interurban lines. Measures introduced in 1909 and 1913 failed to pass. In both years the management of the Los Angeles Railway obtained between 2,000 and 3,000 employee signatures on petitions against the bills, and sent delegations of men at its expense to Sacramento to protest their passage. Testimony before the United States Commission on Industrial Relations in September, 1914, revealed that the carmen actually wanted the measures passed but were afraid of losing their jobs if they openly supported them. The petitions against the bills were signed because company inspectors presented them directly to conductors and motormen with the implication "if they didn't sign them to look out." [36] A very few carmen opposed the bills because they believed that the shorter hours would not be accompanied by any increase in hourly wages and thus would reduce their take-home pay. A serious accident on the Pacific Electric Railway in 1913 caused the *Record* publicly to support reduced hours and better wages for carmen. In a series of editorials it pointed out that fatigue due to excessively long hours had probably contributed to the accident. Recommendations for relief included both union organization to break the grip of the open shop and municipal ownership of city and interurban lines.[37]

The working conditions of conductors and motormen on the Los Angeles Railway in 1914 were publicized in testimony before the Commission on Industrial Relations. There were two groups of employees: 2,248 "regulars" and 222 "extras." The regular men worked from eight to eleven hours on a run, but the problem of peak and off-peak loads meant breaks in their shifts. Thus, as many as fifteen hours might be necessary to complete a shift in any one day. Most runs required between nine and ten hours on a car platform without any regular days off. Men could work 30 days a month and 365 days a year if they wished, as vacations with pay were unknown. Those who worked Sunday runs usually took about two days off each month. Runs that did not have a Sunday schedule were considered choice assignments. About 700 cars were operated daily during the week from five division points, the choice of runs being decided on the basis of seniority within each division.[38]

All platform employees had to buy their own uniforms at a cost of $18 each. At the time of hiring, about half the men also had to purchase a watch, costing approximately $25, which would meet minimum time standards; cleaning of this timepiece was required every fifteen months. A physical examination by a company physician was mandatory for an applicant; if he passed, he was charged $1 and placed on a waiting list. He also had to pay 50 cents for a photograph to be included in his personal record. When an applicant started training for platform work, he was required to take out a $500 bond, at a charge of $2.50 each year, and to make the initial monthly contribution of 50 cents to a company-operated health fund, which gave him some hospitalization protection. He was not paid while learning to operate the car, the average time required for this process being twelve days. After running the gauntlet of these preliminary charges, the newly employed motorman or conductor was entitled to a beginning wage of 25 cents an hour for the first year, as indicated in the following schedule of hourly rates for platform men on the Los Angeles Railway in 1914:[39]

1st year	25¢
2d year	26
3d year	27
4th year	28
5th year	29
6th year and thereafter	30

Although these wages seemed low, they were not out of line with those paid in other large cities. In St. Paul, Minneapolis, Chicago, Denver, and Portland, hourly wages ranged from a minimum of 23 cents for the first three months to 32 cents in the sixth year of employment. In San Francisco and Seattle the starting pay was 25 cents, but in Oakland it was 30 cents; the maximum was 35 cents in the ninth year in San Francisco, 31 cents in the fourteenth year in Seattle, and 40 cents in the eleventh year in Oakland. Lower wages were paid in Los Angeles, however, than in the three California cities where effective carmen's unions were functioning. Except for the San Francisco municipal line, which was on an eight-hour day, all regular platform employees in the unionized cities worked nine- or ten-hour shifts and put in between sixty and seventy hours per week—schedules similar to those in Los Angeles.[40]

Most of the complaints concerning wages and working conditions on the Los Angeles Railway came from the "extra" or "stand-by" men. These were the most recent employees who hoped to be put on a regular run. Usually they remained in the stand-by category for a period ranging from four months to a little more than a year. H. H. Lyon, an assistant deputy labor commissioner of California, told the Commission on Industrial Relations that extra men usually reported to the carbarns for duty at 4:40 A.M., waited an hour or two for their first assignment, and worked for perhaps four or five hours in total during rush periods and on special runs, possibly finishing their day's work as late as 10 or 11 P.M. They earned about $1.75 per day or less. Some men, kept at the carbarns by the foremen for several hours at 15 cents an hour, sent out on a run for an hour and a half, and then dismissed, earned as little as 90 cents a day. The only law that applied to the length of their workday was one limiting the total hours actually worked to sixteen. A. B. Merrihew, assistant superintendent of the Los Angeles Railway, testified that he sought to keep the number of extra men as small as possible in order to maximize their working hours.

In reply to queries concerning disciplinary procedure, Merrihew stated that the railway used a modified form of the Brown merit and demerit system. A man who broke a rule was spoken to by an official, and his record was charged with either a caution or a notation that he had been given five days' suspension. He did not actually cease work nor did he lose any pay, but the remarks on his record did affect his chances for promotion. According to Merrihew, there was no rule that so many demerits or "Brownies" resulted in discharge; but neither could a man, even if his subsequent record was clear, wipe out his Brownies. It was possible, however, for a man to receive merit credits and to have access to his record. Lyon differed with Merrihew as to the relationship between demerits and discharge, pointing out that two or three Brownies could result in a man's being laid off because there were plenty of others seeking employment.[41]

There was little doubt that in 1914 both the Pacific Electric and the Los Angeles railways were open shops. The question as to whether or not they were antiunion left some room for argument. It was alleged that the Pacific Electric occasionally fired men who had taken part in union activities in Los Angeles or elsewhere. Its president, Paul Shoup, definitely supported the open shop, and was accused by labor leaders of seeking to keep union members in check. In June, 1914, however, about 75 per cent of the 250 train-service employees in the freight division of the Pacific Electric belonged to the Brotherhood of Railroad Trainmen or the Order of Railway Conductors, a fact known to management for some time. In September, 1913, management had instituted examinations covering rules of operation in the freight system, and some of the men who failed the examination had been discharged. Labor sympathizers claimed that the tests were being used as a means of weeding out union men.

Lyon, in his testimony before the commission, ventured the opinion that neither the Los Angeles Railway nor the Pacific Electric would knowingly hire union men. The application blank for motormen and conductors used by the Los Angeles Railway did in fact ask whether or not the prospect had ever been a member of any labor organization and, if so, which one, its location, and the date of joining it. In his testimony G. J. Kuhrts, the company's chief engineer, denied that a man who said he was a union member would not be employed, but he added that the railway management would meet with its employees on grievance matters only as individuals or as representatives of non-union groups within the company. The Los Angeles Railway did have an employee organization, but it was strictly a social club which sponsored smokers, picnics, dances, and discussions. The members were regular employees and department heads.[42] It was the position of management that "As a public service corporation and directly responsible to the community at large, we object to the union organizations attempting to dictate to employees or discipline them without responsibility." [43]

Although most attempts to organize city and interurban railway workers before 1915 failed, the unions would not admit defeat. The stepped-up organizing drives in other trades in the war years encouraged the platform men to continue to seek union recognition. As the Pacific Electric Railway was controlled by the Southern Pacific and had interconnections with the steam lines for the movement of freight cars, its train-service employees logically came under the organizing jurisdictions of the rail brotherhoods. The platform men of the Los Angeles Railway, on the other hand, fell more naturally within the sphere of the Amalgamated Association of Street and Electric Railway Employees. After testimony on wages and working conditions on the streetcar line was presented to the Commission on Industrial Relations in 1914, further attempts were made to organize its employees, but they ended in dismal failure in 1915. The open-shop system was too firmly entrenched to be overcome without a bitter struggle.[44]

In the next three years the Los Angeles Railway granted its platform men a series of wage increases which followed the rise in the cost of living. By the middle of 1918 the hourly minimum of 25 cents and the maximum of 30 cents had been increased to 38 and 44.5 cents, respectively. In July, 1917, the Amalgamated Association of Street and Electric Railway Employees conducted a strike against the United Railways in San Francisco under the leadership of Ben F. Bowbeer, one of its vice-presidents and its Pacific Coast representative. When this strike failed, Bowbeer went to Los Angeles and began secretly to organize a local of the Amalgamated among employees of the Los Angeles Railway who were not satisfied with the wage increases. By August, 1918, the organizing activities were no longer a secret. Estimates of the number of men who had joined Los Angeles Division 835 of the Amalgamated varied from 200 to more than 1,000. On August 10 the new union held an all-night mass meeting at Burbank Hall. The *Times* reported the meeting as a failure, indicating that lack of attendance delayed the opening from 8 until 9:30 P.M., by which time only sixty-seven men were in the hall.[45] The superintendent of the Los Angeles Railway did not take the union activities seriously:

I expected nothing less than this when I learned that Bowbeer had arrived in our midst. The men in our employ are receiving the same splendid wage that is paid by the Pacific Electric Railway. It hasn't been a month since we voluntarily gave the man increase [*sic*], and I am sure they have no grievance to air.[46]

The *Times* had underestimated Bowbeer's effectiveness as a leader. New members continued to enter Division 835; by September 13, it was reported that 60 per cent of the platform men of the Los Angeles Railway had joined the union and had elected their first set of officers. A few weeks later, it was claimed that 75 per cent of them had joined, and shortly thereafter representatives of Division 835 presented a petition to the National War Labor Board requesting an eight-hour day and an increase in wages. At hearings held in Los Angeles in December, 1918, before examiners W. R. Kelley and Raymond E. Swing, the carmen charged the Los Angeles Railway with discrimination against applicants for employment who were members of the Amalgamated. The company denied this and also contended that the board lacked jurisdiction over a purely intrastate firm. After the hearings the examiners took the case under advisement, and the union continued to add members. In April, 1919, the board awarded wage increases to the employees of several street rail lines in the state, including the Pacific Electric and Los Angeles railways, but turned down the request for an eight-hour day. It recommended that motormen and conductors of the Los Angeles Railway be paid 41 cents an hour for the first three months, 43 cents for the next nine months, and 45 cents thereafter. The board, finding that the company did not have a collective bargaining system that permitted the employees free and unhampered discussion of their grievances, also ordered the reinstatement of two men allegedly discharged for union activity.[47]

The hearings and the subsequent decision proved virtually worthless, as the management of the Los Angeles Railway refused to follow the recommendations. A seven-man committee chosen by 700 employees tried to see company officials about the matters in dispute, but its request was denied on the ground that it really represented the Amalgamated. Two months later the railway's linemen, who were members of Local No. 61 of the International Brotherhood of Electrical Workers, struck for an increase in wages from $4.40 to $6 per day. As if to emphasize its open-shop position, the management immediately replaced the strikers and service continued without interruption. At the end of June a letter from Kuhrts, by then general manager, addressed to Roland P. Dix, chairman of the employees' committee, was posted at all division carbarns. The letter made it clear that management would discuss grievances only with its own employees and not with any group representing Division 835 of the Amalgamated. It further stated that any wage increase would be impossible until the State Railroad Commission had finished a survey of the company's financial condition in an attempt to forestall a fare increase through economies of operation. The committee, in turn, pointed out that it had been selected at a meeting of both union and nonunion platform men and was thus truly representative of the employees; moreover, it was not asking for recognition of the union but only for the right to be recognized as a legitimately constituted employee group set up for bargaining purposes. As it was also claimed, however, that 85 per cent of the carmen belonged to Division 835, management could hardly fail to conclude that recognition of the committee was tantamount to recognition of the union.[48]

On July 3, in view of the adamant position taken in Kuhrts's letter, the committee asked for a vote of confidence and received support for the continuance of further negotiations by a three-to-one majority. It also asked the State Railroad Commission whether or not a wage increase had to be held in abeyance pending the financial investigation of the company. The commission's reply denied that the railway had to await completion of the investigation before negotiating on a wage increase, and asked that the company publicize this fact. Shortly thereafter, management announced a 3-cent hourly pay increase effective July 30 for all conductors and motormen, which, in effect, instituted the April wage recommendations of the National War Labor Board. The starting rate was raised to 41 cents an hour and the top of the range to 47 cents instead of the suggested 45. Pointing out that the company thus went beyond the board's recommendations, Kuhrts stated that wages had been raised eight times in the past two years and four months, or an aggregate of 56.6 per cent for those in service three years or more and 64 per cent for beginners. Extra men were guaranteed $100 a month, but many of them earned $130 to $150.

The union, however, still maintained that the company had not met the NWLB recommendations because it remained an open-shop firm and refused to recognize the employees' committee as collective bargaining agent. A letter was therefore sent to Kuhrts demanding 75 cents an hour for platform men, the eight-hour day with time and a half for overtime, a genuine collective bargaining procedure, and a wage increase for car repairers proportionate to that received by the platform men. The letter also stated that a strike would not occur and the demands would be compromised if Kuhrts would meet with the committee and agree to put into effect *all* the recommendations of the board. An answer was requested by August 15 if the company did not want a strike. Kuhrts replied that 75 cents an hour was impossible, but that he would meet with a true employees' committee that did not really represent Division 835. Meanwhile, 50 special officers were sworn in for work with the railway, and about 150 extra men from distant points were trained for duty on the cars in the event of a strike. In view of Kuhrts's reply, the employees' committee conducted a strike vote and at 12:30 A.M. on August 16, 1919, announced that 77 per cent of the 1,590 platform men who cast ballots had voted to walk out at 2 A.M. So began a strike that was also to involve the Pacific Electric Railway as well as employees of the steam lines running into the city.[49]

Although the Pacific Electric and Los Angeles railways faced different labor organizations, their other interests often coincided. For some years both had been opposing the so-called "jitney" buses, passenger motor vehicles usually operated by their owners and not subject to regulation by the State Railroad Commission. They followed routes that often paralleled existing streetcar lines and thus competed with the Los Angeles Railway and, to some degree, with the Pacific Electric. The managements of the roads jointly claimed that by June, 1915, they were forced to lay off nearly 1,000 men because of the jitneys. They charged that the buses obstructed traffic and prevented passengers from crossing from the curb to waiting streetcars, and that the drivers even opened the doors of their obstructing vehicles to encourage passengers to ride with them. The two railways lobbied extensively to have the City Council regulate the jitney buses. In September, 1916, the council turned down proposed legislation requiring jitney operators to post an $11,000 bond, but a month later it placed the buses under the jurisdiction of the city's Board of Public Utilities. To win more support for its antijitney campaign, the management of the Los Angeles Railway told its employees that wage increases would depend, at least in part, on getting rid of jitney competition. At a protest meeting held late in March, 1917, the employees threatened to strike unless city authorities would put the jitneys out of operation. Organized labor leaders called those who attended the meeting "Huntington's street-car slaves," meaning that they were merely tools of Henry E. Huntington in the jitney war, whereas the real solution to their troubles was to join a trade union.[50]

Six weeks later, on May 3, 1917, the Los Angeles Railway gave its platform men a cost-of-living increase of 7.5 per cent and promised them a like amount when jitney-bus competition would be curbed. It complained that it was losing more than $750,000 a year to benefit 350 jitney drivers, at the expense of its own 3,500 carmen. The management also alleged that it was limited by law to a 5-cent fare and thus could not raise its rates to cover a wage increase, implying that removal of competition would permit higher pay. In October the City Council refused to place on the November ballot a proposed ordinance that would have permitted an extension of jitney-bus operation on downtown streets. In the remaining months of the war, as noted above, the Amalgamated Association of Street and Electric Railway Employees sought to organize the platform men to seek improvement in their wages and working conditions directly, rather than through support of jitney-bus regulation. Although management was thus no longer able to utilize employees in the antijitney campaign, the Board of Public Utilities on July 15, 1918, eliminated jitney-bus operation over routes paralleling streetcar lines, effective August 1. The main reason, however, was to reduce economic waste during the war rather than to help the railways or their employees. The latter sought solution of their grievances through the unions, which were steadily growing stronger and which were to reach their apogee in the strike of August, 1919.[51]

More than two years before, or early in 1917, the Pacific Electric Railway had unsuccessfully requested a fare increase from the State Railroad Commission on the ground that its gross income was a million dollars below expenses, largely because of jitney-bus competition. In the next eighteen months, however, unlike the Los Angeles Railway, the Pacific Electric did not try to use its employees in the antijitney campaign as a way of forestalling formation of Lodge 808 of the

Brotherhood of Railroad Trainmen (BRT). Instead, the company opposed the union directly and maintained the open shop by discharging, for allegedly unsatisfactory service records, men who were strong union supporters. But the unionists were not to be denied. Like their fellow carmen on the Los Angeles Railway, and indeed like rail workers all over the nation, they wanted redress of their grievances and found their best prospect in the encouragement given to labor organizations in the war years. In May and June, 1918, therefore, the BRT, under the leadership of A. B. Miller of the Cleveland Lodge, made rapid strides in organizing the platform men of the Pacific Electric, despite the hostility of management.

The company sought to retard the union's efforts by granting a wage increase of approximately 3.5 cents an hour early in June, but the men believed they could get 12.5 cents more through their organization. Paul Shoup, president of the railway, in a desperate attempt to head off the union, presented his views on unionization to 1,500 employees at the Pacific Club on the evening of June 4. Pointing out that the company had granted wage increases totaling 10 cents an hour since the previous December, he said that another boost in pay only awaited action by the State Railroad Commission. Thus the basic rate for new men had been increased from 25 to 35.5 cents an hour in six months. Shoup did not believe "that those of us placed in a supervisional position were indifferent or not inclined to help. . . . Personally, I hardly know whether I would rather be a freight motorman or president of the company." [52]

On July 1, 1918, full-page advertisements in the city's newspapers contained a letter from Shoup to his employees. He asserted that union activity leading to a strike would aid the Germans, cripple the transportation system of the Los Angeles area in time of war, and harm army and navy operations at the harbor. He pointed out that wages had been fixed on the exact basis adopted by the director-general of the federalized railroads, even though the Pacific Electric, as an intrastate line, was not subject to federal regulation. Shoup continued:

You have been asked by outside steam line union agitators to strike, with no reason except to secure recognition of unions. . . .

Your wages have been raised five times voluntarily in thirty months—you who were in service in December, 1915, are getting on the average more than 40% increase since that date.

You are making on the average in street car service $125 a month; interurban passenger service $135 per month, and in freight service $167 per month.[53]

On June 29, just before publication of Shoup's letter, the union had taken a sealed-ballot vote on whether or not to strike for recognition, with the further proviso that a wage increase would also be sought if the company locked out its employees. Organizers for the brotherhood claimed the support of nearly 1,000 of the 1,500 motormen and conductors currently employed, though the actual membership of Lodge 808 was 655 men. The results of the ballot, announced early on July 2, favored a strike beginning at 7 P.M. that day if Shoup failed to recognize the new local lodge, as requested in a formal demand to be served on him at 1:30 P.M. The demand was signed by J. A. Farquharson, a vice-president of the Brotherhood of Railroad Trainmen, and W. E. Montgomery, an assistant to the grand chief of the Brotherhood of Locomotive Engineers, who was helping in the organizing effort. Referring to previous futile efforts to secure a conference with Shoup, Farquharson and Montgomery stated that employees of the Pacific Electric had been forced to seek union help because of vigorous persecution by the management. They accused the company of paying wages so low that its men could not earn a living without working excessively long hours, and of following an established policy of locking out its union employees. The two organizers denied that a walkout would harm the war effort, for the shipbuilding firms at the harbor were also served by steam lines that would not be affected by a strike.[54]

At 7 P.M., five and a half hours after the formal demand was served on Shoup, the 400 men then on duty on Pacific Electric trains began walking off their jobs when they reached their terminals. A few minutes after the strike started, however, the company's legal division obtained a temporary injunction from Judge Benjamin F. Bledsoe which, in effect, forbade continuance of the strike. The judge declared that employers had the right to conduct their businesses as they wished without outside union, or third-party, interference; that the Pacific Electric, through years of adherence to an open-shop policy, had the legal right to protect that policy as well as to resist any interference with it; that the employees had a right to quit work, but they had long accepted the open shop as a tacit condition of employment by the railway; and that therefore instigation of a strike to unionize the company by a third party such as the union was equivalent to forcible entry into the house of a private citizen. The judge also held that it was impossible to conduct a strike without violence and intimidation, and that this walkout, in particular, would interfere with shipbuilding and thus be unpatriotic. The injunction was made returnable on July 10, at which time it would be decided whether or not to make it permanent.[55]

The Pacific Electric, the city police, and the armed services were all prepared for the strike. When union men left their jobs, most of their places were immediately filled by nonstrikers, largely imported strike-breakers; extra men; or office employees familiar with the work. The last group comprised operators, assistant superintendents, dispatchers, agents, and others who had been promoted from the ranks of trainmen. City and interurban traffic in some places, such as the Santa Monica Bay district, San Bernardino, and Glendale, was badly hampered, but most trains on other lines were kept running. Just before 7 P.M., Los Angeles police detachments had been placed on a twenty-four-hour reserve basis; vacations and days off had been canceled and men on vacation called back. Those on duty were ordered not to take sides but only to preserve order and protect life and property. The city prosecutor stated that the antipicketing ordinance would be construed leniently as long as there was no violence or undue trouble.

On being advised of the imminence of a strike, Commander H. C. Poundstone of the submarine base at Los Angeles Harbor, senior officer on duty at San Pedro, had taken steps to ensure adequate service between Los Angeles and Long Beach, San Pedro, Arcadia, and Redondo Beach, where federal activities or military bases were located. At 6:30 P.M., just before the walkout, four armed sailors from the naval training station were placed on every operating red car, two at each end; each man was equipped with a rifle with fixed bayonet and a revolver. By 8 P.M. more than 250 such guards were on the cars, and naval officers were in charge of passenger stations at the outer harbor and Long Beach. Commander Poundstone also posted conspicuous notices at division points to the effect that the government intended both to ensure the free movement of mail, troops, munitions, and military stores, and to prevent any interruption of shipbuilding. As a result, only a few demonstrations occurred. In Los Angeles about 150 union men sought to keep shipyard workers from starting for San Pedro in a special car. Yelling "Don't ride scab cars. You take your lives in your hands . . . ," they succeeded in discouraging a few workers. Similar action was taken at 11:20 P.M., when the regular train left for San Pedro. Unionists employed in harbor shipbuilding plants tried to picket the Long Beach Pacific Electric station, where about 2,000 of the curious had gathered to watch the goings on, but the sailors on duty kept the crowd moving and prevented disorder.[56]

When news of the injunction reached a late evening meeting of the strikers, they decided to call off the walkout until after a federal investigation, despite fear that the delay would give management time to consolidate its position. Accordingly, the strike was lifted at 11:30 P.M., four and a half hours after it began, and the next day, July 3, the men returned to their jobs. That same day Governor Stephens appointed a committee of local citizens to make an immediate investigation of the dispute. The committee, composed of Dr. John R. Haynes, former senator Frank P. Flint, and Seth Brown, president of the Central Labor Council, met that afternoon with union officials and representatives of the railway and then telegraphed its findings to the governor. The National War Labor Board also entered the dispute on July 3 in the person of a federal mediator, Captain Charles T. Connell. After acquainting all parties involved with the methods and procedures of the board, Connell sought to begin mediation.[57]

Meanwhile, officials of the Brotherhood of Railroad Trainmen asked Judge Bledsoe to lift the temporary injunction. The judge replied that if they would appear with their attorneys on July 5, after first giving legal notice to the Pacific Electric Railway, he would reconsider the injunction. When the union and management representatives appeared before him, he listened to their arguments, but three days later reiterated his earlier stand. On July 10 he made the injunction permanent, basing his decision on the Hitchman Coal and Coke Company case of 1917. "A company has the right of law and the right of property just as much as it has the right to exist," declared Bledsoe, "and it has the right to conduct its business as an open shop if it chooses to do so." He also remarked that peaceful persuasion was not forbidden so long as a strike or other interference with the company's operations did not ensue.[58]

President Shoup, however, had no intention of accepting mediation when a union was involved or of ceasing to operate his company as an open shop. He stood firm on his interpretation of President Wilson's proclamation of April 4, 1918, concerning the National War Labor Board, which he construed to mean that "an employer not heretofore recognizing unions need not do so during the war and that coercion shall not be used either to make the employees join unions or secure recognition." Shoup was supported by a strong tide of public opinion against the strike. The Long Beach draft board, for example, asked for the names of all strikers under a "work or fight" mandate, even though the union claimed that it had made arrangements for the Southern Pacific and Salt Lake railroads to transport shipyard workers during the dispute. After assessing the situation, therefore, union leaders decided to delay further direct action, but to continue their organizing activities and prepare their case for presentation to the National War Labor Board.[59]

Shortly after the injunction was made permanent, complaints that some strikers had not been rehired reached the ears of Judge Bledsoe. He thereupon wrote to Herbert D. Gale, attorney for the strikers, that if they were not taken back he would enjoin the company from such conduct as a condition of continuance of the previous injunction, as his only aim was to insure uninterrupted rail operations during the war. Shoup countered with the argument that only eleven strikers had not been reinstated and that each had a right to make a personal appeal to him, but he would continue to refuse to work through a federal mediator such as Captain Connell so long as his employees were represented by a third party. All the strikers were reinstated by the middle of August, however, and, effective October 16, train crews were given a wage increase ranging from 1.5 to 4 cents an hour, depending on length of service. Passenger service men now received from 38 to 44 cents an hour in the city and from 40.5 to 46.5 cents an hour on interurban runs. Freight and work train motormen, conductors, and foremen were paid 50 cents, and brakemen and switchmen 45 cents an hour.[60]

The hearings on the dispute were held in the winter of 1918–19 by the same NWLB examiners who were investigating labor conditions on the Los Angeles Railway. Testimony was taken on alleged low wages, long working hours, and discrimination against union members by the interurban line, and a rumor began to circulate that the board might recommend increased pay for platform men. The Pacific Electric made it clear, however, that it did not necessarily plan to abide by the board's rulings. In December the company distributed a circular to its employees and to residents of Los Angeles, Riverside, and Orange counties, stating that wage payments had been increased voluntarily by $584,000 in the past year. It pointed out that an additional increase of $2 million would force it to ask for a 50 per cent raise in freight and passenger rates. Although officials of the company claimed that its wages were higher on the average than those of most electric railways in the nation, employee witnesses at the labor board hearings testified that they had joined the union because collective bargaining was the only way to secure reasonable hours of work and pay equal to that on other roads.

The recommendations of the National War Labor Board, announced in April, 1919, were of little significance, for the Pacific Electric, like the Los Angeles Railway, did not consider itself bound by them. Shoup had no intention of establishing a collective bargaining system involving a union such as Local No. 808 of the BRT, and he believed wage scales were management's business. Nevertheless, dissatisfaction of the employees with the increase of from 1 to 3 cents an hour recommended by the board caused the Pacific Electric voluntarily to raise wages an average of 3 cents an hour, effective August 1, for men who did not take an annual twelve-day vacation with pay; otherwise the increase was 2 cents. The company pointed out that the new scale of from 40 to 52 cents an hour, depending on the length and kind of service, represented an 80 per cent increase over 1913 rates, and had been given despite the fact that the railway would be unable to meet its bonded indebtedness in 1919.

The wage boost, however, did not answer the basic question of freedom of collective bargaining. The employees asked for recognition, not of the union, but merely of their elected committee without reference to whether or not its members were union men. Both union and nonunion men voted for a strike if the management would not recognize this committee, which they had set up for collective bargaining purposes. An ultimatum to this effect was delivered to H. B. Titcomb, vice-president of the railway, at 10 A.M. on August 15. Additional demands were for wages of 75 cents an hour, a minimum monthly guarantee of $180, and an eight-hour day based on a run of 150 miles with overtime for any excess mileage. Titcomb immediately sent his refusal, warning that strikers would lose seniority rights, annual and family pass privileges, and all other special concessions. Moreover, if a walkout occurred, all known agitators would be weeded out from those men eventually desiring reinstatement. Titcomb's position was echoed by Kuhrts of the Los Angeles Railway; nevertheless, the employees of the Pacific Electric's red-car system decided to join the platform men on the yellow cars in the strike which began at 2 A.M. on August 16, 1919.[61]

About 700, or roughly a third, of the platform employees of the Los Angeles Railway struck along with approximately half, or 1,500, of the carmen working for the Pacific Electric. The injunction issued by Judge Bledsoe in the Pacific Electric strike of the previous year was still in force, but union leaders were not certain whether or not it would be used in the current dispute. They had therefore submitted their strike ultimatum to Titcomb through the employees' committee, indicating that the walkout would actually be a peaceful withdrawal from employment. Such a precaution was not taken with respect to the Los Angeles Railway, however, as the injunction did not apply to its employees.[62]

The strike had an immediate impact upon the service given by both lines. The hope of Los Angeles Railway officials that normal operations could be resumed within twenty-four hours of the walkout did not materialize. For the first two days all runs were discontinued at 8:30 P.M., ostensibly in the interest of public safety, and only 50 to 75 per cent of normal service was possible during the day because of the manpower shortage. The management claimed that no inexperienced men were being used to operate the streetcars, and that even some union men had not joined the strike. It pointed out that as of July 1, 1919, the average length of service of all its platform men was 6.24 years and that 1,117 out of 2,151 had been with the company five years or more.

Service on the Pacific Electric was more seriously disarranged than that on the Los Angeles Railway. It ran no cars after 8 P.M. for the first few days, and service was at 50 to 80 per cent of normal efficiency. Most beach and other interurban traffic was cut about 50 per cent, except for cars to Long Beach, Santa Ana, and San Pedro which were maintained almost on regular schedule. Commuters were late for work, theater crowds were forced to use cabs, sight-seeing buses were pressed into service, jitney buses on regular schedules were permitted to detour and pick up passengers where streetcar service was poor, and vacationists were stranded at Camp Seeley in the San Bernardino mountains. Automobile owners were asked to give lifts to persons without cars in an effort to reduce the strain on the electric lines as well as on taxicab companies.[63]

Before the strike started the Los Angeles Railway had had fifty special officers sworn in for police duty, and had broken in 150 extra men imported from other areas for platform duty. The Pacific Electric procured the services of thirty special deputy sheriffs the day the strike began. The Los Angeles County Civil Service Commission appointed 300 special deputies who were employed and paid entirely by the two railway companies during the strike. Besides these private guards, the city police were kept on the alert for some time, and a reserve squad was maintained at Central Station. But, despite such precautions, demonstrations occurred early in the dispute. On the third day, August 18, a streetcar phone box at Sixty-first and Moneta was smashed, several cars on South Main Street were spotted with tomatoes, a striking motorman was fired on by a special deputy in an argument, and several men were injured in fights with strikebreakers.

A group of strikers unsuccessfully tried to mob the Pacific Electric station at Sixth and Main. Most of the incidents that affected the Los Angeles Railway occurred on the East Seventh Street, South Main Street, Central Avenue, and Maple Avenue lines. Management placed its most belligerent carmen on the lines where pickets and strikers were most likely to be found. On August 19 hundreds of strikers and sympathizers blocked traffic at Sixth and Main streets during rush hours, seeking to persuade working platform men to join the walkout. Unsuccessful efforts were made to induce linemen and substation operators for the Southern California Edison Company to shut off power to cars. Strikers greased the tracks at several points, broke the windows on one Pacific Electric car, and attempted to derail the Catalina boat train by placing an iron pipe across the rails. Mexican track workers for the Pacific Electric joined the walkout, demanding $2.72 for an eight-hour day; time and a half for overtime, Sundays, holidays, and nightwork; and a legitimate collective bargaining procedure.[64]

In the first two days no strikers were arrested. By August 18, however, the mounting number of incidents resulted in several arrests and the issuance of an injunction authorizing the Los Angeles Railway to protect its property. Pacific Electric officials reminded the strikers that the injunction issued the preceding year was still in force, but neither restraining order seemed to have much effect. So long as the railways continued to run their cars, the strikers were determined to interfere with their operation. Alleged verbal threats to dynamite cars running late at night, coupled with acts such as the pouring of cement into the pistons of a switching steam engine at El Segundo, caused the companies to request additional arrests and to seek active police protection. The ban on service after 8 P.M. was reinstituted by both lines for several weeks, supposedly in the interest of public welfare, but undoubtedly the move was partly dictated by the lack of sufficient personnel willing to take risks. Buses were given thirty-day emergency licenses to carry passengers between Los Angeles and Santa Monica, Ocean Park, Venice, Hollywood, and Edendale, in an effort to maintain service and reduce attacks on streetcars.

The *Record,* in sympathy with the strikers, demanded mediation of the dispute and proposed that, if the railways refused, the city take over the lines as public utilities. Pressure was put on Mayor M. P. Snyder to appoint a special committee to investigate the situation, but instead, on August 18, he established the Mayor's Industrial Mediation Board, consisting of seven prominent citizens: Dr. Byron H. Wilson, a Methodist minister; S. B. Silverwood of Silverwood's; Bishop

John J. Cantwell; Mrs. Frances Noel, a member of the Women's Union Label League; W. A. Barker, president of Barker Brothers; Seth Brown, president of the Central Labor Council; and Henry Louis of the Brownstein-Louis Company. L. P. St. Clair, an independent oil producer, replaced Barker before the board started hearings on August 21.[65]

Meanwhile the dispute took a more serious turn. On August 20 nearly 3,000 strikers and sympathizers gathered at the Avenue 28 carbarns of the Los Angeles Railway. A riot began when members of the group jeered at platform men taking cars to the barns and pulled a trolley off the overhead wire. In the ensuing battle between strikebreakers and strikers, the company's superintendent, E. L. Lewis, was attacked and knocked down. Forty-seven policemen were required to restore order. In other riots later in the evening, carbarns were damaged but injuries to participants were minor. Steam railroad employees had entered the dispute in its early stages by refusing to handle freight cars at the interchange point shared by the rail lines with the Pacific Electric Railway. By August 20, about 200 loaded freight cars destined to be turned over to the electric line for delivery had been sidetracked at remote points on the Santa Fe, Southern Pacific, and Salt Lake railroads, while some twenty-five freight cars were on Pacific Electric tracks awaiting delivery to the steam lines. The next day 800 yardmen, switchmen, and other train handlers of the three steam lines struck without warning in a sympathetic walkout.

The fear that this was the beginning of a nationwide strike was based on unrest among railroad workers throughout the country with regard to both wage schedules and the prospective return of the steam roads to their private owners. The Brotherhood of Railroad Trainmen was conducting the Pacific Electric strike, under the leadership of F. L. McDowell, general chairman of its Pacific Coast District, and in coöperation with Division 835 of the Amalgamated, which represented the striking carmen of the Los Angeles Railway. It soon became clear, however, that the work stoppage was strictly local, and had not been officially authorized by the national brotherhoods. In their memorandum on the walkout, the local steam railroad men were careful not to use the words "strike" or "organized labor," referring to themselves as individual employees rather than as union members.[66]

When the dispute spread to the steam railroads, the city's 600 policemen were placed on twelve-hour shifts and flying reserve squadrons were organized at all police stations. The officers were ordered to break up all gatherings of strikers and strikebreakers in the interest of protecting lives and property and of maintaining peace. They were, however, required to be impartial, for Mayor Snyder's administration had been elected with the support of organized labor. By this time, through the use of strikebreakers, daytime interurban and streetcar traffic was beginning to approach normal, though it met only about 75 per cent of the usual requirements at peak periods. The Pacific Electric found some replacements by advertising in all the principal daily papers of San Diego, Orange, Riverside, San Bernardino, and Los Angeles counties. Strikebreakers were started at 44 cents an hour instead of the usual 42 cents, plus a 20 per cent bonus, and were guaranteed $5 a day with board and lodging.[67]

The Mayor's Industrial Mediation Board held its first meeting with strikers and representatives of the electric lines on August 21, the day the steam line employees walked out. Company officials claimed there was nothing to mediate as the men had voluntarily left their jobs. The strikers contended that the dispute had been precipitated by the railways' refusal to accept the decision of the National War Labor Board the preceding April, but said they would return to work on a prestrike basis if the companies would agree to arbitrate. When management rejected arbitration as well as mediation, the meeting reached an impasse.

The next day the strikers on the steam railroads presented their demands to William Sproule, district director for the United States Railroad Administration. They included (1) satisfactory settlement of the demands of the Pacific Electric strikers, removal of all strikebreakers, and reëmployment of all strikers; (2) similar action with respect to the strikers on the Los Angeles Railway; (3) the discharge of office workers and others who assisted in making up trains and handling cars at the steam railroad yards when the regular employees struck on August 21; and (4) the restoration of strikers to their former positions with the steam railroads. The men did not seem to expect acceptance of the third point, but insisted on the other three.[68]

The steam railroads were badly handicapped for ten days after their yard crews walked out. Officials and office workers were barely able to get out a train a day on each of the three lines. Freight piled up at local depots. When, beginning on August 22, Salt Lake enginemen refused to haul trains made up by nonunion crews, traffic in and out of Los Angeles on that line came to a virtual halt. The next day brakemen joined the ranks of striking yardmen. By this time Pacific Coast representatives of the brotherhoods of trainmen, conductors, engineers, and firemen had become alarmed. Meeting on August 23 with J. H. Dyer, general manager of the Pacific System of the Southern Pacific, they stated that the walkout was unauthorized and that they were trying to get their men back to work.

Nevertheless, the strike continued to spread. Shopmen on the Southern Pacific walked out at Los Angeles and Colton, and switchmen on the same line struck in Santa Barbara. As trains arriving in Los Angeles from the East could not be sent out again, all available yard trackage gradually became filled with idle cars. A third of a million dollars worth of produce in refrigerator cars which could not be re-iced started to rot on the tracks in the warm sun, while a hundred carloads of cattle suffered from lack of food and water. On August 24 neither the Santa Fe nor the Salt Lake turned a wheel in Los Angeles. The Southern Pacific ran but one train; all its freight crews between Santa Barbara, Mojave, and Barstow were on strike, and on August 25 its freight handlers struck. Santa Fe crews began abandoning their trains at Barstow, forcing passengers to seek other transportation into Los Angeles. Although the strikers permitted some mail to move, it, too, began to pile up at local stations. By this time an estimated 12,000 men connected with one railroad or another in Los Angeles were out, and the city's rail connections with the rest of the country had been severed. The situation was so serious that the Central Labor Council urged its constituent organizations not to join in any sympathetic strike unless so authorized by their national headquarters. AFL organizer J. B. Dale, fearing the development of a general strike, threatened to cancel the charters of unions whose members walked out without permission.[69]

By August 26, however, conditions began to improve on the Pacific Electric; freight service was restored though cars were still not operated at night. The company announced that it had added 905 new men to its payroll since the beginning of the dispute. Claiming that many of these were thugs, the strikers asked that the police cease permitting the appointment of such men as deputy constables. On the same day 1,100 Southern Pacific shopmen marched to the Labor Temple, carrying banners inscribed with slogans demanding government ownership of the railroads; but the next day 500 of them returned to work on learning that their strike was unauthorized. This desire for government ownership of steam roads reflected the national point of view of rail workers at this time, but local citizens expressed a similar idea by asking that the city take over the electric lines and put the strikers back to work pending wage adjustments.

But even as conditions looked brighter for the Pacific Electric management, steam railroad yardmen in San Francisco and Oakland joined the walkout. Because national labor leaders seemed unable to control the strike, Los Angeles businessmen appealed to the federal government to intervene, and the Central Labor Council telegraphed President Wilson to ask for fair play for the strikers. Late on August 27, the heads of the Big Four railroad brotherhoods told their men that they must return to work within twenty-four hours or lose their membership. As a result yardmen in the San Francisco area went back to their jobs at midnight. The next day the director-general of the United States Railroad Administration served notice that the government would undertake to restore full service by 7 A.M. on August 30, and that anyone impeding such action would be committing an offense against the United States. Similar ultimatums were sent by the four railroad brotherhoods, indicating that they would coöperate with the government in seeing to it that the trains moved.

On August 29, therefore, in a stormy meeting, local strikers from the steam railroads who belonged to the Brotherhood of Railroad Trainmen voted to return to work by a majority of 363 to 146. BRT members who were striking against the Pacific Electric opposed this action because it weakened their position, but they were powerless to stop it. Thus steam trains started to move in and out of the city at 7 A.M. on August 30. As a precaution, agents from the Los Angeles office of the United States marshal were on hand to ensure compliance with the order of the director-general of the railroads. Even the freight cars at the Pacific Electric interchange started to move. As a last act of defiance, however, 23,000 workers marched in the Labor Day parade through the streets of Los Angeles, demanding government ownership of the nation's railroads.[70]

The strike against the two electric lines was still in effect. Just before the steam railroad workers capitulated, General Manager Kuhrts of the Los Angeles Railway had reaffirmed management's adamant position. Strikers who wanted to be rehired would have to apply as individuals; the company reserved the right to refuse to take back any men who had verbally or physically abused loyal employees or members of their families or had encouraged such action. On August 29 the strikers offered to submit the question of their return to work to a vote of the platform and car-repair men who had been employed before August 15. The company rejected this offer. Through R. P. Dix of the Amalgamated, the strikers then asked the mayor's mediation board to try to resolve the dispute. The railway again said there was nothing to mediate. It planned to keep its strikebreakers as permanent employees and needed only a few hundred additional men to reëstablish full operations. On the same date 2,000 leading citizens and members of the city's twenty-two largest civic organizations held a mass meeting at Trinity Auditorium to pledge aid to the government in ending the steam strike; they also passed resolutions in favor of maintaining the open shop. Several days later 200 Los Angeles Railway strikers met at the Labor Temple and voted to remain out, but this was no more than a futile gesture in view of the termination of the sympathetic walkouts. Day service was rapidly approaching normal on both electric lines, and night service was gradually being restored. Thus the strikers desperately seized upon a new proposal put forward by the mayor's mediation board to end the dispute on the yellow lines. The board recommended that (1) the Los Angeles Railway take back all striking employees who wished to return; (2) the strikers make individual applications for employment; (3) every man be restored to his seniority; (4) the company have the right to suspend any man without pay; (5) any man suspended have the right of immediate arbitration and, if found innocent, be paid his wages retroactive to the time he applied for reëmployment; (6) the arbitration board consist of five men—two from the railway company, two from the strikers, and one appointed by both groups.

The mediation board, however, could only make suggestions, and the management of the railway chose to ignore them. Service was now nearly normal as strikers returned to work without seniority. Mayor Snyder and the City Council seriously considered a proposal to take over the Los Angeles Railway but decided the cost would be too high. The idea had been initiated by labor leaders and was strongly urged by Councilman Ralph Criswell, former president of the local printers' union. Although Snyder advocated municipal ownership of public utilities, he would not support a high-cost acquisition. Labor sympathizers then circulated a petition to have the streetcar franchise revoked and jitney service restored if the strike was lost, but nothing came of this. Mayor Snyder made a last-ditch effort to gain concessions for the strikers on September 22, when he called a conference of the managements of the electric lines, strike leaders, city councilmen, the mediation board, and the assistant city attorney, but company officials refused to meet with any committee of strikers.[71]

There was little left to do except acknowledge that the open shop had won another round. By the end of October fully 80 per cent of the Los Angeles Railway and Pacific Electric strikers were employed elsewhere. On October 30, when the dispute against the Pacific Electric was declared officially ended, the company announced a pay increase effective November 1 for those workers in its employ. Service was now back to normal, for the places of all strikers had been filled. Several weeks later, by a vote of 37 to 9, Division 835 of the Amalgamated Association of Street and Electric Railway Employees called off its strike and, as the year ended, gave up its quarters in the Labor Temple, a beaten organization.[72]

4. THE SWITCHMEN'S AND THE SHOPMEN'S STRIKES, 1920–1922

The sympathetic walkout of steam railroad employees in Los Angeles on August 21, 1919, was a prelude to a national strike of railway switchmen in April, 1920. Both disputes reflected the mounting unrest among railroad workers which developed during the war and the immediate postwar period. The unrest was based on resentment over the federal government's failure to raise wages sufficiently to meet all the increase in the cost of living. The government's promises further to improve working conditions on the federalized roads seemed empty in the light of wage increases won by other trades through strike threats. Because railroad brotherhood officials, though concerned, seemed too conservative to seek better pay, not a little of the resentment was directed against them as well. Yet the nearly thirty months of federal control were golden years. The Wilson administration was sympathetic to labor and desired to keep the railroads operating effectively during the European conflict and the subsequent adjustment period. Substantial wage increases were granted in 1918, followed by further upward readjustments in the first months of peace. Although these increases were not considered adequate by railroad workers, they did encourage the idea that nationalization of the railways might be better than a return to private ownership.

By 1920, however, the return to private control seemed inevitable. As no action on wage increases could be expected from brotherhood leaders, dissatisfaction among the rank and file became so intense that only a spark was needed to ignite it into open rebellion. That spark was struck among switchmen and yard employees on April 1, 1920, when John Grunau, a foreman in the Chicago yards of the Chicago, Minneapolis, St. Paul and Pacific, was removed from his position when officials of the Brotherhood of Railroad Trainmen claimed that, because of a change in the type of train, his job should be held by a road conductor. Normally so minor a matter would have been adjusted without a walkout. Grunau, however, was a leader in a newly formed independent union known as the Yardmen's Association of Chicago, representing men who were dissatisfied with the conservative leadership of the Switchmen's Union of North America and the operating brotherhoods. His discharge sparked a virtually leaderless, rank-and-file walkout of switchmen and yard employees throughout the country, within some areas of which, however, there was evidence of the work of the Industrial Workers of the World.[73]

Grunau was removed from his job on April 1. Four days later 9,000 switchmen were on strike over the nation, and the walkout was gaining momentum. The railroad brotherhoods quickly labeled it an "outlaw strike," pointing out that the Yardmen's Association had no status before the railroad adjustment boards or the Railroad Labor Board. The latter had just been established by the Transportation Act of 1920, which, among other things, had returned the roads to private hands effective March 1, 1920. The division chairmen of the Brotherhood of Railroad Trainmen on twenty railroads and three of the union's national vice-presidents told the strikers to get back to work by April 7 or face expulsion and loss of seniority, but little heed was paid to the warning. The BRT thereupon began to furnish strikebreakers for the Chicago area. Nevertheless, the walkout rapidly spread to Los Angeles, Jersey City, St. Louis, Kansas City, Omaha, and Detroit. In all these areas a significant number of firemen, engineers, and conductors began to join the switchmen. Obviously the leaders of the Big Four brotherhoods, as well as of the Switchmen's Union, had lost control of their men. In urging the return to work, they expressed the fear that employers would interpret the walkout as a breach of contract and would use it as a means of breaking the railroad unions.[74]

A week after the strike started in Chicago, 1,200 men concerned with the operation of transcontinental trains to and from Los Angeles walked out. The Southern Pacific placed an embargo on the acceptance of perishable freight for shipment, effective April 8. Strike spokesmen claimed that 1,400 men, mostly switchmen and members of yard crews, had struck without notice on the Southern Pacific, Salt Lake, and Santa Fe railroads in Los Angeles, with another sixty out at Colton, and that not a boxcar moved in Los Angeles on April 8. Passenger trains were in operation, but were switched by administrative and office personnel. Fortunately, less than fifty carloads of perishables were left in the local yards when the men walked out, and livestock loads were moved to corrals before yard engine crews quit their posts. The strike seemed spontaneous in Los Angeles, as in Chicago and other areas. Local brotherhood officials, supported by the city's AFL representatives, denounced the walkout just as on the national level.

By April 12 the only freight that moved in and out of the city was shipped by truck. Passenger trains still ran and the mails were moved, though with some delay. A new problem arose when engineers, firemen, conductors, and brakemen on the Southern Pacific and the Santa Fe began to refuse calls for duty; of those who did report for work, some refused to haul trains made up by nonunion switchmen or by railroad personnel, even though the companies continued to pay all trainmen who were involuntarily idled by the striking switchmen. Passenger trains, however, never completely ceased moving in and out of Los Angeles during the course of the dispute.[75]

On April 13 crews deserted three westbound Santa Fe trains at Winslow, Arizona, stranding about 500 travelers. In effect, this move completely tied up the Santa Fe's eastern lines out of Los Angeles, for five trains going in both directions had previously been stalled beyond Barstow. All switchmen on this road at San Bernardino, Barstow, and Needles went out on the same day, as did seventy-five check and receiving clerks in the Southern Pacific freight house in Los Angeles. The strikers made no attempt to attack or obstruct trains.[76] The switchmen held daily meetings in Los Angeles and summed up their position in a statement published in the *Times* on April 14:

Our present scale of wages is: for foremen, $5.44; helpers, $5.11, and on account of the extraordinary increased cost of living, the failure of the Director General of Railroads, to keep the promises made to us, that if the cost of living did not decrease, we would be given at least a living wage, and we know that . . . it has been, and is, ever on the increase; the failure of our grand lodge officers to obey the repeated instructions given them by our conventions, and committees and our membership, and inasmuch as no relief has been afforded us, and there is none in sight, we have taken the only course left open to us, and have left our employment until such time as we can return and do justice to ourselves and our families.

The strike was felt unevenly over the nation. Estimates of the number of men out at the peak of the dispute ranged from 30,000 to 40,000. In some cities, especially in the West, traffic moved almost normally, while in other areas additional switchmen were going on strike. Los Angeles was one of the more heavily hit metropolitan centers, possibly because the dispute represented a chance to aim a blow at the open shop, but also because the men had gained strike experience in the 1919 walkout in sympathy with the Pacific Electric trainmen.

On April 14, 1920, O. W. Karn, general chairman for the Pacific Coast District of the Brotherhood of Locomotive Engineers, tried to persuade his men to stay on the job. Although he obtained an affirmative vote, some members remained beyond the reach of telephones calling them to work. On the same day the blockade of the Santa Fe at Winslow was lifted briefly to permit the mail to go through, but it was lowered again on April 16. Some improvement was noted in Los Angeles the next day, when firemen, engineers, conductors, and brakemen who had previously been inaccessible started to respond in increasing numbers to calls for duty. Only firemen on yard engines declined to return for switching duty. At Needles, California, and Winslow, Arizona, all railroad men, including the "outlaw" switchmen, returned to work on the Santa Fe. By April 19 the Southern Pacific succeeded in running six freight trains in and out of the city, and about half of the seventy-five receiving clerks on strike asked for and obtained their old jobs back, though without seniority; the rest were replaced and thus lost their positions. On the same day the federal grand jury in Los Angeles found twenty-nine of the strike leaders guilty of violating the Lever Act, which made it unlawful to hamper the transportation of food and other necessities during a war or national emergency. Both railroad officials and brotherhood representatives testified against the men, among whom were conductors, firemen, switchmen, and engineers.

The Brotherhood of Railroad Trainmen revoked the charter of its Los Angeles local and told striking members to go back to work by 8 A.M. on April 21 or quit the union. Enough returned to permit the local railroads to begin accepting freight, subject to delay. Some brakemen did not comply, however, declaring they wanted to force the BRT to demonstrate its power. Approximately a third of the normal number of switching crews went back to work, thus permitting the movement of some freight without the assistance of office and supervisory personnel. After April 21 railroad officials hired switchmen without regard to brotherhood affiliation, selecting only the best men among all the applicants. Strikers not back at work by that date were no longer protected in their seniority rights by their unions.[77]

Several factors accounted for the return of most strikers, except for a number of switchmen and brakemen. Perhaps the most important was the entrance of the federal government upon the scene. The strike hastened the appointment by President Wilson of the new Railroad Labor Board under the Transportation Act of 1920. Four days after its appointment on April 20, the board began hearings on brotherhood demands, but it refused to listen to the Yardmen's Association of Chicago or to similar "outlaw" organizations in other cities. Moreover, the Brotherhood of Railroad Trainmen and the Switchmen's Union of North America actively recruited strikebreakers for the railroads and passed on individual applications for reëmployment, thus weeding out the more active rebels. Few brotherhood members could sit back idly and let their jobs slip out of their grasp as a result of active strike-breaking by their own unions. A statement by the Department of Justice that alleged Communist William Z. Foster was behind the walk-out influenced additional strikers to return to work. Finally, the arrest of John Grunau and twenty-two other leaders in Chicago on Lever Act charges similar to those set forth in Los Angeles hampered efforts at the national level to keep the men on strike.[78]

The twenty-nine Southern Pacific, Santa Fe, and Salt Lake men indicted in Los Angeles under the Lever Act were ordered to stand trial on June 1, 1920, as United States District Judge Bledsoe had overruled a demurrer challenging the constitutionality of the law. Although the worst of the walkout was over, normal service still had not been completely restored in the Los Angeles area or elsewhere, and public opinion ran against the strikers. Local brotherhood officials were again willing to testify against men who had defied the authority and threatened the contracts of legitimate unions. In August the jury announced a decision: all the men, except twelve on whom it disagreed, were fined $1,000 each. Five of the group elected to appeal the decision, but a year later, on October 3, 1921, the United States Supreme Court upheld their conviction. The fines were paid from a special assessment levied by the Switchmen's Union of North America.[79]

In June, 1920, while the trial was going on in Los Angeles, "outlaw" strikes broke out again at various points in the country, including Baltimore and Philadelphia, allegedly led by Communists or Wobblies. Brotherhood leaders as well as railroad officials urged President Wilson and the Railroad Labor Board to expedite action on wage issues in view of the continued general unrest among the men. In July the board awarded a wage increase of $600 million to 1,800,000 railroad employees. Although the brotherhoods were disappointed in not getting more, they accepted the decision. In the same month the United Association of Railway Employees of North America, an industrial union with John Grunau at its head, was formed at Chicago. Threatening continuance of the strike, Grunau demanded that all strikers be restored to their status before the walkout, including full seniority rights. As his union had no standing in the eyes of the Big Four, the government, or the railroads, his ultimatum was ignored. On September 13 a majority of association members voted to return to work, forcing Grunau to announce the strike officially ended as of the following day. His new union failed to gain a foothold in the railroad industry. The victory, if any, was the wage increase granted by the Railroad Labor Board and the attention directed to the pressing need for a better system of handling industrial disputes and employee grievances on the nation's rail lines.[80]

A similar outcome was in store for a nationwide strike of railroad shopmen—including machinists, boilermakers, blacksmiths, sheet metal workers, coppersmiths, pipesmiths, electricians, and car repairers— which followed the walkout of yard workers and switchmen. Like the switchmen, the Los Angeles shopmen came into conflict with the open-shop philosophy prevalent among commercial and industrial interests. Although the strike did not occur until 1922, the grievances behind it arose out of World War I. During the war the AFL began to organize railroad shopmen into effective bargaining units. The first evidence of this activity in Los Angeles was seen in the Southern Pacific shops in February, 1918. These efforts were not successful, though they received some publicity because of a public protest meeting held by the metal trades. It was claimed that the railroad had ordered the more active union supporters to other cities under the pretense of insufficient work. Another attempt in May to organize the shopmen of all three railroads in the city under the auspices of C. F. (Curly) Grow, president of the Metal Trades Council, enjoyed greater success, and unions were formed among sheet metal workers, blacksmiths, machinists, boilermakers, and car repairers. The subsequent agitation for an improved wage scale, especially by the sheet metal men who desired the rate paid at the shipyards in San Pedro, was temporarily checked by a federal order which became effective on August 1, 1918. It established the eight-hour day in railroad shops throughout the nation, and granted a wage increase retroactive to the preceding January 1.[81]

The rising cost of living, however, remained a source of discontent. Just as on the national level, local shopmen favored government ownership of the railroads in the belief that it would bring them higher wages. They therefore joined the Big Four in a parade supporting such a program, held in Los Angeles in February, 1919, and continued their organizing activities. When the strike against the electric lines of Los Angeles broke out on August 16, the shop crafts in the roundhouses of the Santa Fe, the Salt Lake, and the Southern Pacific were reasonably well organized and sympathetic to the cause of the platform men. As previously noted, 1,100 Southern Pacific shopmen contributed their bit to the strike by marching to the Labor Temple carrying banners in support of government ownership.

At the same time their national leaders appealed to the federal government for further increases in pay. President Wilson refused, however, asking instead for their coöperation in checking the rise in the cost of living. The shopmen's answer was an affirmative strike vote, but the walkout did not occur then. A period of watchful waiting ensued during which the railroads were returned to their private owners and the new Railroad Labor Board took over the settlement of grievances between unions and employers under the Transportation Act of 1920. Continued unrest among shop employees resulted in a hasty decision by the board on July 20, 1920, increasing their pay 13 cents an hour. Moreover, agreements concluded the preceding September between the United States Railroad Administration and the unions, providing that no changes in wages were to be made except by the joint decision of the carriers and their employees, were continued in effect.[82]

A business decline in the fall of 1920 caused railroads to start cutting shop forces in order to reduce costs. Further savings were made by contracting work to outside shops which did not come under the July wage award. Labor complained that 40 per cent of the shopmen were soon unemployed, and hearings before the Railroad Labor Board began on January 10, 1921. The board was a tripartite body of nine members representing equally the interests of management, labor, and the public. As the three public members appointed by President Harding after his inauguration were allegedly partial to management, railroad labor leaders believed it unlikely that the board would render a favorable decision on wages. Their fears proved justified when the board abrogated the national agreements of September, 1919, between the U.S. Railroad Administration and the unions, thus throwing open the door for each railroad management to deal freely with its own employees. Then, after the January hearings, the board ordered wage cuts of from 5 to 18 cents an hour and called on the workers to coöperate during the period of postwar adjustment. The reduction was rejected by the shop unions, which were banded together in the Federated Shop Crafts, a part of the Railway Employees' Department of the AFL.

Although the railroad managements did not put the wage cuts into immediate effect, they continued to reduce labor costs by contracting more work to outside firms. The shop unions therefore began to accumulate funds for an eventual showdown with the roads. Other decisions of the board reduced the hourly pay of 400,000 maintenance-of-way men from 1 to 5 cents an hour and slashed shop wages even further, with both cuts to be effective on July 1, 1922. Immediate strike votes taken by the shop unions and the maintenance-of-way men overwhelmingly favored a walkout, which was announced for the same day as the effective date of the wage cuts. The workers were convinced that they were being treated unfairly; they had been one of the last occupational groups to receive cost-of-living increases because of wartime inflation, and now a government agency dominated, they believed, by management was forcing them to become one of the first to take wage cuts.

The shopmen's walkout was 90 per cent effective, but the maintenance-of-way men did not strike. In light of the affirmative strike vote, the president of the maintenance-of-way union had asked for a rehearing by the Railroad Labor Board, which the latter gladly granted. The board made a small adjustment in the previously announced wage cut for the maintenance-of-way men, and they remained on the job although their action weakened the strike of the shopmen. Benjamin Hooper, chairman of the Railroad Labor Board, labeled the shopmen's work stoppage an outlaw strike and publicly urged the roads to form company unions and replace the men who had walked out. The Big Four brotherhoods officially took a neutral stand, further jeopardizing the shopmen's chances of success.

Although disappointment in not securing government ownership of the roads and rebellion against the old-line leadership of their unions may have been factors in the shopmen's overwhelming support of the walkout, the immediate causes of the strike stemmed from the recession of 1920–1922, with its wage cuts and unemployment. A further reason was the companies' refusal to abide by a decision of the Railroad Labor Board in May, 1922, outlawing the contracting system. Some railroad managements looked upon the strike as far from an evil; it gave them an opportunity to break the back of the shop unions, and this they set out to do.[83]

In Los Angeles the strike was preceded by the same unrest evidenced at the national level, as layoffs of men at the shops of the Santa Fe, the Southern Pacific, and the Salt Lake took place in 1920–1922. Machinists Local No. 311 and the unions belonging to the Railway Shop Federation of Los Angeles passed resolutions against the layoffs, but to no avail. Unemployment was further aggravated because work was contracted to outside firms. Agitation for acquisition of the railroads by the federal government continued even after they had been returned to private hands. Much of it was stirred up by socialists who addressed local shopmen on this issue as well as on the merits of industrial unionism. Even after the strike began on July 1, 1922, William Z. Foster, later to be a leading figure in the Communist Party of the United States, discussed these subjects in the Labor Temple.[84]

The walkout in Los Angeles was peaceful. Estimates of the number on strike, according to the railroads, varied from 50 per cent of the shop employees of the Southern Pacific and the Santa Fe to 70 or 80 per cent of those working for the Salt Lake, now a part of the Union Pacific. The unions claimed that 95 per cent of the men "hit the bricks." The actual number was approximately 4,000, including 3,300 from the Southern Pacific, 286 from the Santa Fe, and 388 from the Salt Lake. The shopmen had little money to finance the strike and not even a complete roster of those who had walked out. Through the efforts of two local Methodist ministers, E. P. Ryland and G. Bromley Oxnam, about $500 was obtained each week to feed the strikers. A sum of nearly $250,000, borrowed with the help of Mrs. Kate Crane Gartz and Dr. John R. Haynes, civic leaders and philanthropists, was used to save the homes of men who were unable to make mortgage payments during the strike. The local leader of the strikers was George E. Killmer, secretary of the Railway Shop Federation in Los Angeles. At daily meetings held in the Labor Temple, local and outside speakers sought to maintain the morale of the men in the early weeks of the strike. Los Angeles County Sheriff William I. Traeger tried to prevent violence by impartially hiring an equal number of union members and employer representatives as guards to protect railroad property. The city police force under Chief Louis Oaks interceded only when violence was threatened.[85]

During the first week of the strike on the local scene, picketing proceeded peacefully and few incidents were reported, though this was not true of other points in the state, notably San Bernardino and Fresno. The Southern Pacific issued a statement that all shop employees who returned to work by July 7 would be reinstated with full pension and pass privileges as well as their seniority ratings. But a majority of the men remained out, and all the railroads began to recruit new employees. Most trains continued to move, as yard workers, maintenance-of-way men, and members of the operating brotherhoods stayed on the job. Moreover, Hooper's earlier pronouncement on the walkout permitted the hiring of strikebreakers in Los Angeles and elsewhere without any limitations. To the *Times*'s opposition in the name of the open shop were added the voices of other newspapers over the country, which denounced the walkout as a revolt against the legally established machinery for wage adjustment. Union carpenters in Los Angeles, on the other hand, sympathized with the strikers and refused to build stockades around shop areas.[86]

The ranks of the strikers over the nation were augmented in the second week by 10,000 stationary engineers, members of the International Union of Steam and Operating Engineers. In Los Angeles, officials of the struck railroads announced that their shops were functioning quite normally without the strikers, none of whom they expected to rehire. The first arrests in the city occurred when police took three men into custody near the Southern Pacific shops under the 1910 antipicketing ordinance, suspecting that they were about to foment trouble. The governor refused to call out the militia to guard railroad installations in California, in the well-founded belief that local authorities were well able to keep overt acts under control. Both local and national railroad executives claimed that the dispute was between the Railroad Labor Board and the unions, but AFL spokesmen said that the walkout resulted from unsatisfactory conditions of employment and could be settled at any time by bargaining between the railroad managements and the unions.[87]

Late in July Judge Bledsoe of the U.S. District Court in Los Angeles issued a temporary restraining order which prevented the strikers from interfering in any way with the operation of Salt Lake trains and shops. On the national scene, however, prospects began to look a little brighter when Daniel Willard, president of the Baltimore and Ohio and a leader of the less antagonistic managements, indicated his willingness to conclude a separate peace. Nevertheless, the strikers refused on the ground that it would constitute desertion of their fellows. On July 31 President Harding proposed that the strikers return to work and the issues be submitted to the Railroad Labor Board without prejudice. The managements balked at this idea because it would mean reinstating men who had refused to work, with seniority over those hired to replace them. From then on, therefore, the purpose of the strike was restoration of seniority rights rather than redress of the original grievances. Negotiations between union officials and railroad representatives in August, at both national and regional levels, proved fruitless. In Los Angeles, the Church Brotherhood issued a statement blaming management for the chaotic labor conditions. On the open-shop side, the Farmers' and Merchants' Bank attacked Sheriff Traeger for having appointed striking shopmen as deputies, and the *Times* predicted failure for the unions. Trains in and out of Los Angeles continued to operate, though maintenance problems restricted the roads to less than normal schedules.[88]

On September 1 the shopmen's cause suffered a telling blow when, upon the petition of United States Attorney General Harry M. Daugherty, federal Judge James H. Wilkerson of Chicago issued a temporary injunction, setting the hearing for September 11. The defendants included the Railway Employees' Department of the AFL and its officers, the six shop craft brotherhoods, and the 120 system federations, as well as their presidents and secretaries. The order restrained the defendants from issuing interviews or statements, using their funds to carry on the strike, picketing, holding parades, or urging friends to quit railroad employment. So sweeping an injunction was a shock to the strikers. Daugherty had argued that the nation was faced with collapse of its rail transport if the strikers were not stopped under the provisions of the Sherman Antitrust Act. Judge Wilkerson responded in kind. Organized labor all over the nation expressed its resentment by threatening a general strike, which AFL leaders managed to discourage. Instead of stopping the dispute, however, the injunction solidified the strikers and their sympathizers. The Los Angeles Central Labor Council assessed each member of its constituent unions 25 cents a week to support local strikers, and a mass meeting held on September 21 at the Labor Temple, with the Reverend E. P. Ryland presiding, protested the action of the Attorney General. Speakers included the Reverend G. Bromley Oxnam and John S. Horn, secretary-treasurer of the Central Labor Council.

On the national level, Daniel Willard of the Baltimore and Ohio, supported by executives of railroads interested in a reasonable and early settlement of the strike, made a proposal which was accepted by the Shop Crafts Policy Committee of the AFL. B. M. Jewell, president of the AFL Railway Employees' Department, publicly stated the main provisions of the agreement as follows:

1. All men were to return to their positions as of June 30.

2. Future disputes were to be referred to a commission which would have final authority in the matter concerned.

3. The commission was to consist of six representatives from management and six from the unions.

4. Reference was not to be made to previous decisions of this commission in effecting settlements in later controversies that might arise.

5. Neither side was to intimidate or oppress employees who remained at work or who went on strike.

6. All pending lawsuits arising from the strike were to be dismissed.

As a result of this agreement, negotiations got under way for settlement of the strike between the unions concerned and the individual railroads, bypassing the Railroad Labor Board. By the middle of October 98 roads owning 75,000 miles of track had ended their participation in the dispute and were back in normal operation. Eventually the jobs of 225,000 striking shopmen were returned to them along with their seniority status. The remaining 175,000 shopmen on strike were forced to yield to the more "hard-boiled" managements, led by executives of the Pennsylvania Railroad. Most of the shop brotherhoods on these roads were broken, being replaced by company unions which prevailed until the renaissance of organized labor in the 1930's and, on the Pennsylvania, until 1949. The Railroad Labor Board established in 1920 became for all practical purposes a powerless organization. The more moderate managements dealt with the shop unions directly; the less moderate ones controlled company unions and thus did not require the services of the board.[89]

The Western Pacific was the only railroad entering California which signed an agreement with the shopmen. At its annual convention on October 22, the California State Federation of Labor recommended that all unions in the state collect contributions of 25 cents a member to aid the 15,000 shopmen still on strike, but little financial help resulted from this plea. On January 2, 1923, eight trainmen who had abandoned their Santa Fe passenger train with 300 persons aboard in August, 1922, in protest against inadequate maintenance standards and the presence of armed guards on cars, were sentenced to an aggregate fine of $10,000 or terms in the San Bernardino jail. The press had branded the men as heartless, deserting their passengers in the burning wastes, but actually the train had been left at a station with plenty of food and water. The main inconvenience was a four-day travel delay.

As 1923 rolled on, the strike continued in Los Angeles with no settlement in sight, for by this time it had become a lockout. Men who had spent their working lives on the roads, unable to return to the local shops of the three lines entering Los Angeles, were forced to find other employment. Nationally, the membership of the International Association of Machinists fell 75 per cent between the end of World War I and 1925, largely as a result of the disastrous shopmen's strike. Losses to the roads and to shippers in California from the walkout were estimated at $3,997,704. In Los Angeles, however, the open shop gained another victory.[90] The achievement of the strikers, if any, lay in the emasculation of the Railroad Labor Board as a factor in industrial relations and its eventual supersession by the more effective railway labor acts of 1926 and 1934, which provided a more successful system of settling disputes without the constant threat of interruption of the nation's rail transportation.

IV. LABOR AND THE WAR, 1915–1919

THE UNREST among the workers on the steam and electric railroads in Los Angeles and in the nation during World War I and immediately thereafter was mirrored locally in other trades and industries as well. The year 1914 marked the end of a four-year period of darkness for organized labor in Los Angeles. The period from 1915 to 1917 witnessed signs of a revival, in the form of strikes, among shipyard crafts, garment trades, bakers, laundry employees, and maritime unions. The stepped-up tempo of activity continued during the months of American participation in the conflict, as butchers and meatcutters, bakers, reed and rattan workers, ice wagon drivers, and others gained the strength to sponsor walkouts in order to enforce their demands. Additional stoppages occurred after the war when groups such as the shipbuilding crafts and telephone operators sought to catch up with the rise in the cost of living, consolidate gains made during the war, or extend their organizing activities.

A number of factors were important in both the local and the national renaissance of organized labor in 1915. Possibly the major element in the country as a whole was the improvement in business under the impact of increased orders from Europe. Heavy foreign borrowing and purchasing in the United States, coupled with a lack of immigration to these shores, increased the demand for labor as production rose, and consequently improved the bargaining position of organized workers. The entry of the United States into the war in April, 1917, accentuated this trend as men were withdrawn from productive activity for military service. From the industrial centers in the East, the pickup in business spread gradually westward to the Pacific slopes and southern California, though at a somewhat diminished pace. Los Angeles, by virtue of its rather isolated location, was less affected by war industrialization than were cities of comparable size in areas nearer the Eastern ports of embarkation. But Los Angeles had a harbor and it proved expedient to locate some of the war-induced shipbuilding activities there, with a consequent impact on the related iron and steel fabricating firms of the city and a fuller utilization of the local labor supply.[1]

Two additional factors encouraged the growth of organized labor in Los Angeles as well as throughout the nation. The first of these was the rise in the cost of living brought about by the inevitable inflationary pressures of domestic war financing at a time when there was little in the way of unemployed resources. As noted earlier in connection with wartime rail problems, the conflict between sticky wage rates and rising family budgets was a major cause of unrest. At its peak in 1918, the war absorbed about a quarter of the national output, yet the income generated by such production remained largely in private hands and thus was disposable at the option of consumers. As a consequence of their spending in the face of civilian goods shortages, the level of retail prices in that year rose to a point about 18 per cent higher than in 1917. By November, 1918, the retail price level was approximately 50 per cent higher than it had been in July, 1914, a month before the outbreak of hostilities in Europe.[2]

The second additional factor aiding the labor movement during the war period was the desire of the federal government to keep production machinery rolling smoothly without interruption. Thus certain concessions were made to organized labor in return for no-strike pledges by its leaders. Among the most important were the right of organization for purposes of collective bargaining, equal pay for equal work by women, the acceptance of the concept of maintaining minimum living standards for workers, and the idea that the basic workday was one of eight hours. Labor leaders were appointed to the governing boards of various agencies for war administration. The most significant of such appointments was that of Samuel Gompers to the Council of National Defense. Organized labor was also represented on the National War Labor Board, which was charged with the peaceful adjustment of disputes over wages, hours, and working conditions, particularly in war-related industries. The general principles on which board policies were based included the right of workers to organize and bargain collectively through their chosen representatives without interference from employers.[3]

The beneficial effects of the war on organized labor may be seen in the membership statistics for the period 1915–1920. The number of union members rose by almost 2.5 million in these years, more than the entire gain between 1897 and 1914. AFL membership alone increased from 2,072,702 in 1916 to 3,260,168 in 1919. The greatest gains were in industries such as transportation, shipbuilding, metal fabrication, building construction, and machinery. The clothing-manufacturing trades were also quite thoroughly organized. Even in Los Angeles, city of the open shop, the number of workers belonging to unions grew substantially. In 1915 it was variously estimated at between 15,000 and 17,000, and by the middle of 1916, 2,000 more had been added.[4] As the increase continued into 1917, a report from F. C. Marsh, vice-president for District No. 2 (Los Angeles area) of the California State Federation of Labor, reflected renewed optimism:

Los Angeles, at last, can be placed near the top of the column as an Organized Town. After many years of hard struggling, we are proud to make that assertion, and if the union men coming to this town had placed their cards where they belonged, it could be easy work to organize Los Angeles. . . . The spirit of organization is everywhere in Los Angeles. Men are coming into the different organizations without being solicited.[5]

By the end of 1917 an additional 2,500 members were reported, and before another year had passed, predictions were being made that after the war Los Angeles would be among the best-organized metropolitan areas in the country. The report made to the State Federation of Labor in late 1918 revealed a net addition of 10,000 new members since the 1917 convention, and in February, 1919, the Central Labor Council set the increase in membership among its affiliates at 6,889 workers for the preceding year. An annual increment of 12,000 new members in Los Angeles unions was claimed in October, 1919, at the state federation convention, bringing the strength of the city's labor movement to about 40,000. Although this figure was probably an exaggeration, there is little doubt that local unions gained considerable strength in the war years.[6]

1. THE WESTERN FRONT

The optimism of the Los Angeles labor movement during the war years was in sharp contrast to the situation in 1914, when pessimism prevailed and the failure of organizing drives in the prewar depression still rankled. Although some of the antagonism against organized labor resulting from the 1910 bombing of the *Times* building disappeared during the war, the publisher of that newspaper did not let the public forget his interpretation of "industrial freedom." The trials of Matthew A. Schmidt and David Kaplan on charges of participation in the dynamiting of the *Times* provided General Otis with ample opportunity in late 1915 and 1916 to hammer home his open-shop philosophy. The convictions of the two men were played up by the *Times* as evidence of what could be expected in Los Angeles if labor leaders got out of hand, but the public was apathetic. A war was being fought in Europe, whereas the trials of the alleged dynamiters pertained to events that had happened more than five years before. Attempts of the *Times* in 1915 to smear the reputation of Joseph Scott, one of the attorneys in the 1911 McNamara case, backfired when Scott, winning a series of libel cases against General Otis, obtained nearly

$70,000 in damages. This did not deter Otis from thundering his denunciations of organized labor, its supporters, and its leaders from his office at First and Broadway until his death in July, 1917, but the community's interest was temporarily diverted, at least in part, to other matters.[7]

The increase in the strength of organized labor after the low point of 1914 was tied closely to the business recovery that began to develop in 1915 and 1916. By September, 1915, it was clear that the worst of the depression was past. As the year came to a close, the Los Angeles Stock Exchange witnessed the heaviest trading that had ever occurred on any one day and completed six months of consistent price advances for listed securities—local evidence of an improved outlook for business. Los Angeles continued to be the fastest-growing city on the Pacific Coast, posting an estimated increase in population in 1916 as against 1915 of 35,631 persons, and reaching a total of more than 550,000 residents within its corporate limits. This growth was matched by industrial development which expanded private payrolls in the city by approximately 25 per cent in the same year. The trend continued in 1917, when more than $13 million were added to the industrial capital of the city and an additional 13,000 workers were employed in enterprises ranging from steel foundries to fish canneries. In Los Angeles, value added by manufacture increased from $44,517,197 in 1914 to $118,364,712 in 1919, and the number of industrial establishments, from 1,911 to 2,540. Water-borne commerce at Los Angeles Harbor rose from 1,739,548 tons in the fiscal year 1914–15 to 3,528,280 tons in the fiscal year 1919–20. One of the most phenomenal economic developments of the war period was the growth of motion picture production; in 1918 it became the fifth largest industry in the nation, and most of it was centered in Los Angeles and its environs.[8]

The recovery of business and the effects of the war did not alone cause the expansion in organized labor which occurred in Los Angeles before the United States entered the conflict in 1917. Active efforts to take advantage of the more propitious circumstances for union organization were necessary if gains were to be made in the face of the predominant open-shop philosophy. Such efforts were not long in developing as an outcome of the attention that began to be focused on Los Angeles by national and state labor leaders. In August, 1915, the national convention of the International Typographical Union was held in the city, with an address by Secretary of Labor W. B. Wilson. Two months later the California State Federation of Labor, at its annual convention in Santa Rosa, took action to initiate an organizing campaign in Los Angeles. George E. Bevan, its delegate to the AFL convention held in San Francisco a few weeks later, successfully appealed for assistance from the national body. Joshua B. Dale, veteran AFL organizer in the state who was named to head the drive, immediately recommended that every international union send an organizer to Los Angeles for four months. In a brief visit to the southern city after the San Francisco convention, President Gompers himself lent encouragement to the plans for renewed activity.[9] The *Times* did not fail to note the mounting tempo of local preparations for the campaign:

> Militant labor-unionism is rallying for what observers who are competent to speak on the subject declare may be the most vicious attack yet directed against this community, its prosperity and its industrial ideals. . . .
> The faces of these professional trouble-fomenters light with a wicked rapacity at the thought of being in a position to pillage this free and prosperous city. The sagging mouths of their strong-arm bullies and heelers water with the lust for a fray with the free, self-respecting workingmen of this Southwest metropolis. Their fingers itch for the spoils. . . .
> Already the skirmishers are here . . . scowling, bull-necked loafers who are only awaiting the great mobilization and the order of attack to begin their infernal business of cracking skulls.[10]

Referring specifically to Gompers' visit, General Otis editorialized:

> After three days of joy-riding in autos and hours of dalliance with large, cold bottles and small, hot birds, Sammy . . . has departed for San Diego whence he will return to his lair in Washington. . . .
> . . . without compelling a single employer of non-union workers to make of his establishment a closed shop, Sammy took his leave. . . .
> Little as Sammy knew of the *Times* he knew enough to hate it. . . . "We persuade ourselves that had he known us better he would have hated us more." [11]

Although Gompers was called a "grafting scab" by the *Times,* the spark of his leadership ignited the smoldering coals of local union interest. Under Dale's direction, twenty-one AFL organizers representing sixty-nine international unions opened the membership campaign on January 3, 1916. Six months later Dale was able to report to the Central Labor Council that eight new organizations and 2,000 new members had been added to the local labor movement. At the same time the Council proudly noted that fifty-five unions were recognized at its regular meetings through their accredited representatives.[12]

Dale was a thorough and effective leader. Organizers working under him met once a week to discuss plans and compare notes. Although the original intent had been to keep him in the city for only four

months, so successful were his efforts and so necessary did he become
to the continued advance of the campaign that he was assigned to Los
Angeles for an indefinite period. F. C. Marsh reported to the state
convention in October, 1916, that sentiment in favor of organized
labor in Los Angeles was more encouraging than it had been in the
past ten years. He gave much of the credit to Joshua Dale. In 1917
Dale himself reported to the convention that every craft in Los Angeles
had felt the stimulus of organization since the start of the campaign
nearly two years earlier. Intensive organizing activities were continued
in the next two years, when circumstances were much more favorable
to the growth of unions under the prevailing win-the-war philosophy
than they had been from 1915 to 1917.[13]

Dale's success was achieved in spite of great odds against him,
especially in the early months of the campaign. His difficulties were
by no means limited to the dominance of the open shop and the
opposition of the *Times*. In 1914 the local labor movement suffered
from internal dissension, general apathy, and inadequate financial
reserves. In fact, so serious was the internecine warfare that it was
surprising that any progress was made in the next several years in
chartering new organizations or in bringing in new members. The
conflicts were mainly over revenue-raising schemes to reduce the debt
on the Labor Temple. The campaign of 1913–1914 to increase the
sale of stock to union members had largely failed because of depressing
business conditions and the low morale of the labor movement. Total
indebtedness rose from $95,000 in 1913 to $109,055.19 in October, 1915.
Not enough stock was being sold. Vacancies in the Temple were
mounting, as unions found themselves unable to pay their rent and
commercial enterprises on the first floor failed through lack of patronage. Action was imperative if eventual foreclosure was to be
avoided.

Accordingly, a "festival of industrial peace" in the Labor Temple
was proposed for May 20–30, 1916. Plans were laid for a display of the
city's products as well as for a roster of speakers which would include
Governor Hiram Johnson and national labor leader John W. Mitchell.
On April 27, 1916, a labor delegation led by T. D. ("Red") Fennessy,
president of the Union Labor Temple Association, appeared before
the Los Angeles County Board of Supervisors to ask for $1,000 to
initiate the festival. Display space was to be sold to exhibitors regardless of whether they were union or nonunion, as long as their products
were not unfair. On getting wind of the idea, the *Times* opposed it as
a plan to bolster the finances of the Temple, and was indirectly sup-

ported by a number of Central Labor Council members who objected
to the showing of nonunion goods. Although the festival was endorsed
by the Central Labor Council, the City Council, and the County
Board of Supervisors, the proposal was abandoned because of internal
dissension over the question of requiring the union label.[14] Fennessy
had indicated that this might happen when he appeared before the
Board of Supervisors: "I doubt very much whether we will be able to
pull it off, even if you appropriate the $1,000, because the old troubles
will be stirred up. . . . If organized labor is foolish enough not to
embrace this opportunity, we'll be the sufferers—and that's likely to
happen." [15]

Failing to raise money for the Temple by this means, Fennessy next
sought to sell stock again, this time in blocks of twenty shares at $1.50
each, for which payment was to be made in twenty monthly installments. The money was to be deposited in a bank to earn 4 per cent
interest pending its eventual application against the mortgage. It was
hoped that successful sale of the stock, now that business conditions
were better, would make it possible to pay off all indebtedness by
Labor Day, 1918. The project received a lift when it became known
that one of the earliest subscribers for 100 shares was Dr. John R.
Haynes, eminent civic leader and frequent supporter of organized
labor and liberal movements generally. The stock sale still went too
slowly, but proceeds from this source were bolstered by income from
the labor paper, the *Citizen,* which had just been purchased by the
Union Labor Temple Association. The *Citizen* formerly had been
owned by the Union Labor News Company, whose president was Fred
C. Wheeler, member of the carpenters' union for thirty years and an
incumbent city councilman. It was a profitable enterprise, the revenues
from which had long been coveted by the Temple Association, and
it was the center of considerable dissension during the months before
its change of ownership. This dispute, rather than the open shop,
actually provided the primary hurdle for the organizing campaign
initiated by the appointment of Joshua Dale in the fall of 1915.[16]

Although the *Citizen* seemed to be the main source of contention
during 1915 and 1916, it was more of a rallying point than a cause of
dispute. Evidence that other internal conflicts were brewing first came
to the surface in August, 1915, when the painters withdrew from the
Central Labor Council, followed by Carpenters Local No. 158 in
December. It was in the latter month that the Union Labor Temple
Association made its initial overtures to acquire the *Citizen,* in accordance with resolutions to this effect passed by both the Building

Trades Council and the Central Labor Council. Agreement could not be reached with the Union Labor News Company at this time, and the attempt failed. Then the organizing campaign was "kicked off" early in January, 1916. It met immediate opposition from several unions, including those of barbers, garment workers, bakers, floor layers, tile layers, web pressmen, and ironworkers, all of whom resented the interference of the AFL and their own internationals in local affairs. Two-thirds of the membership of Bricklayers Local No. 2 had revolted against the Building Trades Council in October, 1915, and had formed the Bricklayers Mutual Benefit Association, evidence of their objection to the campaign plans. Their action was followed by withdrawal of some of the tile layers and, later, of a group of floor layers. Disgusted with this opposition, Dale threatened to drop the campaign if the three councils—Central Labor, Building Trades, and Allied Printing Trades—did not close ranks and settle the rebellion. He was further incensed by the refusal of Garment Workers Local No. 125 to go along with a one-cent per week per capita assessment for a period of six months to further the cause of union-made goods in Los Angeles.[17]

When the Labor Temple Association failed to induce the Union Labor News Company to sell the *Citizen* in December, 1915, the incident became a catalyst that brought the internal dissension to a white heat. The paper's staff included J. E. Timmons of Iron Workers Local No. 51, which opposed Dale and his international organizers. The *Citizen* began to reflect this attitude and was soon accused of partiality in representing only the opinions of the minority group of unions which were against Dale. Consequently the three labor councils, expressing the sentiment of the majority of the unions in favor of the organizing drive and acquisition of the *Citizen* by the Temple Association, passed resolutions that resulted in the establishment of a rival news organ, the *Labor Press*. It began publication in January, 1916, under the editorship of Francis Drake, formerly a contributor to the Los Angeles *Record*. Profits were to go to the Labor Temple.

In the same month elections were held for Central Labor Council offices. As was to be expected, the basic issue faced by the candidates was support of the Dale campaign and the *Labor Press* as against the *Citizen* and its coterie of opponents of outside organizers. Final ballot tabulations gave the Dale supporters the two most important offices: for president, Seth Brown (Typographers No. 174) with 85 votes to 35 for C. D. Shields (Bakers No. 37); for secretary-treasurer, C. L. Myers (Machinists No. 311) with 92 votes to 54 for J. E. Timmons

(Iron Workers No. 51), incumbent president of the council. After winning the election the majority group, led by Red Fennessy, Curly Grow, Lemuel Biddle, A. B. Hassel, James Gray, J. R. Walker, A. J. Mooney, and L. W. Butler, expelled five opposition locals—Garment Workers No. 125, Bakers No. 37, Barbers No. 295, Web Pressmen No. 18, and Iron Workers No. 51—from the council. Although support of the *Citizen* rather than the *Labor Press* seemed to be the point at issue, the real complaint was their failure to coöperate in the organizing campaign.[18]

Another facet of the internal dissension within the labor movement brought the California Trade Union Liberty League, an antiprohibition group, into conflict with the *Citizen*. During 1915 and 1916, a campaign against two ballot propositions favoring state-wide prohibition was conducted by the League and those trades and industries that stood to lose if liquor abolition laws became a reality. The *Citizen*, backed by a number of locals, refused to give editorial space to the so-called "wets." Because of this stand the members of the board of directors of the Union Labor News Company were summoned to a conference with several of the city's influential labor leaders and requested to vacate six of their positions if they wanted the continued support of the labor movement. Their places were to be filled by appointees of the Central Labor and Building Trades councils. As the Union Labor News Company was an autonomous organization, the directors made a counterproposal that those desiring control should purchase it in a legitimate transaction. The *Citizen*'s continued refusal to support the "wets" in its editorial columns caused the local Joint Executive Board of the Hotel and Restaurant Employees and Bartenders International League to join the majority group in favor of the *Labor Press* when that paper was established. Al Hassel, a leader in the opposition to the *Citizen* and in the expulsion of the five unions from the council, was secretary and business agent of Bartenders Local No. 284. In 1914 Hassel had been defeated for the presidency of the council by J. E. Timmons of the *Citizen* staff. Timmons, in turn, was defeated in January, 1916. Curly Grow, likewise associated with anti-*Citizen* forces at the time of the election, was appointed later in 1916 as a delegate from the Central Labor Council to the Los Angeles branch of the antiprohibition California Trade Union Liberty League.[19]

To make matters more complicated, the Labor Forward League was involved in the internal dissension for several months of the same period. Formed to promote wider use of the union label, the League was favored by the *Citizen*, whose editor, Stanley B. Wilson, was a member of the organization. As the League met in the homes of its members and was openly supported by Wilson in the columns of the *Citizen,* it was not long before it was accused of working secretly to undermine the *Labor Press* and Joshua Dale's organizing campaign. The fact that many of the more active members of the League belonged to unions that supported the *Citizen* served to increase the criticism. There were even suspicions that League meetings were in reality planning sessions for the purpose of overthrowing the newly elected council officials.[20]

Tired of the squabbles and anxious to get ahead with his campaign, Joshua Dale, instead of resigning, finally took the initiative to bring the warring factions together. It was obvious that the local labor movement could not support two papers, much less expect revenue from the *Labor Press* to help reduce the Temple debt. Dale arranged a conference at the Labor Temple on April 21. Those attending included Fred Wheeler, president of the Union Labor News Company, Stanley Wilson of the *Citizen,* and other representatives of the varying shades of opinion in the different disputes. Seventeen speakers addressed the gathering on the need for labor unity in the face of constant opposition from open-shop employers. It was agreed to sell the *Citizen* to the Union Labor Temple Association for $5,000 and to merge its staff with that of the *Labor Press.* Francis Drake was named editor, assisted by Grow and Tom Barker. The first issue of the *Citizen* under the new arrangement was published on May 5, 1916. The Central Labor Council followed up the merger by voting, 44 to 19, to reinstate the expelled unions, though the latter did not all accept the palm of peace. Dissatisfaction with council leadership lingered for a number of months until differences were forgotten in the increasing tempo of business and the war.[21]

The Union Labor Temple Association operated the *Citizen* for less than a year and a half. On August 21, 1917, the Joint Executive Board of the Central Labor, Allied Printing Trades, Building Trades, and Metal Trades councils recommended that the newspaper be transferred to the administrative jurisdiction of the Central Labor Council in order to place its control in the hands of organized labor as a whole. The recommendation was adopted, a down payment was made, and the change of ownership took place on October 1. The remainder of the purchase price of $5,000 was to be paid to the Temple Association in thirty-three monthly installments of $100 each, plus 6 per cent interest on the outstanding balance. In addition, it was agreed that the entire profits of each subsequent Labor Day celebration would go to the association and it would have *Citizen* support in its annual midwinter carnival. So profitable was the newspaper, however, that on October 14, 1918, the final payment to the association was made twenty months ahead of schedule, and the governing board declared a dividend which was split among the four councils. Early in 1919 the *Citizen* boasted of having the largest circulation ever achieved by any labor paper in southern California.[22]

The sale of the *Citizen* gave the Labor Temple Association revenue for a short period after October, 1917, as the monthly installments were paid. Additional income was still necessary, however, for the second mortgage of $16,500 was due and payable early in 1920. In January, 1918, union members were asked to donate a day's pay toward liquidation of the Temple debt, and through this program the mortgage was reduced to $10,265 by the end of the year. Additional receipts of $1,588.34 from the Labor Day picnic of 1918, and a further drive to sell stock to unions, finally provided sufficient funds to pay off the second mortgage in August, 1919. The mayor of Los Angeles, Meredith P. Snyder, participated in the mortgage-burning ceremony. The *Citizen*, meanwhile, continued its successful operations and turned over its entire profits for the year 1920 to the Union Labor Temple Association as a start on a fund for an annex and a modernized printing plant.[23]

2. POLITICS AS USUAL

Councilman Fred C. Wheeler, president of the Union Labor News Company when the *Citizen* was sold to the Temple Association, had been elected to his city position in June, 1913. Before that date the organized labor movement had suffered politically from the defeat of Job Harriman, socialist and labor attorney, in the 1911 mayoralty election held immediately after the McNamara confessions of the bombing of the *Times* building. George Alexander had won this election with the support of an organization called the Good Government Group (known to General Otis as the "Goo Goos") and the temporary assistance of the *Times*. Otis was definitely more interested in fighting organized labor by opposing Harriman than in aligning himself with the Good Government forces, and his truce with the "Goo Goos" did not last beyond the election. Mrs. Stimson tells the story of the 1911 campaign and its aftermath in her volume on the early history of the Los Angeles labor movement.[24]

Although little was accomplished by labor in the arena of practical city politics in 1912, its interest did not flag. Ben C. Robinson, former president of Typographical Union No. 174 and a member of the city's Fire Commission for the year 1909–10, was sent by the Central Labor Council as a delegate to the local chapter of the Select Societies of American Municipalities, then studying the commission form of government. In addition, eight unsuccessful attempts were made in 1912 to have the City Council pass an ordinance creating a plumbing commission. Here the unions ran afoul of the *Times* and other open-shop adherents, who feared that the mayor might appoint a majority of union members to such a commission and that nonunion men would then be prevented from working at their trade by preferential regulations. In 1913, however, organized labor became more effective in politics by virtue of its support of Henry A. Rose against John W. Shenk in the final election for mayor that year. Rose won, as did socialist Fred Wheeler in his race for the City Council. This was the first time in Los Angeles history that a socialist had won a significant elective post in the city's government.[25]

In the same year the City Council appointed a citizens' committee to investigate labor conditions. It was composed of George H. Dunlop as chairman, Douglas L. Edmonds as secretary, Mrs. Frances N. Noel of the Women's Trade Union League, the Reverend George A. Henry, Professor Charles E. Seaman, the Reverend Stanley Ross Fisher, and Mrs. M. E. Johnson. Representatives of the Central Labor Council presented testimony on living conditions and the cost of living. The commission established bench marks by defining a subsistence income as not less than $2 a day and a living wage for a breadwinner with one dependent as not less than $4 a day. It noted that the lowest wages in the city were paid in canneries, clothing factories, laundries, restaurants, department stores, dry goods shops, and groceries. Seventy per cent of the women workers in laundries received less than $2 a day, and in department stores 64 per cent were under the subsistence level. The major conclusions of the commission were fuel for the hearings of the United States Commission on Industrial Relations, which met in the city in September, 1914. The local commission recommended the establishment of a permanent industrial fact-finding and mediation board in Los Angeles with a legal constitution and financial backing; the passage of an ordinance prohibiting the employment of children under twelve in the sale of newspapers or merchandise on the streets; and the adoption by the municipality of the provisions of the state workmen's compensation act. Little came of the recommendations at this time, although the council did instruct the city attorney to draft a model ordinance establishing a permanent industrial commission.[26]

Wheeler was not long in making his presence felt in the City Council, where his first demands concerned the wages of city employees. He requested extra pay for overtime labor by municipal workers and then proposed an ordinance requiring the payment of union wage scales to all craftsmen on city projects. In the latter he was supported by the Central Labor Council, which asked in addition that the union scale be established for unskilled laborers employed directly or indirectly by the city regardless of their union status. Open-shop contractors quickly opposed these proposals, which were subsequently turned down because several councilmen did not want to be "dictated to" by any outside group like the Central Labor Council. Labor leaders then called upon the Los Angeles County Board of Supervisors in June, 1914, asking for consideration of substantially the same proposals. Although organized labor was not represented on the board, an ordinance was passed in October requiring the payment of the union scale to all workers employed on county projects.[27]

Perhaps the most significant political event in labor circles on the eve of the European war was the split with the Socialist Party. Unionists and socialists had been closely associated in support of Job Harriman for mayor in 1911. Harriman tried again for the office in 1913, but was defeated in the primary election. Unionists were increasingly concerned that the Socialist Party was more interested in political ends than in economic objectives, and consequently relations between the two groups became strained. Finally, in March, 1914, the local socialist organization declined to adopt a Central Labor Council resolution that every nominee of the party must be a member in good standing of his appropriate craft union or, if an employer, must be fair to organized labor. Upon the socialists' refusal, the council adopted another resolution advising all union members not to vote for socialist candidates. As Wheeler did not go along with his party on its failure to endorse the stand of the Central Labor Council, the socialists called for his resignation. Their action, in turn, was condemned by the council, which continued to support Wheeler as the only member of the party favorable to organized labor.[28]

In 1915 Wheeler ran for reëlection and was returned to office at the same time that Ralph L. Criswell, former president of the printers' union, also was elected as a councilman. These victories were interpreted as a real gain for organized labor in city politics. Furthermore, an industrial commission was established along the lines recommended in 1913. Among others, the City Council appointed Mrs. Frances Noel, a member of the original investigating body, to the new

permanent commission, along with Mrs. Daisy Houck of Garment
Workers Local No. 125. On the other hand, organized labor did not
fare so well in the election of a board of freeholders to revise the city
charter and in the appointment of new members to the County Civil
Service Commission. Charles D. Shields, endorsed by the labor movement, failed to win a place on the board, and John B. Reeves, sup-
ported for the commission by organized labor and political boss Edwin
T. Earl, publisher of the Los Angeles *Express,* ran afoul of the *Times*
and allegations of influence peddling in connection with city offices.
Reeves was exposed as a Canadian who had not been naturalized until
April 21, 1914, and who was put forward as a candidate for appointive
office as the result of a deal among County Supervisor R. H. Norton,
Earl, and several labor leaders. When Reeves was turned down, Stanley
B. Wilson, editor of the *Citizen,* was advanced as a candidate, but he
was openly accused of running a "red" paper by General Otis of the
Times. Tim Spellacy, a local businessman, Democrat, and former state
chairman of his party, was finally appointed to the post early in
January, 1916.[29]

At the State Federation of Labor convention in October, 1915,
Joshua Dale warned Los Angeles labor about plunging too deeply into
partisan politics. Attributing some of its internal problems to its
former tie with the Socialist Party, he recommended a return to the
nonpartisan political viewpoint of Samuel Gompers. At first little heed
was paid to Dale's warning because of divided opinion over the desirability of his running an organizing campaign in the Los Angeles
area. In fact, the Building Trades Council went so far as to propose a
state labor party early in January, 1916, but this idea was scotched by
the much stronger San Francisco labor movement. Political interest
remained high, however; a few months later the Central Labor Council endorsed the proposed new city charter submitted to the voters
on June 6, 1916, specifically because it provided for paid holidays for
city laborers and authorized legal assistance in the collection of wages
unjustly withheld by employers. When the charter failed to pass, the
mayor appointed Councilman Ralph Criswell to meet with labor's
Joint Executive Board to secure agreement on amendments to be
included in another proposed revision of the charter. In November
Criswell ran as a Democratic candidate for Congress in the Ninth
District, but failed to be carried into office by the victory of Woodrow
Wilson.[30]

Although Los Angeles labor gained in numerical strength in 1917,
it fared badly in politics. Criswell was reëlected to his old seat on the

City Council, which he had vacated in the hope of winning a congressional post the previous fall, but Wheeler was defeated because of his stand on an antibillboard proposal on the ballot. Fearing that a ban on billboard advertising would result in unemployment, he had joined four other council members in opposing the proposition. As a result he lost the backing of the *Record,* normally a supporter of labor candidates, and faced the opposition of the other newspapers in the city which stood to gain through increased advertising linage if billboards were banned. The proposal won; Wheeler lost. The same ballot carried a $12 million power bond proposition, endorsed by the Central Labor Council, the Building Trades Council, Electrical Workers Union No. 61, and Machinists Local No. 311. Passage of the bonds would have meant more employment for members of local unions and, in addition, was a move toward extension of public ownership in the utility field which the labor movement approved, but the *Record* went against organized labor on the issue and the measure failed. A further defeat occurred in connection with a proposal to ban jitney buses, which was supported by the Pacific Electric and Los Angeles railways, as noted in the previous chapter. Labor leaders ostensibly were concerned about the possible loss of employment by jitney-bus drivers but, in reality, opposed the ordinance as a device to rid Henry Huntington's open-shop Los Angeles Railway of a competitor. The ordinance passed, however, and the jitneys were soon on their way out.[31]

The second year of America's participation in the war did not find local labor faring much better in politics. Among other issues in 1918, the City Council spent many hours discussing the pros and cons of a Sunday closing law. Organized labor was divided on the merits of the debate. The Building Trades Council found itself with a strange bedfellow, the Merchants' and Manufacturers' Association, in opposing a law to close commercial establishments on the Sabbath; the barbers, on the other hand, wanted a day of freedom from their shops. This lack of a common political front was criticized by the editor of the *Citizen,* who suggested that a *modus operandi* for the local labor movement in politics could well be to support whatever the *Times* opposed. This pattern was subsequently followed in connection with the labor endorsement of John S. Horn, a member of the beer drivers' union, in his 1918 campaign for the state assembly. It was not a policy that guaranteed victories in politics, however, and Horn failed to get elected.

The year 1919 was politically brighter for organized labor, even though the war was over and employment conditions were not so favorable for membership gains. In the biennial city elections, the unions supported Meredith P. Snyder for mayor and Ralph Criswell and Fred Wheeler for councilmanic seats. All three were elected as well as nine other candidates of the fifteen endorsed by organized labor. Snyder, a Democrat, was thrice mayor of Los Angeles. Although not a union man like Wheeler and Criswell, he was sympathetic to the wage earner and had originally obtained the necessary funds to buy the lots on which the Labor Temple was erected. Labor leaders were so encouraged by their apparent political success in 1919 that shortly after the city election the Central Labor Council appropriated $2,400 for the establishment of a precinct organization to maintain and strengthen its position. In a letter addressed to all union members, the council secretary announced that John Horn of Beer Drivers Local No. 227 had been put in charge of this organization. Its objects were to investigate the so-called "injunction" judges in connection with the street and interurban railway strikes of 1918 and 1919, help to bring in new union members, notify unionists of boycotts, and present a unified political front on candidates for office. Each precinct was to have a captain, with a district manager in charge of every ten precincts. The captain's main function was to pass on to every unionist in his jurisdiction information pertinent to the organization's objectives.[32]

The "love feast" with the city administration was not to last long, for organized labor broke with Mayor Snyder before the end of 1919. The first sign of a rift appeared when Seth Brown, president of the Central Labor Council, and Mrs. Frances Noel of the Women's Trade Union League resigned as members of the municipal board of mediation because of the mayor's alleged lack of coöperation with it in the attempted settlement of the Los Angeles Railway strike. Francis Drake, editor of the *Citizen* and one of Snyder's first appointees, resigned from the Fire Commission after the mayor sent a communication to the chief suggesting that firemen drop their membership in a newly organized fire fighters' union. The Joint Executive Board thereupon resolved that no unionist should accept a position on any municipal body so long as Snyder was mayor. Drake and other labor leaders considered Snyder's letter a major factor in causing men to drop out of the firemen's union, thus forcing the eventual relinquishment of its charter. On October 29, as a symbol of their feeling about the mayor, they placed at the entrance of the Labor Temple an imitation casket covered with cabbages and other vegetables, with a sign reading, "Here lie the remains of the City Fire Fighters' Union, stabbed in the back by Mayor Snyder—M. and M. Snyder." [33]

3. The Open Shop and the Shipyards

Although the Los Angeles labor movement, like its national counter-part, was concerned with events in the political arena, it was still primarily interested in winning economic objectives. The organizing campaign headed by Joshua Dale had to be implemented at the level of the individual local, however, if it was to be a success. Further, it was only a preliminary bout before the main event, which was the serving of specific demands on employers once sufficient strength had been achieved. The basic issue in Los Angeles as an open-shop town was necessarily that of recognition. Though wage questions were sec-ondary to this issue, they closely followed it under the pressure of economic necessity resulting from the impact of inflation on the workers' wallets. As noted earlier, the war did not affect Los Angeles as much as Eastern cities; nevertheless it brought a rapid and diversi-fied growth in local manufacturing industries, including metal fabri-cation, and the establishment of considerable new shipbuilding capac-ity. The opportunities to win recognition and wage improvement were better than they had been for years; thus the unions sought to take advantage of them.

Open-shop supporters were not asleep during the war period any more than they had been in the four years following the bombing of the *Times*. Their spokesmen continued to be General Otis, until his death in 1917, and then his son-in-law, Harry Chandler, both of whom used the editorial columns of the *Times* to express their view-points in positive language. The previous arguments against any shop but an open one were supplemented by the accusation that unions were restrictive of output during a war emergency and hence were unpatriotic. It was also claimed that wage boosts were not necessary in Los Angeles, where the cost of living was low. As usual, this con-clusion depended on the statistics used. A study by the U.S. Bureau of Labor Statistics indicated that in the period 1913–1918 the prices of six basic food items rose less in Los Angeles than in the nation as a whole. Professor William F. Ogburn, surveying ninety-one cities in the United States with respect to high food costs in 1918–1919 for white families with total incomes ranging from $1,200 to $1,500, placed the southern California community eighty-fourth on the list. The *Times,* of course, gave considerable space to such findings. In the Midwinter Edition of January 1, 1917, for example, Alma Whitaker, one of its columnists, pointed out that a person could live with more grace in Los Angeles than in most other cities; a minimum of winter clothing was needed, a hat was a nuisance, clothes were easy to wash, house rents were cheap, fuel bills and utilities were low, and the simple pleasures of life like a streetcar ride to the beach were within everyone's reach. With respect to rents, however, the advantage in favor of southern California was not nearly so marked as in food. Among the ninety-one cities studied, Los Angeles ranked thirty-sixth, and in another survey of forty-five communities the "City of the Angels" was eighteenth.[34]

Thus, although Los Angeles was not one of the leading cities in the nation in terms of the rise in the cost of living, arguments for wage increases could be justified on the basis that some inflation had occurred. Further, it was difficult to prove that living costs had risen less in open-shop Los Angeles than in unionized San Francisco. In fact, though the increase was apparently not so sharp in Los Angeles as in the nation as a whole, it was larger than the rise in San Francisco. As shown in table 2, the difference was not significant, but it did

TABLE 2

Cost of Living in Los Angeles as Compared with
San Francisco and the United States, 1914–1919
(December, 1914 = 100)

Date	Los Angeles	San Francisco	United States
December, 1914	100	100	100
December, 1915	98.1	99.0	101.9
December, 1916	107.0	107.5	113.5
December, 1917	126.7	125.6	134.7
December, 1918	154.7	152.9	162.5
December, 1919	182.1	175.9	186.4

Source: California Department of Industrial Relations, *The Cost of Living in California, 1914–22 and 1939–41* (Sacramento, 1941), p. 4.

indicate that the open-shop status of Los Angeles had little bearing on inflationary pressures. Obviously they existed, and gave local workers a reasonable basis for pressing for wage increases in the war-time years.[35]

The industrial disputes of employees of shipbuilding establishments at Los Angeles Harbor over recognition and wages received wide publicity in Los Angeles newspapers. There were a number of reasons for this: the industry grew rapidly in the war years until it employed more than 10,000 workers; among shipbuilding employers were several of the strongest supporters of the open shop, notably John F. Craig and Fred L. Baker; and federal war contracts awarded to shipbuilding firms aroused the patriotic interest of the public. The last major strike in the harbor industry had occurred at the Craig Shipbuilding Company on June 1, 1910. It had been coördinated with the metal trades strike in Los Angeles and had likewise been a failure; it ended in February, 1912, and the men returned to work under an open shop. Only seventy-five men had been involved in this dispute; but by 1914, a depression period, Craig employed some 150 men, with a normal work force of about 400.

The growth of the shipbuilding industry in Los Angeles, as in other ports, brought with it a number of problems that were never completely resolved and were distinct causes of industrial unrest. These included the lack of physical facilities to accommodate the rapidly expanding labor force; the shortage of adequate housing near the harbor and the limited transportation available; the tendency of shipbuilding wages to lag behind those of other industries (the high wages advertised to attract workers turned out to be maximum rather than average payments); the refusal of employers to concede the principle of collective bargaining with outside unions; and their endeavor to maintain either open or mixed shops. Many other factors encouraged employee grievances: managements were often new to the industry and unused to handling large, fast-growing work forces; eight-hour-day and overtime agreements were frequently violated; contractors were inclined to hire and fire at will; the national labor policy pertaining to shipyards tended to be indecisive, and wage decisions of federal shipbuilding agencies therefore failed to satisfy the workers; and skilled and unskilled employees, thrown together on the same job, frequently did each other's work. In addition, there was an undercurrent of discontent among Los Angeles shipbuilding workers as a holdover from the unsuccessful 1910 strike. All these factors resulted in a high labor turnover and one of the worst strike records of all the war industries.[36]

The first wartime dispute in the local yards developed on April 30, 1916, at the California Shipbuilding Company, successor to the Craig Shipbuilding Company. It was engineered by unions that had suffered from the 1910 defeat. The specific issues were recognition of the International Association of Machinists (IAM) as the collective bargaining agent, higher wages, the closed shop, an eight-hour day, and reinstatement of five skilled workers allegedly dismissed because of their union affiliation. All the men involved were working a nine-hour day except for those on government contracts, who were on eight-hour shifts, as required by law. The government work on the ways at this time included five submarines, one lighthouse tender, and three torpedo boats. More than 300 men left their jobs, including machinists, blacksmiths, boilermakers, patternmakers, iron shipbuilders, ship fitters, steam fitters, and foundry employees and helpers. Pickets were posted in the streets leading to the plant and also on a boat in the channel near the drydock in order to prevent the entry of strikebreakers either by land or by sea. W. C. Foley, manager of the company, refused to operate except as an open shop and consequently would not meet with any committee composed of union representatives. Under these circumstances Curly Grow of the Metal Trades Council and Walter Webster, organizer for the IAM, found it impossible to negotiate with Foley, and the plant remained closed.[37]

Secretary of Labor William B. Wilson appointed a federal mediator on May 3, but after several fruitless conferences with Foley and a committee from the Metal Trades Council, he was released from his assignment. By May 20 California Shipbuilding had resumed partial operations with the help of strikebreakers and some returning employees, though Grow stated that strikers were not going back to their jobs. By June 147 strikers were back in the plant and the dispute was all but over. As the pickets gradually melted away during the summer months, normal activities were resumed under open-shop conditions.

Meanwhile the strikers had requested financial assistance, and donations began to pour in from all over the United States and from as far away as the Canal Zone. They continued to be received for months after the end of the strike. The Los Angeles Central Labor Council voted an assessment of one cent a month per member to assist the strikers, and the *Record* published a constant stream of articles supporting the workers' side of the dispute and accusing the California Shipbuilding Company of cutting contract prices to get government work, and then keeping wages down in order to make a profit. The newspaper also charged that the firm employed inferior Japanese labor to maintain its operations; hence it advocated government ownership of all munition and shipbuilding establishments. Although the Metal Trades Council and the IAM failed to organize the company, they claimed final victory when the firm's contracts to build submarines were canceled on January 9, 1917. The *Citizen* alleged that this was because a government inquiry had discovered that the concern could not build submarines with inexperienced nonunion men.[38]

The period of American participation in the war witnessed no serious disputes in the local shipbuilding industry. Facilities were expanded when the Los Angeles Shipbuilding and Drydock Company was organized in 1917 under the leadership of Fred L. Baker of the Baker Iron Works and open-shop fame. It built thirty-five ships for the government in Los Angeles Harbor. The absence of a federal labor policy in the industry resulted in the establishment of the Shipbuilding Labor Adjustment Board, also called the Macy Board after its chairman. It was set up on June 19, 1917, in accordance with an agreement between Secretary of War Newton D. Baker and President Samuel Gompers of the AFL. In essence, the agreement provided for an open shop in the yards in exchange for union scales of wages and hours. It was signed by the internationals concerned, the most important of which were the machinists, the boilermakers, and the iron shipbuilders, and by the Building Trades Department of the AFL, but it was rejected by the carpenters who would not acquiesce in the open-shop principle. The board had jurisdiction over yards on both coasts. Its main duties were to hear grievances and to establish wage scales, hours, and working conditions. Wages were to be changed only as the cost of living shifted.

The absence of serious walkouts at Los Angeles Harbor in the months of actual hostilities did not mean that the board was successful in maintaining peace in the west coast shipbuilding industry. In yards located at San Francisco, Seattle, and Los Angeles, there were complaints that wage increases were not keeping pace with the rising cost of living. The unrest at San Francisco caused 24,000 men to strike on September 17, 1917. At the local harbor the Metal Trades Council took advantage of the dissatisfaction to set about organizing the Los Angeles Shipbuilding and Drydock Company; such action was not prohibited even though labor leaders could not force the recognition of unions during the war. In an effort to stave off strikes and threats of walkouts, the Macy Board granted a 31 per cent wage increase for west coast yards, which became effective in Los Angeles on November 26, 1917. This figure was chosen because data indicated the cost of living had risen by that amount since July, 1916. The basic wage rate for the shipbuilding trades was now $5.25 a day.[39]

The wage award did not bring peace. San Francisco shipyard workers alleged that it did not match the rise in living costs and again went out on strike. Complaints poured into Washington from workers and their union representatives. As a result, a temporary 10 per cent "war service premium" was awarded to all shipyard craftsmen working a full forty-eight hours in any consecutive six days. This was converted into a permanent increase after February 1, 1918, which meant a basic wage of $5.80 for an eight-hour day in Los Angeles yards, though it was claimed that some local employers were not yet paying even the $5.25 rate. Additional seeds of strife were sown at Los Angeles Harbor in the form of allegations of graft made by labor leaders against the Los Angeles Shipbuilding and Drydock Company. Grow, at this time president of the Metal Trades Council, stated that jobs were being bartered for lots at the harbor: a man could not get a job with the shipbuilding concern unless he held a lot purchased from the W. I. Hollingsworth Company, a real estate firm. He also charged that shipyard employers paid less than the Macy Board wage scales, discharged men because of their union affiliation, and failed to make adequate provision for transportation and housing. Landlords in water-front cities near the harbor were accused of rent profiteering, charging as much as $35 a month for tent houses with two rooms. Rents allegedly had trebled at Long Beach by July, 1918. In September a controversy arose over a rate increase by the Pacific Electric Railway, which coincided with efforts to organize its platform men. Several shipyard employees were arrested for riding the cars and refusing to pay their fares. The basic issue was that the commuter's rate of $6.50 for fifty-four rides was raised to $9.20 for sixty rides. The shipyard unions were behind the complaint, but little came of the attempt to force a reconsideration of the increase.[40]

Meanwhile the Macy Board wage award made earlier in the year had expired in August. Conferences held in Washington and Philadelphia by the board and the Emergency Fleet Corporation of the U.S. Shipping Board resulted in a new award in October, 1918, which on its face provided a 20 per cent wage increase. Accompanying reclassifications of labor, however, actually resulted in lower rates for some trades and no change for workers in the highest-paid crafts. Approximately 15,000 workers were affected at the local yards. Los Angeles delegates to a convention of the Metal Trades Pacific Coast District Council in Seattle on November 7 lodged a protest against the award, demanding a basic wage of $1 an hour for mechanics and $6 a day for helpers and laborers; but they achieved nothing. The constant unrest and stream of complaints strengthened the various unions at the yards, however, as the men sought a medium to express their displeasure with current hours, wages, and working conditions. Among the unions that gained members were Ship Carpenters, Caulkers and Boat Builders Local No. 1654; Blacksmiths Local No. 160; Plumbers, Steam Fitters and Helpers Local No. 616; Ship Fasteners Local No. 2040; Ship Riggers Local No. 38A–17; and Shipyard Laborers and Helpers Local No. 38A–18. The last two were associated with the International Longshoremen's Association. Fearing a rash of strikes now that the war had ended, Charles Piez, director-general of the Emergency Fleet Corporation, ran two full-page advertisements in the *Times,* the *Examiner,* and the *Record,* as well as in other Pacific Coast newspapers in February, 1919, to remind shipyard workers of the federal arrangement for settling grievances then in effect. He asked for their coöperation in accepting the necessary postwar reduction in overtime and Sunday work, pending a review of the entire government shipbuilding program by Congress.[41]

Piez' efforts were futile, for strikes had already broken out in Seattle and other Pacific Northwest ports, as well as in San Francisco, over the reduction of overtime; displeasure with the wage award of October, 1918; and the desire for higher hourly pay scales. A strike vote taken among the metal workers in the shipyards of San Pedro and Long Beach in February, 1919, was negative, however, largely because of a failure of Boilermakers Local No. 285 to ratify the proposal to walk out. A short strike not sanctioned by any union occurred on February 8 at Southwestern Shipbuilding Company over the discharge of a union steward, but it was only indirectly connected with the underlying dissatisfactions. In March the boilermakers reversed their previous stand and asked for a pay scale of $1 an hour and a forty-four-hour week at the Los Angeles Shipbuilding and Drydock Company, claiming that these had been in effect for months in northern yards. As attempts were made in subsequent weeks to avert a general walkout at the plant, the basic issues began to center more on the closed shop and the personnel of the three-man employee committee that handled grievances with management. The company was open shop but had been dealing amicably for some time with this committee, which was elected by the shop chairmen of the twenty-three crafts working in the yard. In the spring one of the members of the committee, H. G. Grimes of the machinists' union, lost his spot to G. W. Lawless of the pipe fitters. Grow, immediate past president of the Metal Trades Council and business agent for the machinists, refused to trust the three-man shop committee now that Grimes no longer was a member. He sought to deal directly with the company for the union, but management officials rejected his overtures.

A strike precipitated by the machinists soon followed, with both day and night crews, totaling more than 6,000 men, walking out on May 2. The prime issue was the closed shop, which Baker, the firm's president, had no intention of granting. As Henry W. Morse of the Emergency Fleet Corporation managed to get the machinists to withdraw their demand, all the men returned to work two days later. But the flames of strife broke out again on May 20, when 600 machinists quit because of alleged discrimination against union men. The strikers claimed that the graveyard shift had been dropped and that about 10 per cent of the employees had been dismissed the previous week. Some of the men laid off were old employees with seniority rights, a number of whom had previously served effectively on the shop committee.[42]

Six days after the machinists' walkout, other crafts joined the dispute, but the strike could hardly have been called at a more inopportune time. Because of the reduction in shipbuilding activities, Baker simply shut down the plant instead of replacing the strikers. Federal shipping officials conferred with union representatives and the company. The Los Angeles City Council passed a resolution urging settlement, and even the mayor offered his services as a mediator, but to no avail; Baker stated that the plant would remain closed until the men were ready to resume work under the old conditions. He indicated his willingness to deal with an employee shop committee but not with strikers or outside union officials.

By June 1 many of the strikers had found jobs elsewhere in the metropolitan area or had gone to northern yards seeking employment. Although the other shipbuilding firms at the harbor remained open, they had no need to hire men who were unemployed because of the walkout. As the month progressed, several conferences were held between company representatives and strikers. A settlement was almost reached at a meeting on June 23, but company officials wished to make certain that employee representatives selected to serve on a new shop committee were not elected by the unions. Though the latter had dropped their demand for formal recognition, they insisted that the election of the committee members be held at the Labor Temple; management wanted it held at the yard in order to guarantee that nonunion men had a chance to vote. Union spokesmen pointed out that the pre-strike shop committee had been elected at union meetings held outside the plant and that 90 per cent of the men were members of the locals concerned. The company refused to concede this point, however, and the conferences collapsed.[43]

Two weeks later, on July 9, 1919, Baker secured a restraining order against a total of fifty labor leaders and organizations, including the Los Angeles Metal Trades Council, the boilermakers, and the machinists, preventing them from picketing or interfering with workers going to and from the plant or molesting them at interurban stations. Seeking then to reopen the plant, the company placed advertisements in newspapers requesting the strikers to return to work and welcoming inquiries from interested prospects. When the plant officially opened on July 10, the union claimed that only 70 former workers returned to work; according to Baker, the number was closer to 250 or 300. At any rate, by the end of the month the number of employees had reached 1,500.

The following November, officials of the machinists' locals that had initiated the walkout asked the Metal Trades Council to call off the strike. The company agreed to reinstate any men still out who wished to return to their old jobs, to recognize seniority rights, and to deal with an elected shop committee but not directly with the unions. Thus the strike ended with the reëstablishment of essentially the same conditions that existed before it began. As the walkout had never been officially sanctioned by the AFL, there was little sense in prolonging it without such support in the face of the company's success in reopening the plant. A further reason for terminating it was that Grow, a key leader of the machinists at the start of the strike, had since aligned himself with a left-wing faction at the national AFL convention and had largely lost the confidence of all but the more radical members of the Los Angeles labor movement.[44]

Meanwhile, another strike had been initiated at the two other major shipbuilding yards in the area as well as at other Pacific Coast ports. The local firms were the Southwestern Shipbuilding and Long Beach Shipbuilding companies, the latter having absorbed the California Shipbuilding Company in 1917. The basic issue was the existing wage structure at coastal yards. The Macy Board award of October, 1918, had been extended to October 1, 1919. Conferences held before the latter date to establish a wage scale were not successful from labor's viewpoint, as government representatives would permit an increase only if the additional expense was not passed on to Uncle Sam. Pressure was strong in government circles not to approve raises that might further push up the cost of living, for President Wilson had already asked railroad workers over the nation to postpone their wage demands for this reason. The government's attitude was expressed in the repudiation by the Emergency Fleet Corporation of an 8-cent-an-hour increase to which it had originally agreed on July 21. Southern California yards had never accepted this increase; but several northern firms that planned to put it into effect on October 1, 1919, reversed their positions after the EFC announcement.

Feeling that they had been double-crossed by the government and recognizing that employers would gladly accept the EFC wage decision, the workers walked out on October 1 from yards located in ports from Los Angeles to Seattle. Locally, 4,000 men struck at the Southwestern Shipbuilding Company and 1,800 at the Long Beach Shipbuilding Company. Los Angeles strike leaders theorized that the "Steel Trust" was behind the failure to grant the wage increase that the men thought they deserved on the basis of higher living costs. They believed that the steel managements wanted the walkout because 327,000 of their workers were out on strike in the East, and a shipbuilding work stoppage would ease the developing short supply of steel.[45]

During the walkout Long Beach Shipbuilding continued to operate with about half of its force; Southwestern shut down until November 10, when it reopened, again as an open shop. Officials of the Metal Trades Council, who had assumed direction of the dispute, failed to hold the participating unions together as the strike progressed. On November 4 the pipe fitters adopted a resolution to allow members to return to work and still retain their union standing. The boilermakers at Southwestern voted not to follow suit, but those at Long Beach Shipbuilding decided to return to their jobs. When Southwestern opened its doors, 2,000 men went back to work and 1,500 others filed applications for employment. The company continued the same shop committee system for grievances as before the walkout, except that elections were held at the yard rather than at the Labor Temple, thus further reducing the influence of the craft unions. On December 19 a majority of the unions still on strike at the Long Beach yard voted to end the walkout, an action in which the Metal Trades Council concurred, although the dispute continued in San Francisco.

The announcement of the end of the strike in Los Angeles attracted little notice; it had really been over for a month and a half. The unions involved had for weeks been torn by internal strife because of the "scabbing." In addition, an industrial union sponsored by the Industrial Workers of the World had begun to make headway with some of the strikers. This further complicated the problem of strike discipline and increased the desire of old-line craft union leaders to terminate the dispute in order to reduce the men's exposure to the industrial union concept. The annual convention of the California State Federation of Labor blamed the strike's failure on poor planning and the utter destruction of all discipline. The end result, however, was dictated by economic inevitabilities: Congress had to cut wartime appropriations for ships and shipyards had to reduce forces as contracts ran out. Under these circumstances, strikes could hardly succeed. Further, the shipyard operators at Los Angeles Harbor, who were old hands at the open-shop game, added up the facts to the usual conclusion that postwar strikes presented an opportunity to keep the unions where they belonged—outside the plants.[46]

4. THE METAL TRADES—DIRECT BENEFICIARIES OF WAR

The war boom in local shipyards placed emphasis on steel fabrication in Los Angeles, and this would inevitably give new life to unions that had been relatively dormant since the failure of the metal trades strike of 1910. In the first two and a half years of the conflict in Europe, however, there was little union activity outside the shipyards. Pile Drivers Local No. 181 was chartered in March, 1916, with thirty men, some of whom had formerly been with old Local No. 51. Molders Local No. 374 continued to struggle against the open-shop Founders' and Employers' Association. Wages ranged from $2.475 to $3.60 per day without extra compensation for overtime. Unionists complained that it was necessary to obtain a working card from the association in order to apply for a job and that, to get such a card, a man had to swear he was not a member of any union. Metal Polishers Local No. 67 engaged in a short strike in November, 1916, but only eight men were involved. The union also reported considerable organizing success, tripling its size by the end of the year and securing employment for all its members.

On November 30 Golden State Lodge No. 3 of the Amalgamated Association of Iron, Steel and Tin Workers went out on a brief strike at the Southern California Iron and Steel Company. The union had decided to take in the open-hearth workers employed in the mill, but the day after they joined several of them were discharged. When union officers were denied a hearing by the company, the work stoppage occurred. After two days management officials notified the union that they were willing to adjust the matter and the men went back to work. Two weeks later the Llewellyn Iron Works was damaged by fire. As this plant had been wrecked by a bomb explosion in the 1910 metal trades dispute, allegations immediately were made that the fire was of incendiary origin and possibly caused by union workers; but an electrical short circuit turned out to be the real culprit.

In 1917 conditions improved in the metal trades, as the Founders' and Employers' Association voluntarily introduced the eight-hour day into the city's fabrication plants with no reduction in wages. Although this helped to quiet complaints about working overtime without pay, continued organizing difficulties revealed no lessening of the domination of the open shop.[47]

Reorganization of the Metal Trades Council in 1917, coincidental with the entrance of the United States into the war, marked the beginning of a strong surge of activity among all affiliated unions. The geographical limits of the council were extended to include Wilmington, Long Beach, and San Pedro, in addition to Los Angeles, thus officially taking in the shipbuilding yards in the harbor area. By this time the direct impact of the war was being felt in southern California; employment was good and locals were increasing in membership. The unions tried to use this opportunity to strengthen their bargaining positions, and most of the organizing efforts were reasonably successful. Engineers Local No. 72, with about 300 members, faced competition from the Stationary Engineers' Association, backed by the Merchants' and Manufacturers' Association, but it still managed to make headway.

The most important dispute in 1917 began on November 1, when Golden State Lodge No. 3 of the Iron, Steel and Tin Workers again walked out at the Southern California Iron and Steel Company. The immediate cause, according to management, was the discharge of an intoxicated employee, which in turn led to demands for union recognition and the closed shop. The underlying reasons, however, were the union's belief that management was systematically eliminating its members from the plant and a desire to improve general working conditions, particularly to reduce work hours from twelve to eight with no decrease in pay. The plant, located at Fourth and Mateo streets, normally employed 400 men. One hundred were directly involved in the dispute, including fifteen open-hearth employees whose affiliation with the union late in 1916 had brought on the short strike of that year.[48]

At first the union tried to reach a peaceful agreement with management through the services of federal mediator Captain Charles T. Connell. By November 15, however, it was clear that the strikers' places were being filled and that the union would have to pursue another tactic. Pickets were therefore stationed at six or seven strategic locations around the plant in an attempt to persuade workers to join the ranks of those on strike. Their efforts were successful enough to cause the firm to become shorthanded and thus to seek an injunction against Local No. 3, its officers, and some of its members. On January 19, 1918, the company obtained a temporary injunction, which Superior Court Judge Frank G. Finlayson made permanent on February 26. Seventy-five defendants personally appeared at the hearing. Officials of the firm testified that it was operating day and night to fulfill contracts for steel products to be used in constructing ships for the

Emergency Fleet Corporation. According to A. C. Denman, the company's president, from thirty to forty men were picketing the plant, particularly during shift changes, and his employees had been threatened with physical violence. The actual occurrence of violence, however, could not be proved, though testimony indicated that some strikers had called on the wives of workers in an attempt to persuade them to get their husbands to quit their jobs. The union sought to demonstrate that all such persuasion had been peaceful and friendly, but its efforts were to no avail. Appealing to the patriotism of the strikers, the court declared that the nation faced the most serious crisis in its history and every possible means should be taken to avoid interference with the manufacture of war supplies. The strike was lost, as the injunction virtually stopped the picketing and all attempts to persuade employees to join the walkout.[49]

The strike at Southern California Iron and Steel was minor compared to another metal trades walkout in 1918. Fred L. Baker, chief executive of the Los Angeles Shipbuilding and Drydock Company, found himself in the middle of this dispute in his capacity as president of the Baker Iron Works. His open-shop firm was a supplier of shipyard steel, though it did not have direct government contracts. Trying to organize his plant in the spring of 1918, Molders Local No. 374 found itself up against the alleged discriminatory discharge of union men. The local was also seeking to obtain the same wage as was paid by the shipyards under the standard set by the Emergency Fleet Corporation, but it was the dismissal of nine molders on June 5 which actually precipitated the strike. Although the company claimed that the walkout on June 10 was without warning, the Metal Trades Council had apparently tried to reach an agreement on wages as early as May 2, but had received no reply to its request for a meeting. Federal mediator Connell, who entered the dispute on May 31, likewise could not arrange a meeting between union representatives and Baker. The latter had no intention of dealing with his men except as individuals. The firm followed the eight-hour-day policy of the Founders' and Employers' Association, and, according to Baker, its shop conditions, hours, and wages were the best possible under its production contracts. As his actions and statements provided no alternative to a strike, the union men followed up the discharge of the molders by voting to walk out.[50]

A total of 156 out of more than 500 employees struck. Connell discussed the issues with the principals in a three-hour conference, but Baker stood firm in his open-shop position. Curly Grow of the Metal

Trades Council collected 200 signatures to a petition demanding that the government take over the plant. Copies of the petition were to be forwarded to Secretary of Labor Wilson, the Emergency Fleet Corporation, and the Navy Department. Grow also gave the dispute a novel twist by declaring that the strike had a patriotic objective; if the government took over the plant in order to maintain peace, output would rise and more shipbuilding steel would be delivered. He claimed that Baker was unpatriotic in replacing molders on strike with Mexicans who could not speak English. Baker countered Grow's charges by asserting that he had the full loyalty of those employees still on the job. As proof, he said that all his workers attended a noon meeting on June 15 in his pattern shop and gave him a standing vote of confidence when he stated that the Baker Iron Works would always remain an open shop. According to Baker, the nine molders had been laid off because of lack of work in their departments, not because of their union affiliation. He was well aware that granting the strikers' demands would involve, at the least, the establishment of EFC shipyard wages, reinstatement of the nine molders with back pay for lost time, and an arrangement to provide for wage increases. Though he could still employ nonunion men, Baker believed that any agreement with the union would in fact mean recognition and the eventual establishment of a closed shop.[51]

The strike dragged on for months. The men who had walked out obtained employment elsewhere, but Molders Local No. 374 and the Metal Trades Council were not willing to give up. Finally, in December, the War Labor Board held a hearing on the issues under examiner Raymond Swing. Testimony by John Oller of the Emergency Fleet Corporation, who was stationed at the Baker Iron Works, supported Baker's contention that the nine molders had been laid off as a result of lack of work in the casting department. Management further pointed out that the men had been chosen for dismissal on the basis of efficiency, that those selected had been marginal employees, and that it would have been difficult to institute layoffs without including some unionists because sixty-four of the eighty men in the foundry were union members. WLB officials explained that it was standard board policy not to insist that a company recognize a union if it had not done so before the war. Thus the hearing ended without coming to conclusions satisfactory to the Metal Trades Council or the union. The Baker Iron Works in effect won the dispute and continued as an open shop. The final epitaph on the strike was written a year later, in December, 1919, when the Metal Trades Council authorized members of its constituent locals to accept employment at the Baker Iron Works without fear of union censure so long as they were returning to work to organize the employees.[52]

In contrast with the molders, the two boilermakers' locals made excellent progress in 1918. Seaside Local No. 285 was composed of iron shipbuilders working in the harbor area, whereas the membership of Local No. 92 came from firms in the city, including the railroad shops. Except for the 1919 walkouts in the shipyards, the boilermakers were able to adjust their grievances amicably with the companies that employed them. The locals grew very rapidly after the entrance of the United States into the war; in mid-1917 there were only twenty union boilermakers in Los Angeles County, but eight months later there were 2,600 men in the two unions, and by February, 1919, Local No. 285 alone had approximately 5,000 members working in the yards at the harbor.[53]

The organized machinists, like the boilermakers, quickly increased in number as the harbor's shipyards expanded in 1917, with Local No. 1306 of Long Beach and Local No. 311 of Los Angeles enjoying most of the growth. Before the war the latter had also benefited from the increased use of automobiles, succeeding in organizing garage mechanics at a number of repair shops throughout the city. By February, 1919, No. 311 was the largest organization affiliated with the Metal Trades Council and was growing at the rate of 250 new members a month, though it was soon to have its wings clipped by the unsuccessful shipyard strike later in the year. At the end of 1919 a new local, No. 1422, was established in Los Angeles for railroad shop workers, and shortly thereafter it became involved in the strike called by the shop unions. The greatest single leader of the machinists during these difficult war years was Curly Grow, but in December, 1919, ill health forced him to resign as business agent of Local No. 311. Ever since the near demise of the metal trades unions after the strike of 1910, Grow had been indefatigable in his efforts to bring them back to a position of importance in the local labor movement.[54]

Among the other metal trades organizations, Metal Polishers Local No. 67, Sheet Metal Workers Local No. 108, and the Metal Platers Union were probably the most active in 1918 and 1919. Most of the polishers worked in small shops scattered throughout the city. In September, 1917, they reported that they were 90 per cent organized, and in the following year they participated in a series of small strikes against thirteen firms. Although the open shop still prevailed, the polishers won a wage increase of $1 a day in most firms where union members worked. The sheet metal workers likewise continued to fight the open shop and made some headway in obtaining wage increases as well as in gaining members among workers in the railroad shops. By September, 1919, they were getting $7 a day; this was increased to $8 in February, 1920, and to $9 effective on June 1. The newly organized platers, on the other hand, did not fare so well. On January 14, 1918, they struck seventeen firms which were members of the Job Plating Association of Los Angeles, an open-shop organization, in an attempt to increase their wages from $4 to $5.25 for an eight-hour day. The association stood firm, however, and the struck firms closed down for the duration of the dispute. They were able to outlast the strikers and reopened a short time later under the same conditions that had existed before the walkout.[55]

5. THE BUILDING AND ALLIED TRADES

The war did not help the building trades unions so much as it did those in the metal trades. Although shipbuilding required the services of carpenters, the crafts employed in metal fabrication were far more important; the impact of the war in Los Angeles was felt mainly by firms connected with shipbuilding or engaged in the manufacture of products not readily procurable from the East during the emergency. The dissension within the Building Trades Council over Joshua Dale's organizing campaign and the fund-raising schemes of the Union Labor Temple Association simmered down by the middle of 1916, but the battle with the open shop continued. The withdrawal of two-thirds of the membership of Bricklayers Local No. 2 in opposition to Dale to form the independent Bricklayers Mutual Benefit Association in October, 1915, was construed as an open-shop scheme. To counteract its influence, Local No. 2 organized dummy contract firms to bid for business even at a loss, the difference to be made up by the bricklayers' international union. A number of important contracts were secured before the *Times* exposed the program as a device to permit the gradual introduction of the closed shop. Thereafter open-shop contractors refused to allow the union-organized firms to bid on bricklaying jobs, and the plan made no further headway.[56]

The Building Trades Council sought to better its position vis-à-vis the open shop by supporting the Central Labor Council in forming a Joint Executive Board in the fall of 1915. The following year it elected a strong group of officers, including J. B. Bowen as president and Tom Barker as secretary and business agent, and reëlected them in 1917 as a result of their successful efforts to strengthen the building trades unions. Organizing activities during the war centered on the carpenters as the key union group. Carpenters Local No. 158 had withdrawn from the council in 1915 in disagreement over internal administrative policies, but it rejoined in February, 1916. Its reaffiliation permitted the initiation of an active membership campaign which extended throughout 1916 and 1917 and involved, in addition, Carpenters Locals No. 2516, 46, 426, and 884, the last being composed exclusively of millmen. Although the carpenters were occupied on the national level with a jurisdictional fight with the metal trades over the use of metal trim, and on the local level with the beginning of a long struggle with the International Alliance of Theatrical Stage Employees in the Hollywood studios, their growth in Los Angeles was basically a matter of their ability to combat the open shop in building construction. The organizing campaign reached a peak in the summer of 1917 when initiation fees were temporarily reduced to $5 in the hope of reaching a goal of 2,000 new members. In addition, the entire front page of the *Citizen* for July 9 was devoted to the carpenters' campaign.

The goal of 2,000 was not reached, but 1,000 new men did join the various carpenter unions, which could then claim that 85 per cent of Los Angeles County carpenters were organized. They felt strong enough to ask the Master Builders' Association for a conference in order to discuss wages and other demands. The construction carpenters wanted a $5 day, Saturday afternoons off, double pay for Sunday work, and a closed shop; the cabinetmakers' demands were the same except for a wage of $4.50 for an eight-hour day. Most of the latter were employed by a few large firms, including Peck and Hills Furniture Company, Pacific Sash and Door Company, Southern California Hardwood and Manufacturing Company, and the Hammond Lumber Company.[57]

C. L. Peck, president of the Master Builders' Association, countered the demands of the carpenters by pointing out that the members of his group had recognized the rise in the cost of living over the past year by increasing wages from $3 and $3.50 a day to the current $4 and $4.50 effective in September, 1917. Refusing to meet with the unions, Peck in effect challenged them to strike by indicating that limited building activity made it a poor time to walk out. The construction carpenters and the cabinetmakers accepted the challenge, but only 300 struck on two major jobs. A compromise was soon worked out; on September 23 the Master Builders' Association agreed to give the men part of their wage and hour demands but not union recognition. The millmen struck separately on October 11, 1917, against the Southern California Mill Owners' Association when the latter failed to sign a conciliation agreement submitted to it by federal mediators Charles Connell and Harris Weinstock. Although the operations of four large firms and twenty smaller mills were noticeably slowed down by the walkout, the employers won this dispute. Nonunion replacements were found in spite of active picketing, and the strikers were soon walking the streets looking for jobs.[58]

On September 11, 1918, the construction carpenters struck the Wilson-Willard Manufacturing Company, which was erecting a new factory building. Thirty-two men walked out, demanding a $6 day, a forty-four-hour week, and Saturday afternoons off. The attempt to break this open-shop job did not succeed, however, and the building was completed six weeks later. After launching a new organizing campaign in January, 1919, the carpenters demanded a $6 wage, an eight-hour day, and a forty-four-hour week. The lack of change in the unions' demands with regard to working hours during the entire war period indicates that they failed to gain from contractors a uniform acceptance of their aims along these lines. Under such circumstances, a claim that 85 per cent of the carpenters under the Los Angeles District Council were organized as early as the summer of 1917 seems dubious. The *Times* disputed this claim a year later when it stated that only 700 of 6,000 carpenters were then union members. The further fact that carpenters were still genuinely concerned about unsatisfactory working conditions in 1919 gives support to the *Times's* statement that they were not nearly so well organized as they were wont to claim in their published reports. Although the union scale was finally raised to $7 a day in August, 1919, success still did not crown their efforts to achieve shorter working hours.[59]

Unlike the carpenters, the electrical workers were organized into one union, IBEW Local No. 61, consisting largely of linemen, at the outbreak of the war in Europe. The unemployment caused by the depression of 1913–1914 had largely abated by the latter part of 1915 and, as the war progressed, two additional locals were organized to take care of the increase in membership: No. 370, telephone and signal workers, and No. 83, inside wiremen and building trades electricians. By September, 1916, the leaders of Local No. 61 believed that the union was strong enough to challenge the Pacific Power and Light Company on the issue of alleged discrimination against union members. They therefore called a strike against the utility, but it soon turned into a lockout as the company continued to operate successfully without the assistance of the 110 men who had struck. Attacking from another quarter, a three-man committee appointed by the Central Labor Council sought an audience with city authorities in a futile attempt to persuade them to buy out the company. The committee, alleging that the utility's equipment was in bad shape, argued that the city should spend large sums to get the plant into condition to give adequate service to the community. Although the only immediate issue was the company's refusal to allow its employees to be union members, charges of labor exploitation were also made, as the linemen's wages were $1 to $1.50 per day less than those paid elsewhere on the Pacific Coast. In December local unionists made a door-to-door appeal to customers to use less electricity or to refrain from dealing with the firm, while the *Citizen* urged them to patronize the municipal power and light company. But all efforts were in vain and the strike was lost. Nevertheless, during 1917 the linemen had some success in organizing members of their craft employed by the city, mainly because a number of the foremen belonged to the union and refused to employ new linemen unless they also were affiliated with Local No. 61. Formal union recognition by the city was not achieved, however, in spite of at least two strike threats.[60]

Another futile, though widespread, attempt to enforce demands by striking a public utility occurred on February 21, 1918, when Local No. 61 joined with several other southern California electrical workers' unions in a walkout against the Southern California Edison Company. The unions had tried to settle the dispute without a strike, but concessions made by the company were not sufficient to satisfy the labor negotiators. The basic issues were the alleged discriminatory discharge of five men at the Mill Creek plant and the refusal of management to meet with union representatives and federal mediator Connell to discuss questions of wages and hours. Connell stated publicly that he thought the Edison concessions were fair, that the unions apparently wanted a closed shop, and that they were setting a dangerous precedent by striking in wartime, in the face of urgent requests to the contrary from their national president. Their specific demands were a 20 per cent increase in wages for employees paid by the month, $1 a day more for men on day duty, and eight-hour shifts.

Initially, as Local No. 61 struck before seeking the sanction of the Central Labor Council, the latter did not support the walkout. Superintendent B. F. Pearson of the utility quickly labeled the strike a fizzle, claiming that only 28 of 1,340 men had left their jobs, although the *Record* stated that 75 per cent of the local union linemen had walked out. Six days after the strike began, Central Labor Council officials met with officers of the company in an attempt to find a way of settling the dispute, but the management refused arbitration. Pearson asserted that the men at Mill Creek were not union members at the time of their discharge and did not join until a week later. Other management officials made it clear that a labor surplus existed, and the strike had thus saved the company the chore of firing unneeded men. As management became increasingly adamant, the Central Labor Council endorsed the strike early in March, requested donations for the strikers, and put the utility on its unfair list. But the company had the last word; the strikers were replaced and labor lost the dispute. Finally, in September, 1918, the Southern California Edison Company was dropped from the unfair list of the Central Labor Council at the request of Local No. 61.[61]

IBEW Local No. 83 was formed by inside wiremen from Local No. 61 in January, 1917. By June it had 300 members, and was expanding in the electrical contracting industry of the city. Although the wiremen did not engage in any major disputes during the war, by 1919 they were earning $6.40 for a day of eight hours and working a forty-four-hour week, with double time for holidays. In contrast, IBEW Local No. 370, composed of telephone and signal workers, became involved in a serious dispute with the Southern California Telephone Company, a subsidiary of the Pacific Telephone and Telegraph Company, in the year after the Armistice. The members of No. 370 were telephone linemen, switchmen, and installers, who, in turn, assisted in launching another union of operators in 1917 known as Local No. 52-A. A strike of telephone workers against the Pacific Telephone and Telegraph Company in the latter part of 1917 in several cities of the Pacific Northwest had not spread to Los Angeles. The 1919 dispute was the result of nationwide dissatisfaction among telephone employees over existing wages and the lack of free collective bargaining through their unions. During the war telephone and telegraph services had been placed under the general jurisdiction of the Postmaster General. They were slated for return to private hands on August 1, 1919, which meant that, for the most part, the open shop would again prevail. Telephone workers believed that their chances for redress of their grievances would be better under government supervision than they would be after the turnover date. At the same time, however, the workers had not been pleased with their relations with the Postmaster General, who had been less than receptive to the idea of union recognition and the subsequent negotiation of wage demands.

At the end of the war telephone operators received $1.50 to $2.25 per day, or basic weekly wages ranging from $9 to $14. Early in 1919 local operators joined others up and down the coast in demanding union recognition and daily wages ranging from $2 to $4, depending on experience. They were joined by the telephone linemen, switchmen, and installers of Local No. 370, who wanted from $4.75 to $6.40 per day. About 900 telephone workers and 600 female operators were involved locally, though some 9,000 girls were behind the demands in all the territories served by Pacific Telephone and Telegraph and a few small independent companies. The Postmaster General made an effort to meet their demands by asking the officers of the utilities involved, including the Southern California Telephone Company, to appoint someone to discuss the complaints with employee representatives. As a result of his failure to act directly on wages, strike threats in California cities became actual walkouts, with Los Angeles telephone workers and operators initiating such a step on June 16, two days before other communities.[62]

On the first day of the strike, Miss S. L. Griffin, president of Local 52-A, announced that 1,200 rather than 600 operators and about 500 male workers had actually left their jobs. The company immediately began to fill the vacancies by hiring former workers who had left to get married and by recruiting some new personnel. In order to reduce the chances of conflict with pickets during shift changes, arrangements were made to feed and house the strikebreakers in telephone offices. Those desiring to go to and from their homes each day were given police protection. In the meantime, small groups of girl strikers visited business firms and sought to talk with their private exchange operators. On being denied entrance, they called in repeatedly by telephone, trying to persuade the private switchboard girls to quit and occasionally using abusive language and threats. Public telephone service throughout the city was impaired during the first few days of the walkout because of a lack of qualified operators. In addition, strikers made the situation worse by using pay phone booths to place long-distance calls to fake numbers in an effort to harass the girls on duty. To stop this practice, the company plugged out pay stations early in the dispute, thus further inconveniencing the public.[63]

Although the strike quickly spread from Los Angeles to other cities, it was largely confined to the states of California and Nevada. Conferences in San Francisco between union officials and company representatives were watched closely by Pacific Northwest locals, but their members did not actually walk out. L. C. Grasser, vice-president of the

International Brotherhood of Electrical Workers, publicly stated that the walkout was illegal. He pointed out that on June 14 the Postmaster General had granted workers the right to bargain collectively with the companies through employee committees, and that actual meetings had been scheduled to begin on June 19, three days after the strike occurred. According to Grasser, a strike cancellation order had been issued when collective bargaining rights had been secured, but some Western locals had ignored it, stating that they were going to strike and remain out until they obtained a satisfactory increase in pay. Striking Los Angeles operators were as good as their word in this connection, and they also visited outlying towns to persuade other telephone girls to walk out. So successful were they that complete tie-ups in service developed in towns such as Fullerton, Upland, Seal Beach, San Bernardino, Colton, Highland, Rialto, and even as far away as Calexico.

Nevertheless, C. F. Mason, general superintendent for the Pacific Telephone and Telegraph Company in the southern California area, admitted only that there were some slight "disaffections" in service, and the *Times* flatly stated that the strike had been virtually broken two days after it began through the employment of new operators. The strike was deemed of sufficient importance, however, for the City Council to pass a resolution urging arbitration and for the police and the mayor to refuse to permit the strikers to parade in downtown streets. Although little disorder was reported except for some name calling by pickets and the throwing of rotten eggs at strikebreakers on June 20, the *Times* recanted its statement that the strike was over by noting on June 21 that the walkout was still effective and normal service not yet restored. Further evidence of the strike's effectiveness was the issuance of a temporary restraining order on June 20 by Superior Court Judge Dana R. Weller, which prohibited picketing by telephone workers and operators.[64]

The pickets disappeared in response to the injunction, and service began to improve as more workers were employed without fear of reprisals by strikers. Some of the girls who had gone out began to return to their jobs, but the mechanical departments continued to operate with only minimum maintenance as a result of inadequate male personnel. Other Los Angeles unions gave financial assistance to those remaining on strike. In an effort to induce the telephone company to improve the wages of operators, the members of Local No. 370 offered to lower their demand from $6.40 to $6 a day and to return to work if the girls were granted their requests. Community pressure to end the strike was placed on the company at the end of June when a group of residents circulated petitions demanding a cut in phone bills during the walkout because of the inadequate service. Shortly thereafter, the utility announced a new wage scale for operators effective July 1, starting at $2 a day for beginners and reaching $19 a week after five years. The old scale did not reach a peak until an employee had worked for seven years. The new wage schedule did not quite meet the demands of the union, which wanted $2 for beginners on the day shift with a top of $4 after two years of employment, but it was better than the old one. A new wage scale also was posted for technicians, which ran from $6 a day for repeater men, line and station repair personnel, inspectors, cable testers, linemen, station installers, and switchboard repair employees, to $6.50 for cable splicers. In addition, charges were reduced to subscribers who had had intermittent service during the walkout.[65]

On July 11 the company put hundreds of pay stations back into operation as service began to approximate normal. As the strikers' funds were running low, some support for a back-to-work movement developed when management announced that the new wage scales would be made retroactive to January 1. The officers of the IBEW and federal government officials added force to this movement by asking the local strikers to return to work on the basis of the wage compromise. Accordingly, on July 20, the latter voted to do so by a margin of 285 to 115. The following day 900 operators and 361 telephone workers went back on the job without discrimination. By July 23 all strikers south of the Tehachapi were at work and the strike was over in the Los Angeles area. A week later the federal government turned the utilities back to private control.[66]

The termination of the strike, however, did not end the dissension, for on August 21 local telephone workers voted against the compromise agreement; but the balloting was an expression of dissatisfaction rather than a walkout threat. The workers were better off than they had been, though their full demands had not been granted. In addition, they charged that reëmployed strikers were being discriminated against contrary to the express statements of company officials. A number of the ex-strikers complained of being hired only for half shifts instead of the full days they had been working before the walkout. Nothing came of the complaints, however, and by the end of the year Telephone Operators Local No. 52-A had all but disappeared, giving up its quarters in the Labor Temple to seek a smaller meeting place at a lower rent. The telephone company retained its open-shop character, for collective bargaining rights were not granted either to the operators or to the technicians who were members of Local No. 370.[67]

Unlike the electrical workers, who exemplified a strong spirit of coöperation, the floor layers were torn by dissension emanating from the 1916 organizing campaign. Opposition to outside organizers resulted in a secession movement from Floor Layers Local No. 1612. A substantial number of members withdrew in the course of a strike of ninety workers on May 3, 1916, against a group of hardwood flooring contractors. The new union formed by the secessionists, the Independent Hardwood Floor Workers Union of America, was closely associated with the local Bricklayers Mutual Benefit Association, which had been similarly established. The separation, however, did not last very long, as Floor Layers Local No. 1612, together with some members of the independent union, merged with Local No. 426 of the United Brotherhood of Carpenters and Joiners in 1917.

Hod carriers, building laborers, and hoisting engineers were also involved in the internal disputes of 1916 within and between the Building Trades Council and the Central Labor Council, but their wartime activities were not particularly noteworthy. Local No. 42 of the wood, wire, and metal lathers was similarly quiescent, except that its members did join with the plumbers of Local No. 78 in a threat to strike for higher wages on July 3, 1919. Both groups wanted a wage increase from $6.50 to $7 per day. The sheet metal workers also made demands at the same time, threatening a walkout on July 14 if they did not receive a raise from $6 to $7 a day. Because the postwar construction revival in Los Angeles put the building trades unions in a strategic position to make wage demands, the requests of all three groups were granted, with only the lathers actually being forced to strike.[68]

The painters and paper hangers were among the most active crafts in the building trades during World War I. They were organized into Locals No. 267, 350, 202, 1063, and 511, the last being established in October, 1916. Art Glass Workers Local No. 636 also was associated with the painters and paper hangers. An aggressive membership campaign was instituted among nonunion painters in 1917 under the leadership of Gus Uhl, an international organizer for the union, who attempted to strike a bargain with the employers' Master Painters' Association. The latter was supporting a proposed city ordinance to require the licensing of painting contractors. The locals agreed to back the ordinance if the employers would grant a closed shop, but these terms were too drastic for contractors who were used to open-shop conditions. Apparently the establishment of restricted entry or semi-monopolistic conditions by a licensing procedure was considered appropriate for contractors, but there was no desire on their part to provide the same privileges for unions.

Failing in this attempt to gain their ends, the painters continued organizing until, early in 1918, they believed they had sufficient power to request the closed shop, a wage increase from $3.50 to $5 a day, and a half shift on Saturday. These demands were presented to the Master Painters' Association in February, with a strike threatened for April 1 if they were not met. Spokesmen for the association came to an agreement with Painters Council No. 36 to establish a $4 day for journeymen, with a gradual increase to $5, and the forty-four-hour week, but they refused to grant the closed shop. The compromise was enough to forestall the strike, and the $5 day became effective in September, 1918, though Barker Brothers refused to institute the forty-four-hour week and was struck the following November. Further demands to raise wages from $5 to $6 for an eight-hour day were made on the Master Painters' Association early in 1919. The employers offered an increase of 50 cents a day with a similar increment three months later, but this compromise was not acceptable. The painters wanted the $6 minimum under a closed-shop contract without delay and struck to get it on April 2. Some thirty-five to forty contractors were affected by the walkout, but they had previously agreed not to accede to the union demands. As usual, the six-week strike ended with a victory for the open shop, though a few establishments did sign contracts.[69]

Among the remaining building trades unions, the plasterers, the plumbers, the roofers and shinglers, and the tile layers showed the most life in 1915–1919. Plasterers Local No. 2 began to stir from its apathy under the impetus of the 1916 organizing drive, but did not achieve much in the way of job control. Although by 1919 it was seeking to gain an $8 day, the closed shop, and a five-day week, it actually had very little strength in the city. In an article in the *Times* that year it was estimated that about 20 per cent of the plasterers belonged to the union. Even if this figure is doubled, it does not indicate adequate job control. Plumbers Local No. 78, on the other hand, strengthened its position during the war. Its wage demand in company with the lathers in 1919 led to the granting of a $7 day, effective July 1, for unionized jobs, and an $8 day with a forty-four-hour week by the end of the year. As for most other building trades unions, the revival of construction after the war, until the onset of the postwar depression, aided the plumbers in achieving a high level of employment, though they did not have a complete closed shop. Because many employers were former union members, job control was easier for the plumbers than for crafts like the lathers, the plasterers, and the carpenters.

In contrast with the plumbers, the roofers and shinglers had to rebuild their organization virtually from the ground up during the war years. Union activity was negligible for all practical purposes until 1917, when J. M. Cameron, an international organizer, came to the city and revived Local No. 21. In October of that year the roofers threatened to strike for a wage increase. Some employers partly acceded to their demands, raising daily wages to $5 for foremen, $4 for journeymen, and $3.50 for kettlemen, but others flatly refused. The ensuing eight-day strike was ended when federal mediator Connell persuaded all the employers to grant the compromise wage scale and the men to return to work on that basis. Further disputes in 1918 and 1919 failed to make a dent in the open shop, though wages were raised to $7 for foremen and $6 for journeymen by September of the latter year. Like the roofers, the tile layers were faced with a strong open-shop system. In addition, they were deeply involved in the internal labor dispute of 1916, when a large number of them refused to follow the leadership of outside organizers. Before the year was over, however, they were back in the fold and embarking on a drive for new members. Because of hard-core employer opposition, the tile layers' membership growth was frustratingly slow. Although they achieved a wage of $8 a day for journeymen by the end of 1919, it applied only to the few union men in Local No. 18, not to all the craftsmen in the city.[70]

6. THE WAR AND OTHER UNIONS—PROGRESS AND DISAPPOINTMENT

The printing trades engaged in no unusual activities in the war period. Several events occurred, however, which gave additional support to the local open-shop opposition to the printing unions. In 1915 the annual meeting of the Board of Governors of the Open Shop Division of the United Typothetae and Franklin Clubs, organized in 1912 to fight the battles of the parent organization against unionization, was held in Los Angeles. This was symbolic of the city's reputation as the stronghold of the open shop, which developed from General Otis' struggle with the printers' union in 1890. The second event of significance to labor was the reorganization in 1919 of the Printing Trades Division of the Merchants' and Manufacturers' Association. The new president of the division was Irwin Rice, an open-shop employer, who was to lead it effectively in its avowed purpose of dominating the local printing industry. One of his first acts was to establish an employment service to find nonunion craftsmen for the division's members, though other activities characteristic of a trade association were also carried on under the direction of Seneca C. Beach. A third development in 1919, the organization in Cincinnati of the International Joint Conference Council, composed of employer organizations and unions in the printing industry, did not initially seem to strengthen the hand of the open shop. Its aim was to adjust controversies through voluntary agreements achieved by means of a board of conciliation. In its first major action, the Joint Conference resolved to institute the forty-four-hour week in the printing trades on May 1, 1921, but the long and bitter struggle that ensued before the change was made belied the peaceful objectives of the organization.[71]

Without displaying any notable aggressiveness, some of the printing trades unions achieved real gains in the war years. The members of the typographical, mailer, web pressmen, stereotyper, pressmen, and press feeder locals were able to obtain regular wage increases as the cost of living rose. After a year and a half of negotiations, Mailers Local No. 9 gained a victory in September, 1917, when the *Tribune,* the *Examiner,* the *Herald,* the *Express,* and the *Record* signed wage agreements covering union members in their employ. Similar success had been achieved by Typographical Union No. 174 six months earlier in negotiations with the Publishers' Association for a higher wage scale to replace the one that had expired. The printers won another new agreement at the end of the war, effective on January 1, 1919. It provided $34 a week for day work and $37 for night shifts on the city's newspapers. Before the year was out, most job offices followed suit in raising wages, though their rate was $32 a week. Of the daily newspapers, only the *Times* continued to refuse to enter into any agreement with Local No. 174.[72]

International Ladies' Garment Workers Local No. 52, Journeymen Tailors Local No. 81, and United Garment Workers Local No. 125 provided most of the activity in the clothing trades during World War I. Local No. 52 engaged in a series of sporadic strikes from 1915 to 1922, and after the war was accused of harboring left-wing political adherents. A two-month strike occurred in 1915, but there were conflicting reports on its success. Although ILGWU leaders claimed that they had won a closed shop from the employers' Cloak and Suit Protective Association of Los Angeles, open-shop supporters alleged that the places of all strikers were filled with nonunion workers. This dispute was minor, however, compared to a walkout of members of the local in August, 1917. The issues then were a forty-four-hour week, pay for six holidays, the replacement of gas flatirons with electric appliances, and wage increases averaging 15 per cent. Conferences with the employers' association delayed the actual walkout and resulted in some compromises, including the employees' offer to forfeit pay for observed Jewish religious holidays if full wages were received for legal and popular national holidays. In spite of the compromise, agreement was not achieved; thirteen shops were struck on August 28 and pickets were placed at the entrances. The *Times* labeled the dispute an attempt to find a breach in the open-shop front. After three days a settlement provided for a 7.5 per cent wage increase, but not much else. The strikers found the employers too firmly entrenched in their open-shop position; in addition, expected aid from the San Francisco Central Labor Council failed to arrive. ILGWU leaders were convinced, however, that the employers would deal justly with the strikers if they called off the dispute and returned to work. Consequently, a twelve-month wage agreement was ratified by both sides, to remain in effect until August 1, 1918.[73]

As the expiration date of the agreement approached, both sides began to jockey for a superior bargaining position. They published accusations and counteraccusations concerning employment conditions and other issues; minor grievances became brief work stoppages or lockouts. Finally, in September, 1918, a five-day strike of 350 employees resulted in a new agreement covering seventeen firms and providing for a union shop as well as a 15 per cent wage increase. But peace was only temporary. In June, 1919, disputes broke out again in shop after shop until fifteen establishments and 375 workers were involved. The new demands were a 40 per cent wage increase and a forty-four-hour week, both of which the employers refused to consider. Violence developed as one employer was assaulted and others were threatened with the dynamiting of their shops. After ten weeks of conflict an agreement was signed on August 25. It provided for a two-year contract, minimum weekly wages for women ranging from $18 to $42 according to skill, pay of from $40 to $50 for operators, and a forty-four-hour week. Even after the settlement the union had difficulty maintaining peace, partly because of the IWW element within Local No. 52 which periodically blew up minor grievances into work stoppages. Although it was estimated that only about 10 per cent of the members were Wobblies, they regularly attended meetings and took advantage of the apathy of the remaining 90 per cent. IWW and other left-wing influence continued to plague Local No. 52 for some years after the war.[74]

Like many Los Angeles unions, Tailors Local No. 81 had the assistance of an outside organizer in its membership drive in 1916. It gained 200 new members and unionized eight firms. Peaceful organizing activity continued during 1917 and 1918, marred only by a strike in the latter year at Foreman and Clark, a men's ready-to-wear store, before an agreement was signed. In 1919 open-shop forces reasserted their determination to thwart union agreements with custom tailoring firms, men's shops, and other retail clothing outlets. The first phase of the struggle began when bushelmen, tailors who handled alterations in ready-to-wear stores, demanded $30 a week, the eight-hour day, and the right of collective bargaining. Upon rejection of their demands, 100 of them struck just before Easter at such stores as Mullen and Bluett, Silverwood's, Desmond's, Harris and Frank, Scott Brothers, Wood Brothers, and the Hub and Nebraska Clothing companies. All these firms were backed by the Merchants' and Manufacturers' Association in their stand against the union. Pickets were placed in front of the stores, but there was no violence as police officers kept them moving and prevented interference with sidewalk traffic. The struck firms were willing to grant all the demands except recognition and collective bargaining. Their obduracy on that issue and their ability to employ strikebreakers cost the bushelmen a victory after more than three months of fruitless picketing.[75]

Meanwhile, a strike was brewing among other members of Local No. 81, including pressers, machine operators, tailors, and helpers employed by custom tailoring shops in the city. Their agreement was due to expire on September 1, 1919, and open-shop employers in the trade were determined to block its renewal. Union demands for the new contract included $44 per week for tailors, pressers, and machine operators, $39 for helpers and trimmers, $29 for women assistants, a forty-four-hour week, time and a half for overtime, double time for Saturday afternoons, a workday from 8 A.M. to 5 P.M. with an hour for lunch, and six holidays with pay. The employers offered a top wage of $36 a week and an eight-hour day. The union believed it had the whip hand because of its job control in the craft and a shortage of tailors resulting from the war and from strict apprenticeship rules which had deterred young men from entering the trade. As a compromise was not achieved before expiration of the contract, union members walked out on August 30 under the slogan "Forty-four and forty-four, or we won't do a darn stitch more." Employers organized as the Los Angeles Merchant Tailors' Exchange promptly countered with a lockout, so that 700 to 900 tailors found themselves out of jobs. As the dispute was coast-wide, this number was increased by strikers in Portland, San Francisco, Seattle, and other cities. Estimating that 8,000 men were out, Sam G. Levy, president of the employers' Pacific Coast Merchant Tailors' Association, stated that the entire custom tailoring business on the coast was almost at a standstill. The struck firms remained closed for more than two months, and then reopened on November 10 as open shops. Tailors on strike had the option of returning under these conditions or of seeing their places gradually taken by strikebreakers. They chose the former, with the result that the union lost its bargaining position after having had agreements with most of the employers for nearly ten years. It was a serious blow for the tailors and one of the most outstanding victories for the open shop in Los Angeles in the first year after the war.[76]

In contrast with the tailors, United Garment Workers Local No. 125 continued to maintain a strategic position in the manufacture of work clothing. Reasonably good relationships existed with most of the employers, including signed agreements and regular wage increases. Although several minor strikes against single firms occurred between 1915 and 1919, they were far from being industry-wide. Most of the members were women, many of them foreign-born. In an effort to help them acquire citizenship, Local No. 125 worked out a plan to give classes in the required subjects in the Labor Temple in July and August, 1917, with volunteer teachers. Shortly thereafter, the city Board of Education was persuaded to establish a regular public evening school in the Temple, which was attended by 200 union members who wanted to become citizens.[77]

The brewery trades, like the garment workers of Local No. 125, had the advantage of producing a workingmen's item, but they faced an even more formidable foe than open-shop employers—prohibition. In 1914 the brewery unions represented, by and large, the only 100 per cent organized crafts in the city. Only the bartenders, who were associated more closely with the culinary trades, were not completely organized, though about 90 per cent of them belonged to the union. In the preliminary skirmishes between the "drys" and the "wets" in 1916, the Central Labor Council supported the brewery trades because of the threat to employment if a law against alcoholic beverages was passed. Although the prohibition struggle waxed hotter in 1917, the brewery unions continued to maintain job control in Los Angeles and won a new four-year contract which provided for wage increases of from 25 to 75 cents a day, depending on the craft involved. But they came to the temporary end of the road when the manufacture of beer ceased as of midnight on November 30, 1918. Approximately 2,000 workers in forty-five California breweries were affected by President Wilson's proclamation banning the use of grains for the manufacture of alcoholic beverages. Although the breweries were permitted to sell already manufactured beer until July 1, 1919, they immediately began to dismiss their production employees and shut down most of their operations for an indefinite period, which turned out to be fifteen years.[78]

The bartenders were similarly affected by prohibition. After the abolition of saloons in 1918, they became soft-drink dispensers and changed their union's name to fit the nonalcoholic beverages they served. During the war years the other unions in the culinary trades endeavored to strengthen their organizations through membership campaigns and an amalgamation of Cooks Local No. 27, Waiters Local No. 17, and Waitresses Local No. 333 into a Culinary Alliance. A few minor skirmishes with individual employers included one unsuccessful walkout of forty waiters, members of the independent Southern California Cooks and Waiters Association, against the Jonathan Club, an open-shop stronghold. By 1919 union leaders believed that their members were ready for a determined effort to dent the open-shop front. Their first action was to absorb the Southern California Cooks and Waiters Association and then to demand a minimum wage scale of $40 a week for first cooks and $32.50 for second cooks in eating houses employing its members. Surprisingly enough, most of the employers went along with the demands even though they refused to concede union recognition. Thus, only a few cafés were struck. One cook was arrested and prosecuted under the antipicketing law when he hawked the *Citizen* in front of a struck café, but there were no other demonstrations.

With this encouragement, organizing activities continued into early 1920 when a full attack was made by the waiters against downtown cafés, including the so-called "smart" restaurants, which did not recognize the union. The surface issue was wages and tips, with the employers claiming that the latter averaged from $6 to $15 a day, whereas the waiters stated that the normal figure was closer to $3.50. The unionists wanted a firm wage scale that would provide a decent living without dependence on tipping. The *Times* indirectly sided with the waiters in urging abolition of the tipping system in favor of straight wages, but it pointed out that the real issue was the establishment of a closed shop. The waiters soon discovered that they had overestimated their strength, and the strike failed after two weeks. The culinary trades, like most of their fellow union groups, thus entered the decade of the 1920's dominated by the open shop.[79]

The daily bread served by members of the culinary trades was still manufactured largely by nonunion bakers who were employees of the city's major bakeries. Bakers Local No. 37 continued to have some organizing success in the smaller establishments but failed to make an impression on the so-called "bread trust" firms. One of the most violent disputes in the war period was the struggle against Gordon's Bakery in 1916. G. B. Gordon had at one time been a member of the bakers' union, but for the preceding eight years had operated a wholesale bakery on East Santa Barbara Avenue. In May, 1916, union representatives asked Gordon to discharge a foreman who was delinquent in his union dues and allegedly had been expelled by his local. Gordon refused to enter the dispute and several days later, on May 29, three of his men struck in protest. When the strikers were replaced by nonunionists, forty pickets took up posts around the plant. In June a number of Gordon's nonunion employees were kidnaped and beaten, one of his drivers was carried to the desert near Saugus before being released, and a strikebreaker claimed that he was held prisoner in the Labor Temple. Management also charged that tires were slashed on Gordon trucks, electric wires in the plant were cut, and acid was thrown into baskets containing bread. Warning that further violence would not be tolerated, the police chief permitted the hiring of armed guards to travel on Gordon vehicles.

Officials of the Central Labor Council did not believe that union men had imprisoned any baker in the Labor Temple; the committee they appointed to investigate the charge concluded that it was untrue and that the alleged mistreatment was the responsibility of nonunionists who had voluntarily joined the strike against Gordon. Although reports of violence continued to be played up in the *Times,* the members of Bakers Local No. 37 refused to end the strike. They even requested that all unfair bakery employers be dropped from the Central Labor Council's "we do not patronize" list except Gordon, thus permitting the centering of boycott efforts on this firm. But Gordon was supported by the open-shop Southern California Bakers' Association, and the union proved no match for a combination of large employers.[80]

The fight against Gordon was only part of a total effort to unionize "bread trust" bakeries. The bakers were well aware that the more efficient large firms furnished extremely effective competition for the smaller organized shops. If better wages and hours were to be gained in the latter, the larger units would have to be brought under union job control. Accordingly, in 1918, a strike was conducted against Bradford Bakery in an attempt to force union recognition, an improved wage scale, and the eight-hour day, and additional strikes were called against other "bread trust" firms in the summer of 1919, but all to no avail. The big shops replaced the strikers with nonunion workers so easily that the public was hardly aware of the disputes. Although the local organizing efforts against the large bakers were part of a Pacific Coast drive sponsored by the international union, the open-shop "bread trusts" maintained their supremacy in Los Angeles after the war.[81]

The butchers and meatcutters had a similar lack of success in organizing large firms. Local No. 265 of the Amalgamated Association of Meat Cutters and Butcher Workmen obtained a weekly minimum wage of $22.50 effective December 24, 1917, as a result of a conference with the Meat Dealers' Association under the general supervision of Dr. John R. Haynes and federal mediator James A. Conaty. At this time the union had more than 500 members, who worked ten hours daily for five days a week and eleven hours on Saturdays. Although several members of the association subsequently failed to live up to the agreement and left the employer group, a strike did not develop. In August, 1918, Local No. 265 demanded a wage increase in the form of ten hours' pay for eight hours' work at the Los Angeles branch plants of Armour and Swift, stating that this was the wage scale in Chicago. When about 100 men walked off the job in an effort to enforce the demand, their places were immediately filled. Strike leaders sent telegrams to the War Labor Board in Washington claiming that they had been locked out, but this proved to be untrue. The men were ordered back to work by their international officers and were rehired without discrimination. In March, 1919, the WLB handed down a back-pay award which benefited 800 Los Angeles packinghouse workers, but the union did not succeed in organizing the local employing firms.[82]

While bakers and meatcutters were winning union recognition from small employers, the laundry workers battled the open shop in all quarters. As they were mainly unskilled women, many of whom were of foreign extraction, the struggle proved uphill and often well-nigh hopeless. One bright spot, from labor's viewpoint, was a successful strike at the harbor in the spring of 1916 against the Golden State Laundry, which did a large volume of maritime work. Although the Merchants' and Manufacturers' Association backed the firm, its management succumbed to the union, granting a 20 per cent wage increase, the union shop, and the use of the union label. Undoubtedly the victory was due in large part to pressure on the laundry from organized marine and shipyard workers in the harbor area. A second bright spot for the laundry workers was the announcement by the California Industrial Welfare Commission that a minimum wage scale for women would go into effect on January 14, 1918. It provided a sliding wage scale for beginners, bonus-rate workers, and cripples among the women and girls employed by laundries and dry-cleaning establishments. The minimum weekly wage for beginners was set at $8 for a day of eight hours for the first six weeks, after which it was to be raised to $9. Not more than 25 per cent of the employees of a firm could be classed as beginners. Bonus workers were to be paid a minimum of $10 a week. Partially incapacitated women and girls could be paid less than the minimum wage upon certification of the Industrial Welfare Commission. The union soon accused Los Angeles employers of firing able-bodied women in order to hire cripples and thus lower wages under the impetus of the intense price competition in the industry.[83]

Laundry truck drivers, unlike the workers in the plants, were under the organizing jurisdiction of the teamsters. In 1915 only about 38 of the estimated 7,000 drivers of all kinds of commercial vehicles in Los Angeles belonged to Teamsters Local No. 208. Little occurred in the life of the union until 1918, though the membership increased several fold. Wages did not improve, remaining at almost the same level as in 1906. The daily scale in that year ranged from $2.25 to $3.25, whereas in 1918 it was $2.50 to $3.50 with a majority of the drivers working twelve to fourteen hours a day. In 1918 Michael Casey, president of the San Francisco teamsters' union, came to Los Angeles in an attempt to inject some life into the local organization. As in 1913, the *Times* greeted his arrival with a lurid editorial in which "Bloody Mike" Casey was accused of trying to bring in his own methods of organizing nonunion men, including the breaking of arms over truck wheels and the smashing of heads against pavements. The organizing campaign did not proceed very rapidly as the membership rose to only about 200 by July, 1919.

The influence of the teamsters, however, increased more quickly than the membership. A meeting of 1,500 organized and unorganized teamsters on July 15 discussed the question of striking for a minimum wage scale of $3.50 to $5.50 a day and an eight-hour shift. This would have meant increases in the current wage scale of from 25 cents to $1.50 a day. The strike did not occur, but the large trucking companies of the city subsequently announced a pay increase of 25 cents for a day of nine hours, though they remained open shops. In December, 1919, the teamsters began to agitate for a strike for the eight-hour day. Paul Scharrenberg, secretary of the California State Federation of Labor, however, stated in Los Angeles that they would not have the support of other unions. In his opinion organized labor could not take a chance on an unsuccessful strike by the teamsters because radicals within and on the fringes of the city's union movement at that time could well use such a situation to their own advantage.[84]

The ice wagon drivers were alone among the teamsters in striking to break the dominance of the open shop in the war period. Their struggle began on June 20, 1918, when twenty-one drivers of the Ice Distributing Company, delivery firm for several cold storage companies, claimed they had been laid off although they had been working from fourteen to sixteen hours a day. Spokesmen for the firm indicated that in reality they had walked out to enforce demands for a nine-hour day and 40 cents an hour for overtime. The plant superintendent made it clear that no man who entered the Labor Temple during the dispute would be rehired. Although the walkout began as a minor skirmish, within two months it developed into a major strike against the large ice companies of the city. Captain Connell served as federal mediator but, failing to bring the parties together, announced on September 5 that he would have to turn the problem over to the United States Food Administration if the strike was not settled within a few days, as large quantities of food were spoiling in the hot summer weather. Union demands centered on a nine-hour day, wages of $115 and $100 per month for drivers and helpers respectively, and 60 cents an hour for overtime. J. W. Grafford was appointed as the union's representative while B. F. Alfs acted for the companies, but the latter did not have the authority to negotiate freely. As the September heat continued, customers began picking up their ice at the plants, the City Council under the urging of Ralph Criswell started to think in terms of municipal ownership, and employees on strike expressed their desire to return to work. This combination of forces proved strong enough to bring an end to the dispute, with both sides accepting arbitration.[85]

Although the ice wagon drivers found the local and federal governments keenly interested in their dispute because of the wartime need to prevent food waste, they were not involved so directly in the defense effort as were the commercial telegraphers. Telegraph communication was under the Wire Control Board during much of the war, but after the Armistice the operators' dissatisfaction with their wage scale and working conditions began to manifest itself through the Commercial Telegraphers Union of America. This organization was strongest in the Postal Telegraph Company because Western Union had an effective employees' association which kept its workers from establishing a labor union to express their economic aims without company interference. After some preliminary skirmishes, the Telegraphers Union called a nationwide strike, which began in Los Angeles at 8 A.M. on June 11, 1919. Demands included the right to organize for collective bargaining, wage increases, and better working conditions. The union charged the wire services with discriminating against its members in firing employees.

It was clearly evident at the outset that the walkout was not uniformly effective throughout the country. In Los Angeles, union leaders reported that all the Postal Telegraph night force went out on strike. Management representatives pointed out, however, that Western Union was not affected so that wire service was still available. Further, though Postal Telegraph branches in the city were closed on the first day of the dispute, they began to reopen that evening. During subsequent days the strike continued to wane, particularly after the Postmaster General informed the companies that under Wire Control Board regulations they had to reinstate workers discharged for their union affiliation but not those who were out on other grounds. In his judgment the strikers had violated the rules of both the Wire Control Board and the War Labor Board in not seeking redress for their grievances through still effective wartime channels. Union leaders, realizing that they would have to fight the government as well as the employers, called off the strike as of July 1. The granting of a retroactive pay increase of 15 per cent from July 1, 1918, to December 31, 1918, and one of 5 per cent from January 1 to July 1, 1919, helped assuage the strikers' disappointment over their inability to obtain union recognition and the right to bargain collectively.[86]

Among the more active miscellaneous unions in the war years were Barbers Local No. 295, Cigar Makers Local No. 225, the Leather Workers Union, the Retail Clerks Union, the Reed and Rattan Workers Union, Musicians Local No. 47, and Motion Picture Operators Local No. 150. The cigar makers struggled against the large national distributors, known to them as the "cigar trust," which were beginning to force independent shops out of existence in Los Angeles and elsewhere through the use of female and child labor. The union sought unsuccessfully to boycott these large firms, on the theory that workingmen were heavy smokers and would refuse to buy cigars made by sweatshop labor. Although the leatherworkers won agreements with several Los Angeles firms, they failed miserably when they tried to beat the open shop by establishing a coöperative factory. Despite continued efforts, the retail clerks also made little headway. The reed and rattan workers, on the other hand, became strong enough in late 1917 to strike a number of firms and won a nine-hour day, daily wages of $3.50, time and a half for overtime, and double pay for Sundays and holidays. The musicians were numerically the strongest organization affiliated with the Central Labor Council in 1917 and 1918. They continued to maintain contracts with the city's leading theaters but did not have a uniform union-shop arrangement. Their working associates in Motion Picture Operators Local No. 150 participated in the city-wide organizational campaign of 1916, and in 1917, through a strike against six theaters, won new contracts providing for wage increases.[87]

Under the impetus of the war a number of new unions were organized in Los Angeles. These included Broom and Whisk Makers Local No. 28, which was 100 per cent organized by 1919; Cannery Workers Local No. 14757 at Los Angeles Harbor; Egg Inspectors Local No. 14934, first of its type on the Pacific Coast; Jewelry Workers Local No. 23; the Office Employees; the Textile Workers; the Fruit and Vegetable Workers; the Soda Dispensers; Brotherhood of Motor Bus Owners and Operators Local No. 300; and Transfer and Baggage Drivers Local No. 626. Except for the broom and whisk makers, few of them achieved any significant job control in their crafts because of the strength of the open-shop movement.[88]

One of the most obvious demonstrations of the effectiveness of the open shop involved the teachers in the city school system. The administrators and the teachers had formed three independent organizations—High School Teachers' Association, City Teachers' Club, and Principals' Association—designed to consider problems of interest to them. Such a problem arose in 1918 when a proposed decrease in the county tax rate threatened to lower their salaries. To aid the teachers fighting this proposal, the Central Labor Council named a committee consisting of P. D. Noel, Francis Drake, and C. L. Myers. In addition, Superintendent of Schools Albert Shiels backed the teachers in a request to the Board of Education for a salary increase. As a result, they won a flat increase of $300 a year, and the Central Labor Council found itself in a position to initiate organization of a local of the

American Federation of Teachers. The issue of a teachers' union came to a head in the summer of 1919, when A. B. Matteson, a vocational teacher at Jefferson High School, learned that his contract would not be renewed. His principal stated that the reason was inefficiency, but Matteson claimed he was being released because of his membership in the International Association of Machinists. Meanwhile, the charter for Local No. 77 of the American Federation of Teachers had arrived. By this time, however, the city's instructors had largely forgotten about the support they had received from organized labor in their salary fight, and members of the teachers' and principals' associations went on record as firmly opposing the new local. In addition, the Board of Education refused by a four-to-three vote to reëmploy Matteson.

The response of local labor leaders was that they would recommend rejection of the next school bond issue. As tempers rose during the fall months, the teachers' local sought to gain new members and the Board of Education considered the implications of having a union in the educational system of an open-shop city. Finally, on December 9, 1919, the board announced that all teachers were barred from joining outside unions because of the possibility of divided loyalties. Those teachers who had joined Local No. 77 were ordered to give up their membership, though the board actually had no way of knowing who had affiliated with the union. But the ultimatum was enough to stop the union from making further progress, and the teachers remained in the same unorganized public servant category as firemen and policemen.[89]

Reference has already been made to attempts to form a firemen's union. Like the teachers' local, this was attacked on the principle of divided loyalties as well as on the ground that it might call a strike that would leave the city without adequate protection from fires. The firemen's basic reason for establishing Local No. 112 of the International Order of Fire Fighters, AFL, was a desire for wage increases to recoup their losses in purchasing power during the war. Realizing that this rather than an interest in collective bargaining was the underlying cause of unrest, the Merchants' and Manufacturers' Association began to support a movement to raise salaries. When the city fathers subsequently showed more concern for their welfare, the firemen voluntarily relinquished their union charter in October, 1919. Salary increases were granted the following month.[90]

The city's policemen had a similar experience. As employees on a fixed salary they too had been vulnerable to the inflationary impact of the war, and organization of a union seemed at least a partial answer to their problem. Though they received a salary increase in March, 1918, they sought another one a year later. The City Council was slow in acting on their request because of the opposition of business to the tax increase that would be necessary to support a raise. Moreover, many members of the force had formerly been affiliated with one or the other of the Big Four railroad brotherhoods. Local brotherhood leaders and AFL organizer Joshua Dale therefore began meeting with representatives of the policemen in the late summer of 1919 in an effort to persuade them to set up a union to secure their wage demands.[91] The *Times*'s reaction to the possibility of a policemen's union was one of horror: "No man's home, no man's wife, no man's children will be safe in Los Angeles if the police force is unionized and made subject to the orders of the red unionite bosses. . . . What is a police force for? Why do we have police? To protect law-breakers?" [92]

The response of the City Council was to initiate action to draw up an ordinance providing for a wage increase. Representatives of the policemen indicated that they wanted the following monthly pay scale:

First year	$100 to $120
Second year	107 to 130
Third year	115 to 140
Fourth year	120 to 150

The council believed that the only way to obtain the necessary revenue to raise city salaries was to levy a license tax on some 200 lines of business. Reluctant to impose this tax, it dillydallied for several months. Rumors that the policemen had received a charter from the AFL began to circulate, while the *Times* berated the council for playing politics instead of providing a raise to head off the union. An attempt to pass an ordinance was made in November, but it failed to get the necessary unanimous ratification. Further efforts to write one that would pass achieved success early in January, 1920. The new salary ordinance, formally adopted on February 1, provided wage increases for both firemen and policemen. It also placated other restless city employees by awarding proportional increases to all who received less than $175 per month.[93]

In a sense the policemen and the firemen epitomized the general status of most workers in Los Angeles at the beginning of the postwar decade. The majority were still unorganized, yet had received some wage increases after complaining about wartime prices. The organized workers had similar success in this respect but, with only a few exceptions, had failed to secure recognition of their unions as collective bargaining agents. The more important exceptions were the United Garment Workers in the manufacture of work clothing, the printers of ITU Local No. 174 in commercial and newspaper typographical work exclusive of the *Times,* and Bakers No. 37 in many of the numerous small bakeries. The building trades unions, especially in bricklaying and plumbing, temporarily achieved some recognition under the impetus of the immediate postwar building boom, but for the most part their success lay in employer acceptance of certain of their wage and hour demands rather than in actual recognition. Even these achievements were largely dissipated in the postwar depression of 1920–1922.

In some respects the wartime experience of organized labor in Los Angeles was not too different from that of the rest of the nation. In both instances, unions grew in number and in membership. Further, locals tended to go along with their national counterparts in supporting the government in the conflict. But whether or not unions were entitled to recognition as collective bargaining agents in return for giving up their right to strike was not clear, and employer attitudes on this issue created a difference between Los Angeles and other metropolitan areas with respect to labor's organizing success.

Early in the war the Council of National Defense stated that neither labor nor management should take advantage of the conflict to change the prevailing situation as to union recognition. Though the National War Labor Board, established in 1918, took a more positive stand in recognizing the right of workers to organize and bargain collectively, this seemingly clear position was soon clouded by the board's statement that workers should not use "coercive" measures of any kind to force employees to join unions or employers to bargain with them. Additional pronouncements that an employer was not required to bargain with worker representatives who were not in his employ, unless this had previously been his practice, further retarded union organization. Los Angeles open-shop supporters took greater advantage of these later statements of the National War Labor Board than did employers in many other cities. As few firms had had collective bargaining contracts with unions before the war, management saw an opportunity to continue on this basis with official government sanction. Organizing activities of unions, even though unaccompanied by violence, were frequently judged as coercive and were restricted by injunctions, which were also used effectively against walkouts.

Thus, though organized labor in Los Angeles increased in strength during the years 1915–1919, actual union recognition was seldom achieved. With the end of the war and the decline of government participation in labor relations, the initiation of the national open-shop drive under the so-called "American Plan" in the early 1920's, and the sharp impact of the depression of 1920–1922, organized workers in Los Angeles, like their counterparts elsewhere in the country, found their numbers decimated in a very few years. The open shop again reigned locally, for it had never been completely unseated in the war emergency. In other cities over the nation new antiunion groups were formed, but this was not necessary in Los Angeles. The prewar open-shop machinery had not been dismantled, and when it was brought back to full operation, the flames of wartime labor organization were quickly reduced to smoldering embers.[94]

V. THE CHANGING TIDES—MARITIME
WORKERS, 1911–1933

1. UP FROM THE DEPTHS

THE YEARS of World War I were the most prosperous yet experienced by workers who made their livelihood from seafaring and related activities. The maritime unions at the harbor were not affiliated directly with the Los Angeles labor movement; union men in the city, however, supported longshoremen and sailors financially and morally in their disputes with shipowners and other water-front employers. Thus the story of organized labor in Los Angeles would not be complete without some pages devoted to the unions of workers on ships and piers.

Few of the significant activities of organized maritime workers were confined to one area of the Pacific Coast. A strike against a single port usually proved ineffective because ships simply used other harbors. Hence the Los Angeles aspects of a maritime strike cannot be isolated from a larger picture.

Maritime workers are divided into ship and shore categories—seafarers and longshoremen. Longshore work is casual, as jobs are available only when a ship is in port. Work at sea, on the other hand, has always been under fixed conditions, for a vessel is a sailor's home as well as his place of employment. Although the longshoreman and the sailor are both dependent on the ship for employment, the different circumstances of their work have frequently led to a failure to coöperate in disputes. In Pacific Coast ports jurisdictional conflicts between seamen and longshoremen often developed over the loading and unloading of steam schooners engaged in the coastal lumber trade. Traditionally, from sailing-ship days, sailors held jurisdiction over this work, but as early as 1880 longshoremen sought to gain full control of the loading activities and to keep the ships' crews from participating in dockside operations. This struggle continued until schooners, with the decline of their competitive efficiency in the 1930's, eventually disappeared. An additional factor that often exacerbated relations between sailor and longshoreman was the strong personalities heading their respective unions; these dynamic individuals, who had worked up the hard way through the ranks of their organizations, often came into conflict.[1]

Although the uphill battles for union organization and recognition were similar to those experienced in other trades, maritime workers faced an unusual array of opposing forces. Three employer organizations were lined up against them: the Merchants' and Manufacturers' Association, the Los Angeles Chamber of Commerce, and the Shipowners' Association of the Pacific Coast. Moreover, the unions were plagued by their own internal bickering as well as the dissension caused by the Industrial Workers of the World, especially during and immediately after the war. By arousing dissatisfaction with working conditions, the Wobblies were able to bore within the harbor locals of the two major groups—the seamen and the longshoremen—and assume positions of leadership at the most opportune times for the propagation of their syndicalist philosophy. They also formed an organization —the Marine Transport Workers Industrial Union—for capturing the members of other locals, as well as influencing unorganized maritime employees.

The sailors on the Pacific Coast had formed the Coast Seamen's Union in San Francisco in 1885, and a branch of this union was established at Los Angeles Harbor that same year. In the period between 1885 and 1915, the nation's seamen gained in status and strength through the efforts of two forceful personalities, Andrew Furuseth and Robert M. La Follette of Wisconsin. Furuseth, taciturn and dedicated president of the International Seamen's Union, convinced Senator La Follette of the great need for improved working conditions and wages for merchant sailors. After the election of Woodrow Wilson as president in 1912 and the consequent increase in labor's influence in Congress, Furuseth through La Follette was able to secure legislation that made sailors something more than second-class citizens. Congress passed the La Follette Seamen's Act of 1915 over the opposition of shipowners and despite the appeal that better living conditions for sailors would raise costs, encourage cheap foreign competition, and drive the American flag from the seas. The most important sections of the act provided for abolition of imprisonment for desertion in a safe harbor, with forfeiture of personal effects on board to be henceforth the only penalty for such action; abrogation of desertion in a foreign port as a cause for the arrest and return of a seaman to his job; improvement of living and working conditions aboard ship; prevention of abuses in the payment of wages; and a variety of safety measures.[2]

The Seamen's Act gave new hope and, for a time, new power to sailors' unions on both the Atlantic and Pacific coasts. In the meantime, the war in Europe had stimulated the movement of goods from Atlantic ports to countries engaged in the conflict, but harbors on the Pacific Coast were slow to feel any effect. Wages remained the same as before the war until May 1, 1916, when they were raised by agreement to $55 a month for sailors on steam vessels. Sailing vessels that went along the Pacific Coast and to Mexico and Hawaii raised monthly wages to $50, while all other offshore ships continued to pay $40.[3]

Like the seamen, the longshoremen had a Pacific Coast history that began in the nineteenth century, but their early unions had achieved little success. The first dispute involving longshoremen at San Pedro after the bombing of the *Times* in 1910 occurred in 1912 under the impetus of the IWW. Wobblies drifting into San Pedro from the free-speech fights in the San Diego area began to organize Italian dock workers in the summer of that year. On July 18, some twenty-five IWW members succeeded in halting work on the steamer *Klamath* which was loading cement for Portland, while others, including Lee McCoy, one of their able leaders, harangued longshoremen along Front Street in San Pedro, urging them to join in stopping all cargo activities in the harbor. At 8 A.M. on Sunday, July 21, McCoy and his associates presented their demands to the foremen at the various wharves: an increase in wages from 35 to 40 cents an hour for regular time and from 50 to 60 cents for overtime, an hour for all meals, and the discontinuance of a small hospital fee. At the same time about 200 longshoremen, most of them Italians, walked out. The rest of the dock workers, however, refused to follow the IWW mandate and continued on the job, so that there was little delay in unloading ships. The strikers concentrated on the E. K. Wood Lumber Company, though also striking the Crescent Wharf and Warehouse Company and the Banning Company, the last being one of the largest employers of longshoremen at San Pedro. By July 25 it was obvious that the strike was a failure because of the lack of coöperation from non-Italian dock workers and lumber handlers. Only a few orators remained on Front Street, and the IWW strike leaders soon left the town to three years of relative peace.

In that period Local No. 38–43 of the International Longshoremen's Association was formed at San Pedro. By 1915 it had 600 members and had reached an agreement with employers providing for time and a half for all work after 5 P.M. as well as that done on Sundays and holidays, plus other benefits. But it had not settled a problem peculiar to the San Pedro area: the relationship between lumber handlers and longshoremen. San Pedro, as the port of a rapidly growing metropolitan area, received a large inflow of lumber from the north by means of steam schooners. As noted earlier, the seamen were in constant conflict with the longshoremen over the former's traditional right to load and unload these ships. Furthermore, the dock workers contested the jurisdiction of the men employed by the lumber companies to transfer the cargoes into port yards for storage or shipment by rail to Los Angeles and other cities. The major lumber companies, particularly the E. K. Wood, Hammond, and Kerckhoff-Cuzner firms, operated as open shops, and readily took advantage of jurisdictional difficulties in order to maintain this system of industrial relations. Thus, as the longshoremen entered the war period, they had a union capable of holding their craft together, but they faced problems that were to cause the eclipse of their organization from the early postwar years until 1934.[4]

2. SEAMEN, THE WAR, AND THE OPEN SHOP

The war's effect on sailors' unions was more marked on the Atlantic than on the Pacific Coast because of the volume of tonnage moving from east coast ports to Europe. A year after the wage increase of May 1, 1916, the United States Shipping Board, the Atlantic Coast Steamship Owners (shipowners on the Shipping Committee of the Council of National Defense), and the International Seamen's Union formulated the Atlantic Agreement, the first such tripartite statement of national wartime policies concerning seamen. Although applying primarily to Atlantic and Gulf Coast shipping, the agreement was subscribed to by Pacific Coast shipowners and, to some extent, by those on the Great Lakes. It deserved at least partial credit for the absence of seamen's strikes in the war period. The agreement, made public on May 8, 1917, provided for the union scale for all classes of workers within its jurisdiction as well as a standard wage for all others, a 50 per cent bonus while traveling in the war zone, $100 compensation for the loss of personal effects by sailors through a war-caused event, relaxed apprenticeship regulations to permit 40 per cent of a deck crew to be ordinary seamen or boys, rapid instruction in seamanship to novices by the union, and free access to docks and vessels by union representatives.

The Atlantic Agreement made possible the rapid expansion of the American merchant marine necessitated by United States participation in the war. The effect on seamen's unions, however, was mixed. Unions on the Atlantic, not yet as well organized as those on the Pacific, were strengthened. Pacific Coast seamen, approximately 95 per cent organized before establishment of the Atlantic Agreement, had much less room for expansion. As before the war, agreements on wages and conditions continued to be made between Pacific Coast unions and shipowners, and were duly recognized by the United States Shipping Board. Labor dilution through the use of nonunion ordinary seamen and boys in deck crews occurred, however, so that Pacific Coast sailors actually witnessed a decline in the percentage of their number who were union members.[5]

Increased shipping activity sent wages up on both coasts. Even though Pacific Coast sailors were not so directly involved in war-induced shipping as those in the Atlantic service, the need for more men on the east coast reduced the number available on the opposite side of the continent, and thus caused a shortage of seamen in Western ports. As a consequence, in May, 1917, wages on all vessels and in all trades rose by agreement to a minimum of $60 a month. By March, 1918, the scale had risen to $75 on both coasts but still did not increase so rapidly as freight rates. On the Pacific, wages continued to rise after the war, to a minimum of $90 a month for sailors, $95 for boatswains, and $105 for carpenters, because the return of tonnage to that area after the slackening of war needs on the Atlantic coincided with a temporary lack of adequately trained personnel in west coast ports. In the same period Western sailors also achieved an eight-hour day in port and at sea in steamers, and overtime pay of 75 cents an hour for ship work and 90 cents for cargo labor. By August, 1919, sailors and quartermasters were getting $1 an hour for working cargo on overtime.

Like the seamen, the officers of steam schooners wanted higher pay, and they sought to secure it through the National Organization of Masters, Mates and Pilots, which called a strike on August 15, 1919. They asked for monthly wages of $175 for first officers, $160 for second officers, $1 an hour for overtime, and employment of a third mate on all ships. The dispute tied up eleven lumber schooners with their cargoes for a short time in Los Angeles Harbor. As water-borne lumber tonnage was running at a high level, particularly because of the postwar building boom in Los Angeles, steam schooner owners quickly compromised the issues.[6]

Although maritime shipping remained prosperous during most of 1920, a decline developing before the year was out became very serious by the spring of 1921. The slump was caused partly by the postwar depression, but also by the increasingly heavy competition of foreign ships able to hire crews abroad at wages much lower than those paid to American seamen. The wartime agreements between the seamen and their employers were slated to expire on May 1, 1921. The reduction in shipping activity in late 1920, coupled with a fall in living costs and a surplus of war-trained sailors, led the United States Shipping Board to agree with vessel operators that conditions justified a wage cut. Official proposals made to the International Seamen's Union and the Marine Engineers Beneficial Association as early as January, 1921, included a wage reduction of 25 per cent, or to $72.50 a month, for seamen, the elimination of overtime pay, and a requirement that sailors work with any longshoremen regardless of union status and not leave the ship until the cargo had been discharged. The wage cut was changed to 15 per cent upon complaints that 25 per cent was too steep, but the elimination of overtime would still mean a net decline in earnings of 40 to 60 per cent for men working under wartime schedules. On April 19, 1921, eleven days before expiration of the war agreements, the Shipping Board issued a revised set of recommendations which added several items to the previous proposals, including abolition of the three-watch system, withdrawal of the privilege given union representatives to enter the docks or board vessels in port, and elimination of preference to union men in hiring.[7]

The reduction in wages and the elimination of overtime pay were severe blows, particularly to seamen on the Pacific Coast, because the crews of coastwise lumber vessels did much of the cargo work on an extra-time basis. Although the Shipping Board substituted equivalent periods off for overtime in excess of eight hours, the seamen preferred the pay to the leisure. A strike was therefore called by the International Seamen's Union, the Sailors Union of the Pacific, the Marine Engineers Beneficial Association, the Marine Cooks and Stewards Association, the Marine Firemen, Oilers, Watertenders and Wipers Association, and the National Organization of Masters, Mates and Pilots for May 1, 1921, when the war agreements expired. At the last minute several of the unions asked for arbitration of the issues; when the shipowners refused, the strike was on. All American shipping on the Atlantic and Gulf coasts was immediately affected, and the walkout gradually spread to the Pacific, reaching Los Angeles Harbor about a week after it began. Ten ships were tied up there by May 8, but the owners lost no time in hiring nonunion crews. Ironically enough, the first struck ship to sail from Los Angeles Harbor with a nonunion crew was the United States Shipping Board freighter *West Himrod*, bound for the United Kingdom. The federal government thus became a strikebreaker because the Shipping Board opposed the walkout. A dozen lumber schooners, caught in the local port at the start of the strike, unloaded their cargoes and sailed for San Francisco to await the end of the dispute. Most of the lumber schooners were owned by members of the Shipowners' Association of the Pacific Coast, but the American Steamship Association, the Pacific American Steamship Association, and the United States Shipping Board were the employing organizations most deeply concerned in the strike. The lumber schooner owners made little effort to operate during the walkout, leaving the conduct of the strike to the board and the larger employers who belonged to the other associations.[8]

The strike had been under way less than two weeks when it obviously became a battle to restore the open shop, especially at Los Angeles Harbor. At its local peak thirteen vessels were tied up and some 500 seamen were out, refusing to return to their ships until arbitration was accepted or the wartime agreements were extended. Of this number 300 were sailors; 95 were marine cooks, stewards, or messmen; 40 were marine firemen, oilers, or water tenders; and the rest were masters, mates, or engineers. In an attempt to put more ships at sea, the Shipping Board obtained injunctions against strikers in various ports on the nation's coasts. Much bitterness was engendered in Pacific Coast unions by the use of University of California students as strikebreakers.

Violence was not long in developing at Los Angeles Harbor, as tempers on both sides rose when strikebreakers began to move ships with the support of their private owners, the Shipping Board, and local open-shop organizations. On May 11, three crew members of the steamer *President* were attacked and two strikers were subsequently arrested for the action. Two days later a boatload of men boarded the General Petroleum tanker *Yorba Linda* late in the evening; in the ensuing fight one crewman was seriously hurt and several others received minor injuries. The assailants were not captured, though the company posted a $2,500 reward for the arrest and conviction of any person who had participated in the attack. On June 20 a riot developed between strikers and nonstrikers at Fifth and Front streets in San Pedro; two Chinese seamen were beaten and robbed of $250. Another fight between crew members and strikers on June 22 involved the Shipping Board vessel *Silver State*.

By this time, however, it was evident that the strike was lost. Even by May 20 nonunion crews had been recruited from the surplus of war-trained sailors for most of the vessels tied up at Los Angeles Harbor, only six oil tankers remaining without personnel. The situation was similar at other ports. The Shipping Board sent more vessels to sea with nonunion crews than did private employers. This development was extremely irritating to the seamen, who alleged that the government was using ships paid for by liberty bonds to fight the battles of shipowners.[9]

Attempts to end the strike were marked by prolonged negotiations and premature announcements of settlements. Several local maritime labor leaders, including Harry Ohlsen of the Sailors Union of the Pacific (SUP), Ernest F. Pegg of the Marine Engineers Beneficial Association (MEBA), and Patrick Flynn and George Clark of the Marine Firemen, Oilers, Watertenders and Wipers Association, went to Washington early in May to participate in negotiations with private shipowners and the Shipping Board. These men made it clear that working conditions, not wages, were the primary problem. Negotiations were terminated on May 9 when the shipowners refused to give preference to American citizens in selecting crews. Before the month ended, however, W. S. Brown, national president of the Marine Engineers, signed an agreement with the Shipping Board, to be effective until April 30, 1922. It provided for a 15 per cent wage cut and eliminated overtime but did not cover private ship operators. Pacific Coast members of the union, including the local at San Pedro, at first refused to accept the terms, claiming that the agreement was negotiated by Eastern leaders without their concurrence. The resulting disaffection almost split the MEBA into Eastern and Western divisions.

On June 25, after this first breach in the seamen's front, the Masters, Mates and Pilots agreed to return to work on Shipping Board vessels without an agreement. As yet none of the unions had settled with private employers, and the Shipping Board still remained on the unfair list of the SUP, the Marine Firemen, and the Marine Cooks and Stewards Association. Private vessels operating on the Pacific Coast functioned with strikebreakers, while union engineers, mates, and masters worked only on vessels under the jurisdiction of the Shipping Board. On July 14, 1921, striking seamen's locals at San Pedro voted to continue the walkout regardless of settlements elsewhere, whereupon the Shipping Board and employers' associations immediately announced that they were suspending all negotiations.[10]

The tide was thus ebbing rapidly for the sailors, and it soon became evident to their national leaders that they would have to grasp at straws to survive. On July 21 the Shipowners' Association of the Pacific Coast decided to begin moving lumber cargoes that had piled up at various ports. Breaking away from the other employer groups, it offered deck sailors $77.50 a month, 60 cents an hour for overtime, the maintenance of union working conditions, a requirement that sailors work with longshoremen regardless of the latter's union status, and an informal open-shop agreement for one year. Andrew Furuseth, head of the seamen's union, wired local unions from Washington to accept the proposals. His reasons were that the steam schooners operated by the Shipowners' Association employed half of the seamen on the coast who were the backbone of the SUP, the union would be able to maintain its strength under the conditions offered, and the desertion of the MEBA had already dangerously weakened the strikers' position. He pointed out that the requirement that seamen work with longshoremen in unloading cargoes was a condition that had long existed in the lumber trade. The Sailors Union, however, voted against returning to work. Furuseth thereupon rushed to San Francisco to make an impassioned plea at a special meeting of the membership. The sailors in attendance voted 1,272 to 481 to return to work under the conditions set by the shipowners and without a formal agreement. At about the same time the marine firemen and the cooks and stewards also went back to work.[11]

The restoration of peace, however, did not quiet the unrest within the Sailors Union of the Pacific. The settlement was far from satisfactory to all concerned, especially at Los Angeles Harbor where the return to work was under stringent open-shop conditions. One of the leading members of the Shipowners' Association was A. B. Hammond, president of the Hammond Lumber Company in Los Angeles and a strong opponent of unions. He issued orders that all deck and engineer officers on his schooners must sever connections with their unions before they would be placed back on vessels. Although a few companies had made concessions to the SUP soon after the walkout began, Hammond had stood firm and was given much credit for forcing an end to the strike and making it possible for operations to be resumed on an open-shop basis. His ships put to sea at the end of July with completely nonunion crews, thus setting an example for other steam schooner operators and extending the influence of the open shop to other ports up and down the coast. It was not long before private shipowners other than lumber operators began to use nonunion crews, to initiate black lists, and otherwise to discriminate against union men who refused to desert their locals. The hiring of nonunion men was facilitated at Los Angeles Harbor through the coöperation of the Merchants' and Manufacturers' Association, the Pacific American Steamship Association, and the Shipowners' Association, which jointly established a Sea Service Bureau managed by Captain J. J. Meaney.

Steamship companies as well as the Shipping Board, thus able to secure crew members without reference to their union affiliation, could ignore the employment bureaus set up by the maritime locals.[12]

The fires of dissatisfaction with the open-shop outcome of the strike were fanned by the supporters of industrial unionism within the Sailors Union. Before the walkout Furuseth, lifetime secretary of the SUP as well as its international president, had been fighting two groups within the union which wanted to deviate from the traditional craft position he advocated. One group was represented by the IWW Marine Transport Workers Industrial Union, which first secretly and then openly sought to capture the Sailors Union for the purpose of using its mobile membership to spread the propaganda of class warfare and to tie up water transportation on the west coast as a demonstration of its economic power. The second group favored industrial unionism over the craft form as a more effective means of increasing the bargaining power of all sailors and longshoremen in dealing with employers. In 1921 this group organized the Marine Transport Workers Federation, with branches in San Pedro, San Francisco, and Seattle. Its initial objective was to achieve closer coöperation between sailors and longshoremen by negotiating contracts for both that would expire on the same date, and by providing a card transfer system between their respective unions. The aim of the latter idea was to eliminate jurisdictional controversy over steam schooner cargo operations, but Furuseth believed it was a device to enable longshoremen to take over such work from sailors, who had traditionally handled it. Therefore, during the months immediately preceding the 1921 strike, the Marine Transport Workers Federation was to Furuseth the most disturbing organization among the seamen. It was led by J. Vance Thompson, editor of the *Seamen's Journal* and long-time member of the Sailors Union. Thompson had narrowly defeated Paul Scharrenberg, a sailor and secretary-treasurer of the California State Federation of Labor as well as a supporter of Furuseth, in a race for the editorship in 1920. He was not a Wobbly but firmly believed that industrial unionism was the answer to the organizing problems of sailors and longshoremen and would, indeed, be the means of keeping them from left-wing influence.[13]

At the 1921 convention of the International Seamen's Union, with which the SUP was affiliated, official support was withdrawn from the *Seamen's Journal* as evidence of Furuseth's opposition to Thompson and in anticipation of a change in editorial policy in favor of industrial unionism. By the time the 1921 strike was well under way Thompson was openly advocating industrial unionism and criticizing conventional union policies in the conduct of the walkout. He opposed the proposals of the Shipowners' Association to end the strike, particularly the requirement that sailors on lumber schooners work with nonunion longshoremen in handling cargoes. Even though such activity was traditional, Thompson called it "scabbing" on the organized longshoremen and wanted union sailors to refuse to do it. His influence within the Sailors Union was evidenced by the membership's original rejection of the employers' proposals. It was this action that brought Furuseth to San Francisco in July, 1921, when he obtained a reversal in favor of returning to work. Furuseth believed that the strike had been lost when members of the Marine Engineers Beneficial Association went back to work on Shipping Board vessels and thus broke the seamen's united front. He further saw that he would lose control of the Sailors Union if the dispute was permitted to continue, a situation that would play into the hands of either Thompson's group or the IWW.[14]

Furuseth did not stop with his victory over Thompson on the strike issue. He continued to put pressure on the editor through a new publication launched in the fall by the International Seamen's Union in opposition to the *Seamen's Journal*. It published only four issues, all of which attacked Thompson and the IWW. By November, 1921, feeling against Thompson was running so high that Furuseth was able to get him expelled for disobedience by a two-thirds vote of the union membership. Selim A. Silver, a Furuseth man, succeeded him as editor of the *Seamen's Journal*. A number of other insurgents, who belonged to the IWW, were expelled at the same time for violating the rule against dual membership. Furuseth was again in complete control of what was left of the west coast branch of his organization, but it was a hollow victory. The International Seamen's Union, with a membership of 100,000 on the eve of the strike, was reduced to barely 50,000 by the end of the dispute. The decline continued during the following two years until, by 1923, the national membership was but 18,000.[15]

Furuseth's troubles after the strike were accentuated by the activities of IWW members, who made considerable headway among longshoremen and sailors in Los Angeles Harbor. Seamen who were disgruntled over the treatment accorded Vance Thompson and the return to open-shop conditions were ripe for the philosophy espoused by the Marine Transport Workers Industrial Union. The Wobblies gained enough strength to launch a weekly paper called the *Marine Worker* at Los Angeles Harbor. Shipowners there, concerned about the growth of IWW influence, refused to permit the Sea Service

Bureau to hire any known holders of so-called "Red" cards indicating affiliation with the MTWIU. Any seamen already on ships who were known to belong to the organization were summarily fired. In response to the discharge of card carriers, the refusal to hire known IWW sympathizers, and maintenance of the open-shop Sea Service Bureau, the *Citizen* ran a series of articles attacking the shipowners. It was alleged that the nonunion men employed were so incompetent that the reported disappearance of several vessels and the wrecking of others were to be expected.[16]

The open shop, however, was not retarded by this opposition. In February, 1922, members of the Shipowners' Association reduced the wages of able seamen on their lumber schooners from $72.50 to $65 a month, and the Pacific American Steamship Association cut wages to $55. Nearly all local maritime employers hired men through the Sea Service Bureau, which became known as the "slave market." As the effects of the postwar depression wore off and shipping increased at San Pedro and other coastal ports, wages rose again, but control remained in the hands of the shipowners. Before the year was out, the AFL seamen's union at the harbor had relinquished its charter.

The members of the IWW did not give up so quickly, even though the energetic campaign to eliminate them from the ships and the water front of Los Angeles Harbor continued in full swing. In November, 1922, foot-loose Wobblies were asked by their leaders to go to San Pedro to help battle the open shop and to sacrifice themselves to the state's criminal syndicalism law as they had done in the free-speech fights of earlier years. On December 18 police arrested sixty-five members of the organization at the San Pedro hall of the Marine Transport Workers Industrial Union, and ninety more were taken into custody in the next few days, many of whom were later tried. Still the IWW group continued to grow. Its most effective weapon was the "quickie" strike pulled just before a ship left port. The demands were usually for overtime pay or the three-watch system, and the employers often granted them just to get their ships under way. The net effect was to keep the harbor area in constant turmoil.

Most of the IWW activity, however, involved the longshoremen rather than the seamen. A strike on April 25, 1923, at Los Angeles Harbor drastically limited the loading and unloading of ships for several weeks until it was broken through effective police action and the use of strikebreakers. The seamen were, for the most part, only indirectly concerned in the dispute. Not until the 1930's did their unions regain strength, either locally or nationally.[17] In the words of Edward Levinson,

With the . . . passing of Andrew Furuseth as an active figure, the 90,000 American sailors had no union to speak of. The sailors' life, romantic but never economically satisfying, dropped to new depths during the depression. Most of them [were] with no homes and with no more security than the next voyage offered. . . . Most sailors had something of that defiant self-reliance in them, and it was all the more surprising that they should have submitted to the type of labor leadership which traded on Furuseth's name from 1920 to 1936. Several officials became the willing recipients of shipowners' favors. They operated what was left of the union somewhat in the manner of a cheap employment agency.[18]

3. THE LONGSHOREMEN IN WAR AND PEACE

Except for a brief period in World War I, the longshoremen's history was similar to that of the sailors from 1915 through the Great Depression. In fact, it was not until 1948 that they were able to achieve a reasonable amount of stability under the auspices of the International Longshoremen's and Warehousemen's Union. Their chief opponents were shipowners and the operators of wharves and lumber yards, and when these formidable foes were combined with internal union dissension created by the IWW at Los Angeles Harbor in the early 1920's, the almost complete eclipse of the International Longshoremen's Association for the ensuing decade is quite understandable.

Local longshoremen were divided into two groups: those who loaded and unloaded the ships, and those who mainly handled lumber to and from the docks and within the yards. The latter were employed by the large lumber companies such as E. K. Wood, Kerckhoff-Cuzner, Hammond, and San Pedro, which were strongly open shop and had the backing of the Merchants' and Manufacturers' Association and the Southern Pacific, Salt Lake, and Pacific Electric railroads. As a consequence, efforts to unionize lumber handlers were more likely to incense open-shop supporters than were attempts to organize general dock workers. Likewise, the inclusion of lumber handlers in the longshore union meant greater vulnerability in the event of a strike, because the lumber companies were able to apply direct economic pressure against their employees. Longshoremen in other coastal ports, where the open shop was less effective and the ratio of lumber handlers to total longshoremen was smaller, were in a stronger position. In coast-wide strikes, Los Angeles longshoremen experienced difficulty in winning a settlement comparable to that obtained at other ports.

The first significant maritime dispute of the war period in which local longshoremen participated occurred in June, 1916. On May 16, after New York longshoremen struck for an eight-hour day, union recognition, increased wages, and a share of the profits on war traffic, Pacific Coast longshoremen, in convention at Seattle, voted to strike all coastal ports unless wages were raised from 50 to 55 cents an hour for straight time and from 65 cents to $1 for overtime. The employers refused, and on June 1, 12,000 dock workers up and down the coast walked out. Of this number, according to various estimates, between 1,500 and 1,700 struck at Los Angeles Harbor, a third of whom were lumber handlers.[19]

The longshoremen at Los Angeles belonged to Local No. 38–18 of the International Longshoremen's Association. Lumber handlers were in a separate ILA local, No. 38–43; they received only 27.5 to 35 cents an hour under open-shop conditions in the harbor lumber yards and docks. When the strike was called, hurried efforts were made to organize more of the lumber handlers, and they walked out along with the longshoremen. The millmen at the yards also struck in sympathy with the handlers. The lumber companies claimed that they had not received any demands before the walkout and that they could not pay longshoremen's wages to the handlers, but in spite of their protests the harbor at San Pedro was tightly closed. Secretary of Labor Wilson appointed Henry M. White as federal mediator, and negotiations to end the dispute were initiated in San Francisco. By June 9 all long-shoremen were returning to work at ports other than Los Angeles under a truce agreement which granted the requested wage scale pending final settlement. Local longshoremen were also given the op-portunity to go back to work under the truce, but the employers refused to include handlers in the agreement. As a third of the strikers were handlers, the dock workers were unwilling to desert them and remained out.[20]

The *Times* attacked the longshoremen, alleging that the men had walked out in violation of an agreement signed by their leaders and representatives of the steamship companies which provided for sixty days' notice of a strike. The *Record,* on the other hand, supported the longshoremen and accused the Merchants' and Manufacturers' Associa-tion of deliberately trying to stir up trouble. Representatives of the M and M and the stevedoring companies met with union leaders on June 13 under the auspices of federal mediator White, but they failed to reach agreement. The bone of contention was still the lumber firms' refusal to recognize their yard employees as longshoremen entitled to the higher wages of regular dock hands.

In view of the deadlock, these companies began to recruit strike-breakers in order to reopen for business on June 19. No lumber had reached the city through the port for almost three weeks, excepting a small amount unloaded at Redondo Beach and shipments received by rail. The actual reopening on June 19 was not successful, as few men reported for work, but it strengthened the longshoremen's determination to prevent effective operation of the yards and thus precipitated violence. On June 19 an employee of the E. K. Wood Lumber Company was beaten, and two days later a foreman of the Kerckhoff-Cuzner Lumber Company was similarly assaulted. In San Francisco, meanwhile, the killing of a longshoreman by a nonunion dock worker led to a threat that the truce would be repudiated unless all nonunion employees were dismissed. When this was ignored, the strike was resumed in other large ports along the coast on June 22. In Los Angeles Harbor on that date several hundred strikers attacked strikebreaking employees of the Consolidated Lumber Company at Wilmington as they left work, injuring about twenty men, several seriously. A lesser disturbance on the same day at the yards of the Hammond Lumber Company caused this plant to close down again.[21]

These threats to industrial peace could not long be ignored by the Merchants' and Manufacturers' Association; President E. G. Judah demanded that the Public Safety Commission of the Los Angeles City Council appoint 500 special policemen to keep order in the harbor district. When Councilman Fred Wheeler challenged the need for such action, both men lost their tempers and almost came to blows. The Public Safety Commission decided to investigate before authorizing the employment of men who would cost the taxpayers $1,500 a day. In the meantime, however, fifty extra patrolmen were detailed from the Los Angeles police force to help maintain peace at the harbor. On June 23 the commission reported that it did not see any need for 500 extra men and recommended that the City Council turn down the request, although Judah pointed out that the fear of violence kept nonunion employees from going to work. The council then authorized the employment of 100 emergency policemen, but failed to appropriate funds for their wages. The chief of police nevertheless declared he would use such men, if necessary, and let the council worry about the source of funds. His determination to maintain the peace encouraged lumber company officials, who announced that they would again try to reopen their yards on June 27. In response, Secretary J. W. Quinn of ILA Local No. 38–18 stated that the unions disapproved of violence and would oppose reopening only through peaceful means. Eight striking longshoremen were appointed to help the police maintain order, and no violence developed for several days after the yards began to operate with a few nonunion employees.[22]

But the strike had been under way for nearly a month, and many of the men were getting restless. Some strikers found themselves unable to secure additional credit at food stores; funds were needed if the men were to hold out much longer. Although food was donated by other unions and the Los Angeles Central Labor Council held a benefit dance for the strikers, these were only stopgap measures. The men participating in the walkout were well aware that the yards had to be kept from full-scale operations if the dispute was to be won. As peaceful picketing was not enough to restrict operations, it was almost inevitable that some strikers, seeing their jobs taken by others, would resort to violence. On July 2 about fifty strikers attacked two truck drivers of the Wood Lumber Company and made a bonfire of their vehicles and cargoes. This did not deter the lumber companies, however, from importing additional nonunion men and stepping up operations. The *Record* alleged that many of them were armed and led by the notorious Denver Mitchell, a professional strikebreaker. So tense did the situation become that by July 7, 200 Los Angeles policemen were on duty around the docks and yards. The *Citizen* pointed out that such conditions could lead only to trouble, as the armed strikebreakers would tend to assault unionists in an effort to bring even more police into the dispute. The *Times* claimed that the strike was really over, for the presence of the policemen was enabling a large number of lumber handlers to return to work.[23]

Whether or not the strike had actually been broken, its end was not yet in sight, for still more violence was to develop. The *Times* was not slow to report incidents and to imply that the strikers were at fault regardless of whether or not their participation could be proved. On July 10 a group of 200 men attacked 30 workers at the Hammond Lumber Company with stones, clubs, and fists. A number of men were arrested for shooting at ships in the harbor with a rifle. The following day another group was alleged to have beaten a watchman at the Wood Lumber Company while a rescuing policeman was held at bay. An attempt to burn the Sunshine Inn where twenty policemen were quartered was credited to strikers, but turned out to be the work of two Italians with personal grudges against the owners.

Whatever the truth of the stories on violence, they made it possible for the San Pedro, Blinn, Hammond, Consolidated, and Kerckhoff-Cuzner lumber companies, as well as the Pacific Wharf and Storage, Crescent Wharf and Warehouse, and Banning companies, to obtain an injunction, on July 11, against the longshoremen's unions, their officers, and some eighty members, restraining them from picketing, name calling, and other obstructive activities. Under its protection six of the lumber companies were able to extend their operations, with a total of 485 employees, most of whom were strikebreakers. Within a week the work force had doubled and the lumber handlers still on strike were ready to give up, though sporadic violence continued to break out. Local labor leader C. F. Grow accused the Municipal Employment Bureau in Los Angeles of sending men to San Pedro to take the jobs of strikers and of being under the domination of the *Times* and the Merchants' and Manufacturers' Association, but the superintendent, Harry Donoho, claimed that he had only followed the instructions of the City Council. He made it clear that he was opposed to the practice of furnishing strikebreakers per se, and that the men who went to the lumber companies for jobs were aware of the strike. The fact that Councilman Wheeler, always prolabor, did not object to the bureau's activities suggests that Grow was incorrect in his accusation. In any event, apparently no more than half a dozen men were sent.[24]

Meanwhile, conferences continued in San Francisco in an attempt to resolve the coast-wide walkout. Judah of the M and M wired San Francisco and Seattle water-front employers that any settlement that would strengthen unionism would not be accepted in Los Angeles regardless of what occurred at other ports; local companies were operating on an open-shop basis and intended to continue that way. On July 15 a vote was taken among the longshoremen at all ports on the question of returning to work under the old conditions until a compromise wage scale could be drafted at a conference scheduled for August 1. San Pedro dock workers unanimously voted to continue the strike, even though by now both the docks and the lumber yards were operating fairly efficiently with nonunion help. San Francisco long-shoremen chose to return to work, but strikers at a number of other ports followed the lead of San Pedro. Additional violence occurred in Los Angeles as the month of July drew to a close. Several fires were set on wharves and in lumber yards; a brick was tossed through the window of a grocery store which sold provisions to strikebreakers, and its deliveryman was stoned; various cases of assault by unionists were reported. But time was running out for those still on strike. The lumber companies were almost on a normal basis with the help of returning strikers and new men. On July 26 the wharf and warehouse companies announced that their crews also were approaching normal, and that any strikers wishing to return individually and at the old wage rate had better hurry.[25]

At the end of July, as the strike seemed to be over, a verbal battle developed between the chief of police and several members of the City Council over the discharge of emergency police at the harbor. The council, still paying the bill to the tune of $750 a day, wanted the force reduced as soon as possible. The chief made it clear, however, that he took orders only from the mayor and would not accede to these demands; hence the discharge of the emergency men occurred at a slower pace than the council desired. Early in August some 200 union millmen voted to return to work in harbor yards as individuals under the open shop. Only about half of them found jobs, however, as employers refused to fire nonunionists hired during the walkout. The few lumber handlers still out also voted to return under the old conditions as employment permitted, leaving only the longshoremen officially on strike. Nine hundred dock workers and approximately 600 lumber handlers had answered the original strike call, but only about 275 were still out early in August, the rest having either returned to work, taken other employment, or left the harbor area.[26]

In San Francisco the longshoremen won a closed-shop agreement. Locally and at other coastal ports, however, water-front employers sent men to work without reference to their union status and without fear of the few remaining pickets. At San Pedro, Local 38–18 continued to be officially on strike, but this made little difference to the employers. Before the end of August they closed the commissaries where they had been feeding strikebreakers, who were henceforth to be treated as regular employees. During the subsequent months employment conditions were reasonably good, with a continuing demand for skilled longshoremen. Local No. 38–18 did not die even though it had lost the strike, and did not declare it officially over until March 1, 1917. By June, 1917, most of the men who had struck a year earlier and were still in the harbor area were in the union and back at work on the docks, earning 5 cents more an hour than before the walkout. The few members of Lumber Handlers Local No. 38–43 who had not deserted their union were added to the rolls of Local No. 38–18.[27]

The war, though increasing the troubles of the longshoremen, also enabled them to make membership gains. The troubles included a dual union controversy with the Industrial Workers of the World, as well as a number of other disputes. On July 17, 1917, the Wobblies formed an independent union of 300 dock workers, a forerunner of difficulties for AFL longshoremen at San Pedro which reached their peak in the early 1920's. This particular IWW union, however, did not have a long life, as its membership gradually drifted into the jurisdiction of ILA Local No. 38–18. By November, 1917, the latter reported 350 members, and increased its strength the following month when Local No. 38–40 of Redondo Beach merged with it. Although the union was operating under open-shop conditions, it was strong enough to participate in a number of minor disputes in 1917. These were primarily local in character, with one exception. This involved the wage differential between Los Angeles and San Francisco, where waterfront employers paid a scale of 75 cents an hour and $1 for overtime. In Los Angeles the rates were 55 and 85 cents, respectively. Local longshoremen believed they were entitled to the same pay for the same work under wartime conditions as were their fellows in closed-shop San Francisco. Their dissatisfaction became serious enough to bring a federal mediator into the dispute, and in December, 1917, they were granted a 33⅓ per cent increase.[28]

Although Los Angeles Harbor was not so much benefited by the war as east coast ports, employment for longshoremen was steady throughout 1918 and 1919. The shipyards absorbed any excess dock workers, and several substantial wage increases were granted by local stevedoring companies. Though union recognition was not formally conceded by all the firms, Local No. 38–18 was able to function without much interference from open-shop employers during the national emergency until the Armistice changed dockside labor relations into industrial warfare. The basic issue was an effort of the San Pedro Chamber of Commerce in 1919 to restore complete open-shop conditions. It passed a resolution to this end which, in effect, threw down the gauntlet to the organized longshoremen. Local No. 38–18 responded by publishing a statement in the San Pedro newspaper asking all friends of organized labor to withdraw from the Chamber of Commerce and to cease patronizing stores that had joined in its open-shop resolution. On October 14 the union called a strike for a wage increase against the Outer Harbor Dock and Warehouse Company as a test case. Violence quickly erupted as several men reporting for work at the struck firm were beaten, allegedly by strikers. The evidence was sufficiently strong to enable the company to secure an injunction against picketing or any other interference with its employees. When other dock companies joined the struck firm in reinstituting a strong open-shop policy, the handwriting on the wall became clear. Matters were further complicated by IWW infiltration into the longshoremen's ranks, which caused a subsidiary union, ILA Laborers Local No. 38A–18, to surrender its charter and move into the Marine Transport Workers Industrial Union. The strike was not successful, and the Outer Harbor Dock and Warehouse Company soon claimed to be handling more cargo with nonunion longshoremen than it had processed for years. It also stated that the minimum wage paid to the nonunionists was $40 a week, with some men earning as much as $70.[29]

Local No. 38–18 maintained a tenuous existence after the strike. Like the sailors, the longshoremen were easily converted to the IWW because they were dissatisfied with the AFL union's lack of success against the open shop. The postwar depression also aided the IWW cause, as the old-line craft unions failed to develop policies to lessen its impact on employment. A further boost for the Marine Transport Workers Industrial Union was the consent of the Sailors Union of the Pacific, at the conclusion of the 1921 seamen's strike, to work lumber cargoes with nonunion as well as union longshoremen.

But the event that finally broke the back of Local No. 38–18 began in 1921 in Seattle rather than in Los Angeles. This was the establishment of a company-controlled hiring hall by Frank P. Foisie, later president of the Waterfront Employers' Association of the Pacific Coast. This hall kept a central registration of all men eligible to work on the docks as longshoremen, from which employers selected the employees they wanted for steady work. The balance of the men on the list composed a reserve pool which was theoretically available for the peak needs of the port but in practice was limited to the number the industry believed it could employ on a reasonably steady basis. Thus, in addition to facilitating the open shop, the Seattle decasualization scheme had the advantages of providing a more stable work force for which steady employment was available and of permitting employer resistance to IWW infiltration. The Seattle program was initiated in Los Angeles through the Sea Service Bureau, but it was not adopted in San Francisco, where employers dominated the Longshoremen's Association, or so-called "Blue Book" union, which in turn controlled the water front. Although the establishment of a hiring hall for longshoremen at Los Angeles Harbor in May, 1922, provoked a strike threat from both the ILA local and the IWW industrial union, neither had the strength to resist. San Pedro became an open-shop town for both dock workers and sailors, and Local No. 38–18 gave up its charter.[30] IWW members, however, were not quite ready to quit in San Pedro. The harbor was growing rapidly and employment opportunities were good, even though largely controlled by employers. Disruption of Local No. 38–18 by IWW activity had not displeased the employers, but once the AFL organization was eliminated, the left-wingers became *persona non grata*. Efforts to keep them from dock employment, however, were not successful. As noted earlier, members of the IWW were asked to go to San Pedro in November, 1922, both to fight the open shop and to test the California criminal syndicalism law, a wartime measure that remained in effect during the "Red scare" of the 'twenties. In spite of mass arrests of the Wobblies, unrest on the water front continued; in fact, persecution seemed only to strengthen the Marine Transport Workers Industrial Union. Although few sailors belonged to this union, enough of them coöperated in the Wobblies' "quickie" strikes to keep many ships from sailing on time and to maintain constant turmoil on the San Pedro water front in the early months of 1923.[31]

Under these circumstances employers would soon have had to take stronger countermeasures, but the Wobblies themselves forced a showdown. On April 25, 1923, shortly after the Los Angeles County Grand Jury held hearings on violations of the criminal syndicalism act, San Pedro Local No. 510 of the MTWIU called a strike and effectively tied up the port for several days. The walkout was national in scope, with its pivotal points in New York and Los Angeles; it brought out 5,000 men on the east coast and probably 1,500 locally, with estimates at San Pedro ranging as high as 3,000. It had little effect at other Western ports, however, though a number of Pacific Coast lumberjacks and oil workers participated and the independent Federation of Marine Transport Workers also joined with the Wobblies. Members of the Sailors Union of the Pacific refused to support the strike, not only because it was IWW-inspired, but also because they were already "working the oracle" or, in other words, conducting a slowdown with some success. The strike itself was a peculiar combination of an ordinary economic walkout and a political maneuver. In its nationwide aspects, it sought to secure the release of political prisoners, particularly those accused of sedition against the federal government or held under the California criminal syndicalism law. Locally, the specific demands included the release of all so-called "class war" prisoners, pay increases, a three-watch system, the same food for licensed and unlicensed personnel aboard ships, clean bed sheets on vessels each week, and recognition of the Marine Transport Workers Industrial Union.[32]

The walkout tied up about ninety ships in Los Angeles Harbor. Police quickly started to round up known IWW agitators, thus depleting the ranks of strike leaders and permitting some ships to get under way. Twelve vessels in the offshore trade, manned by seamen sympathetic to the IWW, suffered the longest delays. The thirty-seven lumber schooners in port were largely manned by nonunionists or members of the Sailors Union. Nevertheless, the cargoes of a number of them had to be discharged in rotation at the piers by the ships' officers because of the shortage of dock hands. By May 2 ship movement had improved, but lumber vessels still had to rotate their cargo handling and so were delayed in port. Strikebreakers had not yet been brought in to replace striking longshoremen. IWW leaders held frequent meetings to keep up the strikers' morale. The most colorful of these occurred on May 1 at Fourth and Beacon streets in San Pedro. It was addressed by Leo Stark, a recently arrested strike leader who was out on bail, and the Reverend Fred R. Wedge, an ex-lumberjack and former pastor of the Terminal Island Congregational Church. Many of the 2,000 persons in attendance wore red flowers in their buttonholes. A red airplane with the word SOLIDARITY painted on it circled overhead dropping leaflets, and a red automobile carrying an IWW placard drove around in the streets below. A fast launch distributed strike literature to ships in the harbor.[33]

On the same day, IWW leaders persuaded approximately 450 of 2,200 men to strike at refinery construction jobs two miles north of the harbor, and it seemed likely that the dispute would spread beyond the water front. Employers therefore decided to take immediate action both to prevent this and to move ships more rapidly. Negotiations with the longshoremen, however, foundered on their demand for their own hiring hall and the abandonment of the Sea Service Bureau, or "Fink Hall," controlled by the stevedoring and shipping firms. Some 1,200 longshoremen voted to remain out until the employers met this basic request. As further conferences seemed futile, local representatives of the Shipowners' Association held a meeting on May 4 on board the *H. F. Alexander* and decided to import strikebreakers, who would be housed in the outer harbor and brought to and from work in launches in order to minimize the chances of contact with pickets. About 140 extra patrolmen and 20 detectives were dispatched to the docks by the Los Angeles Police Department to maintain order in the event of a showdown.[34]

When officials of the Federation of Marine Transport Workers, fearing the importation of strikebreakers, asked the federal government to intervene, they were told that this would be possible only if the strikers returned to work. Nevertheless, on May 5 its members voted to remain out, though making it clear that they were not Wobblies. On the same day more than 100 strikebreakers arrived and were immediately put to work. Two hundred more were scheduled to begin employment on May 8 and an additional 750 were due a few days later. By May 10, 1,500 longshoremen were at work, of whom 350 were imported strikebreakers. The extra police force was increased to 250, largely because of a fire on May 9 which had obviously been the work of an arsonist. The fire had been discovered on a railroad bridge leading into the harbor and could have caused the destruction of millions of board feet of dry wood in the yard of the Kerckhoff-Cuzner Lumber Company. Although definite proof was lacking, the *Times* quickly blamed the IWW. On May 11 the independent federation again voted to remain out, but disaffections were appearing in its ranks as well as in those of IWW Local No. 510. Most of the longshoremen on strike were former ILA supporters. According to one estimate, not more than 250 of the strikers were Wobblies, but the IWW leadership was effective enough to keep 1,500 men out for several weeks. Its power was waning by May 12, however; many strikers were becoming restless, as there seemed to be little hope of settlement and operations at the harbor were beginning to approach normal. About forty-nine gangs were working offshore vessels, 600 men were handling cargoes on lumber schooners, and 400 were laboring in dock warehouses. Although efficiency was below normal and congestion existed at the docks, cargoes were being moved more rapidly every day.[35]

As the strike entered its fourth week, the police cracked down even harder on the Wobblies. The latter began to look on the dispute as a free-speech fight and continued to hold meetings near the water front at a point known as Liberty Hill, a privately owned parcel of land used with the permission of the owner. Local sympathizers and members of the American Civil Liberties Union joined the IWW leaders in seeking to maintain rights of free speech. They included such prominent Los Angeles and Pasadena figures as Upton Sinclair, Mrs. Kate Crane Gartz, Mrs. F. O. Ellsworth, Pryns Hopkins, John C. Packard, J. H. Ryckman, and Hunter S. Kimbrough. Sinclair was particularly vocal, accusing the Los Angeles chief of police, Louis D. Oaks, of attempting to kidnap him and subsequently deny him the services of an attorney. He also claimed that Oaks was the medium through which the Merchants' and Manufacturers' Association expected to end the walkout. He had been in the office of I. H. Rice, president of the M and M, when the latter received orders from the management of the Hammond Lumber Company to break the strike. On May 15, when Upton Sinclair, to test Oaks's determination to end the dispute, read the Constitution of the United States on Liberty Hill, he was promptly booked for disturbing the peace. Three days later, seventy-one alleged IWW members were arrested and jailed. So effective was police action against strike leaders that the Shipowners' Association declared the walkout over on May 18, when eighty-five vessels were loaded or unloaded by 2,800 longshoremen for the busiest day in port history. Fifty policemen were immediately returned to Los Angeles for regular duty, and 500 strikebreakers were given permanent employment.[36]

Although the future looked bleak, IWW leaders were not yet ready to give up. Four hundred of their associates were in jail. Others had left town to look for jobs elsewhere. The efficiency of longshore operations was improving each day. Strikers who were not proven Wobblies were returning to work through the open-shop Sea Service Bureau. But still the walkout continued. On May 21, 3,000 posters announcing a meeting at Liberty Hall in San Pedro on the evening of May 23 were distributed in the harbor area. The meeting was to be addressed by Upton Sinclair and a number of other speakers under the auspices of the American Civil Liberties Union. Noting this, the *Times* published a statement signed by W. E. Townsend, an FBI agent, and John Dymond of the district attorney's office, purporting to show that the ACLU was the defense branch of the IWW. The meeting drew 5,000 people, but there were no fireworks, as police were present to ensure that it was peaceful. Copies of *Solidarity*, the official IWW organ, were distributed and Oaks and his men were figuratively roasted by the speakers for their brutality, but little else occurred. The next day a general meeting of 600 longshoremen, most of whom were not Wobblies, voted to "transfer" the dispute back to the job, and the walkout was officially ended.[37]

Like the strikers who had returned to work earlier, those seeking jobs after the dispute's termination had to apply for employment through the Sea Service Bureau, which was still being used to prevent the reëmployment of IWW members. In an effort to catch any Wobblies who might have slipped through the bureau, it was announced that a complete reregistration of all longshoremen at Los Angeles Harbor would begin on May 31. This blow against the IWW was partially offset several days later by an official statement that only 10 of more than 400 prisoners held in Los Angeles jails as a result of the strike would be tried. The others were subsequently released with only a warning. At least one national observer of the events accused the Merchants' and Manufacturers' Association of seeking to keep the criminal syndicalism law on the state's books in order to thwart the formation of labor unions among longshoremen and seamen rather than to protect the port against revolutionary agitators.

Early in June a preliminary report on the longshoremen's dispute was presented to civic organizations at San Pedro by a "Committee of Eleven," whose chairman was the Reverend Thomas Grice, pastor of the First Methodist Church at the harbor. The committee members had been chosen from fraternal and civic organizations in the area to investigate the causes of the dispute and to suggest a means of establishing industrial peace. The report gave little comfort to organized labor, for it recommended continuation of the employer-dominated hiring hall and failed to probe the fundamental causes of the walkout. These were a wage scale lower than that in effect at other coastal ports and the lack of free collective bargaining. Had these issues been met squarely by water-front employers, the IWW might have been less successful in fomenting unrest.[38]

The pronouncements of the Committee of Eleven did not contribute to labor peace. Before the end of June harbor police suspected that a new longshore strike was in the offing, again under the sponsorship of Local No. 510. Posters were once more appearing in conspicuous places, IWW literature was being distributed in large quantities, and street orators were becoming more active along the water front. A sample poster read as follows:

To all liberty-loving people: Boycott all California-made goods and moving pictures until that State has released all class-war prisoners jailed under the criminal syndicalism Act. Yours for free speech.

Marine Transport Workers, No. 510[39]

The possibility of a strike was strengthened on July 11, 1923, when twenty-seven IWW members, including Leo Stark, were convicted in a Los Angeles court on charges of criminal syndicalism. All were given from one to fourteen years or an opportunity for probation if they would quit the IWW. They chose imprisonment rather than probationary freedom. The convictions were the signal for a meeting held at the harbor that same evening and attended by 1,200 water-front workers, who voted to walk out the next day at 10 A.M. Police arrested three men including the leader of the meeting, Fred Miller, who had recently arrived from Seattle to direct IWW activities at the harbor. Estimates indicated that no more than 300 dock workers were Wobblies, but additional IWW members were reported to be arriving from elsewhere in the country, thus causing uncertainty as to their total strength. Under these circumstances, even though little trouble was expected, it seemed prudent to place harbor police on an alert status with twelve-hour shifts.[40]

The strike occurred on July 12 as scheduled, but only about 200 longshoremen actually walked out, along with approximately 100 sailors and firemen from coastwise lumber vessels. It was more of a political protest than an economic dispute, as its primary aim was to advertise the allegedly unjust treatment of Wobblies in the courts. Its lack of economic success was forecast the first day, when there was actually a surplus of maritime labor available through the Sea Service Bureau and sporadic attempts at picketing were broken up by the police, seventy-five of whom had just been transferred to the harbor force from other Los Angeles precincts. Rumors that more Wobblies were heading for Los Angeles on steamers from Atlantic ports had little basis in fact. On the second day, further attempts at picketing resulted in the arrest of one striker. An afternoon meeting at Liberty Hill under a broiling sun attracted only 200 onlookers, who listened to speakers upbraid them for their apathy with respect to the twenty-seven convicted men. At an evening meeting in the same location, 2,000 gathered to hear denunciations of judges, juries, and particularly the Los Angeles court that had tried the Wobblies. One speaker, E. F. Moffett, a self-styled contractor, was arrested by the police. Just before the meeting two alleged IWW members had been removed from a tanker on its arrival in port. Several days later, two others were arrested at the request of the captain of the steamer *Miskianza* which had just arrived from Mobile, Alabama. It had taken two months to complete a voyage normally requiring seventeen days. The mutinous spirit fostered by the seamen concerned had twice forced the ship into port en route to repair machinery allegedly damaged by sabotage.[41]

On July 16 the Sacramento County Superior Court, on the petition of the United States Attorney General, granted an injunction that prevented the IWW from operating in California. The following day the strike was declared at an end, and a large number of IWW members left the port for other areas. Water-front operations proceeded with less disturbance and unrest than they had for months. Police estimated that more than 500 men, on orders of their national leaders, left for Port Arthur, Texas, to combat the Ku Klux Klan, whose activities there had caused the death of several Wobblies.[42]

Despite this exodus, the peace that settled over the water front at Los Angeles Harbor was short-lived. The new unrest centered on the Sea Service Bureau. A final report by the Committee of Eleven early in September placed the blame for the deterioration of industrial relations at the harbor on a lack of understanding between maritime workers and employers. Hours and pay were secondary issues, according to the committee, and although many disputes would have been eliminated or adjusted amicably if the IWW had not deliberately misled workers into believing their unions had issued strike calls, the real problem was the need for changes in Sea Service Bureau operations. Certain members of the bureau's staff did not understand the relationship between employer and employee and thus tended to make the workers hostile to management. On the other hand, the report did not recommend abolition of the bureau, but instead commended employers for already making some of the personnel changes needed to improve the situation.[43]

Even as the Committee of Eleven made its report, events at the harbor seemed to be shaping up for another walkout. This time leadership for the threatened strike was furnished by the Federation of Marine Transport Workers, which was also active at other Pacific Coast ports. An intensive recruiting campaign during the last ten days of August had brought in several hundred new members, some of whom probably had participated in the earlier activities of IWW Local No. 510. Although Los Angeles Harbor seemed to be the pivotal point for the union, its activities had spread to San Francisco, Coos Bay, Portland, and Seattle, and allegedly involved a total of about 10,000 dock workers. On August 31 its leaders made demands on coastal waterfront employers for abolition of the black-listing of participants in the IWW strike at Los Angeles the previous May; elimination of employer-dominated hiring halls at Pacific Coast ports; a flat wage boost from 80 cents to $1 an hour; a 20 per cent increase in straight-time pay for working with such hard-to-handle commodities as sulphur, pig iron, and coke; and up to $2 an hour exclusive of overtime for loading or unloading a number of objectionable items. Bulletins containing these demands were posted at union halls up and down the coast, and waterfront employers were given until September 15 to meet them or risk a strike two days later. The employers flatly rejected the demands, thus challenging the union to call its strike. But the Federation of Marine Transport Workers lacked the strength to back up its demands with a show of force, and instead of striking it asked for a conference with water-front employers. After prolonged negotiations, a 12.5 per cent wage increase was agreed to on December 23, 1923, but the Sea Service Bureau remained. The wage increase made Pacific Coast longshoremen supposedly the highest-paid dock workers in the world, even though most of them were employed under open-shop conditions.[44]

Through the columns of the *Times,* open-shop supporters sought to demonstrate that the Sea Service Bureau leaned over backward to be fair to dock workers by operating an "Industrial Relations Committee" or "Industrial Court." It was composed of five members familiar with maritime labor problems, all of whom were appointed by water-front employers. Sessions of the court were held every Tuesday evening, and maritime workers with grievances appeared to state their cases. Open-shop supporters pointed out that no complaints had been received concerning a single decision handed down by the court, but this was to be expected when employers controlled the hiring hall. Men who had been black-listed for participation in strikes led by the IWW were forced to seek reinstatement through the court. Eugene A. Mills, president of the San Pedro branch of the Shipowners' Association and founder of the Industrial Court, stated that the longshoremen had opposed it at first but were now in favor of this system of handling grievances. He also pointed out that dock work was now being efficiently done by 2,200 men registered at the Sea Service Bureau in place of the 3,500 who had worked on the same wharves before its establishment. This reduction in force in the face of increased tonnage had been made possible by the institution of new cargo handling equipment. It had permitted the elimination of troublemakers from among the dock workers without jeopardizing the accomplishment of harbor longshore work.[45]

The Wobblies who remained in the harbor area continued to have trouble with open-shop forces as well as with groups infected with the anti-Red hysteria of the early 1920's. On the evening of March 1, 1924, a crowd of nightshirted Ku Klux Klan members and hangers-on, variously estimated at up to 3,000, circled the IWW hall at Twelfth and Center streets in San Pedro. No acts of violence were committed but there was no mistaking the intended warning. A little more than two weeks later, a squad of police raided the hall while a meeting of the Oil Workers Industrial Union was in progress. Entering with drawn revolvers and no search warrant, they went upstairs and ordered the occupants to line up against the walls while they arrested three leaders of the group. At the same time, nightshirted men who had followed the police into the building either removed or destroyed everything of value on the first floor. Although it was claimed that the Hammond Lumber Company was responsible for the raid, this could not be proved. The worst blow hit the Wobblies three months later, on June 14, when 300 men, women, and children were in the IWW hall attending a benefit for the families of two members of the group who had been killed in a railroad accident. A cavalcade of cars stopped before the hall and attacked without warning. Windows were broken and the furniture was chopped up. The adult males at the meeting were put in trucks, driven away, and tarred and feathered. Local newspapers the following day generally excused the action of the mob, but the incident made the atmosphere on the water front very tense. The situation became even more serious when an anonymous note sent to the hall after the incident threatened the Wobblies if they did not leave town.[46]

The American Civil Liberties Union then held street meetings to protest the treatment accorded the Wobblies. At first these were tolerated by the police, but finally, on July 6, 1924, E. F. Moffett and Leo Gallagher, an attorney for left-wing organizations, were arrested while speaking at Fourth and Beacon streets. Gallagher was criticizing the district attorney and the police, charging that the latter had participated in the kidnaping and tarring of IWW members on June 14. Police interference with the ACLU street meetings temporarily immobilized a significant source of help for the IWW in the harbor area. By January, 1925, the *Industrial Worker,* organ of the IWW, had to admit that all active members of the group had left the harbor and that the local branch would have to be rebuilt. Contributory factors included the persecution of IWW members under the criminal syndicalism law and the recognized inability of the organization to better the conditions of maritime workers. Its failure in this regard caused many longshoremen henceforth to refuse to affiliate with any union under its auspices.[47]

The ILA maintained skeleton locals in nearly every Pacific Coast port during the rest of the 1920's and the early 1930's, but they won few economic gains for their members and were largely ignored by employers. Los Angeles Harbor proved to be no exception, and the open-shop Sea Service Bureau continued to dominate water-front hiring procedures. Even the great increase in tonnage at both Los Angeles and Long Beach harbors during the 'twenties did not aid the maritime unions. In 1919, 1,967 ships entered the combined harbors carrying 2,380,622 tons of cargo valued at $86,481,490. By 1930 the number of ships had increased to 8,633, and tonnage carried had risen to 25,920,-159, with a value of $1,055,808,494. In the latter year, Los Angeles Harbor was first among ports in the United States in intercoastal tonnage (much of it in oil), second in export tonnage, and third in total commerce.[48]

The basic grievances of the men during the prosperity of the 'twenties continued to center on the Sea Service Bureau. In spite of the Industrial Court, working conditions gradually deteriorated in the later years of the decade and became rapidly worse in the subsequent depression. Dock workers were often required to work twenty-four to thirty-six hours at a stretch. The speed-up was encouraged in order to reduce overtime. Competition among workers was developed by dividing the longshoremen into star gangs and casuals. The former constituted about a fourth of the labor force, receiving preferential treatment and relatively steady work, but they had to keep up a rapid pace and labor long, consecutive hours in order to maintain this status. After the stock market crash in 1929, competition for the fewer available jobs was intensified. More and more regulars became casuals, the use of the speed-up became more general, larger loads were handled by smaller gangs, the accident rate increased as the men hurried faster, machinery to handle disputes and complaints virtually disappeared, and favoritism increased. The last problem was especially evident in the petty bribery indulged in by some foremen and supervisors who received kickbacks from men selected for jobs. Low and irregular earnings also led the men to patronize loan sharks, who took advantage of their economic status to keep them in perpetual debt at high interest charges. By the end of 1932, after the announcement of a 10-cent-an-hour wage reduction, regular dock workers received only 65 cents for straight time and $1 for overtime, while hatch tenders and winch drivers were paid a regular rate of 85 cents with $1.20 for overtime. Conditions were ripe for a rebellion on the docks, but it did not develop until 1934.[49]

VI. LABOR'S DARKEST YEARS

1. FROM WAR'S PEAK TO DEPRESSION'S DEPTHS, 1920–1932

THE YEARS after World War I sorely tested organized labor in the nation as well as in Los Angeles. The high hopes with which labor leaders faced the postwar decade, as a result of substantial wartime gains in membership, gradually dwindled. For a time the unions were forced to give up the battle against the open shop, until their revival in 1933 under the shelter of the National Industrial Recovery Act.

It is difficult to ascribe the decline of the labor movement over the country to any one cause. There seem to have been a number of operative factors: a general rise in real wages; a failure to consolidate membership gains made during the war; the inability of AFL leaders, dominated by a craft-union philosophy, effectively to organize the mass-production industries; the depressions of 1920–1922, 1924, and 1929–1933; and, perhaps most important, the powerful open-shop campaign carried on under the guise of the American Plan or welfare capitalism. Although the last was not new to Los Angeles labor leaders, it assumed greater importance than ever before on the national scene, particularly in the first half of the postwar decade.

The American Plan was, in part, a reaction against the militant attitude of labor created by its wartime successes and against the strike patterns of 1919–1923, especially those evoking violence. In part, it was an expression of a "return to normalcy" philosophy, which resulted in the misinterpretation of labor's goals of recognition and collective bargaining as Communist-inspired. The structure of the American Plan, based on the plant committee system of the National War Labor Board, lent itself to the development of company unions. Employers were able to use these company organizations as channels to substitute direct guarantees for conditions sought through outside union bargaining.

Though the exact causes or effects of the American Plan are not clearly discernible, there is no doubt that union membership fell during the years right after the war. Four-fifths of the loss from 1920 to 1923 occurred in unions that had accounted for three-fourths of the increase in membership from 1915 to 1920. Although the decline was not so rapid after 1923, it nevertheless continued until 1933. During these ten years the supporters of the open shop maintained persistent pressure on labor unions over the country.[1]

Internal dissension among AFL leaders contributed in no small

[193]

measure to their inability to provide effective resistance to the American Plan. This was particularly evident in the dispute between the United Brotherhood of Carpenters and Joiners of America, led by William L. Hutcheson, and the AFL Executive Council over the National Board for Jurisdictional Awards, formed in 1919. Hutcheson refused to accept the board's decision granting jurisdiction over the installation of metal trim to sheet metal workers. This led to the expulsion of the carpenters' union from the AFL Building Trades Department and eventually to the establishment of dual building trades councils and carpenters' unions in many metropolitan areas of the country, including Los Angeles. In essence, Hutcheson bartered building trades unity for dissolution of the board, and he won, though not until 1927. Meanwhile, the open shop had made substantial inroads in the building trades.[2]

Not all the internal dissension, however, was between old-line craft-union leaders within the AFL. Some of it found the conservative AFL leadership pitted against Communists and members of the Industrial Workers of the World. Although the Wobblies were not a significant power after World War I and the early 1920's, the Communists were a persistent thorn in the flesh of established unions well into the 'thirties. The first programs and platforms of the two main Communist groups in 1919, the Communist Party and the Communist Labor Party, called for the support of industrial unionism and the building of new revolutionary unions, thus rejecting any association with AFL organizations. By the middle 'twenties, however, the Communists had shifted to tactics of entering established unions and boring from within. The AFL, under Samuel Gompers and then William Green, took a militant stand against the radicals, whether IWW or Communist. Although this policy was meritorious in keeping the labor movement within the framework of American social institutions and spared the AFL leaders even stronger maledictions from open-shop supporters, it took its toll in time and effort that could have been spent in opposing the American Plan.[3]

Despite seemingly overwhelming odds, the labor movement won a few battles in this period. Among these was the printing trades' fight for the forty-four-hour week. The International Typographical Union inaugurated the shorter workweek idea in 1919. In subsequent years it gradually whittled away employer opposition until, by 1927, the forty-four-hour week was common in the commercial printing trades, even in Los Angeles.[4]

After the printers' victory, it was not long before other trades, both organized and unorganized, began to achieve a shorter workweek despite the efforts of such employer organizations as the National Association of Manufacturers to stop what may have been the inevitable. In October, 1927, at its annual convention in Los Angeles, the AFL established the five-day week as a major objective. Unfortunately, it took a depression to gain this aim. In 1931 even the Los Angeles *Times* favored the shorter workweek as a spread-the-jobs measure. By 1933 the forty-hour or forty-four-hour workweek was the general rule in most metropolitan areas of the country, including Los Angeles. The victory had been almost completely won, but at a severe cost in employment.[5]

Until the Great Depression workers and businessmen in general fared reasonably well after World War I. The development of automobile, electrical, and chemical manufacturing provided new employment opportunities, even though the craft-dominated AFL was not interested in organizing the workers in these new centers of economic activity. Industries such as agriculture, coal mining, textiles, and clothing manufacture, which did not share in the prosperity, tended to be the exception rather than the rule. Many businessmen became convinced that the combination of welfare capitalism and the Federal Reserve System would make panics impossible. Increased productivity and the rise in real income in the 1920's seemed to support the thesis that an economic millennium was starting. Under such conditions, what was the need of unions? Was there any useful role for organized labor to play?

Residential building reached an all-time high in the 1920's. For the first time American investors found an outlet for saving in foreign investments (a continuation of a World War I trend). There was a tremendous growth of consumer credit. The expansion of the auto industry fostered a sustained increase in the related areas of rubber, oil, glass, steel, road equipment, and cement. Public construction financed by heavy state and federal borrowing moved at a high level. Statements in the Los Angeles *Times* in 1926 and 1927 carried assurance that good times were here to stay and that workers were benefiting from a rise in the purchasing power of the dollar.[6]

But time was running out for both business and labor. Some observers of the economic scene saw signs of the end of prosperity as early as 1926, but little credence was given to their statements. After the stock market's "Black Thursday" in October, 1929, followed by a continuing decline in market activity and employment in late 1929 and 1930, it became evident that American capitalism had overextended itself. Although employers had succeeded in keeping organized labor on the run during most of the predepression decade, they had not corrected the faults of the economic system.[7]

Unemployment proved to be the best index of the times. By early 1931, 7,160,000 workers were seeking jobs, more than double the January, 1930, figure. By January, 1932, 10,197,000 were unemployed. The depression caught the federal government without any organized system of unemployment relief. President Hoover and the Congress initiated a series of steps designed to halt the unemployment trend, but all proved to be "too little, too late." Among these were the November, 1929, conference of leading industrialists; the Smoot-Hawley Tariff of June, 1930; the reduction of discount rates by the Federal Reserve System; an increase in federal spending for construction; the formation in October, 1930, of the President's Emergency Committee for Employment; and the appropriation in December, 1930, of $116 million for emergency public works. But unemployment continued to rise.[8]

In 1931 federal emphasis shifted to work relief. A "Give a Job" campaign was launched in which citizens were asked to hire the unemployed for yard duties, housework, and a variety of odd jobs, but this approach also proved fruitless. People were hoarding their dollars, not expending them on jobs they could do themselves. In February, 1931, Congress passed the Employment Stabilization Act, the first definite step in the planning of public works by the federal government. Throughout the year President Hoover continued to urge that private enterprise aid in ending the depression. He asked for job assurance programs from large firms; appointed sixty national leaders as an advisory staff to handle unemployment problems; and suggested job rotation, a three-day workweek, and six-hour shifts.

The first significant federal aid to the states in the public works area did not come, however, until 1932, when the Emergency Relief and Construction Act was passed. It established the Reconstruction Finance Corporation for the purpose of making loans to banks, agricultural credit agencies, insurance companies, railroads, and other businesses as well as public agencies. Though criticized by its political opponents for helping business instead of the unemployed, it went into effect and continued operative far beyond the 1930's. In August, 1932, President Hoover gathered many of the nation's leaders in Washington, D.C., to say that the crisis was over, but unemployment figures belied his statements. The peak in these figures was reached in March, 1933, by which time a new occupant was in the White House and a new era in the development of organized labor was about to begin.[9]

2. THE POSTWAR YEARS IN LOS ANGELES

The picture in Los Angeles in 1920–1932 was similar to that throughout the nation except for stronger open-shop overtones. The first two years of the postwar period were marked by a comparable inflation and building boom, which aided in the growth of the construction trades but stimulated only minor activity in most of the other unions. The combination of a housing shortage, a large tourist influx, and high rents led to record-breaking building activity in 1920. Ten thousand new homes were built as Los Angeles became the third city in building growth in the United States. This development resulted in membership and wage increases for practically all building trades unions. Bricklayers, plasterers, and floor layers received $10 a day, and cement workers were paid $9. Carpenters, painters, and electrical workers got $8 for a day's work. The Los Angeles Building Trades Council reported a 100 per cent increase in affiliated membership during the year.

These gains were not without cost, however, as the Merchants' and Manufacturers' Association actively opposed the building trades unions. It not only joined the open-shop Associated General Contractors of America, but also purged itself of one of its own member firms which had violated the spirit of the American Plan. The expelled member was the Brownstein-Louis Company, an affiliate of the M and M for more than two decades and operator of a union factory for twenty-three years. Brownstein-Louis was a clothing manufacturing firm which advertised for contractors to put up a new building with union labor. The Los Angeles Master Builders' Association, a chapter of the Associated General Contractors, was kept from bidding on the new structure because of its open-shop policy. This gave rise to a complaint and resulted in the ousting of Brownstein-Louis from the M and M.[10]

The association also sought to prevent the growth of unions in other trades in 1920, but its influence at this time was minimal. The depression that struck the Los Angeles area later in the year hurt unions more than did the M and M. The latter, however, again became an important factor as the decade advanced.

The most significant walkout in 1920, from the standpoint of numbers, occurred at the Southern California Telephone and Telegraph Company, an affiliate of the Pacific Telephone and Telegraph Company. Los Angeles Local No. 370 of the International Brotherhood of Electrical Workers participated in the coast-wide dispute, which was directed from San Francisco. The walkout in Los Angeles began on

February 14 and ended thirteen days later. It affected 400 to 500 men, who demanded $7 per day for journeymen and better working conditions. The strike failed because of the unexpected strength of the company union, which prevented its members from defecting to Local No. 370. The latter lost rather than gained members, and was forced to merge with IBEW Local No. 61, forming a new organization known as Local No. 18.[11]

By 1920 the metal trades as well as the electrical workers began to feel the effect of postwar layoffs in the shipyards and railroad roundhouses. They tried to organize in other areas as a compensatory action but failed in their attempts. The most important of these efforts were made by Machinists Local No. 311 at the American Can Company and the molders at the Martin Iron Works. These open-shop firms proved too strong for the unions and successfully resisted their demands.

A similar situation prevailed in the culinary trades, where the M and M backed up firms struck by the Southern California Waiters Association. The union members demanded recognition and wage increases from a number of large downtown hotels, insisting that they could not support their families on their low wages. The strike brought out several hundred unionists, who were replaced by strikebreakers and permanently dismissed. A number of them later deserted the association and joined Waiters Local No. 17.[12]

A few union groups enjoyed success in 1920. As noted earlier, the local printing trades began their campaign for the forty-four-hour week in this year. The teamsters gained at least a partial victory when approximately 100 stage drivers struck in August, 1920, for higher pay for out-of-town trips to Bakersfield, San Diego, and way points. The men who struck owned their own vehicles, which they leased to the companies, receiving a certain sum of money for each trip they made. The walkout was accompanied by some violence against drivers who refused to go out; a few strikers lost their licenses for assaulting men who had not walked out or had gone back to work. The strikers demanded $36 to $40 per trip, but the dispute was compromised after a few days at $35, a $3 increase over the previous rate. Enough of the drivers accepted the terms to end the walkout and get the stages back into operation on regular schedules. The companies—Motor Transit, Pickwick, United, and White Star stage companies—then asked the State Railroad Commission for rate increases in southern California and were granted a 10 per cent raise before the year was out.[13]

A number of other unions also engaged in strikes in 1920: Marble

Workers Local No. 14, members of the International Ladies' Garment Workers, Millmen Local No. 884, and the Fruit and Vegetable Workers Union. None of these was successful, least of all the walkouts conducted by members of the last union against the wholesale fruit and vegetable terminal and, in particular, John Nix and Company. Four days after representatives of this company had refused to grant pay demands, its buildings, as well as those of the Los Angeles Lumber and Box Company, were burned down. The M and M offered a reward for information leading to the arrest and conviction of the person or persons starting the fire, but there were no takers. The finger of suspicion was pointed at the union, however, and this fact together with the extensive employment of Japanese strikebreakers decimated the strikers' ranks.[14]

Organized labor's general lack of success on the strike front in Los Angeles in 1920 carried over into the political arena. The Central Labor Council appropriated $2,400 on June 6, 1919, for the purpose of establishing an effective precinct organization in the city to aid the unions in their political ambitions. John S. Horn headed the organization, and some 7,000 names of persons known to be prolabor had been catalogued by the end of the year. The effectiveness of the system was tested in the elections of 1920, with completely unsatisfactory results from labor's standpoint. Candidates endorsed by the labor movement were soundly beaten. After the election officials of the Metal Trades Council roundly criticized the precinct organization for supporting a broad ticket rather than concentrating its efforts on a few candidates.

A further reason for the defeat lay in the lack of unity within the local labor movement. "Curly" Grow, long-time leader in the city's metal trades unions, announced his support of the American Labor Party at the 1920 AFL convention in Montreal. A number of Los Angeles labor organizations followed his example, thus diminishing their political strength. In addition, the American Labor Party was endorsed by local left-wing groups such as the Socialist Party, the Committee of 48, and the Plumb Plan League. Grow's support of the Labor Party was only one sign of dissatisfaction with the allegedly conservative leadership of Seth Brown, president of the Central Labor Council, and C. L. Myers, its secretary.[15]

The short depression of 1920–1922 had some impact on the local labor movement, but it was more a financial than an industrial crisis. It began in the middle of 1920 and lasted until early 1922. Bank debits fell, as did the cost of living, but rents remained high. The severity of the depression in Los Angeles was mitigated by continued building activity, the growth of the motion picture and consumer service industries, and oil discoveries in Los Angeles County. Residential building, in particular, proceeded at a steady pace because the continuing influx of immigrants created a housing shortage. Business activity picked up in late 1921 and went on to a peak in Los Angeles in 1923, with the construction industry remaining in the lead. A labor shortage actually occurred in the building trades, particularly among common laborers. Wages rose so high that the local chapter of the Associated General Contractors conducted an active advertising campaign in Eastern papers in an attempt to draw building tradesmen to southern California. Many of the structures that were to mark downtown Los Angeles for the next three decades were constructed in this period, including the Biltmore, Mayflower, and Roosevelt hotels; the Orpheum, United Artist, and Loew's theaters; and the Pershing Square, Subway Terminal, Mercantile Arcade, and Pacific Mutual buildings. Employment increased 13.7 per cent during 1922, reaching a point where there was less unemployment than there had been at any time in the preceding ten years.[16]

In 1924 the business cycle again headed downward. Unemployment rose sharply in the building trades as building permits declined in number. Bank debits fell and oil production dropped off. A surplus in the labor supply developed, in contrast with the shortage of 1923. The year was marked by a low total rainfall, which had an impact on crop success. A hoof-and-mouth-disease scare caused a decline in cattle marketing and a subsequent rise in unemployment among packing-house workers. The downturn did not appear to be so severe as in the 1920–1922 crisis, but it was felt in labor circles and it limited organizational activity in the face of rising unemployment. By 1925, however, the crisis was over and indexes clearly showed a pickup in business.[17]

The brief span between the two recessions was a period of reorganization for the Merchants' and Manufacturers' Association. The open-shop idea was combined with a spirit of intense patriotism in a new group known as the Better America Federation, whose slogan was "100% Americanism." Although this organization was ostensibly an independent association of men and women dedicated to inspiring citizens to a greater responsibility in their communities, it was not long before its leaders were attacking labor unions in Los Angeles as being red-tinged. The Better America Federation numbered among its members many of those who were most active in the Merchants' and Manufacturers' Association. In 1921 the M and M established an industrial relations department and a placement bureau. Thus it formally entered the industrial relations field with the staff organization necessary to coöperate with the growing nationwide campaign for the American Plan. The interest of the business community in the work of the M and M during these years was evidenced by the fact that the association doubled its membership between 1920 and 1923.[18]

Labor leaders in Los Angeles and throughout the state were not caught napping by the activities of open-shop supporters. The California State Federation of Labor took steps as early as 1920 to oppose the American Plan and the growth of the Better America Federation. Resolutions were passed to ferret out employer spies in unions; editorials in labor papers hammered against welfare capitalism in all its forms; organizing drives were launched by unions in the state's major cities. But all these activities had little apparent success in halting the growth of the open shop anywhere in the state, least of all in Los Angeles. In that city efforts were made to restrict the open shop by continued political activities. Labor leaders claimed that the votes of unionists swung the mayoralty election of June 7, 1921, in favor of George Cryer. Labor-backed candidates took seven of the nine seats on the City Council and seven places on the Board of Education. Ralph Criswell, a strong labor supporter, was elected to the presidency of the City Council the following month.

All looked well for union political interests, but subsequent events proved disappointing. Mayor Cryer refused to sign a labor-sponsored ordinance on November 9, 1921, which was designed to create a board of electric examiners. This body would have controlled the licensing of electricians and curbed the use of nonunion labor. The City Council failed to do anything of positive benefit to the labor movement except appropriate a fund of $2,000 for the purpose of conducting an investigation of industrial unrest. In 1922 the Joint Executive Board of the local labor movement, the Central Labor Council, a number of separate unions, and the Federated Railway Shop Crafts united to battle the Better America Federation on any political issue on which the latter took a stand, but the results were far from decisive. The factors hampering organized labor in its fight against the open shop on the national level—particularly inept leadership and jurisdictional conflict—were very much in evidence in Los Angeles. The effort to create a unified front was further frustrated by a short-lived local independent labor party formed by Curly Grow at the Labor Temple in 1923. Labor did chalk up one victory, however, in this period. In 1923 John Horn, then secretary of the Central Labor Council, was elected to the fifteen-man Board of Freeholders which was to draft a new city charter. As chairman of the committee empowered to draft sections affecting labor, Horn was primarily responsible for the inclusion of a "prevailing wage" provision, designed to bring the wages of city employees into line with those paid by private employers.[19]

Labor also attacked the open shop by establishing coöperatives, a number of which were successful as business operations but not as weapons against employers. One of them, the Southern California Cooperative Association, formed on June 24, 1921, was designed to assist the unemployed as well as to compete with nonunion business firms. Coöperatives were also established in baking, broom manufacture, auto painting, laundering, and banking. All these enterprises became virtually extinct in the three years following the depression of 1924, although several, including the laundry and the bank, were absorbed by or were turned into firms that had no connection with the labor movement. The most noteworthy of the coöperatives was the People's Bank and Trust Company, founded in 1924 after thorough study by representatives of the Central Labor Council, the four departmental councils, and the Southern California Cooperative Association. The basic pattern was borrowed from a successful San Bernardino coöperative banking institution. As a railroad center, San Bernardino had been a logical place for the establishment of a bank under the auspices of the Brotherhood of Locomotive Engineers, which was already in the banking business in Cleveland, Ohio. It was hoped that the Los Angeles bank would provide some profits to assist labor in its fight against the open shop, and would prevent workers from becoming the victims of allegedly unscrupulous, antilabor financial houses.[20]

The bank was financed through a stock-selling program under the auspices of the Central Labor Council. Shares, priced at $125, were purchased on installment contracts, which required a down payment of $50 with the balance paid over a six-month period. No individual could own more than 100 shares, thus encouraging a broad distribution of stock and the purchase of ownership interests by workers. The bank opened on April 26, 1924, under the managership of Dr. Walter F. McCaleb and with a capitalization of $1,000,000, a surplus of $250,000, and paid-in cash of $625,000. Deposits in the amount of $158,000 were made on the opening day, when more than 600 accounts were established. Each purchaser of stock signed a seven-year proxy agreement in which he turned over his right to vote to a seven-man board of trustees, composed of three appointees of organized labor, three business or professional men, and McCaleb. The trustees, in turn, elected the twenty-one members of the board of directors. The bank limited dividends in order to have sufficient working capital, established a profit-sharing plan, and provided a loan service for small borrowers. On June 1, 1925, it received a national bank charter and became the People's National Bank and Trust Company. Its operations over the next several years were financially successful, but effective control gradually slipped away from organized labor. By 1928, though a majority of the stock was still owned or controlled by unions and their members, actual operations were in the hands of a syndicate of businessmen. In May of that year all the labor directors were retired, excepting John Horn. Changing its name to the National Bank of Commerce, the institution retained only a sympathy for the workingman and his financial problems. In 1932 it closed its doors after paying off all its depositors in full. Thus ended organized labor's most successful local venture in the coöperative field. As a bank it was a success; as a weapon in labor's fight against the open shop and "big business" it was only marginally useful.[21]

During the same period that the local labor movement was engaged in this constructive effort to present a unified front, it demonstrated a basic disunity in connection with the dispute between the United Brotherhood of Carpenters and Joiners and the National Board of Jurisdictional Awards. This conflict, whose national aspects have already been discussed, became particularly acute in open-shop Los Angeles, where anything that disturbed organized labor's unity worked in favor of the *Times* and the M and M. The local conflict developed into an internal war that threatened the existence of the *Citizen* and seriously damaged the strength of the building trades unions, at this time the backbone of the Los Angeles labor movement.

The California State Building Trades Council supported the brotherhood against the AFL Building Trades Department. The latter countered by forming dual carpenters' unions in a number of cities, but the most significant local struggle revolved around the Los Angeles County Building Trades Council. The county council operated under a state charter granted to it in 1908, and so aligned itself with the state body and the brotherhood against the AFL. In 1923 the Los Angeles carpenters had the largest union membership in the building trades and hence the largest representation in the Central Labor Council. This had been a source of friction within the council for some months before the dispute between the carpenters and the AFL department began to assume importance locally. Other building trades unions believed that the numerical strength of the carpenters gave them too much power in the Central Labor Council as well as in the Los Angeles County Building Trades Council. In March, 1923, a number of AFL officials came to Los Angeles in an attempt to smooth over the differences. They decreed that all building trades unions must affiliate with the Los Angeles County Building Trades Council or face expulsion from the AFL. Before the county council could accept such unions, however, it had to comply with a number of charter changes which, in effect, would have impaired its status with the California Building Trades Council. When it refused to do this, the national department revoked its charter and established a dual Los Angeles, California, City and Vicinity Building Trades Council, AFL. The old Los Angeles County Building Trades Council, dominated by the carpenters, retained its affiliation with its California parent body and remained in operation.[22] Officers of the county council then applied for a restraining order against the new city body and its sixteen constituent unions, claiming that it was operating under a voided charter which had not been cleared through the California State Building Trades Council. The request was denied, however, and both building trades councils continued to function.

The final rift between the county council and the Central Labor Council, in association with the new city building trades council, occurred over the splitting of the annual yearbook profits in 1923. Usually this fund was divided equally among the Building Trades, Allied Printing Trades, Metal Trades, and Central Labor councils. When the share that previously had gone to the Los Angeles County Building Trades Council was distributed to the new city building trades organization, the unions affiliated with the older body decided to publish a newspaper and a yearbook of their own. In addition, several of these unions, especially the painters, were dissatisfied with AFL and Central Labor Council action in severing connections with the Federated Press Service on the ground that it leaned too far toward the political left. The malcontents planned a new paper in order to continue the Federated Press Service, present the viewpoint of the carpenters in their conflict with the National Board of Jurisdictional Awards, and help sustain the Los Angeles County Building Trades Council.[23]

The announcement of the new newspaper and a companion yearbook sponsored by the county council through the Los Angeles District Council of Carpenters reached the public in the form of a letter:

To Our Friends:

This personal letter to your firm is written to acquaint you with the fact that the District Council of Carpenters of Los Angeles County, counting a membership of 17,000 carpenters, had withdrawn its support and cooperation from the "Citizen Company."

We will now publish our own yearbook, and also a newspaper which will be known as the Southern California Labor Press. This newspaper and its annual yearbook will be owned, controlled and edited by union labor, and they will serve as our mediums of communication in matters pertaining to union affairs.

Do not be deceived in regard to any claims that may be made regarding any other so-called "yearbook," or any credentials which are not signed by the District Council of Carpenters. The signatures of this council alone will be authentic evidence of the reliability of any set of credentials concerning publications of interest to the carpenters of Los Angeles county.[24]

The secession movement cut off 5,500 subscribers from the *Citizen* and made them charter clients of the *Southern California Labor Press*. All of them were mandatory subscribers as members of building trades unions, which had required receipt of the *Citizen* as a condition of membership. This requirement was now transferred to the new paper. As if such a loss was not enough for the *Citizen* to bear, three members of its staff also left, including its editor, Francis Drake, who assumed the same position on the *Labor Press*. The first edition of the new paper hit the streets on February 29, 1924, and publication continued on a weekly basis in competition with the *Citizen* until January 27, 1928. The initial funds were supplied by Carpenters Local No. 158, which contributed $1,500 as an investment. There was no stock issue nor were there ever any assessments. Unions belonging to the Los Angeles County Building Trades Council and the Los Angeles District Council of Carpenters were required to enter subscriptions for a majority of their members at 10 cents a month per person. Earnings were distributed annually among the unions according to the number of paid subscriptions. Voting at the annual meetings was on the same basis.[25]

The *Southern California Labor Press* was not quite the same in outlook as the *Citizen*. Emphasis in the news was heavily weighted in favor of the building trades unions, especially the carpenters. Further, the *Press* subscribed to the Federated Press Service and took a more liberal political position than the more conservative *Citizen*. Although the two papers did not duplicate each other in every respect, it was not long before Los Angeles labor leaders discovered that the city could not support more than one union newspaper. Moreover, the existence of two papers provided clear evidence to open-shop supporters of labor's lack of unity. Amalgamation of the two newspapers and the two building trades councils was suggested at the 1925 AFL convention, but nothing came of the proposal. In 1926 District Council of Painters No. 36, which represented all union painters, paper hangers, and decorators in the city, passed a resolution favoring a single building trades council in Los Angeles as a means of effectively fighting the M and M and the Los Angeles Chamber of Commerce. In the same year, at the national level, the carpenters and the metal workers agreed to Hutcheson's terms—abolition of the National Board for Jurisdictional Awards—for ending their jurisdictional dispute. The carpenters thereupon rejoined the AFL at its 1927 convention, and it was only a matter of time before the two local building trades councils buried their differences and consolidated the *Southern California Labor Press* with the *Citizen*. The first issue came out on February 3, 1928, with Harvey E. Garman as editor.

The new *Citizen* immediately began to prosper with the increased subscription list, and warfare against the open shop was stepped up, not only in Los Angeles but throughout the nation. According to the *Citizen*, the National Association of Manufacturers admitted that the open-shop gains of 1921–1927 were partly wiped out across the country by the effective union campaigns that followed revitalization of the AFL when it was rejoined by the strong United Brotherhood of Carpenters. It was not long, however, before the depression clamped down on the activities of both open-shop supporters and unions, and the *Citizen* found itself in straitened circumstances as workers were unable to afford the luxury of subscriptions.[26]

The internal dispute between the two building trades councils in Los Angeles did not preclude all organizing activity. Although the open shop was dominant in building operations during 1921–1924, wages were good and some gains were made by a number of construction unions. Labor was in relatively short supply during the building boom. This shortage helped the unions to maintain wage scales, even though they could not consistently capitalize on it to organize workers because of open-shop opposition and their own disunity. The carpenters conducted several strikes for a closed shop, one of which was county-wide and became effective on May 1, 1923. The M and M aided struck contractors in replacing the 175 men who walked out, and the dispute was quickly terminated. A few of the strikers apparently won a $9 daily wage, but little more than this was achieved. Similar results marked another organizing campaign conducted in 1924 as part of a Pacific Coast offensive by the carpenters.[27]

In 1922 IBEW Local No. 83 tried to obtain a union- or closed-shop arrangement with the principal electrical contractors in the city. Efforts made in the summer to interest employers in a national arbitration program sponsored by the international evoked a negligible response. The lack of coöperation by employers sparked a demand for a wage increase from $8 to $10 per day. When the contractors refused to grant it, a strike was called on December 16 and 400 men walked out. Contractors immediately hired strikebreakers, importing a number from outside the city. The union sought to stop this action by requesting the City Council to set up a board of examiners to check the qualifications of and to license all electricians, thus weeding out incompetent men, but it failed to make any headway. The strike eventually tapered off and the men gradually returned to work without gaining their specific demands. It was officially declared ended by the union in October, 1923. A similar victory was gained by open-shop supporters in 1921 when marble workers and granite cutters tried to increase their job control. The marble workers actually lost ground when P. Carney and Sons Company, formerly a closed shop, refused to have any further dealings with the union.[28]

The painters were no exception to the general rule of the open shop in the building trades. Two hundred house painters struck on April 1, 1921, for an $8 day, five-day week, and time and a half for overtime, when their employers, members of the Master Painters' Association, declined to renew a previous agreement. The strike, which lasted a week, was marked by some sabotage of jobs, including the throwing of electric light bulbs filled with acid against newly painted surfaces. The employers refused to compromise, however, and the strikers gradually returned to work under an open-shop system. In contrast, the bill posters became an exception to the open-shop rule when they won a three-year contract in 1924 with Foster and Kleiser, outdoor advertisers. It provided for a forty-four-hour week and wages of $1 an hour.[29]

Other locals besides the building trades unions took advantage of the several years of prosperity between the two recessions to strive for gains in spite of the American Plan or the application of welfare capitalism by employers. Musicians Local No. 47, for example, became embroiled in a dispute with the Theater Owners' Association which resulted in a strike on October 8, 1921. Thirty-five theaters were struck in an effort to resist a 10 per cent wage reduction. Fourteen of the theaters declared for the open shop, but the remainder worked out a compromise two-year contract providing for the discharge of all nonunion men on condition that Local No. 47 accept a 2 per cent wage reduction effective until September 1, 1922, followed by a 5 per cent cut the second year. Peace was only temporary, however, as the musicians continued to fight the open shop over the next two years. Prominent theaters such as Clune's and the Follies were placed on the unfair list. Antiunion forces were incensed by the refusal of thirty-one musicians to play at the Monroe Doctrine Centennial Exposition on July 24, 1923, unless their demands for back pay were met. The musicians walked out, but were immediately replaced by the Hollywood Post American Legion Band. Tight job control by Local No. 47 in the Los Angeles area, however, enabled the union to make gains, so that by 1924 it claimed to be the largest labor organization in southern California.[30]

The motion picture projectionists, like the musicians, had some success in opposing the open shop. The growing popularity of the moving picture as an inexpensive form of entertainment gave them support in demands made in January, 1921, on downtown theater owners for a seven-hour day and a six-day week, with a $14 weekly wage increase. In a compromise, the union accepted the seven-day week but gained a 15 to 20 per cent increase in wages. By 1924 Motion Picture Projectionists Local No. 150 was crowing over a 12.5 per cent increase in membership in the preceding twelve months.

Little crowing was possible for the brewery trades, however, as the effective demand for their product was severely curtailed by prohibition. The unions made some wage gains in dealing with brewers of near beer in 1923 and 1924 and also won a forty-four-hour week, but their preprohibition closed-shop status was not completely restored.[31]

The clothing trades unions were among those hardest hit by the open-shop drives of the 1920's. In Los Angeles, Amalgamated Clothing Workers of America, Local No. 278, was opposed by employing merchant tailors who were actively backed by the M and M. All efforts to gain a forty-four-hour week, time and a half for overtime, recognition, and the abolition of piecework in the 1921–1924 period were unsuccessful. Abe Plotkin, local manager of the union, was arrested under the criminal syndicalism law. Also, a court issued an injunction against interfering with nonunion workers. The ILGWU was only slightly more successful than the ACWA in battling the open shop. It struck against employing firms in 1921, 1922, and 1923; but the M and M supported the employers, and the injunction was again used effectively. Some marginal headway against a few open-shop employers was made by Local No. 52 in September, 1923. A strike for union recognition and a wage increase was called against thirty-two cloak and suit manufacturers, only thirteen of which acceded to the demands. Not even a minor victory could be claimed by Tailors Local No. 81. Torn by dual unionism that had all the overtones of Communist infiltration, the union failed to present a common front to employers.[32]

The metal trades suffered from the decline in shipbuilding which began after World War I, the American Plan offensive, and the failure of the 1922 shopmen's strike. The Founders' and Employers' Association, which became the Metal Trades Manufacturers' Association of Southern California in 1924, continued to pursue an open-shop policy during the early 1920's. In May, 1923, for example, the boilermakers called a strike against a number of firms for a wage increase from 90 cents to $1 an hour, but lost out when nonunion replacements were brought in. The Amalgamated Association of Iron, Steel and Tin Workers also was unsuccessful in a strike against a long-time opponent, the Southern California Iron and Steel Company. Only Sheet Metal Workers Local No. 108 met with some success in resisting wage cuts from $9 to $7.20 a day.[33]

Among the other unionists active in the early postwar years were the culinary, furniture, and maritime workers. The culinary trades battled wage cuts in 1921 and engaged in a number of boycotts the following year. Cooks, waiters, and waitresses reported generally good employment conditions in 1922, but there seemed to be few union shops despite energetic organizing campaigns. The furniture workers were hurt by the importation of Chinese reed goods, which had become fashionable. Furthermore, prison rehabilitation programs resulted in an output of furniture that was sold in the public market. The Reed and Rattan Workers, weakened by this competition, withdrew from the Central Labor Council in 1924. The upholsterers' unions continued to function, though they lost their battles to maintain wage scales in 1921–1922 and failed to eliminate piecework wage systems. The maritime workers at San Pedro, plagued by the IWW during the early postwar years, were firmly under the domination of a company-union system by 1924 (see chap. v).[34]

Unlike most Los Angeles unions, the printing trades organizations made some headway against the open shop during these years. Participating in the national campaign for the forty-four-hour week, to become effective on May 1, 1921, they assessed their memberships to cover possible unemployment contingencies. When about half the Los Angeles job shops refused to accept shorter hours, their linotypers and compositors walked out. The M and M assisted the firms by financial grants as well as employee recruitment. Shops adhering to the forty-four-hour-week agreement were worked to capacity because of the shutdown of a number of noncomplying firms. The Allied Printing Trades Council, with the aid of the Central Labor Council, began a boycott of opposing employers in an effort to counteract the latter's black list. The union men stood together without defections and gradually began to convince more and more shops to adopt the shorter week. The assessment on working unionists' wages was reduced from 10 to 7 and then to 5 per cent, and by May, 1923, it was almost negligible. In 1925, when ITU Local No. 174 celebrated its golden anniversary, the tide was definitely running in favor of the forty-four-hour week, though a number of important job or commercial printing shops were still holding out. Three years later the Allied Printing Trades Council announced that the M and M was no longer of any significance in the printing trades, and that the shorter workweek was almost universally effective in the city.[35]

The printing trades were exceptions to the rule, that, by and large, the open shop reigned in Los Angeles throughout the 1920's. So effective was its hold on the city that very little effort was devoted to the formation of new unions in areas heretofore unorganized. One of the few noteworthy efforts was made in 1923 by a group of courthouse reporters, representing the Los Angeles metropolitan dailies, who met at the City Hall with John Horn and J. W. Buzzell of the Central Labor Council. The reporters wanted to reduce their long working hours and increase their wages. Unexpectedly, among the opponents of their possible unionization was the International Typographical Union, whose opposition was based on its failure to organize editorial personnel elsewhere in the United States. The printers believed that efforts to organize reporters in Los Angeles would be futile and, meanwhile, would be a drain on their local. Hence the reporters did not go ahead with their union plans, but instead formed what became the Los Angeles Press Club, a fraternity of reporters and other newspaper people with almost purely social objectives.[36]

A number of other unions were active enough to receive some publicity in this period. Bakers Local No. 37 continued to pursue a boycott against the larger baking companies, a number of which belonged to chain organizations, but with little success. The broom makers struck for a 10 per cent wage increase in 1923, but accepted 5 per cent as a compromise. They also dabbled briefly in a coöperative broom-manufacturing firm. The unions in meat packing suffered severely after the "Big Five" packers declared themselves to be open shops and announced wage cuts in 1921. Company unions were very effective in the Los Angeles plants of the packing companies. Moreover, the 1924 hoof-and-mouth-disease scare frightened the buying public, temporarily reduced the consumption of meat, and caused some unemployment. Cigar Makers Local No. 225 suffered from unemployment, wage cuts, and lockouts. A continued trend toward the elimination of the chain cigar store hurt the trade, making it difficult for the union to prevent the use of cheap labor in the manufacture of cigars distributed through varied channels. The California State Federation of Teachers tried to organize a Los Angeles local but could not overcome the opposition of the Board of Education. Steam shovel operators, egg inspectors, jewelry workers, produce workers, dredgemen, and clerks also were active, but reported little in the way of gains. Successes were offset by losses as the American Plan gained momentum in the city during the early 1920's.[37]

3. THE LAST BIG PUSH OF THE DECADE

The revival of business in Los Angeles after 1924 encouraged labor leaders to strike out again at the open shop and to seek to rebuild union memberships. The period from 1924 to 1929 witnessed the rapid development of outlying shopping centers and building programs, such as the "Miracle Mile" along Wilshire Boulevard. The last six months of 1926 were particularly prosperous in the city, with all the earmarks of a boom. Although national AFL membership figures showed a downward trend during the late 1920's which was not arrested until the initiation of the NRA in 1933, the California and Los Angeles labor movements made minor membership gains in 1926–1928 before the decline of the depression years.

There were two significant general organizational drives in Los Angeles after 1924. The first one began in 1926, taking its cue from a national drive initiated by the AFL in May of the preceding year; it was continued until 1928, when it tapered off and was abandoned. The second campaign was mounted in 1929 but quickly came to nought as the depression hit California in 1930 and 1931. Major organizing efforts were concentrated on musicians, cleaners and dyers, culinary workers, taxi drivers, engineers, teamsters, barbers, machinists, butchers, garment workers, and building tradesmen.[38]

The 1926 campaign was made possible, in part, by the increased willingness of some of the disaffected building trades locals to cooperate in the struggle against the open shop. Moreover, nearly all elements of the local labor movement had become annoyed with the radical fringe and wanted to close ranks against it. By 1926 the radicals were either being purged or were quite clearly identified as such, so that the more conservative elements could join together in a common effort.

In the campaign, labor leaders made a concerted effort to take advantage of all the propaganda media available. In addition to publicity in the *Citizen* and the *Southern California Labor Press,* labor went on the air through radio station KGEF. Later in the campaign the various labor councils of Los Angeles, Glendale, Long Beach, San Pedro, Pasadena, and Santa Monica were coördinated through monthly meetings to which each group sent three representatives. The purpose again was to create the unity of a common front against recalcitrant employers bent on maintaining open shops. Relatively large sums of money were funneled into Los Angeles for several years beginning in 1926. As both Los Angeles and Detroit were strongholds of the open shop, the AFL was determined to beat down the opposition in both areas. One estimate indicated that as much as a million dollars a year was spent in Los Angeles at the peak of the campaign.[39]

As an aid to the organizing drive, the AFL held its 1927 convention in Los Angeles. At first it seemed that gains were being made against open-shop employers. In his 1926 annual report the secretary of the Central Labor Council reported that eighty-nine organizations were affiliated with the city central body. A year later the number had increased to 105, with a membership gain of 3,049. By 1928, however, the impact of the drive had lessened and not one manufacturing firm in Los Angeles could be reported as 100 per cent organized, with the possible exception of two or three in the garment industry. The membership losses in this year were at least partly due to developing unemployment in the metal industry and a number of miscellaneous trades. But this did not completely discourage Los Angeles labor leaders, who soon made plans to launch a new organizing drive in 1929.

The master plan for the 1929 campaign called for the appointment of a central committee and the parallel organization of neighborhood circles. The committee, with 125 members, consisted of union delegates to the Central Labor Council, representatives of locals without delegates, and organizers stationed in the city. Its members addressed locals in their particular trades which, in turn, set up committees to talk with nonunion men in their crafts. After the interviews had been completed, a questionnaire was filled in with pertinent data about each nonunion man interviewed. This was turned over to the Central Labor Council, and a reference card was sent to the appropriate craft local to which the man would belong if he joined the labor movement. Members of the local then called on the prospect and sought to persuade him to join the union. The Central Labor Council followed up to make certain that the interview was satisfactorily completed.[40]

The neighborhood circles were organized at the same time as the committee of 125 unionists. To set them up, the Central Labor Council ascertained the residences of about 20,000 craftsmen, union and nonunion, whose names were placed on addressograph plates. These names were divided into groups of eighty persons, all of whom lived within circles ranging from three-quarters to one and a quarter miles in diameter. Each circle contained a neighborhood shopping center, and each was further divided into four sections of twenty names each. Members of the Women's Union Label League were then asked to organize the sections into neighborhood groups. It was hoped that this structure would not only bring more nonunion workers into the fold but would also permit the placing of pressure, under threat of a boycott, on businesses in the neighborhood shopping centers to use only union-labeled goods.[41]

The progress of the 1929 organizing drive was watched with interest by Los Angeles labor leaders. After a month of the interview system, only about a hundred cards had been returned to the Central Labor Council. The neighborhood-circle plan was limited by available funds; although every union in the Central Labor Council was to contribute $2 a month in 1929, the income was not enough to finance this aspect of the drive. Nevertheless, Secretary Buzzell of the council reported a net membership increase of 5,000 in the twelve months preceding June, 1929. But the campaign was doomed by the depression that spread over the country in late 1929 and became definitely noticeable in California by 1930. Moreover, it is doubtful that the drive was so successful as Buzzell claimed, for the unions were fought every step of the way by individual open-shop employers, the All-Year Club, the *Times*, the Chamber of Commerce, and the local chapter of the Better America Federation, which saw in unionism a threat to basic American freedoms.

Furthermore, welfare capitalism was making a strong stand throughout the city in the form of employee benefit plans. Many companies, such as Los Angeles Gas and Electric, Young's Markets, and the Los Angeles Railway, had a Christmas bonus program. Others, including

Southern California Edison, Shell Oil of California, Union Oil, and California Petroleum, sponsored group insurance and other fringe benefits. Holsum Bakery had a profit-sharing plan; Goodyear and several other firms instituted an employee representation program; Barker Brothers, among others, utilized the stock purchase idea; Pacific Electric operated a recreation center for its employees in the San Bernardino Mountains. Company unions were also established in many industrial plants, and conferences were held for foremen on the subject of better human relations. Even had the depression not come along, there is little doubt that the open shop would have remained the dominant system of industrial relations in Los Angeles, in spite of the 1929 organizing drive.[42]

Harold N. Sturgeon, a member of Mailers Union No. 9 and delegate to the Central Labor Council, exposed the threat presented to Los Angeles labor by the American Plan and welfare capitalism in his poem, "The Company Union," published in the *Citizen* in 1929, with apologies to Tennyson:

> Have a Union, have a Union,
> Help yourselves onward.
> All in the company Union
> Went the six hundred.
> "Forward," the bosses bade,
> "Sign on the line," they said:
> Into this bondage they went—
> All the six hundred.
>
> "Forward," the bosses bade.
> Was there a man delayed?
> No, though they dreaded to,
> Not one had blundered.
> Theirs not to make reply,
> Theirs not to reason why,
> Theirs but to get by;
> Into this yellow deal
> Signed the six hundred.
>
> Spies to the right of them,
> Spies to the left of them,
> Spies in front of them,
> Among the six hundred.
> Stormed at by boss and sup.,
> Speeded by an efficiency troupe
> Worked with a willing hand
> But could not understand
> Though oft they had wondered.

> When will this mockery stop,
> When will the false mask drop—
> Where there's no dues to pay
> Then soon will come the day,
> This farce will be sundered.
> Out from the yoke they'll come,
> They're shy on guts, not dumb—
> All the six hundred.[43]

Organized labor demonstrated a surprisingly strong influence in city politics during the late 1920's in spite of the strength of the open shop. The interest in politics, as always, was deliberate and a part of the organizing drives of these years. The labor vote played a significant role in the city election of May, 1925, when eight of eleven union-supported candidates for the City Council were elected to office. Mayor George E. Cryer, who was endorsed by the city's labor leaders, was reëlected to office at the same time. The mayor publicly admitted the importance of labor's support in the outcome of the election, while union leaders rejoiced that a political victory had been won over the open-shop front, including the *Times* and the Better America Federation. Before the election John Horn had been appointed by Mayor Cryer to fill a vacancy on the Civil Service Commission. After the election he was appointed to the Board of Public Works, from which vantage point he could influence the use of union men on public projects. In September, 1925, his power was increased when he became vice-chairman of the board. J. W. Buzzell of the Central Labor Council replaced Horn on the Civil Service Commission.[44]

Labor soon made its influence felt in city administrative affairs. Horn introduced a charter amendment requiring that all workers on city projects be citizens of the United States; it was passed at the 1926 election over the opposition of the *Times* and the Chamber of Commerce. In the same year twenty-three of thirty-seven candidates endorsed by labor for various offices were elected. Open-shop supporters became increasingly concerned about the effectiveness of Horn and Buzzell in city affairs when, in 1926, many departments began to pay craftsmen the union wage scale, and the forty-four-hour week with no wage reduction was introduced for a large group of city electrical workers. The *Times,* as the mouthpiece for open-shop employers, strongly attacked labor's influence in 1926 and 1927. It alleged that city electrical inspectors were discriminating against the work of nonunion electricians; that Buzzell was trying to organize all city employees; and that labor was seeking to buy the votes of civil service workers. Charges of corruption in the Cryer administration implied that labor leaders and their roles in the machine were partly responsible. Certainly wages were increased all down the line in 1926 and 1927, whether or not because of the efforts of Buzzell and Horn. Craftsmen were not the only beneficiaries, as key supervisory and administrative personnel also received salary increases.[45]

The combination of the *Times*'s antiunion publicity and Buzzell's boldness contributed to the downfall of labor's political power, beginning with the city election in May, 1927. Buzzell overplayed his hand by seeking to use both his executive position on the Central Labor Council and his place on the Civil Service Commission to attack candidates for public office. His most flagrant action was to mail a letter to 8,000 city employees on the eve of the election, urging them to vote against office seekers who opposed unionism. The move boomeranged, and all four union members running for the City Council lost, including Ralph Criswell, long-time labor supporter. Buzzell was condemned for his letter writing by the Personnel and Efficiency Committee of the city government, and a resolution was introduced into the City Council to have him dismissed from the Civil Service Commission. The resolution was pigeonholed, but he was not reappointed when his term expired in 1927. Later he became the subject of a legislative inquiry at Sacramento because of asserted attempts to intimidate Assemblyman W. E. Badham into supporting prounion legislation.[46]

The 1927 defeats, however, did not discourage local labor leaders from participation in city politics. In 1928 they opposed a city school construction bond issue because there was no assurance that union wages and union-shop conditions would prevail, or that American citizens would be employed. When the bonds lost, labor officials claimed credit for a victory. Shortly afterward, the Central labor Council lobbied before the City Council for a wage increase for laborers employed on city projects. Whether or not as a result of this plea, the wages of laborers were increased, effective July 1, from $4.75 to $6.25 a week. In 1929, however, most of the labor endorsees were badly beaten at the city polls, and John C. Porter became mayor without union support. Nevertheless, he appointed Francis Drake, former editor of both the *Citizen* and the *Southern California Labor Press,* to the Police Commission over the opposition of the *Times,* thus softening the feelings of labor leaders against him. Local labor supporters also lost ground on the state political front because a reapportionment

of Los Angeles County seats in the Assembly gave the county delegation, which was generally antilabor, control of more than 25 per cent
of the eighty votes in the Assembly. Thus, as the local labor movement
entered the period of the Great Depression, it found its political wings
badly clipped.[47]

While the Central Labor Council dabbled in politics and served as
the nucleus for organizing activities, individual unions continued to
fulfill the function of front-line troops in the battle against the open
shop. A number of unions went their independent ways, notably those
in the amusement trades. Although in sympathy with the organizing
drives of 1926–1928 and 1929, their members seemed more interested
in their own problems than in a coördinated effort to defeat open-shop
supporters in Los Angeles. In 1925, before the first campaign started,
Musicians Local No. 47, Stage Employees Local No. 33, and Motion
Picture Operators Local No. 150 joined together to demand wage
increases from the members of the Theater Owners' Association and
to seek an agreement. All three locals, after negotiations, made some
gains. A number of the theaters, however, refused to become union
shops: the Banner, Rosslyn, Lark, Wonderland, Columbia, and Dalton
houses. But they later signed two-year agreements raising the pay of
their employees in order to placate the amusement locals and thus
retain the services of their skilled members.[48]

The musicians also showed an interest in radio broadcasting in
1925, when they unsuccessfully demanded a 35 per cent wage increase
during the time an orchestra was on the air, whether or not it was
playing from a café or a hotel. They claimed that a radio orchestra
must have a larger repertoire. This demand placed them in direct
opposition to the *Times,* which controlled KHJ, one of the best-known
stations in the Los Angeles area. The union hit at the *Times* by forbidding its members to broadcast over KHJ after October 15, 1925,
but the order did not stand long, as the station immediately was
turned into a propaganda weapon against Local No. 47. Even termination of the boycott after three weeks did not end the matter for the
Times. The newspaper attacked the musicians as examples of the worst
in unionism, and criticized Local No. 47 for the refusal of its members
to play at a charity Christmas party for a thousand newsboys because
they would not receive extra pay for some additional chores requested
of them. On December 28 the local declared a last-minute boycott of
the Pasadena Tournament of Roses Parade if any nonunion bands
were permitted to march. The action was aimed specifically at Harold

Roberts' Golden State Band, which was nonunion. The band was prevented from participating in order to keep a majority of the musicians in other bands in the line of march. The *Times* gave maximum publicity to this and other activities of the musicians which it interpreted as being against the public welfare.[49]

Early in 1926 the musicians opened their new five-story headquarters building on South Georgia Street. In the same year they conducted a sympathy walkout in connection with a nationwide strike against the theaters of the open-shop Orpheum circuit. In 1927 the two-year agreement with downtown theaters came up for renewal. Again the musicians, the stage employees, and the projectionists made common cause and threatened the Theater Owners' Association with a strike unless wages were increased. The employers wanted a three-year contract, whereas the unions insisted on a one-year arrangement. A compromise settlement provided for the longer agreement and wage increases.

Peace did not yet reign in the amusement trades, however. In 1928 the projectionists of Local No. 150 came into conflict with three open-shop theaters. The throwing of stink bombs and the subsequent arrest of the perpetrators provided further fuel for antiunion forces. With the advent of sound the musicians began to feel the impact of "canned music" in theaters, but this did not slow down their organizing efforts. In 1929 they successfully struck the Hollywood Bowl Concert Series when the management refused to hire a union electrician. The amusement unions constituted one of the strongest craft groups in the city on the eve of the depression.[50]

The brewery trades continued to be hurt by prohibition and the consequent unemployment, except in the manufacture of near beer. Their relations with local near-beer breweries, except for Pabst, were generally amicable. The brewery trades won a small victory in 1925 when Schlitz became a union shop. They also signed a one-year contract with a number of brewers, providing for an eight-hour day and a five-and-a-half-day week with a $3 weekly wage increase. This contract was renewed in 1926 and again in 1927. The second renewal was for three years and covered bottlers, brewers, beer drivers, coopers, engineers, firemen, and machinists working in breweries. In essence, even though the consumption of near beer was less than that of beer in preprohibition days, the brewery trades gradually regained job control in the late 1920's.[51]

Although the building trades resolved their internal difficulties and participated in the organizing campaigns of 1926 and 1929, they were not able to achieve the same job control as the brewery unions. They were hampered not only by the open shop but also by the decline in construction after the early 1920's, caused partly by rising costs. In 1920 it cost an average of $4.09 per square foot to construct a building, but by 1926 the figure had risen to $5.10. The oversupply of workers created by the decrease in activity made it difficult for the building trades to enforce union wages, hours, and conditions. They made some gains, however. In 1927–1928, for example, the City Hall was constructed with union labor. But for the most part the unions were unsuccessful, particularly after 1927, when the decline in construction caused unemployment in the building trades unions in advance of the general drop in business which began in the winter of 1929–30.[52]

In 1925 an attempt had been made by unionized Los Angeles building tradesmen, in conjunction with San Francisco unionists, to boycott the construction of the local baseball park, but to no avail. The park was largely completed under the supervision of the Llewellyn Iron Works, an old-line, open-shop firm. In the same year the efforts of tile setters and helpers and marble setters to secure short-run gains received considerable publicity in the *Times*. The tile helpers struck on October 30 for an $8 day and union recognition. As the tile setters could not work without helpers, they joined the strike, demanding $11 a day. The setters gained their demand and returned to work, but refused to lay tile with nonunion helpers. The contractors, organized as the Tile Contractors' Credit Association and the Southern California and Southwest Tile Contractors' Association, threatened to go open shop if the helpers did not get back to work with the setters by November 5. As the threat seemed real, both the setters and the helpers returned to their jobs on that date, but the latter went back unrecognized and under their old wages of $6 a day.

Marble Setters Local No. 24, which was a part of the bricklayers' union, fared no better when its members struck against nine principal Los Angeles contractors in December in an attempt to force the closing of an apprenticeship school operated by contractors. They were joined by both the bricklayers and the tile setters, who walked out in sympathy on several jobs in January, 1926, when nonunion marble setters were employed to replace those on strike. When open-shop contractors, most of whom were members of the Pacific Coast Marble Dealers' Association, stood firm and obtained nonunion help, the strike petered out, with many of the unionists returning to work by March under open-shop conditions.[53]

Hardwood Floor Workers Local No. 2094 also faced an adamant

employers' organization in August, 1925, when it struck against demands that its members take a pay cut of $2 a day and go on a piecework basis. The Los Angeles Hardwood Floor Contractors' Association, with the support of the Chamber of Commerce and the M and M, was able to force the union to back down.

The next year, however, open-shop contractors found themselves up against more dedicated opponents than the hardwood floor layers. As part of the organizing campaign of 1926, twenty-nine carpenters' unions in Los Angeles County decided to join in a common effort to establish the closed shop. Besides, the carpenters and other building trades unions wanted to enforce union working conditions in the reconstruction of the city of Santa Barbara, which had been badly damaged by an earthquake the year before. A. W. Muir, a general organizer for the United Brotherhood of Carpenters and Joiners, and twenty other union representatives were sent from the East in May, 1926, to aid in the campaign. The drive was coördinated with similar campaigns in Santa Barbara and San Francisco. The carpenters claimed a victory in Los Angeles by September, pointing out that they had added 1,500 men to their rolls and $10,000 in initiation fees to their treasury in the preceding seven months. But in Santa Barbara the open shop won the battle.

Another drive, started a year later on the eve of the AFL convention in Los Angeles, centered on the construction of the new $4 million Goodrich plant, allegedly the largest industrial addition in the city in eight years. The Goodrich management replaced the fifty-odd carpenters who struck, along with a few bricklayers, and built its plant under open-shop conditions. In 1928 the carpenters, suffering from wage cuts and a serious labor surplus, were unable to mount another campaign as the nation pointed toward a depression.[54]

Jurisdictional conflict was not entirely absent from the building trades in Los Angeles in the middle and late 1920's. There was some evidence that dissension between the carpenters and the sheet metal workers continued until 1928; the plasterers and the bricklayers also became embroiled in jurisdictional difficulties. These unions, together with the painters, the lathers, the electricians, the ironworkers, and other building trades organizations, supported the campaign of 1929, but were largely ineffective. By 1929 most of the unions that had withdrawn from the Los Angeles Building and Construction Trades Council, as a result of either the carpenters' and the sheet metal workers' dispute or other jurisdictional differences, were back in the fold. However, the decline in construction, as shown by building permits, meant that the near future held little for them in terms of economic advancement.[55]

Although the culinary and furniture workers did not face a decline in the demand for their products, nevertheless they were unable to make much headway against the open shop. Unionists in culinary work coöperated in the general 1926 organizing campaign, but with little success. Seeking to organize the major hotels, they soon discovered that it was easy for management to replace strikers with nonunion men. Only the waitresses seem to have gained in membership during the next several years. The cooks, the waiters, and the beverage dispensers (formerly the bartenders) either lost members or remained approximately stationary. Because of the continued high turnover among culinary workers in hotels and eating houses and the small size of most establishments, the open-shop system remained very strong in this service industry. The furniture workers, particularly Upholsterers Local No. 15, were quite active in the years just before the depression. Consistent attempts were made to organize the many small units in the industry, with occasional success, and to obtain union-shop agreements. An industry-wide strike by the upholsterers against twenty-five firms in 1929 coincided with the general campaign of that year. A few firms signed with the union, but the larger ones were able to withstand its demands. By October, moreover, a new opponent emerged— the Communist-dominated Trade Union Unity League.[56]

Communists also were active in the clothing trades in the decade, particularly after 1925. Radicals in the state found rallying points in the famous Sacco and Vanzetti case in Massachusetts and the California criminal syndicalism law, held to be constitutional in 1927. Locally, the Communists were especially active in the International Ladies' Garment Workers Union. The effects of an industry-wide strike in New York City and of the breakdown of the unions there under the impact of Communism reached Los Angeles in 1927. In the preceding two years the Los Angeles ladies' garment industry had been strengthened by the exodus of firms from strife-torn New York. By 1926 about 60 per cent of the Los Angeles firms were organized under the jurisdiction of ILGWU Local No. 52. The increase in Communist activity, however, soon left its mark on the local, which reorganized in 1928 in an effort to eliminate card-carrying party members. Local No. 52 was dissolved and replaced by newly chartered No. 65, which was able to retain some of the gains made by its predecessor but found itself weakened by the constant battle against Communists on the one hand and open-shop employers on the other.

Amalgamated Clothing Workers Local No. 278, Millinery Workers Local No. 26, and Tailors Local No. 81 engaged in a number of small strikes in the late 1920's. Union contracts were won in some instances, but victories were few and far between. United Garment Workers Local No. 125 was more successful, since the union label was important in the manufacture of work clothes. A label campaign was supported extensively in 1924–1926 because prison-made overalls were being placed on the market. In 1925 the District Council of Garment Workers was organized in Los Angeles, composed of UGWA Locals No. 125 and 36 as well as Local No. 69 of Ontario. In contrast with the rest of the clothing industry, UGWA relations with employers were generally good, and contracts were maintained with Brownstein-Louis, Cohn-Goldwater, P. A. Newmark, and several other manufacturers.[57]

Another industry concerned with clothing had a very different experience. In late 1924 a long, three-cornered battle began in the cleaning and dyeing industry among route men, an association of wholesalers, and independent retailers. It developed when the wholesalers complained that the route men, who collected and delivered on a 40 per cent commission basis, were taking the bulk of the profits. The issue seemed to be resolved when the route men, members of Cleaners and Dyers Local No. 176, raised prices to the public, thus making possible an increased payment to wholesalers. Independent retailers, who solicited their own business and operated their own plants, did not raise their prices, however, and they began to get the bulk of the trade. In attempts to force them out of business, their drivers were beaten up, trucks were rammed, windows were broken, patrons' clothing was ruined by acids, employees were threatened, and shops were bombed. It seemed that the tactics of Chicago gangsters were being introduced into Los Angeles; at one time Al Capone, operator of a cleaning and dyeing racket in Chicago, was escorted out of town by "Roughhouse" Brown of the local detective force. But the battle was carried to Long Beach, Santa Monica, San Pedro, Pasadena, and other nearby cities.

The M and M backed the independent retailers, and tried to prevent the wholesalers from reaching closed-shop agreements with the unionized route men, but with little success. Violence and periodic strikes against retailers, as well as efforts by both unionists and organized wholesalers to keep recalcitrant members in line, marked the years until 1929. In January of that year the arrest of a number of unionists on charges of plant sabotage temporarily halted the violence, but it started again in July. As prosperity began to fade, the open shop prevailed among the independent retailers, while most of the wholesalers remained tied closely to the organized route men under union agreements.[58]

Although the route men were perhaps the best-organized truckers, the teamsters showed other signs of life in this period. There were a large number of "for hire" vehicles in the city which were owned by the drivers, and the living was not easy. In late 1924, 600 of these independent truckers banded together and struck for $30 a day, but life was too competitive and defection from the cause was too easy to permit the winning of a strike. Organizing also took place among cab drivers, milk wagon men, intercity bus operators, and municipal truckers, though none of them made permanent gains. The key union during these years was Truck Drivers Local No. 208, which conducted a campaign to organize the vehicle operators of Arden, Sanitary, Gold Seal, Burr, and California Cooperative creameries. Little headway was made, in spite of union claims that the drivers were held responsible for credit extended to customers, had to put up bonds, and had only two days off per month.[59]

The metal trades were even less successful than the teamsters, for they continued to be plagued by strongly entrenched employers who had adopted the American Plan and by an oversupply of labor, especially in those trades most used in shipbuilding during World War I. The prosperity of 1926, however, coupled with the organizing drive of that year, temporarily eased the unemployment problem, particularly for Machinists Local No. 311 and Engineers Local No. 72. The former, although not affiliated with the Metal Trades Council, continued to be the most prominent union among the metal trades. Iron Workers Local No. 51 was harassed during these years by a dual left-wing organization, but finally launched an organizing drive in 1929, only to see it halted by the depression. The patternmakers made perhaps the most progress in job control, and so won a wage increase and the forty-four-hour week in 1926.[60]

The bakers also continued to face strong open-shop opponents. Bakers Local No. 37 struggled against the fast-growing chain organizations, especially Continental Baking Company, which by 1925 owned Holsum, Ward, and several other local units. Some success was achieved in this area, and by the end of the decade the local claimed that its members were enjoying better conditions than at any time since 1918, although, as most of the large bakeries were still unorganized, this was an idle boast. Jewish Bakers Local No. 453 actually lost ground to the open shop. With the help of the M and M, sixteen of their most important employers organized the Hebrew Bakers' League in 1926 and declared for the open shop. The union struck, but its members were replaced with nonunionists. When the strike was settled in May, ten of the employers refused to sign agreements and ousted the union.[61]

Most unions in other trades were hard put even to maintain themselves in the late 1920's. The barbers participated in the organizing campaign of 1926 and added to their ranks by unionizing a number of shops. The butchers organized a new Jewish local, but gained little in other membership drives. Led by Meat Cutters Local No. 421, they unsuccessfully sought to reduce their long hours by prohibiting Sunday work and employment after 6:30 P.M. on weekdays. By 1928 the membership of Local No. 421 was declining, and the trend continued into the depression. The cigar makers held mass organization meetings in 1926, with meager results. Although they made strong efforts to hold the line in their trade, the continued decline of the cigar store, the mechanization of manufacture, and the severe competition of the cigarette during these years aided open-shop employers in opposing the union. The Beauty Operators' Association of America tried to organize employees in this trade in 1927, but even though it was becoming more customary for women to have their hair done outside the home, the M and M was too strongly entrenched in the many independent shops of the city. A similar state of affairs prevailed among auto mechanics, though a few of them were union members.[62]

The broom makers found their existence increasingly precarious because of the marketing of prison-made products in the Los Angeles area. Egg Inspectors Local No. 14934 survived until 1929, when it was cut adrift by the termination of its agreement with the large Poultrymen's Cooperative Association. Though the jewelry workers joined in the 1926 organizing campaign, their weakness forced them to withdraw from the Central Labor Council the following year in order to reduce their per capita tax obligation. The laundry workers, never a strong organization, were practically dormant by 1927, and the same situation prevailed with respect to Retail Clerks Local No. 406.

Thus, either because of the strength of the open-shop American Plan or for such reasons as inadequate leadership, internal dissension, or jurisdictional disputes, the Los Angeles labor movement, with but few exceptions, followed the national pattern of decline in the late 'twenties. By 1929 unionism both in the nation and in Los Angeles was already experiencing a depression so far as organizing success and membership gains were concerned. The trend of events after the black days in the fall of that year merely reinforced what was already established.[63]

4. THE DARK HOURS

As Los Angeles union and open-shop leaders entered the never-to-be-forgotten years of the Great Depression, they carried batons passed to them by men who had been extremely active in the struggle for and against the American Plan. On the open-shop side, Felix J. Zeehandelaar, long-time executive secretary of the M and M and bitter union foe, had passed away in 1924. Charles K. Walrath, prominent employer in the printing trades and strong supporter of General Otis, had died in 1926. The following year Fred L. Baker and Henry Huntington went to their respective rewards. Baker had headed the Baker Iron Works and other enterprises in the metal trades, whereas Huntington had been a power in California railroad and political circles. Both men had been implacable foes of unions and, in particular, of the AFL. On labor's side, the most significant loss was the death in 1929 of Joshua B. Dale, a senior AFL organizer in the state and a man who, at times, had almost singlehandedly maintained the morale of a local labor movement that believed itself so completely the underdog that at times it was ready to give up the battle. Labor lost a number of other men from the old guard that had faced General Otis and the open shop. Not the least of these was C. R. Gore, a long-time leader in the local building trades unions, who committed suicide in 1925. Thus the leadership on both sides changed in the 1920's, as men who had been in the front lines almost from the beginning of the open-shop struggle in 1890 were replaced by younger ones who had not experienced the bitterness of those early years.[64]

As local labor leaders looked back on the decade, they had little for which to be thankful. The organizing drives of 1926 and 1929 had proved unrewarding; union membership again was declining after a brief spurt in the middle 'twenties; leadership seemed to be increasingly ineffective; the open-shop American Plan and welfare capitalism were riding high in the saddle. It was not long, however, before it became evident that welfare capitalism could not sustain economic progress in the nation. October, 1929, caught it overextended economically and ideologically. Although the decline in labor's strength may have resulted in greater industrial freedom from the employers' point of view, it contributed little to correcting the faults of the American economic system. As unemployment deepened after the stock market crash, it became increasingly clear that this was no temporary crisis. By January, 1930, as noted earlier, 3,216,000 men were out of work. The figure doubled to 7,160,000 a year later, and rose to 10,197,000 by January, 1932.[65]

The inadequate measures taken by the Hoover administration in 1930 and 1931 have already been described. It was soon apparent that reliance on "natural forces" and local action, with minimal assistance from the federal government, would not effect recovery. William Green, president of the AFL and heretofore a follower of the Gompers philosophy of letting economic forces work themselves out, began to urge some kind of unemployment insurance. Attrition in AFL ranks was becoming serious enough to threaten the very existence of the organization. To many, a break with the past seemed necessary for survival, and finally, with the passage in 1932 of the Emergency Relief and Construction Act as well as a bill to provide credit for home construction, the federal government recognized that it must play a more positive role in restoring the nation's economy. As far as labor was concerned, however, the bottom of the depression was not reached until early in 1933, when unemployment hit its peak, with nearly a third of the nation's productive workers on the streets.[66]

In California the impact of the depression was delayed because of distance from the East and less heavy industrialization. The state's unemployment problem was complicated, however, by the influx of unemployed from other parts of the country, out-of-work migratory agricultural workers who headed for the cities, and the large population of Mexican nationals at the bottom of the skill ladder, especially in Los Angeles. In 1930 the problem became so serious that Governor C. C. Young appointed the California Unemployment Commission to study the situation and recommend remedial legislation. In March, 1931, the State Federation of Labor advocated a plan for unemployment relief to include insurance, a ban on immigration, the five-day week coupled with a shorter workday, immediate grants to those in serious need, and better coördination among state, county, and municipal agencies. Five months later the state and local chambers of commerce proposed what became known as "The California Plan," a spread-the-work program based on voluntary action on the part of employers. Although supported by President Hoover and the United States Chamber of Commerce, it was not enough to brake the continuing decline of business. In November an unofficial state committee was formed to develop a state-wide program to offset the influx of jobless into California, which was estimated at 1,000 a day. Although the committee was backed by the mayors of San Francisco and Los Angeles, its voluntary and unofficial status made it largely ineffective. Moreover, the depression was a national problem which could not be solved at a state or local level. In 1932 the California Unemployment Commission held hearings and investigated the over-all labor problem in the state, while the state chamber of commerce pushed its job-sharing plan; but economic conditions continued to worsen.[67]

In the Los Angeles area also, initial programs to aid the unemployed at the county and city level were voluntary in nature. Little was done before late 1930 other than to administer the usual relief. In November the Los Angeles County supervisors formed a committee to map a plan of action. From its recommendations developed what became known as the Employment Stabilization Bureau, headed by Harvey C. Fremming, a deputy state labor commissioner and president of the Long Beach Central Labor Council. With the support of a committee of labor, business, and civic leaders, Fremming went to work early in January, 1931, to register all the unemployed in the unincorporated areas of the county. The bureau proved to be one of the more successful organizations in relieving unemployment in the county, finding jobs and procuring aid for 30,516 persons in the first six months of its existence. Its achievements resulted in its continuation during the rest of the year and on into 1932 and 1933. Fremming eventually resigned after several years as the director, convinced that the political machine of Supervisor Frank L. Shaw was using the bureau as a means of getting votes to maintain itself in power.

Other programs advocated to solve county unemployment problems in 1931 and 1932 included the Los Angeles Chamber of Commerce's "Buy Los Angeles County Products" campaign and Supervisor Shaw's "Man-A-Block" plan. The latter envisaged giving one man in each block a job for ten weeks with pay of not less than $15 per week to be raised by his neighbors, but it proved worthless. A more effective program was the establishment by the unemployed of self-help cooperatives in 1932. Their importance increased in 1933, and they continued for a number of years until the need for them declined with the expansion of federal relief and eventual improvement in employment prospects.[68]

Private organizations, of course, gave relief to those in need, including the American Legion, the Union Rescue Mission, the Midnight Mission, Goodwill Industries, the Salvation Army, the Red Cross, the Parent-Teachers Association, and the Community Chest. Their funds were limited, however, and could not stem the tide of cases. By May, 1932, the Community Chest had exhausted its funds and other organizations could take care of only the most destitute.

Work camps for single men were established by the city and the county in 1931 in an attempt to aid the migratory unemployed as well as to ascertain whether or not they really wanted jobs. Those refusing to contribute labor in exchange for room and board were charged with vagrancy or shoved out of town. The police did the recruiting for the program by meeting incoming freight trains in the Los Angeles yards.[69]

Beginning in 1930, the city and the county also undertook to provide direct relief. In 1931, however, the county welfare budget had to be cut as funds were running out. The Board of Supervisors therefore used funds allocated to other county activities in an effort to continue relief, but even this was not enough. By June, 1932, the supervisors were urging that the state and federal governments step in to help the sorely pressed Los Angeles area.

In the meantime, some public works expenditures began to trickle into commercial channels. Late in 1930 work was begun on a $38,800,-000 water bond construction program in southern California. The next year Los Angeles County launched a program of road work which gave employment to a few hundred men. Two thousand were put to work on dam projects in San Gabriel Canyon. The federal government began to construct post offices in various communities. The largest project was the new federal office building in Los Angeles, costing $5,850,000. In late 1932 both the city and the county turned to the Reconstruction Finance Corporation for help, and even the *Times* admitted that local measures were insufficient. The most significant grant made by the RFC in southern California was $40 million for the Metropolitan Water Aqueduct. Its purpose was to bring water from the Colorado River to southern California cities, but its main object at this time was to give employment to an estimated 10,000 men over the next six years.[70]

The increase in unemployment among Los Angeles residents, coupled with the in-migration of the jobless from other areas of the country, gave impetus to the activities of left-wing organizations. The Socialist Party organized an unemployment conference in the city in 1931 and unsuccessfully sought a permit for a parade of the unemployed to City Hall. Other hunger marches took place in the city in 1930–1935. Most of them were poorly organized and, lacking a permit from the City Council, were broken up by the police. A large number of unemployed Los Angeles citizens joined a national hunger march organized by the Trade Union Unity League and the Communist Party, which entered Washington, D.C., in December, 1931. Left-wingers also continued their agitation in labor unions in these years. Although Communists, the IWW, and similar organizations were condemned by the AFL leadership, their boring-from-within tactics harassed a number of locals, especially in the clothing trades. The apathy of the membership, together with the distress of unemployment, gave the radicals an opportunity to control and, in some instances, virtually destroy certain unions.[71]

The radical elements would not have made so much headway, however, had the local labor movement entered the depression in better financial shape and with a larger membership. In a sense the open shop actually contributed to the success of left-wing activity by keeping AFL unions constantly on the defensive and, often, in a weakened condition. After the depression began to be felt in Los Angeles, many unions became virtually inactive, and some of them disappeared. By 1931 the Central Labor Council was in financial straits because of the drop in per capita tax income and the added expense of maintaining a representative at sessions of the state legislature. Similarly, the Union Labor Temple Association encountered difficulties when many unions reduced the number of meetings held in the Temple in order to lower overhead expense, and others either used smaller meeting rooms to cut costs or moved to other quarters outside the Temple. In 1931, in order to make ends meet, the ULTA requested and received the proceeds of the Labor Day celebration as well as the meager profits of the *Citizen* and the *Official Yearbook*.[72]

Organized labor in Los Angeles seemed to have more success on the political front from 1929 to 1933 than in the economic arena. The appointment of Francis Drake, former editor of the *Citizen* and of the *Southern California Labor Press*, to the Police Commission in 1929 by Mayor John C. Porter, in spite of opposition from the *Times*, was considered a victory by local labor leaders. In 1931 five assemblymen endorsed by labor in the Los Angeles area were elected to office, and in April, 1932, Mayor Porter appointed A. W. Hoch, a prominent figure in both local and state labor circles, to the Civil Service Commission. Possibly the greatest political setback for organized labor in these years also occurred in 1932, when James E. Davis was appointed police chief. Davis was known to be antilabor and a strong supporter of the open shop, and soon after his appointment the antiunion and anti-radical activities of the Red Squad under Captain William Hynes were intensified. This appointment was somewhat offset when A. C. Denman, former president of the antiunion Better America Federation, was turned down as a candidate for the Police Commission by the City Council.[73]

But political victories were of little moment when compared with failures on the economic front. In 1929–1932 steady decline marred the effectiveness of unions in the Los Angeles area as well as over the nation. Because most unions entered the depression in 1929 from positions of relative weakness, they were almost impotent by 1932. Mere survival was so difficult, for both business and labor, that little in the way of energy and resources was left over for industrial conflict. The brewery trades furnish an example. New contracts were signed in 1930 for one or two years, depending on the particular trade concerned, but with virtually no change in detail. Renewals were made in 1931 and 1932 more or less automatically, except for a wage reduction accepted by the engineers. There was little inclination to argue on either side. The *status quo* was accepted, with employers reducing costs by cutting the number of employees rather than debating contract provisions. Little attempt was made to organize the unorganized.[74]

The building trades were probably more severely hit by the depression than any other group. The decline in employment which had begun in the mid-'twenties because of the fall in building construction in the city was accentuated after 1929 and continued well into the 1930's. The carpenters suffered more unemployment than any other union in the Building Trades Council. The corresponding drop in membership resulted in the merger of Locals No. 158, 426, and 738 as early as 1930. The severity of the depression's impact caused both withdrawals from and a dearth of new affiliations with the Building Trades Council. By 1932 the unions of bricklayers, tile setters, carpenters, and plasterers were all independent of the council, which became hardly more than a shadow organization. The electrical workers sought to strengthen their position through an ordinance setting standards of performance for men in their craft, but the City Council rejected the measure, perhaps because the *Times* interpreted it as a move to control employment in the electrical field. By the end of 1932 at least 50 per cent of the workers in the building trades were unemployed in spite of the lowering of union wage scales in the depression years. Public works gave them some hope, but relatively little employment was available even in this area as 1932 drew to a close.[75]

The amusement trades were not hit quite so hard. Musicians Local No. 47 was still the largest union in California in 1930, but was beginning to suffer from "canned" music in the theaters and feared the eventual results of mechanization. Such fears were not unfounded, for the combination of sound and the business downturn greatly increased unemployment for musicians by 1931. Although conditions continued poor during 1932, the union, by making several concessions, renewed all existing contracts with theaters. Houses that had long fought the union, however, were not organized. The American Federation of Musicians held its annual convention in Los Angeles in June, 1932, but this failed to lend significant strength to organizing efforts in the face of adverse economic conditions.[76]

In the early months of the depression the motion picture projectionists had some success in moving out into neighborhood theaters from the downtown section where they had maintained most of their strength. Evidences of racketeering, however, brought them trouble. Stench bombings of theaters, beginning in 1928, continued sporadically in succeeding years and reached a peak of seventy-three in the first ten weeks of 1932. As the theaters so victimized were open-shop houses, the *Times* placed the blame on Motion Picture Operators Local No. 150. A grand jury investigation and subsequent arrests indicated, however, that the union was not behind the bombings but, rather, that Eastern racketeers were seeking to establish a dual union or force members of Local No. 150 to capitulate to their control.

The projectionists were also in the public eye in 1930–1931 in connection with the city's antipicketing law. While they were on strike to organize the Rialto Theater, long an open-shop house, several unionists were arrested for selling the *Citizen* in front of the establishment. Because the paper contained a story of the strike, the newsboys were construed as union pickets. Labor leaders charged that freedom of the press was being violated. In the trial, Judge Walter S. Gates held that the arrests did violate the freedom of the newsboys and enjoined the police from interfering with the hawking of the *Citizen* before the

Rialto or any other theater. But further arrests by the police and an appeal to a higher court brought a reversal of the original decision. In effect, the unionists were declared to be within the purview of the anti-picketing law inasmuch as they were not simply hawking newspapers, but were advertising a theater as unfair. Here the matter rested, but it was not altogether a defeat for the unions. In August, 1932, Local No. 150 arrived at a settlement with the Rialto, Olympic, and Broadway theaters which ended a two-year dispute and removed them from non-union status.[77]

The motion picture projectionists suffered some unemployment in the early 1930's, but as the theaters most affected by the depression were in outlying districts where organization was weak, the net effect on the union was not too damaging. For the most part, the major downtown theaters where unionists were employed continued to operate. For quite different reasons, a similar situation prevailed among the members of the ILGWU. The impact of the Communist issue had so disrupted the union in Los Angeles and throughout the nation by 1929 that the depression caused little immediate harm. As a matter of fact, membership actually increased after 1932 because of the extension of union activities into the women's dress industry, settlement of much of the left-versus-right-wing trouble, and, finally, the effect of the NIRA.

Cloakmakers Local No. 65 was the dominant ILGW union in Los Angeles during the early depression years. It called a strike in the fall of 1930 in order to ensure equal division of the work in slack times, a definite minimum wage scale, the forty-four-hour week, establishment of conditions to help stabilize cloakmaking, and union recognition. The walkout hit sixty-three firms, but all workers struck at only thirteen of them. Attempts to continue operations by a number of open-shop employers led to the roughing-up of some nonunion workers as well as the arrest of pickets. An explosion in a building in the garment center on October 17 resulted in injury to forty-eight garment workers. At first it was attributed to Local No. 65, but investigation revealed that escaping gas was the cause and that most of the injured were union members who were engaged in dressmaking and hence were not involved in the cloakmakers' strike. By the end of October thirty-five of the struck shops had signed with the union, thus placing about 70 per cent of the local's members under contracts. The strike was therefore deemed a success despite the depression and some harassment from left-wing elements.[78]

By 1931 Los Angeles was becoming recognized as a leading clothing-manufacturing center. Most of the unions in this field were active throughout the year. Cloakmakers Local No. 65, now quite well organized as a result of its 1930 strike, was still plagued by Communists. A strike in 1931 against a number of open-shop firms was hampered by left-wingers who openly scabbed on the unionists. Gloveworkers Local No. 74 also struck an open-shop firm, but failed to make any gains. Early in 1932 Local No. 26 of the ACWA was involved in a strike-lockout with the L.A. Cap Company. A compromise was worked out providing for wage adjustments satisfactory to the firm, and it continued as a union shop. The year 1932 was the worst for the clothing trades in terms of unemployment. Before the year was out, however, the movement of shops from New York in search of lower wage scales and more freedom from union interference enlarged the industry in Los Angeles. In the fall of 1932, according to one estimate, the 250 shops operating in the Los Angeles area were employing 12,500 workers. Deliveries allegedly were two to three weeks in arrears, with the plants doing twice as much work as in 1931. This augured well for both the unions and the industry in future years.[79]

The culinary, furniture, maritime, and metal trades generally were in bad shape throughout the early years of the depression and, unlike the clothing unions, could see little about which to be optimistic for the future. The culinary workers were hurt by numerous failures in the restaurant industry, which was marked by a high rate of business turnover even in normal times. By 1932 all the separate unions in the culinary trades had combined into one organization for survival. The furniture workers were in similar straits. They faced severe unemployment, as consumers cut down on purchases of high-priced items in the recession period, and could scarcely hold together even the framework of a union. The maritime workers continued under the open-shop system of the Marine Service Bureau (or Sea Service Bureau) established early in the 1920's. Both the longshoremen and the seamen suffered from the decline in freight traffic. The seamen in particular had to rely on help from such organizations as the Salvation Army, the Seamen's Institute, and the Sailors' Rest Mission to keep body and soul together. The Marine Service Bureau also contributed to sailors' relief, operating a hotel and a food kitchen in San Pedro for those without work. The metal trades were likewise hit by heavy unemployment after 1929, caused by the drop in building construction and sharp cutbacks in heavy industry. Although it was claimed that union wages were maintained where contracts prevailed, admissions by union leaders that 50 per cent of the members of the metal trades unions were unemployed by 1932 lend credence to the suspicion that hourly pay scales were maintained at the expense of employment.[80]

The printing trades continued to be relatively strong during the depression, especially the typographers. But even effective job control within certain trades could not prevent employers from discharging men and women in an effort to cut labor costs. By the end of 1931 from 10 to 40 per cent of union members were unemployed, and by 1932 printing trades unemployment in Los Angeles was at its highest level in twenty years. The absorption of the *Express* by the *Herald* in that year, and the merger of the *Hollywood News* and the *Hollywood Citizen* into the *Hollywood Citizen-News* in 1931, displaced a large number of printing craftsmen. The International Typographical Union held its national convention in Long Beach in 1932, but the delegates saw no improvement in the employment or the wage situation in southern California. Although the printers won new agreements with the *Herald-Express,* the *Record,* the *Examiner,* and the *Daily News* in 1932, they were forced to take a wage cut of more than 63 cents a day.[81]

As the depression deepened, railroad workers also suffered wage reductions. In 1930 the open-shop Los Angeles Railway had secured a fare increase and raised the wages of platform men, but two years later it was necessary to cancel this action by imposing a cut of up to 10 per cent. The operating brotherhoods tried to lessen the impact of unemployment on their memberships by shortening hours, but this was of negligible effect. The decline in rail traffic necessitated wage reductions for all workers on the railroads, including those entering Los Angeles. The Southern Pacific management took the lead by cutting the wages of its white-collar workers 10 per cent in September, 1931. On the national scene railroads sought to persuade the brotherhoods to accept wage reductions voluntarily. Although the unions resisted at first, most of them saw the need and compromised the issue. The cuts took effect locally for shopmen and other blue-collar workers in February, 1932.[82]

Nor did the unions in truck transportation fare well in Los Angeles in the early depression years. Truck Drivers Local No. 208 continued its efforts to organize dairy drivers, but Arden locked out all union men in 1930 and most of the other large establishments remained open shop, though some headway was made among the drivers in smaller dairies. A milk wagon drivers union was finally organized in 1931 with 150 names on the charter, but its existence was extremely tenuous. Some success was achieved in organizing cab drivers at two small companies. Taxi Cab Drivers Local No. 640 also signed up the California Cab Company, one of the larger firms, in 1931. Union drivers were employed for a time by Red Top Cab Company, but Yellow Cab, Brown Cab, and Peerless remained open shop. Red Top joined the latter group just before the capitulation of California Cab to the union.[83]

A number of other unions showed some signs of life in Los Angeles in the early 1930's. These included bakers, asbestos workers, butchers, barbers, egg inspectors, elevator operators, cigar makers, and cleaners and dyers. The last were again involved in racketeering and outbreaks of violence, including the usual acid throwing and application of chemicals to vats of clothes. In May, 1932, the union struck against United Cleaners and Dyers, a firm that was in receivership. The places of strikers were quickly filled with nonunionists, and the federal receiver secured an injunction restraining those dismissed from utilizing their knowledge of customers' lists to solicit United's clients. After the institution of a boycott by the union and further negotiations with the receiver, an agreement was reached under which the strikers were rehired. The nonunion employees were released, and a small wage increase was obtained for unionists returning to work.

In addition to this activity there were rumblings of unionization among the aircraft workers, but nothing developed. It would take World War II, with its impact on airframe manufacture, to give unions in this industry the base for highly successful organizing efforts. The bakers retained their organization during these years but their membership declined, for the combination of layoffs at several large bakeries and the demise of a number of small ones, where they were strongest, put a large number of unionists out on the street. Helms Baking Company, soon to become one of the largest bakeries in the city as a result of its official status as baker for the Olympic Games held in Los Angeles in 1932, was the outstanding open-shop firm on the unfair list of Bakers Local No. 37.[84]

All in all, organized labor had little reason for optimism as 1932 drew to a close. Throughout the nation an atmosphere of gloom enveloped the movement, with only a gleam of success here and there to keep alive the hope that the future might be better. The passage of the Norris-LaGuardia Act promised some relief from the worst abuses of the injunction and yellow-dog contracts. Occasionally a strike was won or a wage cut successfully resisted, but these were only pinpoints of light in a blanket of darkness. The AFL had reached a membership peak of 4,078,740 in 1920, followed by a gradual decline throughout the decade. With the onset of the Great Depression, unemployment dragged membership down very rapidly until, early in 1933, it dropped below 2,200,000 workers for the first time since before World War I. Membership similarly declined at state and local levels.[85] By 1933 survival was a question of genuine concern. The prevailing feeling was aptly expressed at the 1932 convention of the California State Federation of Labor when Vice President Clyde H. Isgrip spoke for the Los Angeles area as follows: "The widespread apathy apparent among wage earners toward organizations designed to better their economic conditions in this district is appalling and is indicatory of dire consequences, which will retard both organized and unorganized workers alike." [86] A new day was soon to come for organized labor, but the first streaks of its dawn were yet to appear. The darkest hours still prevailed.

VII. RENEWAL OF THE STRUGGLE

1. 1933—BOTTOM OF THE DEPRESSION

THE OPENING of a new year brought little hope for an upturn in the national economy. Business and bank failures were continuing apace. The White House would have a new occupant on March 4, but no one was certain whether or not this would make much difference in the over-all economic picture. The total membership of the AFL had dropped to the lowest figure since World War I—2,126,796 workers. Organized labor was ready to accept federal action in the economic sphere, especially in the form of unemployment insurance, but had not yet proposed a workable plan. The Congress, recognizing the gravity of the problem, had passed the Emergency Relief and Construction Act in 1932, which authorized the lending of $300 million to state and local governments for the emergency relief of destitute persons, primarily through employment projects. It was yet too early to see any positive results.[1]

Although California was not affected by the depression so early as the eastern seaboard states, by 1933 it was feeling the full impact of straitened economic circumstances. As pointed out in the preceding chapter, the state's relatively lighter industrialization initially cushioned its economy, but California soon became burdened with the unemployed and the homeless from other sections of the country, as well as with many of its own unfortunate citizens. Southern California, in particular, was in the depths of the depression by 1933. Many people in this area normally worked in service industries, earning their livelihoods from the tourist trade and the expenditures of retired people. The severity of the business downturn had reduced and, in many instances, eliminated retirement incomes. Likewise, regular tourists had less to spend or could not afford to come to southern California. In their places a new type of tourist entered the area and began to add to the relief burden of the southern counties. They came on foot, in old cars, and via "side-door Pullmans." They knew that a person was unlikely to freeze during the winter in California and expected that some sort of relief would probably be forthcoming. The new tourists were often unemployed industrial workers, but many were penniless farmers from Midwestern states.[2]

California residents were not prepared for tourists who came to receive and not to give. The citizens of many communities resented the intrusion, and made it evident to the newcomers that they were not

[237]

wanted. Further, the state had a history of opposition to undesirable immigrants. In the early days of the gold rush there had been an outcry against Chinese coolies who had left the mines and gone into other types of work. A special tax levied against aliens in the mines in those years became so burdensome that many left the state. To some extent, this antagonistic viewpoint had continued down through the years. In 1931, for example, the legislature passed an amended law requiring three years of state and one year of county residence to be eligible for relief, including medical care and hospitalization. The unemployed continued to pour in, however, in spite of hostile laws and a cool reception, and established their shanty villages on the outskirts of towns in the central and southern areas of the state. County officials soon found their funds inadequate to support the residents who were out of work, much less the new migrants. As special state funds likewise were too small, the Golden State began to receive money allocated by federal action. By June, 1933, it was the second largest recipient of such aid, which could be used for both resident and migrant unemployed. The Federal Emergency Relief Act of 1933, in particular, earmarked certain funds for the support of transients, further easing the burden on the southern counties.[3]

Economic conditions in Los Angeles in 1933 were like those in any other large city in that depression year. The resident relief load of the city was the heaviest in its history, and, in addition, Los Angeles was a mecca for many migrants. In January, 1931, Los Angeles County officials had sought to ease the relief problem by establishing the County Employment Stabilization Bureau headed by Harvey Fremming. It had soon registered more than 200,000 unemployed, classifying them as common laborers and making them available for county and municipal projects at a flat rate of $3.20 a day. The protest of the Los Angeles Central Labor Council that this system would mean the employment of skilled union men at the common labor wage went unheeded.[4]

The Employment Stabilization Bureau functioned until May, 1933, when its jurisdiction over unemployment and relief funds allocated by the Reconstruction Finance Corporation was transferred to the Los Angeles County Welfare Department. This change was effected because an official investigation had tended to substantiate the allegation that, under the bureau, relief work was being conducted so as to further the candidacy of County Supervisor Frank L. Shaw for mayor. After the transfer, RFC funds were spent for various park beautification projects, the cutting of wood to be used as fuel by the unemployed, and the maintenance of county camps for unemployed men which had been established in 1932. Further appropriations for these same purposes were later received from the Federal Emergency Relief Administration and through the public works provisions of the National Industrial Recovery Act.[5]

The financial burden of city and county relief in Los Angeles was also partially eased by money received from the State Emergency Relief Administration. This organization distributed funds to employable residents who were unable to find jobs, operated relief and work camps for single men, and later assumed other duties in liaison with federal agencies. By constitutional amendment, the State Emergency Relief Administration was reorganized in 1934 as the State Relief Administration, and in 1935 was placed under the provisions of the California Unemployment Relief Act.[6]

The problems of relief administration were more than financial. On August 17, 1933, for example, Earl E. Jensen, superintendent of charities in Los Angeles County, narrowly averted a strike among unemployed relief workers. A week earlier a shortage of funds had made it necessary to decrease the workday from eight to four hours in order to spread the available work among the approximately 100,000 unemployed. The workers then threatened to strike, but were persuaded to elect a committee of three which, with Jensen, compromised on a six-hour day, to be effective on August 22. But on that date some of the workers, unwilling to accept the compromise, walked out in a one-day strike. The strikers were well led and peaceful, but made the following demands on Jensen: $4 for a six-hour day; seven days of work out of thirty as a minimum for single men; ten days of work out of thirty as a minimum for married men, with two extra days for each dependent; 2.5 per cent to be added to all wages to cover the state sales tax; free transportation to and from jobs where the transportation cost was more than 14 cents; immediate abolition of all unpaid labor, such as that done by prisoners; official recognition of the Relief Workers Protective Union, two members of which were to be chosen by the workers to represent them on the County Welfare Board; full pay for the day of labor lost because of the strike; no misappropriation of relief funds for espionage work among relief workers; an immediate answer to the demands; and an audit of the income and the expenditures of the Los Angeles County Welfare Department.[7]

County officials claimed that not more than 4,000 of the unemployed actually went on strike, but the walkout was effective in stopping relief work for the day. Several thousand strikers congregated at the old Plaza, where the questions at issue were discussed, as well as others such as freedom for Tom Mooney, one of the men convicted of the 1916 San Francisco Preparedness Day bombing. Efforts were made to secure more members for the Relief Workers Protective Union through the solicitation of a 10-cent initiation fee, and some Communist literature was distributed. Several arrests were made on the ground of failure to have a city license for such activity. The strikers gained little except newspaper publicity and the attention of the police. Their demands were not granted; the six-hour day went into effect and the wage rate remained 40 cents an hour. Superintendent Jensen recognized that the strikers did have legitimate grievances, one of the more important being that, with a shorter workday, transportation cost to and from the job became a proportionately larger expense for the worker on relief. He insisted, however, that a six-hour day was necessary in order to provide work for a larger number of eligible unemployed and destitute persons, as funds were limited. In subsequent years additional strikes were called, most of them under the auspices of the Workers Alliance, a union for workers on relief in the late 1930's, but the dispute of 1933 was the first walkout conducted by the unemployed in Los Angeles.[8]

In November, 1933, additional relief funds were forthcoming after the federal Civil Works Administration was organized. It established a work program for 4 million unemployed over the nation. By December 15, 1933, some 58,000 unemployed men and women in the Los Angeles area were benefiting from it. Most of them were from the rolls of the Los Angeles County Welfare Department, which had been supporting them through the distribution of work relief made possible by previous federal, state, and county appropriations. The payment of prevailing wages for the varying grades of labor used on the public projects under the CWA quickly exhausted the available funds, causing cancellation of the program in April of the following year.[9]

City and county officials were also assisted in unemployment relief by the Civilian Conservation Corps. Angeles National Forest gave employment to approximately 4,000 youths under this program. Although not all of them were from the Los Angeles area, a large proportion came from the immediate vicinity, as the initial CCC quota for the county was 4,400 recruits. By August, 1933, 8,700 young men from southern California were at work in the nation's forests, 4,500 of them remaining in local areas.[10]

The unemployment relief problem in Los Angeles was lessened to some extent by the activities of the self-help coöperatives set up in the early years of the depression. These organizations assumed two major forms. One type was limited to the exchange of the labor of members for surplus commodities of all kinds to be used by the whole group. The other promoted the barter of one commodity for another between individual members of the coöperative or between a member and the organization. There were approximately forty-five local units of the first type in Los Angeles County, about twenty-three of them within the city limits. The first one was set up in 1932 at Compton; by March, 1933, about 125,000 persons in southern California were in 103 such organizations and were partly dependent on them for support. The barter-type coöperative had at least four units in Los Angeles County with a total membership of 7,600 persons. The largest unit was the Los Angeles Cooperative Exchange with 5,600 members.[11]

Despite all efforts by officials of the city and the county of Los Angeles to assist the needy unemployed, many individuals and organizations protested about the way relief was administered and the amount of help given to those in want. Complaints about alleged inefficiencies in the administration of various programs were frequent in 1933 and later years. There is some evidence to support the charge that those affiliated with the political machine of Supervisor and later Mayor Frank L. Shaw administered relief funds so as to aid in maintaining themselves in public office. Further, various groups of unemployed objected to the relief programs in a demonstrative fashion in 1933. On January 4 one of these groups was accosted by Los Angeles police at Fifth and Towne while attempting to marshal recruits for a "hunger march" to Sacramento. Although the men claimed that they were peacefully organizing to present demands to the state legislature on January 10, the police alleged they were agitators spreading Communist propaganda. Several were arrested and charged with criminal syndicalism under the state law, and the rest were dispersed by the use of tear gas. Again, on March 4, a group of the unemployed, under the auspices of the National Federation of Unemployed Workers League of America, arranged a demonstration in honor of President Roosevelt's inauguration, but the police, led by Captain William F. Hynes, were present to disband the participants. Captain Hynes, as head of the Intelligence Bureau of the Police Department, commonly called the "Red Squad," had the uncanny ability of appearing inopportunely with his men at the meetings of groups likely to disturb the peace or with objectives contrary to those of supporters of the open shop. Members of the Red Squad also frequently supervised the conduct of picket lines and other public demonstrations by individuals and organizations. The squad was heartily disliked by local labor leaders, who were often arrested for disturbing the peace while conducting strikes.[12]

2. THE BLUE EAGLE

Although relief was given to the unemployed regardless of their union affiliation, organized labor was more interested in getting men back to work in legitimate, productive jobs than in perpetuating federal and local aid programs. During the first two years of the depression national labor leaders had believed that the decline in business activity was only temporary, and that prosperity would return as a result of the automatic operation of economic laws. Most AFL officers had opposed federal relief for the unemployed, calling it a "dole." Even as late as the spring of 1933, Matthew Woll, an AFL vice-president, had opposed the establishment of a minimum wage, insisting that unless similar legislation applied to workers in other countries who manufactured goods imported by the United States, such action would result in increased unemployment for American workers. By 1933 the majority of AFL leaders were not in complete sympathy with Woll, however, believing that some positive action would have to be taken by the central government to aid in restoring prosperity. Hence organized labor gave limited support to the emergency measures taken by the new administration of Franklin D. Roosevelt after it took office in March, 1933. As noted earlier, most of these were temporary, such as the various acts for relief of the unemployed. Others were destined to have far-reaching effects in establishing precedents for government action in various fields of economic life. Among these was the National Industrial Recovery Act, which represented an effort to reconstruct the economy of the nation by assuring reasonable profits to industry and a living wage to labor, and by reducing so-called "chiseling" competitive practices. The act also required employers to grant recognition to those workers desiring to organize and bargain collectively. This, indeed, was an effort to legislate industrial democracy.[13]

The National Industrial Recovery Act was well timed. Not only were many labor leaders ready for it, but there was also a widespread public belief that it was time for the government to do something about a depression that did not seem to respond to self-generating forces of economic recovery. Even persons like Matthew Woll, who opposed anything that resembled economic planning, were beginning to state publicly that there was some need for balancing production and consumption. Business failures, coupled with price and wage reductions, revived old notions that competition was destructive and "predatory" and needed to be curbed. Further, in the decade following World War I, a number of economists had developed theories from their studies of contemporary conditions and ideas. Some stated that the rapid technological advances of the years preceding the depression had led to a significant displacement of men by machinery which made it necessary to devise some means of spreading the available work. Others believed that current income in the hands of the consuming public was insufficient to permit the purchase of the output of an advanced industrial system, and that consumers should therefore be given more purchasing power. In addition, economists advocating partial or complete economic planning supported the idea that a great depression marked the time to make such a plan operative.

Early in 1933 organized labor's exponents of governmental intervention in the economic field urged that immediate action be taken to end the depression. Testifying before the Senate Committee on Finance on February 17, John L. Lewis and Sidney Hillman advocated an extensive governmental program to revive the economy. Many of their ideas were incorporated in the National Industrial Recovery Act, which was passed by Congress on June 13, 1933, and signed by the President on June 16. Title I of the act had direct significance for organized labor through its famous Section 7(*a*), which encouraged workers to organize into unions for the purpose of bargaining collectively. Donald Richberg, one of the men who had drafted the law, stated that a major intent of the framers was to provide for worker participation in the self-government of industry, and that the satisfactory labor relations necessary for this in modern enterprise could not be achieved without permitting some form of labor organization. Noting this objective, the AFL leadership laid plans for an organizing campaign when the act became effective. As soon as it was signed by the President, the 30,661 AFL local unions acted as nuclei for organizing activities, and a period of intensive labor unrest began. The summer of 1933 saw more than 200 new strikes each month, a figure that had not been reached since 1923. In the year as a whole, more than a million workers engaged in strikes, seventeen of which were supported by 10,000 or more persons.[14]

In 1933 the California Legislature passed the California Industrial Recovery Act, designed for integration with the NIRA. It provided for the establishment of codes of fair competition for persons, firms, or corporations in intrastate commerce which were not subject to the national act. In effect, the act brought the state's industry under the national law. When the California Recovery Act became effective, labor unions were given full recognition as spokesmen for workers in hearings on violations of state codes when other employee representatives did not appear. Further, whenever a federal code was established covering a field of business activity heretofore under state authority, the former was given priority over the latter, thus avoiding possible code conflicts.

The passage of both national and state recovery acts, together with a slight increase in employment, made organized labor in California more optimistic than it had been for years. This was very evident at the annual convention of the California State Federation of Labor held at Monterey in September, 1933, even though a net loss of 9,100 members in affiliated unions in the previous twelve months left only 82,100 in good standing. Paul Scharrenberg, secretary of the organization, reported that the entire labor movement in California had a total strength at this time of 140,000. This figure, however, included railroad brotherhoods as well as AFL union members whose dues were delinquent. The convention supported the NIRA and the California Recovery Act, requested that both laws be made permanent, and expressed the belief that the worst of the depression was over.[15]

Labor leaders in Los Angeles welcomed the NIRA with open arms. It represented an opportunity for them to regain the membership losses of the 1920's and the depression, as well as to make some headway against the open shop. The local labor movement was barely intact in the spring of 1933. The Central Labor and the Allied Printing Trades councils continued to meet regularly, but those of the metal and building trades were extremely weak. The Metal Trades Council had only a few members and existed primarily as an adjunct of the Central Labor Council, partly because there had been very little employment in the foundry trades the previous year and competition for available contracts had been intensified by an increase in the number of small job shops which would take work at any price. In addition, the locals of boilermakers, blacksmiths, and machinists were not affiliated with the council at this time, thus diminishing its numerical strength. The Building and Construction Trades Council likewise had so small a membership that it was hardly more than a paper organization. Several of its affiliated locals, including the bricklayers, the carpenters, the electrical workers, and the steam shovel engineers, had suffered severe membership reverses because of unemployment and the competition of newly arrived craftsmen who were willing to work for less than union wages. The council's secretary received a very small salary and only enough petty cash to pay for stationery. At various times in the depression years, there had been only enough money in the treasury to maintain a telephone.[16]

As of May 31, 1933, on the eve of passage of the NIRA, there were seventy-five unions in good standing in the Central Labor Council. Per capita tax figures revealed a total membership of 11,139 workers, a decrease of 1,590 from the previous year. The true paid-up strength of organized labor in Los Angeles at this time, however, was probably slightly under 20,000, including the railroad brotherhoods and unions not affiliated with the central body. The council had not been in a sound financial condition for some time, and in the early months of 1933 was desperately in need of funds. Its two main sources of revenue were per capita tax receipts and an annual or semiannual dividend from the *Citizen*. The tax receipts had shrunk drastically in the preceding two years, and the Board of Publishers of the *Citizen* had suspended the dividend because the newspaper also was in serious financial straits. The Central Labor Council consequently had to borrow operating funds from the Farmers and Merchants National Bank and the Allied Printing Trades Council, using Labor Temple mortgage redemption notes as security. Strong measures were taken to pare expenses: the secretary returned to the treasury one week's salary out of each month's pay, the assistant secretary was discharged, all transportation expenses except automobile liability insurance were curtailed, and rent payments to the Union Labor Temple Association were allowed to lapse. These economies permitted the reduction of the bank loan to $150, and, beginning in June, an assessment of $1 a month on each affiliated local was collected for the rest of the year. The *Citizen* also was adversely affected by the depression, which had reduced the income of many subscribers and advertisers. Beginning in January, 1933, therefore, the staff of the paper contributed one day's pay each week to its general fund, and the number of pages was reduced to economize on paper.[17]

The National Industrial Recovery Act was less than two weeks old when a large group of local union officers gathered under Central Labor Council auspices on June 29, 1933, and organized the Industrial Recovery Act Committee, with J. W. Buzzell, the council secretary, as permanent chairman and Collins Hardin of the *Citizen* as secretary. The program adopted pointed to the old problem of the need to counteract the open shop. Local labor leaders believed that many employers would endeavor to establish National Recovery Administration codes without consulting their employees, and, by instituting company representation plans in order to conform to the law, would keep AFL unions out of their plants. The program therefore requested that all industrial codes in Los Angeles provide for a five-day week and a six-hour day, as well as the establishment of a weekly union wage for thirty hours which was not less than seven-eighths of the scale of the trade concerned for a week of forty-four or forty-eight hours in 1928. Table 3 compares union wages scales in Los Angeles in 1933 with those in 1913 and 1929. Although little change is evident between 1929 and 1933, the figures are misleading as income data because there was more unemployment in 1933 than in 1929.

In addition to the wage request made in the program, all members

TABLE 3

UNION WAGE RATES AND WORKING HOURS
OF SOME PRINCIPAL TRADES IN LOS ANGELES,
1913, 1929, AND 1933[a]

Occupation	Rate per hour (in cents)			Hours per week		
	1913	1929	1933	1913	1929	1933
Bricklayers	75.0	137.5	100.0	44	44	40
Building laborers	34.4	62.5	62.5	44	44	40
Carpenters	50.0	100.0	100.0	48	44	40
Cement finishers	62.5	125.0	100.0	48	44	44
Compositors						
Book and job	46.9	106.8	106.8	48	44	44
Newspaper (day work)	62.5	117.8	109.6	45	45	45
Electrotypers						
Molders	50.0	113.6	104.2	48	44	48
Finishers	50.0	113.6	104.2	48	44	48
Granite cutters, inside	62.5	112.5	106.3	48	44	40
Inside wiremen	50.0	100.0	100.0	48	44	44
Painters	43.8	100.0	100.0	48	44	40
Plasterers	75.0	150.0	112.5	44	40	40
Plumbers	56.3	112.5	112.5	48	44	40
Sheet metal workers	56.3	112.5	112.5	44	44	44
Structural ironworkers	50.0	112.5	112.5	48	44	44
Typesetting						
Book and job, mach.	58.3	120.5	120.5	48	44	44
Newspaper, mach.	62.2	117.8	109.6	45	45	45

[a]The figures represent the minimum wage and the maximum hours found in collective bargaining agreements between unions and employers.

SOURCE: "Union Scales of Wages and Hours of Labor in 1933," *Monthly Labor Review*, XXXVII (Sept., 1933), 660–673.

of unions were forbidden to meet employers as individuals, but were instructed to ask that an official labor representative be selected to conduct negotiations with employer groups. Subcommittees were established on publicity, organization planning, general presentation and negotiation, and group representation, as well as a committee on committees. The results of the meeting of June 29 were then sent to the secretaries of all unions in the city and county. These officials, in turn, were instructed to prepare for employers their specific trade recommendations on wages, hours, working conditions, and union rules for insertion in the respective codes.[18]

While this activity was going on, Buzzell telephoned A. G. Arnoll, executive secretary of the Chamber of Commerce, requesting a conference of committees from their two organizations for the purpose of working out a system to establish NRA codes in the city. Upon receiving Buzzell's confirming letter, Arnoll wrote to Edgar R. Perry, general manager of the Merchants' and Manufacturers' Association, requesting his participation in such a conference. Perry replied on July 12 that the members of his organization did not believe it was necessary to deal with organized labor under the NIRA. Arnoll thereupon informed Buzzell that the proposed meeting was not feasible, though he personally saw no harm in getting the viewpoint of organized labor.

As Buzzell had anticipated this reply, delegates to the Central Labor Council meeting of July 7 had been warned that each union probably would have to push its own demands for representation on the various industrial committees that were formulating codes. At the same time a large number of unions had reported a marked increase in attendance at their meetings. With this evidence of support, local labor leaders decided to carry on an organizing campaign in spite of the apparent lack of coöperation on the part of the M and M and the Chamber of Commerce in the establishment of NRA codes. The second meeting of the Industrial Recovery Act Committee was held on July 13, and the subcommittees began to function. Four days later Buzzell forwarded a copy of the plan of action to the Los Angeles Chamber of Commerce. This communication pointed out that workers had the right to organize and bargain collectively through representatives of their own choosing, a fact that chamber officials did not deny.[19]

After receiving organized labor's plan of action, the Chamber of Commerce in turn sent its proposal for coöperation under the act to the Central Labor Council. Called the Joint Conference Plan, it set forth a model of the agreement that should be established between employer and employee. It was basically a company representation plan which provided for mutual understanding and coöperation between labor and management, thereby fulfilling the provisions of the NIRA but eliminating the necessity of establishing new AFL locals. The Chamber of Commerce did not oppose the general recovery program and, in fact, welcomed the abolition of unfair practices. Its members, however, did not want to be forced to negotiate with AFL unions under Section 7(a) of the act. The chamber had opposed Section 7(a) as early as June 1, 1933, when the NIRA was known only as Senate Bill 1712. In July, after passage of the law, the M and M published a bulletin stating that nothing in the wording or spirit of the act made it necessary for an employee to join a union or an employer to sign a trade agreement.[20] The bulletin read, in part:

Employers operating under the act should point out to employees their full legal rights as stated in Sec. 7, and should further emphasize that there is less necessity for an employe to join American Federation of Labor ranks than ever before, because the administration has guaranteed them decent living wages and shortened working hours. . . .

Employees should be advised that it will not be necessary for them to obtain work through business agents or organized Union Labor offices. Employers should tell employees that within any industry or business operating under a Federal code, they may set up and join an organization of their own, which will include all workers within their business classification. The worker can then be assured of being properly represented.[21]

This statement clearly advocated the establishment of company representation plans by Los Angeles employers in order to prevent the growth of AFL unions, while adhering to the provisions of the NIRA. One of the first firms in the city to follow this procedure was the Los Angeles plant of the Goodyear Tire and Rubber Company. The company union in the local branch was established on July 1, and was modeled after the employee representation plan in effect at the main plant in Akron, Ohio. Local branches of other national rubber companies organized similar unions.[22]

Although a majority of Los Angeles employers signed the President's Re-employment Agreement in July, 1933, labor leaders discovered that a number of them were failing to abide by the spirit and the letter of the law, for they released some employees when wages were increased and hours were shortened. The Central Labor Council therefore appointed a committee to sift reports received from unions of such violations of the NRA codes. Proved abuses of this character were then reported to the California State Federation of Labor and to President William Green of the AFL for appropriate action. Other abuses occurred when some individuals took advantage of the NIRA by charging an honorarium for a speech to a labor group, organizing workers on a commission basis, requesting exorbitant attorney's fees for representing labor groups before NRA officials, requiring large initiation payments for entrance into nonexistent unions, and other similar practices. All these activities were repudiated by the established AFL unions.[23]

As the weeks passed, the bustle around the Labor Temple incident to the renewed interest in organizing activities reminded many veteran unionists of the more active days during and immediately after World War I. Many workers came to the Labor Temple unsolicited to request admission into a union, and numerous charters were issued. According to one estimate, at least 6,000 men and women joined Los Angeles unions in the first few weeks of July. Organizers were at such a premium that they were sought by newspaper advertisements. Even lawyers, doctors, screen writers, newspapermen, movie directors, and social workers, groups heretofore not considered suitable material for unions, wanted to be organized. The number of organizers sent into the field in July contrasted sharply with the few in Los Angeles in the months before the NIRA. The latter usually had their offices in their hats, doubled as business agents for the unions, and often received wages as low as $15 a week.[24]

The organizing drive moved apace throughout the summer with no perceptible diminution under the auspices of the Central Labor Council's Industrial Recovery Act Committee, which continued to meet and coördinate the campaign. Its executive committee was in frequent session as local problems arose and new unions came into existence. The Labor Temple's meeting halls began to be much in demand. Old unions outgrew their quarters and had to rent larger offices. Among the groups making the most substantial numerical gains during the summer were teamsters, clothing workers, bakers, packinghouse workers, butchers, cleaners and dyers, culinary workers, printing craftsmen, glass workers, and barbers. The flint glass workers were 100 per cent organized by July, 1933. In contrast, the laundry workers were unable to organize more than one local in the entire industry in the city, primarily because of the effective opposition of their employers. By September seventeen new locals in various crafts had been organized in Los Angeles and twelve more were in the process of formation. C. J. Hyans, an official of the Central Labor Council, believed that approximately 15,000 workers had joined unions in the first six weeks of the organizing drive. Further good news came from General Hugh S. Johnson, administrator of the NRA, who wrote, in answer to a letter from Secretary Buzzell, that an open hearing would be held before any codes were adopted, even though local employers might have ignored the unions during their preparation. Many locals forwarded suggested codes to Washington, D.C., for consideration by NRA officials along with those sent by employers.[25]

While labor leaders sought to spread the gospel of union membership, the editors of the *Times,* true to their policy of opposition to the closed or union shop, advocated an interpretation of Section 7(a) which would encourage workers to organize and bargain collectively but not through AFL unions. In furtherance of this policy, the newspaper supported the Chamber of Commerce and the Merchants' and Manufacturers' Association in their efforts to offset the organizing activities of the local labor movement. Its editorial columns pointed out that "union promoters" were misrepresenting the letter and the spirit of the NIRA by declaring that workers must join the AFL in order to have organization and collective bargaining rights under the act. On August 30 the *Times* alleged that the AFL was making a special effort to use the NIRA to increase the economic influence of unions in Los Angeles, the "pioneer open-shop city of America, as it has always been the chief stronghold and outstanding beneficiary of that system of industrial relations." The editorial continued: "If, as all experience has gone to indicate, there can be no closed shop without coercion and violation of the rights of individuals, then the closed shop has no place among free American institutions and must go." [26] Similar statements were made in the *Times* on August 31 by Carrol A. Stilson, manager of the Metal Trades Manufacturers' Association of Southern California, and on September 1 by W. C. Pridham, ex-president of the Community Chest, organizer and for four years president of the Chamber of Commerce, a leading director of the M and M, and a former chairman of the Los Angeles County Board of Supervisors.

Taking note of the *Times* editorials, labor leaders declared that Los Angeles unions were making the greatest organizational headway in years and that this was responsible for the renewed emphasis on the virtues of the open shop. They pointed out that union leaders were not preaching that workers had to join unions under Section 7(a), but were saying that until employees established locals free from company domination, they would have no chance to improve wages, hours, and working conditions under the NIRA.[27]

3. THE FIRST WALKOUT UNDER THE BLUE EAGLE

In Los Angeles, as in the nation as a whole, the organizing drives that took place after passage of the NIRA had two distinct phases. The first began shortly after the act was passed and continued until early 1934, when labor leaders realized that NRA officials lacked power to enforce its provisions. The second, less evident phase began in the summer of 1934 and lasted throughout most of the winter. During this period organized labor relied on its own economic strength rather than on government officials to take advantage of the rights granted it under the act. Each of the two phases in Los Angeles was marked by an increase in the number and frequency of strikes, and at least one dispute of a major character.

The International Ladies' Garment Workers provided the major walkout that occurred in the first phase of the organizing drive in the Los Angeles area. As early as the first months of 1933 the union began to grow steadily in most cities of the nation where it had locals. This growth was the result of increasing job control gained by means of shrewd organizing efforts backed up by strikes where necessary. Members of the ILGWU manufactured almost every type of women's and children's wearing apparel. Dues and initiation fees were low, arbitration machinery was in operation, and various educational and cultural programs were sponsored. Functioning in a highly competitive industry subject to the mutations of style, changes in climate, and seasonal cycles, by 1933 the ILGWU had checked, to a certain extent, those factors leading to job insecurity for its members by accepting joint responsibility with management for the maintenance of stability in the volume of output and, consequently, in employment. Los Angeles, however, was an exception, as the union there had not yet achieved economic stability. Local No. 65, established in 1928 as an outgrowth of Local No. 52, was numerically and economically weakened in 1929 when the Communists withdrew from it and established a dual Needle Trades Workers Industrial Union, which existed until 1935 as an adjunct of the Trade Union Unity League. Moreover, workers whom employers suspected of affiliation with Local No. 65 were subject to discriminatory discharge.[28]

In the spring of 1933 a general rise in employment in the clothing industry led to increased organizing activities by the ILGWU. A new union of cutters, Local No. 84, was established with Harry Scott and Jack Hass as manager and secretary, respectively. In September, 1933, the international sent Rose Pesotta as an organizer to help in the Los

Angeles membership drive. She was assisted by William (Bill) Busick, who had just joined the union as an organizer at this time although he was not a garment worker. Most of the several thousand dressmakers in Los Angeles garment factories still were unorganized and worked in some 175 small companies. About 75 per cent of the cutters and the pressers and a large number of the cloakmakers were organized, but the activities of their unions were strenuously opposed by a group of manufacturers who wanted to maintain the open shop. Miss Pesotta and Busick, assisted by the leaders of Locals No. 84 and 65, immediately initiated their organizing campaign. A local Spanish cultural society gave them radio time to be used in reaching the Mexican workers who constituted a majority of the dressmakers. Leaflets were passed out to these workers in order to arouse their dissatisfaction with the poor working conditions in the industry, the discriminatory discharge system, the unequal distribution of work by foremen who played favorites, the low earnings, and the long hours. Attention also was called to the fact that the state minimum wage law for women, stipulating $16 a week for forty-eight hours, was often violated, as was President Roosevelt's Re-employment Agreement under the NIRA. Moreover, the dressmakers were informed of the existence of a black list and of the encouragement of a certain amount of labor turnover by employers in order to prevent a stability in employment conducive to the growth of unions. As most of the manufacturing operations could be learned in a short time, the training period was negligible.[29]

On September 25 a mass meeting of all cloakmakers was held at Walker's Orange Grove Auditorium. A one-and-a-half-hour work stoppage had been called for 3 P.M. that day in order to facilitate attendance, and the hall was overflowing. The workers present authorized a general strike if employers would not sign union contracts. Two days later, at a second meeting, the dressmakers, as yet not organized in a separate union, gave a like authorization. Both meetings were publicized in newspaper headlines, and a few employers indicated their desire for a settlement. The demands of the two groups included union recognition; a thirty-five-hour week; a guaranteed minimum wage for each craft in accordance with the pending NRA dress code; a five-day week; regular hours from 8:30 A.M. to 4:30 P.M. with an hour for lunch; no home work; the shop chairman and the price committee to be elected by the workers of each shop; no punching of time cards except when actually entering or leaving factories; and all disputes to be adjusted by a committee composed of the shop chairman, a union representative, an employer representative, and an impartial arbitrator selected by mutual consent. Copies of these demands were immediately sent to all employers, many of whom were working with the Associated Apparel Manufacturers of Los Angeles in an effort to maintain the open shop and promptly began to discharge more workers because of their union activities. The mediation committee of the State Recovery Board held three meetings with representatives of both sides in an unsuccessful effort to prevent the walkout. By October 6 ILGWU officials in Los Angeles knew a general strike in the industry would be necessary if the dressmakers were to achieve their objectives.[30]

The union kept the date of the walkout secret, hoping thereby to prevent employers from taking countermeasures and to keep the Communists of the Needle Trades Industrial Union from interfering with the strike. The Central Labor Council sanctioned the strike and pledged support. At 5 A.M. on October 12 the walkout began. For the first time in Los Angeles history dressmakers were approached by pickets in front of the buildings before eight o'clock in the morning and asked to strike. The results were heartening to the ILGWU leaders, for by 11 A.M. the strike headquarters, a three-story building near the garment center, was crowded with women. In a few hours the 200 members of the organization committee had distributed, to unionists and nonunionists alike, more than 10,000 copies of the strike declaration printed in both English and Spanish, asking workers to proceed to union headquarters at 1108 South Los Angeles Street instead of to their jobs. On arrival at the headquarters, the strikers were registered and then organized into shop groups, each of which elected a chairman. Each striker was given an identification card and could thus obtain meals in the commissary, grocery bags, and a weekly cash benefit. Finally, picket lines were organized. By the end of the first day a large proportion of the dress industry had been shut down.[31]

The police arrived shortly after the strike was called, and under their protection a number of factories resumed operations with nonstrikers. Numerous demonstrations occurred during the walkout, and a large number of pickets were arrested. ILGWU leaders charged the police with deliberately placing strikers under arrest in the afternoon so that they could not have police court hearings until the next day, thus forcing the union to bail them out in order to prevent their staying in jail overnight. The disorders on the picket line were publicized in the *Times*, which also sought to minimize the impact of the walkout by quoting Captain Hynes of the Red Squad to the effect that only about sixty plants were affected by the strike, with 1,375 workers out "on the bricks" and 1,095 on the job.[32]

The local NRA office entered the controversy almost at its inception. Campbell McCulloch, executive secretary in Los Angeles for the State Recovery Board, brought representatives of both sides together on October 13, the second day of the strike. Garment manufacturers agreed to deal with union officials if shown that a majority of their employees were members of the ILGWU. McCulloch thereupon wired for permission from the National Labor Board to hold an election to determine the ratio of union to nonunion workers in the shops. Arthur Booth, executive secretary of the manufacturers' association, stated that the demand for union recognition was the only point of difference between the employers and the union, but the strike committee replied that this was only one of the demands, as 40 per cent of the girls and women in Los Angeles dress-manufacturing shops received less than $5 a week. It offered to produce hundreds of checks in amounts of $3 and $4 for a week's pay in support of this contention.

In the midst of these charges and countercharges, the cloakmakers signed an agreement with the Associated Apparel Manufacturers of Los Angeles which granted the union shop and all other demands, and withdrew from the dispute. They gave moral and financial support, however, to the dressmakers, who remained on strike. On October 15 McCulloch arranged a tentative, three-month compromise plan to end the walkout. Its provisions permitted the union to represent only its own members in grievance matters and allowed the manufacturers to obtain employees from the open market if a proposed union-operated placement bureau proved unable to fill requests for workers in a manner that was satisfactory to management. Both sides rejected the plan. Labor leaders were afraid that, if accepted, it would permit the manufacturers, who would have access to the open market, to discriminate against union members in employment. This would ultimately force unionists to accept unfavorable terms of employment.[33]

Meanwhile, the State Recovery Board appealed to Washington for instructions on further strike settlement procedure, supplementing a previous request of its Los Angeles regional office. On October 19 the Associated Apparel Manufacturers of Los Angeles appealed to President Roosevelt to authorize an election to determine whether or not the employees wanted a union to represent them in dealing with employers. The situation was growing more serious. Minor riots were occurring almost daily, with strikers hurling epithets at nonstrikers and the latter reciprocating with fists, sticks, or any other handy weapon. On October 20, for example, a total of fourteen clashes occurred between strikers and nonstrikers in the garment district.

This district contained the majority of the city's dressmaking establishments and was in an area bounded by Seventh Street on the north, Tenth Street on the south, Broadway on the west, and Maple Avenue on the east. The police sought to maintain peace, but the strikers threw tacks in the streets near the strike area, thus hampering the operation of police cars.

On October 21, NRA officials in Washington, noting the deteriorating situation, requested that the dispute be settled by arbitration before impartial parties. Two days later both sides agreed to this procedure, though the union would not call off its strike during arbitration proceedings unless the manufacturers closed their shops. As they would not do so, the strike continued. More police were assigned to the garment district, bringing the total on duty there to nearly 100. The size of this force did not deter strikers from blocking loft-shop entrances at Ninth and Broadway by mass picketing, but the end of the strike was in sight. On October 26 McCulloch announced that three persons had been approved by both sides for an arbitration panel, and by October 31 a board of five members was seated.[34]

Arbitration proceedings began on that date at the Los Angeles City Hall before the board, which consisted of Rabbi Isadore Isaacson of Hollywood, Father James F. Cunningham of West Los Angeles, Dr. J. L. Leonard of the University of Southern California, Campbell McCulloch, and Mrs. Frances Noel. Both sides agreed to abide by the results. The hearings lasted until November 4, the date the new NRA dress code was announced. In the course of the hearings Charles J. Katz, attorney for the Wool and Silk Dress Manufacturers' Association, stated that at least 1,339 employees of the forty-two manufacturers still affected by the strike were nonunion and represented a majority of the workers. He reiterated the employers' demand for an election to determine whether or not a majority of the workers were union members. Union representatives, in turn, described a whispering campaign conducted against the ILGWU by the employers, claimed that a black list was in existence, charged that workers were dismissed for union activity, and pointed to the meager earnings of many of the female strikers for long hours of work—a violation of both the state minimum wage and maximum hour laws for women. On Saturday, November 4, after hearing both sides, the board arrived at a temporary solution. It provided for the employers' acceptance of the wages and hours embodied in the dress code. Pending final decision by the arbitration board, the workers were to be returned to their jobs without prejudice with status as of October 12, 1933, and all picketing was to cease. Any disputes that arose were to be submitted to the board by a union representative and an employer agent, and any nonunion employee was to be permitted to have union officials represent him in a complaint.[35]

The strikers approved the truce by a vote of five to one on November 6, and most of them returned to work the next day. The union leaders did not find the terms entirely satisfactory, but they were afraid of adverse publicity if they did not accept them. As the truce had not been signed and there were no enforcing provisions, both employers and union leaders recognized that infractions would probably go unpunished. Unfortunately, when the strikers returned to their jobs, there was little work in the shops. Numerous grievances subsequently arose, among the most common of which were complaints that employers took advantage of the lack of work and refused to hire the more active union members, some manufacturers would not discharge workers hired during the strike, unionists refused to work beside nonunionists, and the work was not distributed equitably. By November 9 the unionists were considering another strike to effect compliance with the truce provisions, and about twenty small dress manufacturers were being picketed for failing to acknowledge the agreement. To complicate matters further, the Needle Trades Workers Industrial Union was distributing pamphlets to workers accusing the ILGWU leaders of "selling out" to the employers under an unsatisfactory truce arrangement. By November 16, however, nearly all picketing had ceased pending final settlement of the dispute by the arbitration board. A few disgruntled workers paraded before two shops on Los Angeles Street, but otherwise all was quiet. The trial of thirty-nine pickets arrested in the course of the strike for violating the city's ordinance regulating picketing had been postponed from November 7 to December 5. Union leaders continued to lodge complaints against manufacturers with NRA officials, charging noncompliance with the truce in rehiring strikers, but the employers countered by stating that there was insufficient work for all workers.[36]

Meanwhile a separate headquarters was set up for the newly organized dressmakers in a vacant warehouse. The unionists elected a nineteen-member executive board and, with the arrival of a charter, Local No. 96 of the ILGWU was established. After further conferences among representatives of the union, employers, and the arbitration board, a final award was announced on December 6, to be effective until August 1, 1934. Both sides agreed to abide by the decision, whose provisions were:

1. Strikers were to be reinstated on the basis of individual employment as it existed just before the walkout.

2. If additional workers were hired, preference was to be given to former employees who had been on the payroll since August 1, 1933.

3. Employers were to have the right to discharge employees without notice for insobriety, dishonesty, and willful neglect. Questions of competency were to be given a hearing. Complaints of workers concerning discharges were to be submitted within two working days of the termination of employment.

4. The scale of remuneration and the working-hour schedule were to be as provided in the national dress code, less 15 per cent in wages, until a final decision on pay for the Western area was embodied in the NRA agreement. This meant that the workweek would be thirty-five hours, with weekly wages varying from $14 to $45 and hourly from 50 to 90 cents, depending on trade and skill, less the 15 per cent Western differential.

5. Representatives of the cloak and dressmaker unions, Locals No. 65, 84, and 96, were to have access to all shops where members were employed in order to observe working conditions, provided that proper application was made to employers.

6. Disputes over wages, working conditions, wrongful discharge, or abandonment of employment were to be submitted initially to Father James F. Cunningham as impartial arbitrator. He agreed to serve in this capacity without compensation for no more than three months.

The agreement went into effect officially on December 28. About sixty firms signed it, but only forty-one were significantly affected by its terms. Although the provisions of the award were not entirely acceptable to either side, the strike had been costly and the trade volume needed to be increased. The new dressmakers' union, Local No. 96, launched a program that included educational and recreational activities for its members. Most of the trials of strikers arrested in the dispute took place in December, 1933. Twenty-three defendants received suspended $25 fines for violating the city's antipicketing ordinance. Seven others demanded and received a jury trial before Judge Clement D. Nye after he had dismissed charges of blocking the sidewalk which had been levied against them. The Reverend Wesley G. Nicholson, pastor of the Westwood Hills Congregational Church, was tried and acquitted of charges of picketing and blocking the sidewalk for a brief period in the strike. Two employers went on trial in January, 1934, on charges of attempting to bribe a police officer to intimidate strikers by beating them. Two strikers successfully appealed their convictions under the city's antipicketing law, as some of the alleged acts did not constitute a lawful foundation for a criminal prosecution. Aside from these legal activities, however, there were no further disputes in the ladies' garment industry for the period of the agreement.[37]

4. NEW LIFE FOR SOME UNIONS

The International Ladies' Garment Workers was not the only union to be given new incentive to engage in organizing activities after passage of the National Industrial Recovery Act. Other locals within and without the clothing industry followed the leadership of the Central Labor Council, seeking to gain new members and to sign contracts. Within the garment manufacturing industry, Local No. 278 of the Amalgamated Clothing Workers, under the leadership of Louis Stark and, a short time later, of Jack Blumberg, bestirred itself to participate in an aggressive organizing campaign. Stark had instituted a spread-the-work policy after 1929 and was able to form the union into a cohesive organization in the early depression years. Earnings were usually under $1 an hour, but unemployment was not a serious problem for a small local composed of expert workmen. During the NRA period of 1933 to 1935 it was able to participate in the national growth of the Amalgamated from 125,000 to 150,000 workers. In the fall of 1933 the leaders of Local No. 278 began to organize small manufacturing shops in the men's clothing field. Various employers, not desiring to be unionized, asked for police protection against union organizers and pickets.[38]

The only serious strike in late 1933 and early 1934 was against Kurtzman Brothers, which had signed a contract with Local No. 278 on September 2, 1933. Three months later Kurtzman Brothers repudiated the agreement and locked out members of the union. According to union leaders, the immediate cause of the strike was the management's desire to reduce wages 20 per cent below the prevailing scale. On December 3 Manager Jack Blumberg of Local No. 278 called out 860 workers at other plants in the city to support the 45 men involved in the Kurtzman dispute. The sympathetic strikers returned to work on December 8, but the Kurtzman employees remained out. Regional officials of the National Labor Board tried to settle the dispute, while the day-to-day picket line clashes belied descriptions of the strike as a "peaceful" walkout. On March 9, 1934, the board handed down a decision outlining settlement terms. Officers of the local were willing to submit the terms to arbitration, but the firm's management refused to accede in view of the union-shop demands of the Amalgamated.

On March 27, however, after almost seventeen weeks, the strike was settled. Blumberg and the company's representatives agreed on nearly all points, leaving the final decisions to Campbell McCulloch of the Regional Labor Board. In essence, the final settlement reinstated the agreement signed the preceding September, and Kurtzman Brothers continued as a union shop.[39]

Among other local groups active in 1933 were the culinary workers. They began a membership drive on March 1 as part of the nation-wide organizing campaign of the International Alliance of Hotel and Restaurant Employees and Bartenders International League of America. The legalization of the sale of beer in Los Angeles on April 7 gave impetus to the campaign as new restaurants and cafés opened to dispense the beverage, but the major part of the drive came in July and August after passage of the NIRA. During these months the culinary workers' unions in the city doubled in membership, mainly because Leighton's Restaurants, numbering ten establishments, signed contracts on August 29 with Waiters Union No. 17, Beverage Dispensers Union No. 284, Cooks Union No. 468, and Waitresses Union No. 639. Thus, by the stroke of a pen, approximately 300 workers were added to union rolls.[40]

On May 23, 1933, about forty cleaning and dyeing wholesale plants were struck by Cleaners and Dyers Union, Local No. 17954. Thirty plants were closed, and ten continued operations using nonunion employees. The immediate cause of the walkout was the attempt of the employers' association to establish a weekly wage of $15 for all cleaning and dyeing drivers, plus a 5 per cent commission on total trade above $100 each week. Union officials, contending that many employees received as little as $5 a week and worked up to sixteen hours a day, counterdemanded an eight-hour day, a five-day week, and minimum weekly wages of $18 to $40, depending on skill. On the request of Secretary Buzzell of the Central Labor Council, Mayor John C. Porter offered to arbitrate the dispute, but the employers stated that there was nothing at issue as they were replacing all employees who had walked out. The strike was adjusted by June 9, however, when union officials agreed with individual plant owners to accept the conditions prevailing before May 15, the date the wage cut for drivers was to go into effect. The settlement did not end the troubles of Local No. 17954, as Communists endeavored to organize the workers in the cleaning and dyeing industry in late 1933 and 1934. The issue of Communist infiltration in the Los Angeles local became sufficiently important to be brought to the attention of the 1934 AFL convention in the form of a resolution to investigate its extent and influence. Communist attempts to establish a new local in the trade, as well as to gain control of Local No. 17954, reduced the latter's membership and its influence in a highly competitive industry subject to periodic price wars, during which employers often tried to compensate for lowered revenues by salary reductions and long work hours.[41]

Like the cleaners and dyers, the Los Angeles Building and Construction Trades Council had a small membership and little control over employment in 1933 and early 1934. Little building was being undertaken in Los Angeles at this time, and, as the construction field was a chief market for steel, brick, wood, paint, and glass, the lack of activity therein was partly responsible for unemployment among workers in the latter industries. In addition, the influx of unemployed building craftsmen into Los Angeles in the early years of the depression increased the problems of the construction unions. Many an unemployed individual had a knowledge of one or more of the skills of a building craftsman and was willing to work long hours at low wages in competition with union men for the little work available. Even union members often hid their identification cards and buttons in order to get work at any wage.

Where union wage rates did prevail, they varied considerably by trade. They were based on a workday of eight hours with time and a half for overtime or for work on Sunday or seven enumerated holidays. Although overtime was discouraged as part of a spread-the-work philosophy, it was permitted by union contract under extraordinary conditions. Daily wage rates varied from $4.50 for a truck driver to $12 for a sprinkler fitter foreman. Carpenters were paid $10 for an eight-hour day and worked a thirty-two-hour week. The state prevailing wage law of 1931 was of assistance to building craftsmen in Los Angeles at this time in maintaining reasonable wage scales in public employment, as labor leaders were able to convince the public authorities of the wisdom of paying wages based on union rather than nonunion prevailing wage rates. The Los Angeles County Board of Supervisors and a few other public agencies, which were doing nearly all the building in the city and vicinity, were abiding by the law.[42]

In the fall of 1933 an effort was made to organize an independent carpenters' union outside the jurisdiction of the Los Angeles Building and Construction Trades Council. R. C. Cramer, alleged nonunion carpenter, contractor, and foreman, held an organizational meeting on October 10, 1933, at Polytechnic High School, but union members, learning in advance of these plans, packed the auditorium and gained control of the conference. Cramer was forced to relinquish the chair to several carpenter union business agents, who then took the remaining time to discuss the merits of "bona fide unionism" under the AFL as a means of taking advantage of the right to organize and bargain collectively granted by Section 7(a). Although union leaders called Cramer's effort a phase of the employers' campaign to maintain the open shop, a more basic reason was the policy of the national government to call on unions for skilled craftsmen to work on public projects. Carpenters not affiliated with the AFL believed that they could get a larger share of this work if an independent union was organized in the city.[43]

The meat-packing industry evidenced more activity after the NIRA went into effect than did the construction trades. An organizing drive initiated by the Amalgamated Meat Cutters and Butcher Workmen of North America in January, 1933, gained impetus soon after passage of the recovery legislation in June. In late July the two unions involved, Abattoir Workers Local No. 244 (packinghouse employees) and Meat Cutters Local No. 421 (butchers in wholesale and retail markets) reported gains of more than 800 new members in the previous sixty days. By October it was estimated that Local No. 421 had 1,200 members, while Local No. 244 had nearly 1,000. On October 27 international organizer George J. Hobart called out Local No. 244 in a strike against the Wilson Packing Company. The strike vote had been taken at a regular meeting of the union the preceding evening, and had been reported to company officials by a spy. About 130 Wilson employees allegedly were union members, although approximately 450 walked out. Union officials ascribed the strike to the firm's refusal to allow plant workers to choose their own representatives for the local meat-packing code hearings.[44]

On October 28 the Los Angeles NRA Compliance Board conducted a vote of Wilson workers to determine their spokesman in negotiations with company officials. A. E. Peterson, plant manager, refused to recognize the results of the balloting, however, as he claimed the company had no notification of the procedure. He therefore proceeded to hire strikebreakers, most of whom came from an employment office established before the walkout by the Merchants' and Manufacturers' Association. Although pickets were placed about the plant the first day of the strike, they made no effort to interfere with the movements of strikebreakers in and out of the premises for a few days. When union leaders saw that the Compliance Board officials would not be able to settle the walkout, they held an election on November 9; the vote favored a general strike against the seventeen larger plants in the Los Angeles meat-packing industry. All packing plant operators were given an opportunity to sign the state and national recovery codes, as well as union agreements providing for recognition of Local No. 244 as collective bargaining agent for their employees, before a partial walkout in a number of plants was ordered on November 17. H. B. Newcomb, manager of the southern branch of the Institute of American Meat Packers, described the strike as relatively ineffective, as less than 200 men were off their jobs, all Los Angeles plants were operating on a normal basis, and only two or three small concerns were being picketed. But George Hobart of the union claimed that between 600 and 700 workers were on strike, with all but two Vernon plants affected by the walkout.[45]

About three weeks after the strike was called, the men out of jobs and on the picket lines began to get restless, and violence soon developed when attempts were made to detain delivery trucks. In one instance an effort was made to throw oil on a load of meat near the Cudahy plant. Twice it was reported that bricks were thrown through the windows of the homes of nonstriking employees. Union officials denied that strikers had participated in these activities, stating that they had warned union members not to encourage disturbances, but the violence continued. Police arrested eighteen persons for throwing light globes filled with kerosene into a meat company truck in Alhambra. Similar acts were reported in Long Beach, Huntington Park, and Wilmington. Management officials took precautions in the face of these disturbances. Tear gas was purchased although it was not used, and armed guards were placed on all meat delivery trucks. Strikebreakers continued to be hired and operations within the plants began to assume a more normal schedule, though picketing was maintained in front of the seventeen struck firms.

Meanwhile, the Los Angeles NRA Compliance Board was replaced by the newly organized Regional Labor Board. The latter called representatives of both sides together for a peace conference on November 24. As a result of the conference Local No. 244 called off the strike on November 29, and the men were told to apply for their old positions, the packers agreeing to reëmploy them as rapidly as possible. The companies concerned had, in the interim, signed the NRA codes and both sides had agreed to abide by the decision of the Regional Labor Board. The hearings conducted by the board were marked by charges and countercharges. Officials of the packing companies stated that they were abiding by the codes; union leaders denied this. The latter also said that strikers were not being rehired, and that the companies were refusing to deal collectively with their employees and were cutting wages. Because of the conflicting testimony and the refusal of both sides to compromise the issues, the Regional Labor Board was unable to arrive at an agreement that was satisfactory and workable. The packing plants were thus able to continue to operate as open shops, for the union lacked strength to resume the strike.[46]

Like the unionists in the meat-packing industry, the upholsterers were encouraged by the NIRA to launch an organizing drive in June, 1933. Members of Local No. 15 started the campaign by picketing the Universal Furniture Manufacturing Company for several days, but they failed to gain recognition of the union. On June 13, therefore, as a demonstration of strength, a one-day holiday was called in all union shops. The men returned to work the following day, except in one plant where forty men remained out. Coincident with the demonstration, employers were asked to consider demands for a minimum wage of 75 cents an hour and a forty-hour week. Hourly wages at this time ranged from 20 to 80 cents and work was so scarce that many employees had only fifteen to twenty hours of employment each week. Organizing activities continued throughout the summer, and in October a strike of about 850 workers was threatened unless wages were increased and the union was recognized. When employers compromised with the union, the strike did not take place.

Officials of Local No. 15 claimed that nearly all upholstering shops in the city were 100 per cent union with respect to their upholsterers and seamstresses. But because unemployment was high, wages were low, and hours were short, the union had less bargaining strength than might have been expected. Furthermore, it was hampered by jurisdictional disputes with the Furniture Workers Industrial Union, an affiliate of the Communist-dominated Trade Union Unity League. Thus, though there was an upsurge in the activities of Local No. 15, it did not establish a bargaining position strong enough to force Los Angeles employers in the upholstering field to consider it a major factor in labor relations.[47]

The teamsters had more success under the impetus of the NIRA than did the upholsterers. Two of their locals were active in metropolitan Los Angeles in early 1933. Local No. 208, consisting of miscellaneous truck drivers, was the oldest teamster union in the city. Local No. 521, composed principally of milk wagon drivers, had been formed on May 1, 1931. Both groups initiated organizing campaigns after passage of the act. Previous to that time the employers of the milk wagon drivers had opposed their union by discharging its leaders whenever they were found at work in any of the large dairies. After the NIRA became effective, the union men discovered that employers were suspending their leaders on petty traffic violations instead of firing them. International organizer W. J. Conboy of the teamsters was sent to Los Angeles and remained for some time, principally to help the milk wagon drivers overcome employer opposition. In spite of Conboy's presence, however, Local No. 521 failed to add many new members and the dairy industry remained open shop until 1938.[48]

Lack of success in organizing the milk wagon drivers did not deter the teamsters from moving in other directions. A new local, Ice Wagon Drivers No. 326, was established after passage of the NIRA when some employers, particularly the Union Ice Company, attempted to support company-dominated unions. As part of its organizing campaign, Local No. 326 placed appeals in the *Citizen* asking unionists to insist that their icemen carry a union card. The intensity of the membership drive evoked criticism from the *Times,* which accused unionists of using threats to frighten icemen into joining the local and paying dues. A new local of laundry drivers was established at about the same time. Designated as Local No. 322, it became one of the city's larger unions, claiming more than 500 members by September, 1933, three months after its establishment. This represented the peak of its power, for the open-shop laundry employers quickly regained the initiative and, as a consequence, the union was relatively weak during the rest of the decade. To obtain better coördination between these two new unions of icemen and laundry drivers, as well as Bakery Salesmen Local No. 276, and the older locals, organizer Conboy established Joint Council of Teamsters No. 42 in the fall of 1933. By January, 1934, most of the teamster locals in the Los Angeles area were affiliated with it.[49]

Like the teamsters, the two unions in the baking industry, Locals No. 37 and 453, began membership campaigns in July, 1933. Officials of Local No. 37 were especially aggressive and sent a suggested code of fair competition covering the Los Angeles baking industry to the NRA headquarters in Washington. By the end of November this local had more than 300 new members, as well as 100 more signed applications awaiting union action. In December its officers persuaded the leaders of one of the new teamster unions, Bakery Salesmen Local No. 276, to join it in demanding a change in working hours and wages in several bakeries, under threat of a strike. They reported that a number of nonunion plants kept their men working twelve to sixteen hours each day under adverse working conditions and low wages. McCulloch of the Regional Labor Board intervened, however, and had the strike indefinitely postponed.[50]

Local 453, consisting of Jewish bakers, was probably the first union in Los Angeles to force a firm to lose its NRA emblem or "blue eagle." In July, 1933, this union entered into an agreement on wages, hours, and working conditions with the Heirshberg Rye Bakery, which supported the NRA and displayed the official emblem with the words "We Do Our Part." A few days after signing the agreement, however, Heirshberg suddenly notified William Gewirtz, business representative of Local No. 453, that he would no longer comply with the union contract. Members of the union walked out on strike, but Heirshberg continued to operate his business and display the blue eagle, notifying his customers that he was abiding by the spirit of the act. Officials of Local No. 453, unable to negotiate with Heirshberg, appealed to the local Compliance Board which, upon investigation, validated their complaint and sent it to Washington. After months had passed and further investigations had taken place, a telegram arrived from Washington on February 2, 1934, ordering the removal of the NRA emblem. Local No. 453 continued its drive against the bakery by urging customers to cease patronizing it. The boycott was sufficiently effective to cause the bakery to move to another location, where it signed an agreement with Local No. 453 on December 14, 1934.[51]

A number of other locals were likewise aroused to increased activity by the more favorable organizing atmosphere created by the administration of President Roosevelt and the NIRA. In mid-1933 the Communist-dominated Needle Trades Workers Industrial Union participated in a strike against Golden Brothers Millinery Manufacturing Company. In September Local No. 48 of the United Hatters, Cap and Millinery Workers was organized out of the remnants of a union that had become inactive in the 1920's. In the same month hosiery workers at the Mission Hosiery Mills struck and secured a working agreement. Other strikes took place at several leather goods manufacturing plants, a fur shop, and a cigar store. The Bill Posters Union threatened a strike against Foster and Kleiser, an outdoor advertising concern in Los Angeles, but the dispute was settled.

These and other activities all indicated that life was stirring in Los Angeles unions. President A. W. Hoch of the California State Federation of Labor announced in October, 1933, that trade-union membership was increasing very rapidly in Los Angeles. He called attention to recent editorials in the *Times* which had expressed apprehension concerning the future of the open shop in the city. These alone were evidence to organized labor that the NIRA was a substantial aid in revivifying the cause of unionism in the open-shop citadel. By the end of 1933 Los Angeles labor leaders were jubilantly proclaiming the rapid expansion of the local movement, which then had 13 departmental councils, 152 locals, 14 women's auxiliaries, and an estimated total membership of 70,000. Officials of the Central Labor Council claimed that 106 unions with an estimated membership of 60,000 were affiliated with the central body. They had pointed out in the middle of October that 30 new charters had been issued since July 1 and that 15 more were pending. Undoubtedly the total membership figures were somewhat exaggerated. The true paid-up membership was probably closer to 30,000, but labor leaders in Los Angeles could hardly be blamed for indulging in some exaggerations at the close of 1933. For the first time in nearly a decade and a half, prospects for victory over the open shop looked reasonably good, but subsequent months were to reveal that it was not to come so quickly as anticipated.[52]

VIII. THE BLUE EAGLE, 1933–1935

1. And Still Depression Everywhere

THE TWO YEARS of the National Recovery Administration did not witness the end of the depression that covered the land. Upon the termination of the Civil Works Administration in the early part of 1935, the state governments, including that of California, coöperated with the Federal Emergency Relief Administration in the establishment of a program that completed many of the projects left unfinished. The new program gave jobs only to those on relief, but direct assistance continued to be extended to persons not employed on projects. "At one time during the winter of 1934–1935 almost three million people were being taken care of through the federal extension of direct relief, and over two million others were provided for through general relief." [1] As FERA grants would certainly be exhausted by mid-1935, Congress passed the Emergency Relief Appropriation Act, and President Roosevelt signed it on April 8. It provided for the disbursement of $4,880,-000,000 and the establishment of the Works Progress Administration to create jobs for the unemployed. Other relief organizations were continued under the auspices of the national government in 1934 and 1935, including the Civilian Conservation Corps. In 1934 a total of $173,800,000 was paid in wages by the CCC, a share of which was placed in circulation in southern California trade channels through the medium of the men in the forest camps of the area. On August 14, 1935, President Roosevelt approved the Social Security Act, which provided for old-age assistance, unemployment compensation, maternal and child welfare, and aid to the blind. The unemployment insurance provisions of the law were of particular interest to workers, organized and unorganized, even though they were applicable to the future rather than to the 1930's. [2]

In California, 1934 and 1935 were years of tension between labor leaders and employers. A contemporary writer described the situation in colorful terms:

If ever a revolution was due, it was due in California. Nowhere else has the battle between labor and capital been so widespread and bitter, and the casualties so large; nowhere else has there been such a flagrant denial of the personal liberties guaranteed by the Bill of Rights; nowhere else has authority been so lawless and brazen; nowhere else has the brute force of capitalism been so openly used and displayed; nowhere else has labor been so oppressed; nowhere has there been a falser or more poisoned and poisoning press. It was time for some sign of rebellion. But the final victory is not yet won. [3]

The San Francisco general strike in mid-1934 released some of the tensions that had accumulated in the state during the early depression years. They were due to various factors: the growing labor unrest common to the whole country; California's peculiar large-scale farming system and migratory labor force; the increasing response to the political campaign of Upton Sinclair and the appeals of certain utopian groups; the alleged intensification of Communist propaganda, which was vigorously opposed by the Hearst press, the American Legion, and various employer groups; and the continuing influx of people into California. The strains were evident in the agricultural valleys of the state in the fall of 1934. Fruit growers and other farmers feared low prices and the prospect of having to sell their crops for less than the cost of raising them. This fear was reflected in their bitter opposition to the increasing number of strikes for higher wages, and led to bloodshed, criminal syndicalism trials, and anti-Communist hysteria. The agricultural workers, many of whom were from cities or drought-stricken areas, needed only effective leaders to encourage them to rebel against their poverty.[4]

The 1934 campaign of Upton Sinclair for the governorship of California on the Democratic ticket was another sign of the times. Sinclair advocated a "production-for-use" plan to support the unemployed. The scheme was designed for the entire nation, but Sinclair hoped to apply it to California in order to prove its validity. Its basic tenet was to put the unemployed to work for themselves. Through state-owned exchanges the products of their labor would be so distributed as to support them, thereby taking them off public relief rolls. Under the popular title of EPIC, which officially meant "End Poverty in California," Sinclair's plan and political campaign appealed to California's restless, insecure, unemployed population because he offered a program to relieve their poverty. His humanitarianism and his vision for the solution of the problem of unemployment won him the backing of many labor leaders in the state, including the political endorsement of the California State Federation of Labor. With this and other support Sinclair swept the primary election of August 28, 1934, winning the Democratic nomination. He was opposed in the final election by Frank F. Merriam, the incumbent Republican governor. Sinclair was defeated in November, after a bitterly fought campaign, but his followers supported the production-for-use principle for a number of years. Political adherents of the plan attained various state offices in subsequent elections, and production-for-use clubs survived until the final years of the decade.[5]

Los Angeles reflected the labor unrest of the state at this time. It was estimated that one out of four residents needed some form of public or private relief from economic distress in 1934. Periodic appeals for parade permits to hold "hunger marches" were denied by city authorities, who believed they were Communist-inspired. The open-shop question invaded the area of relief for the hungry when a dispute centering on this issue arose early in 1934 in connection with the Civil Works Administration program. Officials of the Central Labor Council accused the Merchants' and Manufacturers' Association, the Chamber of Commerce, and the Associated General Contractors of bringing influence to bear upon the local citizens' group named to handle the CWA program in the city. This influence, they declared, was resulting in the arbitrary establishment of wage scales and discrimination against union members in hiring on federal projects. Telegrams and letters demanding an investigation were sent by various unions to officials in Washington. When the leadership of the local CWA offices was changed several weeks later, labor officials claimed the credit. Army officers replaced the civilian officials. An investigation by a federal grand jury also was initiated in order to verify reports of discrimination against union members. Finally, in February, 1934, Secretary of the Interior Harold L. Ickes and CWA Director Harry L. Hopkins issued instructions that there was to be no discrimination against workers because of their economic views or union affiliation.[6]

The self-help coöperatives organized among the unemployed workers of the Los Angeles area in 1932 and 1933 continued to be of assistance during the next two years, supplementing the aid received from federal sources. By December, 1934, Los Angeles County contained nearly 45 per cent of all the self-help units in the United States, which undoubtedly reflected the severe economic distress of many of the residents or recent migrants to the area. It was estimated that at the height of the movement in Los Angeles County about 75,000 workers' families received up to 50 or even 75 per cent of a minimum food budget through this system.[7]

Radical activities among the unemployed as well as those with jobs were a source of irritation in the community. The Trade Union Unity League, an arm of the Communist Party, took advantage of the unrest caused by the depression to try to organize a number of firms, including the General Cable Corporation, then under contract to supply the cable for the Hoover Dam power line. Chief of Police Davis, through the Red Squad under Captain Hynes, endeavored to control these radical activities. Not only was the Red Squad present at all strikes, but an elaborate spy system was put into operation and means were contrived for police representatives to attend meetings and conferences of designated radical groups as well as of AFL unions. Union leaders accused the Red Squad of being so zealous in arresting strikers that AFL pickets were frequently jailed as radicals. Secretary Buzzell of the Central Labor Council protested to Mayor Shaw, and a formal request was made for abolition of the Red Squad, but to no avail. A subsequent protest to the grand jury was rejected on the ground that this body did not have jurisdiction over the Los Angeles Police Department.[8]

2. POLITICS AND ORGANIZING PRESSURE

The Los Angeles Central Labor Council, as in previous years, continued its political efforts in order to offset any influence that open-shop partisans might have on city and county government officials. In municipal affairs one of the items of greatest concern to labor leaders in 1934 was the school bond issue. In March, 1933, an earthquake had wreaked considerable havoc on many poorly constructed school buildings in the city. To secure funds for reconstruction, a $20 million bond issue was proposed for a vote on March 20, 1934. The Board of Education long had been accused by labor officials of letting contracts for school construction to contractors who discriminated against union labor and paid less than prevailing union wage scales. Early in 1934, therefore, committees from the Central Labor Council called upon the Board of Education to request that a union clause be inserted in all contracts for the reconstruction projects to be undertaken if the bond issue passed. The request was backed by a threat that, if union labor was not given preference, organized workers in Los Angeles would vote against the proposition. Open-shop advocates countered that preference for unionists on construction projects was unfair and illegal, because nonunion as well as union men had children in school. After hearing both sides and the advice of legal counsel, the Board of Education passed a resolution against a union clause, taking what labor leaders chose to call an open-shop stand.[9]

The Joint Executive Board of the organized labor movement, representing the Metal Trades, Building Trades, Printing Trades, and Central Labor councils, immediately recommended that the bond issue be opposed. It publicly declared that union members would not permit the M and M or the open-shop Associated General Contractors to violate the rules of the Public Works Administration, which prohibited discrimination against any workman because of race, creed, or economic group affiliation. The Board of Education had announced previously that it would ask the PWA for $31 million if the bond issue passed, and hence its rules would govern the construction. Violation of PWA rules was not the real issue, however, for the basic aim of Central Labor Council officials was a union-shop or closed-shop clause in all construction contracts. The Board of Education refused to grant this clause as it, too, would have been a violation of PWA rules. The board pointed out that all construction contracts would provide for wages commensurate with union scales, a thirty-hour week except in an emergency, and, whenever possible, employment of workmen residing within the Los Angeles school district. The bond issue was supported by a number of organizations that favored the open shop, including the M and M, the *Times,* the Chamber of Commerce, and the Associated General Contractors. This support was not enough, however; the bonds failed to win the required two-thirds majority at the March 20 election, though they did receive a preponderance of the votes cast. As might be expected, unionists claimed much of the credit for the defeat.[10]

Later in the year union members were asked to support the recall of three members of the Board of Education at a special September election. These three, William E. Beaudry, Arthur W. Eckman, and Letitia J. Lytle, were alleged to be affiliated with the open-shop political machine which, according to labor officials, had controlled the board for nearly thirty years. Three union members were nominated as candidates to oppose them: J. W. Buzzell, secretary of the Central Labor Council; C. B. Hamner, member of Mailers Local No. 9; and Ralph McMullen, business representative of Plumbers Local No. 78. When election day arrived, organized labor did not get out the vote. Less than 30 per cent of the registered voters cast ballots, and the recall did not succeed.[11]

In 1935 the Joint Executive Board approved a full slate of candidates for the April city primaries. Although all those endorsed did not win, a majority were able to enter the final election in May. The victory at that time of John F. Dalton, head of International Typographical Union No. 174 and former president of the California State Federation of Labor, in his campaign for the Board of Education was heralded by labor leaders as a political achievement. It was the first time in the city's history that a union man had been elected to the board, which was one of the largest employers in the area and long accused by organized labor of paying less than union wages in the building trades. A few months later union members were asked by their leaders to support three bond issues to be presented at the polls the following November.

One of these was for the school rebuilding program that had been rejected the previous year. This time organized labor supported the bonds, believing that Dalton would try to ensure the payment of prevailing union wages in employment that was badly needed by unionists in the building trades. The bond issue passed and labor again rejoiced in its political success.[12]

Another victory was gained in 1935 when, for the first time in many years, a union man was chosen to serve on the Los Angeles County Grand Jury. Labor leaders had long suspected, although they could not prove, that open-shop supporters had tried to prevent the selection of unionists as members of that body. Hence the appointment of Oliver E. Burns, president of Electrotypers Union No. 137, was considered another political achievement. Other gains included the reëlection of A. W. Hoch, former president of the Central Labor Council, for four terms president of the California State Federation of Labor, and a member of Machinists Local No. 311, as vice-president of the Board of Public Works, and Luther S. McGahan of ITU No. 174 as president of the City Health Commission. Labor officials thus believed they were again securing spokesmen on their behalf in city political circles, as they had just before and during World War I.[13] Even executives of the State Relief Administration indirectly aided local unionists when they ruled that a "member of an established Trade Union will not be separated from the rolls if he declines to accept work at a rate of pay the acceptance of which would subject him to loss of his Union membership." [14]

Although "the goose was hanging high" for organized labor in political affairs during 1934 and 1935, the same could not be said with respect to union activities in general. Cracks in the optimism that prevailed in labor's ranks during the first six months after passage of the NIRA began to appear in late 1933 and early January, 1934. One reason was the lack of preparation among AFL locals in Los Angeles for the unexpectedly heavy demands of workers to join unions, but the intensified efforts of the M and M to maintain the open shop also were significant. Edgar R. Perry, dynamic manager of the M and M, kept reiterating his organization's interpretation of the NIRA in speeches before public groups and through the medium of the *Times*. This theme basically was that the act was not inconsistent with the open shop, as labor representation under Section 7(a) did not have to come through outside unions, and that such representation actually was hindering the NRA. Perry also pointed out that the Regional Labor Board, established in Los Angeles in the fall of 1933, had no authority to order elections but, rather, that this was a matter of employee privilege on request.[15]

Labor leaders in Los Angeles were aware as early as November, 1933, of the adverse effect on union membership of the open-shop campaign, though the initial gains of the organizing drive were retained. The Industrial Recovery Act Committee reported a lag in the response to their appeals for increased union membership. At the Central Labor Council meeting of December 1, the delegates noted that the Regional Labor Board was not able to enforce its decisions and that local NRA compliance agencies were often ignored by employers summoned before them for code violations. By the middle of December the *Citizen* reported that many of the largest firms in the city were openly ignoring union efforts to secure collective bargaining representation through Labor Board elections. The council received reports every day that employers who originally had made no objection when their employees joined outside unions were now demoting, laying off, discharging, and otherwise discriminating against AFL union members.[16] "Candor compels the admission they have made much headway, but it is possible it will be only temporary."[17] The *Citizen* further noted that the impetus given to the Los Angeles labor movement by the Recovery Act had stimulated the M and M to increased activity. This was in contrast with its previous decline in influence during the early depression years, when organized labor was weaker and little effort against closed or union shops was necessary.

At the Central Labor Council meeting of December 15, 1933, no additional unions were affiliated for the first time in many months. Secretary Buzzell reported that the M and M was encouraging employers to establish complete rosters of union members, with the evident intent of black-listing them. The council therefore called a meeting of business agents of all Los Angeles locals to lay plans to offset these open-shop activities. In an effort to get favorable publicity, a joint conference of the Methodist ministerial association, several citizens' groups, and representatives of the Labor Council was held at the First Unitarian Church on December 16. Leaders of the conference were Dr. E. P. Ryland and the Reverend A. A. Heist. Both were prounion Methodist ministers, and Ryland was a former delegate to the Central Labor Council from the Ministerial Alliance. Ryland was made the head of a committee that sponsored several additional meetings to bring before the general public the viewpoints of labor leaders concerning application of the provisions of Section 7(a).[18]

By the new year, labor spokesmen in Los Angeles had definitely concluded that the national government through the NRA was not going to be of much assistance in the effort to eliminate the open shop. But, determined to continue the campaign, they held a mass meeting in the Labor Temple on March 1, 1934, under Central Labor Council auspices, as the first step in a scheme to revive the membership campaign in Los Angeles. It was claimed that about 6,000 persons were present in the halls of the Temple and in the street outside. Union members were urged to sign cards pledging their full support of the new campaign. At the conclusion of the meeting the audience stood and took this oath:

Believing that there is nothing in this world that is so important as the rights of Labor, and with the full understanding that Labor will not accomplish its place in the world until it becomes fully organized, I, (insert name), solemnly promise that I will dedicate myself to the task of bringing into the fold of the American Federation of Labor and its International Unions, every worker with whom I come in contact.

That I will never let a day go by without doing something to make the Labor movement in Los Angeles stronger and better. That I will help to put over the program of the Labor movement in this city, and I will not cease my efforts until Los Angeles becomes a union city. I so dedicate myself to this work and give my word of honor to carry it through to the end.[19]

The regular gathering of the Central Labor Council on the following night, March 2, did not retain the enthusiasm of the mass meeting, as many of the delegates were unable to attend two meetings in succession. On March 15 an assemblage of members of union women's auxiliaries and women unionists was held in the Labor Temple for the purpose of gaining their support, but the attendance was smaller than had been anticipated. In the meantime, nine committees of nine members each, as authorized by the March 1 mass meeting, started the organizing drive. These eighty-one unionists represented the total number of paid officers in the AFL movement in Los Angeles at this time. A proposal to raise the per capita tax to the council from 5 to 20 cents in order to ensure that each paid-up unionist would receive the *Citizen* was rejected by the members of the locals affiliated with the council.

The organizing campaign was successful only in holding the membership gains of the previous year. Some new unions were established in 1934, but the total paid-up membership of all locals affiliated with the AFL in Los Angeles probably did not exceed 30,000 in this year, or at any time under the NIRA. Not until 1937 and 1938 were local labor officials able to initiate so successful an organizing campaign as that of the first few months under the act. At the end of 1934 the Los

Angeles labor movement as a whole comprised thirteen departmental councils and approximately 171 locals. The total membership of the city's unions was estimated to be about 70,000, the same as in December, 1933, but it seemed closer to 40,000 in terms of paid-up unionists, including organizations not affiliated with the AFL.[20]

The maintenance of a larger paid-up membership in the Central Labor Council in fiscal 1933–34 enabled its officials to pay all its expenses as well as pay back money loaned by the Union Labor Temple Association early in 1933. Although no new staff members were added to the council in 1934, full salary payments were made to those already on the payroll. In contrast, the *Citizen* continued to need a financial transfusion because of the defeat of the per capita tax proposal. If the tax had been increased from 5 to 20 cents, not only would each unionist have received a paid subscription, but the paper would have been more secure with a larger circulation. As it was, the small subscription list and the loss of advertising patronage in the depression kept the *Citizen* on a minimum survival basis.[21]

Bare survival was not enough, however, in the opinion of the Central Labor Council, for local unionists who were forced to accept relief through the federal Works Progress Administration, established after passage of the Emergency Relief Appropriation Act in 1935. Using the California prevailing wage law of 1931 as a basis of argument, council officials tried to obtain union rates for all skilled workmen employed on WPA projects, instead of the subsistence wage contemplated by the national government. They believed that if rates were lowered, open-shop employers in Los Angeles would reduce wages in the building trades as well as in other industries. They failed with the Los Angeles City Council, but succeeded with the Los Angeles County Board of Supervisors for WPA jobs in unincorporated county areas. The failure with respect to municipal projects was reported to officials of the California State Federation of Labor, who had been receiving similar complaints from other areas. At its annual convention, the federation passed a resolution that members of California labor organizations would henceforth refuse to work on WPA projects requiring skilled labor unless prevailing union wages were paid.[22]

Meanwhile, officials in Washington took the position that the California prevailing wage law did not apply to the WPA, a federal agency. Yet local labor leaders continued to meet with county WPA authorities in an effort to reduce the number of hours worked in a given period with no decrease in the total wages paid. Similar conferences were held elsewhere in the nation, and persistence finally brought victory when the WPA authorized state directors to reduce hours worked without changing the total wages paid to an individual. On December 18, 1935, Frank Y. McLaughlin, WPA director in California, issued the following order:

> 1. The state administrator has been authorized to permit a reduction in working hours and an adjustment of earnings for skilled and semi-skilled workers on construction projects, including construction laborers, so as to result in the payment of wages equivalent approximately to local prevailing hourly wages in any locality. The total number of persons thus exempted from the standard schedule of monthly hours and earnings cannot exceed 10 per cent of the total number of workers employed on projects in the state, but may exceed 10 per cent of the number of persons employed in any locality and/or an individual project.
>
> 2. The provisions of this order shall apply only to those skilled and semi-skilled trades, including building construction laborers, for which a prevailing wage scale has been well established.[23]

Local labor leaders rejoiced. Not only would the order help to maintain union wages in the building trades, but the national government had set an example which they believed would discourage the payment of open-shop wage rates in all industries.

Because these and other activities necessitated frequent conferences, the Central Labor Council began, on February 1, 1935, to meet weekly instead of twice a month, as it had in the depression years. Renewed activity under the NRA and the consequent expansion of membership also necessitated the assignment of another AFL organizer to the Los Angeles area in 1935, and developed an interest in seeking further publicity outlets. A proposal to establish a radio station to be known as KCLC, the "Voice of Labor," was presented to the council on March 22, 1935. It seemed to be a "heads I win, tails you lose" proposition for the Central Labor Council, which would not be required to cover any erection or operation costs, but only assist in securing a permit for KCLC from the Federal Communications Commission. If the permit was obtained, officials of Los Angeles unions would be given a certain amount of broadcasting time each day to acquaint the listening public with the aims and activities of their organizations.[24]

The offer had been made by one Abe Corenson, who was organizing the station and had filed an application with the FCC under the name of the Metro Broadcasting Company. Corenson apparently wanted to establish the station as a business venture, and desired the support of the local labor movement in order to justify the existence of a new radio station in the city. Public officials and labor leaders were asked to write to Anning S. Prall, chairman of the FCC, to urge favorable consideration of the application, and individual unionists were asked to send postcards. The campaign was supported by such influential persons as Senator Hiram Johnson of California and numerous judges in city and county courts. The Central Labor Council also heard that congressmen, senators, central councils, local unions, and international union officials in different parts of the country had all written to the FCC in favor of the radio station. Nevertheless, the application was rejected when examiner Ralph C. Walker reported that there were inadequacies in the financial statements of Abe Corenson and the Metro Broadcasting Company, and that a large number of stations were already operating in the Los Angeles area.[25]

Labor spokesmen in the city, claiming that antiunion interests had influenced the FCC, again urged union members and persons high in political office to write to Washington and request a rehearing. Delegates to the AFL, California State Federation of Labor, and California State Building Trades Department conventions in 1935 passed resolutions in favor of a new hearing, which was subsequently granted. Examiner P. W. Seward, who made the second investigation, also recommended denial of the application on substantially the same grounds as before. An appeal was then made directly to Prall, and Secretary Buzzell accompanied Corenson to Washington for a hearing before the commission on February 6, 1936. They were informed that the FCC felt that representatives of the labor movement in Los Angeles, rather than Corenson, should apply for the permit and assume the responsibility for operation of the radio station. The commission seemed convinced that the application was more a matter of Corenson's desire to set up a radio station for profit rather than to serve organized labor by providing a publicity medium.[26]

After the Washington hearing, in an effort to meet the FCC objections, title to the application passed to the Central Labor Council through a voting trust agreement entitled "Voice of Labor Stations, Inc." The officers of the trust were Harry Sherman, J. W. Buzzell, and Abe Corenson. Sherman was president of the council as well as of the new trust. A final hearing was held before the FCC on June 23, 1936, but no positive action satisfactory to organized labor was taken and the application never became effective. The unions in Los Angeles did not have the funds to operate a station and therefore needed Corenson's capital. The commission did not consider Corenson legally, financially, or technically competent for such a venture, but he was not willing to relinquish ownership of his funds to the officers of the Central Labor Council in order to obtain approval for the new station. A short time later he gained control of XEBG in Mexico and gave the council some broadcasting time from 10:30 to 11 P.M. daily, beginning on November 11, 1936, as token payment for its coöperation in the unsuccessful KCLC affair.[27]

3. NEW LIFE FOR OLD UNIONS

Like the Central Labor Council, individual unions were encouraged by the favorable atmosphere created by the Recovery Act to continue their efforts during 1934 and 1935. Even though the "honeymoon period" of the first six months of organizing activity under the law was over, the spirit of new life remained in many of the unions in Los Angeles and carried them forward for the next two years. Specific evidences of vitality were especially noticeable in the clothing trades, but other unions also participated in the upsurge of organizing activity.

In mid-1934, in continuation of their aggressive tactics, Los Angeles Locals No. 65, 84, and 96 of the International Ladies' Garment Workers Union initiated an organizing drive which led to the formation of a new union of pressers, Local No. 97, and a new agreement for its members. A special effort was also made to organize all the 7,000 employees of the dress-manufacturing industry in the city. In June, when a measure of success was achieved, the ILGWU leaders demanded a forty-hour week and a minimum wage of $18.50 for cotton dress workers. They claimed that wages were as low as $3 for forty-eight hours and that homework brought the weekly total up to sixty and seventy hours. An extension of the contract for silk and wool dress workers beyond August 1 also was requested, with a strike threatened on that date if it was not granted. There was a serious question as to whether or not the strike proposal had the support of all the workers. The union leaders seemed reluctant to submit the issues to the Regional Labor Board, and they would not agree to shop elections to determine proper collective bargaining representatives. Moreover, various committees of workers asked Mayor Shaw and Chief of Police Davis to prevent a strike, stating that Eastern officers of the ILGWU were causing the dispute.[28]

At conferences held in July under the auspices of the Regional Labor Board, with Father James F. Cunningham presiding as impartial chairman, employers and union representatives worked out an agreement that was to be effective until July 1, 1936. It provided for union recognition and specified the wages fixed by the NRA code for the dress industry, subject to the differential between the east and west coasts. The parties agreed not to strike or lock out for the duration of the agreement, but to submit all complaints to an arbitration committee established for that purpose. Group death and disability insurance was provided, with the costs divided between both sides. The workday was to be seven hours, and the workweek, five days. The agreement was a genuine victory for the union. It was celebrated in October when David Dubinsky, international president of the ILGWU, visited Los Angeles and was tendered a banquet sponsored by the Joint Executive Board of Locals 65, 84, 96, and 97. At this affair it was pointed out that the ILGWU in Los Angeles had grown from a membership of 35 in 1930 to more than 2,000 in 1934, although 5,000 workers in the ladies' garment–manufacturing industry still were not organized. Working under a two-year contract, organized garment workers firmly believed that the open shop would soon be abandoned in favor of union-shop agreements.[29]

Five months later, in March, 1935, the total strength of the ILGWU in Los Angeles was reported to be 2,460 members, 1,100 of whom were in Local No. 96. Contracts were in effect with 112 manufacturers of cloaks, dresses, blouses, shirts, and sportswear, but all was not peaceful within the locals. The disbandment of the Needle Trades Industrial Union of the Trade Union Unity League on orders of the Communist Party was causing trouble. Communists had been told they were no longer to form separate unions but were to bore from within existing locals. Hence they joined the ILGWU and other labor organizations. They began to filibuster at meetings, get jobs in the best shops, and occupy key positions on important union committees as well as the front seats at all union assemblies, but they were unable to slow down the renewed organizing campaign of the garment workers in Los Angeles during 1935.[30]

Early in the year a majority of the employees working in cloak shops apparently were organized. A new agreement was signed in June, 1935, when the old one expired after being in effect more than a year and a half. The Cloak Manufacturers' Association, part of the Associated Apparel Manufacturers of Los Angeles, agreed to a closed shop, said to be the first in the city in twenty years. The contract, covering approximately 1,300 employees, was to run for two years and, in addition to the closed shop, provided for a thirty-five-hour week; minimum weekly wages for finishers, operators, and cutters of $22, $29.75, and $45, respectively; five paid holidays each year; no discharge of new workers after a ten-day trial period; reinstatement of any employee unjustifiably discharged, with pay for all time lost; equal division of work in the slack season; selection of retained workers by lot, if a shop was reduced in size; no contracting or subcontracting by manufacturers without the consent of the union; all disputes to be settled by an enforcement committee composed of two manufacturers and two union representatives, with an impartial chairman in the event of disagreement. The membership of Cloakmakers Local No. 65 increased 18 per cent in the two months following the signing of the agreement, making this part of the clothing industry almost 100 per cent organized. A few of the small cloak-manufacturing establishments in the city remained open shop, and several firms endeavored to escape the jurisdiction of the local by moving to nearby communities, but the union continued its efforts to organize their workers.[31]

The ILGWU drive also reached out among the cotton dress and underwear workers in 1935. These employees belonged to one of the few branches of the ladies' garment–manufacturing industry not under the jurisdiction of the union. Organizers also sought new members among the silk and wool dressmakers. In addition, attempts were made to maintain fair-trade practices among dress manufacturers, and strikes were called against several firms not operating under agreements. The strikes resulted in the arrest and subsequent trial of several unionists accused of disturbing the peace, but a number of dress manufacturers signed contracts with the union. One firm, the Fashion Frock Company, which refused to capitulate, was forced out of business by a boycott and strike. It was better to do this, ILGWU leaders claimed, than to permit a nonunion, price-cutting establishment to lower the morale of union workers and reduce the business volume of union shops. The union also tried to organize the workers in knitting mills and the new sportswear industry, but with little success. Most of the firms in these two industries remained open shop until later in the decade.[32]

Like the ILGWU, the Amalgamated Clothing Workers continued the organizing campaign initiated in Los Angeles after passage of the NIRA. The contract signed with a number of firms in the fall of 1933 expired in 1934, and the officials of Local No. 278 were forced to threaten a strike in order to focus attention on their demands. Their main requests included a 10 per cent wage increase, a few minor changes in working conditions, and an extension of the contract for another year. The employers claimed that the pay increase would have to be passed on to consumers in the form of higher prices and that, because of the elasticity of demand for men's clothing, this would lead to substitution of ready-made for tailor-made suits and so to unemployment for union members employed by merchant tailors. The unionists answered by voting a strike, but before it started both sides agreed to submit the dispute to the Regional Labor Board. The settlement in November, 1934, favored the union.[33]

Both the Amalgamated and the ILGWU moved to larger quarters in 1935 as a result of their growth in membership, but their troubles were not over. When Title I of the NIRA was declared unconstitutional in May, 1935, a few manufacturers of men's clothing reduced wages and lengthened hours in violation of their agreements. When the contracts expired in November, 1935, Local No. 278 of the Amalgamated, in order to stop these practices and obtain new agreements, called a strike in coöperation with Local No. 81 of the Journeymen Tailors Union. On November 14 more than 500 workers walked out and established picket lines. Police immediately were called to strike duty, and the Regional Labor Board entered the controversy. Agreements signed the next day covered most of the struck plants. They provided a 10 per cent wage increase, a thirty-six-hour week, and time and a half for overtime. Because of the satisfactory results of this strike, the unions continued the policy of working together in securing contracts.[34]

Not all the strikes in the clothing trades were successful in 1934 and 1935. A failure occurred when approximately 250 members of Local No. 43, American Federation of Full-Fashioned Hosiery Workers, AFL, struck on March 30, 1934, against the Mission Hosiery Mills. Early in the month a request by union officials for the maintenance of a wage scale in the thread-manufacturing department which the management considered too high had been taken before the Regional Labor Board. After an audit of the firm's books, the board had decided against the union. The latter continued its organizing campaign within the company, however, and the management allegedly began to discriminate against union members. The strike was called, according to union officials, because eight women members of Local No. 43 were discharged for union activity. At the inception of the walkout a regular police detail was assigned to maintain order on the request of the firm's owner. A boycott was established by the union members in retaliation, and the brands manufactured by the company were placed on the unfair list. The management hired strikebreakers, many of whom were imported from the hosiery mills of Greensboro, North Carolina. They were housed in the Coliseum Hotel at Figueroa Street and Santa Barbara Avenue, which also was immediately put on the unfair list of the Central Labor Council.[35]

The strike continued throughout April, with most of the strikers dependent on charity in order to make ends meet. Early in May several pickets were arrested and convicted for referring to strikebreakers in opprobrious terms. On May 7 a committee of strikers asked Mayor Shaw to intervene, but he was unable to bring the parties together. Three days later the management of the Mission Hosiery Mills filed a suit in the Superior Court claiming a trade loss of $10,000 as a result of the dispute and denying the union charges of discriminatory discharge. According to the company, the eight women had been released in a slack period because of their lack of seniority when dismissals were necessary, and would be rehired when vacancies occurred. The court granted a temporary injunction against picketing, the use of derogatory language directed at strikebreakers, and the sale on the picket line of the union's publication, the *Hosiery Worker*.

With such restrictions, and with the continuing replacement of union members by strikebreakers, violence was almost inevitable. In June four union members were arrested on charges of battery and robbery, and nine strikebreakers were booked on charges of carrying concealed weapons. On July 12 five men were injured in a riot that took place in front of the plant after two workers had been beaten by pickets. As similar outbreaks continued throughout August and into September, union spokesmen accused the police Red Squad of manhandling pickets. The attempt of the Regional Labor Board to mediate the dispute was fruitless, for the union insisted on a closed shop and reëmployment of all strikers, and the employer refused to grant these demands, though he made numerous compromise offers.[36]

Failing to get satisfaction on the local level, the strikers sent three of their number to Washington to lodge a protest with the National Labor Relations Board and the Executive Council of the AFL, but neither body took action. Local No. 43, lacking both local and national support, decided to terminate the strike on September 10. As the plant had continued to operate most of the time on an open-shop basis, the management refused to take back all those who had walked out. It gave a few their old jobs and promised to reëmploy others as rapidly as trade conditions permitted, but the leaders of Local No. 43 were not brought back into the plant. The union soon fell apart and was disbanded in 1935. Its demise was made official when the Central Labor Council wrote off the $348 contributed to the local in the 1934 strike as a poor investment.[37]

In contrast with the hosiery workers, the employees of firms manufacturing headgear were reasonably successful in their organizing efforts in 1934. On March 20 Local No. 48 of the United Hatters, Cap and Millinery Workers International Union, AFL, signed a one-year agreement with employers representing about 75 per cent of the industry in Los Angeles. They belonged to the Millinery Manufacturing and Jobbers' Association. The union, though failing to get a closed shop, made some gains: the workweek was reduced from forty to thirty-seven and a half hours; wages were increased to $18, $24, and $30 a week depending on the skill of the worker; and an arbitrator was appointed to handle all future disputes. International President Max Zaritsky and International Vice-President Carolyn Wolfe worked with the Regional Labor Board in achieving the settlement and averting a strike, which had been called for March 20. A year later, however, the manufacturers refused to renew the agreement, and Local No. 48 called a strike on March 20, 1935. Picketing of millinery establishments began almost immediately, but seventy policemen and a cold rain kept the picket lines orderly on the first day. As usual, there were conflicting reports concerning the number of strikers. Police officials stated that about 295 workers actually were out, but union spokesmen claimed that 675 had signed the strike rolls. The most important issue, from the viewpoint of the union, was the unwillingness of the manufacturers to arbitrate a closed-shop demand, but after the strike began, union members discovered that it would be a struggle merely to maintain the wages and working conditions existing under the old contract.[38]

J. L. Leonard of the Regional Labor Board was unable to negotiate an agreement, for neither side would give in on the closed-shop issue. Pickets, most of them women wearing bright new hats, continued to march in front of some forty plants, but the response to the strike call began to weaken after only a few days. As manufacturers were able to obtain replacements for the strikers, total hat production remained almost normal and those on the picket line began to fear for their jobs. Violence soon developed when a nonstriking hat blocker was beaten by strikers on March 25, and a unionist was accused of throwing a rock through the window of a strikebreaker's car. The Regional Labor Board tried to stem the violence by arranging a settlement, but the effort was in vain. Zaritsky charged that the employers were violating the NRA code for milliners and demanded an official investigation. He claimed that apprentices were being used instead of journeymen in many operations, that women workers could not live on their average weekly pay check of only $9, and that hat blockers were trying to support families on a weekly wage of $18 in a millinery-manufacturing season averaging only fourteen weeks a year. On April 1 the Regional Labor Board finally induced both sides to compromise, under an armistice that favored the employers. The manufacturers consented to rehire all strikers within a week without discrimination if the union would not try to organize the workers in any nonunion shop for a year.[39]

The armistice was short-lived, as officials of Local No. 48 soon filed complaints with the Regional Labor Board that employers were discriminating against unionists. Employers declared that a reduction in sales volume had lessened the need for workers, but the union contended that they wanted to maintain open-shop establishments. Petitions were therefore filed with the board requesting a separate collective bargaining election in each of twenty-one establishments. Max Feingold of the Millinery Manufacturing and Jobbers' Association asked instead for one unified election in all the shops. He believed that the union would be defeated in a general election but that, if individual shop elections took place, it might gain representation rights in several establishments. Hearings were held, and on May 10 the board issued its order. All strikers not yet employed were to be returned to work by May 15, an impartial arbitration board was to be established, and employees were to choose their own collective bargaining representatives. But soon thereafter the NRA was declared unconstitutional. Conditions in the industry quickly deteriorated, and discrimination against union workers continued. In July a new organizer, Fred E. Carrano, was assigned to Local No. 48, and he was able to strengthen the union numerically in the latter part of 1935. A few agreements were signed covering male workers and operators, but most of the women trimmers remained unorganized.[40]

Of all the unions in the garment trades, the milliners and the hosiery workers were the least successful in the NRA years, largely because of open-shop opposition. Communists sought to gain positions of influence within both unions, but, for the most part, they remained in the background. This was not true of Local No. 81 of the Journeymen Tailors, which faced direct Communist competition in 1934 from a branch of the Needle Trades Workers Industrial Union known as the Custom Tailors Union. Two hundred members of this organization, most of them employed in about fifteen high-priced custom tailoring establishments, walked out on April 6, 1934, demanding a thirty-five-hour week, a minimum wage scale, and equal division of the available work. The strike was opposed by Local No. 81, and the employers refused to recognize the walkout. The Regional Labor Board endeavored to effect a settlement, but it was successful only with respect to the firm of Charles Levy and Sons, where Local No. 81 won the right to represent the workers. Members of the Custom Tailors Union continued picketing despite an injunction obtained by the company. Some overt acts took place in the course of the strike. Three men were arrested for throwing acid on merchandise; one was convicted and sentenced to ninety days in jail. Other arrests were made on charges of blocking the sidewalk, pushing customers in front of stores, name calling, assault with deadly weapons, and the like. But these devices failed to prolong the strike, and the pickets were removed in June when the Communists faded away.[41]

While the garment unions were providing a degree of excitement for downtown Los Angeles, with their colorful picketing and milling crowds of workers, the culinary trades, including Waiters Local No. 17, Cooks Local No. 468, Waitresses Local No. 639, and Bartenders Local No. 284, engaged in some of the most bitter and highly publicized disputes with open-shop supporters in these years. The Brown Derby strike of 1934 was particularly noteworthy because the restaurant was a favorite of the Hollywood motion picture colony. The walkout occurred on March 1 after the head of the firm, Robert H. Cobb, allegedly reduced the wages of twenty-seven waiters from 23 cents an hour to 90 cents per day of nine or more hours. Twenty-five cents a day had to be paid from this sum to the bus boys, and the waiters were required to maintain their own uniforms. Spokesmen for Waiters Local No. 17 demanded minimum weekly wages of $15 for waiters and $21 to $40 for cooks, as well as an eight-hour day and a six-day week. In addition, the waiters were to be permitted to keep their tips, which often were substantial. When the strike was called, the Brown Derby management hired a new culinary crew while the strikers established picket lines at both the Beverly Hills and Hollywood restaurants. Police were immediately assigned to the dispute, and the Central Labor Council initiated a boycott against the firm. Special editions of the *Citizen* were sold by the pickets at the Hollywood restaurant in order to advertise the strike, but this was hardly necessary in view of the wide coverage in all the local newspapers.[42]

The Brown Derby management asked for a temporary injunction against the Central Labor Council, Secretary J. W. Buzzell, Waiters Local No. 17, two officers of the union, and a large number of John Does. The charges included intimidation of customers and employees, which, it was claimed, had caused a $10,000 loss of trade. On March 14 Superior Court Judge Frank C. Collier granted the restraining order on ex parte evidence. The defendants claimed that open-shop advocates were supporting both Judge Collier and the Brown Derby management. The hearing on a permanent injunction began on April 10, but on June 2, before the case was settled, the strike was terminated. The management granted a small increase in wages, recognized Waiters Local No. 17, agreed to hire future help through the union, and returned the striking workers to their jobs. Letters were then dispatched to movie stars to the effect that the Brown Derby again was fair, the boycott was dropped, and the pickets went back to work.[43]

On July 11, 1934, Sardi's, another restaurant catering to the Hollywood colony, was struck after the breakdown of negotiations for union recognition. The walkout ended on July 20 with the granting of all the strikers' demands, including equal pay for waiters and waitresses doing the same work, an eight-hour day, and the hiring of all culinary help through the unions. But this was not the end of the matter, because Sardi's had broken away from the Southern California Restaurant Association in acceding to these demands. At this time the association was endeavoring to maintain the open shop in Los Angeles cafés and restaurants and thwart the aggressive organizing drive of the culinary trades. In fact, that very month the Southern California Hotel Association and the Southern California Restaurant Association had jointly established an emergency fund and an employment agency in order to assist member firms in opposing the unions. Sardi's had received $721.30 from this fund and had procured strikebreakers through the agency. Under these circumstances the quick capitulation of the firm was unexpected, and the employers' association initiated action to recover the money it had supplied.[44]

The day the walkout ended at Sardi's, the culinary unions struck against Levy's, an old Los Angeles firm with one branch in downtown Los Angeles and another in Hollywood. Demanding a closed shop, the unions claimed that employees were compelled to work broken shifts, were charged 50 cents for their meals, received pay of only 28 cents an hour, remitted 35 cents a day each to the bus boys, and thus netted an average of only 83 cents for a six-hour day. Picketing was initiated and became sufficiently effective to cause the restaurant management to secure a temporary restraining order on ex parte evidence. This did not stop the unionists, however, and a number of the pickets were cited for contempt of court for throwing on the ground the papers served on them for violation of the restraining order. On July 27 Judge Emmet H. Wilson rendered a decision of not guilty of the contempt-of-court charges, modified the restraining order, and set a date for a new hearing. The strikers were permitted to picket peacefully if they did not block the entrance to the restaurants. Two days later Al Levy, owner of the firm, signed a complaint that union news vendors selling the *Citizen* in front of his restaurants were disturbing the peace. The case came up for trial on August 16, but the charges were dismissed.

In the meantime, Levy took advantage of the emergency fund of the open-shop restaurant and hotel associations and also obtained workers through their employment agency in order to continue operating. Under these circumstances, the culinary unions decided to spread the strike to Simon's dairy lunch and coffee shops, with which Al Levy was affiliated. As the months passed, the dispute became a stalemate. Another craft became involved in April, 1935, when Mike Lyman, an official of Simon's, opened a new restaurant on Hill Street in Los Angeles. He found himself unable to hire musicians, as members of Local No. 47 refused to work in his establishment so long as the culinary unions were on strike. Finally, in June, 1935, the strike was compromised and the unions were recognized, with some small increases in wages.[45]

The restaurant industry was characterized by small units or firms which were forced to band together in an association in order to meet union organizing campaigns. A similar situation prevailed in furniture manufacturing, but here the start of union activities in 1933 was further complicated by the Communist issue. The Independent Furniture Workers Union of the Trade Union Unity League was organized in 1933 by seven workers. In July, 1934, claiming to have 750 members, it threatened to strike unless employers agreed to recognize the union and raise wages from an average of 34 cents an hour to 45 and 50 cents, depending on skill. The Regional Labor Board averted the walkout at all except one of the larger firms, the Gillespie Furniture Manufacturing Company, which refused to compromise. On August 6, 200 of its employees walked out. Under cover of police protection, the strikers were replaced and operations were continued at the factory in spite of picketing. The Regional Labor Board finally negotiated an agreement which was accepted by the managements of Gillespie and ten other firms. The strikers were to be reëmployed as rapidly as trade volume permitted, and a few concessions were made to the union on working conditions, but recognition was not achieved.[46]

The agreement turned out to be more a truce than a settlement. Communist control of the union was relinquished early in 1935, and in March the Independent Furniture Workers Union became Local No. 1561 of the United Brotherhood of Carpenters and Joiners of America, AFL. In April the members of the union voted 1,265 to 72 to call a strike for hourly wages of 75 cents for skilled workers and 50 cents for unskilled. The employers, organized as the Furniture Manufacturers' Association, were given until May 1 to meet the union demands, which affected approximately sixty establishments and 3,000 employees. Spokesmen for the companies said they could not possibly meet the wage demands because of competition with other manufacturing areas. Los Angeles was the fourth largest furniture-manufacturing center in the country. Of the 65 per cent of its output sold outside the state, 40 per cent was distributed east of the Rockies in competition with Eastern companies. The Regional Labor Board, represented by Towne J. Nylander, failed to bring both sides together in a satisfactory compromise before the dead line. Consequently, on April 29 the union struck the Los Angeles Period Furniture Company and the C. R. Kayser Company. Employees in other plants walked out the next day. Though the Labor Board continued its efforts, the employers decided to take matters into their own hands. By May 8 at least ten plants were operating in spite of union pickets while others remained shut down; but an equal number of firms employing about 1,000 workers decided to settle with Local No. 1561. They temporarily agreed to an hourly wage of 60 cents for skilled and 40 cents for unskilled employees. This was an increase over the 50 cents and 34 cents specified by the NRA code for the furniture-manufacturing industry.[47]

By May 10 some 1,100 unionists were back at work under temporary agreements, but violence broke out when pickets attempted to prevent the employment of strikebreakers at several firms that had refused to settle. There were still 400 men on strike at eleven plants. Officials of Local No. 1561 were quite certain by this time that the holdouts were led by the Gillespie management. They claimed to have evidence that Gillespie had made an agreement with a number of other manufacturers under which each had posted a $1,000 bond, the bond to be forfeited by any employer who recognized the union as collective bargaining agent for any of his employees. They also charged that, prior to passage of the NIRA, Gillespie's company had paid as little as $1 for a nine-hour day, but that M and M officials had forced it to raise the figure to $1.50. With the eleven holdout manufacturers adamantly in support of the open shop, events were shaping up for a protracted dispute. In July a committee from Local No. 1561 visited the largest retail furniture stores in San Francisco, Oakland, San Diego, Los Angeles, and several other cities in the state, which promised not to purchase the products of the struck plants. The employers, in turn, advertised for skilled workers in order to maintain production quotas, and representatives of the Chamber of Commerce and the Merchants' and Manufacturers' Association tried to get retail stores in Los Angeles to buy furniture from the eleven plants. Products of these firms were featured at a furniture show held the week of August 29, but pickets paraded in front of the building and sold copies of the *Citizen* listing the names of the unfair manufacturers.[48]

In September violence broke out anew at the Morris Furniture Company, when workers armed with hand tools attacked twenty pickets, injuring five of them. Some gains were made by the union before the month was out, however, when five plants operating under temporary agreements entered into permanent contracts covering 830 men. Three of the five agreed to a closed-shop clause and the following hourly rates: helpers, 40 cents; skilled finishers, 50 cents; skilled cabinetmakers, 55 cents; highly skilled cabinetmakers and finishers, 60 cents; and operators of complicated mill machinery, 75 cents. After hearings conducted by the Regional Labor Board, three more plants signed union contracts in November, but the strike continued into 1936. By January ten firms had signed closed-shop contracts, and eight others had agreed to pay the union wage scale—a substantial achievement for the union. The eleven open-shop manufacturers led by Gillespie continued to hold out, however, and on January 16 the members of Local No. 1561 decided to call off the strike. Pickets were withdrawn and only a boycott remained against the products of the open-shop manufacturers.[49]

Closely related to the furniture workers were the members of Local No. 15 of the Upholsterers International Union of America, AFL. They had failed to achieve sufficient strength in 1933 to bargain with their employers, but this did not deter them from calling a strike on October 8, 1934, as part of a coast-wide dispute in their craft. Some 400 men went out in Los Angeles, asking for a minimum hourly wage of $1 and a thirty-five-hour week in about thirty-five upholstering shops and furniture factories. Police officials had advance notice of the walkout and furnished patrolmen for strike duty almost at once because of a suspicion that Communists were active in Local No. 15. The Regional Labor Board quickly entered the dispute and gained the consent of union leaders to a tentative agreement under which the strikers would return to work pending arbitration on a coast-wide basis, but the employers refused to concur. Los Angeles union leaders therefore decided to seek a separate settlement apart from other Pacific Coast locals. Thus, when employers in the city agreed to arbitration, to begin October 25, the strike was terminated in Los Angeles. The peace continued during 1935 except for a few minor disputes at several small plants, with the union reporting a membership of 750 workers.[50]

Although the NIRA provided some impetus to organization among the furniture workers and the upholsterers in 1934 and 1935, it did very little for the building and construction trades. Their hope lay more in the initiation of government projects than in a revival of private construction and the adoption of codes. Only the 300 members of Roofers Local No. 36 threatened a walkout in 1934 unless the employers, who belonged to the Southern California Roofers' Bureau, would agree not to hire more than one helper for every three journeymen roofers. The Regional Labor Board brought the disputants together and negotiated an agreement containing such a clause as well as continuance of the 1929 wage rate of not less than $7 per day for journeymen and $8 for foremen, an eight-hour day, and a forty-hour week.

As 1934 ended, optimistic predictions of more employment in the building trades were made by a number of union officials. They believed that the various work relief programs and a prospective housing plan sponsored by the federal government would end the long drought in work, and this proved to be true. The annual report of the secretary of the Central Labor Council for 1935 indicated that the combination of federal work relief projects, the construction of several breweries after the repeal of prohibition, and the rebuilding of schools damaged in the 1933 earthquake gave the building trades unionists greater stability in employment in that year than they had experienced in the preceding five years of depression. This still did not mean that jobs were plentiful, for construction remained at a level far below that of the 1920's. Moreover, the unions were forced to counteract what they considered efforts of open-shop contractors to lower wages in 1935. A number of employers, for example, were accused of advertising in newspapers to the effect that there was a shortage of building trades mechanics in Los Angeles. This, labor leaders believed, was a deliberate attempt to increase the labor reserve by attracting workers from other areas and crafts and thus force wages down.

Table 4 shows the union rates per hour and the hours worked per week in the more important building trades in the city in 1934 and 1935. Building trades unionists were in the forefront of efforts to establish these prevailing union wages on WPA projects in the city and the state. The applicable subsistence wage scales provided for monthly payments of from $55 to $65 to skilled craftsmen for a five-day week and a seven-hour day. Thus, unemployed building tradesmen received approximately $3.75 a day for work on WPA projects for which they were usually paid $8 by private employers. As noted earlier, this dis-

TABLE 4

UNION WAGE RATES AND WORKING HOURS
IN THE BUILDING TRADES, LOS ANGELES,
1934–1935

Occupation	Rate per hour		Hours per week	
	1934	1935	1934	1935
Asbestos workers	$1.25	$1.25	40	40
Bricklayers	1.00	1.00	40	40
Building laborers	.625	.625	40	40
Carpenters	1.00	1.00	40	40
Cement finishers	1.25	1.25	44	44
Elevator constructors	1.125	1.125	40	40
Elevator constructors' helpers	.788	.788	40	40
Hod carriers	.75	.75	40	40
Inside wiremen	1.00	1.00	40	40
Lathers	1.25	1.25	30	30
Marble setters	1.00	1.00	40	40
Painters	1.00	1.00	40	40
Plasterers	1.25	1.25	30	30
Plasterers' helpers	1.10	1.10	40	40
Plumbers	1.125	1.10	40	40
Sheet metal workers	.875	.875	40	40
Steam fitters	1.25	1.25	40	40
Stonemasons	1.00	1.00	40	40
Structural ironworkers	1.125	1.125	44	44

SOURCE: "Union Scales of Wages and Hours in the Building Trades in 1934 and 1935," *Monthly Labor Review*, XLI (Nov., 1935), 1166–1177.

pute was resolved by reducing the number of hours worked each month so that the total payment of $55 to $65 was obtained at the prevailing hourly wage rate in the community.[51]

Among the building trades unions only the millmen engaged in a walkout of any importance in 1935. Millmen Local No. 884 of the United Brotherhood of Carpenters and Joiners was one of the larger unions of the city. Most of its members worked in cabinet and store fixture manufacturing, an industry in which employer open-shop feelings ran very high. After an organizing campaign early in the year, the membership of Local No. 884 demanded a wage scale ranging from 40 cents up to $1.16⅔ per hour, depending on skill, and a five-day, thirty-hour week. To avert a walkout, the Regional Labor Board, with the coöperation of the union and the twelve most important firms, set up a five-man arbitration board. But at this point the publisher of the *Times* jumped into the fray. He interpreted the move as an attempt to unionize the workers of an open-shop industry comprising more than 300 mills, most of which were small and employed only a few men. The unionists, immediately deciding to show that they meant business, called a strike at a few firms as a warning that a general walk-out would ensue if their wage and hour demands were not met. Arbitration proceedings were postponed several times, as some employers could not be persuaded to participate. Because a union agreement covering only a few mills would place the unionized concerns in an unfavorable competitive position, further negotiations seemed useless. Leaders of Local No. 884 thereupon decided to extend the walkout, and 700 men "hit the bricks" on June 4, 1935, temporarily paralyzing the operations of the fifteen largest firms in the cabinet and store fixture industry of Los Angeles.[52]

When, on June 6, another 300 employees joined the strike, bringing the number of closed plants to twenty, the employers began to lay plans for reopening their establishments. Eleven of them formed an informal open-shop organization which was to be incorporated later as the Cabinet and Store Fixture Association of California. Members of the M and M gave their support to the group, and Chief of Police Davis informed them of their legal rights in a labor dispute. Captain William F. Hynes, on leave from the Police Department, advised the employers concerning the proper protection of their property and nonstriking employees. These actions did not deter picketing, but they undoubtedly reduced the possibility of violence. Union officials believed that the invalidation of the NRA had given the employers courage to resist arbitration and establish battle lines for an open-shop showdown. Nevertheless, the strike was firmly prosecuted and agreements were reached with a number of mills. These provided for hourly wages of 85 cents for unskilled labor and $1 for skilled work, including the installation of equipment. Overtime was set at $1.10 an hour. This break in the open-shop front brought other employers into line. By August fifteen of the largest firms had signed with the union and had granted wage increases ranging from 80 cents to $2 per day, on the basis of a sliding scale for different operations. Although the union did not win all its demands, its officers, claiming that working conditions and wages were better than before the dispute, hailed the strike as a decided victory over the open shop. Events of the next year, however, were soon to prove that it was only an armistice following a minor skirmish which really marked the beginning of a major open-shop battle.[53]

The building trades locals were not bothered by Communist activities as were other unions, particularly in the clothing industry. A similar situation prevailed among the teamsters, who successfully ignored the Communists during 1934 and 1935. The twelve teamster locals, functioning under the general jurisdiction of Los Angeles Joint Council of Teamsters No. 42, had attained a total membership of more than 1,000 by February, 1934. Special but unsuccessful organizing campaigns were initiated in 1934 by Milk Wagon Drivers and Dairy Employees Local No. 521 and Ice Wagon Drivers Local No. 326. The latter's continuing efforts to organize the Union Ice Company were no more successful than in the preceding year. The coöperative organizing drive launched in 1933 by the members of Bakers Local No. 37 and Bakery Truck Drivers Local No. 276 continued quite steadily throughout 1934 and well into 1935. On January 3, 1934, both unions won an agreement with the Armstrong Baking Company, which was believed to be the first formal written contract with the teamsters signed by a Los Angeles employer. The next month officials of Local No. 276 also signed contracts with the Basso, Barbara Ann, and Bradford bakeries, but failed to reach agreement with the Langendorf Baking Company. Langendorf had been operating under a contract with Bakers Local No. 37, but in September, 1934, the management, having broken nearly every section of the agreement, terminated it without the required thirty-day written notice. Local No. 37 called a strike, but the company answered it with a discriminatory program which caused most of its employees to leave the union. A boycott against Langendorf was instituted in April, 1935, and the firm was placed on the unfair list of the Central Labor Council, although its branch plants in San Jose, San Francisco, Oakland, and Seattle were unionized.[54]

The most important activities of the teamsters were in the field of general trucking. An organizing campaign started in 1934 extended over several years, reaching its apogee in 1937 and 1938. Its most obvious aspect in 1934 was teamster support of the longshore strike, which became strong enough to force open-shop truck operators to establish a convoy system between Los Angeles and the harbor district in the summer. Police guarded the convoys, which consisted of six to eight trucks. When the longshore strike ended, the teamsters continued to concentrate their organizing efforts on harbor traffic, and a new local of truck drivers was established at San Pedro in 1935. The tactics adopted by the teamsters were to stop trucks on trips between Los Angeles and the harbor and request the drivers to show their union cards. Those who did not have cards were given a warning to join up or expect unpleasant consequences. As a few drivers required actual physical persuasion, the Los Angeles Police Department reëstablished the road patrols used during the longshore strike in an effort to keep the highways to and from the harbor free of union organizers, but the locals of general truck drivers continued to grow.[55]

The printing trades unions also made gains in contracts and membership in the NRA period. Unlike most other crafts in the city, they enjoyed close coöperation under the NRA codes from the majority of employers with whom they had contracts. Though not launching special organizing drives in 1934 and 1935, the printing trades locals did support the general membership campaign of the Central Labor Council. Members of International Typographical Union Local No. 174 benefited by an hourly increase in the commercial wage scale, effective on May 1, 1934, of about 5 cents for operators and 7½ cents for floor men. One firm, the Compton Printing Company, at first refused to pay the new scale, but reluctantly complied when a strike was threatened. A change in the publishing wage scale, effective on October 8, 1934, for one year, really represented the restoration of a 7.5 per cent reduction made in October, 1932, and reëstablished daily rates of $9.33⅓ for the night shift and $8.83⅓ for day work. Stereotypers Local No. 38 negotiated similar changes in its agreements with several newspaper publishers, restoring a 10 per cent wage cut instituted in 1932. Employment for printing trades unionists improved in both 1934 and 1935, except in bookbinding. Bookbinders Local No. 63, meeting strong opposition to its organizing efforts, could do little to improve either working conditions or wages. Experienced bindery women received a minimum wage of 33⅓ cents an hour, and inexperienced apprentices were paid $12 a week in nonunion shops. In most of the printing crafts, however, there was an increased use of the union label, and wage reductions initiated in the earlier years of the depression were restored. The largest of the printing unions, ITU Local No. 174, with more than 1,000 members, celebrated its sixtieth anniversary in 1935.[56]

In contrast with the stability of employment and gradual improvement in working conditions in the printing trades, the members of the Amalgamated Meat Cutters and Butcher Workmen of North America had to struggle for very marginal gains. After failing to organize the large packing plants in 1933, the union's organizers directed their efforts toward the workers employed by poultry-killing and processing firms, most of which were small and hired only a few employees. They succeeded in establishing Poultry Workers Local No. 323, whose members then proceeded to make demands on their employers. When the demands were ignored, 250 men struck 175 plants on March 27, 1934. The Regional Labor Board entered the dispute with the approval of officials of the Retail Poultry Dealers' Association and international organizer George Hobart of the union. As a result, most of the workers returned to their jobs by 1:30 P.M. on the same day with improved wages and hours. Killers and scalders were granted wages of $32 per week, while all other poultry workers except apprentices were given weekly wages of $26. The workweek was reduced from sixty and eighty hours to a maximum of forty-eight. In May, however, 200 poultry workers struck because of the alleged failure of four wholesalers to abide by the NRA code. The Regional Labor Board submitted the dispute to arbitration while the workers returned to their jobs. The arbitration decision, announced in September, provided a forty-hour week with pay ranging from a minimum of $20 a week for pieceworkers to $37.50 for foremen.[57]

The meatcutters also tried to organize meat markets in the city during these years. The campaign, conducted by members of Local No. 421, attained some success; by June, 1934, contracts had been negotiated with the owners of thirty-five markets, and more agreements were signed later in the year. Although this number was very small when compared with the aggregate of markets in the Los Angeles area, it did give some encouragement to union meatcutters. The campaign began to lag in 1935, however, and little further progress was made. Paradoxically, the only strike that affected the meat markets in this period was not part of the strategy of Local No. 421. In April, 1935, a group called the United Conference Against the High Cost of Living struck some forty retail shops operated in Hollenbeck Heights by members of the Kosher Retail Butchers' Association. The strike lasted only a few days and the shops reopened on April 10 under police protection.[58]

While the meatcutters were having their troubles, the rubber workers were seeking to gain a foothold in the four major plants in this industry. The meatcutters were primarily up against small, locally owned employing units, whereas the rubber workers had to tackle plants that were, for the most part, branches of national concerns. Organizing attempts, begun in 1933, accomplished little during that year. In February, 1934, the Los Angeles Police Department investigated the possibility that Communists were at work in the city's rubber plants, but found no conclusive evidence to that effect. The same month, the officials of Tire and Rubber Workers Local No. 18304, AFL, tired of trying to overcome the opposition of managements determined to maintain open shops rather than endure the interference of labor unions, appealed to the Regional Labor Board for help in establishing collective bargaining at the Goodrich and Firestone plants. The appeal was granted and an election set for February 21, but before that date unionists complained that the firms were promoting company unions and that workers were being given time off their jobs to assist in the formation of such organizations. On the day of the election, according to union officials, three general department foremen and the personnel officer of the Goodrich plant remained at the voting booth all day, writing down the names of those who dared to vote. Nevertheless, the results went against both companies. At Goodrich, 209 workers voted for the AFL union, whereas only 21 supported the company plan. The workers at Firestone were equally decisive, voting 695 to 80 to have Local No. 18304 represent them. In spite of this, the managements of both plants refused to recognize Local No. 18304, and the Regional Labor Board found itself powerless to enforce the election decision.[59]

In July, Local No. 18304 was split into four unions, one at each plant, in accordance with the program of its parent body, the newly formed United Rubber Workers, but organizing work did not proceed with any greater facility. Management opposition continued and, in October, officials of the local plant of the United States Rubber Company supported a company union and refused to sanction the Regional Labor Board election that was held to determine the proper collective bargaining agent. Similar conditions prevailed at the Firestone and Goodrich plants. The Regional Labor Board, unable to enforce its decisions, referred the cases to the National Labor Relations Board, which, after due consideration, decided against the unions at Goodrich and Firestone on the ground that the change in identity of Local No. 18304 in July, when it split into four separate organizations, had invalidated the election of the preceding February. The new locals were not considered direct successors of the old union so far as collective bargaining rights were concerned, and new elections were deemed necessary. However, the board held that the local management of the United States Rubber Company had violated Section 7(a) of the NIRA in not recognizing Local No. 19747. This did not terminate the company's antiunion activities; it immediately filed an injunction suit in Washington, D.C., against the removal of its blue eagle emblem and continued to refuse to recognize the local. The case, in effect, was won by management when the NRA was invalidated in May, 1935. By the latter part of the year the rubber workers' locals in Los Angeles had virtually disappeared. The opposition of employers and the inability of the NLRB to enforce its decisions were primarily responsible for this state of affairs, which lasted until the early months of 1936 when a representative from the parent United Rubber Workers set about reorganizing the locals.[60]

Unlike the rubber workers, the cleaners and dyers did not have a continuous corporate existence during 1934 and 1935. The local that had been active in 1933 after passage of the NIRA was disrupted by Communists and subsequently disbanded, and the new Cleaners, Dyers and Pressers Union No. 19989, AFL, was organized on April 15, 1935. A membership campaign was initiated and an agreement requested from the Cooperative Plant Owners' Association. The Regional Labor Board averted a possible strike by assisting in drawing up a contract, which provided a closed shop, stipulating that retail shop owners would trade only with wholesale plants employing union members and vice versa; a maximum workweek of forty hours instead of up to seventy hours; and a 20 per cent increase in wage scales. Unionists acclaimed the agreement, pointing out that it covered 75 per cent of the employers and 90 per cent of the employees in the industry. Its main purpose was to end the price cutting that had resulted in low wages and long hours in this highly competitive industry, but open-shop advocates argued that it deprived the public of low, competitive prices for dry cleaning. Towne Nylander of the Regional Labor Board was specifically accused of engaging in practices designed to stifle competition and of aiding the growth of illegal commercial procedures through employer-union collaboration. Little came of this criticism, however, and in May the members of Local No. 19989 picketed about twenty wholesale and retail plants in an endeavor to force their owners to sign the agreement. Fourteen of the firms signed contracts, and on June 7 the union joined the Central Labor Council, but it still had problems. Communists continued to plague the local throughout the year, thus contributing to instability within the union and in its relationships with employers.[61]

Instability also marked efforts to unionize the employees of the aircraft industry of Los Angeles, but for a different reason. In this instance the cause lay in the newness of the industry itself and in its lack of previous experience with unions. The aircraft-manufacturing industry in southern California dated from 1912, when Allen and Malcolm Loughead designed and, with the assistance of one mechanic, assembled a biplane in Los Angeles County. In subsequent years three airplane plants were established in the area and began to produce custommade commercial aircraft. Early in 1934 the first definite efforts were made to organize workers in the industry, and in August the employees of the Douglas Aircraft Company voted for a plant representation plan and against the United Aircraft Mechanics Union, AFL. A branch of the latter was established at Lockheed Aircraft Corporation, however, and covered a small group of its employees. Organizing activities continued during 1935 in all the aircraft firms, forming a base from which there developed the campaigns of 1936 and 1937 at the Lockheed, Douglas, and Northrop plants.[62]

4. TROUBLE ON THE STREET AND INTERURBAN RAILWAYS

The disputes engaged in by employees of the street and interurban railway systems of Los Angeles in 1934 and 1935 were among the most widely publicized labor events of the time in southern California, partly because the workers' organizing activities reopened wounds dating from the World War I period. The managements of the Los Angeles and Pacific Electric railways strongly supported the open shop, and had successfully fended off all attempts in the intervening years to organize their employees and secure recognition for outside unions. Under these circumstances labor officials did not expect the companies to be guided by the spirit of Section 7(a) of the NIRA. Thus, when management called a mass meeting of Pacific Electric workers for the evening of August 13, 1933, the employees foresaw only a reiteration of the company's intention to remain an open shop. But at the meeting, to their great surprise, D. W. Pontius, president of the company, read an order removing all restrictions against union membership. He stated that Pacific Electric's former policy of dealing with employees individually had been abandoned in order to comply with the purpose of Section 7(a) in permitting employees to organize as they pleased.[63]

At the conclusion of Pontius' talk the 2,000 employees present voted for one large company union which would include all crafts. After the meeting, however, the platform men, representing about 1,400 conductors and motormen in the system, held a separate conference and decided to affiliate with the Brotherhood of Railroad Trainmen (BRT). As the interurban lines of the Pacific Electric Railway radiated from Los Angeles into adjoining communities and counties, thus covering a broad geographic area, the trainmen believed that a railroad lodge would be a better form of organization. By the end of 1933 Pacific Electric Lodge No. 912, chartered by the BRT, was functioning with a membership of approximately 1,000 men. Unions also were formed by other crafts. The telegraphers affiliated with Southern Pacific System Division 53 of the Order of Railroad Telegraphers and, on

September 16, 1934, won the first union agreement ever negotiated with the Pacific Electric. This contract covered agents, assistant agents, ticket agents, assistant ticket agents, and tower men. It provided a pay increase effective from January 1, 1934, time and a half for overtime, and improved working rules. The agreement was for one year, though the wage question could be reopened on January 1, 1935. The various shop craftsmen united to form Sunset Lodge No. 410 of the Brotherhood of Railway Carmen, and the signalmen affiliated with the Brotherhood of Railroad Signalmen (BRS).[64]

In the spring of 1934 the Pacific Electric Railway was declared subject to the Railway Labor Act of 1926. Negotiations had been in progress since the first of the year among representatives of the BRT, the BRS, and the management in an effort to reach agreement on wages and hours. When a deadlock developed, the National Mediation Board entered the dispute. The brotherhoods of trainmen and signalmen won the elections held to determine proper collective bargaining representatives, whereupon the board requested their leaders to postpone a threatened walkout as time was needed to compromise the dispute. When union officials agreed, federal mediator William F. Mitchell, Jr., attempted to bring the parties together, but failed. Then, in compliance with the Railway Labor Act, arbitration was proposed. When it, too, was rejected, the matter was referred back to the National Mediation Board in Washington. Officials of the BRT immediately conducted a strike vote, which favored a walkout by a majority of 1,052 to 62. The members of the BRS local also voted in favor of a strike, though less than 100 signalmen were involved.[65]

Leaders of both unions and D. W. Pontius of the company then wired the National Mediation Board to request President Roosevelt to appoint an emergency fact-finding board under Section 10 of the Railway Labor Act, which would avert a strike for sixty days. Pontius pointed out that his major objection to the union demands concerned the proposed wage change. The management, he said, was complying with all the provisions of the NRA code and had restored all wage cuts made in the early years of the depression. Train service employees thus were guaranteed $90 a month, but most of them were paid substantially more. All other workers were receiving pay as high as they had ever obtained in the history of the company. Pontius further claimed inability to raise wages because the 1934 payroll for employees in train service would total about $1,990,000; the wage increase, if granted, would amount to $1,014,000 per year, or about 51 per cent, because of penalty rules; if similar demands were made by workers in other departments, the total annual wage increase would be $1,750,000. Furthermore, the company had not earned its operating expenses and taxes in 1933 by $156,985.56, and in the first ten months of 1934 it had failed by $240,087.29 to cover such costs. No dividend had ever been issued on the capital stock of the company, and no bond interest had been paid for two years. Lee R. Smith, international vice-president of the BRS, and D. A. MacKenzie, international vice-president of the BRT, countered that the pay rates for Pacific Electric signalmen were 15 to 20 per cent below those of other railroads in the area, and that trainmen also were receiving lower wages than those paid by comparable Western lines. The strike was therefore called for 2 A.M. on November 24, but it was postponed to Monday, November 26, upon the request of the national headquarters of the respective unions.[66]

The National Mediation Board then asked for an indefinite postponement, which the union leaders granted. Three of the board members immediately came to Los Angeles to act as a fact-finding committee in an effort to settle the dispute. From December 3 to December 12 daily conferences were held by the board members, representatives of the Pacific Electric Railway, and union officials to consider data submitted by the parties to the dispute, municipal officials, and the California Railroad Commission. Three days later representatives of the BRT offered to reduce their wage demands for conductors and motormen in local service from 75 to 62 cents an hour, with a proportionate reduction for other employees except freight service trainmen at Los Angeles Harbor, who were to remain on a wage parity with workers doing similar tasks on steam lines. The management of Pacific Electric at first insisted on a maximum of 53½ cents for trainmen, but on December 19, in joint conferences with union officials and Mediation Board members, it raised the figure to 56 cents and indicated its readiness to make additional wage concessions, if necessary. An agreement reached the next day ended the strike threat and set up the following wage schedules:

1. Freight employees to receive standard steam train rates of pay, an eight-hour day, and time and a half for overtime—an increase of more than $2 a day in some classifications.

2. Fourth-year and older employees on the interurban lines receiving 55½ cents an hour to be raised on January 1 to 60 cents, and on July 1, 1935, to 63 cents.

3. Fourth-year and older employees on local passenger lines receiving 52½ cents an hour to be raised to 56½ cents on January 1, 1935.

4. The eight-hour day to apply, with time and a half for overtime beyond nine hours.

5. In most instances pay to be raised by half the agreed amount on January 1, 1935, and by half six months later.

6. Operators of all one-man carriers, including buses, to receive 4 cents an hour more than members of two-man crews, the eight-hour day being applicable over a spread of twelve hours, with time and a half effective at nine hours.[67]

The signalmen obtained corresponding adjustments in their pay schedules, hours, and working conditions. Their net wage gain averaged 7.5 per cent and ranged from 1 to 17 cents an hour. All parties concerned were pleased with the agreement and signed an interim pact on December 21 which remained effective until March 9, 1935, when the final contract was sealed. Although the agreement was for only one year, it provided for automatic continuation unless either party desired to open it for modification. In subsequent months Pacific Electric signed contracts with the Brotherhood of Railway Carmen, the Brotherhood of Maintenance of Way Employees, the Brotherhood of Railway Clerks, the Association of Public Utility Employees, and the Union Electrical Railway Employees, the last being a company union. By the end of 1935 all the operating employees of the system belonged to one union or another.[68]

The willingness of Pacific Electric to reverse its long open-shop record was not echoed by officials of the Los Angeles Railway. When the NIRA was passed in 1933, leaders of the Amalgamated Association of Street and Electric Railway Employees began to organize the operating employees of that railway, including motor coach drivers, conductors, motormen, and substation employees. By December a local known as Division No. 997 had been formed, with a claimed membership of approximately 2,000 men, and charges filed with the Regional Labor Board alleged a violation of Section 7(a) in the fostering by the railway's management of a controlled company union. The board called a representation election for January 4, 1934, and University of Southern California students were placed in charge of seven polling places at which the 2,366 eligible operating employees were to cast their votes. The management refused to consent to the election, stating that the board did not have jurisdiction over an intrastate firm, but it did not prohibit the employees from voting. Election results revealed that of 2,120 votes cast, 1,290 were for Division 997 and 767 for the company union, known as the Los Angeles Railway Employees Association. Sixty-three ballots were void. Management officials promptly announced that they would not abide by a majority ruling, but would recognize all minority groups as well as individual employees in collective bargaining.[69]

A few weeks later union leaders filed charges with the Regional Labor Board alleging that seven substation employees had been dismissed in violation of Section 7(a) for minor rule infractions and union activity. The company denied the charges, stating that the dismissals were for inefficiency. After eight hearings, during which lawyers for the corporation filed fifty-one affidavits answering the plaintiffs and both sides were given ample opportunity to testify, the board decided against the union. Meanwhile, leaders of Division 997 continued their organizing activities, and in the fall of 1934, still failing to gain recognition, they again appealed to the Regional Labor Board. They charged not only that the company refused to recognize the union as the majority representative of the operating employees in accordance with the election of January 4, but also that the management had failed to negotiate with sincere intentions of reaching an agreement on wages and working conditions. They intimated that the union would call a strike and demand the removal of the NRA emblem unless the company yielded. J. Stuart Neary, legal adviser to the corporation, questioned the jurisdiction of the NRA in the case and supported the position taken by management in recognizing all groups as well as individuals in collective bargaining.[70]

On October 31, 1934, the board announced its decision: the management of the railway must recognize the union as sole collective bargaining agent for platform men, motor coach operators, and substation employees within the seven days following November 1, 1934, and signify within the same period its intention to bargain in good faith. Union officials thereupon presented the company with a contract providing for a pay increase of 12 cents an hour, a forty-eight-hour week, time and a half for overtime, an eight-hour day, union recognition, and arbitration of all questions in dispute during negotiations or other conferences. The management secured a delay in replying to the union demands, during which time P. J. O'Brien, international vice-president of the Amalgamated, arrived to assist in negotiations. In subsequent conferences with union officials and the Regional Labor Board, railway representatives pointed out that the wage demands would increase company expenses $1,500,000 a year, which it could not afford without an increase in fares, and that a pending investigation by city officials as to whether or not it could purchase new equipment would reveal its financial status. In addition, they argued that recognition of the union would itself violate the NIRA, as it would force a large group of employees into an organization they did not voluntarily choose as their collective bargaining agent.[71]

As the company seemed to be adamant on the recognition issue, union officials requested arbitration, but Neary countered by asking that the state's railroad commission appoint an impartial fact-finding board to investigate the financial status of the railway. The management also claimed that approximately 1,400 employees in the company union did not want a strike, but supported the right of workers to join a labor organization of their own choosing and settle employment issues through peaceful negotiations. After hearing both sides, the Regional Labor Board recommended impartial arbitration of all the points involved, but the company rejected this, leaving Division No. 997 in the position of having to call a strike in order to enforce its demands. Nylander tried to prevent a strike vote by calling a meeting of the disputants late in the afternoon of November 23, but he could not break the deadlock. At 2:30 the next morning a mass meeting of members of Division No. 997 voted for a walkout by a majority of 1,840 to 60. At 4 A.M. the strike was on.[72]

Officials of the Los Angeles Railway, believing the strike almost inevitable, had already made preparations for it. Company agents known to labor as "stool pigeons" had been mingling with the unionists long before the strike, a fact borne out by management's advance knowledge of union activities. Arrangements had been made to purchase tear gas and equipment for the use of the Los Angeles Police Department; Federal Laboratories, Inc., delivered $430 worth of such items a few days after the walkout began. Police officials had also laid plans for action in the event of a strike: officers in fifteen divisions and the central detective bureau went on twelve-hour shifts for the duration of the dispute; a special force of 600 policemen began patrolling carbarns, powerhouses, terminals, and substations; 16 officers experienced in mob fighting were kept in mobile reserve; 100 detectives were stationed at other strategic points; the entire motorcycle division of 107 officers was placed on strike alert; and ten radio cars from the county sheriff's office patrolled terminals in unincorporated areas. Even the city attorney's office was prepared to give twenty-four-hour service to the police if there were arrests. Municipal and county authorities were determined to prevent violence.[73]

The demands of the union leaders, which were widely publicized when the strike was called, included a closed-shop clause providing for complete job control. Open-shop adherents claimed that the basic issue really was complete unionization of the yellow-car lines under an association that had its headquarters in the East. Articles in the *Times* requested the public to support the workers who were not on strike, including the 1,400 members of the "street-car workers own local organization, the Los Angeles Railway Employees' Association," who disapproved of the dispute.[74] Although union officials did not deny that they were working for a closed shop, they claimed that their wage demands were reasonable, pointing out that at the height of prosperity in 1928–1929 the Los Angeles Railway had paid 57 cents an hour to motormen and conductors. In 1929 management had been authorized to raise fares, and it had then granted a wage increase of 1 cent an hour and instituted an insurance and retirement plan to which employees had been forced to contribute. With the coming of the depression, according to the union, the company had abolished certain minimum guarantees of monthly earnings to regular employees, such as pay for waiting time when men were on duty at division barns but not on cars, and had also instituted a 10 per cent wage reduction.[75]

Just before 4 A.M. on November 24, company officials posted a notice that the positions of all union men would be considered automatically vacated if they voluntarily left the employ of the railway. Although the union claimed that enough men had walked out to cripple rail and bus service, this seems to have been only temporary. Less than 500 men, or about a third of the claimed membership of the union, actually struck. President Samuel M. Haskins of the railway would not even admit to this figure, stating that on the morning of the strike 828 of the required 839 men reported for duty and normal service was restored by noon. Many of those at work, he said, were Division 997 members who did not support the strike. All vacancies were filled by extra men, pensioners, and retired carmen from other cities.[76]

Violence began late in the evening of the first day of the strike, resulting in injury to seven persons. More than a score of reports of rock throwing were filed with the police as pickets began to march around terminals in order to enlist or to heckle workers remaining on duty. On November 25 other reports mentioned such incidents as the greasing of rails, the disconnecting of a bus gas line, the beating of several nonstriking conductors, the placing of rocks on the tracks, the throwing of beer bottles, and the firing of rifles and pistols at streetcars. Mayor Shaw, disturbed by these events, sent a telegram to President Roosevelt requesting that every possible effort be made to end the walkout. The police arrested twenty-six strikers who participated in violent acts on the first day, but the officials of Division 997 disclaimed sanctioning the use of force. They stated that Communists as well as company spies were taking advantage of the situation to join union picket lines, encourage violence, and distribute handbills, but that they were being disavowed whenever they were discovered. Regardless of who was at fault, the company decided to protect its property by hiring private guards, and took extra precautions to prevent injury to passengers, particularly school children. Police officials substantiated the statements of union leaders that Communists were active in the strike, but said that unionists or other organized groups were also inciting violence by deliberately stoning streetcars.[77]

The significant strike disturbances of the following days occurred in the late afternoons and early evenings when homeward-bound workers crowded the streetcars. On November 26 the police were forced to use tear gas to disperse a rioting crowd at Seventh and Broadway which had yanked trolleys off the wires and was removing the valves from air brakes. Passengers, spectators, unionists, and car crews suffered from the effects of the gas and traffic became jammed for blocks, remaining tangled for two hours, but no one was seriously injured. Strike violence continued throughout November, but gradually lessened in December and January. A streetcar was overturned at the busy intersection of Pico and Vermont; another was derailed by an automobile axle; an attempt was made to burn a car at Third and Bixel streets. Several downtown riots required the use of tear gas, and in one area a dynamite stick was removed from the tracks. The consequent arrests resulted in a number of trials in which a few strikers were found guilty, mainly of felonious assaults on nonstriking crewmen. After January, however, all violence ceased as the strike waned.[78]

Local mediation efforts began on November 26 when Mayor Shaw held a peace conference in his office, but Haskins refused to reinstate the strikers in their jobs without prejudice pending an investigation by a fact-finding agency, claiming this action would discriminate against loyal workers. The Regional Labor Board also failed in a mediation attempt the next day. Company officials refused to acknowledge the board's jurisdiction, stating that striking members of Division 997 had left the employ of the railway voluntarily and that union leaders had disavowed unionists who had remained on the job. The management was clearly determined to follow an open-shop policy and not abide by the "majority rule" interpretation of Section 7(a). The dispute was definitely over as far as railway officials were concerned, though they had been willing to bargain simultaneously with three groups of employees—Division 997, the company union, and individuals—before the walkout. In their view, Division 997 no longer represented any of the employees, as it had disowned all its members who had remained at work. The attitude of the company and the failure of local efforts to settle the walkout brought the Pacific Coast supervisor for the NLRB, P. A. Donoghue, into the picture. His suggested truce, under which the company, over a period of ninety days, would reëmploy approximately 100 men not identified with acts of violence, was rejected by the union. The NLRB in Washington thereupon assumed jurisdiction in the case and arranged a hearing for December 20.[79]

In the meantime the strikers continued to picket the properties of the Los Angeles Railway and to hold daily mass meetings at the Labor Temple. The company intensified the training of new crews and promoted extra men to fill the vacancies created by the strike, so that the transportation system continued to operate. Union officials claimed that a 20 per cent wage bonus was being paid to nonstriking platform men, despite representations that the company could not afford an increase. With the strike obviously going against the union, officials of the Central Labor Council called a meeting of business agents on December 11 and laid plans to support Division 997 by raising funds, sending letters to all member unions requesting financial and moral support, organizing a public mass meeting of sympathizers, and launching a campaign against one-man cars and in favor of a municipal bus line. On December 21, through the medium of the *Citizen,* an active boycott was instituted against all those firms whose names were published in the *Times* as contributors to a "scab turkey fund." The fund had been started by the publisher of the newspaper in order to provide Christmas turkeys for all employees of the railway who had remained on the job.[80]

The mass meeting organized by the Central Labor Council was held at the Olympic Auditorium on December 27 under the auspices of several organizations, including the Epic League, the Municipal League, and the Workmen's Circle. The proceedings were broadcast over radio station KNX in an effort to give the strikers' cause wide publicity. Among the principal speakers was Allan E. Wilson, a former railroad commissioner in Nebraska, who outlined the cost and revenue situation of the streetcar lines. Wilson declared that the company should not have recorded any depreciation expense in 1933 because of the wear and tear on equipment. Without that item, net profit would have been $1,281,749, from which sum the wage increase demanded by the union could have been paid. According to Wilson, the increase would have amounted to $486,000 in 1933. Company officials asserted, however, that $1,455,698 was properly charged to depreciation expense, leaving the corporation with a net loss of $173,949. At the mass meeting, cards were passed out containing a pledge not to ride on transportation equipment belonging to the Los Angeles Railway. Other cards also were distributed which were to be signed and sent to Mayor Shaw; they complained of the alleged discriminatory attitude of the Police Department and called for a public hearing on a program seeking redress of grievances. Finally, it was announced that petitions were in the process of preparation and would be circulated early in 1935 requesting the initiation of a municipal motor coach system with a 5-cent fare.[81]

The NLRB, which had begun hearings on December 20, issued its decision on December 24. It held that the railway officials had violated Section 7(a) of the NIRA and must recognize Division 997 as collective bargaining agent for their employees. The management was given ten days to comply with the order and reinstate the men on strike. On December 28, the day after the Central Labor Council's mass meeting, the company again denied the board's jurisdiction, and claimed it was complying with the intent of the act in recognizing all organized and unorganized employees who wished to bargain collectively. It refused to abide by the decision. As Division 997 no longer had any members working on the rail line, the company union, organized a few days after Division 997 in August, 1933, now was the largest employee organization. The strikers, in a meeting held immediately after the company's announcement, voted in favor of the continuance of picketing, support of petitions for municipal buses, and action to initiate repeal of the law forbidding the operation of jitney buses. The latter, it was believed, would provide enough competition seriously to curtail the income of the Los Angeles Railway. On December 29, a midnight show was given by a number of unions in the entertainment field at the Million Dollar Theater for the benefit of the strikers, many of whom were in genuine need.[82]

On January 5, 1935, the NLRB requested the Recovery Administration to remove the blue eagle emblem from the Los Angeles Railway because of its noncompliance with the board's order. The management protested, reiterating its two main arguments: (1) it was operating an intrastate business and (2) it had complied with the letter of the law. In its opinion, the only valid way to take away the blue eagle was by due process of law through the federal courts. Nevertheless, the symbol of the NRA was removed on February 1, 1935. Although it is doubtful that this action alone caused much loss of business, the railway was feeling the financial pinch occasioned by the dispute. Open-shop supporters pointed out that the 485 men who had lost their jobs had given up approximately $75,000 in wages as of January 8, but the cost to the railway was also significant. Later investigations revealed that the company spent $333,481.49 in 1934 on items directly related to antiunion activities. This total included a payment of $7,393.68 to Captain Hynes of the Police Department Red Squad for his work in connection with the strike. Hynes was on leave from his position during this period in order to advise the management of the railway in its efforts to resist the organizational activities of Division 997.[83]

In January the strikers became more desperate. The international officers of the Amalgamated seemed to feel that the strike was lost, but the local union officials were determined to prolong it. Mayor Shaw acknowledged receipt of many of the postcards distributed at the mass meeting of December 27, but stated that, as the strike was under the jurisdiction of the NLRB, he would not interfere. In spite of the protests of Division 997 and the Central Labor Council, more one-man cars appeared on the streets and were approved by the city's Board of Public Utilities and Transportation. Labor leaders declared that the cars were a safety hazard and pointed to numerous accidents as proof of their statements. Company officials replied that all the motormen were trained and that the accidents were primarily a result of the activities of strikers and Communists who heckled the operators, hurled missiles through windows, removed the valves in air brakes, and placed objects on the tracks. The publicity given to these acts did not help the cause of the strikers, but they continued to hold union meetings in the Labor Temple and to serve meals to those of their number in greatest need. Members of Division 997 also tried to raise funds by holding a home talent show at the Temple.[84]

In January and February, 1935, more than 500 men and women, most of them affiliated with Division 997, circulated petitions requesting repeal of the city's ordinance against jitney buses and asking for their reëstablishment. At the same time the Central Labor Council asked the City Council to withhold approval of the purchase of new equipment by the Los Angeles Railway, inasmuch as petitions to establish a municipal bus line were being circulated by a group called the Municipal Bus League. Both petitions were filed with the city clerk in March and were rejected by the city's voters on May 7. Consequently, overenthusiastic members of Division 997 instituted their own jitney bus system on May 27, 30, and 31. Using a score of automobiles bearing the sign "Paper 5 cents, Ride Free," they carried passengers over the No. 3 streetcar route. No fare was charged but a newspaper was sold.

The police arrested seven of the drivers, charging them with operating buses without a permit, bond, or insurance. Four of the seven received sentences of a $100 fine or fifty days in jail, and the other three were put on probation.[85]

Early in February, 1935, the protective screens placed on the front windows of streetcars and buses were removed because most of the violence had ceased. On February 9 the NLRB reversed the decision of the regional board in the 1934 case of the seven substation employees, which had been appealed by Division 997, and issued an enforcement order. The national board found that six of the seven had been dismissed for union activity, which was discovered by means of undercover agents employed by the management. There was insufficient evidence concerning the seventh man. The board ordered reinstatement of the six within ten days. If compliance was not effected within that period, the case was to be turned over to California Recovery Act authorities for enforcement. The railway's management chose to ignore the order, and considered the threat to refer the case to state authorities an admission of the NLRB's lack of jurisdiction.[86]

The strike dragged on through March, though the union cause was obviously hopeless. Weekly dances to raise money were sponsored by Division 997. The strikers wrote protest letters to newspapers, visited the meetings of other unions to urge continued support, and made an ineffective attempt through Nylander to obtain an audience with company officials. The NLRB also made a final effort to secure compliance with its orders of December 24 and February 9. Mrs. Beatrice M. Stern, assistant executive secretary of the board, arrived in Los Angeles from Washington and requested City Attorney Ray L. Chesebro to prosecute the officials of the Los Angeles Railway under the California Recovery Act for their defiance. As the federal Department of Justice had declined to prosecute the railway, the management regarded Mrs. Stern's trip as a desperate face-saving effort on the part of the board. Chesebro questioned the legality of her request because a number of courts had declared Section 7(a) invalid when applied to intrastate commerce. J. J. Morgan, secretary of Division 997, threatened to take the case to the state attorney general if Chesebro failed to act, but this had little effect. The city attorney refused to prosecute the railway under the statute of limitations, which provided that an indictment for any misdemeanor must be found or a complaint filed within one year after its commission. In this case, the railway management had refused to bargain with representatives of Division 997 on January 5, 1934, more than fourteen months earlier. Robert B. Watts, special counsel for the

NLRB, also asked Chesebro to take action against the company. Watts declared that federal authorities had exhausted their resources in the case and that prosecution was now a matter for local and state authorities. When Chesebro rejected this request, the case was dropped.[87]

Members of Division 997, however, remained on strike for several months. They reduced the number of their delegates to the Central Labor Council and frequently requested additional funds from other unions, though most of them had applied for relief or found other jobs. In August, 1935, the strikers gave two of their officers power of attorney to sue for a share in the distribution of the "Los Angeles Railway Employees' Provident Fund," instituted in 1930 to provide pensions for loyal employees. Three per cent of each worker's pay check had been placed in the account, together with a similar amount contributed by the company. Early in 1935, when company officials decided to liquidate the fund, the strikers sought to participate in the distribution of the reserve that had accumulated while most of them were employed by the railway. Through their attorneys they secured a restraining order against further liquidation of the fund, pending adjudication. The strikers' case was lost, however, in a trial before Superior Court Judge Maurice Dooling. This was a blow to many of them who had been on State Emergency Relief Administration rolls since the latter part of December, 1934. In June, 1935, SERA officials attempted to transfer some of the strikers from direct relief to work relief, but a protest to federal relief officials in Washington by officers of Division 997 stopped this move. Similar action by the SERA in October also was appealed and subsequently canceled. The unionists claimed that forcing strikers on direct relief to work on public projects would mean that a government body was functioning in a strikebreaking capacity.[88]

The last action taken by the members of Division 997 before the union passed from the scene pertained to the operation of one-man cars. A fire on a one-man trolley at Fifth and Main streets in the fall of 1935 brought the issue before the City Council, and a series of lengthy debates ensued concerning the safety and comfort of passengers on such conveyances. The union induced the Central Labor Council to pass resolutions against the cars and in favor of the licensing of all streetcar and bus operators, and the council officers were instructed to appear before the city fathers on these issues. The real intent of the resolutions was eventually to force the Los Angeles Railway to place two men on all cars as well as to begin an expensive training program which would increase its operating costs. The City Council did not take the action desired by Division 997, and in a few months the local surrendered its charter.[89] Employees of the Los Angeles Railway remained free of the influence of outside unions for a number of years, but the one-man car and municipal bus issues continued to be subjects of public discussion and petitions for the remainder of the decade.

5. THE END OF THE NRA

The blue eagle aided other unions in their organizing campaigns in 1934 and 1935, but their efforts were little publicized. Among these were shoe workers, bill posters, handbill distributors, moving picture projectionists, musicians, stage employees, barbers, fur workers, borax workers, brewery employees, and coopers, all of whom showed more life than they had evidenced in many years. There was little question that the NIRA was responsible for this renewed activity, but the effectiveness of the act diminished as the months passed.[90]

The actual operation of the act was seriously hampered by disagreement over interpretation of its provisions and by the lack of authority of the labor boards. Both these factors were especially evident in open-shop Los Angeles. As originally organized, the Los Angeles Regional Labor Board had ten members, an impartial chairman, and an executive secretary. Five members represented organized labor and five were industrial spokesmen. The first chairman was Joy L. Leonard, a University of Southern California professor, with Campbell McCulloch as the full-time, paid executive secretary. A delay in lining up employer representatives postponed the first meeting of the board until November 28, 1933, at which time it established its policy and procedure regarding the holding of hearings. The regional board functioned under the National Labor Board, an agency authorized by the NIRA. Although periodic executive orders of President Roosevelt extended the jurisdiction of both the national and the regional boards, these bodies never had the full support of NRA officials in Washington and were unable to enforce their decisions by legal processes. Labor union officials interpreted the executive orders and statements of the President so as to infer an advantage for organized labor, but his early declarations apparently were intended only to clarify the prohibition in Section 7(a) against employer interference in workers' rights to organize in any way they desired, and they indirectly tended to give encouragement to company unions in Los Angeles and other open-shop cities.

On February 1, 1934, President Roosevelt issued an executive order calling for a "majority rule" interpretation of the results of representation elections held by the National Labor Board for collective bargaining purposes. Local and national labor leaders believed that this order would outlaw the interpretation of the act under which many employers continued to deal with representatives of company unions and minority groups of employees, as well as with the outside organization designated by the majority of the workers, but they were wrong. The regional boards were unable to enforce the "majority rule" order in Los Angeles and elsewhere. When the National Labor Board was dissolved on July 9, 1934, and replaced by the National Labor Relations Board, the problems of employer-dominated company unions and of enforcement of the majority representation rule still remained. Los Angeles locals thus continued to be hampered in their organizational efforts by company organizations and splinter representation groups, which were weapons used to maintain the open shop.[91]

Another aspect of the NRA which concerned Los Angeles labor officials was the relationship between the Chamber of Commerce and the local blue eagle offices. When the Recovery Act was passed, chambers of commerce, representing cross sections of the business population, were called upon to establish local offices of the code agency. In Los Angeles, chamber officers thus assisted in starting the NRA organization, stating that it was the duty of everyone to help support the President's program. Local NRA officials were housed in the same building as the chamber and soon had a reputation of close association with it. As the Chamber of Commerce supported the open shop, and many M and M members belonged to it, Los Angeles labor officials were suspicious of the local NRA body, though they believed that the Regional Labor Board functioned somewhat apart from the rest of the organization. This was borne out by the board's consistent rulings against the practice adopted by some employers of discharging union members when a controversy arose and then claiming they were no longer employees and thus not entitled to representation or consideration. The lack of enforcement authority made the rulings of little effect, but they indicated an attempt on the part of the board to abide by the spirit of the NIRA regardless of the local strength of open-shop supporters and their continued efforts to keep out labor unions.[92]

The ineffectiveness of the NRA in Los Angeles was admitted by Secretary Buzzell of the Central Labor Council in his annual report in June, 1934. He pointed out that Los Angeles employers were in almost complete control of the seventeen local compliance boards and had largely ignored union suggestions with regard to the codes.[93] A similar situation prevailed throughout the state, according to reports made at the convention of the California State Federation of Labor in September, 1934. President A. W. Hoch stated in his annual report:

In reviewing past events, we find that Section 7-a of NRA has not yet proven sufficient, for it has been widely evaded by employers.

Regional labor boards throughout the country have been overwhelmed by the number of grievances placed before them for adjustment. Such complaints have been filed more rapidly than they could be disposed of. They constitute the massed evidence that many employers, not negligently or unknowingly but deliberately, have determined to ignore and violate the labor provisions of NRA and of approved code. Workers have been compelled to use strike measures in order to force employers to concede the exercise of a right guaranteed them by this law.

Certain employer groups have been organized for the purpose of fostering and developing an anti-union, anti-collective bargaining campaign. These associations have within their active membership much of the personnel of the code authorities. Such collective bargaining may have been necessary to protect wage earners welfare prior to the NRA but, under codes, collective bargaining is no longer necessary. . . .

Should the labor policy of the employers be successful, it will mean that the intent and purposes of the NRA will be destroyed.[94]

Hoch was a member of the Los Angeles labor movement and had been a firsthand observer of the operation of the NRA in that city. President William Green of the AFL and other national labor leaders likewise pointed out that the economic and psychological barriers against unionism remained, even though legal obstacles had been removed. Like local union officials, they specifically criticized employers for their lack of coöperation in code making, their evasions of the law, and their failure to provide adequate wage and hour clauses in the codes which might have made possible a net increase in employment. A number of labor leaders were sufficiently clairvoyant in late 1934 to predict the demise of the act the next year.[95]

While these criticisms were being leveled at the NRA, the Los Angeles Regional Labor Board was having its troubles. In September, 1934, Towne J. Nylander, a professor of economics at Occidental College, replaced McCulloch as secretary of the board. In that month the board faced a crisis when five of its employer representatives quit without warning. Ostensibly the reason was a lack of harmony between them and the employee representatives on the board, all of whom were members of or formerly affiliated with labor unions. As only a minority of southern California workers were unionists, it was not surprising that dissension should develop over the issue as to whether or not the employee representatives should all be union sympathizers. The *Citi-*

zen alleged that the resignations were submitted on order of M and M officials who were seeking to discredit the Regional Labor Board, but this could not be proved. The resignations and the allegations of bias did not torpedo the board, however, and it continued to function after being reorganized in October as a subsidiary of the new National Labor Relations Board. By November it was again handling disputes arising under Section 7(a), as well as assuming the role of conciliator to avert threatened strikes.[96]

Meanwhile, the National Labor Relations Board informed President Roosevelt that its lack of power to issue subpoenas and to enforce orders was invalidating Section 7(a). Senator Robert Wagner of New York urged the passage of new legislation designed to correct these and other deficiencies of the NIRA. In his opinion Section 7(a) had been weakened because the managements of large corporations continued to deny collective bargaining rights to workmen organized in AFL unions. The opportunity to pass a new law dealing with this problem came on May 27, 1935, when the United States Supreme Court declared the code-making authority of the statute unconstitutional. Shortly thereafter, on June 14, Congress repealed Title I and voted to extend the remainder of the NIRA until April 1, 1936. Labor leaders throughout the nation were dismayed by the Supreme Court decision, even though they had been critical of the act. They immediately urged the adoption of legislation that would legalize that portion of the old law contained in Section 7(a) and provide means for the enforcement of its provisions. Their hopes were realized by the passage of the National Labor Relations Act (NLRA or Wagner Act), which was signed by the President on July 5, 1935. Thus workers experienced only a momentary setback in recognition of their legal rights to organize and bargain collectively without fear of intimidation or discrimination.[97]

The NLRA did not regulate wages, hours, or working conditions. Section 7 of the new law incorporated the essential features of the old Section 7(a), thus guaranteeing employees the right to organize and bargain collectively. Section 8 prevented employer interference in the rights established under Section 7. The act also enlarged and strengthened the enforcement powers of the National Labor Relations Board, which was authorized to issue a cease-and-desist order against an employer found guilty of committing any of the unfair labor practices itemized in the law. Such an order could be issued only after a complaint had been made to the board and a fair hearing had been held. Certain affirmative actions also could be required of the employer, and the board had the power to petition for an enforcing order from the United States Circuit Court of Appeals or, under certain circumstances, the United States District Court, in the circuit or district, respectively, in which the offense occurred. The existing national board, which had been established on June 29, 1934, was continued by an executive order until a new board could be organized under the NLRA. In the summer of 1935 President Roosevelt nominated three persons to be the members of the new NLRB, and they were confirmed by the Senate on August 24. All regional boards and field personnel were subsequently transferred to the new organization.

In spite of these changes, employers, particularly in open-shop centers like Los Angeles, were no more ready to submit to the provisions of the new law than they had been to comply with the NIRA. Many of them believed that the legislation did not have to be obeyed until it had been reviewed by the Supreme Court, and they were quite certain that it would then be invalidated. Hence, until 1937, when the law was declared constitutional, it continued to be difficult for the national and regional labor boards to enforce their decisions. Often employers not only ignored the boards, but also obtained injunctions against their orders. Company unions also continued to expand during these two years. After the NLRA was sanctioned by the Supreme Court, however, employers began to comply with board decisions. Hence labor leaders, discouraged at first by the act's initial lack of success, found it to be at least a partial fulfillment of their hopes for legislation guaranteeing workers the right to organize and bargain collectively.[98]

The experiences of the labor movement over the nation in this transition period were mirrored to a large extent in Los Angeles. Neither the local nor the national movement was seriously affected by termination of the NRA, though there was a lull in organizing activity in Los Angeles throughout the summer of 1935, after the Supreme Court decision. Numerous reports of pay reductions, increases in the length of the workweek, and price cuts were sent to the Central Labor Council, but there were actually very few changes in hours, wages, and working conditions in larger firms and in companies where strong unions were active. Most of the reports originated in small concerns whose managements had a record of consistent opposition to the NIRA. Members of the building trades unions ran into some difficulties on several small jobs where the contractors notified their men that they must work longer hours with no provision for overtime pay. The garment-manufacturing and printing trades, on the other hand, were in the forefront of those industries maintaining the wages and hours specified in the NRA codes.[99]

Several efforts were made locally to assess the effect of the end of the NRA on the labor movement and to gather support for the proposed legislation which was to become the NLRA. On June 6, 1935, members of Local No. 278 of the Amalgamated Clothing Workers sponsored an open mass meeting in the Labor Temple which was attended mostly by unionists in the garment trades. After considerable discussion, those present decided that the Supreme Court decision had not caused any significant deterioration in labor relations policies in clothing manufacturing. A second mass meeting, this time under the auspices of the Central Labor Council, was held on June 13 in Trinity Auditorium. Its purpose was to demonstrate the numerical strength of the labor movement in Los Angeles and give support to the AFL legislative program aimed at passage of the Wagner bill. Speakers on the program included C. J. Haggerty, secretary of the Los Angeles Building and Construction Trades Council; William W. Busick, an organizer for the ILGWU; John F. Dalton, president of ITU Local No. 174 and a member of the Los Angeles Board of Education; Paul Scharrenberg, secretary of the California State Federation of Labor; and J. W. Buzzell, secretary of the Los Angeles Central Labor Council. Postcards were distributed for unionists to send to their congressmen asking them to support legislation providing for social security, a thirty-hour week, and the right of workers to organize and bargain collectively without interference from employers. Union members were also urged to write separate letters to their congressmen asking, in particular, for passage of the Wagner bill. Local labor leaders believed that this proposed legislation would give them a strong ally in their battle against the open shop.[100]

When the NLRA became law in July, 1935, the fears of Los Angeles labor leaders that the demise of the NRA might sweep away all organizational gains made since 1933 were dispelled. In subsequent months the Regional Labor Board was again reorganized and Nylander reappointed as its executive secretary. Union activity continued much the same as before, and on December 31, 1935, Secretary Buzzell reported little change in the strength of the local labor movement. At that time organized labor in Los Angeles was composed of 15 councils and boards, 4 departmental bodies, 165 local unions, and 20 women's auxiliaries. This count excluded company, independent, and railroad unions. The total membership of the movement was estimated to be about the same as at the end of 1934, or 70,000, but this figure must be discounted as optimistic. The total paid-up strength seemed to be slightly more than reported a year earlier, or about 45,000. Thus, as local labor leaders looked toward 1936, their confidence was bolstered by the fact that the change in national legislation in 1935 apparently had caused no serious damage to the movement—certainly not in terms of numbers. Although the struggle against the open shop was no closer to a successful conclusion than it had been in 1933, at least the battle front seemed to be stabilized. The next several years were to see a climax in the struggle, as unionists sought to take advantage of the NLRA and open-shop supporters regrouped to prevent the demise of a system of industrial relations for which the city had been famous since 1890.[101]

IX. UNION SUCCESS
IN THE MOVIE INDUSTRY

1. UNIONIZATION IN THE MOVIES

THE EARLY 1930's witnessed signs of the coming of age of unions in the motion picture industry. The National Industrial Recovery Act gave an impetus to organization in Hollywood, not only among skilled and unskilled workers but also among the talent groups which normally would not have been expected to show an interest in unions. Yet what happened in these depression years cannot be completely understood without looking back at some of the earlier developments in labor relations. Unions had long been interested in the effective organization of movie lots. Collective bargaining victories in the studios would certainly contribute to organized labor's prestige because of the economic importance of the film industry in a southern California dominated by the open shop. The characteristics of the industry, however, were such that most of the work in its studios, shops, and offices had little connection with the activities of unions elsewhere in Los Angeles, even those in the same craft. The movie moguls employed heterogeneous groups of workers who were faced with dissimilar problems: technicians with differences in skill, status, and earning power; guilds of creative talent such as artists, actors, writers, and directors; skilled professionals such as make-up men who were tied closely to the studios; and craftsmen such as carpenters, electricians, and similar artisans with the same abilities as their fellows outside the lots. Employers were very conscious of certain factors peculiar to movie making, which, in turn, affected their attitudes toward their employees. These included the speculative nature of the industry—every picture was a gamble until the box office proved it otherwise—a flexible cost structure, rapid technological and economic change, and casual employment for many of the workers.[1]

Most of the early development of the industry occurred in New York City before World War I. As Eastern employers took a less adamant stand on the open shop than did their counterparts in Los Angeles, unions did not at first encounter strong opposition in the studios. The climatic advantage of Hollywood for motion picture manufacture soon became evident, however, and forces were set in motion which changed the sleepy agricultural crossroads into the screen capital of the world. By 1920 Hollywood had attained a supremacy in "flicker" manufacture which was never again seriously challenged. Its subsequent development was a major factor in the industrial growth of Los Angeles, and its large payroll was a challenge to the unions. Open-shop adherents in Los Angeles feared that the combination of Eastern control and physical separation from the heart of the city would make the industry a tempting plum for union organizers.[2]

Stagehands and musicians were largely unionized in the legitimate theater by 1916. It was only to be expected that there would be a desire to transfer this success to Hollywood. Because movie producers were used to dealing with unions in the East and were not closely tied to downtown Los Angeles business interests, union leaders believed that their chances of success would be quite good. At first local producers presented a uniform front for maintenance of the open shop through the Motion Picture Producers' Association. By 1922, however, this organization had been supplanted by the Motion Picture Producers' and Distributors' Association, headed by Will Hays and headquartered in the East. As the new association had nothing to do with labor directly, it formed an affiliate in Hollywood under the leadership of Pat Casey, known as the Association of Motion Picture Producers, to handle industrial relations problems. The organization of the movie crafts was beginning to be significant in Hollywood in the early 1920's, although the union shop still did not prevail. As Casey's staff conducted negotiations with unions, some standardization of contracts was achieved. At the same time, all agreements were signed individually by the member studios in the association. Uniformity of policy was thus obtained, but each studio was individually responsible for the enforcement of its agreements. By 1926 the craft unions, along with the musicians, had made extensive inroads in the industry. These groups were parties to what became known as the Studio Basic Agreement of that year. It stipulated recognition of the unions and the institution of procedures that gradually replaced the vestiges of the open shop among these workers.[3]

The creative talent categories were not similarly organized. In recognition of this fact and in an effort to forestall unionization, the producers established the Academy of Motion Pictures Arts and Sciences (AMPAS) in May, 1927, with five branches representing the most important divisions of motion picture production: producers, writers, directors, actors, and technicians. Through democratic processes, each branch elected an executive committee to function as its governing body, and the branches were equally represented on the Academy's board of directors. Every effort was made to make the AMPAS a prestige organization, above the status of a labor union. Individuals were selected for membership by invitation, which was ostensibly based on distinguished accomplishments in film production. This method of selection, however, kept the control of the organization in the hands of a few, so that it took on many of the aspects of a company union.[4]

Thus, organization in the motion picture industry was spotty and incomplete until the 1930's. Only the craft groups had legitimate unions, and even here there was no consistent tie with their fellow craftsmen in the Central Labor Council. Their work differed from that done by their counterparts in the building trades, as they worked primarily on sets or in maintenance. Because set work required extremely close coördination among the skills, frequent jurisdictional disputes arose, some of which lasted for long periods and were marked by bitter controversy. Furthermore, much of the work done by the crafts as well as the talent groups was casual in nature, providing a different pattern of employment from that prevalent in downtown unions. Executives handling craft and talent employees in the industry had to recognize and cope with these characteristics of employment. The problems incident to achieving job satisfaction for highly trained employees, some of whom were casual whereas others were on contract, at times seemed almost insurmountable. They required special handling, and if this was not successful, disputes occurred which often bore little relationship to what was going on simultaneously in the rest of the labor movement in the Los Angeles area.[5]

2. Organization among the Crafts

The motion picture industry has long been divided into three fields of operation: production, distribution, and exhibition. The exhibition branch was the first to be unionized because of the strength of unions in the amusement trades in the legitimate theater before the introduction of movies. The International Alliance of Theatrical Stage Employees (IATSE) and the American Federation of Musicians (AFM), both affiliated with the AFL, were the two strongest unions in the amusement field when films first made their appearance. The motion picture machine operators soon came under the jurisdiction of the IATSE, and the musicians who played during silent movies were considered suitable prospects for the AFM. The IA subsequently changed its name to the International Alliance of Theatrical Stage Employees and Motion Picture Machine Operators.[6]

Union organization moved from the theaters to the production end of motion pictures, where the Alliance became a powerful force long before the talent workers had any effective unionization. Basically the

IA developed into a horizontal combination of locals of crafts closely related to the building trades, plus a few other groups such as the motion picture machine operators, the property men, and grips. Because it cut across a number of crafts, and because set construction was such that lines of demarcation were not always clearly defined, a quasi-industrial type of union organization began to emerge at studios and theaters. This trend was resented by the AFL craft union internationals with which the backstage locals were affiliated, even while they were also members of the Alliance. The resentment was particularly acute in the Los Angeles area, where most of the motion picture production was centered. Its roots went back to 1908, when the IATSE first asserted its jurisdiction over motion pictures and established two locals of projectionists in Los Angeles. The 1912 IATSE convention decided that film sets were similar to stage sets and therefore should be made only by members of the organization. IA leaders realized that the projectionists could play a key role in the organization of production employees through their power to resist the showing of "unfair" films made by non-Alliance workers.[7]

In Los Angeles the IA carried on basic organizational work in the motion picture industry through its local of theater stagehands. Its attempts to organize carpenters, electricians, and other trades in the studios as well as to use the projectionists as a weapon to this end angered the internationals with jurisdiction over these crafts. Their officers saw the movie studios as opportunities to strengthen their own locals in the face of downtown open-shop opposition. Their resentment spurred numerous attempts to expel members who also belonged to the IATSE. Unfortunately, both the craft unions and the Alliance competed to supply manpower to the studios by offering lower wage rates and currying the favor of foremen and managers. Consequently, for many years before the 1930's neither wage rates nor working conditions were stabilized in the film industry. Wage scales, in fact, were often less than in downtown Los Angeles. Thus unionism could not uphold its frequent claim that it eliminated unfair competition through the standardization of employment conditions. The combination of jurisdictional troubles within the studios and competition between IATSE and non-IATSE locals to furnish manpower often led to disputes and walkouts which put the studios squarely in the middle. Furthermore, the producers lacked power to stop the controversy except through temporary recourse to open-shop conditions, and this only aggravated the situation.[8]

The IATSE had first appeared on the Los Angeles scene in 1893, when Local No. 33, consisting of stagehands, was chartered. Through the efforts of this local, as noted above, the IA spread to movie projection in 1908 and, finally, to general studio construction activities four years later. The Los Angeles Building and Construction Trades Council began dispatching carpenters to the studios in 1914 when they seemed to be developing as a source of employment, but it was not until 1916 that the AFL took official cognizance of them by sending Jim Gray out from the East to organize the industry. The result of Gray's visit, however, was not a clear victory for the AFL. Organizing efforts led to three significant strikes in the next five years, awakened producers to the existence of a labor problem in the studios, caused them to organize the open-shop Motion Picture Producers' Association comprising seventeen studios, and marked the beginning of a unified labor policy in film production.[9]

The IATSE sent its own organizers into the studios in late 1917 and early 1918. The subsequent campaign included closed-shop demands, boycotting of movies, and attempts by the stagehands' local to unite all studio mechanics in one union. The last action soon generated jurisdictional trouble, especially with the carpenters. While the stagehands were affiliated with the IATSE, they did not belong to an AFL craft international. Hence the Los Angeles Building Trades Council appealed to the federation for clarification of the situation and requested support from the Central Labor Council. Committees from the two councils and the Alliance sought to iron out the conflict, but were unsuccessful. The Los Angeles District Council of Carpenters then voted, on March 4, 1918, to unseat all delegates from carpenters' unions affiliated with the IATSE. Thus began the jurisdictional conflict that was to plague the studios and hamper organizing efforts for many years to come.[10]

The IATSE continued its activity among studio craftsmen, and in July, 1918, called a strike against twenty-five motion picture producers. The demands included a $6 day to meet the rising cost of living, time and a half for overtime with double pay on Sundays, and a closed shop. Halfhearted efforts were made to enforce the demands over the nation by allying with the Sunday closing and film censorship movements, and by urging the institution of sympathetic strikes in theaters. A number of the studios were closed for varying periods of time, while others continued operating by hiring strikebreakers. These were not too difficult to procure in set construction, as the United Brotherhood of Carpenters urged its members to stay on the job and also to fill the places of IA carpenters who walked out. The strike ended in a compromise on

September 10. The wage scale of $6 a day was granted, but not union recognition. The overtime issue was settled later by arbitration.[11]

The IATSE increased its strength in the studios over the next six months, reporting 930 new members by February, 1919, most of whom came from unions affiliated with the Building Trades Council. Hence the jurisdictional issue again flared up and remained unresolved, despite further conferences called by P. H. McCarthy, AFL representative from San Francisco. On September 15, 1919, the IA struck against twenty-six producers, demanding recognition and a union shop as well as contracts with individual studios rather than a blanket agreement. Approximately 400 carpenters, electricians, stagehands, property men, and technical directors walked out. The Building Trades Council and the Brotherhood of Carpenters again supplied strikebreakers, and in the theaters the International Brotherhood of Electrical Workers (IBEW) agreed to replace projectionists who refused to show pictures produced by studios on strike. Thus the studios could resume operations without attempting to resolve the dispute, and the question of jurisdiction remained unsettled.

At the AFL convention of 1919 the IBEW sought to have the IATSE charter revoked, and the Los Angeles Building Trades Council lodged complaints the following year. As a result, the AFL Executive Council directed the IATSE to relinquish its claim over carpenters, painters, plasterers, and other building trades and to disaffiliate these crafts from its organization. The Alliance was given jurisdiction over projectionists and set electricians, but the IBEW was to handle the laying of conduit and electrical installations. Although the newly elected IA officers agreed to this decision, it did not end the strife. Complaints were made at the 1921 AFL convention that the IA was in fact not complying with the decision. When investigation revealed this to be true, the Executive Council ordered compliance by August 1, 1921, under penalty of loss of its charter. The IATSE thereupon made specific written agreements with the building trades unions involved, thus temporarily resolving the jurisdictional conflict.[12]

Meanwhile, events were shaping up for the most important dispute of 1921 in Los Angeles outside the printing trades' struggle for the forty-four-hour week. In the wave of the postwar deflation movement, eleven studios decided to lower the wages of craftsmen by $1 to $3 a day even though motion picture production was enjoying a high level of activity. They also began to pay straight-time rates up to ten hours rather than eight, and took a stand for the open shop. To enforce these policies, the producers locked out between 800 and 1,200 craftsmen on July 8, 1921, and hired nonunion men to take their places. The unions concerned immediately turned the lockout into a strike by picketing the studios, forcing them to shut down for periods that varied from a week to a month because of interference with their operations. To support the strikers, the Central Labor Council aligned itself with the movement to close theaters on Sundays and threatened to circulate petitions to this end. It also endorsed film censorship and asked workers in other industries to call sympathetic strikes and to boycott the films of the struck studios, which were placed on a nationwide unfair list. As would be expected, the *Times* and the M and M supported the producers. M and M members were asked to refuse to sign petitions for a Sunday closing law, while the newspaper sought to stir public opinion against the strikers by alleging that John S. Horn of the Labor Council had accused the American Legion of furnishing strikebreakers.[13]

The Central Labor and Building Trades councils formed the Joint Studio Committee to direct the strike under the chairmanship of Vern Ostendorf. Federal mediator Charles T. Connell sought to bring the parties together, but failed in all attempts. By August the strikers were concentrating on four major studios: Famous Players–Lasky Corporation, William Fox Productions, Goldwyn Productions, and Christie Comedies. The electricians imposed levies on working members in an attempt to raise funds to continue the struggle, and in November the Labor Council initiated an assessment of 50 cents a month against its membership. In the same month Samuel Gompers asked the studio owners to meet with AFL organizer Joshua Dale, but they refused. As they were able to operate with strikebreakers, they were not inclined to deal with the unions. In a final desperate effort, Gompers arranged a meeting in New York City at which he discussed the issues with William F. Brady, Jesse L. Lasky, Winfred Sheehan, Samuel Goldwyn, and D. W. Griffith, but little came of the conference. By the early months of 1922 it was obvious that the strike was lost. Although the Joint Studio Committee tried to continue its world-wide boycott against the films of the principal studios, it had little effect on movie attendance and the lots remained open shop.[14]

In the next several years the studio craftsmen became increasingly dissatisfied with the fluctuating employment conditions within the industry. Jurisdictional strife continued, but it was overshadowed by the desire of craftsmen to lessen their job insecurity. Growing numbers of them therefore turned to their respective unions. Though the producers did not discriminate against union men in hiring, a good many of their needs for technicians were met through a placement bureau on South Hill Street rather than through union halls. In 1925 the IATSE compromised its jurisdictional differences with the carpenters, and in 1926 with the electrical workers. A united front among the studio unions, whether affiliated with the AFL alone or with both the Alliance and the AFL, was achieved before the end of the year. Demands for a closed shop, a readjusted wage scale, the eight-hour day, pay for six holidays a year, and extra compensation on Sundays were then made on the major studios, which were grouped together as the Association of Motion Picture Producers. The employers found themselves faced with a solid craft-union front and a threatened closure of the theaters by the projectionists. In November, 1926, therefore, they agreed to a contract, effective December 1, which became known as the Studio Basic Agreement.

Though the Basic Agreement did not provide for a closed shop, it granted recognition to the IATSE and the unions of carpenters, painters, electrical workers, and musicians, most of which were loosely connected through the Studio Mechanics Alliance, the agency that coördinated the activities of the IA and the separate AFL unions. The agreement was not primarily concerned with working conditions, but it did provide for an eight-hour day, higher wages for Sundays, overtime periods, and enumerated holidays. It also established two committees, one composed of five producers and the other of the international presidents of the five unions involved. These committees were to meet together periodically for the purpose of settling all disputes that might arise. In this way the producers hoped to eliminate jurisdictional disputes by bypassing local business agents. In practice, however, the secretaries of the two committees actually settled many of the minor difficulties. Disputes they could not resolve were referred to the committee chairmen and, as a last resort, to high executives of the unions and the studios in the East.[15]

The original two-year Studio Basic Agreement, though renewed several times, was not a complete success. Its operation was hampered more by lack of coöperation among labor representatives than anything else. Minute job divisions made in an effort to reduce jurisdictional strife actually were the principal causes of friction among the unions. They led to a number of halts in production in the next five years, but to few extreme actions. The onset of sound movies fed the jurisdictional fire, as the IBEW and the IATSE both sought to organize the sound technicians. Nevertheless, the period from 1927 to 1933 was marked by unprecedented increases both in the number of new unions formed and in the membership of individual locals, despite constant opposition from the *Times* and other open-shop supporters. An organizing campaign in 1928 and 1929 resulted in almost complete unionization of the different mechanical trades as well as of several additional groups such as wardrobe workers, costumers, engineers, and cameramen. The introduction of sound aided Musicians Local No. 47, as many instrumentalists migrated to the West. By 1930 this union was the third largest in its trade in the United States.[16]

The Studio Basic Agreement was renewed in 1928 for three years. It provided for a 25-cent increase in daily wages for craftsmen each year until November, 1931. Negotiations were for the most part confined to New York meetings beyond the reach of the *Times* and the M and M. A two-year extension negotiated in 1931 continued the agreement through November, 1933.

In this period a number of smaller studios organized the Independent Motion Picture Producers' Association. One of its members, Like Ltd., was faced with a strike of IA sound technicians on July 20, 1932. These workers had no contract with either the major studios or the independents, and they considered Like an easy target to hit in an effort to gain recognition. The strike ended two days later with both sides claiming victory. Agreement was reached on a wage scale totaling $225 per week for a three-man sound crew working on a seven-day basis without overtime. The producers believed that they were the winners in this arrangement because the sound men had wanted $100 more than this sum. On the other hand, the IA union had achieved recognition under a two-year agreement, though not a closed shop.[17]

In the meantime, the depression had begun to make inroads on wages, hours, and employment in the studios. By late 1930 all members of the Studio Mechanics Alliance reported increasing irregularity of employment and membership turnover. RKO-Pathé adopted a six-hour day in 1931 in order to spread the work, and a number of other studios followed suit. Paramount cut salaries in April, 1932, but union workers were exempt under the Basic Agreement. The same year all studios went on a five-day week in further support of the share-the-work movement. In spite of these cuts, motion picture craftsmen were generally in better financial circumstances in 1933 than were their counterparts on the outside. This did not mean, however, that the producers were in good shape. Box-office receipts declined rapidly after 1930; employment opportunities shrank for everyone from stenographer to star; the studios found themselves saddled with properties, such as lavish production facilities and ornate theaters, which had been acquired at inflated prices in the pre-1929 real estate boom. By 1933 a number of the studios were on the brink of a disaster that soon bankrupted Paramount, forced Fox to reorganize, threw RKO into receivership, and pushed several others into oblivion.

Under the economic exigencies of the times, including the bank holiday which caught the studios without ready cash, the major producers announced an eight-week salary slash in March, 1933. It was to be a 50 per cent cut for all workers receiving $50 a week or more regardless of talent, skill, or position, except that the minimum income was set at $37.50. Weekly wages of less than $50 were to be cut by 25 per cent, but not below $15. Although most of the nonunion craftsmen were willing to accept the reduction, it was rejected by stars, directors, writers, and other contract people; stenographers and similar low-pay white-collar workers; and a number of the IATSE and other locals. The opposition of both union and talent groups caused the studios to reconsider. A strike seemed probable if some adjustment was not made in the original proposal, particularly as it affected the lower-paid employees. Consequently the studios proposed an alternate arrangement providing for graduated cuts, the size of the reduction to depend on the salary or wage received, with no reduction for employees paid $50 or less per week. Four of the IA unions refused to accept the new proposal, but agreed to continue work while the matter was discussed in New York between international and producer representatives. The salary cut subsequently proved to be a mistake. It antagonized the craft and other skilled employees; it caused the talent groups to start thinking about some form of labor organization; and it marked the beginning of the end of the usefulness of the Academy of Motion Picture Arts and Sciences in the labor relations field. Executives of most of the major studios soon realized their error and restored full salary scales before the end of the eight-week period, but the damage had been done.[18]

Another factor influencing the talent groups to organize was Academy action in connection with the National Industrial Recovery Act. Producers worked through the Academy in attempting to get into the NRA code certain provisions regarding the licensing of agents and the control of salaries, all of which were opposed by the artists and made the Academy suspect as a company union. The NIRA, in effect, marked the beginning of the guild movement among the talent groups and the end of harmonious relations between screen actors and producers under Academy auspices.

As far as the studio craftsmen were concerned, the NRA lowered hours and increased pay per hour. Employment was improved through spreading the available work. The more competent employees, however, disliked sharing their employment with marginal workers, and the studios claimed that the shorter workday decreased productive efficiency and thus raised labor costs. By and large, union leaders were happy with the NRA as it provided for a six-hour day, kept the formerly unemployed members reasonably contented, and gave the locals large paid-up rosters through membership rotation in jobs. The NRA code also provided for standard wage rates in all skill classifications and time and a half for overtime. In addition, it placed foremen on a weekly salary, enabling the studios to keep them on call over a seven-day week and work them unlimited hours. This was qualified, however, by a provision that only one foreman could be assigned to a producing unit, thus preventing the hiring of a number of artisans on a weekly rather than hourly basis for the purpose of lowering costs. A bipartisan committee was appointed under the NRA to adjust all studio labor disputes except those pertaining to actors, writers, directors, supervisors, and extras. After months of bickering over its official status, this committee finally became effective and was able to adjust most complaints arising from the labor provisions of the code.

But perhaps the greatest service of the NRA was to the unorganized workers. Before its establishment, only the parties to the Studio Basic Agreement and other recognized unions had standardized wages and working conditions. The industry code established minimum rates and codified wages, hours, and conditions for all workers. Now those who did not belong to unions had an opportunity to discuss grievances with management, a privilege heretofore reserved for signatories to the Basic Agreement.[19]

The NRA also brought to a head the long-standing feud between the IATSE and the IBEW over the sound technicians. These workers had not been included in the 1926 Studio Basic Agreement because they had not yet become a factor in the studio labor picture. In the period 1926–1933 both the IA and the IBEW sought to organize the sound men. The former was the more successful, but it could not obtain recognition for the craft in the major studios until the international presidents of the two organizations settled the jurisdictional issue. In 1932, as previously noted, the IA sound men signed a contract with several independent producers who were not parties to the Basic Agreement. In July, 1933, the Alliance tried to force Columbia Pictures into this same mold. The studio refused on the ground that, even though it was not signatory to the Basic Agreement, it was bound thereby because of its membership in the Association of Motion Picture Producers. On July 24 all IA members at Columbia walked out, an event that was not entirely unwelcome to the producers. At this time, IA Local No. 695 had a membership of about 600 sound men, whereas IBEW Local No. 40 could claim hardly a tenth of that number. The latter and other building trades locals immediately started to coöperate with the producers in replacing the strikers. The Alliance found that it was helpless to use its traditional weapon against the producers —the threat of a sympathetic strike of IA projectionists in theaters across the country—for the depression had made too many inroads in their ranks. The IA therefore appealed to President Roosevelt and the National Labor Board, and on August 23 obtained a decision that ended the walkout.

All strikers were to be rehired without prejudice or discrimination because of union membership, if jobs were available. The AFL was asked to settle the issue of jurisdiction between the IATSE and the IBEW, but it was now too late to help the Alliance. As its leaders had violated the provisions of the Studio Basic Agreement by calling the strike without polling the membership, it had had to withdraw from that agreement a few hours after the walkout began. Hence the members of the other AFL unions felt justified in acting as strikebreakers. When IA members saw their jobs being taken by other unionists, they had little recourse except to quit the IA and scramble for their positions. The membership of the Alliance fell from about 9,000 before the strike to less than 200, and for several years the organization had little influence in Hollywood.[20]

This did not mean that the IA did not attempt to fight back. In subsequent NRA hearings in Washington its leaders charged a conspiracy between the producers and the IBEW to wreck the Alliance. In signed affidavits, they alleged that strikers were refused reëmployment unless they joined the IBEW. It was also noted that AFL carpenters had replaced grips and prop men who struck. In addition, the IA filed suit for damages in the amount of $3,950,000 against the IBEW and the United Brotherhood of Carpenters and Joiners on conspiracy grounds as well as for violation of the 1925–1926 jurisdictional compromise, but it was thrown out of court. The Studio Basic Agreement continued until 1936 with the IBEW, musicians, carpenters, and teamsters as signatories, the latter having been admitted in 1933.[21]

The IATSE returned to power in 1935 under the leadership of George E. Browne, who had become its international president in 1934. His personal representative in Hollywood was William (Willie) Bioff, who, in effect, controlled the IA locals in the movie capital until 1940. The means by which the Alliance made its comeback was again the power of the movie projectionists to darken theaters. An intensive organizing campaign after the 1933 debacle enabled it to make a show of strength by striking the Paramount theaters in Chicago in 1935. The immediate issue was the studio's refusal to grant location employment in New York to an IA cameraman who did not also have an IBEW card. The IA leaders threatened to tie up all major theaters in the United States by December, 1935, if the organization was not granted recognition in Hollywood. Faced with this kind of ultimatum at the box office, the producers succumbed and signed a five-year agreement on December 8. It provided for readmission to the Studio Basic Agreement the following January and for a closed shop for IATSE crafts through the requirement that former Alliance members had to present IA cards as a condition of employment. Jurisdictional troubles with the IBEW were resolved by a decision that Local No. 40 of the IBEW would become part of the Studio Mechanics Alliance and have jurisdiction over outside permanent installations at the studios. Temporary work on the stages was to belong to the IA, which was also to have jurisdiction over all cameramen except the first man, over still photographers, lamp operators, grips, stage carpenters, laboratory technicians, and film editors and operators. The problem of distinction between permanent and temporary electrical installations presaged later jurisdictional difficulties, but the 1935 agreement eclipsed the IBEW, with the result that the IATSE membership quickly grew to 12,000. The new agreement also virtually eliminated the Academy of Motion Picture Arts and Sciences from the industrial relations field, and gave impetus to the guilds that were formed after 1933 to seek closed shops for the talent groups.[22]

But trouble was looming from another direction. In 1932 the unions not included in the Studio Basic Agreement had formed an organization known as the Federated Motion Picture Crafts (FMPC) under the leadership of Charles Lessing, who represented the Brotherhood of Painters, Decorators and Paperhangers. The painters had been a party to the original agreement but had been forced out because of their tenacity in holding on to the make-up artists against an IATSE claim to jurisdiction over them. The FMPC was composed of painters, plasterers, stationary engineers, plumbers, molders, cooks, scenic artists, boilermakers, studio utility employees (common laborers), make-up artists (part of the painters' union), hair stylists, and set designers. The organization's desire for recognition flared up in the form of a strike threat in 1937, which was complicated by the jurisdictional struggle over the make-up artists. Browne and Bioff wanted to absorb the FMPC unions rather than permit them to remain as separate entities competing for membership with IA locals.

About 6,000 workers were involved in the FMPC strike for recognition, which began on April 30, 1937. The Federated Crafts had the indirect support of the Screen Actors Guild (SAG), which also was seeking recognition and originally planned to strike at the same time. Browne and Bioff went to the aid of the SAG, however, threatening the producers with an IA sympathetic walkout in favor of the screen actors. This action forestalled a strike by the SAG at that time and took some of the sting out of the FMPC walkout. In addition, the IA leaders disrupted the studio utility employees' local by convincing the producers that they should raise the hourly wages of common laborers under a new classification within IA Local No. 37 from 75 cents to 82½ cents an hour. As the striking studio utility employees were asking only 75 cents an hour, many of them quit the walkout, joined the IA, and returned to work for 82½ cents. The make-up artists and hair stylists then abandoned the walkout by accepting a new charter from the IA, thus leaving the remainder of the FMPC locals, except the painters, to end the strike as best they could on June 14. The unions and the studios tentatively agreed on a contract, but wages and hours remained the same as before, pending further negotiations. The painters held out and won a 15 per cent wage increase and a closed shop. This was the first agreement giving an individual studio craft local direct recognition, as the members of the Studio Basic Agreement were represented by their international officers rather than by local officials. Finally, after further negotiations, the producers informally recognized the other FMPC unions and granted conditions that varied little from those enjoyed by the parties to the Basic Agreement. The outcome was at least a partial victory for the IATSE, however, for the termination of the strike marked the end of the FMPC.[23]

The demise of the FMPC did not mean peace for the IATSE and the Browne-Bioff axis. Some members of the organization, known as the "IA Progressives," were dissatisfied with the policies of the international president and his henchman. Led by Irwin P. Hentschel, the IA malcontents sought to restore democratic control within the locals and force an accounting by Browne and Bioff. IA members had no voice in local affairs, there were no union meetings, nor were there elections; yet the two officers had a free hand in assessing the unions under their control without accounting for the disbursement of the funds so received. Other internal problems faced by Browne and Bioff included a continuation of the old factional trouble with the IBEW and, beginning in 1935, the infiltration of the four Hollywood locals by Communists. Bioff strengthened the cause of the IA Progressives when he admitted to a Sacramento grand jury that he had received a "loan" of $100,000 from a prominent producer. Late in 1937 the Progressives had managed to get a legislative assembly committee to investigate the government of the Hollywood locals, but they failed to secure any indictments. The assembly committee, in fact, gave the leadership a clean bill of health, so that in December, 1937, and January, 1938, the locals concerned voted to retain the international control of George Browne and Willie Bioff.[24]

The assembly investigation and incidental events, however, raised the question of Bioff's usefulness in Hollywood, and as a result he was temporarily transferred to Washington, D.C. This encouraged the Progressives to continue to work for improvements within the locals despite the vote of the membership. The combination of the recession of 1937–1938, the apathy of the majority of the members, and the strong opposition of IATSE officers eventually defeated them. For a time there seemed some hope of success when a 2 per cent assessment levied against union members was dropped, and the IATSE executive board voted to restore local autonomy in September, 1938. This action, however, was followed by a decision to split the key Hollywood local, No. 37, into five parts in order to divide the strength of the Progressives. Hence the reform group had no alternative but to join Herbert Sorrell, militant leader of the painters' union, and the Communists in the formation of the United Studio Technicians Guild (USTG) with CIO help early in 1939. A working arrangement was developed with the Communists still within the IA locals in an attempt to wrest control from the international, but without success. While the USTG constantly attacked the IA on charges of corruption, the forces behind its own formation placed it under indictment as a Communist-front organization tied in with the CIO. It therefore could not obtain the support of other craft unions outside the movie industry or of the Los Angeles Central Labor Council.

Nevertheless, the USTG was not ready to admit defeat. An interim NLRB investigation of bribery charges against Willie Bioff helped to arouse public suspicion that the IA was far from being above approach and was in collusion with the producers, though the latter partly negated this idea among the workers by announcing a forty-four-hour week. The USTG then asked the NLRB for a representation election in the studios, which was set for September 20, 1939. One month before that date, IA officials announced a new five-year agreement with the producers which provided for a closed shop as well as for negotiations on a wage increase. As a result, a 10 per cent increase, retroactive to August 12, 1939, was obtained for all 12,000 IA members. This took the steam out of the USTG bid for recognition. Consequently the election returns on September 20 favored the IATSE, which was then officially certified as the appropriate collective bargaining agent by the NLRB. The USTG leadership claimed collusion between the producers and the NLRB, but in vain. The Los Angeles Central Labor Council, which the IA had often ignored up to this time, also aided in winning the election because of its fear of the Communists and its hatred of the CIO.[25]

The election results made the IATSE the strongest labor organization in the movie industry and eliminated the CIO as a rival in the studios. Had the USTG not been tied in with the Communists and the CIO it might have won the election, for it would probably have had AFL support. Much as the AFL craft unions hated the IA because of their jurisdictional battles with it, they despised the Communists and the CIO more; hence they had little choice but to support the Alliance in its war with the USTG.

After the election Willie Bioff came back into the picture as chairman of a committee to coördinate AFL studio union activities and to fight all unaffiliated unions. The carpenters, the teamsters, and the electricians were expected to join the IA in this new alignment, but the painters decided to go it alone and to strike for a 15 per cent wage increase. Nearly 800 painters of Local No. 644, AFL, were involved in the dispute. The producers, in the meantime, had asked the IA to give up the 10 per cent wage increase awarded a few months earlier, but Bioff had refused, advocating instead the same pay boost for all AFL workers whose unions were not signatories to the Basic Agreement. He was successful in this demand in December, the month in which the studio painters obtained their 15 per cent wage increase retroactive to August 25, 1939, thus raising their wages to better than $9 per day. They also achieved a 250-day minimum work year for 70 per cent of their membership.[26]

But Bioff soon had personal troubles which developed from his past. Westbrook Pegler revealed that the IATSE's Hollywood dictator had almost six months yet to serve on an uncompleted sentence for pandering in Chicago. Bioff persuaded the Central Labor Council to oppose his extradition, but he was forced to go back to Illinois, partly because of the counteropposition of Sorrell of the USTG. The committee of studio unions of which Bioff was chairman refused to accept his resignation, however, and he was reinstated after his return from jail. In 1941 both Bioff and his superior, George Browne, were indicted by the federal government on charges of extorting $550,000 from four large picture producers under threat of strike fomentation in theaters over the nation. Their connection with the IATSE was thus brought to an end. Bioff's racketeering affiliations eventually caught up with him in 1955, when he was blown to bits in Phoenix, Arizona, by a booby trap that was rigged to explode when he entered his car.[27]

IATSE control over most of the crafts working in the film industry after 1937 did not mean peaceful labor relations. While the IA was winning its struggle with the USTG, it was also engaged in another dispute with the actors which had begun in 1937. In that year a Screen Actors Guild extra secured an IA card and went to work while the former organization was on strike. He was suspended by the SAG for this action, and IA leaders subsequently threatened to raid the Guild's extra ranks in retaliation. The SAG took the issue to the Associated Actors and Artistes of America (AAAA), which was composed of eleven actors' unions. The AAAA, with the exception of the American Federation of Actors (AFA), one of its constituent unions, voted to fight the IA threat. The AFA was composed primarily of night club actors and vaudeville performers, led by Ralph Whitehead as secretary. The result of the AAAA decision was a struggle between the talent groups and the crafts over who would control Hollywood. The Associated Actors calculated that this, if ever, was the time to stop the IA from moving outside its jurisdictional area into the talent arena and hence to complete domination of labor relations in the movies. After holding a secret conference with USTG leaders, the actors decided to quit the AFL and join the CIO. John L. Lewis, then CIO president, was consulted, but he refused to issue a charter to the actors until the controversy was over. His decision turned out to be a mistake. President Browne of the IATSE saw what was happening and capitulated to the AAAA a few hours before the NLRB election of September 20, 1939, thus ending the threat of a coalition among the AAAA (less Whitehead's American Federation of Actors), the USTG, and the CIO. Browne's capitulation meant that he would stay out of the talent field, which was thus left to the AAAA.[28]

Actually, however, the story was not so simple as this makes it seem. By refusing to go along with the AAAA in opposing the IATSE, the AFA had become an instrument used by Browne in his attempt to control the talent unions. During 1938 and part of 1939, the IA and the musicians aided Whitehead in building up the AFA, more than doubling its membership. The apparent aim was to gain control of the AAAA through democratic means, but this effort was frustrated through a change in AAAA rules which prevented any one of its constituent unions from controlling more than a third of the votes, regardless of its size. Whitehead's group at this time was presided over by Sophie Tucker, long-time vaudeville actress, and comprised a great many of the variety actors on the stage and in cabarets and night clubs. If it had been able to capture the AAAA, the only actors left outside its jurisdiction would have been a few of the high-priced stars.

The AAAA not only changed the voting rules to end this threat, but also decided to expel Whitehead by filing charges against him for misapplication of funds. Whitehead, with the support of Sophie Tucker, took the AFA with him and obtained a charter from the IATSE. He then appealed to the AFL to settle the jurisdictional problem of control over the actors. The AAAA countered this move by forming a new variety actors' group known as the American Guild of Variety Artists, under the presidency of Eddie Cantor. This new union forced the jurisdictional issue. Whitehead had been cultivating William Green, AFL president, for some time. Because Green apparently liked Whitehead, he found it most difficult to make a decision regarding jurisdiction over the variety actors. Finally, the Executive Council requested the IATSE to return the AFA to the AAAA, but ordered that Whitehead should remain as secretary. The latter action was displeasing to the SAG and its secretary, Kenneth Thomson, who saw in it a future threat to the AAAA. It was at this time that the SAG and the AAAA, under the influence of Thomson, decided that they must stop the IA while it was having trouble with the USTG and was seeking to win an NLRB election. Their shrewdness was evidenced in Browne's agreement to take his hands off the actors in order to prevent SAG and AAAA support of the USTG. Whitehead was removed from the AFA, and the SAG and the AAAA supported the IA in the election of September 20, 1939.[29]

All was still not peaceful on the IATSE craft-union front, although the row with the actors was settled. After its defeat in the election, the USTG under Herbert Sorrell turned its attention to the screen cartoonists, who were organized in an independent union known as the Screen Cartoon Guild. Sorrell, acting as the business agent of the painters, obtained a charter for the cartoonists as Local No. 822 in 1940. In the spring of 1941 the cartoonists went out on strike at the Walt Disney

Studios with the support of machinists, painters, office employees, and film technicians. The Disney management capitulated after about nine weeks, granting recognition to the cartoonists. Meanwhile, the latter also secured recognition at Metro-Goldwyn-Mayer and the Schlesinger studios.[30]

Later in the year the five unions that had struck the Disney Studios formed the Conference of Studio Unions (CSU) and were joined by a number of other important labor groups, such as the carpenters and the electricians. The *raison d'être* behind this organization was the desire for more local autonomy in the settlement of grievances and in the negotiation of contracts, as well as dissatisfaction with the jurisdictional quarrels and the gangsterism that had marked the Bioff regime. The CSU became possible because of the removal of Bioff and Browne from the IATSE on extortion charges. These developed in April, 1941, when Joseph Schenck, chairman of the board of Twentieth Century–Fox, was indicted for income tax evasion, and subsequently implicated the two IA leaders. The subpoenaed records showed that in 1935 Bioff and Browne had been paid $100,000 by Loew's and $50,000 by RKO to avert a strike of the projectionists in New York City. The next year they had demanded $2,000,000 from five major companies under penalty of a possible shutdown. It was estimated that Browne and Bioff actually had collected at least $1,100,000 from the movie industry in the period 1935–1940, in addition to the 2 per cent assessment on IA members in Hollywood, which had netted another $1,500,-000 for which no accounting was available.

The Browne-Bioff combination ended in late 1941, when the former resigned and the CSU entered the picture. This organization set up policies that were in sharp contrast with those of the preceding era. It sought the democratic participation of its members, with at least part of its meetings open to the public. Locals were free to formulate their own policies with reference to wages, hours, and conditions, but were to clear through the CSU in dealing with producers. The principal bargaining power was in the hands of the painters and the carpenters. This did not settle craft jurisdictional issues for all time, however, nor did it mean the end of troubles with producers. The IATSE continued to be a powerful factor in Hollywood labor circles under the leadership of Richard Walsh, successor to Bioff and Browne. Differences between the CSU and the IA soon came to the fore and, after World War II, broke out in an open conflict that was to plague the film industry for many months. But that is another story. Now the spotlight will be turned on the talent groups that were active in the prewar years.[31]

3. Organization among Actors and Extras

The working conditions surrounding the actor in his on-the-job activities have helped to shape his reactions to labor organizations. He is accustomed to direct supervision as a necessary aspect of his occupation in preparation for a play or a film. His working conditions are variable because of the different theaters in which he must play or the changes in location which he must endure in connection with the making of movies. In general, employer-employee relations tend to be clear-cut, enabling a union concerned with actors and actresses to concentrate on setting up minimum employment standards. Thus, even though acting is a white-collar profession and some of those engaged in it receive high salaries, actors' unions can be and have been organized along ordinary trade-union lines. Furthermore, the glamor of the stage and screen attracts a constant flood of new applicants for acting roles, with the consequent threat to those who have long been in the public eye. Hence a union has the added advantage of being an agency for controlling the number of newcomers in the interests of those already on at least the lower rungs of the ladder to fame.[32]

Organizations such as the Actor's Order of Friendship and the Actors Society existed before World War I, but they had little interest in or orientation toward industrial relations. From 1906 to 1913 there was practically no leadership among actors and actresses in favor of any sort of labor union. The first real labor organization among those who trod the boards of the nation's stages was the Actors Equity Association, established in May, 1913. It directed its initial efforts toward obtaining a standard contract for its members which would provide for free transportation to and from New York City, two weeks' notice of dismissal, curtailed rehearsal time, pay for actors dismissed without compensation after more than a week of rehearsal, limitation of extra performances without wages, and pay for all weeks actually played. In 1917 Equity secured its first contract, embodying most of these changes, with the United Managers' Protective Association. Two years later, after the formation of a new producers' group, demands and counter-demands were made which could not be reconciled. Equity thereupon joined the AFL, becoming the first white-collar organization of any size to affiliate with this national labor body.

At this time Actors Equity was composed primarily of rank-and-file actors and actresses. Most of the great stage personalities were members of the Actors Fidelity League, which did not want its members to act like discontented laborers—the great names were above regular unions! The major exception was the Barrymore family, which, along with a few other stars, belonged to Equity. In 1919 Equity built up a war chest by putting on a show in the Lexington Avenue Opera House and then struck against the producers to obtain new demands. The support of the stagehands and the musicians won the day for Equity, which secured recognition on Broadway and became the representative of the legitimate stage as of September 6, 1919. The producers canceled all lawsuits against Equity, recognized it for collective bargaining purposes, granted all wage demands, agreed to a limit of eight performances a week, and eliminated black lists. The actors promised not to engage in sympathetic strikes nor to expect a closed shop. Equity won jurisdiction over all English-speaking performers except vaudeville and burlesque actors, who remained under the American Artists' Federation.[33]

Just before winning recognition in the theaters, Actors Equity through its AFL affiliation had become a member of the Associated Actors and Artistes of America. The AAAA gave it jurisdiction over the Motion Picture Players Union in Hollywood, composed of atmosphere and bit players. The important Hollywood actors and actresses belonged to the Screen Actors of America. The MPPU officially amalgamated with the AAAA in March, 1920, receiving a new title as the Screen Players Association of Los Angeles County. This affiliation, however, did not indicate enthusiasm for unions on the part of film actors, as many of them had no stage experience and little interest in the traditions of the theater. Unionization of the actors was also delayed because there was no employer bargaining unit until Will Hays organized the movie producers in 1922. Further, salaries and conditions for actors, especially the stars who would normally be looked to for leadership, were relatively good.

Equity leaders asked Will Hays, as the representative of the producers, for a standard contract in August, 1922, a few months after the establishment of the Association of Motion Picture Producers. After two years of delays, the request was finally rejected in the summer of 1924. Equity representatives again sought contracts in the period 1925–1927, but without success. In May, 1927, the Academy of Motion Picture Arts and Sciences was established and immediately turned its attention to foiling the efforts of Equity to organize the Hollywood actors. It persuaded the producers to postpone a threatened 10 per cent salary cut for actors, pointing out that this would help Equity, but the latter continued to gain in power.³⁴

On July 28, 1927, at a dinner presided over by Douglas Fairbanks as president of the AMPAS, it was announced that the producers planned a uniform contract for independent or free-lance actors, writers, and directors, and had abandoned any program of salary cuts. The following December such a contract was negotiated. It was criticized by Equity leaders on grounds that it failed to limit working hours and to provide for compulsory arbitration of all disputes. In their opinion it smacked of company unionism. On the other hand, influential actors were not pleased with Equity's attempts to organize and control from 3,000 miles away, and particularly resented the influence of the stage in motion picture labor relations. The Los Angeles *Times* also was concerned over the role of Equity in the film capital. It saw Equity as a true union making a hole in the open-shop dike, and forcing the producers to give in inch by inch until eventually a closed shop would prevail in Hollywood. The AMPAS contract, though taking the steam out of Equity's organizing drive in 1927, did not discourage it from continuing to seek control over filmdom's talent.

The Academy had separate branches for producers, actors, writers, directors, and technicians. Its alleged aim in the area of industrial relations was the coöperative settlement of any disagreements among these branches without recourse to a regular union setup and its accompanying strikes or lockouts. As would be expected, a number of prominent actors were members of both Equity and their appropriate branch of the AMPAS. Equity would gain their undivided attention only when it proved it could do more for the actors than could be achieved through the AMPAS. Further, leading actors were not likely to quit the Academy in favor of a union until they found a lack of good faith in the former and were ready to consider themselves as workers in need of a labor organization rather than members of a professional group who were above unionization.³⁵

Equity leaders claimed credit for pressures that resulted in revisions in the AMPAS standard contract between December, 1927, and 1929. These included clarifications of ambiguous wording and the addition of a voluntary conciliation clause. Equity also claimed that even though it had no official status, it had informally settled many disputes that had arisen from the contract provisions. Meanwhile, the introduction of sound pictures brought many strongly unionized stage players from New York to Hollywood, as the importance of voices came to the fore. These people protested to Equity about filmdom's working conditions, long hours, and the frequent necessity of acting in two pictures at once. Equity leaders calculated that the time was ripe for a show-down in the movie industry and the elimination of the AMPAS as an integer in the Hollywood actors' labor relations equation. Plans were carefully laid for a decisive battle with the open shop. Equity's president, Frank Gilmore, came to Los Angeles to take charge of the campaign. On June 5, 1929, he called a strike and issued an order that no Equity member, except those under a definite contract, could work in a film with actors who were not members of the organization. In addition, he declared that any new contract signed by an Equity member must provide for the closed shop and conditions acceptable to the union. The penalties for violation of these orders were severe. Any actors under contract who violated them were to be fined double the cash value of their contracts and suspended for a year, and extras (actors working by the day) were to be fined their full earnings while in violation and be suspended for four months.[36]

If Gilmore had stopped at this point he might have won. There is little doubt that actors and actresses below the star level were interested in eliminating abuses. These included being forced occasionally to accept a lump sum for a part with no stipulation as to the length of the workday or the engagement, a frequent lack of pay for rehearsals, workweeks that were often as long as sixty to eighty hours, and location employment varying from eight to twenty hours per day without additional bonus. Only a small minority of individual stars received large sums as salaries and controlled their own conditions; no others were assured of continuous income. Equity sought to protect the actors by demanding a forty-eight-hour week, time and a half for overtime, paid rehearsals, no contracts for a part in a picture without a stipulated termination date, Sunday work to be considered as overtime and limited to eight hours in total, only Equity casts for talking pictures, no voice substitution without consent, the workday to start when the actor appeared at the studio, and several other provisions.

But Frank Gilmore overreached himself. He apparently believed that Equity, whose membership was estimated at nearly 3,000 in June, 1929, was strongly enough entrenched for him to extend his orders to all actors regardless of whether or not they were Equity members. Non-members quickly saw that if Equity won its Hollywood struggle, those who had not soon fallen into line would be seriously hurt by the fine and suspension. If they did not pay the fine, they would be through in the film capital. A cry of protest arose against Gilmore from nonmembers as well as from many who belonged to the organization. The producers joined in by announcing on June 6 that they would refuse to be restricted to Equity members, that they would sign on the basis of talent and would continue to use the standard rather than the proposed Equity contract. So far as the *Times* was concerned, the major difference between the two contracts was that the Equity agreement required the closed shop, although the union was not a closed organization. The Academy of Motion Picture Arts and Sciences asserted its neutrality in this struggle because its employer members belonged to the Association of Motion Picture Producers and a number of its actor constituents were associated with Equity. The AMPAS made it clear that it was primarily interested in harmonious relations among the various segments of the industry and in the advancement of the arts and sciences in motion picture production through better technology, review of films, awards for outstanding achievement, and other devices.[37]

As the strike went on during the summer of 1929, a race ensued against this background of disagreement with Gilmore's commands. Equity sought to gain more members, while the producers tried to get more signatures on their standard contracts. Names of actors and actresses spelled out in the bright lights of many a theater marquee were to be found on both sides of the controversy. Equity gained some support from the Los Angeles Central Labor Council by having its Hollywood affiliate join that body. The AFL also furnished some backing, but it was not direct enough to offset the real difficulty—differences among the leading Hollywood players over whether or not they really wanted an Equity shop—in prosecuting the strike. The actual suspension of a number of prominent actors who violated Gilmore's orders during the strike contributed to the turmoil. Early in August several independent studios yielded to Equity, but the major producers continued to hold out. On August 10, at an open meeting, the Equity membership voted for the principle of having a cast composed of 80 per cent Equity members and 20 per cent non-Equity. This change from the closed-shop demand would still give Equity control over any cast. Gilmore presented the new proposal to the producers, who immediately rejected it. Gilmore, concluding that there was no use in pursuing the strike further, called it off on August 17 and returned to New York.[38]

The strike, which had lasted for eleven weeks, represented Equity's last bid for Hollywood domination. It failed for a number of reasons, not the least of which was that influential Hollywood players did not recognize Equity's claim to represent them. They were suspicious of it as a stage actors' organization, particularly those stars who had played in the silent movies and had endured ridicule of the screen by members of the legitimate stage. The clashes of temperamental personalities within and outside Equity did not help the union in its fight with the producers. Although the abuses that had existed on Broadway had not been transferred to Hollywood, Equity behaved as though they had. Equity leaders also underestimated the number of Hollywood actors who would accept attractive terms offered by shrewd producers in their contract negotiations, terms that were a far cry from the working conditions of Equity players before their 1919 strike. In addition, Equity discovered a good deal of defeatism and treachery within its own ranks, stemming from a lack of support by other labor groups associated with it in the theater. Sympathetic strikes by the stagehands and the musicians had aided it considerably in 1919, but these were not in evidence in the later Hollywood dispute.[39]

After Equity's failure to win the 1929 strike, the Academy of Motion Picture Arts and Sciences stepped into the breach to negotiate a new standard contract in February, 1930. Although the AMPAS had remained neutral during the walkout, it was by no means a nonentity in the labor relations field in the period from 1927 into 1933. It helped the actors get a number of demands into the standard contract at a time when they were not ready for unionization. An AMPAS-sponsored adjustment committee for the actors made many decisions, only a handful of which were appealed to an Academy conciliation committee. So successful was the AMPAS on behalf of its actor members that the Screen Actors Guild, which succeeded it as a bona fide labor organization in the 1930's, consulted its interpretations and decisions as a guide in later actor-producer relations.

The 1930 standard contract, negotiated by a committee of twenty-one actors and representatives of all the major producers, provided for compulsory arbitration by the AMPAS conciliation committee of all disputes arising under the contract, a guarantee by the actors not to strike for the period of the agreement, and an eight-hour day with overtime for day players earning more than $15. This contract was renewed in February, 1931, for four years, and in this period the depression hit the film industry. Equity continually charged that the AMPAS was still a company union; that its founding fathers, as charter members, still ran it with the assistance of a few others who were elected to the controlling group; and that they prevented the election of others who were outside this small coterie. In the eyes of Equity's leaders, the AMPAS was far from democratic and was the main force opposing Equity in Hollywood. Actually, however, subsequent events revealed that the AMPAS was not to remain in control of the actors in Hollywood but, rather, that Equity was to lose out to a new union, the Screen Actors Guild, a product of the NRA period.[40]

The extras or players hired by the day were in a somewhat different situation from that of the screen actors. In World War I most of the extras in the newly established film industry came from the legitimate stage, where they had served in a similar capacity. Another migration to Hollywood occurred after the war with the decline of vaudeville and the theater, the return of the ex-service man, and the rise of the movie-struck youngster. Abuses began to develop in Hollywood in the form of unscrupulous acting and make-up schools and dishonest placement agencies, all of which were more interested in grabbing a few dollars than in helping the applicant. Hiring procedure on the movie lots was haphazard, requiring daily visits by the extra to the lot at his own expense and with his own wardrobe. When work was available, the pay was small and the hours were often extremely long.

In 1924 the Russell Sage Foundation sponsored a study of the social and employment conditions of extras. The study was commissioned by Will Hays of the Association of Motion Picture Producers. It revealed a lack of labor turnover records in studios, high fees paid by extras to employment agencies, payments to extras by studios in the form of non-negotiable vouchers, frequent assignment of part of the extras' unearned wages to placement organizations, and an extreme casualization of work. As a result of the findings of this and several other studies, the Central Casting Corporation was established by the major studios on December 4, 1925, and began operations early in 1926. It was quickly successful in providing for better distribution of the available work for extras without the high fees charged by private placement agencies. By the cataloguing of all extras at Central Casting, producers benefited in being able to secure the proper person for a particular need at the right time. Extras also saved themselves time and money by being on call without the necessity of making daily rounds of the studios while carrying expensive wardrobes. One supposedly very great advantage of the new system was that accretions to the labor supply could be limited through Central Casting. This, it was hoped, would permit the development of an expert corps of extras whose jobs would not constantly be threatened by newcomers who would undercut wages in an attempt to break into the movies. Producers likewise could benefit from the increased efficiency of extras, who would become specialists in certain fields. The effectiveness of Central Casting in its first six months is revealed by its total of 113,837 placements.[41]

The advent of sound in the period 1926–1929 intensified the decasualization problems of the extras by increasing their ranks. This occurred in spite of Central Casting because of the need for new categories of jobs such as singers, linguists, and others who could make different sounds at proper times. Then the onset of the depression further impaired the position of extras, as the number of openings decreased while registrations with Central Casting were increasing. Daily placements in 1926–1929 had averaged between 828 and 840; by 1931 the figure had dropped to a low of 606. Although the California State Department of Industrial Relations had been regulating wages and working conditions for women and minors in the movies for five years, employment was not guaranteed. The male extras had no protection, and many of them were family breadwinners who were trying to make ends meet on an average wage of about $9 a day, when they could find work.

The situation finally, in 1933, prompted the Academy of Motion Picture Arts and Sciences to make an investigation. The findings were startling. About three-fourths of the unemployed were drifters, undesirables, or casuals who picked up a day or two here and there in crowd scenes; the rest were genuine extras, many of them with years of service, who were suffering severely from the lack of jobs. Some 44 per cent of the extras hired in the first six months of 1933 were nonprofessionals. Many of them were employed because the studios asked for particular individuals, such as relatives of management officials, unemployed friends of studio mechanics, and unoccupied persons from other industries. These special requests made up from 30 to 80 per cent of nearly all lists submitted to Central Casting by the major studios. Favoritism thus seemed to be quite common, but professional extras told Academy investigators that they feared reprisals if they criticized the system. After further investigation, the AMPAS concluded that the number of professional extras actually needed in 1932–1933 was about 1,800, rather than the approximately 8,000 who were registered. It also estimated that about 3,600 placements a week would be available to these 1,800 professionals. As the average weekly wage of the 1,400 extras on Central Casting lists who received 35 per cent of the available work in the first six months of 1933 was only $8.22, the AMPAS decided that payments would have to be raised.[42]

Nearly all the positive recommendations which came out of the Academy's report on the extras were incorporated in the code set up under the National Industrial Recovery Act. The code authorities, however, ignored the AMPAS in establishing a regulatory agency known as the Standing Committee on Extras. The committee was composed of five producers and five representatives of the extra players. Its first accomplishment was the institution of a minimum wage of $5 a day for miscellaneous crowd extras without any special wardrobe. Other scales were established at higher levels depending on wardrobes and other responsibilities. Employment conditions were also standardized under the code, but the most serious problem facing the Standing Committee was decasualization. After eleven months of work the final list of extras was sent to the code authority in March, 1935, but before any decisive action could be taken the NRA was declared unconstitutional. Nevertheless, the Standing Committee did much to better the status of extras in the film industry. Working conditions and wage rates were improved; favoritism in job placement was somewhat curtailed, as studios stopped asking for extras by name; and 92 per cent of the complaints brought to the Standing Committee were satisfactorily resolved.[43]

Decasualization remained a problem into 1935, even though the Central Casting Corporation had been in existence nearly ten years. Operations were more efficient than under the old haphazard system, but they could have been better had the movie industry wholeheartedly coöperated. Instead, conspicuous publicity was given to the few extras who became stars, and the studios did not discourage enough applicants as they did not want to lose the good will of fans and their friends who came to Hollywood to get into the movies. Private placement agencies were still permitted to operate, and make-up and acting schools continued to thrive. Although Central Casting technically could control the supply of extras in its files, its officials felt that they had to go along with the studios by listing individuals who showed exceptional promise or whose types were in short supply. The new extras, who were registered only if they had an additional source of income, were warned that employment prospects were not good. The producers agreed to help by maintaining code standards for extras after the NRA was declared unconstitutional, and Central Casting representatives were more active in adjusting wage and hour complaints. The Screen Actors Guild (SAG) also helped the extras by pressing constantly for the elimination of practices that were contrary to NRA standards. Two years later the SAG, having won recognition from the producers in May, 1937, was in a much more favorable position in this regard. By enforcing dues of $18 a year and stringent membership regulations for extras, the SAG was able to reduce their number somewhat by 1940, thus raising annual wages.[44]

The SAG took its first step in improving wages at the time of its recognition in 1937, when it obtained an increase in the extras' minimum daily pay from $5 to $5.50, as well as overtime remuneration for all players in the lower wage brackets. When complaints that the minimum was becoming the maximum began to come in, SAG officers decided to have another try at raising wages. The only way to do this was to secure job control for the extras. In 1934 the SAG had set up the Junior Screen Actors Guild for extras and bit players. It was a self-governing organization but subject to the veto of the SAG's board of directors, a power that was seldom used. As members of the Junior Guild could not vote for SAG board members, they had no direct voice in the senior organization. Membership limitation was a key feature of the Junior Guild. Hence, when the SAG decided that the extras needed further wage increases, the logical procedure was to limit the number available through Junior Guild shop control. The SAG therefore declared a closed union for extras as of March 1, 1938. The books were closed to new members except for those considered absolutely essential. A special committee of the SAG then admitted the new candidates only after an examination of their special talents and a determination of their essentiality. Hiring by a studio outside the membership of the Junior SAG was permitted only when an unusual talent, not possessed by a current member, was needed. Detailed files were kept on the abilities, the characteristics, and other features of each member in order to provide for quick and efficient placement on call.[45]

Despite the SAG's assistance in 1939 and 1940, the extras continued to be plagued by alleged placement inequities at Central Casting. The restrictions on membership in the Junior SAG helped to increase earnings, but favoritism remained a problem. There were complaints that extras still had to telephone in several times a day in order to find out if there was work, rather than awaiting a call from the casting office, and that the same faces were seen in picture after picture with no attempt at rotation.[46] The SAG made some progress in the last years of the decade in minimizing some of the problems, especially in increasing the average earnings of extras (see table 5).

TABLE 5

AVERAGE DAYS WORKED AND AVERAGE ANNUAL EARNINGS
OF EXTRA PLAYERS CAST THROUGH CENTRAL
CASTING CORPORATION, 1936–1940

Year	Average number of days worked by individual	Average annual earnings of individual
1936	11.72	$105.63
1937	18.46	187.40
1938	29.77	320.95
1939	28.89	317.26
1940	32.58	361.03

SOURCE: Murray Ross, *Stars and Strikes* (New York: Columbia University Press, 1941), p. 169. The basic data came from the report of the Standing Committee of the Motion Picture Producers and of the Screen Actors Guild, *The Problem of the Extra Player*, October, 1940.

The real problem continued to be the employment of marginal extras. As most of the complaints came from this group of players, the SAG hoped that its membership restrictions, plus normal dropouts over time, would gradually reduce their number and thus solve the problem. An organization known as the Standing Committee of the Motion Picture Producers and of the SAG made a number of recommendations to this end in 1940: (1) retention of Central Casting as the most efficient system of handling extras; (2) establishment of a limited form of seniority for extras; (3) placement of players who had worked more than ten days in 1939 on a preferential list, while those with less worktime would be placed on a supplementary roster and told that the industry had no responsibility to support them; (4) creation of an apprentice system for new players with probationary SAG membership subject to review before the achievement of full status; and (5) development of a more adequate system of work rotation and longer notice by the studios to Central Casting when requesting extras for given pictures. A new contract signed by the SAG in 1941 increased the earnings of both actors and extras and incorporated some of the suggestions of the Standing Committee.[47]

Although the SAG was instrumental in improving the extras' working conditions, it did not achieve this without a struggle over its own status. The rejection of Equity in the unsuccessful strike of 1929 did not result in its elimination from the Hollywood scene, but it had little influence in the relations between actors and producers after that time. As noted above, the Academy of Motion Picture Arts and Sciences was in the saddle during the years from 1929 to 1933. Through its offices, in March, 1930, the producers installed an arbitration board to deal with the complaints of contract actors, gave them assurances that they would be fairly treated, and secured a five-year no-strike pledge which was signed by most of the actors.

The depression changed this apparently amicable arrangement, however, for by 1932 working conditions for actors had so deteriorated that unrest was rife. Terms of contracts for free-lance actors were slashed as much as 50 per cent; excessively long hours were worked by women as well as men; stunt men received no compensation for injuries; and extras on location often stood in the rain or other inclement weather for hours. By this time the actors had decided that there was no use in complaining to the AMPAS, as it was dominated by and favorable to the producers. These and other grievances sparked by the bank holiday in March, 1933, which caused the producers to threaten an eight-week moratorium on salaries, led to the birth of the SAG. Had the salary reduction plan not been proposed, a union might not have developed at this time. Actors were traditionally individualists. Their number was limited by the scarcity of top talent. Incomes of good actors were high by most standards. Under these circumstances a union would normally not be expected to arise. But because the producers, in the opinion of a number of free-lance actors, did not show much concern about their talent employees in early 1933, the SAG was officially established on July 12 of that year. The initial membership roster contained only eighteen names, but included such prominent actors as Alan Mowbray, Ralph Morgan, C. Aubrey Smith, James Gleason, and Boris Karloff. Most of the stars did not join, however, preferring to stay with the AMPAS.[48]

It was the NRA that gave impetus to the growth of the new and inconsequential SAG. Producers saw in the recovery program a possible answer to the problems inherent in the star system which had developed in the studios. Not only had it resulted in high salaries for a relatively small number of top actors and actresses, but it had encouraged strong competition among producers for this talent. Stars were not above breaking their contracts if the producer concerned did not equal other offers made to them. When the initial NRA code was set up, the producers put in clauses to eliminate raiding, curb the activities of artists' agents, and limit high salaries paid to creative talent. The AMPAS assumed the right to represent the stars, an action that was resented by the latter, who no longer had confidence in the Academy's ability to act in their behalf free from the influence of producers. A meeting of all actors and actresses, including stars, to protest the proposed code was called at the home of Frank Morgan shortly after the draft of the code was publicized in September, 1933. The small SAG was invited to present its case for a union for all actors regardless of their salary scales and popularity. Those present liked the proposal, decided to adopt the SAG as their organization, and began to affiliate with it. In a few weeks the membership of the SAG rose from 81 to 3,000.

Under the leadership of the newly elected president, Eddie Cantor, steps were immediately taken to oppose the draft code. A mass meeting held at the El Capitan Theater on October 8, 1933, protested the provisions introduced by the producers in an effort to end the star system and competitive bidding. Resolutions were passed against the code and the actions of the producers, and a 2,000-word telegram of complaint was dispatched to President Roosevelt. Several days later SAG leaders issued a threat to strike any studios that signed the code.[49]

The situation became critical when, several weeks after the mass meeting, NRA administrator Hugh Johnson approved the code. In an effort to resolve the dispute, President Roosevelt invited Cantor to spend Thanksgiving with him at Warm Springs, Georgia. As a result of the meeting, the most controversial provisions were suspended when FDR approved the code on November 27, 1933. These included the salary clause that outlawed "unreasonably excessive" compensation and gave the code authority power to levy fines up to $10,000 for violations, and other clauses relating to antiraiding and AMPAS agreements. As the Academy had lost out at the hearings on the code, it soon ceased to have much influence over the actors in the labor relations arena.

But establishment of the code did not end the problems, for controversy arose as to the proper agency to hear complaints concerning violations of its provisions. Pressure from the SAG brought about the formation of the Actor-Producer Five-Five Committee, composed, as its name implies, of equal representation from each side. In order to name its representatives the SAG held an election in February, 1934, which was open to all actors with screen credits. Those chosen were Robert Montgomery, Claude King, Ralph Morgan, Kenneth Thomson, and Richard Tucker. The producers stalled in naming their representatives to the committee, being reluctant to enter into what was likely to become a collective bargaining relationship implying recognition of the SAG. A similar delay was encountered by the Screen Writers Guild, which had supported the SAG in its criticism of the draft code and was organizing its own Five-Five Committee. The committees were formally established in June, 1934, however, seven months after adoption of the code.[50]

The committees did not bring peace, for the producers did not really want to bargain collectively. In October, after three months of fruitless discussion, the members of the Actor-Producer Five-Five Committee agreed to disagree, and the actors filed a brief of complaints with NRA deputy administrator Sol Rosenblatt. Basically the brief charged the producers with drawing exorbitant salaries and mismanaging their companies, thus creating financial distress; asked for the elimination of the AMPAS supplementary contract which guaranteed continuous employment and a twelve-hour rest period between calls, charging that it was not enforced; claimed that free-lance and day players often overlapped and that individuals shifted between these categories, so that new-type contracts were needed with a set of fair practices covering these actors; and, most significantly, expressed the desire for an enforced eight-hour day. The SAG also referred to abuses existing at a central employment bureau operated by the producers as a means of obtaining free-lance actors. The actors claimed that every call from the studios was recorded, thus giving the producers information on how much work an actor had had and the consequent probable strength of his bargaining power. The SAG further suspected that the producers kept salary data to prevent raises and could reserve certain actors without their knowledge, thus depriving them of opportunities for alternate employment. Because of these and other abuses, the actors desired the abolition of this central bureau and felt that they needed the protection of the NIRA with full and free collective bargaining.[51]

The producers denied that they were so bad as pictured by the actors. They pointed out, for example, that most contract actors had many days off while under salary and that free-lance actors sometimes did not work a full eight hours. The actors did not deny the latter but argued that they often would work four hours the first day, six hours the second day, perhaps three hours the third, and then fifteen hours on each of several succeeding days, without adequate rest periods. In an effort to break the deadlock in the Five-Five Committee, the producers proposed an organization called the Producers Institute. It was to have two branches, one each for actors and writers; however, it did not provide for the incorporation of their respective guilds. The producers agreed to provisions for improved working conditions, but, in the opinion of the actors, an adequate enforcement procedure was not set up. The actors and the writers looked upon the Producers Institute as just another Academy of Motion Picture Arts and Sciences, and so turned down the idea. No further progress was made in getting the producers and actors together before the code provisions of the NIRA were invalidated in May, 1935.[52]

While the Five-Five Committees of the actors and the writers were shadowboxing with the producers, the AMPAS was trying to make a comeback. Although most of the stars had joined the SAG, the Academy still continued to function. In the summer of 1934 the writers' branch announced a new writer-producer code of ethics with a strengthened enforcement procedure. In February, 1935, upon expiration of the old contract, the actors' branch concluded a new free-lance agreement which answered every criticism made of the Academy, except the SAG demand for an eight-hour day. Nevertheless, the new contracts did not win over most of the actors and writers, who continued to distrust the AMPAS and to seek recognition of their independent organizations. But before the Screen Actors Guild would have a free path to recognition, it had to come to terms with Equity. These were negotiated while the Five-Five Committee discussions were under way and the AMPAS was seeking to win back the actors. In November, 1934, Equity gave up jurisdiction over motion pictures to its parent Associated Actors and Artistes of America, AFL, which then issued a charter to the SAG giving it complete autonomy and exclusive jurisdiction over screen actors. The terms of the Equity-SAG agreement also stated that neither organization could call the other out on strike and that stage players could not "scab" on screen actors. The SAG thus became affiliated with the AFL and later with the California State Federation of Labor and the Los Angeles Central Labor Council. Actors who had formerly been affiliated with both Equity and the SAG were required to join only one or the other, depending on whether they earned most of their livelihood in Hollywood or on the legitimate stage.[53]

The arrangement with Equity cleared the boards for a drive to secure recognition for the SAG. Nearly 600 actors and actresses joined the Guild between July 28, 1935, and May 24, 1936. A few stars who refused to go along with the accord between Equity and the SAG in regard to joining one or the other, such as John and Lionel Barrymore, Lionel Atwill, Lloyd Nolan, and Jack Oakie, were suspended. In this period the IATSE gave impetus to the SAG drive by successfully negotiating its five-year agreement of December 8, 1935. The

National Labor Relations Act also helped to stir the SAG to more militant action. The Guild's golden opportunity finally came in 1937 during the jurisdictional controversy between the IATSE and the FMPC. As noted earlier, to keep the actors from supporting the FMPC, the Browne-Bioff IA combine agreed to help the SAG by threatening to close all theaters over the country by calling out the projectionists. As a result, the SAG won its coveted recognition by June, 1937, and secured a contract. It provided for a 100 per cent closed shop for extras, bit players (actors paid by the day), and stunt men, and a 90 per cent closed shop for stars and feature actors which was to become completely closed after five years; a minimum wage of $50 per week for stock players; an increase from $15 to $25 per day for bit players; compensation for all actors while riding to and from locations; abolition of the $3.20 standard wage for the lowest class of extras; a 10 per cent wage increase for all extras earning up to $15 per day with a $5.50 minimum; an increase from $20 to $35 per week for stand-ins or a daily wage of not less than $6.50; a fifty-four-hour week (reduced to forty-eight in 1938); written contracts for free-lance actors; the arbitration of disputes; assured twelve-hour rest periods; and a promise by the SAG not to strike during the life of the agreement.[54]

All was not peace within the SAG for the rest of the decade, but the major goal was obtained with this contract, and there were subsequent membership gains. Other talent unions also were encouraged to pursue more aggressive organizing tactics by the success of the actors. These included the Hollywood Radio Artists Guild; the American Federation of Actors, AFL, which covered variety, night club, and vaudeville entertainers; and the Association of Independent Organizations. The last was a dual union which claimed that the SAG did not really have the best interests of its membership at heart and that its dues were so high that many members could hardly make a living. It achieved little success, however, although it reached the point where it was able to petition the NLRB for a bargaining election over 2,500 actors, extras, and film riders. Jurisdictional disputes within the Associated Actors and Artistes of America, of which the SAG was a member, characterized much of 1939. Edgar Bergen, for example, had to belong to three unions in order to cover radio, movie, and personal appearance work; he had to pay full dues to one union and half dues to two others. To clear up this problem, the AAAA established a procedure under which an actor would be required to have only one set of clearance papers and pay one initiation fee.

By and large, as far as the SAG was concerned, the years after 1937 were marked by good relations with producers. The latter, in turn, seemed happy to have the SAG assume responsibility for the extras. The Guild's contention that fair treatment of the actors was in the best interests of the producers was borne out by events. The negotiations for the 1941 contract were peaceful and the producers were willing to make some concessions. Wage increases totaled $309,000 a year; $10.50 was established as the basic wage for extra work, with limitations placed on $5.50 calls; the minimum weekly wage for free-lance players was increased to $100; the $16.50 daily check for dress extras was unchanged; working conditions were improved; and other wage increases were granted.[55]

4. SCREEN WRITERS, DIRECTORS, AND WHITE-COLLAR LABOR

The Screen Writers Guild (SWG) coöperated with the Screen Actors Guild in a number of organizational efforts, but it did not achieve quite the success of the latter. The actors had a more favorable bargaining position and a more conservative, less militant attitude than the writers. Furthermore, producers apparently desired freer access to the story material market than to acting talent; thus an SAG shop was less of a threat than one controlled by the SWG. Moreover, the SAG had more in common with back-lot workers than did the writers. The status of an actor as an employee was more definite than that of a writer, and he made a more tangible contribution to a motion picture. Hence the collective bargaining contract negotiated by the SAG in 1940 bore closer resemblance to that of the IATSE than did the agreement won by the SWG.[56]

The writers were slow to make the transition to the movies, but longer stories eventually brought them into the fold. For many years they were subject to a number of abuses: copyright laws did not protect them against plagiarism; their stories were often heavily mutilated in the course of production, and they felt themselves unfairly judged by the results rather than by the original manuscript; a general lack of knowledge concerning finance and production operations in the movies worked to their detriment, as did the difficulty of identifying the employer-employee relationship; and, finally, they were unprotected by equitable or enforceable standard contracts.[57]

The writers made the first real attempt to organize in 1912 when they formed the Authors League of America. Most of its members were concentrated in the East and had little interest in motion pictures, which were just beginning to become a source of employment. In 1914 the Photoplay Authors League of America was formed specifically to protect Hollywood screen writers against the growth of correspondence schools purporting to teach how to write for the movies. It also tried to safeguard the copyrights of members by publishing scenarios in a bulletin. Not succeeding in either aim, it ceased to exist in 1919. The Screen Writers Guild was formed the following year by members of the Authors League of America, who were encouraged by the success of Actors Equity at the end of the war. By 1924 it had a membership of 250 writers, but it failed to make any progress toward achieving a standard contract. By threatening to call a strike of scenarists, the SWG coöperated with Equity in opposing the 10 per cent salary cut proposed by the studios in 1927. When the proposal was withdrawn, the SWG claimed at least part of the credit. In the same year the Academy of Motion Picture Arts and Sciences moved into the field of writer-producer relations. The SWG distrusted the AMPAS at first, but when the writers' branch of the Academy voted to recognize the Guild's prior right to handle negotiations and expressed hopes for a standard contract, a period of more amicable relations began. The SWG, lulled by this olive branch, ceased its efforts to establish a minimum basic contract for free-lance scenarists. The AMPAS writers' branch further gained the confidence of the SWG by placing two of the latter's members on its negotiating committee to face two producers against whom the writers had never had a complaint. The fifth member was a director who recognized the importance of the screen writer. Most of the major writers then joined the AMPAS, and the SWG went into eclipse.[58]

The AMPAS dominated writer-producer relations from 1927 until 1933. It adjusted many disputes in this period, with the settlements favoring the writers by a two-to-one ratio, but never arrived at a standard contract. The negotiating committee established to work out such a contract was consistently deadlocked. Then, with the entrance of sound and dialogue, screen writer techniques became so complicated that negotiations were called off until 1931. Finally, a three-point code agreement was signed in May, 1932, by nine studios and more than 200 established screen writers. It covered layoffs and quitting, payments made on delivery of scenarios, and the important issue of screen credits. By this time, however, the depression was in full swing, and the code was loosely administered and violated as often as it was observed. This situation, plus the 50 per cent salary reduction plan of March, 1933, reawakened distrust of the AMPAS. The writers clearly saw that only those unions with definite contracts were exempt from the proposed salary cut; hence they no longer believed that the AMPAS was primarily interested in their welfare. A number of important writers therefore left the Academy, and the SWG was revived.[59]

After the NRA came into existence in 1933, the SWG, looking toward code revisions, agitated for the formation of producer-writer and producer-actor committees in collaboration with the SAG, but without success. In the same period the president of the SWG appointed a commission of twelve writers to handle conciliation, arbitration, ethics, and discipline for its members. Noting the Guild's new life, the AMPAS made a bid to win back the writers in 1934 by obtaining a strengthened agreement from the producers. Then, when the agreement was renewed in late 1935, it was amended to incorporate most of the provisions the SWG had tried to get into the code. These included written contracts for all writers, advance notice of discharge, and certain changes in the screen credit allocation system. The SWG members were not interested in these concessions, however, as their distrust of the AMPAS was too great. They stepped up their efforts to secure an SWG contract apart from the AMPAS by seeking the support of the Authors League of America. They wanted the latter's members to refuse to grant motion picture rights to their stories until the producers had accepted a Guild agreement. This action only compounded their problems, however, as a number of screen writers disagreed with the plan so strongly that they broke away and formed a dual union known as the Screen Playwrights Guild in May, 1936. The new group not only feared that any tie with the Authors League would lead to domination by Eastern writers, but also suspected that Broadway dramatists with little Hollywood experience and with left-wing political leanings were already influential in the SWG. The latter, in turn, declared that the Screen Playwrights Guild was dominated by the producers and was under the too-conservative leadership of Rupert Hughes, known as the "king" of the free-lance writers. There was little doubt that the SWG was hurt temporarily by this defection in its ranks.[60]

The next year the validation of the NLRA brought a shift in power. The SWG asked for representation elections in the studios, a request opposed by producers on the ground that writers were not employees as defined in the act. After months of bickering and a lengthy hearing on the matter, the NLRB authorized elections in eighteen major studios for June, 1938. The Screen Playwrights Guild refused to abide by the ruling and the studios concerned balked at the requirement that they provide the names of eligible voters, thus postponing the election until the 28th of the month. The results favored the SWG by a margin of almost five to one. This did not resolve the issue, however, as the producers dragged their feet during subsequent contract negotiations, and mutual distrust hampered the conferences. The SWG desired a contract for one year, and certainly for no longer than three, whereas the producers wanted a seven-year agreement. The producers were adamant in refusing a Guild shop, nor would they break any existing contracts with the Screen Playwrights Guild. For many months charges and countercharges marked all attempts to arrive at a settlement, until the producers grew tired of the struggle. They finally voided their contracts with the Screen Playwrights Guild and reached an agreement with the SWG in May, 1940. It was a poor substitute for what the SWG really wanted, but it was still an agreement. The six-month contract provided for recognition and an 80 per cent SWG shop. Because the impact of World War II was beginning to be felt, the producers were not willing to sign anything that would increase their costs in the face of a decline in revenue. In November, when the contract expired, the SWG threatened a strike if a better agreement was not forthcoming. As a result, a new seven-year contract provided for an 85 per cent Guild shop for the first three years and a 90 per cent shop for the remaining four years, and established a weekly minimum salary of $125 for all screen writers, effective at the end of the first year. Thus the writers finally acquired status in the studios, though at a later date than the SAG.[61]

The film directors were slower to organize than either the actors or the writers. In the eyes of the public, as well as of their co-workers, they were associated with management and, like the stars, they were relatively highly paid. But technically they were employees. They had little budgetary control and, though they worked closely with producers, in the final analysis they were subject to the latter's dictates. The first attempt to achieve bargaining status was made at the 1931 AFL convention when Assistant Directors Union, Local No. 18096, of Los Angeles asked for help in a drive for recognition by the studios. Assistant directors and production unit managers hoped to overcome alleged mistreatment by producers through the establishment of collective bargaining procedures. On the positive side, they wanted more authority in selecting stories for their pictures, more influence in the film-cutting room, and a percentage of profits. Nothing came of their requests, however, as the depression and the film-code troubles of the NRA period prevented effective action and weakened the local.

Help came in 1936, when about forty top directors, including King Vidor, Lewis Milestone, Frank Tuttle, William K. Howard, and John Ford, bolted the Academy because they were disgusted with producer domination. They formed the Screen Directors Guild (SDG), which also covered assistant directors and production unit officers. Before long the membership reached 100 directors, including most of the big names in the business. Although a number of directors made more money than some of the producers, they wanted to improve working conditions and remuneration for assistant directors and production unit managers along the lines of their 1931 demands.[62]

The producers refused to recognize the new SDG on the ground that directors, their assistants, and production unit managers did not constitute an appropriate bargaining unit. They argued, first, that the third group represented the business interests of producers while directors handled the artistic aspects of production, and, second, that assistant directors were under the directors and thus were not free agents. Accordingly, the producers refused to bargain unless the directors were organized into a separate unit. The directors disagreed, however, and asked for certification by the NLRB. In 1938, while conferences and hearings were taking place, some 300 assistant directors, directors, and production unit managers voiced their desire to unify all independent professional film workers' organizations into one group. This proposal was prompted by what seemed to be an undue delay in securing certification from the NLRB, coupled with the fear that if the board did not authorize collective bargaining by professional film workers, the IATSE would take them over. Not long after this demonstration of unity, certification was obtained by the SDG, and the producers decided to proceed with recognition and grant a contract.

Eventually, in 1939, a nine-year agreement was signed. It provided for an 80 per cent SDG shop; recognized the SDG as the bargaining agent for all directors and assistant directors; established special committees to settle individual disputes and arbitrate abuses of the contract; gave directors a longer period for the preparation of pictures; required that directors be consulted concerning the casts and the cutting of film; provided for compensation for lower-paid free-lance directors who were consulted in connection with casting, cutting, and other chores; gave screen credits to directors on all pictures, with any resulting disputes to be settled by the SDG; and granted assistant directors a 10 per cent pay increase. Other clauses improved working conditions for directors and their assistants. Meanwhile the production unit managers formed a guild of their own for collective bargaining purposes.[63]

A number of other professional white-collar groups were organized in 1935–1940. The most important of these were illustrators, screen publicists, artists, film editors, art directors, set designers, script clerks, and cartoonists. Most of them established guilds after NLRB certification elections, and subsequently won producer recognition and made some material gains. A few had CIO leanings, but they did not join the new industrial union organization because the studio unions were largely AFL-oriented.[64]

Unionization of office employees and semiprofessional workers was slow in starting. Most of these were clerical workers who feared the racketeering they saw in the craft unions under IATSE leadership and, in addition, typically considered themselves somewhat above unionization. Further, their wages were usually higher than those paid for comparable work in outside business firms. Before 1939, therefore, stenographers, switchboard operators, bookkeepers, and general clerks on the movie lots were practically unorganized. Such organizations as did exist were usually office employees' guilds of a company-union type. Concerned with losing privileges that they believed outweighed the gains from affiliation with an independent union, they remained in company-controlled groups during most of the 1930's. As would be expected, they had little effective bargaining power. Although they had employee bargaining committees, final decisions on grievances rested largely in the hands of producers, on whose generosity the workers thus came to depend.

Because the guilds were organized on a company basis, a number of discrepancies soon developed among the different studios in terms of wage scales, conditions, and fringe benefits. Although the workers began to be aware of these differences, they showed no greater interest than before in affiliating with the established AFL office employees' union, which had too long a record of ineffectiveness for white-collar employees to feel that it provided an answer to their problems.

Finally, in February, 1939, the studio clerical workers formed their own independent union, the Screen Office Employees Guild (SOEG). An intensive organizing campaign made headway in all but the 20th Century–Fox, Paramount, and Warner Brothers studios, whose office employees were treated very well, with high minimum wages, good vacations and adequate sick leave, and a fixed scale of salary increases. Opposition from the AFL office employees' union, experienced in the other studios, was overcome and NLRB certification was obtained for all studios except the three indicated above. The lack of organization in these three hampered the efforts of the SOEG to secure recognition from the producers as a body. Even so, the new decade promised to give clerical workers some of the status previously achieved by professional groups and craftsmen in the studios.[65]

Standing on the threshold of the 1940's, the leaders of the movie unions could look back on a decade of achievement which, in part, had its roots in the new economic era that began after World War I. The rise in the per capita standard of living in the 1920's gave the public both the funds and the time to enjoy the silver screen and to encourage its output. The concentration of movie production in the Los Angeles area also helped union leaders in the amusement trades to organize studio employees. By 1939, 89.6 per cent of all workers employed in the production of motion pictures in the United States were located in Los Angeles. Finally, the sympathetic attitude toward organized labor evidenced in the legislation of the 1930's, which encouraged collective bargaining, was of prime significance in sparking the growth of labor unions in the studios.[66]

But the producers themselves had involuntarily encouraged the growth of unions. The Academy of Motion Picture Arts and Sciences had been an innovation in industrial relations, and seemed to be a reasonable idea for successful industry-wide employee representation. Through the Academy a number of talent groups obtained standard contracts and developed codes covering various practices which worked to their benefit. Although the AMPAS was not a true union, it introduced the principle of collective bargaining. Thus, when opportunities to develop labor unions came along, the talent groups were able to use the experience gained in Academy relationships to good advantage in establishing collective bargaining through the various guilds.

The producers also made a number of mistakes that aided in the development of unions. One of these certainly was siding with the leadership of the IATSE during the period of its greatest corruption in the middle and late 'thirties. Employees concerned with ethics in labor relations might have been expected to resent this and to seek to establish other labor organizations. Moreover, a number of producers took sides in jurisdictional disputes or allegedly encouraged such disputes.

This was conducive to turmoil in labor relations and to the growth of new organizations that sought to resolve the jurisdictional difficulties of the established unions. The fact that producers showed more concern for talent groups through the Academy than they did for the crafts lowered the morale of the latter and influenced them to seek their own salvation through outside independent or AFL unions. The tardiness of producers in recognizing that many groups of their employees had hardly enough work in any given year to keep body and soul together further encouraged unionization. For these workers the best recourse was to find some way of limiting the labor available. Unions presented an excellent medium for this purpose.[67]

There seems little question, however, that the unions were often their own worst enemies. Particularly was this true in connection with the jurisdictional troubles that beset the movies. There were not only the well-known and frequently widely publicized struggles among leaders over membership and dues, but also the related clashes caused by the desire to control jobs. At times the differences among unions seemed to be wider than those between producers and their employees. Evidences of graft within the unions, particularly in the Bioff-Browne era, hurt the unions in the eyes of the public and tended to limit their effectiveness to the degree that favorable public relations were important.[68]

As the movie unions entered the period of World War II, certain problems that had been plaguing them for a long time continued to exist. Jurisdictional disputes still remained unsolved, as the AFL had been unable to secure a lasting truce, and the IATSE controlled the industry through its ability to order out the projectionists in theaters over the United States. The decasualization of extras was an outstanding problem, although the Screen Actors Guild and Central Casting had made some progress in this area. In 1940 it seemed unlikely that a complete solution to this difficulty would be found, because of the technical requirements of film production in casting matters. The eventual formation of the Screen Players Union by the extras in 1944, when they left the SAG, did not dispose of the issue but resulted only in continuation of the decasualization campaign by a new organization.

The elimination of Bioff and Browne gave IATSE unions the autonomy they desired, and World War II found most Hollywood labor groups organized into effective unions. As the effects of the defense economy began to be felt in terms of a shrinking of the studio labor force, producers recognized the need for a plan to stabilize employment in the studio crafts. Wage increases totaling more than $5 million a year were therefore negotiated for the crafts. This action helped the studios to retain an adequate labor force and stabilized employment, wages, and conditions during the war years. By the end of the war Hollywood was a union town, with professional, semiprofessional, skilled, unskilled, and semiskilled groups all organized into effective bargaining agencies. Little did either the producers or the movie labor leaders realize that the postwar years and television would bring woes that would force an industry decline even in a period of unprecedented prosperity.[69]

X. REVIVAL AT THE HARBOR

1. THE 1934 STRIKE

UNIONS in the maritime trades on the Pacific Coast, particularly at Los Angeles Harbor, revived very rapidly in the middle and late 1930's. Just as the movie industry was almost completely unionized by the end of this decade, so were the maritime trades. Unlike Hollywood workers, however, the men who earned their living from the sea were largely unorganized as the decade began, although they still had memories of union experiences as late as the years immediately following World War I. In further contrast to craft and talent groups in the movie industry, the maritime occupations were as old as recorded history.

The background for the revival of unions on the water front at San Pedro and other coast cities was composed of a number of factors. Some were sociological in nature, developing from the fact that water-front workers were hardly considered a part of the general community before the 1930's. The casual nature of the job isolated the worker from his employer and kept him from any personal and permanent identification with the maritime industry. As a sometime employee, he found it difficult to become associated with the more stable elements of the community, which was likely to regard him as a transient. It was inevitable, therefore, that these casuals would develop a common bond of self-interest and needed only a union to weld them into an effective economic instrument based on their recognized insecurity and mutual grievances.

In part, the background factors were economic. Some employers apparently wanted to assume no responsibility for the casuals and very little for those who had more regularity of employment as members of longshoring gangs. The unchecked power of the employer after the postwar elimination of outside unions led water-front workers to believe that the only avenue to stability and security was to seize control of the job. Indeed, the workers were inclined to ask why they should feel any responsibility toward an employer who, during the 1920's and early 1930's, had shown little interest in their economic welfare.

Other economic factors contributed to the upsurge of maritime unions. The depression of 1929 accentuated the problem of excess capacity and the consequent rate cutting that developed after World War I in an effort to fill bottoms and keep ships running. Furthermore, foreign competition was exceedingly keen because most nations could hire and maintain crews on a lower standard of living than Americans were accustomed to enduring. Domestic land transportation also made inroads into the available commerce. The pressure on American shipowners to remain competitive inevitably lowered the wages and worsened the conditions of the men in the forecastle and on the docks. The older men who remained on the job despite this situation experienced more difficulty with the onset of the depression, when many young men drifted to the docks and the ships in search of employment. The problem of job retention by the older men, in fact, became acute. Because many of the newcomers were well educated, they at first looked upon their jobs as temporary; but as the depression deepened, they became convinced that they would remain in these lowly occupations for some time and that their only recourse was to seek ways to improve their working conditions. Thus, economic pressures in the industry associated with the increase in labor supply in the face of declining industrial activity and growing competition from foreign ships and domestic rails and trucks led in the early 1930's to a critical situation for maritime labor. The workers eventually saw no solution except organization. Militant unionism could not weaken their position; the worst that could happen was a continuance of their current status.[1]

When the NIRA was passed in 1933, officials of the International Longshoremen's Association (ILA), AFL, under the leadership of Joseph Ryan of New York, sent organizers into all Pacific Coast ports. By September of that year they had established a Pacific Coast District of the ILA with William J. Lewis as president. Similar activities occurred among the seafaring unions. The longshoremen and the sailors joined their respective organizations in large numbers. Among them was Alfred (Harry) Renton Bridges, an Australian-born longshoreman who was to become one of the leaders of the dock workers. In October, 1933, 400 members of the newly established San Francisco local of the ILA struck over the alleged discriminatory discharge of several unionists by the Matson Navigation Company. The walkout ended when the strikers won a National Labor Board award in favor of recognition and against the discrimination, and were reinstated in their jobs. In November officials of the Sailors Union of the Pacific, the Marine Firemen, Oilers, Watertenders and Wipers Association, and the Marine Cooks and Stewards Association presented demands concerning wages, hours, and the closed shop at the NRA shipping code hearings in Washington. Their requests were not granted.[2]

On December 17, 1933, longshoremen in San Francisco Local No. 38-79 of the ILA voted for a walkout if the members of the Waterfront Employers' Association in that city would not agree to a six-hour day, a thirty-hour week, and a minimum wage of $1 an hour. Taking a similar vote, the San Pedro local decided to submit the issues to the Los Angeles Regional Labor Board.

Early in January, 1934, the San Pedro ILA members established a hiring hall in competition with the employer-controlled Marine Service Bureau, which was, in effect, a company union with its own hiring hall. In the same month the Regional Labor Board held an election to determine the collective bargaining agent for the San Pedro longshoremen. The ILA won over the Marine Service Bureau by a vote of 1,262 to 32. Aware that the longshoremen desired their own union and were deadly serious in their demands for improved wages and working conditions, water-front employers authorized a 10 per cent wage increase; several favorable changes in working conditions, including the addition of Armistice Day to the list of holidays requiring the payment of overtime wages; overtime pay for standing by at the completion of a regular shift while waiting for a work call; payment of a 10-cent "penalty wage" to men handling offensive items such as fertilizer, fish, blood or bone meal, green hides, and creosote; travel time to and from jobs requiring the handling of explosives; basic wages of 85 cents an hour for straight time and $1.25 for overtime; hourly rates of 95 cents for regular shifts and $1.30 for overtime for hatch tenders and winch drivers; 75 cents and $1.15, respectively, for front men and dock workers; and maintenance of a 55-cent rate for car workers. Officers of the San Pedro local, with leaders of other longshore unions up and down the coast, continued to press for wages of $1 an hour for straight time, $1.25 for overtime, $1.65 for hatch tenders, and recognition of the ILA as the official collective bargaining agent.[3]

In February a convention of all ILA locals on the Pacific Coast, held at San Francisco, reaffirmed the principal objectives of longshoremen: a uniform coast-wide agreement, union-controlled hiring halls, a six-hour day, a thirty-hour week, and a minimum wage of $1 an hour. These demands were presented to water-front employers, who were given until March 7 to meet them. During negotiations the employers agreed to recognize the ILA and to meet certain other requests, but they refused to grant a coast-wide agreement and a union-controlled hiring hall. ILA representatives were adamant on the latter two issues. In the ensuing coast-wide strike vote, the ILA membership sanctioned a walkout to begin on March 23. San Pedro longshoremen voted for the strike by a majority of 836 to 200, and also favored the establishment of a federation of coast maritime unions. Noting the temper of the men, water-front employers at Los Angeles and Long Beach harbors prepared for conflict. Through the coöperation of Captain Hynes of the Los Angeles Police Department, the Burns Detective Agency was given a contract to furnish guards in the event of a strike. A pool of $85,000 was established by subscription from various steamship companies and held by the Marine Service Bureau at the harbor for disbursement as needed.[4]

On March 22 President Roosevelt intervened in the controversy, and ILA Pacific Coast president Lewis agreed not to call the strike pending the appointment of an impartial fact-finding board. This news was received with enthusiasm by local water-front employers, but spokesmen for the central strike committee of the harbor union felt that Lewis had exceeded his authority. Four hundred workers gathered in and around the local ILA office and ridiculed the announcement postponing the walkout—evidence of the burgeoning discontent with AFL leadership which was to result in the formation of a new union in 1937 under the leadership of Harry Bridges. The impartial fact-finding board appointed on March 26 began a series of conferences with both sides in San Francisco. San Pedro water-front employers refused to send representatives on the ground that employment conditions in their area differed from those in other Pacific Coast ports. At their request a separate fact-finding investigation was conducted at the local harbor in April. Meanwhile, the San Francisco meetings continued. ILA officials insisted that any decisions reached be applied to all Pacific Coast ports and that a closed shop be established. As employers were equally stubborn on these points, the conferences were soon deadlocked.

On April 30 the union filed written notices with water-front employers at Pacific Coast ports that unless definite and satisfactory agreements were arrived at by 8 P.M. on May 7, 1934, the strike would be called shortly thereafter. When further conferences proved futile, on May 9 the longshoremen left their jobs in Seattle, Tacoma, Portland, San Francisco, San Pedro, San Diego, and smaller ports. The only major change in the original demands was a request that hiring halls be jointly operated by the ILA and the employers. Water-front employers were convinced that the strike would not last long because of a number of factors: the reserve of unemployed workers available as strikebreakers; the difficulties of achieving unity of aim and action among the leaders of all the local maritime unions along the coast; the opposition of conservative officials of the ILA, who wanted only a short strike, to the younger militant leaders in the longshoremen's locals; the belief that employers could prevail over the key San Francisco local, thus ending the strike as in 1919; and confidence that the federal government would intervene because it subsidized the merchant marine.[5]

About 30,000 union men walked out, for the longshoremen were joined by members of the seamen's unions who had been dissatisfied with the outcome of the NRA shipping code hearings the preceding November. The seamen wanted wage increases and certain changes in working conditions. Seventy per cent of the crew members on intercoastal common carriers and 37 per cent of the unlicensed personnel in coastwise service, as of June, 1933, received wages of $50 a month or less in addition to their quarters and subsistence.[6]

The strike quickly closed all the largest ports on the Pacific Coast except Los Angeles and Long Beach harbors. Although a majority of the local dock workers, numbering about 1,300, answered the strike call on May 9, members of the Longshoremen's Mutual Protective Association of Los Angeles and Long Beach continued to work. This organization had been formed several days before the strike by approximately 300 dock workers. Officials of the San Pedro ILA local called it a company union and claimed that its purpose was to furnish strikebreakers to load and unload the ships. Attempts by the Waterfront Employers' Association and the Pacific American Shipowners' Association, the two main employer organizations, to continue operations at the local port were supported by open-shop advocates in Los Angeles. They recruited strikebreakers from local colleges and high schools and among the unemployed to swell the ranks of those longshoremen who had remained on the job. In addition to employment offices set up at Vernon and Wilmington, the M and M established a recruiting station for dock workers at the Rosslyn Hotel in Los Angeles, where they were housed before being sent to the harbor. Representatives of the M and M enlisted a total of 5,081 strikebreakers, 1,281 of whom were used in longshore work while the rest manned the ships moving in and out of the port. Most of the strikebreakers doing dock work lived on moored vessels or behind stockades erected for the duration of the dispute.[7]

Negotiations to end the strike were conducted in San Francisco. A. H. Peterson, secretary of the San Pedro ILA local, was sent to the northern city as a liaison representative for his union. The Los Angeles Regional Labor Board tried to settle the strike at San Pedro, but waterfront employers there, backed by the M and M, stood firm in their opposition to the closed shop and the jointly controlled hiring hall. Meanwhile, officials of communities near the harbor assigned police to strike duty, canceling all leaves and placing officers on twelve-hour shifts. Both the water-front employers and the police departments hired special deputies to augment the regular security force. By May 15 more than 300 policemen, in addition to an equal number of private guards and deputies, were on duty in the San Pedro strike area. By the time the strike ended, approximately 700 Los Angeles policemen under the command of Captain Hynes had been used to maintain order. Many of them received additional pay from water-front employers, who also purchased tear-gas equipment for their use through the services of Captain Hynes.[8]

In the first days of the strike, only about 300 pickets walked the dock area. As shipping operations continued, however, this number was increased to approximately 1,800, with union seamen and teamsters joining the picket lines. Although clashes between police and strikers occurred frequently, there was no serious disturbance until the night of May 14, when some 300 strikers stormed a strikebreakers' stockade in the west basin of Los Angeles Harbor. One striker was killed by a special deputy, six were wounded, and a score or more were injured in the melee that ensued. The violence caused the Central Labor Council to pass a resolution protesting the alleged promiscuous arming of strikebreakers and deputies at San Pedro.

On May 14, in an effort to offset the strength of the open shop, the Teamsters Joint Council in Los Angeles voted to support the maritime trades. The refusal of members of affiliated locals to truck cargoes to and from the harbor area made it necessary to convoy vehicles between Los Angeles and the docks under police escort. With the success of this arrangement, carloadings at the local harbor gradually increased. San Francisco, however, remained closed, and ships began to avoid it after the Matson Navigation Company announced, on May 18, that for the duration of the walkout it would not consider the northern city as a port of call. All passengers on Matson ships embarked and disembarked at Los Angeles Harbor, where operations were at almost a normal level by May 27.[9]

On May 28 a tentative agreement to end the participation of the longshoremen in the strike was reached in San Francisco through the mediation of the assistant secretary of labor, Edward F. McGrady, who had entered the dispute on behalf of the federal government. Joseph P. Ryan, ILA president, approved the settlement, but most of the union members in coastal ports, including San Pedro, rejected it, being influenced by Harry Bridges, chairman of the Joint Marine Strike Committee at San Francisco, and other young leaders in the various locals. The major criticism was that, although the agreement recognized the ILA as collective bargaining representative, the wage, hour, and hiring-hall issues were to be decided by arbitration, the results of which might not favor the union. Opposition to the proposed contract also was expressed by Joseph Banning, a Los Angeles shipowners' representative, who reiterated that local water-front employers and vessel operators would accept no settlement reached in San Francisco, but would negotiate only for San Pedro and only with employees who worked there. Such negotiations, he pointed out, would be on the employers' own terms and would exclude the strikers. Other management spokesmen claimed that the strikers wanted to return to work but were prohibited from doing so by their leaders. All such statements were repudiated by union officers. A. H. Peterson of ILA Local No. 38-82 at Los Angeles Harbor blamed the M and M for prolonging the strike there. He charged that open-shop supporters paid many of the strike costs and kept an unofficial representative, Edgar R. Perry, at the San Francisco conferences to oppose any action that might result in the granting of union demands.[10]

Early in June M and M officials criticized the Los Angeles County Welfare Department for furnishing public relief to strikers' families, on the ground that those on strike could work if they would become strikebreakers. The Board of Supervisors replied that the federal government supplied the relief funds and therefore set the policy, over which county officials had no control. A denunciation of the federal ruling was subsequently printed in the *Times,* which characterized it as tantamount to giving relief to the voluntarily unemployed. Maritime employers also were critical of the presence of Communists among the strikers from the beginning of the dispute. As outbreaks of violence continued at various ports, police officials as well as employers claimed that Communist agitators were responsible for prolonging the strike and causing many of the riots and demonstrations. A number of individuals were arrested at Los Angeles Harbor on charges of distributing literature advocating the overthrow of the capitalist system. The ILA publicity committee officially denied the Communist charges, however, stating that local strike leaders were conservative AFL men working for legitimate union objectives and that only a minority of the longshoremen or sailors had any Communist leanings.[11]

Sharp clashes among strikers, strikebreakers, and police occurred in June. Unionists declared that the police used brutal methods, including night sticks, riot guns, and tear gas, and that many strikers had been falsely arrested, beaten, and then held for days. Employers and police officials maintained that Communist leadership at San Pedro made forceful methods necessary to keep the situation under control. ILA members rebutted this by pointing to a vote of confidence in their officers and a resolution against communism, both of which were passed at a meeting of the union longshoremen on June 18. Part of the violence was probably in response to the extension of picketing in June to all shipping operations in the harbor area. This move was precipitated by an announcement by the maritime employers that more tonnage had been shipped in May from Long Beach and San Pedro than in any month since January, 1931. The picketing was also extended to include the private employment offices in Los Angeles which were furnishing strikebreakers. The Los Angeles office of the California Department of Employment, though accused of supplying strikebreakers, was not picketed. Spokesmen for the state agency pointed out that, according to regulations, their actions were permissible so long as those who sought employment were informed of the strike.

Workers at the Los Angeles Shipbuilding and Drydock Corporation backed the striking seamen and longshoremen by refusing to work on ships brought in for repairs during the walkout. In addition, the Los Angeles Central Labor Council voted to support the strikers morally and financially. It sent letters to all its constituent unions requesting voluntary contributions to a strike fund, and assessed employed members of each affiliated local 25 cents a week for the duration of the dispute. Council officials distributed a total of $1,947.89 to the 4,000 strikers participating in the walkout, a sum collected from seventy-seven unions and their individual members. This figure did not include contributions made directly to the longshoremen or funds received from benefit shows and dances sponsored by the strikers.[12]

On June 16 a truce agreement was signed in San Francisco by Ryan for the ILA and by T. G. Plant, president of the Waterfront Employers' Association of San Francisco. Although the longshoremen at San Pedro accepted the truce by a vote of 635 to 584, it was rejected at all other ports and hence was not adopted. Most of the longshoremen objected to the agreement because it did not include the striking members of the various seamen's unions. Ryan was accused by younger rank-and-file leaders of "selling out" to the employers and deserting the members of the other maritime unions. This criticism widened the breach between the older, conservative leaders of the ILA and the younger local officials. The breach was never closed, although Ryan later repudiated the truce. This difference was one of the reasons for the jurisdictional conflict in 1937, through which Harry Bridges and the members of the International Longshoremen's and Warehouse-men's Union eliminated the ILA from representation in all Pacific Coast ports except four small harbors in the Puget Sound area.

In 1934 the first steps were taken to unify all the maritime unions in San Pedro in order to present a common front to employers, and in 1935 a branch of the Maritime Federation of the Pacific was formally established. It was composed of locals of the ILA, the National Organization of Masters, Mates and Pilots, the Sailors Union of the Pacific, the Marine Firemen, Oilers, Watertenders and Wipers Association, the Shipyard Workers Union, and the Scalers and Painters Union. Similar branches were formed in other Pacific Coast cities.[13]

On June 26, 1934, President Roosevelt issued Executive Order No. 6748, which established the National Longshoremen's Board under the provisions of the NIRA. This three-man body was authorized to investigate the continuing strike and to endeavor to settle it. It began its work almost immediately and by July 1 had secured tentative permission from representatives of the longshoremen and the water-front employers to submit the issues to arbitration. The seamen were not to be included in these arbitration proceedings, but officials of coast steamship companies consented to bargain collectively with representatives of their seafaring employees, to be selected in elections conducted by the board. Any controversies not settled by this procedure were to be submitted to arbitration. On July 11 the leaders of the maritime unions agreed to accept these proposals, and their decision was supported by the members in a referendum vote whose results were announced on July 27. The ILA local at San Pedro had favored the initiation of arbitration proceedings by a majority of 1,211 to 149. Open-shop supporters objected to the discharge of strikebreakers at the harbor and the rehiring of strikers, but water-front employers agreed to this procedure in order to end the eighty-three-day strike and facilitate the beginning of arbitration.[14]

On July 31 all the maritime strikers on the coast returned to work, including some 3,000 unionists in San Pedro. Three observers from the ILA were present at the Marine Service Bureau during the reëmployment process to prevent discrimination against union members. The rehiring was orderly in contrast with the violence that had occurred in the weeks just before termination of the walkout. Some of the disturbances took place when police dispersed demonstrations and conducted raids on Communist meetings, including those of the Marine Workers Industrial Union. Officials of ILA Local No. 38-82 coöperated with the police in this endeavor by creating a committee of 100 longshoremen which instituted a campaign to oust Communists from membership in the union. Looking back on the dispute, E. J. Amar, president of the Board of Harbor Commissioners of Los Angeles, estimated that, apart from damages and medical costs resulting from violence, the strike had cost the harbor department alone approximately $60,000 a month because of the loss of pilot, wharf, and dock charges. Although the level of harbor activity had been reduced in May and June, much of the curtailment at San Pedro occurred in July.[15]

On August 3, employers and ILA leaders in San Pedro established machinery to deal with disputes arising in the arbitration period. Some stoppages of work had already taken place, but they were deprecated in a strongly worded statement by officials of the local union. Little did either side realize that work stoppage would become a virtual disease in longshoring operations in subsequent years. Stoppages halting cargo handling for periods of a few hours, days, or weeks became a part of what was known as "job action." They were later used in attempts to gain from water-front employers certain concessions that were not in the award or agreement, or to enforce a particular clause to the advantage of longshoremen. The full extent of job action was not envisaged at this time, however. On August 7 representatives of the employers and of the longshoremen's unions on the Pacific Coast entered into an agreement to abide by the arbitration award when it was made by the National Longshoremen's Board.[16]

Meanwhile, the board began to conduct its hearings in San Francisco. The Regional Labor Board acted as its agent in San Pedro and initiated elections there to select the proper collective bargaining representatives for shipyard workers, seamen, and longshoremen. In a very few days dock operations were normal and ships entered and left the port in increasing numbers. ILA members thanked the Los Angeles County Board of Supervisors for granting relief to strikers' families, and the union commended the Los Angeles Police Department for the efforts of its officers in preventing the spread of violence.[17]

The National Longshoremen's Board inspected most of the major ports in the course of the hearings. San Pedro was visited for several days in September, when conferences were held with both sides. The major point of contention proved to be control of the hiring halls. ILA representatives believed that if employers gained control, an open shop would be maintained. The employers contended, on the other hand, that union control of the halls would remove all matters of hiring, firing, and selection of employees from management's jurisdiction. After due consideration of the arguments presented in San Pedro and other ports by union members and water-front employers, the board announced its decision on October 12. The award granted increases in base rates of pay as well as standardized scales, a six-hour day and a thirty-hour week, improved working conditions, penalty pay for certain types of disagreeable cargoes, arbitration machinery in the form of joint port committees with veto power on each side, and a jointly controlled hiring hall with an ILA-elected dispatcher. The settlement was coast-wide and binding in all the principal ports on the Pacific Coast.[18]

Under the settlement, hiring halls were to be controlled by a joint port committee in each harbor composed of representatives from both sides. The committee's powers included the authority to change the size of the rotated list of men dispatched by the hiring hall. All grievances and disputes concerning working conditions were also to be referred to this committee which, in turn, was to refer deadlocks to an arbitrator designated by the Secretary of Labor. These arrangements, along with the other gains, were generally regarded as a victory by the unionists, though they had failed to win all their demands, including the $1 an hour basic wage and full control of the hiring halls. Harry Bridges in San Francisco seems to have been the only important dock leader who regarded the award as inadequate. San Pedro longshoremen expected to get $30,000 to $40,000 in back pay, for the agreement provided a substantial wage increase retroactive to July 31, 1934. Even the employers seemed reasonably pleased. An editorial in the *Times* stated that the settlement maintained an open shop in the local maritime industry, as the hiring halls were to be jointly administered without union or nonunion discrimination. But open-shop leaders were whistling in the dark, for control was soon to pass to the union.[19]

Before the end of the year the National Longshoremen's Board issued additional awards affecting marine clerks and checkers who were members of the ILA. Representatives of the Sailors Union of the Pacific, the Marine Firemen, Oilers, Watertenders and Wipers Association, and the Marine Cooks and Stewards Association entered into agreements with the largest Pacific Coast steamship companies which became effective on February 25, 1935. These agreements provided only for preference in employment. The unions involved had previously been designated as bargaining agents for unlicensed seafaring men in elections conducted by the board. In later months, similar agreements were signed for licensed personnel represented by the National Organization of Masters, Mates and Pilots and the Marine Engineers Beneficial Association. A final agreement, negotiated between the shipowners and the American Radio Telegraphists Association, designated in earlier elections as agent for the ship radio operators, went into effect on May 7, 1935. The board itself was abolished by a proclamation of President Roosevelt's on March 11, 1935, after its work was completed.[20]

2. ARMISTICE, 1934–1936

Water-front relations were not peaceful despite settlement of the 1934 strike. In 1935 there were 128 strikes and work stoppages which caused from one to fifty-three ships to be idle in Pacific Coast ports for different periods of time. The jointly controlled hiring halls proved to be an illusion for the open-shop forces. Dispatchers would not send out men of questionable union allegiance and sent only the poorest workers to companies in bad standing with the ILA. Many of the old-line longshoremen who had not been in favor of the strike or did not like the younger leadership began to leave the industry. New men ready to do the union's bidding took their places, and were largely blamed by the employers for the subsequent increase in job action, slowdowns, and other tactics designed to harass management in an attempt to gain concessions. The dispatchers in the various ports usually worked from a list of registered longshoremen who were sent out in rotation. The list was enlarged or reduced only by joint action of the union and the water-front employers; the former could prevent the hiring of a nonunionist, and the latter could block the registration of an incompetent man. But all the registered men were entitled to an equal share of the available port work without reference to ability, performance, experience, or other factors. Thus, such personal relationships as had existed between employers and certain favored employees began to break down under the new hiring-hall practices. Although the employers hired the foremen or so-called "walking bosses," these men were mostly unionists who had come up through the ranks and had to keep on good terms with their men; hence they had little power in the face of strong union opposition.[21]

Employers claimed that the practices indulged in by the union after the 1934 strike were illegal and in violation of the October award, but to little avail. The officers of the Maritime Federation of the Pacific, formed in April, 1935, and composed of the largest Pacific Coast maritime unions, recognized "quickie" strikes, work stoppages, and other job action as legitimate means of enforcing the awards and gaining concessions not granted under the agreements. Employers declared that these actions were disrupting schedules, increasing operating costs, and forcing shipping companies into bankruptcy. Port labor relations committees and arbitrators rendered many decisions against the unionists, but these had little effect. Generally speaking, the men would quit before the committee could convene; thus work was delayed until a decision was forthcoming. The port committee was supposed to discipline the men for failing to obey working rules, but its composition made it difficult to achieve unanimity. Usually the violation was dismissed. Further, a man who was fired for an infraction was often sent back on the job by the hiring hall. In other instances a whole gang would quit when one of its members was discharged.[22]

Employers were most concerned, however, over the operation of the hiring hall and the increasing control exercised by the ILA dispatcher. They were used to selecting certain preferred men, but, as already noted, the union dispatcher used a rotation system in order to spread the work. Employers thus had to take what was sent to them, a practice leading, in their view, to production inefficiency and reduced output per man, thereby increasing shipping costs.

A similar situation existed with respect to the hiring of unlicensed seamen. Jointly operated hiring halls had not been provided in the agreements, but the local unions established halls and tried to force the employers to hire the men sent by the dispatchers, thus prohibiting the selection of crews at the dock. The seamen participated in about 250 short strikes in 1935 and 1936 in an attempt to enforce this hiring-hall procedure. As with the longshoremen, shipping employers complained that the lack of coöperation on the part of union officials in effecting the discharge of incompetent seamen weakened discipline among the crews and obscured the employer-employee relationship. In addition, "hot cargo" or secondary-boycott disputes frequently caused ships to remain in port for unduly long periods of time because sailors and longshoremen would refuse to work such cargoes.

The new spirit generated among maritime workers in 1935 and 1936 was aptly expressed by their leaders in reply to employer complaints:

Since waterfront and maritime unions were organized through the 1934 maritime strike and reasonable conditions of employment including hours, wages and working conditions have been established, practically every waterfront dispute has been caused by attempts of employers to weaken the economic and political strength of the unions and to attack conditions established by the unions.

Most of these attacks have taken place under the cover of accusing the unions and their leaders of Communism and the unions of violating their contracts in refusing to help break strikes or work with strikebreakers or han-

dle cargo coming from struck plants, by labor spy activity and agitation in the
unions, by frame-ups of leaders or members of the unions. . . .

Such were their public statements but in reality behind the scenes and
through their various organizations, every attack was directed at a return of
the open shop and employer control of Pacific Coast waterfront labor.[23]

Los Angeles Harbor had its share of strikes and work stoppages in
the maritime industry in 1935. Most of the stoppages in the first few
months of the year occurred because unionists refused to work with
nonunion men. The most important strike concerned tanker seamen.
Leaders of the International Seamen's Union (ISU) suspected oil companies and other tanker operators of trying to weaken the union
through the use of nonunion men, even though the ISU, in January,
1935, had been declared the bargaining agent for tanker seamen by the
National Longshoremen's Board. ISU officials therefore demanded that
tanker operators give union men employment preference, as a pre-
requisite to the arbitration of other issues. When the demand was rejected, the walkout was called on March 9, 1935, against the Associated,
General Petroleum, Richfield, Union, and Standard Oil companies and
the Hillcone Steamship Company in all Pacific Coast ports. A few days
later, members of the Masters, Mates and Pilots and the Marine Engineers joined the strike. By March 19, eleven tankers were idle at the
harbor, with a total of thirty tied up at other Pacific Coast ports.[24]

Meanwhile, the companies took steps to maintain operations: they
began to man their ships with nonunion crews; an employment office
was established in the city at Sixth and Main streets; two power boats
patrolled the oil-loading docks; and a Los Angeles police detail was
assigned to the harbor area. Officials of the Marine Service Bureau purchased tear-gas equipment for use in the event of violence, while the
struck companies hired and armed special police. In April and May,
therefore, tankers manned by nonunion crews moved in and out of the
harbor in larger numbers, and operations gradually became normal despite the heckling of strikebreakers by pickets and acts of violence.
These included beatings of strikers by so-called "beef squads," reciprocal actions on the part of unionists, and the breaking of windows in
service stations operated by the struck firms. A general marine strike
on the Pacific Coast, threatened by officials of the Maritime Federation
of the Pacific in support of the tanker crews, did not materialize because it was opposed by the rank and file of the unions in that organization. By June picketing had dwindled to the point where ISU officers were willing to accept a compromise settlement.

Mediation proceedings had been initiated at San Francisco almost as soon as the strike began. In subsequent months two federal mediation boards tried unsuccessfully to settle the dispute. An offer made on April 8 by the struck companies finally became the basis for termination of the walkout on June 17. The strikers lost three months' pay and many were dismissed permanently from their jobs on tankers. The settlement provided for monthly wage increases ranging from $10 for seamen and firemen to $30 for first officers and chief engineers. These gains, however, were less than half the amounts originally requested by the strikers. A forty-hour week had been demanded, but a fifty-six-hour week was granted. Members of the International Seamen's Union did not obtain preferential hiring, and the companies continued to employ crews on a merit basis regardless of union affiliation.

The seamen's dissatisfaction with the results of the tanker strike, combined with the longshoremen's militancy, kept the harbor area of Los Angeles in a state of unrest throughout the remainder of 1935. Short, sudden strikes, work stoppages, and similar job action developed at frequent intervals. Several strikes of shipyard workers were called. A new local of the Inland Boatmen's Union of the Pacific, AFL, was organized in the same year. Continued disquietude in all coastal ports led to a belief that a general strike would occur upon expiration of the agreements in September, 1935, but the members of the maritime unions voted to extend all contracts for another year. Early in October, in an attempt to secure recognition of the ILA as collective bargaining agent for dock workers at ports on the Gulf of Mexico, all Pacific Coast longshoremen refused to handle cargo loaded by nonunion stevedores at the southern harbors. This dispute disrupted shipping operations at Los Angeles Harbor from November 2 until the strike was settled at Houston, Texas, on December 7, 1935. Although local port activities did not cease, they were severely curtailed by the secondary boycott as a number of ships loaded at gulf ports were tied up in Los Angeles Harbor during the dispute.[25]

Labor unrest on the Pacific Coast continued in 1936. At the beginning of the year sixty-four steam schooners were idle in various coastal ports, including fourteen in Los Angeles Harbor. Their crews wanted a six-hour day, overtime pay, and a new agreement. In February the controversy was settled by extending the existing agreement. In the early part of 1936 San Pedro shipyard workers conducted a number of strikes against their employers and at one time closed all the dry-dock and shipbuilding facilities at the port. Ship joiners, calkers, and carpenters participated in the walkouts, the most important of which involved the harbor local of the Industrial Union of Marine and Shipbuilding Workers, a union founded in 1933 at Camden, New Jersey. After a strike lasting three months, this union won a 10 per cent wage increase and recognition.

Other disputes affecting San Pedro, which were only forerunners of the great strike in the fall of 1936, involved marine clerks, checkers, and watchmen, but agreements were signed providing satisfactory settlements. The Panama-Pacific Steamship Company, an intercoastal line, had several ships tied up when their crews struck for equalization of wages on the Atlantic Coast with the higher Pacific rate. Although the seamen failed to gain their objective, they claimed a victory because of the show of strength and because the strikers were reëmployed without prejudice. A walkout of marine engineers on the Export Steamship Company boats docking at San Pedro, called for similar reasons, was settled after seven weeks of negotiation.[26]

3. THE 1936–1937 MARITIME STRIKE AND BEYOND

The unrest following the 1934 controversy led to a general maritime strike in the fall of 1936. As the root causes of the later dispute lay in the earlier one, the interim months were hardly more than an armistice. Leaders of the 1936 walkout came from among the younger men who had opposed the old-line leadership since 1934; they were militant, vocal unionists determined to get higher wages and better working conditions for maritime workers. Of these, longshoreman Harry Bridges and seaman Harry Lundeberg were the most outstanding. Bridges was often accused of being a member of the Communist Party; definite proof was never obtained, but the circumstantial evidence convinced many. Lundeberg, a Norwegian-born sailor, became the leader of the unlicensed seamen in the 1934 dispute. Like Bridges, he was aggressive and desired to improve the lot of his fellow members in the Sailors Union of the Pacific (SUP), but he was not accused of affiliation with the Communists. Lundeberg, supported by Bridges and his followers, became president of the Maritime Federation of the Pacific (MFP) in 1935. In January, 1936, he was elected secretary-treasurer of the Sailors Union. Seven months later Bridges was elected president of the Pacific Coast District of the ILA, having previously become president of the San Francisco longshoremen's local and of the San Francisco District Council of the MFP. Thus, both Lundeberg and Bridges were in important positions in their respective unions before the general maritime strike began in October, 1936.[27]

The Maritime Federation of the Pacific became the means by which Bridges and Lundeberg directed the west coast maritime unions toward common economic objectives. Although the MFP was not a party to agreements, its officers established the policies of its constituent unions. Therefore, the union leaders were united in aims during negotiations with groups of employers. MFP officials were likewise opposed to the conservative leaders of the ILA and the ISU, believing that they were not forceful enough in their dealings with employers. In January, 1936, at the time that Lundeberg took office in the Sailors Union of the Pacific, the internal conflict within the ISU came to a head when the international revoked the charter of the SUP, causing it to become an independent member of the MFP. The publicized reason for the revocation was the refusal of SUP officers to reinstate Paul Scharrenberg as a member of the union. Scharrenberg was a conservative SUP leader who had been secretary-treasurer of the California State Federation of Labor for more than two decades.[28]

In the early months of 1936 employers and maritime unionists made charges and countercharges concerning the conduct of industrial relations in the water transportation industry, and asked for a federal investigation of the issues involved. The substance of union statements was that the companies desired to lock out and weaken labor organizations. The employers, in turn, claimed that the unionists were consistently violating their contracts and that preventive measures must be devised. As neither side seemed willing to compromise, events were clearly shaping up for a struggle between the Maritime Federation and employers in the larger Pacific Coast ports. The first significant step in this direction was taken on July 29, 1936, two months before expiration of the operating agreement, when the chairman of the employers' coast committee, composed of representatives from water-front employers' associations in San Francisco, southern California, Portland, and Seattle, notified officials of the Pacific Coast District, ILA, of a desire to modify the contract. Management asked for an early conference with union officials and for the arbitration of all issues not settled through negotiation by September 1. In August a similar request was addressed to the officers of unions representing unlicensed shipboard personnel. The first meeting between representatives of the maritime employers and the labor organizations was held on August 18. Management wanted to arbitrate all issues, but union officials refused to accede until they knew precisely what matters were in contention. Six days later it was agreed to put the demands and issues into writing for point-by-point consideration.[29]

The employers claimed that more than 450 unlawful strikes and work stoppages had occurred since the National Longshoremen's Board rendered its awards after the 1934 strike. These interruptions had hurt the competitive position of the shipping industry, despite its subsidies, and had worsened its financial condition. American vessels in international trade had to compete with foreign ships operating with lower labor costs; ships used in domestic commerce had to compete with other forms of transportation. It was necessary, therefore, to reduce operating costs, which were being increased by the alleged inefficiency and low productivity of labor caused by the unionists' job action. The employers' proposals thus were aimed directly at the enforcement of existing awards in order to cut costs by securing uninterrupted service and higher productivity per man. Their specific demands included the adjustment of pay to output, using a base of 95 cents per hour, which was allegedly representative of the productivity levels of 1934; neutral hiring halls impartially administered; penalties to guarantee observance of contract provisions; and the elimination of secondary boycotts. The employers also repeated their original demand that all points not settled by conference should be decided by arbitration proceedings.[30]

Dock worker representatives opposed the effort to base pay on productivity, claiming that it presaged reinstatement of the speed-up system. They also refused to arbitrate the hiring-hall issue, as they would thereby risk the loss of a privilege already possessed by the longshoremen, which enabled the ILA to maintain job control. Nor would they arbitrate the six-hour day granted to them by the 1934 award. In substance, the longshoremen did not want to risk any of the gains won two years earlier, but were willing to arbitrate working conditions, wages, and the limitation of work. Their specific demands included an hourly wage increase of 5 cents for straight time and 10 cents for overtime; uniform differentials on penalty cargoes for the entire coast; preferential employment for union members; overtime pay for all work between 3 P.M. and 8 A.M., and on Sundays and holidays; twelve holidays each year; and the right to refuse to handle hot cargo or to go through picket lines.

The seamen likewise would not arbitrate any concessions gained as a result of the 1934 strike. They stated their willingness to negotiate for a new agreement to replace the contract expiring on September 30, 1936, provided the employers would concur in the continuance of the union-controlled hiring halls; an eight-hour day within a time span of twelve hours; habitable living quarters for marine cooks and stewards; and overtime pay in cash rather than in off-duty hours for seamen, firemen, and deck officers. All other matters were to be discussed in further conferences.[31]

Negotiations collapsed late in August primarily because of the hiring-hall issue. The longshoremen, in particular, insisted on retaining the arrangement set up by the 1934 award, whereas management wanted to arbitrate the problem. The maritime employers sent notices to the union leaders that the agreements would be terminated on September 30, but that shipping operations would continue. Meanwhile, ILA officials polled the members of the Pacific Coast locals on the question of arbitration of the working agreement. An overwhelming majority of the longshoremen voted against the arbitration of any 1934 gains. Just before the agreements expired, however, both sides concurred in a fifteen-day truce negotiated by Assistant Secretary of Labor Edward F. McGrady. The United States Maritime Commission, formed under the Merchant Marine Act of 1936, had requested a longer time in order to investigate the issues involved, and an additional extension carried the truce through October 28. During this period neither union leaders nor employers would budge from their positions. Accordingly, a strike vote was taken, with the majority of unionists supporting a walkout. Rear Admiral Harry G. Hamlet of the Maritime Commission continued last-minute efforts to avert the strike, but his clumsy mediation methods angered both sides. Finally, at midnight on October 29, 37,000 maritime workers left their jobs in Pacific Coast ports, and the industry was shut down.[32]

The unions taking part in the walkout, under the leadership of the Maritime Federation of the Pacific, were the Marine Engineers Beneficial Association, the International Longshoremen's Association, the National Organization of Masters, Mates and Pilots, the American Radio Telegraphists Association, the Sailors Union of the Pacific, the Marine Firemen, Oilers, Watertenders and Wipers Association, and the Marine Cooks and Stewards Association.

The employers were better organized than in 1934. The Coast Committee for the Shipowners represented the offshore shipping firms and the stevedoring companies in all prestrike negotiations. The coastwise shippers were organized as the Shipowners' Association of the Pacific Coast. These two employer groups had coöperated in creating a favorable climate of public opinion before the strike by publicly offering to arbitrate all points and by acceding to all government requests for truce periods in order to facilitate investigations. This reasonableness made union leaders seem uncompromising in their demands. Officials of the Pacific Coast District of the ILA also had made preparations for the walkout by assessing union members $2.50 each for a strike fund. They arranged with Los Angeles teamster leaders, then busy with an organizing campaign, that union teamsters would stop every trucker who was delivering goods to docks in the harbor area during the strike. Furthermore, delegates to the Los Angeles Central Labor Council, even though their unions were not directly involved, declared their readiness to support the maritime workers throughout the dispute.

The Police Department made prestrike plans to prevent outbreaks of violence. As soon as the walkout began, 408 officers were assigned to the harbor under Captain Hynes. Twenty-four police radio cars began patrolling the area, and twenty-six plain-clothes detectives were placed in strategic locations. All the officers were equipped with side arms, tear-gas bombs, and clubs. In addition, officials of the Waterfront Employers' Association of Southern California had made earlier arrangements to hire ship guards, caretakers, and fire watchmen for idle vessels.[33]

On the first day of the strike observers estimated that nearly 5,000 longshoremen and seamen went out at Los Angeles Harbor and that nineteen ships were idled. Twelve hundred pickets began walking the docks, on which all activity had ceased except for the unloading of some mail and other cargo which was declared to be "fair." Several acts of violence had occurred before the walkout, but after it started the employers did not try to move ships, as they had in 1934, and so did not provoke retaliatory action. The Mexican port of Ensenada was a thorn in the side of southern California longshoremen, as it remained open and was used by vessels of the Grace Line and by foreign ships, though the latter also continued to dock at Los Angeles Harbor. Longshoremen made numerous attempts to blockade the Mexican port, but immigration and government officials south of the border barred their passage, even though Mexican workers expressed sympathy for the striking American unionists.

The problem of the removal of perishable foodstuffs from idle ships came to a head at Los Angeles when federal Judge Paul J. McCormick issued an order directing the United States marshal to remove bananas from the steamship *California*. The order was subsequently vacated when it was pointed out that officials of the federal government would have to function as strikebreakers to unload the cargo. A later attempt by employers and importers to unload perishables and thousands of bushels of Argentine corn was halted by union leaders in January, 1937. Tankers continued to move during the strike, and United States mail was loaded and unloaded from foreign vessels docking at the local harbor. At least two exceptions to the ban against unloading general cargoes were made in the Los Angeles port: 800 bags of cocoa beans needed for medicinal purposes were discharged from an idle ship, and the cargo was removed from the Mexican steamer *Sinaloa* after it ran aground in the port.[34]

Negotiations to end the strike were initiated at San Francisco in November, 1936, under the auspices of Assistant Secretary of Labor McGrady. Steam-schooner operators and officers of the Marine Cooks and Stewards Association agreed to a tentative contract in the same month, but did not withdraw from the strike. Editorials in the Los Angeles *Times* in defense of the open shop commented adversely on President Roosevelt's failure to intervene in the dispute upon a request by the mayors of Pacific Coast cities.[35] The *Times,* noting the high cost of the strike to both sides, stated that the "decision of the State Relief Commission that the families of marine strikers are entitled to be supported at the expense of the taxpayers while the wage earners are voluntarily idle, makes the taxpayers of California finance what is sought to be turned into a revolution." [36]

Assistance for the strikers also came from sources other than the state. At a mass meeting on October 31, representatives from all Los Angeles unions discussed various means of raising funds for that purpose. The Central Labor Council levied a 25-cent weekly assessment upon all working unionists, and thus furnished a total of $14,812.19 for the relief of the maritime workers. This figure did not include funds contributed directly to the unions on strike. The San Pedro Joint Central Strike Committee organized two speakers' bureaus which furnished union representatives to address organizations in the Los Angeles area, labor or otherwise, interested in the dispute. The Pacific Coast maritime workers also sent an appeal for funds to unions in all cities west of the Rocky Mountains. In December, members of the striking unions who attended a public mass meeting at the Olympic Auditorium in Los Angeles launched a campaign to gain public support and financial aid. Harry Bridges was the main speaker at the meeting, but Roger Lapham, a representative of the shipowners, also addressed the audience. About $2,000 was pledged to the strike fund by persons in attendance.[37]

The strike had a definite impact on Los Angeles industries, particularly construction, rubber, and citrus. Trucking was handicapped in the harbor area as teamster locals gave the strikers continuous support by prohibiting the trucking of cargoes to and from the docks. Los Angeles merchants, shippers, and manufacturers urged a quick settlement of the dispute, and members of the Foreign Trade Association of the city undertook a publicity campaign to that end. Some department stores in Los Angeles instituted weekly, one-day forced vacations without pay for their employees because of a decreased trade volume. It was estimated that in November the strike cost employers and employees in Los Angeles nearly $75 million. This did not include losses resulting from factory shutdowns, the gradual decline in retail business, lack of trade for importers and exporters, and the increased cost of shipping citrus by rail. Cargo valued at more than $12,750,000 and eighty-three ships were tied up in Los Angeles Harbor before the strike ended. Officials of the Los Angeles Chamber of Commerce estimated that the ascertainable cost of the strike to both sides on the entire Pacific Coast was approximately $830 million.[38]

New attempts to settle the controversy in December, 1936, came to nought when union representatives failed to agree on the terms of the proposals. Strike leaders at Los Angeles Harbor appealed to President Roosevelt to terminate the government subsidies received by the larger shipping firms because they refused to agree to the smaller shipowners' demands for a compromise. As negotiations continued in January, 1937, the hopes of the disputants alternately rose and fell as local and federal arbitrators worked with the leaders of both sides. An apparent split over strike policy developed between Harry Lundeberg and Harry Bridges, but they coöperated until the end of the walkout despite the efforts of employers to exploit the schism during negotiations. This breach between the two men was to lead to disruption of Pacific Coast maritime union unity in 1938. Though employers were better organized than they had been in the 1934 strike, steam-schooner operators and some representatives of the smaller offshore lines tried to make independent settlements. They remained with the main body of employers, however, because of the pressure exerted by the larger firms, including the Dollar, Matson, and American-Hawaiian lines.[39]

In the latter part of January signs of a possible settlement began to appear. Rank-and-file union members manifested an increasing desire to return to work, and employers made more positive attempts to submit offers acceptable to the Maritime Federation of the Pacific. As the labor representatives would not assent to any proposals that did not provide for all seven participating unions, it was necessary to negotiate satisfactory agreements with officials of all the unions before holding a coast-wide ratifying election on whether or not to end the strike. The results of this election (18,406 to 2,604) showed that the maritime workers clearly wanted to return to work. The walkout officially ended at 2:45 P.M. on February 4, 1937, after ninety-eight days of controversy which had idled about 240 ships and thousands of tons of cargo in Pacific Coast ports.

Under the terms of the settlement, wages and working conditions for longshoremen were almost the same as before the strike, with one significant exception. Under the 1934 award, 95 cents an hour was paid for all six-hour work shifts completed between 8 A.M. and 5 P.M. If a gang completed its six-hour shift by 3 P.M., employers could call for relief crews to work at the hourly rate of 95 cents until 5 P.M., when overtime wage rates became effective. In practice, gangs usually were not available for the period between 3 P.M. and 5 P.M., and overtime had to be paid to the old crew, which then worked a total of eight hours. Under the 1936 agreement employers relinquished the right to ask for relief crews at 3 P.M. They paid $1.40 an hour overtime for all hours worked beyond 3 P.M. until 8 A.M. the following day. The hiring hall remained under joint control, which meant that in practice the union-elected dispatcher controlled the supply of workers. ILA officials, however, agreed to discipline union members for misconduct or illegal work stoppages.[40]

The greatest gain for unlicensed seamen was the right to dispatch all men through union-operated hiring halls. The members of the Sailors Union of the Pacific received a 15 per cent base pay increase, amounting to $10, and cash payments instead of off-duty hours for overtime. The basic monthly wage rate was to be $72.50 on deep-sea vessels and $80 on schooners. Seamen affiliated with the Marine Firemen, Oilers, Watertenders and Wipers Association won basic wage rates, working conditions, and other changes similar to those of the deck sailors. The members of the Marine Cooks and Stewards Association obtained a work shift of eight hours within a span of twelve on freight vessels and a nine-hour day within a thirteen-hour period on passenger ships. The basic monthly wage scale of $45 was increased to $55, and cash overtime pay as well as hiring-hall control was granted.

Strikers affiliated with the Masters, Mates and Pilots and the Marine Engineers Beneficial Association received monthly wage increases of $15 for all job classifications, recognition of their respective unions as collective bargaining agents, and cash payments for overtime; but their closed-shop demand was not granted. The members of the American Radio Telegraphists Association, the only other union of licensed personnel participating in the strike, obtained a monthly pay increase of $10 or a minimum wage of $125 a month. They also won a straight eight-hour day along with hiring-hall control.[41]

Shipping operations at the local harbor were resumed immediately, preliminary arrangements having been made to facilitate the movement of strike-bound ships and the 234,000 tons of idle freight. Members of the teamsters' union delayed some longshore work because of a harbor blockade they had instituted as part of their organizational drive. The departure of several ships also was postponed a few days while a new working agreement was interpreted. Otherwise, operations began to assume a normal complexion. Many employers believed that the end of the strike was the beginning of another period of armistice rather than peace. In their opinion, as long as Lundeberg and Bridges were the leaders of the two most powerful maritime unions, waterfront employers would have to expect difficulties in dealing with their employees. Subsequent events proved that they were correct, for labor disputes continued to arise in the maritime industry after termination of the coast-wide strike in February, 1937.

The first dispute at Los Angeles Harbor came almost immediately, when the crews of several ships refused to acquire continuous discharge books as required by the provisions of the Copeland Act. These books, containing a continuous record of service, were to be carried by seamen. In addition, the law required crew members to obtain certificates of efficiency. Sailors, believing the service records to be black-listing devices, referred to them as "fink" books. This dispute was settled in March, however, when Congress passed a bill making it optional for sailors to carry the discharge books.

Through the remainder of 1937 other work stoppages and quickie strikes occurred on ships and docks, and there were a number of walkouts of carpenters, calkers, and unskilled laborers at the shipyards. Because of this uncertain peace, and in order to present a more unified front to the longshoremen, maritime firms formed the Waterfront Employers' Association of the Pacific Coast in March, 1937. Almon E. Roth was elected president of the new group, which comprised shipowners, contract stevedoring companies, terminals, and other employers of seamen and longshoremen. Its officials represented most of the maritime employers on the Pacific Coast in later negotiations with the Maritime Federation of the Pacific.[42]

The most significant local controversy in 1937, however, took place within the labor movement itself. In April the American Radio Telegraphists Association, an MFP affiliate, was chartered by the Committee for Industrial Organization (CIO), which had been established in 1935. The following month Harry Bridges, president of the Pacific Coast District of the ILA, extended his conflict with the conservative leaders of his union by announcing that the 20,000 members in Western ports would probably apply for a CIO charter. A vote on the issue was conducted in all Pacific Coast ILA unions in June. The members of San Pedro Local No. 38-82 voted for the new affiliation, and this proved to be the trend. However, though only a few of the west coast locals chose to continue their connection with the ILA, the issue had not been resolved. Internal factional disputes began to develop when minority groups within several locals that had voted for CIO affiliation, including Local No. 38-82, decided to protest the proposed change. When the San Pedro local joined the newly organized Los Angeles Industrial Union Council, CIO, even before a charter was received from the national body, P. W. Walker and O. M. Benton, representatives of the AFL faction, instituted a suit before Judge Reuben S. Schmidt in Superior Court. They wanted to have a receiver appointed to handle the finances of the union, remove its officers and board of directors, and prevent its permanent affiliation with the CIO. A temporary injunction was subsequently granted which forbade the installation of a CIO charter pending a hearing on the matter.[43]

Meanwhile, Pacific Coast longshoremen voted to extend the contract arising out of the 1936–1937 strike until September 30, 1938. As the agreement had been signed in the name of the ILA, the AFL faction within Local No. 38-82 had some justification for its attempts to control the union. Initially, water-front employers refused to hire men from the CIO faction, which desired to join the newly formed International Longshoremen's and Warehousemen's Union (ILWU), until a court had decided that such action was in accordance with the contract. The CIO group therefore requested the NLRB to hold an election to determine whether the union should affiliate with the ILWU or remain under the jurisdiction of the ILA. The Los Angeles Central Labor Council supported the AFL adherents in the intra-union dispute, and Secretary J. W. Buzzell presented the issue to the 1937 AFL convention. The convention passed a resolution condemning the disloyalty of the CIO sympathizers in their attempts to appropriate the hiring hall, the funds, and the contracts of the ILA.[44]

Early in October the dissident members of Local No. 38-82 received a charter from the ILWU, though it was not installed. This resulted in the filing of another suit by representatives of the AFL faction, who declared that the temporary restraining order preventing affiliation with the CIO had been violated. Judge Schmidt dismissed the case, however, and refused to appoint a receiver for the local. On November 1, 1937, proceedings began in Judge Schmidt's court on whether or not the temporary injunction should be made permanent. CIO-oriented longshoremen within the local wanted to acquire the hiring hall and the funds of the ILA organization and to install the previously granted charter. This would permit them to function as Local No. 1-13 of the ILWU. They supported their case by testifying that a majority of the present members of Local No. 38-82 desired such a move. The court was recessed during the month in a fruitless attempt to reach an out-of-court settlement. Eventually hearings were resumed, and on December 8 Judge Schmidt granted a permanent injunction against affiliation of the local with the ILWU. The judge stated, however, that if the bylaws of the charter under which Local No. 38-82 was incorporated were altered to permit such an affiliation, the injunction would be dissolved. Late in December the CIO faction amended the articles and bylaws of the union's charter in order to permit the legal acquisition of its assets. AFL supporters immediately secured a writ of mandate which prevented the secretary of state of California from accepting the amendments. Later, in a closed meeting of only fifty members, the AFL faction formally expelled from the union nearly 2,000 longshoremen who favored the CIO. A letter was sent to all water-front employers in the harbor area, demanding that they cease employing men from a hiring hall that was really controlled by the ILWU and use only longshoremen who were loyal to the AFL.[45]

During the court proceedings of November and December, the leaders of the CIO group again requested an NLRB representation election. The Los Angeles Regional Labor Board inaugurated an investigation but postponed the hearing pending the outcome of the case before Judge Schmidt. Five days after his decision favoring the permanent injunction, the board began hearings on the question of designation of the proper collective bargaining agent. After only a few days of testimony the proceedings were again postponed until January, 1938, on the motion of counsel representing the AFL element in Local No. 38-82. Several more days of hearings were held in January, but, again, no action resulted and the case was transferred to the national board in Washington. In February the NLRB held public hearings on the matter in San Francisco. The northern city seemed a more logical place for the inquiry because the basic issue was recognition of the ILWU as the collective bargaining agent for most of the longshoremen on the Pacific Coast, rather than in a particular port like Los Angeles. In the following months, hearings were held in other ports.[46]

By January, 1938, only about twelve longshoremen within Local No. 38-82, known to the CIO supporters as "the dirty dozen," remained loyal to the AFL and continued the dispute. In that month the writ of mandate obtained in December, which had prevented the filing of the amended articles of incorporation and bylaws with the California secretary of state, was reversed. Thereupon local ILWU leaders officially recorded the changes at Sacramento. Also in January, Judge Schmidt, in response to a petition from representatives of the ILA, appointed Will Hays, a retired attorney, as the receiver for the assets of Local No. 38-82 and enjoined all efforts to charter the union as Local No. 1-13 of the ILWU. The judge withheld execution of the order, however, when attorneys for the CIO faction made a motion for a new trial. His action presumably was influenced by an affidavit filed with the court and a statement by Bridges in a telegram sent to Secretary of Labor Frances Perkins. In both affidavit and telegram Bridges threatened to call a strike against the entire Pacific water front if the receiver officially became custodian of the assets of Local No. 38-82. To emphasize the threat, local supporters of the ILWU conducted a five-hour work stoppage at the harbor on January 28 and held a meeting in the Wilmington Bowl. The longshoremen present passed a resolution stating that they would work only on jobs secured through a hiring hall under the jurisdiction of the ILWU. Ship firemen affiliated with the CIO also agreed to furnish steam for the operation of loading equipment only to dock crews dispatched by the ILWU. Consequently, the employers hired longshoremen through the CIO-controlled hall, as the twelve or so supporters of the AFL in Local No. 38-82 obviously were not able to work the ships.[47]

On February 2, 1938, Judge Schmidt began hearing the motion for a new trial made by the CIO counsel. The order appointing a receiver continued to be held in abeyance. After three days of testimony the judge placed the motion under deliberation and urged both sides to try to compromise the dispute out of court. On March 18 he set aside the receivership order and injunction, instructed the attorneys for the CIO faction to file an amended cross complaint, and ordered the case reopened on April 7 for further testimony. At the conclusion of this trial, Judge Schmidt ruled that the 2,600 longshoremen at the local harbor could change ILA Local No. 38-82, AFL, into ILWU Local No. 1-13, CIO.

Meanwhile, the hearings conducted by the NLRB on the question of the proper coast-wide collective bargaining agent for the longshoremen were terminated on March 26. Three months later, on June 22, the NLRB certified the ILWU as the exclusive collective bargaining representative for the stevedores in most Pacific Coast ports. The board ascertained that 9,557 of the 18,860 members of the ILA in coastal ports had signed cards designating the CIO union as their bargaining agent. On June 30, therefore, President Roth of the Waterfront Employers' Association of the Pacific Coast declared that the members of his organization would recognize the ILWU in the new contract to be signed on September 30, 1938.[48]

Harry Bridges' threat to strike all Pacific Coast ports if a receiver took over Local No. 38-82 had not remained unchallenged. In addition to Bridges' affidavit, Judge Schmidt had received similar threats from two other labor leaders. Interpreting these as attempts to influence the judge's decision, members of the Los Angeles Bar Association filed charges as friends of the court. Contempt citations were then issued by Judge Schmidt against the persons involved. In March, 1938, Charles J. Katz, an attorney for the ILWU who had filed Bridges' threatening affidavit with the court, was tried on the contempt charge and fined $250. In the same court proceedings Randolph Meriwether, business manager of San Francisco Local No. 97 of the Marine Engineers Beneficial Association, was fined $25, and German J. Bulcke, vice-president of San Francisco Local No. 1-10 of the ILWU, was sentenced to five days in the county jail. Bridges could not be reached immediately for trial, but was apprehended several months later. On September 13, 1938, he was fined $125 by Judge Edward T. Bishop after two of three original contempt-of-court charges had been dismissed. In December Bridges was granted a writ of review by the California Supreme Court. The case was heard in March, 1939, and a decision upholding his conviction by the lower court was announced in October. An attempt by Bridges' attorneys to secure a new hearing in November was denied.[49]

Resolution of the ILA-ILWU controversy did not end the maritime unions' internal troubles. As previously noted, the differences that arose between Lundeberg and Bridges during the 1936–1937 strike came to a head in 1938. Both men were colorful personalities with strong opinions on water-front relations. Lundeberg came from a syndicalistic background, which was modified as his union of unlicensed seamen achieved security. Under his leadership the Sailors Union of the Pacific rapidly became an example of business unionism. Bridges, on the other hand, did not lose his radical aggressiveness, but continued to regard the employer as an enemy. As Lundeberg became more conservative, Bridges increasingly considered him a deserter of the cause. The affiliation of the ILWU with the CIO in 1937 contributed to the disaffection between the two men, particularly because Lundeberg believed the National Maritime Union (NMU), CIO, was a dual organization of

unlicensed personnel and was dominated by Communists. He had refused to affiliate his union with the NMU when it was formed on the
east coast in 1937 under Joseph Curran. The subsequent appointment
of Bridges as west coast director of the CIO only confirmed Lundeberg's determination to stay out of the organization.[50]

Some of the evidence suggests that water-front employers entered the
interunion dispute by encouraging Lundeberg through more generous
settlements than had heretofore been granted the sailors and also
through a willingness to make separate agreements. Whether or not
employers did drive a wedge between the two unions, Lundeberg withdrew his Sailors Union of the Pacific from the Maritime Federation of
the Pacific in June, 1938, when the latter was holding its annual convention. He immediately initiated action to establish a counteralliance,
which resulted in the chartering of the Seafarers International Union
of North America, AFL, in October, 1938. Lundeberg, given the temporary presidency, began to organize seamen as a challenge to CIO
leaders in the maritime industry.[51]

In 1938 the discord between Bridges and Lundeberg became evident
at Los Angeles Harbor through a jurisdictional conflict on the ships of
the Shepard Line. Both the NMU and the SUP were struggling for
control of the unlicensed seamen of this intercoastal steamship company. An NLRB election resulted in the certification of the NMU as
the official collective bargaining agent for the sailors on five vessels of
this line. SUP officials opposed the certification on the ground that the
management had signed a prior contract with them, but the NLRB
ruled that the agreement was void. This action did not end the dispute.
When freighters of the Shepard Line docked in Pacific ports, they were
picketed by members of the SUP who demanded the discharge of
NMU sailors. Bridges' longshoremen, dominating dockside activities
at all but a few Puget Sound ports, supported their parent CIO by
refusing to recognize the SUP picket lines. The first clash occurred at
Los Angeles Harbor on April 23, 1938, when the *Sea Thrush,* a Shepard
Line freighter, was docked in order to load 400 tons of cargo. SUP officials immediately established picket lines. When ILWU longshoremen
ignored the pickets and began to load the vessel, SUP leaders, in
retaliation, removed the crews from nine other ships in the harbor.
Members of the Marine Firemen, Oilers, Watertenders and Wipers
Association (MFOWWA) joined the SUP in sympathy as well as in
protest against the entrance of the CIO into the seafaring field through
the NMU.[52]

The strike was terminated the day after it began, but several days later the *Sage Brush,* another Shepard Line freighter, arrived from the east coast. Officials of the MFOWWA and the SUP again established picket lines because the crew of the ship belonged to the NMU. This time the pickets were joined by members of the Marine Engineers Beneficial Association, who were protesting the refusal of the steamship line to employ engine-room crew replacements from the San Pedro local of the union. ILWU longshoremen again passed through the picket lines and worked the ship. The strike was ended after a few days, only to be resumed on September 21 when a third Shepard freighter arrived in the port. The persistence of the sailors and the marine firemen was rewarded when AFL teamsters came to their aid. The truckers refused to handle cargo unloaded from Shepard Line freighters by ILWU longshoremen. In addition, east coast longshoremen affiliated with the ILA refused to unload any Shepard Line ships so long as NMU sailors were aboard. These actions forced the company to hire AFL seamen and firemen for all its ships which called at Pacific Coast ports. Thus, Lundeberg won a point over Bridges.[53]

The Bridges-Lundeberg controversy was not the only source of conflict on the local water front in 1938. A dispute over the use of lift boards in the loading of cargoes halted most of the shipping operations in Los Angeles Harbor from March 14 to 24. The trouble originally developed on March 9 while longshoremen were unloading a railroad car at a warehouse on the dock of the American-Hawaiian Steamship Company. Freight from the car was being placed directly on lift boards for storage in the warehouse pending arrival of a vessel. The unloading process was interrupted by the sudden establishment of a picket line by warehousemen who, like the longshoremen, were members of the ILWU. As the longshoremen refused to cross a picket line of their fellow workers, unloading operations promptly ceased. Spokesmen for the warehousemen declared that the longshoremen were working in violation of an award made in February, 1935, by Judge M. C. Sloss, a federal arbitrator, in which he ruled that such labor was under the jurisdiction of the unionized warehousemen. They also stated that the continued use of lift boards would result in the displacement of workers. Previously, when freight was unloaded from railroad cars, it was placed directly on the warehouse floor to await the arrival of a ship. After it docked, the cargo was loaded on lift boards or conveyances for movement to the side of the vessel, at which point longshoremen performed the actual cargo-stowing operation. Placing the cargo directly on lift boards rather than on the warehouse floor, when a ship was not in port, meant the elimination of one operation in the handling of the freight and, therefore, less employment for warehousemen. Lift boards could be shifted at a future date by the use of cargo-handling equipment without recourse to additional manual labor.[54]

The longshoremen voted to support the demands of the warehousemen. Members of the port labor relations committee and the Regional Labor Board tried to settle the dispute in order to prevent its spreading to other docks.[55] Representatives of the Waterfront Employers' Association of Southern California entered the controversy directly and countered the arguments of the warehousemen by pointing out that the

longshore practice of unloading onto lift boards, irrespective of whether the freight continues immediately to a ship, has existed here three years at one dock, months at two others, and that employers don't care which union does it.

Employers further stated that the 1937 contract stipulates the men shall work as directed; that there shall be no stoppage of work, but that unions shall arbitrate with employers all controversial points. The employers contend under the contract they have a right to institute labor-saving devices and they object to two operations when one suffices.

Further, they declare, unloading of cars to lift boards whether the item goes immediately to a ship or not is being practiced in San Francisco, Portland and Seattle.[56]

Officials of the Waterfront Employers' Association set the dead-line date of March 10, later changed to March 14, for settlement of the dispute. Mediation efforts were unsuccessful, however, and at 7 A.M. on March 14 the employers concerned ordered all loading and unloading of vessels to cease. Twenty ships and 500 workers became inactive. A few vessels entered and left the harbor after the order was given, but the longshoremen announced that they would continue to refuse cargo requiring the use of lift boards, as their contracts permitted them to unload cargo from freight cars to lift boards only when ships were in port. In all other instances, warehousemen were to unload the freight to the floors of dock shelters. At the time of the establishment of the picket line on March 9, the longshoremen had been unloading a car and placing the cargo on lift boards in the absence of a ship at the dock. This was being done under the provisions of an informal agreement with officials of the Matson Line. The short time spent in port by ships of this company had made the practice of preliminary loading on lift boards very expedient during the past three years. A similar practice had been followed since February 14, 1938, at the docks of the McCormick and American-Hawaiian lines.[57]

Employers and longshoremen agreed to the appointment by Secretary of Labor Perkins of Albert A. Rosenshine, a San Francisco attorney, as federal arbitrator. Rosenshine arrived in Los Angeles on March 23. He immediately proposed a truce during the arbitration period, providing that lift boards could be used only at the Matson pier, unless the freight was moved directly from a ship to a railroad car and vice versa. Both sides accepted the proposal, and shipping operations were resumed at the port at 10 A.M. on March 24. Rosenshine then held hearings, consulted the Regional Labor Board, and personally investigated the circumstances of the dispute. The main problem appeared to be the fear of ILWU officials that the increased use of lift boards at Los Angeles Harbor would eventually eliminate the jobs of approximately 125 warehousemen and 500 longshoremen. After a thorough investigation, Rosenshine issued his award on April 16, containing the following provisions:

1. The matter was subject to arbitration under the agreement of February 4, 1937.
2. Warehousemen had no right to do the work in the controversy, having abandoned the right even though it was covered by the language of their agreement.
3. The warehousemen had violated the agreement of June 21, 1937, in establishing picket lines.
4. The work was being done by longshoremen and warehousemen under an implied contract and with the consent of the employers.
5. Terms of the implied contract covered only wages, hours, and joint operation of the hiring halls.[58]

After publication of the award the officers of ILWU Local No. 1-13 sought to secure a written contract covering the use of lift boards in accordance with the decision. They requested penalty wages in view of the technological unemployment that would result. When a deadlock developed in the negotiations, the Waterfront Employers' Association asked for the appointment of another federal arbitrator to resolve the issue. Although the longshoremen protested that the dispute already had been arbitrated, Dean Wayne L. Morse of the University of Oregon law school was appointed as federal arbitrator and conducted hearings which ended on September 1, 1938. His decision, announced later in the month, provided that employers could request longshoremen to use lift boards in handling cargo under the wages, hours, and working conditions established by the contract of February 4, 1937. This did not completely settle the issue, however, as the lift-board question was not included in the new coast-wide contract signed on the expiration of the old agreement on September 30. Provision was therefore made for the initiation of negotiations on the issue by joint employer-employee committees at each port on the Pacific Coast within sixty days after the establishment of the new contract. This action finally settled the problem at Los Angeles Harbor in favor of the employers, who were authorized to use lift boards in either direct or indirect cargo movement without any change in the wage rates paid to longshoremen.[59]

Still another employer-employee dispute in the local maritime industry occurred in December, 1938. Approximately 305 members of the Marine Clerks Union, Local No. 1-63, ILWU, employed as cargo checkers, threatened to strike on January 1 if a one-year contract which had expired in March, 1938, was not renewed with certain changes. The unionists stated that regular cargo checkers worked 192 hours a month and received $155, or a little more than 80 cents an hour, whereas casual or extra checkers were paid a straight-time hourly wage of $1. They demanded that regular cargo checkers receive $160 for 180 hours and overtime for Saturday afternoons. The local also announced that, after January 1, all cargo checkers would be dispatched through a union hiring hall and be paid a uniform wage on an hourly basis. The Waterfront Employers' Association offered only to renew the old contract. This was not acceptable to union officials, who noted that casual checkers received as much as $175 a month, or $20 more than regular men. The strike was therefore initiated on January 3, 1939. Longshoremen refused to cross the picket lines established by the checkers at many of the docks. Los Angeles Mayor Fletcher Bowron immediately began efforts to mediate the dispute, with the result that the port was reopened under a thirty-day truce, due to expire on February 2. Conciliators from the Department of Labor then conferred with employer and union representatives. On the expiration of the truce, a new agreement was signed. It provided for a monthly wage of $160 for regular men, who were to work 190 hours. Casual men continued to be employed on an hourly basis at $1 an hour for straight time and $1.50 for overtime.[60]

In 1939, cargo-loading longshoremen who constituted the membership of Local No. 1-13 at San Pedro voted to open negotiations for changes in a new coast-wide contract which was to become effective on September 30. Other locals up and down the Pacific Coast followed their lead. The demands of the unionists included increases in pay, strengthening of the clauses in the contract providing for the six-hour day, clarification of the status of picket lines, and certain adjustments in the agreement necessitated by the use of laborsaving devices. The employers, in turn, demanded clauses in the contract which would insure definite penalty rulings by arbitrators for every possible breach of the agreement. Joint conferences between employers and ILWU officials began in August and continued into September. Both sides agreed to maintain the current contract after September 30 and for sixty days following the conclusion of negotiations. Twenty-one days were to be added to the sixty-day period if, at any point in that time interval, a vote on the acceptance or the rejection of a new contract was initiated. This action paved the way for a new agreement which was signed without a strike interruption in November, 1940. The new contract proscribed so-called "quickie" strikes and included a pledge not to interfere with technological advancements.[61]

Representatives of the offshore unions of Masters, Mates and Pilots, Marine Engineers Beneficial Association, Marine Cooks and Stewards Association, and the American Radio Telegraphists Association also agreed to an extension of their old agreements and the continuance of negotiations beyond the expiration period. Officials of the Sailors Union of the Pacific and the Marine Firemen, Oilers, Watertenders and Wipers Association refused to acquiesce in such an extension. A strike of these two unions was prevented in October, 1939, however, when representatives of offshore shipping lines signed a one-year agreement with the SUP and a two-year contract with the MFOWWA. The owners of steam lumber schooners in the coastal trade also signed a contract with the SUP, but they failed to come to terms with the marine firemen. The latter therefore called two coast-wide strikes, the second and more important of which began on November 10, 1939. It ended on November 18, but idled fourteen lumber vessels in Los Angeles Harbor during the eight-day period. Representatives of the employers, organized as the Shipowners' Association of the Pacific, facilitated resolution of the dispute when they agreed to a 20 per cent increase in hourly overtime pay and a $5 raise in monthly wages for the firemen.[62]

A strike of cargo checkers in San Francisco during the last two months of 1939 caused freight and passengers to be diverted to Los Angeles Harbor. At one point, eighty-two ships were reported to be in the local port. Spokesmen for Local No. 1-13 at San Pedro believed that cargo destined for San Francisco was being deliberately unloaded before freight consigned to Los Angeles. They therefore asked Mayor Bowron to investigate, as they did not wish to be in the position of helping to break the San Francisco strike. The mayor appointed a fact-finding committee which looked into the charges and aided in resolving the problem.

Another issue involving arbitration arose in May, 1939, when four gangs of longshoremen who were members of Local No. 1-13 refused to cross a demonstration picket line composed of Chinese. The latter were protesting the loading of scrap iron on two ships bound for Japan. Port arbitrator Irvin Stalmaster declared that the longshoremen had participated in an illegal work stoppage and suspended them for a week. Local No. 1-13 officials decided to ignore the decision and notified Secretary of Labor Perkins that Stalmaster was biased against labor unions. Miss Perkins replied by upholding the arbitrator. The unionists thereupon threatened to call a strike, which Stalmaster averted by deciding to review the case. This action did not change the situation, however, as he subsequently reissued his original decision, including the penalty. Meanwhile, the longshoremen concerned had reported for work as members of their old gangs but were ordered off the docks by the employers. In August they returned to their jobs as members of new gangs, but the employers continued to reject them. Longshoremen who were not involved in the dispute also left the docks, and shipping operations in the harbor were soon curtailed. Water-front employers then appealed to Wayne Morse as arbitrator for the entire Pacific Coast. After studying the case, Morse reversed Stalmaster's decision on the ground that port arbitrators did not have the authority to inflict penalties, as union members were responsible for disciplining one another; thus ended the dispute.[63]

Although the coming of World War II in September, 1939, promised at least a temporary end to some of the economic problems facing the Pacific Coast maritime industry, it did not remove the instability in the labor relations area. Hostility continued to mark the attitude of each side toward the other, and the colorful personalities of the union leaders dominated negotiations. Quickie strikes signaled union efforts to gain short-run goals as well as to make long-run impressions that would be remembered whenever new contracts were negotiated. A student of the problem of maritime industrial relations has characterized the entire period from 1934 to 1948 as follows:

> Minor jurisdictional disputes became major negotiating issues. At the bargaining table, each union pursued aggressive campaigns which would give its settlements a slightly more favorable appearance. The unions played off employers against one another to achieve certain advantages; in turn, the employers capitalized on splits between the unions. Factionalism, intrigue, power politics, and irresponsibility kept the industry in a turmoil.[64]

Not until 1948 were reasonably stable collective bargaining procedures to come to the Pacific Coast maritime industry. A strike in that year began a new period of improved labor relations, with acceptance by both sides of the idea that the other was going to remain very much in the picture. Strikes, lockouts, personal prejudices, third-party settlements, and lawsuits were not completely abandoned, but were so reduced in number as not to be major issues. A new peace was to settle over the water front—but this story has been told by others. It now seems propitious to find out what was happening more directly in the city of Los Angeles in the middle and late 1930's.

XI. 1936—YEAR OF TRANSITION

1. A PRELUDE TO BATTLE

ALTHOUGH 1936 was a showdown year in maritime labor relations, inland unions had not yet progressed to this point. They continued, however, to make solid membership and organizational gains under the protective umbrella of favorable federal legislation. The NIRA had been invalidated in 1935, but the NLRA was operative as its successor, though its provisions had not yet been completely reviewed by the Supreme Court. The economy was making progress in recovering from the worst of the business downturn, yet evidences of the depression remained everywhere. The most widely publicized contest was in national politics, not industrial relations, as Kansan Alf Landon challenged Franklin Delano Roosevelt's New Deal, and lost. Perhaps 1936 is best described as a year of transition in local and national labor circles—an intermission between the acts.

In 1936 the federal government established administrative procedures to manage the social security accounts of millions of wage earners under the program initiated the preceding year. It also continued its general relief policies. By the end of February, approximately 3,800,000 persons, most of them from direct relief rolls, were employed on work projects established with funds allocated by the Emergency Relief Appropriation Act of 1935. Further assistance for the unemployed was supplied by other federal agencies such as the Civilian Conservation Corps, the Farm Resettlement Administration, and the National Youth Administration.[1]

The AFL found itself increasingly challenged at national, regional, and local levels by the Committee for Industrial Organization. The CIO had been formed at the 1935 AFL convention, under the chairmanship of John L. Lewis of the United Mine Workers, in an attempt to persuade the Executive Council to organize workers in the mass-production industries along industrial union lines. Although the new organization sought to remain within the framework of the AFL, the Executive Council suspended it and its constituent internationals. In 1936 the CIO placed special emphasis on the organization of employees in the rubber, iron, and steel industries, which resulted in the affiliation of the Amalgamated Association of Iron, Steel and Tin Workers and the United Rubber Workers. CIO leaders also established Labor's Non-Partisan League, designed to assist in the reëlection of President Roosevelt. The AFL Executive Council, which had consistently rejected the temptation to form an independent political party or organization in 1932, 1933, and 1935, decided not to coöperate with officials of the league during the 1936 presidential campaign. This decision was based in part on AFL opposition to the dual unionism represented by the CIO but it also reflected a belief that Communists were active in the leadership of the new organization.[2]

California continued to be the national mecca for transients, the temporarily unemployed, and drought refugees. The refugees entered the state in increasing numbers in 1936, as compared with 1935. To prevent the entrance of migrants, the Los Angeles Police Department established patrols at the state borders early in 1936, but succeeded in halting them only temporarily. Although this action was widely criticized by officials of other states, labor leaders, and private citizens as a breach of civil liberties, the Los Angeles police had been curtailing the movements of suspected vagrants and transients in the city for many years by means of arrests and jail sentences. The border patrol was merely an expansion of this policy during an emergency period. But lack of public support as well as extensive criticism forced a withdrawal of the city's officers from the boundaries of the state after only two months.[3]

Though California labor leaders watched the border activities of the Los Angeles police with keen interest, they were more concerned with internal organizational problems. The 1936 convention of the California State Federation of Labor (CSFL) was one of the most momentous sessions in the history of the organization. Paul Scharrenberg, CSFL secretary-treasurer since 1909, had resigned in March, 1936, following his expulsion from the Sailors Union of the Pacific, and had become an AFL legislative agent in Washington, D.C. The convention elected Edward D. Vandeleur, then CSFL president, to succeed Scharrenberg. Convention delegates also unanimously opposed the suspension of the CIO by the AFL Executive Council. Resolutions endorsing the CIO were framed in the form of a request that the AFL convention take constructive steps to achieve harmony between the two national organizations. Representatives of forty-eight Los Angeles unions and their auxiliaries joined in this endorsement.[4]

Los Angeles AFL leaders became cognizant of CIO activities in the city in early 1936 when efforts were made to organize rubber and oil workers. It was not until August 21, however, that the AFL-CIO controversy first came up at a Central Labor Council meeting. A resolution passed at this meeting protested the suspension of ten CIO unions by the AFL Executive Council, and requested that action on the mat-

ter be deferred until the annual AFL convention. The *Citizen* refused
to take sides in the dispute, believing that nothing would be accomplished by airing the AFL-CIO controversy in the press.[5]

CIO organizers were not the only visitors to Los Angeles in 1936.
A large proportion of the migrants entering California in that year
came to Los Angeles, thereby aggravating the relief problem as well
as increasing the labor reserve. Members of the Citizens' Relief Committee of the Los Angeles County Relief Administration tried unsuccessfully to have migrants and other workers removed from public
charity rolls if they refused to accept positions at strike-bound plants.
A policy of extending relief to those refusing work where an NLRB-recognized strike was in progress was adopted as a compromise.

The belief of relief workers that their only chance of improving
their economic status lay in organization was reflected in their efforts
to establish unions in 1936. A group of Works Progress Administration
laborers known as the Public Works and Unemployed League organized various demonstrations as well as strikes and made specific demands for economic improvements. The privilege of organizing unions was granted to WPA workers, but such activity in working hours
was not tolerated. In July a state convention of unemployed and relief
workers in Los Angeles resulted in the formation of a local chapter as
well as a state organization of the Workers Alliance of America. Local
WPA officials refused to accept the Workers Alliance as the collective
bargaining representative of any relief workers other than those composing its membership, and also rejected a demand made by its spokesmen for a 20 per cent wage increase.[6]

WPA laborers were merely following the lead of other workers in
seeking to present a common front for positive gains. Los Angeles
labor officials used a similar approach to promote their political objectives, urging unionists to register in order to vote in the 1936 presidential election. Both the AFL and the CIO supported the general
campaign for particular candidates conducted by officials of Labor's
Non-Partisan League. Although national AFL officers castigated the
league as a CIO affiliate, the initial meetings of its Los Angeles chapter were held in the Labor Temple. The league elected John S. Horn,
a member of an AFL brewery trades union, as its temporary chairman
in Los Angeles and established a state committee composed of AFL
unionists. Labor also made a vain effort to unite politically in order
to prevent the reëlection of Superior Court Judge Frank C. Collier to
a new six-year term of office. Collier was a prime target because of the

number of restraining orders he had issued on ex parte evidence against locals and their members in past years.

On the positive side, the Los Angeles AFL Joint Executive Board unanimously endorsed Buron Fitts for the position of district attorney. A Labor Temple political rally was held in his behalf on October 28. Labor scored two victories when Fitts was elected and John F. Dalton was selected as president of the Los Angeles Board of Education. Dalton, head of ITU Local No. 174, was considered one of the outstanding labor leaders in Los Angeles.[7]

Signs of improved economic circumstances and a related increase in membership in the local labor movement were apparent in 1936 in the activities of the Union Labor Temple Association. The annual election of its board of trustees was held early in the year, and the payment of interest was resumed on all its outstanding mortgage redemption notes. The association also paid all interest owed on these notes for former years and liquidated other debts. Some of the debts were paid out of the proceeds from a dance held at the Shrine Auditorium on February 25, which netted $4,500 for the Temple.

The annual Labor Day parade provided further evidence of organized labor's growth. Members of 142 Los Angeles and San Pedro unions marched up Broadway to tunes played by nineteen bands. The estimated number of participating unionists, relatives, and friends was 35,000. The strength of the Central Labor Council at this time also indicated that Los Angeles unions were improving on the membership record of the preceding two years. Representatives of 110 unions were entitled to vote at council meetings. They reëlected a majority of the incumbent officers, including President Harry Sherman, Vice-President H. P. McMurray, and Secretary-Treasurer J. W. Buzzell.[8]

Perhaps no small part of the optimism visible in Labor Council circles in the early months of 1936 was caused by the belief among Los Angeles AFL leaders that the M and M was in a state of decline. An M and M labor placement bureau had ceased functioning effectively in 1935 because of a lack of demand for its registrants and insufficient funds for its maintenance. Taking this as a sign of reduced M and M activity, AFL leaders, under the impetus of the NLRA, decided to embark on a new organizing campaign. No sooner was this initiated, however, than M and M officials saw in it a renewed threat to the open shop and laid plans to combat it. By March, 1936, the labor placement bureau had been reorganized at 105 West Sixth Street under the new name of Free Employment Industrial Bureau. It soon became more a source of strikebreakers than of independent workmen, as the former received more than twice as many referrals as the latter. Open-shop employers also demanded that the M and M itself be reorganized in order to oppose more effectively the rapidly increasing local efforts to organize workers.

This demand was answered in June and July of 1936, when the M and M organized two new bodies: the first was known as the Special Secret Advisory Council; the second, as the Executive Committee. According to Edgar R. Perry, general manager of the M and M before this time, these months marked the resurgence of allegedly reactionary members, who seized control and initiated an aggressive antiunion campaign which was to reach its peak in the following two years. The Special Secret Advisory Council was composed of one representative from each large industry in Los Angeles, and the Executive Committee comprised delegates from the council and the M and M board of directors. The Executive Committee was responsible for carrying out the program of the organization. S. M. Haskins was elected to head the M and M, and J. Stuart Neary became executive secretary and counsel for the Executive Committee. Haskins had served as president of the Los Angeles Railway and Neary as legal adviser during the 1934–1935 strike. The most important aims of the reorganized M and M were to give workers wages equal to those demanded by unionists, to introduce collective bargaining with employees but not through outside unions, to gain the coöperation of law enforcement agencies in maintaining industrial peace along open-shop lines, to persuade the managements of industries not supporting the open shop to favor that system of industrial relations, and to sponsor a guard service for those needing protection against strikers during a labor dispute.[9]

With these preparations, the M and M was ready to launch its counterunion campaign of "maintaining somewhat of an equality with labor and to prevent the domination of labor through the obtainment by organization of this monopoly by the closed shop."[10] Full-page advertisements presenting the principles and the objectives of the M and M began to appear in the daily papers. The *Times* published editorials in the early summer warning against the activities of union leaders. The newpaper phase of the campaign continued into the fall, at which time M and M officials broadened their program to maintain the open shop. They held conferences with representatives of nearly every major industry in Los Angeles, explained their objectives, and offered financial as well as organizational assistance to those who wished to adhere to open-shop principles.

Among the industries that subsequently organized to combat the union drive were banking, store fixture and furniture manufacturing, dairying, candy production, wholesale food and grocery distribution, sash, door, and paint manufacturing, retail clothing, drugs, shoes, and public warehousing. In nearly every instance the employers concerned signed contracts with their respective trade associations in which they agreed to maintain certain minimum wage schedules, maximum hours, and working conditions as well as the open shop. Some of the agreements were to be effective for several years, though most of them were for shorter periods. As a further encouragement to these employers, the M and M assumed the overhead expenses of the Glen E. Bodell Detective Agency from October 22, 1936, until June 10, 1937. This action permitted affiliated firms to obtain guard or spy services at a reduced rate. The M and M also distributed information about how and where to procure company-union plans.[11]

Chamber of Commerce officials likewise were concerned over the status of the open shop in 1936. Realizing that workers in Long Beach, Wilmington, and San Pedro had been extensively unionized after the 1934 maritime strike, they believed that an organizing campaign might accomplish similar results in Los Angeles. Undoubtedly the labor unrest that had prevailed at the harbor after the dispute had spread to the inland unions and had given them much of the basic impetus for their organizing activities over the next two years. In the light of this knowledge, the chamber supported the M and M drive to maintain the open shop. Although the M and M was the more aggressive of the two groups, officials of both organizations were convinced that one of the most effective ways to strengthen the open shop was to develop amicable relations between employers and their employees.[12]

The incorrectly assumed inactivity of the M and M, the influence of the water-front unions, and the impact of the NLRA were not the only spurs to a new organizing effort in 1936. An increasing number of large manufacturing industries, in such fields as rubber, automobiles, aircraft, and clothing, were locating in Los Angeles. These industries brought together big groups of factory workers who, in turn, wanted better working conditions, reasonable hours, and higher wages, and who recognized that unions could help them attain these ends. An additional factor, which had local significance, was the nationwide conflict between the AFL and the CIO. Leaders of the AFL encouraged their Los Angeles counterparts to gather in new members before the CIO became strong enough in the West to act in effective opposition. Further, the possibilities that the NLRA might not be validated by the Supreme Court and that President Roosevelt might not be re-elected in November spurred increased organizing activity on both local and national levels.[13]

Regardless of its causes, the renewed campaign was of undoubted importance. The *Times* called it "the greatest drive in fifty years to unionize and subjugate" the city.[14] Warning that continuance of the open shop was threatened in the motion picture, agricultural, furniture, cabinetmaking, rubber, transportation, garment, building, maritime, and service industries, *Times* editorials gave local organizers a premonition of the battles to come. Well aware by this time of the reorganization that was taking place within the M and M, labor leaders referred to the *Times* as the "organ of special privilege," and claimed that its editorials revealed a fear of the strength shown by the local labor movement.[15]

Organizing activities in the first part of 1936 were conducted primarily by individual unions or groups of locals. Later in the year the Central Labor Council coördinated all these efforts into a single campaign to combat the renewed open-shop drive. At a special September meeting, officers of affiliated unions voted to increase the funds of the council, strengthen mass picketing lines, and place more organizers in the field. In October the Labor Council geographically extended the campaign by establishing a joint council composed of representatives from labor bodies in other Los Angeles County communities. These decisions were immediately implemented by increased mass picketing of unfair firms. Furthermore, on October 16, Section 1 of Article X of the council's constitution was amended to raise the per capita tax from 5 to 10 cents. The larger income enabled the council to move its offices to larger quarters and hire an assistant secretary and two additional organizers, who brought its full-time staff up to six persons. The record-breaking attendance at council meetings in the latter part of 1936 reflected the increased interest of constituent unions in its activities. The list of twenty-seven unfair firms published in the *Citizen* was the longest in the history of the newspaper.[16]

The most direct impact of the revived open-shop opposition came in the form of an increasing number of injunctions against organizing activities. The resultant pressure forced the Labor Council to retain legal counsel. Because of limited funds, however, union officers were not permitted to place firms on the unfair list unless they guaranteed to pay a reasonable share of the expenses incurred if legal action developed. The council could not permit indiscriminate use of its unfair list, as published in the *Citizen,* with the consequent possibilities of legal action, when it was already a too-frequent defendant in suits instituted by employers as a result of offenses committed by members of individual unions.

Legal opposition, however, did not slow the organizing campaign. In fact, local labor leaders considered 1936 the most successful year for the Los Angeles labor movement since the beginning of the depression. They noted that union building tradesmen were employed in larger numbers than in any previous depression year—a sign of improved economic conditions. Less unemployment and expanding memberships were reported by nearly all the unions affiliated with the council.[17] The prevailing optimism was well expressed at the council meeting of December 11: "It is evident from the interest manifested and strict attention paid to what goes on, the men and women who represent the locals of the movement in the Central body, Unionism is at a higher ebb in this city now than for many years, if ever."[18] The Los Angeles labor movement was indeed making progress. Secretary Buzzell's report in June, 1936, revealed that, according to per capita tax figures, council membership had grown to 17,869, as compared with 14,573 for 1935. This was a slightly smaller total than the figure recorded in 1934, but this fact did not disturb Buzzell, who claimed that there really were more than 65,000 members in various AFL locals in the city, some of which were unaffiliated with the council. In 1935 only ninety-seven unions had been affiliated with the council, whereas there were 110 in June, 1936.[19]

2. MAJOR FIELDS OF UNION ACTIVITY

The union upsurge in Los Angeles in 1936 led to fifty recorded strikes involving 10,502 workers. However, the airframe-manufacturing industry, one of increasing interest to organizers, did not experience a strike although in subsequent years it became a major southern California employer. Some members of the United Aircraft Mechanics Union, AFL, were working in airframe-manufacturing plants in Los Angeles as early as 1934, but their total was small compared with the number of employees of these firms who belonged to company unions. In the same year a group of Communists formed the Western Mechanics Industrial Union, which in October affiliated with the UAW-CIO as Local No. 188. Most of its 400 members were employed in small metal trades shops. Organizing committees for various industries were soon established within the union, including the Aircraft Industrial Council, the Jobbing Shop Industrial Council, and the Automobile Industrial Council. In 1936 representatives were sent to the two

Douglas plants in Santa Monica and El Segundo and to North American in Inglewood and Lockheed in Burbank. Before the year ended, UAW Local No. 188 had workers in its fold from all these companies.[20]

Bakers Local No. 37 was just as active as the UAW in attempting to organize nonunion firms in Los Angeles. But, as in the past, union representatives ran head on into the M and M, which furnished guard service and advice to struck plants. Despite this opposition, the local signed agreements with the managements of the Weber and 4-S baking companies. Its officers also negotiated contracts with the Cosmopolitan, Foix, Basso, Los Angeles, and Las Pumas bakeries, but were forced to call two strikes in the process. Further, they won a closed-shop agreement from the Bradley Pie Company after a seventeen-hour strike. The contract, which provided a 5 per cent wage increase, a forty-eight-hour week, a minimum wage of $20 a week, and overtime pay, was the first agreement signed by the union with the management of a pie bakery in the city. Another union, Local No. 453, composed of Jewish bakers, called a strike against the Heirshberg Rye Bakery which lasted for nine weeks. Jacob Siegelman, a charter member of the local, finally bought the company from Heirshberg, signed a union agreement in September, 1936, and began to operate the business.

Similar successes were gained by Cleaners, Dyers and Pressers Union No. 19989, AFL, which signed a contract with the larger wholesale cleaning plants, renewing for one year the working agreement signed in April, 1935. But the renewed agreement was a failure. In a strike called on July 14, in a period of high trade volume and employment in the cleaning industry caused by the Elks' national convention, between 600 and 1,000 workers walked out. Union demands included a 20 per cent pay boost for employees receiving from $16 to $20 per week and small increases for those receiving higher wages. The walkout was directed principally against members of the Cooperative Plant Owners' Association, who were paying wages ranging from $16 to $30 a week. Mayor Frank L. Shaw acted as mediator in the dispute. Late in July the parties finally reached a one-year agreement calling for weekly minimum wages of $25 to $40 for skilled workers, $18 for unskilled employees, and $20 plus a 10 per cent commission for drivers. Provision was also made for the establishment of an arbitration board. Shortly after the wage increase, the price for cleaning suits was raised from 49 to 59 cents.[21]

Building tradesmen took advantage of a similar period of higher employment, reflected in increased membership in AFL construction unions. All locals except the carpenters were affiliated with the Los Angeles Building and Construction Trades Council in 1936. Wages began to rise as the physical volume of construction increased, and soon the delegates to the council had to meet semimonthly instead of monthly because of the larger amount of business to be transacted.

Efforts to improve wages in view of better employment conditions met an old enemy in the form of statements in Los Angeles newspapers that there was a shortage of building craftsmen. In reply, council officials charged that open-shop supporters were responsible for the publicity and were thus attempting to create a large labor reserve by attracting building mechanics from other cities. More tangible opposition developed in the same period in the form of an organization called Allied Building Crafts, Inc. Local AFL officials declared that it was a dual union organized by contractors opposing the closed or union shop, and that its members should be treated as strikebreakers.[22]

The most significant strike sponsored by the Building Trades Council began on March 16, 1936, against a contractor erecting a $2,500,000 General Motors Corporation assembly plant in South Gate. The contractor was charged with paying 1916 wages rather than the higher scales that were more realistic for 1936. Unionists established a picket line and initiated a boycott against General Motors cars. Eventually both actions were extended over much of the nation. Union members displayed cards on their automobiles advertising the walkout. Many of the signs were stolen, however, by small boys who were paid 5 cents for each placard by automobile salesmen. After several months the striking building mechanics decided that it was impossible to prosecute a successful boycott against a firm the size of General Motors. Moreover, they discovered that their jobs were being taken by unemployed craftsmen who were willing to work on a nonunion basis at lower wages. The end of the strike came soon after the struck contractor increased wages for those who had continued to work while the dispute was in progress.[23]

A union closely related to the construction trades was Local No. 884 of the United Brotherhood of Carpenters and Joiners of America. Its members were millmen who challenged one of the most powerful associations of open-shop employers in Los Angeles, composed of the larger firms in the cabinet and store-fixture industry. The two opposing groups met head on in April, 1936, after expiration of an agreement made in 1935. Negotiation conferences held for several months prior to April failed to produce a new contract. The employers steadfastly refused to recognize Local No. 884 as collective bargaining agent for the millmen. Spearheading the fight for the open shop, according to union officials, was the Weber Showcase and Fixture Company. They accused its management of laying off journeymen and hiring apprentices to do the same jobs at lower wages. They also asserted that the larger manufacturers had refused to participate in the arbitration proceedings that were to have followed the 1935 strike. The main union demands in 1936 included hourly wages of $1 for skilled mechanics, 60 cents for laborers, 45 cents for the first six months for apprentices with gradual increases until they became journeymen, and $1.10 on installation work; a forty-hour week with overtime pay rates; elimination of all employment on Saturdays, Sundays, and legal holidays; and recognition of the union as the collective bargaining agent for the employees.[24]

The strike that followed expiration of the agreement stopped nearly all production in the cabinet and fixture industry of Los Angeles for a few days. Approximately 1,200 workers walked out and immediately established picket lines. Within a week 200 of the strikers were rehired at several plants under new agreements, but the larger firms terminated all negotiations and prepared to fight. By the end of May 500 men were still on strike, although sixteen plants had signed agreements. Most of these strikers were picketing seven large companies which still refused to negotiate under any circumstances.

M and M officials entered the dispute at the outset, but were unsuccessful in their first efforts to enlist the coöperation of cabinet and store-fixture manufacturers in their program to maintain the open shop. The latter refused to agree to reasonable hours, working conditions, and minimum wages; to certify that they would abide by certain ethical principles of business upheld by the M and M; or to help bear the expense of eliminating labor controversy. All these conditions had to be accepted before M and M aid would be forthcoming.[25]

In June the seven largest manufacturers in the industry, controlling 75 per cent of the trade volume, agreed to M and M conditions and established the Cabinet and Store Fixture Association of California. The signed agreement provided for maintenance of the open shop for two years, heavy penalties for its violation, and standard wage rates. M and M officials encouraged the new association by urging the managements of various stores using cabinets and fixtures to give orders only to these seven manufacturers. They also tried to induce the executives of companies dealing in building materials to withhold supplies from any firm that signed an agreement with Local No. 884.[26]

The Cabinet and Store Fixture Association participated in fighting what remained of the strike by hiring guards and undercover operatives. All members of the association were able to continue production on a reduced scale by using strikebreakers. In spite of this setback, however, Local 884 successfully maintained mass picketing of stores buying cabinets and fixtures. This form of attack encouraged some stores, including the Atlantic and Pacific Tea Company, to purchase equipment from firms in which the workers were unionized. Officials of the W. T. Grant Company also assured the strikers of their desire to coöperate by buying fixtures with the union label. Several lumber yards employing unionists, yet supplying materials to such struck firms as the Weber Showcase and Fixture Company, were persuaded to cease such deliveries. The result was that a number of open-shop manufacturers experienced difficulties in purchasing some items. The pressure was sufficiently effective to induce the Wheat Cabinet and Fixture Company to resign from the Cabinet and Store Fixture Association after about eight weeks of the strike and become a unionized firm.

Local No. 884 was supported in its dispute by the Los Angeles Central Labor Council, the District Council of Carpenters, and a number of unaffiliated AFL unions. These groups gave financial assistance and backed a boycott of the products of the struck companies through publicity in the *Citizen* and the refusal to handle those products. Fortunately, there were few acts of violence, although the dispute lasted more than a year.[27]

The strike was finally settled in June, 1937. A contract was drawn which provided hourly wages of $1 for skilled craftsmen in manufacturing operations, $1.10 for work at building sites, time and a half for overtime, double time for Sundays and holidays, an adequate apprenticeship system, and recognition of the union as the collective bargaining agent for employees of the struck firms. Although this settlement did not end all union-management problems in the cabinet and store-fixture industry, it was the primary cause of the later dissolution of the Cabinet and Store Fixture Association of California.[28]

In 1936 another union of the United Brotherhood of Carpenters, Furniture Workers Local No. 1561, revived its campaign against the ten manufacturers with whom it had fought a losing battle in 1935. The union continued its boycott against these open shops during the year and requested retail stores selling "unfair" furniture to cease patronizing the struck manufacturers. Under this kind of pressure, a few plants signed union contracts before the end of the year, but counterpressure from the M and M aided in keeping several of the larger factories from succumbing. Mass picketing also was used against retail outlets such as Eastern-Columbia and the May Company in an attempt to force them to stop selling furniture manufactured by open-shop firms, but was of little avail. At the end of the year the Kroehler Manufacturing Company in Inglewood was clearly the leading non-union concern in the industry. Although an active strike was in progress against it, with 200 strikers on the picket line, the firm continued to operate on an open-shop basis.[29]

Furniture Workers Local No. 1561, Sawmill and Timber Workers Locals No. 2607 and No. 2788, and Millmen and Cabinet Makers Local No. 884, all affiliated with the Brotherhood of Carpenters, established the Joint Council of Lumber, Fixture and Furniture Workers in 1936. In subsequent years this new organization would oppose open-shop employers in the woodworking industries of the city.[30]

Los Angeles culinary workers also engaged in disputes with open-shop employers in 1936, in continuation of the organizing drive that started in 1934. Some of the unions involved were Waiters Local No. 17, Cooks Local No. 468, Waitresses Local No. 439, and Bartenders Local No. 284. A strike against the René and Jean cafés, initiated in 1935, was maintained during part of 1936. It was terminated when the management won an injunction ordering the withdrawal of pickets and the discontinuance of sales of the *Citizen* in front of the cafés. But the defeat did not prevent the culinary workers from making some progress in union membership during the year. They also succeeded in establishing a new union, Miscellaneous Employees Local No. 440, composed of dishwashers, bus boys, and cooks' helpers.[31]

Union teamsters, numbering about 2,000 in the Los Angeles area, were active on several fronts in 1936. In May the international union sent organizer Harry W. Dail to the city to supervise extension of the membership drive that had been started at the harbor the previous year to the whole southern California area. The drive was to continue for the next two years. Dail underlined the need for effective teamster organization when he estimated that the hourly wages of nonunion Los Angeles truck drivers ranged from 20 to 50 cents, as compared with union rates of about 75 cents in San Francisco.[32] Table 6 indicates that similar union wage rates prevailed in Los Angeles.

In launching their organizing campaign at Los Angeles Harbor, the teamsters established a blockade of pickets around the harbor area shortly after the longshoremen walked out in October, 1935, in support of the ILA's attempt to secure recognition at ports on the Gulf of Mexico. Union drivers were forbidden to cross the picket lines, and

TABLE 6

WAGE RATES AND WORKING HOURS OF UNION TEAMSTERS,
LOS ANGELES, MAY 15, 1936

Type of driver	Wage rate		Hours per week
	Per hour	Per week	
Brewery			
Bottle beer	$.818	$36.00	44
Keg beer and shipping	.841	37.00	44
General			
Light pick-up, under 2 tons	.600	28.80	48
Road, up to 5 tons	.650	31.20	48
Above 5 and under 10 tons	.700	33.60	48
Low-bed, winch, and rigging trucks and interchangeable series	.800	38.40	48

SOURCE: "Union Scales of Wages and Hours of Motortruck Drivers, May 15, 1936," *Monthly Labor Review*, XLIV (May, 1937), 1253.

nonunion truckers were stopped and, in some instances, told to join the union or be prepared to suffer the consequences. By April, 1936, the M and M was deeply concerned over the blockade's effectiveness. The association called a meeting of common carrier truck line managers to warn them of the menace to the open shop in the industry. Fearing that the teamsters' success in organizing truck drivers in San Pedro would encourage similar efforts in uptown Los Angeles, the *Times,* in a series of articles, warned the public that the trucking unions were controlled by racketeers who beat nonunion drivers, broke the windshields of their trucks, and terrorized the industry by using "beef squads." The real leaders of the union teamsters were declared to be Dave Beck of Seattle and Mike Casey of San Francisco, to whom Harry Dail reported.

Concerned over the situation, the M and M established a special truck fund to pay for guards and extra police officers needed to protect trucks in the harbor area. During the later months of 1936, eight radio cars patrolled the highways leading from the city to the port, and other police were stationed at half-mile intervals along a designated truck boulevard. The police prevented union pickets from stopping trucks, and were so effective that union leaders recognized the futility of making further efforts to organize truck drivers on the harbor highways, although they kept pickets in the water-front area. In December, 1936, therefore, they concentrated on organizing truckers driving vehicles on the main roads from Los Angeles to the north and east.[33]

Within the city the teamsters were especially active in recruiting drivers who worked for food processors and distributors. Allied Food Industries, Inc., representing the more important firms in this field, was formed late in the year partly because of these organizing efforts. The new association vigorously opposed the closed shop and coöperated with M and M officials in resisting the teamsters' membership drive. It also helped to finance guard service on trucks going to and from the harbor area by contributing to the M and M special truck fund.[34]

Teamster organizing efforts likewise aroused the opposition of three dairymen's organizations. At least one of the associations, Dairy Industries, Inc., was formed as a result of encouragement from the M and M. A part of the funds collected from the members of these three groups was spent for publicity campaigns in favor of the open shop.

House-to-house canvassing by teamsters in the latter part of 1936 netted about 135 additional members for Los Angeles Local No. 208 and more than 750 for Local No. 696 at San Pedro. Officials of the Los Angeles Chamber of Commerce, the M and M, and allied organizations such as those of the dairymen predicted that the teamsters' organizing drive would continue in subsequent years. The institution of the M and M special fund, the establishment of associations of open-shop supporters in various industries, and the provision of city police and special guard protection for trucks were at least partly owing to a belief among employers that the union teamsters could reduce the number of open shops in Los Angeles. By controlling transportation, they also could assist officials of allied unions in organizing other industries.[35]

The teamsters did not suffer from Communist infiltration, but this could not be said about the Fur Workers Industrial Union. An attempt to overcome the handicap was made in 1935 when this affiliate of the Communist Trade Union Unity League was dissolved. Most of its members joined Local No. 87 of the International Fur Workers Union. In March, 1936, the local began an organizational drive against open-shop retailers and manufacturers. After several preliminary disputes, its leaders called a general strike on August 1 against employers in the industry. About 400 workers walked out of member firms of the Los Angeles Retail Fur Manufacturers' Association. Their demands included a 20 per cent wage increase, time and a half for overtime, a thirty-five-hour week, and recognition of Local 87 as their collective bargaining agent. The employers refused to accede to these requests, pointing out that the strikers represented only a small number of the total workers in the industry.[36]

As a consequence of the picketing that followed the walkout, the owners of twenty-three small shops signed agreements with Local No. 87 before the end of August, but the larger manufacturers continued to resist. Finally, in September, the rest of the manufacturing wholesalers and eight retailers signed contracts granting the strikers' demands. One large retail furrier, Maurice Ball, refused to sign and, along with several other retailers, continued to oppose the unionists. He obtained a restraining order against the union pickets and prolonged the dispute into 1937. The working members of Local 87 were assessed 5 per cent of their wages to finance the fight against Ball.[37]

Other clothing trades unions were active in 1936. Nationally, the Amalgamated Clothing Workers of America and the Journeymen Tailors Union were combined into one organization under the former's name. In Los Angeles, Tailors Local No. 81 and Amalgamated Local No. 278 formed a joint board, whose function was to coördinate the activities of the two locals.

Local No. 278 struck against Rosenblum, Inc., a Los Angeles garment-manufacturing firm, on August 25 when two unionists were fired and bodily ejected from the shop. One hundred workers walked out, picket lines were established, and demands for a union shop and the undisputed right of Local No. 278 to represent the firm's employees were submitted to the management. Rosenblum was placed on the unfair list of the Central Labor Council, and a systematic boycott was enforced against the firm's market outlets, including Bullock's, a leading Los Angeles department store. Rosenblum executives hired strikebreakers and provided them with taxis, pay increases, and free lunches in an attempt to counteract the union. Local No. 278 officials were certain, from these actions, that the firm was being counseled by representatives of the M and M. They wired the national officers of the Amalgamated that the homes of union members were being raided, unionists were being arrested on false charges, and there was interference with their civil rights.

In subsequent months the union officers sent sworn affidavits attesting to sweatshop working conditions to the firm's suppliers and customers in an effort to curtail its output. Outbreaks of violence were reported, including the throwing of rocks and eggs at strikebreakers' homes as well as beatings of workers on both sides. A number of riots occurring in connection with picketing caused the hospitalization and jailing of several unionists and strikebreakers. After seven months of dispute, Local 278 finally secured an agreement ending the walkout on March 29, 1937. The contract provided for collective bargaining, a thirty-six-hour week, time and a half for overtime, the immediate rehiring of fifteen strikers, and reëmployment of the rest over a period of time.[38]

Another strike of lesser significance was also called by Local No. 278 in 1936 against an old opponent, Kurtzman Brothers. In previous years the management of this firm had been hostile to the union. In 1936 the plant was moved to Vernon and its name was changed to the Kay Bee Sportswear Company. Union organizers went to Vernon, however, and conducted a strike which resulted in an agreement. This ended the long-standing feud and marked a significant victory for the union.[39]

The International Ladies' Garment Workers Union was also active in 1936. Its representatives pursued the task of organizing employees in pajama and underwear manufacturing, an effort they had initiated the preceding year. They conducted strikes against shops in this field and organized and chartered a new union, Local No. 236. The cloakmakers in the ILGWU called a strike against eleven shops in the city early in the year. They were successful in obtaining agreements with most of them, providing for a thirty-five-hour week and the union wage scale.[40]

The most important ILGWU activity was a general strike of dressmakers. Prestrike efforts were made early in the year to consolidate prior gains in union membership among the workers in the silk and wool dress industry and to organize new shops. The union wanted to be designated as collective bargaining agent for all dressmakers when the contract with employers expired on July 1. A few weeks before its expiration, the General Executive Board of the ILGWU met in Los Angeles for the first time in its history and put its stamp of approval on the walkout, if needed to enforce demands.

Preliminary negotiations for a new agreement caused postponement of the walkout. As talks continued, ILGWU representatives, headed by International Vice-President Israel Feinberg, insisted on a closed shop in the industry in addition to wage increases which the employers believed to be excessive. A deadlock developed, and on August 5 nearly 3,000 workers, led by members of Local No. 96, struck and established picket lines under police supervision. The striking dressmakers were assisted by the cloakmakers, who by this time had achieved almost a closed shop in their trade, and by financial contributions from the members of other ILGWU unions in San Francisco, San Pedro, and Los Angeles.[41]

Demonstrations occurred during the picketing, with consequent blocking of streets, hurling of epithets, beatings, arrests, and trials for violators of the city's ordinances governing picketing and maintenance of the peace. A group of nine employers formed the Southern California Garment Manufacturers' Association and fought to retain open shops. M and M representatives assisted the group in securing incorporation. Each member agreed to pay a heavy fine if he recognized or negotiated with any person not on his payroll. The association utilized the services of extra policemen during the walkout, paying a total of $769.50 to Captain Hynes of the Los Angeles Police Department to cover the cost of lunches and dinners for officers on strike duty. In addition, the Glen E. Bodell Detective Agency was paid $1,085.25 in the same period for furnishing special detectives as guards and investigators.[42]

A few days after the strike began, ILGWU representatives signed agreements with fifty-six firms employing 2,650 workers. Each contract provided for a closed shop by November 1, a weekly minimum wage of $28 for women and $35 for men, and a thirty-five-hour workweek. Employers affiliated with the Southern California Garment Manufacturers' Association continued to resist, but the large majority of manufacturers in the dress industry agreed to abide by the contracts.[43]

The retail clerks were not so successful as the garment workers in 1936. Pharmacists Local No. 840 ran into trouble when it called a strike against the Thrifty Drug Company in December. The dispute occurred in the course of an organizing campaign that had been started in the fall of 1935. The Thrifty Drug Company was accused of failure to negotiate for a contract with Local No. 840, and of discriminating against employees who were union members. Union officials stated that 240 registered and assistant pharmacists employed by Thrifty worked as long as seventy hours a week for as little as $25. Local No. 840 therefore asked the management for a forty-eight-hour week, a minimum weekly salary of $40 for registered pharmacists and $32.50 for assistant pharmacists, time and a half for overtime, and two Sundays and fifteen nights off duty each month. When the firm ignored the demands, the strike was called.

Leaders of Local No. 840 claimed that more than 50 per cent of the pharmacists employed by Thrifty were members of the union and took part in picketing. The management countered, however, that unionists composed only 16 per cent of the total number of pharmacists employed, and that none of them were picketing. Union officials retorted that the company tolerated unfair labor practices and used stool pigeons and spies in union meetings. These accusations were subsequently taken to the Regional Labor Board, but were dismissed because the Thrifty Drug Company did not operate in interstate commerce. A temporary restraining order against picketing was secured by the management, and then dropped in March, 1937. The unionists used picketing, boycotting, and an unfair list to advertise the strike extensively during the following months, but their demands were not granted. The dispute was finally discontinued, and on September 24, 1937, the firm was removed from the unfair list of the Central Labor Council.[44]

The printing trades were able to continue the upward trend in employment and membership which started in 1935, though the membership of a few locals remained stationary during these years. By April, 1936, the union label of the Allied Printing Trades Council was being used by about fifty firms, and unionists were employed in a number of other printing houses. The first printers' strike in several years was called by ITU Local No. 174 against the Compton Printing Company when a nonunion foreman was hired. The strike and boycott began in May, 1936, and lasted until June, 1937. The perseverance of the unionists was rewarded, for they obtained a settlement that guaranteed continuance of the closed shop. Local No. 174 also negotiated an increase in the newspaper wage scale which became effective in January, 1937, and remained unchanged for two years. The agreement provided for a daily wage increase of 40 cents for the first year, with an additional increment of 20 cents for the second year.[45]

Among other unions in the city, the rubber workers seemed the most aggressive in 1936. In February George B. Roberts was sent to Los Angeles as a field representative and organizer for the United Rubber Workers, CIO. He also represented the United Automobile Workers and the national CIO. Roberts initiated an organizing campaign designed to revive the rubber workers' local which had virtually disappeared in 1935 and to obtain contracts with the major employing firms. At first, the Los Angeles police suspected him of being a Communist, but he disproved this possibility by his statements and actions. By August, Local No. 44 of the United Rubber Workers had been formed and, in an election conducted by the NLRB, had become the collective bargaining agent for the workers employed at the Samson Tire and Rubber Company. The rubber workers thus seemed to be on their way to new status and the old company unions to be on their way out.[46]

In contrast with the new life experienced by the rubber workers, the meatcutters and butchers became disorganized early in 1936 after maintaining only a marginal existence during the preceding year. The inactivity of the union's leaders caused dissension between them and the rank and file, thus necessitating reorganization. In late 1936 the union initiated a campaign to increase its membership, as many supporters had left the local earlier in the year. Only mediocre success was achieved, and the union remained weak in 1937.[47]

The plight of meatcutters and butchers did not symbolize the status of the majority of the unions in the city in 1936. Even though the NIRA had passed from the scene in May, 1935, and the NLRA had not yet been validated by the Supreme Court, the year 1936 was more than a holding period for Los Angeles labor. On the other hand, the open shop was far from eliminated and was still to make its strongest stand. Although Los Angeles labor leaders did not realize it at the time, in 1936 they were really consolidating the gains of the preceding several years, and were thus better prepared to meet the open shop in new forms and on new fronts. The lack of open conflict between the AFL and CIO factions in Los Angeles during the year contributed to the consolidation process, as it kept the two groups from dissipating their energies in fruitless warfare. The need for this conservation of strength on organized labor's part became evident as the open-shop conflict intensified in 1937.

XII. A NEW OFFENSIVE
FOR THE OPEN SHOP, 1937–1938

1. THE NATIONAL AND THE STATE SETTING

THE NATIONAL PROGRAM of direct and work relief for the unemployed which was functioning in 1936 carried on into the following year. On June 29, 1937, the federal government appropriated $1.5 billion under Public Resolution No. 47 to ensure sufficient funds for relief expenditures, under the direction of the President, for the coming fiscal year. State and local government funds were also used to help support the jobless.

The business decline that began in the late summer of 1937 continued through the early months of 1938. The accompanying distress and suffering reminded the nation that it was not yet out of the depression, and brought back vivid memories of early 1933. On June 21, 1938, the President approved Public Resolution No. 122. Under Title I of this legislation $1,712,905,000 was appropriated for work and general relief, of which $1,425,000,000 was allocated to the Works Progress Administration. The Public Works Administration received a further appropriation under Title II of the act, and a public-building construction program was continued by means of Title III. Other titles authorized expenditures by the Rural Electrification Administration, the secretary of agriculture, and the Housing Authority.[1]

In May, 1937, the Supreme Court declared the federal Social Security Act constitutional, thus removing any doubts as to the law's validity. By August, 1938, all the states, the territories of Alaska and Hawaii, and the District of Columbia had passed unemployment compensation measures, which covered about 25.5 million workers. Twenty-five states were already paying unemployment benefits. For example, California's public assistance plan for aid to the aged, the blind, and children, as well as its unemployment compensation law, had been approved by the Social Security Board by June 30, 1937.[2]

Organized labor gained a victory the same year when the Supreme Court, in a series of five cases, declared the National Labor Relations Act constitutional. Members of a number of employer groups, including the National Association of Manufacturers, demanded revision or repeal of the law. Strangely enough, in the following years their criticisms were supported by others made by AFL officials, although the latter were concerned with the administration of the law rather than with its purpose. CIO leaders were less critical. They opposed basic changes in the law's administration, except for revisions that might be necessary to assure continuance of the industrial union structure. CIO leader Philip Murray charged that AFL officials were attempting to amend the law and to use the National Labor Relations Board to further the designation of craft unions as collective bargaining agents for employees in plants where a majority of the workers had expressed a preference for a CIO local. AFL leaders, in turn, accused NLRB members of discriminating against craft unions in their decisions. They felt that the board should not recognize the CIO because it was a dual organization which had been excommunicated by the old-line craft federation. Furthermore, they believed that recognition of the CIO would undermine the foundations of American democracy, as a number of Communists were leaders in some of its affiliated unions.[3]

The Los Angeles Central Labor Council alleged that some local NLRB decisions in 1938 discriminated against craft unions. Its officers asked all Los Angeles union leaders to report discriminatory actions of the Regional Labor Board, so that such complaints could be forwarded to the AFL Executive Council. Local and national CIO leaders were critical, too, but mainly of the delays in hearing cases under the NLRA. They feared, however, that the AFL criticisms of the act, added to those made by employers, would result in elimination of the provisions relating to collective bargaining. They also expressed concern that the AFL's proposed amendments might make the craft union the only acceptable collective bargaining agent. Consequently, the CIO opposed fundamental changes in the law.

NLRB officials, as expected, denied any favoritism or discrimination against the AFL, stating that they were accomplishing the objectives of the act and saw no necessity for amending it. They declared that their policy of settling jurisdictional disputes by representation elections was one of the reasons for AFL opposition to the law, because the results of such elections often favored a CIO local.[4]

The Fair Labor Standards Act, regulating the wages and the hours of certain classes of workers employed in industries in interstate commerce, was passed by Congress and became effective on October 24, 1938. It was a compromise between AFL and CIO demands for such a law. Under its provisions the hourly minimum wage was to be gradually increased over a period of seven years from 25 to 40 cents. Although the main purpose of the act was to establish a minimum wage, it implemented the spread-the-work policy which the AFL had been advocating for more than five years. AFL President William Green therefore called upon all members of the labor movement to assume responsibility for enforcement of the act.[5]

Favorable national legislation, however, did not bring peace in the industrial relations field. There were more strikes in 1937 than in any previous year in United States history. A substantial number of these stemmed from jurisdictional disputes between AFL and CIO unions. In late 1936, moreover, CIO officials started a campaign, which in 1937 proved to be very successful, to organize the workers in unskilled and semiskilled trades. On December 28, 1936, workers in the Fisher Body Division of General Motors "sat down" and refused to leave the plant until the United Auto Workers was recognized. This struggle was followed by activity against "Big Steel," which signed a CIO contract without a strike on March 2, 1937, prior to settlements with any of the auto manufacturers. In the same month Green provided the necessary impetus for organizing separate city and state CIO organizations when he issued an order instructing AFL regional labor bodies to expel all delegates from locals affiliated with the CIO. The CIO experienced a temporary setback in May, when strikers were defeated in a walkout against "Little Steel." By September, 1937, however, the CIO, thanks to its successful organizing efforts, became the largest national labor organization, with a membership of 3,718,000. In November, 1938, it held its first national convention and formally converted itself into an independent labor federation called the Congress of Industrial Organizations.[6]

Delegates to the 1936 convention of the California State Federation of Labor (CSFL) had originally endorsed the CIO. But since then President Green had ordered all CIO unions expelled from state and city central bodies. This policy was supported by state secretary E. D. Vandeleur, who declared early in 1937 that the CIO was closely allied with Communism. He further condemned the CIO at the 1937 state AFL convention held in Long Beach, accusing its leaders of trying to maintain its membership by influencing officials of the NLRB in their collective bargaining decisions.[7] After long debate, the delegates present finally resolved "that the California State Federation of Labor, in 38th annual convention assembled, definitely repudiate the activities of the Committee for Industrial Organization and all its affiliates and members."[8]

At the request of CIO national leaders in 1938, Harry Bridges, its west coast director, issued a call to establish a state federation in California. A meeting held in Los Angeles on August 20 was attended by representatives of CIO unions and industrial councils from all over the state. John Brophy, CIO national director, was the main speaker. More than 400 delegates representing nearly 60,000 unionists elected P. M. (Slim) Connelly as the first president of the California CIO Council. At the time Connelly was head of the Los Angeles chapter of the American Newspaper Guild.

Sixty-one Los Angeles unions and other labor organizations sent delegates to the 1938 meeting of the AFL state federation. Their main concern no longer was the CIO, but the stepped-up open-shop campaign in Los Angeles which by this time had reached its zenith.[9]

The differences between the AFL and the CIO at the state and local levels also affected their political activities in 1937 and 1938. Labor's Non-Partisan League established a chapter at the Labor Temple in Los Angeles and expanded to become a state-wide organization by 1938. Members of both the CIO and the AFL continued to support it, though it came increasingly under the domination of the former and the condemnation of the latter. Officials of the league invited officers of the California State Federation of Labor to coöperate in the joint sponsorship of certain political measures in 1938, but the invitation was not accepted. Green reiterated his appeal to AFL members to shun the league, which he called a "ventriloquist's dummy for the CIO."[10]

The CSFL shortly thereafter established the first state-wide political organization in its history at a meeting held at Santa Barbara on March 20. Commissioned as the American Federation of Labor Political League of California, it endorsed a full slate of candidates for various state positions, including Sheriff Daniel C. Murphy of San Francisco for governor. Murphy was a candidate in the Democratic primary in opposition to Culbert L. Olson, who was supported by Labor's Non-Partisan League. The endorsements almost caused a mutiny among state leaders of the AFL. Those who were known as "liberals" did not wish to support most of the candidates of the AFL Political League, the majority of whom reputedly were "conservatives" in politics and seemed to be endorsed not for their views on labor issues but because they were opposed by CIO leaders. Secretary Buzzell of the Los Angeles Central Labor Council was influential in inducing the Political League to endorse conservative candidates, and in persuading Los Angeles delegates to support the entire slate.[11]

Gubernatorial candidates Frank F. Merriam, the incumbent Republican governor, and Olson won in the primary elections. Labor leaders regarded Merriam as the candidate of the state's employers. Before the final election in November, Green wrote to Joseph M. Casey, an international organizer for the teamsters in San Francisco, implying his advocacy of Merriam because of his belief that Olson had CIO support. The publication of Green's letter again aroused the ire of many California AFL leaders. CSFL officials and various central bodies and locals all over the state sent letters and telegrams to Green requesting that he withdraw his endorsement of Governor Merriam. These messages pointed out that Merriam twice had called out the militia in labor disputes, that the CSFL was not officially endorsing a candidate for the final election, that most unionists were going to vote for Olson, and that the Republican candidate was supported by the same employers who were advocating the passage of a state-wide proposal, known as "Proposition No. 1," to regulate labor unions. Olson also denounced Green for supporting Merriam, stating that this action had aided the enemies of the labor movement. Although Green held to his stand, Culbert L. Olson was elected the first Democratic governor in California since 1894. State labor leaders believed that for the first time in many years a governor had been elected who would aid them in their struggle against the political influence of employers and landholders in the California Legislature.[12]

In 1938 organized labor also was concerned about two controversial measures which appeared on the ballot as initiatives. Proposition No. 1, aimed at regulating labor unions, was sponsored jointly by a number of employer organizations and will be discussed in greater detail below. The second proposal was called the Retirement Life Payments Act, but was popularly known as "Ham and Eggs" or "Thirty Dollars Every Thursday." Sponsored by several promoters as an old-age pension, it appealed to many of the aged persons in the state. Labor leaders formed an alliance with the supporters of "Ham and Eggs" in order to oppose Proposition No. 1 at the polls. "Ham and Eggs" had further appeal for the young as well as the old because of the in-migration of unemployed workers and drought-stricken farmers from other areas of the nation. Many of these migrants were older citizens who wished to qualify for the highest old-age pension in the country and were likewise interested in increasing it. Younger persons who had enlarged the already swollen unemployed labor supply of the state saw "Ham and Eggs" as a means of removing the competition of older persons for jobs. Meanwhile, both the old and the young added to the already serious relief problems of the state.[13]

2. THE DIE IS CAST

Relief problems were particularly harassing to Angelenos. Organizers for the Workers Alliance were responsible for a number of incidents involving persons on work relief in 1937 and 1938. These included work stoppages, demonstrations at the old Plaza, and a strike against Los Angeles officials of the State Relief Administration. Local WPA executives continued to refuse to recognize the Workers Alliance or any other union as the sole collective bargaining agent on public projects.

The recession of 1937–38 was less severe in Los Angeles than in the nation as a whole. The percentage decreases in department store sales, power output, manufacturing employment, and bank debits were relatively small in the open-shop center because of the expanding foreign market for petroleum and aircraft. These factors, as well as the population growth in the area, hastened recovery. In 1938 the city grew at a rate of approximately 10,000 inhabitants per month. Wage rates moved upward even though employment declined, and this helped to arrest the impact of the recession.[14]

Economic adversity did not end the AFL-CIO controversy in the local labor movement, as Los Angeles unionists followed the national lead early in 1937. Although the CIO unions had tabled plans for a central body of their own in Los Angeles in the interests of local unity, they appointed a temporary committee to coördinate the activities of all the locals that were organizing workers in basic industries. This committee became a permanent city central body after the first open break occurred between leaders of CIO and AFL unions at a meeting of the Central Labor Council on May 14, 1937, when Secretary Buzzell read a letter from Green denying CIO unions the right of representation in AFL city central bodies. The *Citizen* reported what ensued:

After the reading of the communication from President Green, for a second or so there was tense silence. Several delegates made efforts to secure the floor to talk on the matter or perhaps make a motion or a statement. However, President Sherman promptly ruled the matter was not debatable and was an order to be obeyed, and there was no alternative than to declare all locals in the Council coming under the ban, suspended, which he proceeded to do. He thereupon declared the following suspended from membership in the Los Angeles Central Labor Council:

Amalgamated Clothing Workers, 278; locals 65, 97, 96 and 84 of the International Ladies' Garment Workers' Unions, and locals 43 and 44 of the United Rubber Workers. These are the only Internationals of the ten under suspension affiliated with the Los Angeles Central Labor Council. . . .

As the delegates left the auditorium there was a hush, then some hand clapping and several other delegates from locals not affiliated are also said to have withdrew [sic] at the time, whether officially or not remains to be seen.

Many of the delegates who were deprived of their affiliation have been long part of the movement and active in the work of the Council.[15]

CIO members then proceeded to elect officers, establish a headquarters, and adopt the title of Los Angeles Industrial Union Council. On June 14 the new organization, composed of delegates from twenty-two unions, received a CIO charter and began to hold weekly meetings. Among the officers elected were George B. Roberts, president; Charles West, vice-president; and C. H. Jordan, secretary. Support for the council was provided by a 5-cent per capita tax levied on the members of affiliated unions. Later in the year the CIO organization started a newspaper, the *Industrial Unionist,* but it failed to provide income.[16]

The Industrial Union Council took over the conduct of the CIO organizing drive, started at a mass meeting of union representatives on January 31, 1937, to unionize workers in the automobile, aviation, rubber, and steel industries of Los Angeles. On June 14 William Dalrymple, field director for the Steel Workers Organizing Committee, reported that in the preceding five months 45,000 persons had joined CIO unions in Los Angeles and southern California. By September the council allegedly represented 50,000 unionists, but per capita tax data indicated a paid-up membership of only about 17,500. The organizing drive continued until November, when it was curtailed by increasing unemployment as the recession gained momentum.

In the early winter of 1937–38, in accordance with instructions from national CIO headquarters, the council reorganized and subsequently operated a relief office originally instituted by the United Automobile Workers. Unions supported its operation by voluntary contributions of 10 cents per member, and from funds so raised financial assistance was given to unemployed CIO unionists. Despite the increase in unemployment, Secretary Jordan stated that by February, 1938, there were almost 50,000 workers affiliated with Los Angeles CIO unions.[17]

In 1937 the Los Angeles Central Labor Council also resumed an organizing campaign that had been started the year before. A 5-cent increase in the per capita tax provided the necessary funds and also permitted a two-page increase in the size of the *Citizen.* The newspaper, beginning with the March 12 issue, was sent gratis to members of unions affiliated with the council. Special meetings of all Los Angeles AFL union officers resulted in the formation, early in 1937, of "Labor's Committee on Organizing Los Angeles and Orange Counties," which coördinated the drive in the two counties in 1937 and 1938. The results of the campaign soon became evident. In February, 1937, 135 locals, the largest number in Los Angeles history, were affiliated with the council. By March the figure had increased to 138. In this same month the AFL Executive Council appointed A. H. Peterson, former official of the International Longshoremen's Association, as a full-time organizer in southern California. By the end of April twenty-four new unions had been chartered and more than 400 delegates were attending council meetings.[18]

When Buzzell gave his annual report in June, 1937, leaders of Los Angeles AFL unions were convinced that the organizing campaign was the most successful in the history of the Central Labor Council. The largest gains in membership accrued to the unions of clerks, teamsters, and carpenters. Buzzell stated that thirty-one new unions formed as a result of the campaign had joined the council. Despite the suspension of the CIO locals in May, there were 144 unions on the rolls as compared with 110 a year earlier. The council's membership, according to per capita tax figures, had increased during the fiscal year from 17,869 to 34,478, and its finances had never been in better shape.

The organizing drive slackened at the end of the summer, however, when the business depression curtailed AFL union activity. Attendance at the weekly meetings of the council became smaller, and by October was at its lowest point in more than a year. Membership figures for constituent unions, however, remained more or less stable. Competent observers estimated that the total labor movement in Los Angeles city and county, including the AFL, the CIO, and the railroad brotherhoods, comprised approximately 150,000 workers.[19]

In December, 1937, members of Labor's Committee on Organizing Los Angeles and Orange Counties started a new campaign specifically directed against open-shop front organizations that had been formed in 1937 and were expected to increase in number and strength the following year. Although the $75,000 needed to finance the drive was not obtained, enough money was raised to permit the establishment of a public relations office under the supervision of Fred L. Carver. A former newspaper man, Carver had been associated with Mayor Shaw's campaign for reëlection in 1937. He devoted most of his efforts to a half-hour radio broadcast called the "Voice of American Labor." The program, which was started over KFWB on February 14, was presented thrice weekly for thirteen weeks, terminating in May at the request of the station's management, which explained that criticisms of "unfair" firms and products by labor leaders were embarrassing to it. Labor

Council officials, however, believed that the cancellation was requested by open-shop supporters. Labor also sponsored a series of semiweekly broadcasts in opposition to radio programs conducted by an open-shop group known as "The Neutral Thousands." But after seven weeks labor's broadcasts were terminated and the public relations office was closed, largely because of a shortage of funds.[20]

The intensity and the success of the 1937 organizing campaigns started by the AFL and CIO groups in the city may be judged by the responses elicited from open-shop spokesmen. Byron C. Hanna, president of the Los Angeles Chamber of Commerce, later stated: "The year 1937 had witnessed an intense campaign to subject employers, employees, and business in Los Angeles to the domination of labor union bosses, some of whom have conducted their operations with well defined racketeering policies." [21] Labor leaders, believing that organizing opportunities were better than at any time since 1910, predicted that the workers in Los Angeles would be completely unionized by the first months of 1938. Although the prediction was not fulfilled, the force of the 1937 campaigns drove supporters of the open shop into redoubled efforts to oppose unionists, who were attempting to establish closed or union shops in nearly all industries.

M and M officials continued to organize employers into industrial or trade groups, establishing a labor relations committee within each such body. They also adopted new tactics in their fight to maintain open shops. For example, they urged employers to revise wage scales for whole industries wherever practical, and to seek out the weak points in relations with employees which might encourage labor organizers. In addition, the Labor Placement Bureau of the M and M was given increased financial support. Although association officials denied any discrimination against unionists in placing men through the bureau in 1937, the facts are that strikebreakers were hired and that preference was given to unorganized workers. Liaison also was maintained by M and M officials with Chamber of Commerce representatives, though the chamber itself did not actively participate in the campaign. Labor claimed that open-shop advocates even attempted to influence bank officers to refuse loans to employers who had agreed to recognize outside unions as collective bargaining agents for their employees.[22]

As the battle approached its climax in 1937 and 1938, another new employer technique—that of organizing allegedly independent groups to oppose labor unions—came to the fore. One of the earliest of such groups, The Neutral Thousands, was formed in September, 1937. Its leaders claimed that the organization was a voluntary association of housewives who had adopted the slogan "Truth Not Terror" in countering union racketeering which raised prices to consumers. Officials of the M and M and the Chamber of Commerce actually originated The Neutral Thousands, in the belief that an apparently neutral women's organization could aid in creating a public opinion favorable to their cause. Prominent open-shop supporters led by Hanna hired Mrs. Bessie Ochs to head the group, which became known as "TNT." Mrs. Ochs had been lecturing to women's groups under the auspices of the M and M for several months before her appointment, describing how labor racketeers and the activities of unionists in retail and wholesale food concerns allegedly increased the prices of necessities. An importer by occupation and a capable administrator, Mrs. Ochs soon established a publicity campaign directed against union organizing. She publicly declared that she had become interested in workers and unions because of the pitiful appeal of a striker's wife whose husband had been victimized by labor racketeers and was consequently in financial distress.[23]

Shortly after it was organized, TNT claimed a membership of thousands of women. Testimony taken several years later at the La Follette Committee hearings, however, revealed that membership figures were falsified. Of the 109,075 names and addresses listed, only a few hundred were actually obtained from the persons concerned; the rest were copied from direct-mail catalogues, telephone directories, and records that Mrs. Ochs had in her possession from previous business connections. TNT, therefore, seemed to be neither neutral nor thousands. Instead, it was formed to support the open-shop campaign by arousing public opinion against CIO and AFL activities. For example, in the fall of 1937 Mrs. Ochs and her husband conducted a series of weekly radio dramas designed to reveal the adverse economic effects of labor unions on workers and their families. TNT also tried to establish independent unions in various firms in opposition to organizations affiliated with the AFL or the CIO, particularly in 1938.[24]

Of special interest to labor groups was the source of financial support for TNT. Mrs. Ochs publicly stated that it came from voluntary subscriptions. To some extent this was true, as the founding fund of $10,600 was set up through voluntary gifts of Chamber of Commerce members. Later investigations revealed, however, that 88.2 per cent of the total income of the organization, from its inception to its disbandment in 1939, was received from officials of Southern Californians,

Incorporated (SCI), another open-shop group. Only 0.2 per cent of the revenue of TNT came from membership dues. Members of SCI cooperated closely with TNT officers by assisting them in establishing their budget and by providing a liaison representative, J. L. Van Norman.[25]

Southern Californians, Incorporated, had been conceived in May, 1936, when discussions were under way at the Los Angeles Chamber of Commerce regarding the establishment of a general fund to be used to maintain the open shop. The fund was not to be connected directly with any existing organization such as the M and M. Action was not taken to establish such a fund, however, until 1937, when labor's organizing campaigns became a serious threat. A series of meetings held under the auspices of the M and M and the Chamber of Commerce in the early fall of 1937 led to the formation of Southern Californians, Incorporated, with Hanna as chairman. The new organization was to serve as a coördinating agency for all groups dedicated to maintaining the open shop or "industrial freedom," as the *Times* defined it. These groups included TNT, the M and M, the Chamber of Commerce, and various trade or industrial organizations.[26]

Southern Californians, Incorporated, was introduced to the public at a rally held at the Biltmore Hotel on December 13, 1937. Hanna outlined the general purposes of the organization, but declared that the strategy to accomplish them would remain a secret. Labor leaders rightly considered the meeting as part of the open-shop campaign, although Hanna claimed that the members of SCI were not against "legitimate" unions.

Although the 1937 AFL and CIO organizing campaigns had come to a standstill by this time, Labor Council officers were planning renewed efforts. The council and Labor's Committee on Organizing Los Angeles and Orange Counties decided to launch a new drive at a meeting at the Biltmore Hotel on December 23, only ten days after the one held by Southern Californians, Incorporated. About 1,300 persons, including labor union and business firm representatives, and, oddly enough, members of the M and M, the Chamber of Commerce, and SCI, attended the labor meeting. Local AFL officials spoke to the assemblage. Secretary Buzzell, in the main address, outlined a plan for the peaceful settlement of labor disputes, but no action was taken on his proposal. Radio stations KHJ and KFI refused to grant time for Buzzell's address. Open-shop supporters were accused of influencing the stations' managements, and a protest was later filed with the Federal Communications Commission, but to no avail.[27]

Both labor and management thus entered 1938 with the conviction that a showdown over the open shop was imminent. Editorials in the *Times* made it clear that open-shop advocates regarded the situation as serious. "Not since the Times Building was dynamited by the closed shop union terrorists twenty-eight years ago and twenty-one employees murdered, have the people of Southern California been in such danger as confronts them now." [28]

Southern Californians, Incorporated, led the fight to maintain the open shop in 1938. It sponsored an extensive public relations program and conducted research intended to demonstrate the superiority of an open over a closed shop. It gave moral and financial support to the M and M, TNT, Associated Farmers, Farmers' Transportation Association, and Women of the Pacific. The organization of the last group, headed by Mrs. Edwin Selvin, was announced to the public in February, 1938. Mrs. Selvin, who had previously been considered for the chairmanship of The Neutral Thousands, hailed from Seattle, where she had organized Women of Washington during a strike against the *Post-Intelligencer*.[29]

Labor leaders were well aware of the purposes of Southern Californians, Incorporated, when it was established, and their awareness became more acute in 1938. Although SCI did not enter directly into the collective bargaining process, its officials tried to dissuade business executives from signing closed-shop contracts. Occasionally it used economic pressure to accomplish its aims. The affiliation of many SCI members with the M and M indicated the close liaison between the two groups. Dual memberships were encouraged through a reciprocal arrangement for paying dues to the two organizations. Professional men and private individuals could also join SCI. The dues paid by commercial and manufacturing enterprises to SCI were 50 cents a month per employee. Individuals became members by paying an initiation fee of $100; they were not charged dues. By March, 1938, the membership consisted of 320 firms employing 43,703 workers, as well as 89 individuals.[30]

Announcement of the formation of Women of the Pacific, with the unannounced support of Southern Californians, Incorporated, was preceded by a publicity campaign in the *Times* under the title "Industrial Freedom—or Slavery." Mrs. Selvin stated that Women of the Pacific was a housewives' group opposed to trade monopolies and labor rackets, both of which raised the prices of consumer goods. But in publicity issued by Women of the Pacific, most of the monopolies remained anonymous, whereas unions, labor leaders, strikes, organiz-

ing campaigns, and union labels were usually identified. The organization's members allegedly patronized firms whose managements were
experiencing difficulties with union organizers and leaders. But, for
the most part, Mrs. Selvin concentrated on issuing antiunion letters
to the membership, publishing newspaper stories favoring the open
shop, and addressing women's clubs.[31]

The inauguration, in what proved to be the only meeting, of Women
of the Pacific took place on February 28, 1938, at the Shrine Auditorium. It was planned to counteract the efforts of the teamsters to
win a new contract in the milk distribution industry, and the speakers
charged that union racketeers were threatening the milk supply of
the city. The 3,000 women present passed resolutions opposing the
closed or union shop. Labor leaders immediately labeled the group as
antiunion, and Buzzell characterized Mrs. Selvin as "a very sweet,
grandmotherly lady . . . self-appointed president of a mythical organization." [32]

In the following months Women of the Pacific established chapters
in various cities in Los Angeles and Orange counties. One of its major
projects was a petition for a state-wide initiative requiring the incorporation of labor unions and circumscribing the official activities of
their memberships. It chose Flag Day, June 14, as the date on which
186,378 signatures of registered voters were to be obtained in order to
put the proposition on the November ballot. But the one-day campaign for signatures failed. Despite an extension of time for signing
the petitions and urgent *Times* editorials requesting support, the proposal had to be abandoned. It was opposed by labor leaders and was
not supported by officials of TNT and Southern Californians, Incorporated, because they felt it was too extreme.

The *Times* remained the most important publicity medium of
Women of the Pacific throughout 1938. It published editorials urging
financial support as well as increased membership, and undoubtedly
helped to keep funds coming in, in small amounts, from numerous
firms as well as from individuals.[33]

3. THE GAME IS ON

The advent of open-shop organizations soon made it clear that the
battle between unionists and advocates of "industrial freedom" would
reach its climax in 1938. The number of lawsuits in which unions were
defendants began increasing even as early as 1937. In January, California State Federation of Labor officials granted the Los Angeles Central Labor Council the first of a series of $500 monthly stipends to be

used to defray the expenses of court cases. The council previously had retained the law firm of Rosecrans and Emme for $250 a month. Daily fees and court costs were met by the particular unions involved in the litigation. Most of the cases resulted from the issuance of restraining orders against unionists engaged in the intensive organizing campaigns of the period. The increasing number of injunctions and restraining orders in 1937 and 1938 caused the council to cease publishing the names of boycotted firms or products in the *Citizen*. Such publicity gave employers advance notice of boycott and strike proceedings, and enabled them to make preparations to thwart the unionists. Frequently an employer requested an injunction as soon as a boycott or a strike began. Although the injunctions often were not granted, the legal expenses and court costs of opposing the suits were extremely burdensome.[34]

The severity of the injunctions led to the formation, in October, 1937, of a legislative committee by the Los Angeles Industrial Union Council, CIO. The new committee immediately coöperated with Labor Council officials in asking for the removal of Superior Court Judge Emmet H. Wilson. Judge Wilson, presiding over Department 34 of the court, heard preliminary actions involving injunctions and writs of mandate. Labor leaders called him an "injunction judge," declaring that he issued too many unjustified temporary restraining orders against picketing. They arranged a meeting with Presiding Judge Fletcher Bowron of the Superior Court to make formal accusations against Judge Wilson. Called into the conference, Wilson denied any prejudice or discrimination in cases coming under his jurisdiction, and Bowron upheld him. Shortly thereafter, the new presiding judge for 1938, Reuben S. Schmidt, reappointed Wilson to his duties for the following year.[35]

The labor movement won a legal round in 1938 when a number of *Times* executives were cited by Judge Schmidt for contempt of court. Representatives of the Los Angeles Bar Association initiated charges in an affidavit claiming that five editorials in 1937 and 1938 were designed to influence court proceedings in labor cases. The editorial writers had commented on trials involving a number of sit-down strikers at the Douglas Aircraft Company, several members of the teamsters' union who were charged with assault, and three other cases. According to defense lawyers, the contempt action abridged freedom of the press. A. L. Wirin, an attorney for the Los Angeles Industrial Union Council and a representative of the American Civil Liberties Union, appeared for the defendants as a friend of the court. The judge sustained the charges, however, and fined several officials of the newspaper, including its publisher, Harry Chandler.[36]

The most severe opposition faced by local labor leaders in 1938 came from the open-shop groups already described. The M and M continued to be the principal antagonist, closely followed by Southern Californians, Incorporated. M and M officers consistently objected to the lack of responsible leadership in labor unions and to the large number of labor rackets that were allegedly springing up. They pointed out that less than 5 per cent of the labor disputes in 1937 were caused by demands for wage and hour changes, and that only 4 per cent were jurisdictional strikes. Nearly 92 per cent of the disputes were allegedly initiated by demands for a closed shop and/or union recognition.[37]

The Neutral Thousands, in close coöperation with Southern Californians, Incorporated, and other open-shop groups such as the Associated Farmers, reached the peak of its antiunion activity in 1938. One of the major undertakings was issuance of a mimeographed newspaper called *Memo-News,* published every seven to ten days. TNT also sponsored two radio series, the second of which dramatized incidents in the history of the state under the title of "California Caravan." The programs depicted labor unions as being against the best interests of the workers. Local labor leaders, immediately complaining to the Federal Communications Commission that the presentations were biased, brought about discontinuation of one of the programs. After this TNT was less direct in its radio attacks on organized labor.

Perhaps the most damaging TNT activity was the support it gave to the company-union movement. TNT representatives organized a large number of independent groups in late 1937 and 1938 in opposition to AFL or CIO locals. Mrs. Ochs's effective interest in independent unions seems to have dated from her employment of G. L. Huff and Clay C. Rittenhouse, two experienced leaders of the Firestone Independent Rubber Workers Union, in the fall of 1937. Both men became TNT organizers of unaffiliated unions. Many of these company unions were formed in firms that were represented in the M and M and/or Southern Californians, Incorporated, but most of them existed for only a short time. TNT officials claimed they resolved numerous labor disputes in this manner.[38]

As early as August, 1937, before their employment by TNT, Rittenhouse and Huff had helped to establish an organization called the League of Independent Unions. Though it was declared to be a completely independent labor organization, M and M officials gave advice and encouragement to league leaders in the first few months of its existence. When Huff and Rittenhouse accepted employment with TNT, they resigned from the league. Later the league was reorganized, and on February 11 and 12, 1938, it held a state convention at the Hayward Hotel in Los Angeles. Delegates came from more than 400 independent unions; Michael B. Fanning, editor and publisher of the *Independent Union News,* was chairman. Although the delegates insisted that the league was completely separate from the AFL, the CIO, and all employer organizations, they promoted a reciprocal arrangement with TNT in order to prevent jurisdictional disputes between independent unions. The league was disbanded a few months later, but many of its affiliated units survived its demise.

Throughout 1938 TNT representatives continued to organize what local CIO leaders called "termite unions." Southern Californians, Incorporated, was outspoken against this activity because it did not want to encourage unions of any type, but its opposition did not deter TNT officials.[39]

Much of the antiunion effort of Southern Californians, Incorporated, in 1938 was directed toward promotion of a proposed municipal law to regulate picketing. In recent years several communities near Los Angeles had passed restrictive picketing laws, but a coördinated campaign for a more rigid ordinance within the city did not develop until SCI was established. An ordinance regulating picketing had been placed on the books in 1936:

Sec. 41.23 Picketing

No person shall, in or upon any public street or sidewalk, make any loud or unusual noise, speak in a loud or unusual tone, or cry out or proclaim, for the purpose of inducing or influencing any person to refrain from entering any works, factory or place of business or employment; or from purchasing or using any goods, wares, merchandise or other article; or from doing or performing any service or labor in any works, factory or place of business or employment; or for the purpose of intimidating, threatening or coercing any person who is performing, seeking, or obtaining service or labor in any works, factory, place of business or employment.[40]

SCI officials, considering this law not restrictive enough, requested the City Council to pass new legislation, and on December 6, 1937, the council asked City Attorney Ray Chesebro to prepare an amendment to the municipal code. The first hearings on the draft of the new measure were held on December 8. Labor leaders opposed it, as expected, claiming that the existing legislation was entirely adequate to prevent strike disturbances. But open-shop forces were determined to stop organizing campaigns led by men like Harry Bridges on the water front and Dave Beck and others at inland points. After hearing testimony from both sides, the City Council passed the proposed ordinance on December 29 by a nine-to-six vote and sent it to Mayor Shaw.[41] Its more important provisions were as follows:

Only bona fide employees of a firm may picket that firm, and then only if a bona fide dispute exists, relating to wages, hours of work or other working conditions, in the business, or if as a result of such dispute a bona fide strike shall exist on the part of such employees.

Such pickets may not, by either voice or banner, attempt to persuade anyone from entering a place of business, from working there or seeking work, or from buying or selling at the establishment. The measure likewise prohibits intimidation, threats or coercion by pickets.

Banners carried by pickets may not exceed a size of 24 by 36 inches, and may carry only the announcement that a strike is in progress, the reasons therefor, and that the place of business of the employer is being picketed.[42]

In the days immediately after passage of the ordinance, Mayor Shaw received advice from the city attorney, AFL and CIO officials, the M and M, the Super Market Association, Southern Californians, Incorporated, and others. Even a group of Methodist ministers protested the ordinance, claiming that it would prevent peaceful picketing. On January 7, after due deliberation, the mayor vetoed the measure and returned it to the City Council. In his veto message he took the position, contrary to the opinion of City Attorney Chesebro, that the law was not enforceable, and that it was an unconstitutional compromise which evaded the fundamental issues. He stated that it would not eliminate any evils that might develop from the activities of labor organizers and, in addition, would work a serious injustice to employees. The mayor was ready, however, to approve an ordinance that would stop mass and professional picketing, labor racketeers, and gangsters. The City Council sustained the mayor's veto, but several of its members attacked his position on the matter.[43]

Meanwhile, SCI initiated a survey to ascertain public reaction to the proposed regulation of picketing. Central Labor Council leaders, well aware of the implications of the poll, warned unionists against giving a favorable answer to any question that might point toward restrictive legislation. At the conclusion of the survey, President Hanna of SCI announced that nearly 55 per cent of the city's registered voters apparently would support an ordinance prohibiting all picketing. In April, therefore, SCI circulated petitions requesting a special municipal election to pass such a law. Again, AFL and CIO leaders warned all unionists against signing the petitions. In addition, Labor Council officials drafted a counterproposal copied from the Norris-LaGuardia Act, and circulated petitions embodying this proposal in an effort to present a less stringent alternative and to confuse the voters.[44]

All the petitions were filed in June. Supplementary signatures had to be obtained by labor officials when a check of their petitions revealed a shortage of some 13,000 names. Intense campaigns for and against both proposals were conducted during the summer up to the day of the election, September 16. SCI labeled the AFL measure a sham that would not change the existing municipal ordinance, whereas union leaders believed the open-shop version was designed to eliminate all picketing and diminish the strength of the labor movement in the city. Both sides campaigned on the radio for their respective proposals. SCI and The Neutral Thousands, backed by trade associations, bought newspaper space for quarter- and half-page advertisements, and the larger dailies supported the stringent measure in their editorial columns. Organized labor lacked the financial resources for this kind of publicity, but its members carried placards in the Labor Day parade in favor of the counterproposal and mailed thousands of letters to union sympathizers.

The election was complicated by the fact that Mayor Shaw was up for recall on the same ballot. Local AFL leaders interpreted the recall as an attack on the labor movement because of the mayor's veto of the picketing ordinance the preceding January. Although the mayor did not express his views concerning either of the new proposals, the Joint Executive Board of Organized Labor in Los Angeles, AFL, recommended his retention in office. Judge Fletcher Bowron, Shaw's opponent, opposed the proposal sponsored by Southern Californians, Incorporated, and supported the Labor Council measure. He was backed by the CIO for this stand. Most of his support, however, came from a citizens' group known as the Federation for Civic Betterment headed by Clifford E. Clinton, a local cafeteria owner.[45]

At the September election, the open-shop measure was passed by a vote of 198,507 to 152,065, and Judge Bowron was elected mayor. Although he did not approve of the new ordinance, he agreed to enforce it. Southern Californians, Incorporated, had spent $45,646.75 in its campaign to secure passage of the law. In the months that followed, the organization endeavored to protect its investment in connection with test court cases that were instituted by labor leaders. Groups such as Labor's Non-Partisan League, the Municipal League, the Screen Actors Guild, the Lawyers Guild, the American League for Peace and Democracy, and the Progressive Forum coöperated with local AFL and

CIO leaders in opposing the ordinance. Although convictions resulted from several of the cases, the law's constitutionality was not tested until 1939. The success of the ordinance was lauded by SCI leaders, who pointed out that the number of labor disputes in late 1938 and early 1939 dropped by 65.9 per cent.[46]

The effort to control labor organizations and union picketing in 1938 was not confined to the Los Angeles area. The primary purpose of the state-wide Proposition No. 1 was to control picketing, boycotts, and other activities of unionists in California. Maximum penalties for its violation were two years' imprisonment and a $5,000 fine. The planning for such a law seems to have originated in March, 1938, in an exchange of correspondence among officials of several employer groups, including Southern Californians, Incorporated, the Associated Farmers, and the Industrial Association of San Francisco. Most of these groups had previously considered such legislation. Now they formed a coördinating body known as the California Committee for Peace in Employment Relations, headed by State Senator Sanborn Young and composed of prominent industrialists and representatives of employer groups, trade associations, and women's clubs. This committee drew up Proposition No. 1, obtained enough signatures to qualify the measure for the ballot, and launched a campaign to secure its passage at the election on November 8, 1938. The law did not provide for the incorporation of unions and was less restrictive of union activities than the unsuccessful proposal sponsored by Women of the Pacific in June of the same year. Thus it seemed to have a good chance of passing.[47]

The sponsors of Proposition No. 1 planned to use most publicity media in the campaign, yet prevent an overemphasis on the proposal. Advertisements were placed in most of the California newspapers published in large population centers. The *Times* ran editorials stressing the need for its passage. The proposition was also publicized by radio. Organizations such as the California Farm Bureau Federation, the California State Chamber of Commerce, Allied Food Industries, Associated Farmers, the Industrial Association of San Francisco, Women of the Pacific, Southern Californians, Incorporated, the Los Angeles Chamber of Commerce, and The Neutral Thousands disseminated information in its favor. TNT officials endeavored to organize county councils and city committees in support of the measure, as well as to secure the backing of leaders and members of independent unions. SCI was given over-all responsibility for the campaign in the southern part of the state, where it made an unsuccessful effort to obtain the endorsement of the Los Angeles City Council.

On the other side, AFL and CIO leaders throughout the state united to oppose Proposition No. 1. They urged union members not to sign the petitions to put the measure on the ballot, and officials of the State Federation of Labor tried, without success, to have it outlawed through legal action. When the proposal finally qualified for the ballot, the opposition intensified its campaign.[48]

The CSFL, backed by the AFL Executive Council, formed a state-wide committee to work against the proposal, and officials of the AFL Political League of California made its defeat their major objective at the November election. It was at this time that the CSFL arranged a political alliance with promoters of the Retirement Life Payments Act, under which labor agreed to support the pension proposal if its advocates would vote against Proposition No. 1. This alliance seemed realistic because the opponents of the pension plan were the same persons who favored the state-wide initiative.

In Los Angeles the Central Labor Council coördinated the campaign against the proposition. Paul Scharrenberg, legislative representative for the AFL, came from Washington, D.C., to represent the Executive Council in the city and to assist in defeating the proposal. The local council, however, actually planned the drive and established committees to organize and conduct it.[49]

The campaign intensified during the month before the election. The *Citizen* and the *Industrial Unionist* devoted many pages to publicity against the proposed law. Labor leaders made radio addresses warning against the proposal's implications. Unionists carried banners on their cars stating "Vote No on Proposition No. 1." Musicians Local No. 47, ITU Local No. 174, the Los Angeles County District Council of Carpenters, the Los Angeles Building and Construction Trades Council, and other AFL organizations gave moral and financial support. Labor's Non-Partisan League set up a coördinating committee composed of leaders of various unions affiliated with the CIO and the AFL, as well as representatives from different political organizations, which campaigned against the proposition. In October representatives of more than eighty Los Angeles fraternal, civic, religious, and political bodies established the California Committee Against Initiative No. 1. Believing that the loose phrasing of the initiative posed a threat in the form of restrictions that could be placed on their activities, members offered their services to any group desiring speakers or writers to work against the proposed legislation. Mayor Bowron and the Federation for Civic Betterment opposed Proposition No. 1, as did Culbert L. Olson, the Democratic candidate for governor.[50]

This proposition, as well as the "Ham and Eggs" measure, was defeated at the election on November 8. AFL and CIO leaders heralded the defeat of Proposition No. 1 as a setback for an alleged trend toward economic dictatorship in California. The *Industrial Unionist* stated, for example, that the election of Olson as governor and the rejection of the initiative climaxed a revolt against the open shop which had begun in 1934. Los Angeles CIO officials were convinced that the California labor movement, particularly in Los Angeles, was about to begin a period of unprecedented expansion. Although labor leaders claimed that AFL-CIO unity was responsible for the defeat of Proposition No. 1, investigation revealed that more than 70 per cent of the members of some unions had not voted. The obvious conclusion, therefore, was that the measure might have passed had it not been for the coalition among promoters of the Retirement Life Payments Act, organized labor, and liberal political groups. The campaign conducted by Los Angeles AFL officials against Proposition No. 1 cost $29,782.98, but union leaders did not begrudge the expenditure. Feeling that the defeat would prevent further attempts to curtail union activities in 1938 or 1939, they began to institute court cases to test the constitutionality of the new ordinance regulating picketing in the city.[51]

Laws to regulate picketing and control labor unions were not the only evidences of the intensity of the open-shop struggle in the political arena. Nearly all political activities in Los Angeles in 1937 and 1938 were inextricably bound up with the last-ditch effort to maintain "industrial freedom." For example, in 1937 the Central Labor Council had contributed funds toward the maintenance of the Joint Labor Legislative Headquarters, which was basically a lobby against open-shop employers at the state capitol in Sacramento. Further, as was the custom, an annual dinner was given for members of the California Legislature from Los Angeles. At this dinner the Los Angeles legislators were apprised of the political aims of the AFL in the city and of the seriousness of the open-shop conflict.

Early in 1937 delegates from the San Pedro and Wilmington Central Labor Council were admitted to membership on the Joint Executive Board of the Organized Labor Movement of Los Angeles and Vicinity, AFL, in order to provide for a more unified front, particularly on political issues. The board also supported candidates who would be prolabor and anti–open shop. This was accomplished through close liaison with the representatives of such political groups as Labor's Non-Partisan League, California Progressives, the California Continuation Committee for United Political Action, the Municipal League, the End Poverty League, the Public Ownership League of Southern California, and United Organizations for Progressive Political Action.[52]

The Joint Executive Board endorsed candidates for the city primary election of April 6, 1937, and urged unionists to vote. Although it did not make a recommendation for mayor, it supported candidates for the Board of Education, the City Council, and the Superior Court. It also made suggestions with reference to several amendments to the city charter and the offices of city attorney and comptroller. The same procedure was followed with respect to the general election of May 4. Labor leaders were pleased when the final ballot results revealed that John F. Dalton, president of ITU Local No. 174, was reëlected as a member of the Los Angeles Board of Education in spite of intense opposition from open-shop supporters. But a labor-supported initiative ordinance providing for the establishment of a municipal bus line failed to pass. This defeat was offset when Adolph W. Hoch, a member of Machinists Local No. 311, was selected as chairman of the Board of Public Works. Mayor Shaw's victory in this 1937 election was not universally acclaimed by labor leaders, even though he had shown a sympathetic viewpoint toward unions at various times. His reëlection meant the retention of Chief of Police James Davis and Captain William F. Hynes, neither of whom had the reputation of being friendly to organized labor.[53]

Later in the year District Attorney Buron Fitts came under labor's fire in connection with so-called "racketeering" charges. Labor had supported Fitts in his successful 1936 campaign for reëlection. On December 19, 1937, however, in an address over radio station KFWB, he pledged that he would rid the city of racketeers. Fitts was not opposed to organizations of workers, but he wanted to eliminate the illegal methods used by some union leaders in the past year to gain control of the Los Angeles labor movement.

In reality, Fitts was only responding to repeated requests for such a campaign. Earlier in December the *Times* had publicized the attempts of Eastern racketeers to establish a business "protective association." On December 6 Councilman Franklin P. Buyer, representing the harbor district, had charged in a City Council meeting that business protection fees in the San Pedro area were being increased. The council shortly thereafter adopted a resolution to investigate conditions in Seattle, where Dave Beck of the teamsters' union was active in city politics. Beck was believed to be behind the racketeers at San Pedro, although Secretary Buzzell of the Central Labor Council, appearing before the City Council on December 9, had denied the presence of racketeers in AFL unions in Los Angeles; any local labor official engaged in such illegal activities would be removed. These statements were reiterated by attorney A. L. Wirin, speaking as a representative of the Los Angeles Industrial Union Council, CIO.

In succeeding weeks members of political, church, and social groups joined the campaign against racketeers, and many of them also denounced the closed shop. The official formation of a city labor-racket squad on December 22 caused union leaders to believe that Fitts very definitely was a supporter of the open shop. His further actions in 1938 and 1939 brought him under the concerted attack of both AFL and CIO leaders, who accused him of allying himself with open-shop groups, attempting to make felonies from misdemeanors by strikers in order to obtain more severe penalties, causing unionists to incur additional legal expenses, and encouraging antiunion publicity. In October, 1939, the delegates to the state CIO convention initiated action intended to remove Fitts from office, but it was not consummated.[54]

Although Fitts retained his office during the intense open-shop fight in the late 1930's, the election of Bowron and the defeat of Shaw in September, 1938, were interpreted by local CIO leaders as a compensating victory. They hoped that Bowron would abolish the Intelligence Bureau of the Police Department under Captain Hynes's leadership. Their hope was borne out when Mayor Bowron, as one of his first official acts, eliminated the bureau, removed Chief of Police Davis, and campaigned to wipe out graft in the Police Department.[55]

The change in personnel of the city's administration was symbolic of the shift in the fortunes of organized labor in Los Angeles. The formation of open-shop groups such as Southern Californians, Incorporated, and The Neutral Thousands represented a major effort to offset the advantages accruing to organized labor from favorable federal legislation and the increased industrialization of Los Angeles. These factors had enabled unions to make headway with local workers despite the long-standing tradition of "industrial freedom." When the La Follette Committee of the United States Senate agreed to investigate open-shop groups in the city, new hope sprang up among Los Angeles unionists that the grip of the open shop, now nearly fifty years old, was at last slipping. The committee arrived in Los Angeles in November, 1938, and conducted a brief investigation. In 1939, after a lengthy recess, the hearings were resumed.

As 1938 drew to a close, AFL and CIO leaders alike ventured the statement that the future of the labor movement in the city seemed to be the brightest in its history. Similar comments were made at a conference of AFL leaders in southern California and by Secretary Buzzell of the Labor Council in his annual report. These predictions were possible partly because of the victories won by the city's unions against open-shop firms in the preceding two years, but these victories were achieved under the shadow of internal dissension.[56]

XIII. SKIRMISHES ON THE
LOCAL UNION FRONT, 1937–1938

1. BROTHER AGAINST BROTHER

THE STRUGGLE against the open shop in 1937 and 1938 was handicapped by intermittent fighting within organized labor's own ranks. The withdrawal of CIO-oriented unions from the Central Labor Council on May 14, 1937, led to a spate of jurisdictional disputes which worked against the over-all effort to unionize the city. Beatings and other forms of violence frequently marked the fraternal warfare between rival CIO and AFL unionists. Local CIO leaders accused police officers of not interfering when AFL members were winning such disputes, though this charge was denied officially by the mayor and remained unproved. In August, 1937, as one outcome of these conflicts, the Los Angeles Industrial Union Council resolved:

That this Council go on record urging all affiliated unions to carry out the principles of true industrial organization and open their membership to take in truck drivers, and others engaged in the transportation division of their industry, who are clamoring for admittance into the organizations affiliated with the CIO whether such workers now be affiliated with a craft union or are as yet unorganized.[1]

The resolution did nothing to improve relations between the two rival groups. The fratricidal warfare even carried over into the Labor Day celebration. Labor Council officials obtained a city parade permit, thus effectively excluding unions affiliated with the CIO council. The parade was composed of 50,000 AFL unionists and their families, led by Mayor Shaw and other city officials. It went off without a hitch except at the start when a float sponsored by Musicians Local No. 47 would not operate because someone had poured paint into the crankcase. Who had done it? The CIO? Many had suspicions, but no one was sure.[2]

The state-wide AFL-CIO struggle eventually spread to Labor's Non-Partisan League, which had the unqualified support of the Los Angeles Industrial Union Council. A split occurred locally early in December, 1937, when Secretary Buzzell of the Central Labor Council ordered local affiliates to disassociate themselves from the CIO-dominated organization, saying that through it "Lewis and his Communist satellites and allies hope to wriggle their way" into AFL unions.[3] But many officers and members of AFL unions in Los Angeles ignored the in-

[442]

structions. They continued their associations with the league, and sent representatives to its first convention later in the month.[4]

Early in 1938 the league established suborganizations in the assembly districts throughout the city. Many of the members were still from AFL unions despite Buzzell's edict of the previous year. On March 27 and 28, at a mass meeting in Trinity Auditorium, it adopted a political platform. Meanwhile, the league's opposition received support from Dr. John P. Lechner, Americanism chairman of the American Legion County Council. Lechner echoed the charge made by numerous AFL leaders that the league was a Communist-dominated organization. After this the Board of Education prohibited the league from using public school auditoriums for its meetings. Many local residents protested the board's action, but to no avail.[5]

Although the Industrial Union Council was politically unified in its support of Labor's Non-Partisan League, its organizing efforts were hampered by internal troubles. Some of these stemmed from the presence of a Communist faction within its ranks. Members of this group often interrupted the regular council meetings by presenting speakers on national or world affairs. The council's unfair list reflected the delegates' concern over world problems rather than over their own organizing difficulties; for instance, they declared boycotts against all goods manufactured in Germany, Italy, and Japan. At times the very existence of the council seemed imperiled, as the unemployment incident to the 1937–1938 recession took its toll among the members of constituent unions and provided fertile ground for further Communist infiltration. Labor Unions Unemployment Council, a relief office, was organized to help members get aid from the State Relief Administration, but it did little to alleviate the problem of Communist influence or the misery caused by lack of jobs.[6]

In February, 1938, L. H. Michener was elected president of the CIO council, and C. H. Jordan was retained as secretary. Jordan provided temporary leadership stability at a time when the council was sorely pressed, but he resigned the following July to resume a position in the American Communications Association. The weekly *Industrial Unionist*, launched in September, 1937, with $500 in loans and block subscriptions from members of the larger CIO unions, had to be cut from eight to four pages in April, 1938, because of a lack of funds. It continued in financial straits the remainder of the year despite a campaign to widen its circulation. Occasionally an issue failed to appear because of inability to meet expenses or internal conflicts over editorial policy.[7]

The controversy between Communist and anti-Communist factions in the Industrial Union Council came to a head in August, 1938, just before the first state-wide convention of the California CIO, when delegates from the International Ladies' Garment Workers, the United Automobile Workers, the United Rubber Workers, the United Shoe Workers, and several lodges of the Steel Workers Organizing Committee (SWOC), representing 20,000 unionists, left the council. Among their leaders were William Busick of the ILGWU, Richard Coleman of the UAW, and George B. Roberts of the URW. The basic cause of dissension was the 1937 appointment of Harry Bridges as west coast director of the CIO. Bridges had been labeled a Communist by the local press and was considered a liability to the CIO by Busick and his associates. They also accused Bridges of aiding Communists to control the Industrial Union Council by the votes of delegates from nonexistent or "paper" locals, and by appointing party members to executive positions in various unions without consulting their memberships. Moreover, the secessionists objected to devoting so many council meetings to discussions of foreign aid and reports from such organizations as the Abraham Lincoln Brigade in the Spanish Civil War, rather than to the immediate problem of organizing workers in Los Angeles.[8]

The secessionists published a six-point program, in which they made these accusations, and established a separate Los Angeles Trade Union Conference. Their purpose was to prevent Communist domination of the local industrial union movement, not to withdraw from the CIO. But Harry Bridges ignored the revolt and continued his plans for the state convention on August 20 and 21. Likewise, most local CIO unions maintained their delegations in the council. Noting Bridges' aloofness, the leaders of the seceding locals announced their refusal to send delegates to the convention, but when it actually began, only the ILGWU and the URW boycotted it. Ninety-one per cent of the unionists belonging to the SWOC in the city, more than half of the UAW members, and the larger of the two locals of the United Shoe Workers were represented. The revolt ended in the fall of 1938 when delegates to the council agreed to place less emphasis on international politics and more on local labor problems. The seceding unionists, believing their objectives accomplished, again sent representatives to council meetings.[9]

The struggle of brother against brother was seen again in the Labor Day parade of 1938. Although the parade was the largest in the history of the city, not one CIO unionist took part. An estimated 75,000 persons were in the line of march, including members of more than 200 unions and their auxiliaries. The internal struggle also interfered frequently with the activities of the Regional Labor Board, which by 1937 was the second largest branch of the NLRB. Its functioning was complicated when the 1937 State Federation of Labor convention in Long Beach expressed the belief that NLRB representatives in Los Angeles favored unions affiliated with the CIO. Towne Nylander and other local officials of the board consistently denied the charge, proclaiming their neutrality in all labor disputes, particularly in jurisdictional conflicts between AFL and CIO locals. The AFL-CIO dispute undoubtedly aided the growth of the independent union movement during these years through NLRB-supervised collective bargaining elections.[10]

2. ORGANIZING A NEW INDUSTRY

The controversies within the CIO and between AFL and CIO unions did not prevent some locals from making organizational gains. Southern Californians, Incorporated, gave a clue to the volume of organizing activity in Los Angeles in 1937 when the editor of a pamphlet SCI published in defense of civil liberties and civil rights pointed out that labor leaders were endeavoring to organize workers in fourteen different industries. Actually, disputes were occurring simultaneously in at least twelve large firms. The pamphlet emphasized the point by reproducing sixty-one headlines from local newspapers, each headline citing a specific act of violence in a labor dispute. The Intelligence Bureau of the Los Angeles Police Department investigated 188 labor disputes between July 1, 1937, and June 30, 1938, most of which took place in 1937. A *Times* article included an M and M estimate that there was a monthly average of fifteen labor disputes in Los Angeles County from January through September, 1937. The high month was July with twenty-three conflicts; not all, however, were actual strikes.[11]

A declining trend in the number of strikes appeared in the first six months of 1938, as Regional Labor Board member Nylander had predicted. The board partly contributed to the unions' gains by deciding most of the 1,115 cases it heard between its inception and March 1, 1938, in favor of employees and their unions. Evidence of union growth was seen in the developing inability of the Labor Temple to house the headquarters of AFL locals. A number of unions were forced to buy or lease property elsewhere. The reëlection of Harry Sherman and Buzzell in June, 1938, as president and secretary-treasurer, respectively, of the Labor Council was a recognition of the part their leadership had played in bringing about these membership gains. Sherman thus began his seventh year in office, and Buzzell, his fourteenth. In the same month Paul Shoup, vice-chairman of the board of directors of the Southern Pacific Railroad, was elected to replace Byron C. Hanna as head of Southern Californians, Incorporated. Labor leaders declared this change was necessitated by the lag in the campaign to maintain the open shop.[12]

Another side of the open-shop picture was revealed when officials of Southern Californians, Incorporated, used M and M statistics to show that in 1938 there were only forty-one strikes in Los Angeles County as compared with seventy-four in 1937. They attributed much of this decrease, not to organized labor's conquests, but to the agitation for and the passage of a picketing law on September 16, 1938. The economic loss, including wages, caused by strikes in 1938 was estimated at $20,-095,341, approximately 25 per cent of the estimated $84,843,000 lost the preceding year. These data did not include losses from maritime disputes. M and M officials further pointed out that 75 per cent of the strikes in 1938 were caused by closed-shop demands which employers refused to sanction.[13]

Regardless of the validity of claims made by each side concerning its success in the open-shop struggle, there was no doubt that union activity was expanding in 1937 and 1938. Even the Los Angeles Industrial Union Council, said to be in critical danger from Communism within its membership and in acute need of funds, started a new organizing campaign in February, 1938, in the midst of the recession. Eight hundred delegates met at the Odd Fellows Hall on February 22 and approved an educational program, a campaign for delinquent dues, continued support for the members of all unions involved in disputes with employers and AFL locals, and an expansion of the *Industrial Unionist*. The immediate aim was to consolidate the local CIO rather than to solicit new members. Shortly thereafter, Pat Commore, a SWOC organizer, initiated a "Dawn Patrol." Two mornings a week, from 100 to 200 unemployed CIO members stood outside the gates of plants where unorganized workers were reporting for work, passed out handbills publicizing union meetings, obtained signatures on petitions, and signed up new members. The Dawn Patrol functioned for several months until improved employment opportunities curtailed the number of jobless unionists willing to volunteer for such duty and finally forced its abandonment. The following September the CIO began a new organizing campaign. Its goal was to increase its membership in the city to well above 50,000. The drive was conducted by an advisory board composed of state officials of the CIO in southern California and Secretary Michener of the local council. The coincidental improvement in general economic conditions in the latter part of 1938 made the time quite favorable for such a campaign.[14]

The first impact of CIO organizing activities on a specific industry in southern California had been felt in February, 1937, by the Douglas Aircraft Company at Santa Monica. Before this time many of the workers had joined a company union. Others had affiliated with a local of the United Auto Workers, CIO. Officials of the Labor Council had approved an AFL organizing campaign at Douglas in January, 1937, which was conducted by members of the International Association of Machinists and the Pattern Makers League of North America. But very few workers belonged to either of these two outside unions. At this time the hourly pay at Douglas ranged from 40 cents to $1.10, with a thirty-day probationary wage of 35 cents for helpers.[15]

On February 22, 1937, representatives of Local No. 188 of the UAW petitioned the Regional Labor Board for an election to determine the proper collective bargaining agent for the workers at the Douglas plant. They claimed that 3,000 of the 5,600 workers in the factory were members of the local and alleged that the company had discriminated against several employees because of their union affiliation. The next day a group of workers led by William Busick, erstwhile organizer for the ILGWU, began a sit-down strike. About 400 employees remained in the plant, which was closed down immediately. Local CIO officials claimed that the strike was precipitated by the failure of management to negotiate with union officers. The strikers' major demands included a pay increase of 15 cents an hour, recognition of the union as collective bargaining agent for the workers, seniority rights, time and a half for overtime, and the reinstatement of several discharged unionists. Officials of the company union, the Douglas Employees Association, denounced the strike and claimed a majority of the workers belonged to their organization, while the company immediately sought a court order to oust the strikers. District Attorney Buron Fitts secured indictments against the strikers from the Los Angeles County Grand Jury, charging the men with felonious assault and conspiracy to trespass. After conferences among labor leaders, the Regional Labor Board, and members of the district attorney's staff, the strikers agreed to leave the plant on February 26, with the understanding that their grievances would be heard at once by the local representatives of the NLRB. When they left the plant, deputy sheriffs took them to the county jail, but all except twenty men placed on bail were released on their own recognizance.[16]

The Central Labor Council watched the strike because some AFL unionists worked at Douglas. On the day the sit-down ended, council delegates passed a resolution condemning the district attorney; but this action was reversed on receipt of a letter from Fitts explaining the indictments as a defense of the laws of private property. At a later meeting local CIO officials were condemned for calling an ill-timed, premature strike, and were denied financial support. Although CIO leaders did not respond to the criticism at this time, they made the same charge against Busick when he finally left the CIO two years later.[17]

The Douglas plant was reopened on February 29 and most of the employees returned to their jobs with a wage increase of 5 cents an hour. Although picket lines were maintained at the plant for several weeks, employees were not deterred from their work. On March 15 Local No. 188 terminated the strike. Picketing ceased, and 297 strikers were reëmployed after they had signed affidavits stating that they had not participated in acts of violence during the dispute.

Meanwhile, in the greatest mass arraignment in the history of Los Angeles County, 342 indicted sit-down strikers appeared in court on March 9 to enter pleas. A hearing before the Regional Labor Board also was started after UAW officials filed a complaint on February 29. The complaint contained a petition for designation of Local No. 188 as the collective bargaining agent for the employees of the company. It was contested by representatives of the Douglas Employees Association and the AFL unions of machinists and patternmakers. The petition was subsequently withdrawn, but the UAW filed a new complaint on April 13 accusing the company of intimidating and coercing its workers against joining the union, rejecting requests to employ about a hundred former strikers, and refusing to bargain collectively in good faith with representatives of Local No. 188.[18]

The first trial of 294 sit-down strikers—the others having been dismissed—began on May 11 and continued until August when a hung jury resulted in dismissal of the case. In the trial prosecution witnesses had charged that the strikers carried arms with intent to commit sabotage and that Communists were on the scene of the dispute. Union officers denied the accusations, declaring that the strike was planned by the participants, not outside labor leaders, and that the men were sincere, not malicious. They admitted, however, that the strike was premature and badly led. Estimates of the number of Douglas employees who were affiliated with labor organizations varied from a majority, as claimed by one local, to about fifty, as stated by Richard Coleman, organizer for the UAW.[19]

A new trial was begun in October. Less than two dozen of the defendants were present, the others having been released. Each of the defendants was maintained during the trial by the members of a different CIO local. As in the first trial, the prosecution tried to prove the strikers had entered the plant illegally with intent to commit violence and sabotage. The defense denied the charges, although it was admitted that several organizers had entered the plant without authorization. Finally, after one of the defendants had been dismissed, the case again was given to a jury which, after several days of deliberation, found the twenty-two strikers guilty. Superior Judge Thomas L. Ambrose denied defendants' motion for a new trial and passed sentence. Twelve men who had worked in the plant and participated in the sit-down were fined $100 each. The eight members of the strategy committee for the strike were individually fined $300. Andrew Schmoulder and William Busick, leaders of the strike, were each fined $600. The case was hailed as a decision against the legality of sit-down strikes, as the defendants were convicted solely of forcibly holding property.[20]

The hearing conducted by the Regional Labor Board proceeded concurrently with the trial. The important issue was whether or not the company could be compelled to rehire forty-five strikers who had allegedly participated in acts of violence. On the completion of testimony, the case was sent to the NLRB in Washington, D.C., and in 1938 the board decided against the management. Basically, the decision ordered Douglas to reinstate forty-five UAW members, eleven of whom had been convicted of forcibly entering the plant while the strike was going on. In addition, it ordered the management to disestablish a company union known as the Aircraft Workers Union, Inc. The decision was based on charges that the independent union was dominated by the management, the strike had been caused by unfair labor practices within the plant, and the dispute did not result in damage to the firm's property. The board declared that the discharge of the employees was, therefore, unjustifiable.[21]

The Aircraft Workers Union, Inc., allegedly represented 4,200 workers at the Santa Monica plant of the Douglas Aircraft Company. It became directly involved in the aftermath of the hearing in the latter part of April, 1938, when it was the subject of a new complaint made to the Regional Labor Board by officials of the International Association of Machinists. The IAM called it a company union. Donald Douglas refused to accept the NLRB decision. His attorneys were directed to petition the Ninth United States Circuit Court of Appeals at San Francisco to have the entire order set aside. He contended that the board had denied a fair hearing to the Douglas management and had rendered its decision without regard to the direct evidence and the testimony in the case. When the board withdrew the order on May 10, Douglas interpreted the action as evidence of its unwillingness to permit an impartial review by a court. Douglas then reversed his position, and petitioned unsuccessfully for a temporary restraining order to prevent the withdrawal.[22]

Board spokesmen stated that the withdrawal was in accord with its policy of reviewing "all cases in which a skeletonized procedure was adopted which might be subject to court attack."[23] On August 18 the board held another hearing in Washington, D.C., to which the interested parties sent representatives. It reissued its April order on December 8, but required the reinstatement of only thirty-two strikers. It also ordered back pay for thirteen others who had been reinstated earlier or had taken jobs elsewhere. Again the board ordered disestablishment of the company union, and requested the management to cease interfering with the attempts of UAW officials to organize the firm. Douglas petitioned the Circuit Court of Appeals for a modification of the award, but the court did not render a decision until September, 1939, at which time the matter was settled by stipulation. The management agreed to reinstate only one employee instead of thirty-two, and to pay a total of $650 in back wages to eleven other workers who had been rehired during the hearing. It also stated that it would stop discriminating against employees affiliated with the UAW. The company then posted notices that it no longer recognized the Aircraft Workers Union as the collective bargaining agent for its workers.[24]

On another front in 1937, local CIO officials failed in their attempts to organize the employees of Lockheed Aircraft Corporation in Burbank. UAW organizers called an assembly of employees, most of whom attended. The proceedings were ended, however, when workers rose to their feet and praised the management. The minimum wage at Lockheed at this time was 42 cents an hour. A system of regular pay increases, averaging about 10 cents per man-hour per year, helped to keep the employees satisfied. President Robert E. Gross also kept all workers informed about the present and prospective earnings of the company and current problems at the plant by means of mimeographed bulletins. The International Association of Machinists secured a charter for a Lockheed local in March, 1937, but it was not the exclusive bargaining agent for all the plant's workers.[25]

In 1937 AFL and CIO organizers both tried to unionize the 900 workers at Northrop Aircraft Corporation, a subsidiary of Douglas. Late in February, 109 CIO members seized the plant through a sitdown strike, but relinquished control when threatened with arrest. The strikers were promised that a hearing would be conducted by the Regional Labor Board in an effort to determine the collective bargaining agent for the workers. All the strikers were rehired in the interim and production was resumed on March 1. In the board hearings a three-cornered dispute developed among the IAM-AFL, the Western Mechanics Industrial Union of the UAW-CIO, known as Local No. 299, and the Northrop Employees Association, a company union. The representation election held by the board showed that Local No. 299 was preferred by 63 per cent of the voters. The Northrop management therefore agreed to recognize the CIO union, thus terminating the case.[26]

Later in 1937 officials of a branch of the Aircraft Workers Union, Inc., newly established at Northrop, charged that a majority of the employees did not want to be represented by Local No. 299. Another election was therefore held by the board, and again the employees voted for the UAW by a majority of 551 to 138. Local No. 299 then requested a closed shop, which the management refused to grant. Union representatives also complained that seasonal dismissals were made without regard to seniority. As a result of the dispute, Northrop closed the plant on September 7. Employees immediately began to petition the firm to reopen, claiming that a majority of the workers did not vote at the board elections and that the members of Local No. 299 were a minority of the total work force. This back-to-work movement seemed to be initiated partly by representatives of The Neutral Thousands. TNT also assisted the officials of the Aircraft Workers Union in holding a rally of its members on October 4.

The Northrop management wanted to reopen because there was danger that it might incur losses on a United States Army contract for the manufacture of airplanes. Hence the company began to accept applications for reëmployment, but it insisted that the men return as individuals, not as members of unions. Furthermore, it required all applicants to sign a contract including a no-strike pledge before they were considered for jobs. By October 21 nearly all positions had been filled, and operations were resumed.[27]

When the plant reopened, Charles Rogers and Richard Coleman, UAW international representatives, filed charges with the Regional Labor Board alleging that the men returning to work were compelled to sign contracts which, in effect, prevented them from joining a union. Towne Nylander of the board immediately began an investigation, which was followed in February, 1938, by a hearing. Attorney J. Stuart Neary, representing the management, declared that the employment contract had been prepared at the request of a majority of the workers at the plant who were tired of needless labor disputes caused by attempts of UAW leaders to organize them. In Neary's opinion the board did not have jurisdiction over such a voluntary contract. But Thomas H. Kennedy, trial examiner at the hearing, filed a report to the contrary ordering Northrop to void the 1,400 yellow-dog contracts. In his view an agreement providing for a pledge not to strike and establishing a pay forfeiture of $15 from the balance owed any dismissed striking employee was clearly against the intent of the NLRA.[28]

3. FROM BAKERS TO GARMENT WORKERS

The attempts to unionize the new aircraft industry did not diminish efforts to overcome the open shop in the older enterprises of the city. Union activity bestirred the M and M to encourage the managements of various bakeries to maintain open shops and to draw up an agreement establishing uniform reasonable wages and working conditions. This did not prevent Bakers Local No. 37 from continuing with renewed zeal the organizing campaign initiated in 1936. By June, 1937, the union had 720 members. Later in the year it presented an agreement to the wholesale baking industry in Los Angeles, Orange, Santa Barbara, San Bernardino, and Riverside counties. Seventy-five per cent of the larger firms in these areas signed the agreement, almost doubling the membership of Local No. 37. The contract provided for an average weekly wage of $34 and the establishment of a union shop. Organized labor was clearly the victor.[29]

In August, 1937, the Langendorf Baking Company, after being on the Labor Council's unfair list for two years, finally signed contracts with Local No. 37 and Bakery Drivers Local No. 276. Local No. 37 also conducted a sit-down strike against the Brownie Pie Company, but the firm was granted a permanent injunction against such action.

The court order declared the strike illegal and restrained picketing. For the most part, however, the union was successful, and by January, 1938, Local No. 37 had 1,600 members, making it one of the largest labor organizations in Los Angeles. It continued to make headway during 1938, despite strong resistance from the larger bakeries of the city, and enjoyed the coöperation of Bakery Drivers Local No. 276 and Jewish Bakers Local No. 453. The Jewish bakers conducted an intensive campaign to place more union labels on bakery products. Union "harassment" finally caused the owner of the Bradley Pie Company to lock out eighty-five members of Local No. 37 in May, 1938, and close down his plant. Bradley stated that he was tired of accepting the dictates of union leaders. The unionists countered that they had helped him increase his volume of business. After a couple of months the firm reopened as an open shop and refused to renew its contract with the union. The wages and hours of union bakers in 1938 are presented in table 7.[30]

The Los Angeles Building and Construction Trades Council likewise took an aggressive position against open-shop contractors in 1937

TABLE 7

WAGE RATES AND WORKING HOURS IN UNION
BAKERIES, LOS ANGELES, 1938

Occupation	Rate per hour	Hours per week
Hand shops		
Mixers	$ .909	44
Ovenmen	.864	44
Bench hands	.773	44
Machine shops		
Foremen	1.050	40
Mixers	1.000	40
Ovenmen	.950	40
Bench or machine hands	.850	40
Helpers	.750	40
Bench or machine hands' helpers	.675	40
Wrapping and shipping department		
Machine men or checkers	.700	40
Helpers	.600	40
Hebrew bakeries		
First hands	1.313	40
Second hands	1.188	40

SOURCE: "Wages and Hours in Union Bakeries," *Monthly Labor Review*, XLVIII (Jan., 1939), 184.

and 1938. The members planned their campaign to begin in March, 1937. To facilitate the drive, the council set up a speakers' bureau and an organizing committee, and for several months it reduced the initiation fee of constituent unions to a maximum of $25. Building trades unionists donated 10 cents each to a war fund, to which the locals were also to contribute $1 for every new member. At this time about 8,000 men in eighteen locals were affiliated with the council.[31]

The campaign officially began on March 3 at a mass meeting held in the Labor Temple. Advertising literature was passed out for distribution to unorganized building tradesmen, and "flying squads" were organized. Each squad, composed of two or three carloads of unionists from different locals, was assigned to patrol a particular area of the city. Beginning on March 6, the squads investigated all construction jobs within their assigned areas and tried to persuade unorganized workers to join an appropriate craft union. They concentrated on craftsmen employed in residential construction because many of these were not organized. Most of the squads restricted their activities to Saturdays, as they were also endeavoring to enforce a forty-hour week in the construction industry.[32]

Except on rainy days and holidays, the flying squads continued their Saturday organizing work in Los Angeles and nearby communities throughout 1937. Although 250 men participated on March 6, the number reporting in the latter part of the year was often below 100, or less than 5 per cent of the unions' membership. Even so, union officials believed that the squads were effective in reducing the number of weekend construction jobs and in increasing union affiliation. The squad members committed few acts of violence, but they were strongly opposed by the open-shop alignments.

Sunday picketing began on May 23 when several contractors started to work crews on the Sabbath to offset the effective ban on Saturday work. The Sunday picketing, especially in subdivisions being erected by nonunion labor in areas open to public inspection, not only interfered with construction work but hindered the activities of real estate salesmen. The picketing continued until October, despite articles in the *Times* opposing it.[33]

The M and M seems to have been instrumental in establishing a group to counteract these activities. It was known to labor leaders as the Building Protective Association and was composed of open-shop contractors who actively opposed the organizing campaign. Another similar group called the Building Contractors' Association of Southern California nearly signed an agreement with the Building Trades

Council in 1937. The terms of the contract, however, were not entirely satisfactory to the council. M and M officials continually tried to influence the managements of companies building branches in Los Angeles to hire open-shop contractors. Despite the activities of the flying squads, open-shop firms built many of the homes under construction in 1938. Council officials warned the purchasers of these homes that they were jerry-built, but such statements were not substantiated. That the community was not entirely in sympathy with the work of the flying squads was evidenced when one Saturday a squad discovered a nonunion painter working in the home of Mayor Shaw! Nevertheless, the squads continued to function until the latter part of 1938, when increased unemployment in construction took its toll of unionists and diminished interest in organizing efforts.

In the view of labor officials, 1937 was the most successful year for the building trades since 1929. Although eighteen large contracting firms were still on the council's unfair list in December, 1937, a number of sizable companies had come into the union-shop or closed-shop fold as a result of the organizing campaign. Among this group was the William Simpson Construction Company, a long-time open-shop firm, which had granted the demands of the union leaders after a brief strike during the construction of the Columbia Broadcasting System building in Hollywood. This gain and others were made in spite of an estimated 40 per cent decline in dollar volume of construction during late 1937 as compared with 1936. One of the largest meetings in the history of the Building Trades Council was recorded in December, 1937. The thirty-three affiliated unions represented the highest total ever achieved. By early 1938, according to available records, individual membership also reached a new peak. The Los Angeles County District Council of Carpenters showed more than 400 contractors on its fair list. Many of the workers in 100 or more lumber mills, 80 per cent of the Venetian blind industry, 40 furniture factories, and all boat yards and boat shops in the county were members of unions affiliated with the District Council. At this time Carpenters Local No. 15 was one of the largest unions in this craft in the United States.[34]

The District Council of Carpenters had coöperated with the Building Trades Council in the 1937 organizing campaign, and it too made gains. In March two new locals received charters, and Lumber and Sawmill Workers Local No. 2788 signed an agreement with an old open-shop enemy, the Hammond Lumber Company. Three months later No. 2788 threatened to call a general strike after expiration of an agreement previously negotiated with other lumber yards. A new contract was drawn up, however, which provided for a 15 per cent wage increase, a forty-four-hour week, and time and a half for overtime. Representatives of seventy firms verbally agreed to the contract, thus preventing a strike that would have directly affected more than 2,000 workers. A similar agreement was negotiated at San Pedro by Local No. 2607.[35]

The year 1938 was a different story. When representatives of Local No. 2788 tried to make changes in the verbal contract upon its expiration in June, 1938, they were opposed by the Lumber and Allied Products Institute, which was supported by members of Southern Californians, Incorporated. The union requested continuation of the forty-four-hour week, no change in hourly wage rates, time and a half for Saturday work, and a closed-shop clause. When employers proved adamant on the last demand, the unionists referred the dispute to the Regional Labor Board. Meanwhile, on July 5, they initiated a test strike at the Owens-Parks Lumber Company. Although 175 workers walked out and established picket lines, the firm remained open. It placed advertisements in local newspapers to the effect that it would continue to run its business as usual and would oppose a closed shop. After nearly three weeks the strike was discontinued and the workers returned to their former jobs under prestrike conditions. Union leaders withdrew the closed-shop demand and requested the Regional Labor Board to drop the case. A new agreement provided for hourly wages ranging from 65 cents to $1.10, the preferential hiring of union members, an eight-hour day, and time and a half for overtime including Saturdays.[36]

The District Council's organizing drive was stepped up in September, 1938, when eight new organizers were placed in the field. By the end of the year more than seventy new union labels had been assigned to mills, cabinet and fixture shops, and other woodworking firms. The council again experienced difficulty, however, with an old-line open-shop supporter, the Weber Showcase and Fixture Company. Weber had discharged several members of Millmen Locals No. 884 and 1291 for union activity late in 1937. Union officials reported the incidents to the Regional Labor Board, but, deeming more drastic action necessary, called a strike for December 9, almost coincident with the public unveiling of Southern Californians, Incorporated. The unions started a boycott of Weber products and established a picket line around the plant. Owner Karl Weber protested that he was fair to his employees and that a majority of them did not favor a strike. He asked that an impartial citizens' committee be appointed to visit his plant in order to verify these facts. No action was taken, however, and the strike dragged on. On May 4, 1938, Locals No. 884 and 1291 were consolidated as Local No. 721, but the dispute with Weber continued. In the early fall Weber almost signed a contract, but backed down at the last moment. The strike went on until an agreement on wages and hours was finally signed in 1939. As both sides had become tired of the long conflict, they readily approved a pact covering millmen, cabinetmakers, painters, sheet metal workers, and teamsters employed at the Weber plant.[37]

Another union affiliated with the Los Angeles District Council of Carpenters was Venetian Blind Workers Local No. 1763, chartered in 1937. It signed an agreement with six of the seven members of the Venetian Blind Manufacturers' Association of Los Angeles which provided for wages of 50 cents to $1.10 an hour, a forty-four-hour week, and time and a half for overtime. Another agreement negotiated later in the year provided for a forty-hour week, a wage increase of 10 per cent, seniority rights, improved working conditions, and the elimination of piecework. Because Columbia Mills, Inc., refused to sign the first of the two agreements, the union Venetian blind workers struck the plant on October 4. The dispute was marked by violence, including the throwing of acid at a company truck loaded with mail, the puncturing of tires on strikebreakers' cars, and the smashing of plate-glass windows at the plant. Strike leaders denied that members of Local No. 1763 participated in these acts, but later events proved otherwise. After obtaining a temporary injunction against picketing, the company hired strikebreakers and reopened for business. The Neutral Thousands organized an independent union within the firm, and Columbia's management filed a damage suit against the union. Two unionists were indicted and convicted of acid throwing. The dispute ended in January, 1938, when the suit was settled out of court. Although Columbia Mills received nothing for damages, the unionists failed to crack its open-shop position by securing an agreement.[38]

The construction trades were able to coördinate their organizing efforts through the Building Trades Council and the District Council of Carpenters, but this was not true of Cleaners, Dyers and Pressers Union No. 19989, AFL. Its activities were hampered by factional strife. When the 1936 agreement with the larger wholesale and retail plants of the city expired in April, 1937, the union called a strike to obtain a new contract. After eight days the unionists returned to work under the old contract, until a new one was established on May 3. It provided for a blanket 10 per cent wage increase, a forty-hour week, and time and a quarter for overtime. Peace was only temporary, however, as internal problems came to a head soon after Local No. 19989 received a new charter, becoming Local No. 5 of the International Association of Cleaning and Dyehouse Workers, AFL. Factional strife tore the new local asunder in November, when about 150 of its members decided to resist an effort to affiliate it with the CIO. Thomas Porter, president of Local No. 5, declared a state of emergency, and international officers authorized him to suspend the other officials of the union, including Sam Blumenberg, its business agent. Blumenberg obtained a court injunction which forbade Porter to expend union funds or property except to pay necessary utility bills. Porter, in turn, secured a temporary restraining order preventing Blumenberg from acting as an officer of the union. The dispute was then taken to court. After a trial lasting several months, the court handed down a decision in favor of the AFL faction and Porter. Blumenberg left Local No. 5, taking nearly 400 members with him. His request to the CIO for a charter produced quick action, and Local No. 268 of the Amalgamated Clothing Workers of America was established in March, 1938.[39]

But peace continued to elude cleaning and dyeing unionists. Price wars and renewed organizing efforts characterized labor relations in this field during 1938. Local No. 268 and a new Local No. 85 of the United Cleaners, Dyers and Laundry Workers, CIO, were enjoined from picketing plants in a half-dozen instances. Employers also complained that the unions were attempting to force them to raise prices in order to obtain higher wages and closed-shop agreements. An organizing campaign begun late in 1937, when factional strife was high, continued through the first six months of 1938. In this period the windows of many cleaning and dyeing shops were broken or damaged by acid. The victims of these malicious acts were proprietors of independent cleaning establishments who charged low prices and had not signed the 1937 contract. After an investigation the Los Angeles County Grand Jury indicted fourteen men, including Alfred Lushing, a city water and power commissioner, and Deputy State Fire Marshal Frank D. Scovel. The other defendants were described by District Attorney Buron Fitts as "imported Eastern muscle men." They included a number of union officers and their assistants as well as the owners of several plants.[40]

At the time of his arrest Lushing, formerly manager of the Cleaners' Association, was a director of the Association of Wholesale Cleaners and Dyers. Scovel was accused of conniving with representatives of the Cleaners' Association to harass independent operators who refused to accede to the association's demands. As deputy fire marshal, he was able to declare plant facilities unsafe and force owners to install expensive devices for fire protection or else join the association and maintain higher prices. The union officials were accused of coöperating in the conspiracy, because increased prices would mean higher and more stable wages under contracts.[41]

Thirteen of the fourteen defendants were apprehended and went on trial in September. Court proceedings revealed that for many years terrorists had been guilty of assaults, throwing stench bombs, attempts at extortion, bribing policemen, window smashing, placing caustic soda in cleaning vats, hurling acid, and even of murder. The trial also brought out the fact that Chicago hoodlums had been imported to aid in the organizing campaign. If shops refused to charge the higher prices of the Cleaners' Association, union leaders called strikes and placed pickets in front of the stores. The testimony indicated that terrorism had been initiated as early as 1923 and had continued sporadically since then, becoming more frequent in 1937 and 1938. But the charges against five of the defendants, including Scovel, were dismissed for lack of evidence. Lushing and the remaining seven defendants were convicted on one count of conspiracy and five counts of acid throwing. Lushing resigned from his city position and, with three others, was sentenced to one to ten years in San Quentin. Four defendants were placed on probation for five years, with the first twelve to fifteen months of this period to be spent in the Los Angeles County jail. At a later trial in 1939, six other associates in the campaign of terrorism were convicted of the murder of a night watchman in a 1931 price war.[42]

Although the culinary workers, like the cleaning and dyeing employees, were in a service industry, their activities in 1937 and 1938 were not nearly so colorful. The lack of price wars and factional strife, however, did not lessen the seriousness of their continued organizing activities or the severity of their open-shop opposition. Members of the Southern California Restaurant Association, a trade organization formed more than thirty years earlier, established an open-shop group in July, 1937, known as "Group A" or the "Representative Restaurant Group." It functioned independently of the parent body, and its purpose was to oppose the organizing campaign of the culinary unions. Group A was a secret organization which furnished strikebreakers and guards and, according to circumstantial evidence, maintained a black list for the restaurant industry. It was supported by contributions from its members, a part of which was used to maintain Southern Californians, Incorporated. Group A, though not successful in stopping union organizational activity, did retard strikes called against the Mayflower and Beverly-Wilshire hotels, the Los Angeles Athletic Club, the Globe Dairy Lunch, and the Brown Derby restaurants. The culinary unions succeeded in signing union-shop agreements with Mike Lyman's and Levy's restaurants, and chartered a new local known as Oriental Restaurant Employees Union No. 646.[43]

On August 20, 1937, the unions called a strike against the Los Angeles Athletic Club in an attempt to organize its culinary employees. Frank A. Garbutt, president of the club, proved a shrewd opponent. He presented his views on the strike in open letters to the *Times* and simultaneously obtained a temporary injunction against picketing. He also attempted to form an organization called the "Los Angeles Open Shop Party." The strike was terminated before the end of the year because the unions failed to organize the club employees.

Meanwhile, on August 6, 150 culinary workers had struck the Brown Derby restaurants for higher wages and better working conditions. The management secured a temporary restraining order which restricted picketing, and obtained strikebreakers from Group A. The dispute ended when the union and the management signed a new five-year agreement which became effective on February 1, 1938. It provided for improved wages and working conditions, an arbitration system, a union shop, and retention of the strikebreakers as employees of the firm.[44]

Throughout 1938 Group A and the M and M fought the culinary workers' organizing campaign. The open-shop organizations procured injunctions, and a number of restaurants successfully repelled the unionists. The strongest opponent was the Globe Dairy Lunch, a firm composed of six branches located in metropolitan Los Angeles. A union effort to organize its employees had caused the management, in October, 1937, to obtain an injunction against picketing which was not modified until March 1, 1938, and was not vacated until the following August. Although the modification permitted the unions again to initiate organizing activities, they experienced only failure. Globe Dairy Lunch, a member of Group A for a short period, continued to resist the demands of union leaders throughout the year. Officials of The Neutral Thousands aided in this resistance by organizing an independent union, the Globe Employees Association, among employees who refused to join the AFL organizations.

Such opposition, however, did not discourage the culinary unionists, who countered that gains had been made in the city as a whole. In a radio broadcast on April 11, 1938, Waitresses Local No. 639 claimed that it alone had jurisdiction over 5,000 to 6,000 waitresses in the city and that the union was making headway in organizing them. A representative of Waiters Local No. 17 stated that his union had 2,000 members. Although, on the basis of the union's activities, this figure seems too high, sufficient gains were being made against the open shop to warrant considerable optimism on the part of union officials.[45]

The furniture workers did not claim union membership gains like those of the culinary employees, but they actively opposed the attempts of open-shop employers to beat them down. An effort in August, 1937, to renew their agreement, with certain basic changes, ended in a strike against forty plants employing approximately 1,200 workers. The strike was called off when the members of Local No. 1561 were granted a wage increase of 10 per cent, changes in several wage classifications, time and a half for overtime, seniority rights, the shop steward system, and preferential hiring. About 3,000 workers in twelve large plants and a number of smaller firms in the industry were not unionized at this time. In several of these factories, representatives of The Neutral Thousands established independent unions.

The upholsterers, like their brethren in wood furniture manufacturing, had some trouble with employers in 1937. Members of Local No. 15 had been locked out of thirteen firms in September, 1936, when union demands for renewal of an agreement were denied. The unionists opposed the lockout and initiated a new organizing campaign, which resulted in agreements with thirty-five firms by July, 1937. This drive was continued during the remainder of the year in spite of restrictive injunctions, internal dissension between factions sympathetic to the CIO or the AFL, arrests of pickets, several additional lockouts, and acts of violence committed on picket lines. By the end of 1937 agreements effective until August, 1938, had been negotiated with forty-nine firms in which upholstered furniture was manufactured or repaired. They provided for recognition of Local No. 15 as sole collective bargaining agent for the workers involved; a union shop; a forty-hour workweek; time and a half for overtime, which was not to exceed two hours in any one day; equal distribution of available employment; and union wage scales.[46]

The factional warfare between CIO and AFL sympathizers within the unions of upholsterers and furniture workers badly hampered them in their relations with employers during 1938. CIO-oriented unionists had been elected to most of the offices within Upholsterers Local No. 15 in 1937, and had gained control of the union's treasury. They did not report on the financial status of the union for almost a year. In January, 1938, officers of the Upholsterers International Union of America, AFL, sent A. F. Masoero to investigate the local's activities. Later, while he was temporarily absent from the city, the CIO sympathizers called a special meeting to vote on the question of affiliation with the CIO, although only about 350 of the 1,365 members of the union were present. They voted for affiliation by a majority of 230 to 61, and the union's leaders publicly declared that its members favored the action by a ratio of 4 to 1. Officers of newly established Local No. 576 of the United Furniture Workers of America, CIO, then tried to gain control of the membership and the contracts of Local No. 15. Early in 1938 similar events occurred in Local No. 1561 of the furniture workers, which had a membership of more than 1,000. When the members voted at a special meeting on the question of affiliation with the CIO, the reported ratio was 3 to 1 in favor of affiliation, though the actual vote seems to have been 112 to 42. Officers of Local No. 576 then tried, just as they had with the upholsterers, to get control of the membership and the contracts of Local No. 1561.[47]

Intimidation and violence were used in this effort to force the members of Locals No. 15 and 1561 into CIO Local No. 576. For example, in February, 1938, unionists from No. 576 attempted to seize the union hall belonging to Local No. 15. Six members of the latter, led by Masoero, barricaded themselves in the building and resisted the seizure. After a court action, however, members of Local No. 15 agreed to give the hall to Local No. 576 and to establish their headquarters in the Labor Temple. Officials of the CIO local also petitioned the Regional Labor Board for certification of the union as sole collective bargaining agent for the approximately 2,000 workers under union contracts in the furniture industry of Los Angeles. A hearing was never held on the petition, and the jurisdictional trouble continued into 1939. Both sides conducted intensive organizing campaigns throughout 1938, as they tried to win exclusive bargaining rights for their respective unions in various firms.[48]

Some employers tried to take advantage of the factional disputes by canceling their union contracts. Several employers joined with members of Locals No. 15 and 1561 in seeking to discover and discharge employees who were affiliated with CIO Local No. 576. Mem-

bers of No. 576, in turn, picketed the Mason Manufacturing Company
and several other firms in an effort to force their managements to support the CIO, though most of the workers in these establishments preferred to remain in the AFL under existing contracts. Most of the
agreements between Locals No. 1561 and 15 and various furniture
manufacturers expired in September, 1938. Many of them were renewed, but others were replaced by new agreements negotiated by
representatives of Local No. 576. The new CIO contracts provided
for essentially the same wages and working conditions as before, with
the furniture workers' hourly wage scale ranging from 50 cents to
$1.25 and the upholsterers' scale having a maximum of $1.10. Local
No. 576 had negotiated agreements with twelve firms by the end of
September, and continued its organizing drive as part of a national
campaign by its international. Both AFL unions were similarly active
during the remainder of the year. Local No. 15 signed fifteen agreements which provided for closed shops covering more than 500 workers, while Local No. 1561 signed agreements with eight firms and
negotiated verbal contracts with two more. In this same year The Neutral Thousands organized several independent unions.[49]

The AFL-CIO conflict also affected the clothing trades in 1937 and
1938. The locals of the Amalgamated Clothing Workers were among
those suspended from the Central Labor Council in 1937 because of
affiliation with the CIO. In fact, the offices of the ACW at 833 South
Broadway served briefly as the headquarters of the newly formed Industrial Union Council. In May, a one-day strike conducted by the
Amalgamated resulted in a new agreement replacing an expired contract. It covered 1,800 unionists in 120 manufacturing concerns and
provided standard minimum hourly wages in the men's clothing industry of 50 cents for women and 75 cents for men. Skilled employees
were paid up to $1.65 per hour—a 12 per cent increase in wages.
Nearly all workers in the industry were covered by the agreement, as
manufacturers had agreed to abide by its provisions if 60 per cent of
their number favored it.

The ACW experienced few organizing problems in 1938, although
there were several jurisdictional disputes with unionists who belonged
to the United Garment Workers, AFL. Leaders of the UGW were
able to negotiate contracts with the managements of Rosenblum, Inc.,
Kurtzman Brothers, and Paramount Tailors, all of whom had signed
agreements with the ACW in previous years.[50]

The International Ladies' Garment Workers locals were likewise
involved in the AFL-CIO controversy. When the manufacturers of

women's clothing began to employ migrant workers in increasing numbers, the ILGWU locals started an organizing campaign to bring them into the fold. Most of the migrants were American-born whites and Negroes without previous union experience. The drive, begun in January, 1937, was directed primarily at the workers engaged in manufacturing cotton dresses, underwear, and blouses. Shortly thereafter the ILGWU formed Local No. 266, composed of cotton dress workers. But its delegates were refused seats in the Labor Council because the officers of the international and William Busick, a local organizer for the union in Los Angeles, were sympathetic with the aims of the CIO. The snubbing of these delegates led to the withdrawal of all ILGWU representatives from the council.[51]

The organizing campaign caused a number of acts of violence and several riots. The ILGWU, however, negotiated additional contracts, and in July, 1937, the cloakmakers signed a new three-year agreement specifying a 10 per cent increase in wages, a closed shop, and an arbitration system. A new group touched by the organizing drive included workers employed by knitting mills. In one instance, three unionists purchased the Beverly Knitting Mills in order to end a dispute involving fifty-five employees. Considerable violence accompanied the attempts made to organize the employees of the Jones Knitting Mills. Someone hurled bottles of creosote through the bedroom windows of two strikebreakers' homes. An undertaker was sent to the home of the owner of the plant, Hyrum Jones, in order to pick up his body, but Mr. Jones was very much alive! In January, 1938, someone threw a quart milk bottle filled with creosote through a window in the plant. It burst on a work table and caused considerable damage to materials. Other acts of violence included slashing tires on workers' cars and assaulting employees who refused to go out on strike. Jones maintained his resistance, however, and continued operations. The Neutral Thousands actively opposed the ILGWU campaign to organize the knitting mills and cloak and dress firms by seeking to establish independent unions at several plants. The numerous instances of violence were heavily played up in the local press.[52]

Although not involved in the AFL-CIO issue, Los Angeles millinery workers faced a constant struggle against sweatshop conditions. Their efforts were rewarded in 1937 in the form of several new contracts, and officials of Cap Makers Local No. 22 renewed a working agreement with a number of manufacturers in the city. Numerically, however, the union millinery workers were quite weak, as evidenced by their inability in April, 1938, to secure a contract with the Golden

Brothers Millinery Company. When, at the request of Local No. 41 of the Hatters, Cap and Millinery Workers International Union, the Regional Labor Board conducted a collective bargaining election at Golden, the union was rejected.[53]

The CIO was active in two other areas of the city's clothing industry. In August, 1937, the officials of Local No. 87 of the International Fur Workers, CIO, renewed their 1936 contract with representatives of the manufacturers' association in the fur industry of Los Angeles. This agreement remained in effect during 1938, providing for a thirty-five-hour week, time and a half for overtime, pay for legal holidays, the closed shop, and a 5 per cent increase in the minimum wage rate. Seven independent fur wholesalers and retailers also signed new contracts embodying the same provisions. The only serious holdout in the fur industry was the firm of Maurice Ball, against which a strike had been called in 1936. Finally, in November, 1937, the firm signed a contract granting union recognition, a 15 to 20 per cent increase in wages, a workweek of thirty-five hours, and time and a half for overtime.

Local No. 99 of the Textile Workers Organizing Committee, CIO, also supported an organizing campaign, but was not really active in Los Angeles until 1938. After a strike that lasted two weeks, it won a union shop for several hundred workers employed at the California Mill Supply Company. Efforts also were made to organize the workers in plants manufacturing bags and in the Mission Hosiery Mills.[54]

4. TRANSPORTATION TROUBLES

Workers in clothing and textiles thus made some headway against the open shop, although their efforts were hampered by the AFL-CIO controversy. The same could not be said of the employees of the Los Angeles Railway. After the strike of 1935, some of the workers had joined independent company unions within the utility. In September, 1936, Samuel M. Haskins resigned from the presidency of the firm and was succeeded by Lucius S. Storrs. This change meant little for either AFL or CIO unions, however, except a continued desire on the part of management to maintain the open shop. In 1937 some of the employees joined a newly established independent labor organization, the Transportation Union of California, Incorporated. Another independent union, Transportation Operators and Affiliates, was continued. Both organizations negotiated agreements with the Los Angeles Railway in May, 1937. The Transport Workers of America, CIO, tried to obtain recognition, and even filed a complaint with the Regional Labor Board alleging discriminatory practices against its members. Little came of the action, however, and the CIO failed to get a foothold in the company.[55]

The situation was different on the Pacific Electric Railway, where unions had established a bargaining position several years earlier. In 1936 a wage dispute developed which was not negotiated to the satisfaction of union representatives. In July, 1937, the Brotherhood of Railroad Trainmen voted to strike if their wage requests were not granted. The unionists demanded hourly wages of 80 cents for conductors and motormen on two-man cars, 90 cents for the operators of one-man cars, and a minimum work shift of eight hours within a ten-hour period. The company countered by offering to raise the existing pay rate of 56½ cents an hour to 62½ and 67½ for crew members on two- and one-man cars, respectively. The strike was to become effective on August 28, but it was twice postponed at the request of the National Mediation Board. When the board failed to settle the dispute, the brotherhood set another strike date. Before this call took effect, however, President Roosevelt appointed an emergency fact-finding board under the provisions of the Railway Labor Act. Early in November, 1937, the three-man board heard testimony from representatives of both sides, and on the 22d the disputants reached a one-year compromise agreement specifying wage increases of 15 to 25 per cent. Officials of the Pacific Electric estimated that the wage changes would add $500,000 to the annual payroll, but the agreement nevertheless went into effect, retroactive to August 1 for passenger trainmen and to October 1 for freight crews. In December approximately 1,750 unionized clerks, telegraphers, signalmen, shop craftsmen, maintenance-of-way men, and substation attendants demanded increases in wages. Federal mediator William F. Mitchell, Jr., arranged an agreement that provided a pay raise of 5 cents an hour, retroactive to August 1.[56]

Another group of transportation workers, the teamsters, were troubled by disputes between managements and unions in 1937 and 1938. The members of various teamster unions had supported the longshoremen in their 1936–1937 strike by setting up a blockade of the roads leading to the harbor. Although the police interrupted the blockade late in 1936, unionized teamsters began a new organizing campaign on the port highways in February, 1937. The M and M then established a hiring hall to furnish nonunion swampers for trucks going to and from the docks. M and M officials sent hundreds of telegrams to its members encouraging them not to patronize union trucking concerns, and secured signed pledges to maintain the open shop. Teamsters picketed the docks serviced by vehicles from open-shop trucking companies until the end of February, when such activity was terminated because employers threatened to institute injunction proceedings against the union. This picketing hampered the resumption of harbor operations after settlement of the maritime general strike, as the longshoremen refused to cross the teamster picket lines. Early in March, 1937, Mayor Shaw appointed a three-man committee to study this recurring problem, but it found no solution.[57]

At the end of March, Local No. 208 of the teamsters called a strike against Pacific Freight Lines, one of the largest intercity trucking concerns in Los Angeles, as part of the campaign to organize drivers working north and east of the city. M and M officials were alarmed, for if Pacific Freight recognized the union, the open shop in the Los Angeles trucking industry would be doomed. The M and M therefore urged shippers to patronize the Pacific Freight Lines. It also furnished guard service and secret operatives through the Bodell Detective Agency. After the anticipated violence broke out, the firm's management obtained injunctions against a large number of overt acts committed by union members, but intimidations, beatings, and such actions as the firing of rifles at tank trucks on the Ridge Route proved to be persuasive tactics. Even though, according to the M and M, only about a tenth of the employees of the trucking line were unionized when the strike began, the company could not hold out against the strong union offensive. The strike ended on June 2 when an agreement was negotiated providing for arbitration of the dispute and reinstatement of the strikers. Though a closed shop was not granted, the settlement was a sign of the times. On June 16 representatives of the teamsters and the Truck Owners' Association of California negotiated a wage scale and agreement. In November another agreement, amended in January, 1938, was established with the Motor Truck Association of Southern California. By means of these and other agreements, the teamsters were able to control employment on many intercity trucks operating in southern California.[58]

The teamsters also put on a drive in 1937 to unionize workers in milk distribution. Their main opposition came from members of Dairy Industries, Inc., which furnished guards for Arden Farms during a short dispute in May. This association was disbanded in October, 1937, however, because a majority of its members had signed contracts with Milk Drivers and Dairy Employees Union Local No. 93. These agreements, mainly negotiated in August and September, covered the employees of thirty distributing firms and trucking companies in the dairy industry. All the contracts expired on February 1, 1938, but new agreements were not forthcoming. The open-shop Associated Farmers vigorously protested the renewal of agreements covering 75 per cent of the city's milk distribution industry, and threatened a boycott if new ones were signed.[59] The *Times* took up the cudgels with statements like these:

> Milk now. Vital food of infants. At Christmas it was pleasurable anticipations of childhood. Dave Beck, "The man who tried to kill Santa Claus."
>
> Davebeckism now seeks to impose closed-shop tribute on every bottle of milk distributed in Los Angeles County.
>
> Today milk. Tomorrow—what? [60]

Early in 1938 dairies in the Los Angeles area formed a new organization called the Associated Dairymen, in an attempt to negotiate as a group with the union. Although the old agreement had expired, the dairies continued for several months to abide by its provisions. At the same time they tried to evade the demands of the union leaders for a new contract. At first Local No. 93 did not press for renewal, though it distributed copies of a suggested contract to the firms involved.[61] The *Times,* suggesting that this peace was only on the surface, stated that in reality Local No. 93 was instituting a reign of terror:

> Some of the drivers who have refused to join the Beck union have reported that in some instances when they left milk on doorsteps or other exposed places, the milk had been uncapped and fouled with cigarette butts and dirty sticks.
> Housewives have reported they have been told they may find poison in their milk if they take from milk men who are not members of the Beck union.[62]

The antiunion Women of the Pacific was particularly prominent in urging the maintenance of an open shop in milk distribution, but it failed to get assurance from dairy representatives that they would not sign contracts with the union.[63]

In July, Einar Mohn, a representative of the Western States Dairy Employees Council of the Brotherhood of Teamsters, arrived in Los Angeles and renewed the campaign for a contract between Local No. 93 and dairy product distributors. On November 15, after months of negotiations, followed by a strike threat, Local No. 93 signed a contract with members of Milk Products Industries, Inc., and several other dairy distributors. (By this time, the Associated Dairymen had passed out of the picture.) The agreement was not publicized, did not provide for a closed shop, and was considered by the employers to be less restrictive than the one that had expired the preceding February. It covered details concerning wages, working conditions and hours, vacations, arbitration of grievances, and the maintenance of a union shop.[64]

The attempts to organize the dairymen brought the open-shop Associated Farmers onto the Los Angeles industrial relations scene in 1938. The Associated Farmers did not want unionism to spread from market and dairy employees in the city to the drivers of farm trucks, and thence to ranch workers. The M and M coöperated very closely in the attempt to maintain the open shop on farms and on farm-to-market roads. Early in 1938 the Associated Farmers formed a subsidiary called the Farmers' Transportation Association, which attained its primary purpose of blocking the unionizing of truck drivers engaged in hauling farm products from Imperial Valley to Los Angeles. In March officials of the Los Angeles County Farm Bureau announced that, under an agreement made with representatives of the teamsters, a farmer, his son, or a farm employee hauling exclusively for his employer could unload a truck in the city without joining a labor organization. The agreement did not apply to a farmer who was operating a commercial truck line.[65]

The line drawn between farmers and commercial truckers was clearly seen in the organization in 1937 of Local No. 630, Wholesale Produce Market Workers Union, by union teamsters. In the same year its officers won union-shop agreements at three of the large wholesale markets in the city. Many of the new members were of Japanese extraction. The union was better known as Produce Drivers Local No. 630, as many of its members hauled fresh fruits and vegetables on a commercial trucking basis. The agreements made in 1937 were renewed for a year in February, 1938. The teamsters then directed their offensive toward the unionization of icemen. As a result of their success, Local No. 630 became the Produce and Ice Drivers Union, with a membership of 1,500 by the end of the year.[66]

Young leaders in the teamsters' union conducted much of its organizing work. Dave Beck, regional representative in the eleven Western states, had watched these younger, local leaders in their successes, but he became increasingly concerned over the progress made after 1935 by their counterparts in the International Longshoremen's Association. This union also sought to organize truckers and warehousemen in coastal cities. In February, 1937, the teamsters were granted jurisdiction over all warehousemen except those working on docks in harbors. A few months later the members of ILA locals in most of the larger ports on the coast voted for affiliation with the International Longshoremen's and Warehousemen's Union under the aggressive leadership of Harry Bridges, and began to move into inland warehouses, thus coming into conflict with Dave Beck and his teamsters. The result was a series of jurisdictional battles among the warehousemen in coastal cities.[67]

These jurisdictional disputes began in Los Angeles in the summer of 1937 after a June convention of the Western unions of the Brotherhood of Teamsters. There were acts of violence as well as several street riots. Local ILWU leaders appealed to the Los Angeles County Grand Jury for protection against what they called "teamster goon squads," while open-shop supporters repudiated both unions. Despite this trouble at the inland warehouses, union teamsters and warehousemen coöperated at Los Angeles Harbor. For example, longshoremen refused to load furniture that had been delivered to the dock by non-union truckers for shipment on the steamship *Catalina* until it had been carted away and returned to the pier by union teamsters. On other occasions in 1937 and 1938, the ILWU refused to handle cargo delivered by the employees of open-shop trucking firms.[68]

Meanwhile, the teamsters continued their organizing campaign among the workers in drug and paper warehouses, milling companies, and fruit-packing concerns of the city. The manager of the Vernon Nussbaum Company, which packed dried fruits and nuts, applied for an injunction against picketing by members of Grocery and Warehousemen Local No. 595. In November, 1937, officials of The Neutral Thousands had established an independent union among the Nussbaum employees, and acts of violence had subsequently occurred at the company's two plants. The firm was granted a permanent injunction against picketing, but failed to collect damages of $10,000 which it had also requested.[69]

In September, 1937, a jurisdictional dispute between General Warehousemen Local No. 598, chartered by the teamsters the preceding June, and ILWU Local No. 1-26 at the warehouse of the Zellerbach Paper Company caused a street riot. An election held the following December to determine the proper collective bargaining agent for the firm's warehousemen gave neither side a majority, the first time this had happened in the history of the local Regional Labor Board. The longshoremen continued their efforts to organize the firm, however, and soon requested another election. In the balloting in February, 1938, ILWU Local No. 1-26 was designated collective bargaining agent for Zellerbach warehousemen in a clear victory over the teamsters. The latter likewise lost out at the Los Angeles Drug Company. After a seven-day strike, the firm recognized Local No. 1-26 as bargaining agent for its warehousemen. The CIO union also organized the workers at the drug warehouse of McKesson and Robbins, although here again it was opposed by members of Local No. 598, who continued periodically to picket the firm.[70]

The following months saw no letup in the rivalry between the CIO and AFL unions. Warehouse workers at the Blake, Moffitt and Towne Paper Company chose Local No. 598 as their collective bargaining agent in an NLRB election. Another teamster affiliate, Flour, Feed and Cereal Warehousemen Local No. 757, tried without success to organize the workers at the V-O Milling Company. Its tactics included beating employees, throwing bricks through truck and show windows, and other acts of violence. The local did manage to secure recognition at the California Milling Company, but this success was only temporary. Early in 1938 approximately fifty-five of its members at the company joined the CIO and were locked out of the plant. In an April election conducted by the Regional Labor Board, a majority of the firm's employees voted for ILWU Local No. 1-26. Although a contract was signed, The Neutral Thousands entered the plant in May and established an independent union. The resultant controversy raged for several months until Local No. 1-26 obtained a new contract in December and ousted the company union.

Other jurisdictional conflicts occurred in 1938 at the Taylor and V-O milling companies, but by the end of the year Local No. 1-26 had signed contracts with the managements of the California, Globe, Capitol, and Universal mills. These companies produced more than half of the total output of the Los Angeles feed and grain industry. This local had also signed an agreement on August 25 with the managements of seven drug warehouses in the city. The provisions of the contract included a pay increase ranging up to 10 cents an hour for 20 to 30 per cent of the workers, recognition of the principle of preferential hiring, plant-wide seniority, and shorter apprenticeship periods for women.[71]

At the harbor, members of the teamsters' unions were accused of siding with AFL longshoremen in the factional dispute late in 1937 which finally resulted in the ILWU's becoming the dominant dockside labor organization. At one point the jurisdictional conflict between the teamsters and the ILWU at inland warehouses almost spread to the harbor area. CIO leaders accused the International

Longshoremen's Association of trying to establish a coalition with the teamsters in order to keep the ILWU out of the harbor by means of a blockade. Teamster officials denied the relationship, however, and continued to coöperate with the longshoremen regardless of their affiliation.[72]

The teamsters penetrated a number of other commercial fields in 1937 and 1938, including gas stations, parking lots, automobile sales, and magazine distribution. On November 30, 1937, teamster organizers were said to be working in sixteen different industrial classifications in Los Angeles in an effort to unionize "everything on wheels." A union of automobile salesmen was formed in April, 1937, and in July Local No. 20548, Gas Station and Parking Lot Attendants Union, was established. By mid-1937 more than 10,000 workers were reportedly affiliated with various teamster unions in Los Angeles city and county. In October 3,000 delegates from teamster locals in the eleven Western states and British Columbia attended a convention in Hollywood. At the meeting Dave Beck derided charges made by open-shop supporters that he had come to destroy the commercial activity of the city. But he did inaugurate a new organizing campaign, which reached its apogee in 1938 and struck fear into the hearts of open-shop advocates, judging by editorials in the *Times* in the fall and winter of 1937–38. Seattle, Washington, was cited as an example of a city ruled by Dave Beck, where building costs had become prohibitive, jurisdictional disputes had caused unemployment, the shipping industry was declining, and major firms were going bankrupt. Moreover, it was alleged that the principal and interest on municipal bonds had been defaulted, the citizens were discouraged and pessimistic regarding the future of the community, and the press was censored by Beck.[73]

The efforts of open-shop forces to oppose Beck and the teamsters centered on a dispute at the May Company, a large Los Angeles department store. On December 1, 1937, the teamsters placed pickets around the firm's warehouse and the truck entrance to the store, and inaugurated a boycott against all products sold by the firm. Officials of Locals No. 389 and 589, under the leadership of Harry Dail, an international organizer, were in charge of the strike. The cause of the dispute was the failure of the May Company to recognize the union as the sole collective bargaining agent for the truckers and warehousemen it employed.[74] According to Dail, the drivers wanted a wage of $6 for an eight-hour day with time and a half for overtime, and the warehousemen wanted to negotiate a scale predicated "on the competitive conditions existing in the Los Angeles area."[75] Dail said the teamsters had no complaints against other department stores and would not interfere with their parcel deliveries during the holidays.[76]

Within a few days after the beginning of the strike, twenty-seven of the leading downtown stores coöperated in publishing quarter-page ads in the newspapers asking patrons to carry small packages instead of using the free delivery service. The merchants charged the teamsters with threatening the continued existence of the open shop and destroying the spirit of the holiday season. On December 11, however, having made known their unity on the open-shop issue and having publicly accused labor racketeers of not respecting the significance of the Christmas season, the merchants restored full delivery service. Other open-shop groups also rallied to the cause. The *Times* published editorials and articles, and spokesmen for The Neutral Thousands, the M and M, the Chamber of Commerce, and Southern Californians, Incorporated, made clear their stand in the dispute. Women's groups such as the Republican Study Club, the Presidents Civic Association, the Friday Morning Club, the Hollywood Women's Club, American Women, Inc., Women's Law Observance Association, and others passed resolutions against "davebeckism," the symbol of labor tyranny publicized by the *Times*. Most of these resolutions stated the willingness of the women to patronize stores against which strikes were being waged, to carry their own parcels, and to oppose the teamsters' attempt "to defeat Santa Claus." Various groups of church women as well as several pastors also opposed the organizing campaign and the strike against the May Company.[77]

Violent acts occurred shortly after the strike began. Several non-striking employees were beaten and stones were thrown at May Company trucks, breaking the windshields. Several trucks were struck by steel ball bearings fired from slingshots, and a number of drivers were cut by flying glass. Two teamsters were arrested, tried, and convicted of making these assaults. The May Company store and warehouse remained open, however, and the firm continued to deliver merchandise, having hired replacements for the small number of workers who had walked out. To protect its employees, the company hired guards from the Bodell Detective Agency, while city police patrolled the strike area. Delegates to the Los Angeles Industrial Union Council and the Central Labor Council endorsed the strike and the organizing campaign, though the CIO council opposed the use of "goon squads" by the teamsters. Officials of Joint Council of Teamsters No. 42 distributed circulars throughout the city, stating their viewpoint concerning the dispute. May Company representatives countered by arguing that salaries were being paid and working conditions had been granted which equaled the union's demands; thus, in effect, the sole issue was the closed shop.[78]

On December 4 the May Company's management obtained a temporary injunction prohibiting mass picketing, and nine days later instituted a suit against the teamsters' union. It asked for damages of $250,000 as well as for a permanent injunction against the picketing. In the trial, company attorneys presented evidence to show a decline in trade volume, the existence of violence against nonstriking employees and the property of the store, and the good faith of the management during prestrike negotiations. The court granted a permanent injunction against mass picketing, but refused to award damages. The union was allowed to place one picket at the truck entrance of the store and one for each fifty feet of warehouse frontage. The strike continued well into 1938. On March 15 Beck announced that thus far it had cost the union $50,000, and he threatened to spread the dispute to May Company stores in other cities. He also requested the members of all unions under his jurisdiction in the eleven Western states to support the strikers. In April he put uniforms on the pickets in order to attract more attention. The dispute was finally settled on July 30; the strikers returned to work on August 1 and the strikebreakers, many of whom had been hired through the Labor Placement Bureau of the M and M, were discharged. The agreement was not publicized in the newspapers, but representatives of both sides publicly expressed satisfaction with the settlement.[79]

Meanwhile, trouble descended upon the teamsters from another direction. In January, 1938, Harry Dail announced that the Department of Justice and the La Follette Committee had been asked to conduct an investigation of alleged illegal labor practices on the Pacific Coast. An investigation followed, but it was conducted by Los Angeles County officials rather than federal officers. It officially began on April 18 when representatives of the district attorney raided the headquarters of Local No. 208 at 730 South Grand Avenue and seized its records. After the raid, District Attorney Buron Fitts presented evidence to the Los Angeles County Grand Jury, through the testimony of witnesses, concerning acts of violence committed by "goon squads" from the local. The grand jury subsequently indicted eleven men, including Harry Dail; Thomas L. Pitts, secretary-treasurer of Local No. 208; George A. Schultz, a former officer of the same union; and Dexter L. Lewis, president of No. 208. The charges included a felony conspiracy to commit twenty-three overt acts, five counts of assault, and one of extortion. Warrants were therefore issued for the arrest of the eleven men. They were arraigned after ten of them failed to escape trial by filing demurrers in which they challenged the validity of the true bill on grounds that it was vague and general and did not indicate a direct violation of the law.[80]

Labor leaders in Los Angeles reacted to the arrests in various ways. Dail claimed the indictments were sponsored by open-shop supporters to discredit the aggressive members of Local No. 208. CIO leaders favored the arrest of the "goon squad" members, but they were afraid that the coming trial would support the campaign for an ordinance to regulate picketing. Many members of Local No. 208 seemed to approve the arrests because, they alleged, terroristic methods had been used against them to maintain a dictatorship within the union.[81]

The selection of a jury began on July 13 before Superior Court Judge Clement D. Nye, but the actual trial did not start until August 2. A large number of witnesses testified concerning Dail's control of Local No. 208, assaults on both unionized and unorganized truckers, and extortion of money from employers. During the trial two of the defendants became witnesses for the prosecution, although the defense attempted to discredit their testimony. Efforts also were made to have the case dismissed or the jury instructed to return an advised verdict. Several of the defendants pleaded that they had acted only in self-defense. Dail and Lewis denied that a dictatorship existed and disclaimed any responsibility for issuing orders to commit violent acts.

The case was given to the jury on October 11. Two days later, four of the defendants were found guilty and the rest were acquitted. Lewis and Dail were placed on probation for ten years and were given jail terms of eighteen months for conspiracy in planning and directing a campaign of violence against trucking concerns, unorganized truck drivers, rival unionists, and recalcitrant members of Local No. 208. Two "goon squad" members were convicted of simple assault misdemeanors and were given six months in jail on each of two counts.[82]

Another trial involving teamsters occurred shortly after five members of the union were arrested in March, 1938, on charges of beating an automobile salesman with a baseball bat. The salesman, an employee of the Homer C. Thompson Nash agency, had refused to join the union. At the completion of the trial, four of the five unionists were convicted and sentenced to jail.[83]

There is little question that, in spite of the trials and adverse publicity, the teamsters made headway in organizing warehousemen and truckers. The membership campaign of 1937 and 1938 was considered by teamster officials as the most successful drive in the city's history. In fact, they estimated that there were 25,000 to 30,000 members of the union in the Los Angeles area by the middle of 1938. Spokesmen for Joint Council of Teamsters No. 42 declared that most of the large trucking companies in southern California had signed or agreed to abide by contracts negotiated with the various unions of truckers.[84]

5. Renewed Vigor on Other Fronts

The publicity attendant upon the trials of teamsters on charges of inciting violence was matched by that accorded the activities of the American Newspaper Guild, CIO, when it struck against the *Hollywood Citizen-News*. Although the international had been started in 1933, efforts to organize a local chapter were not initiated until the following year and did not really bear fruit until 1936. Members of the Guild were employed by most of the large daily newspapers of the city except the *Times*, though collective bargaining contracts had not been established. When the American Newspaper Guild was suspended by the AFL Executive Council in 1937, delegates from the Los Angeles chapter were expelled from the Central Labor Council. The union later affiliated with the Los Angeles Industrial Union Council. The Central Labor Council immediately established a rival union called the American Federation of Newspaper Writers and Reporters No. 1, chartered directly by the AFL. It soon became involved in a jurisdictional dispute with the Guild at the *Examiner*. As most of the members of the new AFL union were employed by the *Examiner*, it was recognized as their collective bargaining agent. Before the end of 1937, however, the Guild won agreements with the *Evening Herald and Express*, the *Daily News*, and the *Evening News*.[85]

Efforts to organize the *Hollywood Citizen-News* in 1938 met with more difficulty. The Guild called a strike after Harlan G. Palmer, publisher of the paper, discharged several editorial employees who were active members of the union. He refused to accede to requests made by Guild officials for reinstatement of the unionists, explaining that they were discharged in order to reduce expenses and that he reserved the right to select his editorial workers. Union officials claimed the employees were fired because of their activities on behalf of the Guild, which had been endeavoring to negotiate a contract with the *Citizen-News*. Palmer explained the coincidence of the discharges and the negotiations by stating that plans for a reduction in the newspaper had been completed simultaneously with, but independently of, the conferences with Guild representatives.[86]

The strike began on May 17, when more than twenty editorial employees who were members of the Guild walked out. The Guild immediately established a picket line and demanded reinstatement of the discharged employees and a provision in a new contract that there would be no further dismissals as a result of the agreement. The picket line was not universally respected, particularly by members of the Printing Trades Union, Inc., an independent labor organization composed of printing tradesmen employed at the *Citizen-News* who refused to support the strike. The Los Angeles Industrial Union Council gave full backing to the strike, however, and placed the newspaper on its unfair list. Other groups of unionists, including the San Francisco Industrial Union Council, CIO, took similar action. Several AFL unions also joined the fight, as the *Hollywood Citizen-News* had been on the Central Labor Council's unfair list for several years because of the management's failure to employ union printing craftsmen. Members of International Typographical Union, Local No. 174, AFL, aided the strikers financially and urged unionists to discontinue their subscriptions to the paper. The Screen Directors Guild, AFL, also contributed money to the strike fund, while members of the American Federation of Teachers, AFL, as well as unionized longshoremen and auto workers, served as pickets. The strike marked one of the few instances of unity between AFL and CIO unionists in southern California in 1938.[87]

Harlan Palmer was considered a liberal by members of many left-wing political groups, but when he refused to accede to the Guild's demands, leaders of these organizations branded him a hypocrite and an advocate of the open shop. Members of such groups as the American Student Union, the American League for Peace and Democracy, and the League of Women Shoppers joined the picket lines on different occasions. A number of prominent members of the movie colony, including actors, actresses, and writers, also served as pickets at various times, giving the strike a touch of glamor. Famous Hollywood characters such as "Peter the Hermit" often joined the march. One day eight state assemblymen paraded in the picket line with their names printed on placards pinned to their chests. One afternoon Frank Scully, a writer, held a cocktail party on the curbstone for pickets. On another occasion, pickets wearing green visors covered with stickers walked two and three abreast selling copies of the *Holly-*

wood Citizen-News Striker. Those supporting the strike attempted to reduce the circulation of the *Citizen-News* by encouraging subscribers to purchase other newspapers. Guild members also tried to curtail the amount of advertising in the paper. On one occasion, for example, 225 pickets marched in groups in front of three drugstores and a clothing firm, requesting the managements to withdraw their advertising from the *Citizen-News.* By June 6 spokesmen for the Guild claimed that more than eighty-three advertisers had canceled their contracts with the newspaper. Palmer also lost the contracts for printing *Daily Variety,* a moving-picture trade periodical, and the programs for the Hollywood Bowl.[88]

Legal action inevitably accompanied the dispute. Attorneys for Sontag Chain Stores Company, Ltd., and Schwab's Men's Store, establishments that were being picketed and boycotted because they advertised in the newspaper, filed a suit for $25,000 damages against the Guild and certain of its members, and requested a permanent injunction prohibiting these union activities. After holding a hearing, Superior Court Judge Emmet H. Wilson ruled that the secondary picketing of advertisers in the *Citizen-News* was illegal, and issued a permanent injunction against it. Later on, six men were cited for contempt of court for continuing to picket the advertisers after the permanent injunction had been handed down. They were declared responsible for stopping the movement of vehicles on Hollywood Boulevard in front of the Egyptian Theater on July 9 by conducting a demonstration against the newspaper. The case was dismissed after termination of the strike. The most significant case, in the view of open-shop supporters, began on June 24, when three strike leaders were arrested for distributing handbills in front of a Hollywood market in violation of a city ordinance. The defendants demanded a trial in order to test the constitutionality of the ordinance, and filed a request to enjoin interference by the police in such an activity. At the conclusion of the trial Municipal Judge William R. McKay declared that the ordinance was unconstitutional because it violated freedom of speech and of the press. The three members of the Guild were acquitted. The Appellate Department of the Superior Court, however, upheld the constitutionality of the ordinance.[89]

Early in the strike officials of the Los Angeles Newspaper Guild filed a complaint with the Regional Labor Board, alleging that five members of the editorial staff of the *Hollywood Citizen-News* had been discharged because of their union activities. At the subsequent hearing Palmer again maintained that he had been planning to curtail expenses because of a reduction in his business volume. Guild representatives, however, presented evidence purporting to show that Palmer was prejudiced against national labor organizations and that this was the reason for the dismissals. In an intermediate report filed after the end of the strike, the board found Palmer guilty of the charges. He was ordered to reinstate with back pay four of the discharged employees, to reinstate nineteen other striking employees, and to bargain in good faith with Guild representatives.[90]

Palmer continued to publish his newspaper during the strike, and to print editorials presenting his side of the argument. But finally he decided to compromise, and the walkout officially ended on July 30 with the reinstatement of the twenty-three dismissed strikers. The question of back pay for the strikers was decided in a later NLRB award. A contract was signed, but it did not provide for the closed shop. The strikers were given a vacation of two weeks with pay before returning to work, and were protected against dismissals until January 1, 1939.

Another contract signed in the same period with the *Huntington Park Signal* was the first closed-shop agreement secured by the American Newspaper Guild in California. It covered employees in the editorial, advertising, business, and maintenance departments and established a new and higher schedule of wages for these workers.[91]

The butchers' activities were not so colorful as those of the newspapermen in 1937 and 1938. Amalgamated Meat Cutters and Butcher Workmen of North America, Local No. 421, AFL, started an organizing campaign in the latter months of 1936 which continued for the next two years. By the middle of 1937, 1,200 workers belonged to the local, and before the end of the year union officials claimed a membership of 4,000. Most of the opposition to the organizing drive came from members of Allied Food Industries and the Super Markets' Association who supported the open shop. Allen and Huck markets, an affiliate of the association, successfully withstood a seven-month strike by the butchers and meatcutters in 1937. All the strikers were replaced and the pickets were restrained by means of an injunction. A number of other markets similarly opposed the demands of the unionists. In the same year Local No. 421, with the coöperation of other union butchers in southern California, managed to obtain agreements covering the meat departments of Safeway Stores, Inc., in Los Angeles; but another union, Packing House Butchers Local No. 563, AFL, failed to organize the employees of the Cudahy Packing Company, some of whom belonged to a company union. Local No. 563, aided by a teamsters' affiliate, Meat and Provision Drivers Local No. 626, AFL, established a boycott and picketed the firm's plants in Los Angeles, Fresno, and Salt Lake City. But Cudahy employees, satisfied with the firm's wage and hour policy, refused to join the AFL unions.[92]

One of the more unusual happenings on the local labor scene in 1938 occurred on March 2, when 1,200 members of Local No. 421 approved a voluntary reduction in wages from $40 to $35 for a fifty-four-hour week as a means of coöperating with their employers during the business recession. This arrangement apparently continued throughout the year, for in December Safeway Stores, Inc., signed an agreement with Local No. 421, as well as with the unions of bakers, warehousemen, teamsters, confectionery workers, and clerks, which guaranteed meatcutters a minimum wage of $35 for a fifty-four-hour week, and an annual vacation of one week with pay after one year.[93]

In 1938 Packing House Butchers Local No. 563, despite several jurisdictional disputes with the Packing House Workers, CIO, became one of the largest unions in the city. A Regional Labor Board election at the Cudahy plant late in 1938 gave the local certification after its failure of the year before. In a strike against the Cornelius Packing Company, the union won a thirty-two-hour week and a wage increase of 10 to 15 per cent. No. 563 was also certified as the collective bargaining agent for the workers at Armour and Company. Everything considered, 1938 was a good year for the AFL butchers and meatcutters, perhaps the best in the history of their union in Los Angeles.[94]

The printing trades unions made progress in 1937 and 1938, increasing their memberships and gaining new contracts. The Neuner Printing and Lithographing Company, an open-shop firm for fifty years, became a closed-shop establishment in February, 1937. A month later the Los Angeles Allied Printing Trades Council, AFL, disclosed that total union employment in commercial print shops was the highest since 1929. By the end of May Secretary Buzzell of the Central Labor Council was able to report that the electrotypers and the stereotypers had unionized almost all the workers in their trades, and that the unions of bookbinders, pressmen, and photoengravers were growing. The membership of ITU Local No. 174 showed an all-time high in November of 1,201 printers.[95]

Unemployment, which began to increase in the printing trades after July, 1937, became quite severe by the end of the year as the recession ate into the available jobs. As 1938 moved along, however, more opportunities for work appeared, and several new unions were formed. By the end of the year, spokesmen for the printing trades locals reported that few unionists were unemployed, and eleven locals were affiliated with the Allied Printing Trades Council. To aid an intensive campaign to increase the use of the union label, the members of ITU Local No. 174 voted an extra per capita assessment of 5 cents a month. Some success was achieved as more union labels were in use at the end of 1938. Possibly the major failure of Local No. 174 was its inability to organize the workers in the composing rooms of the *Hollywood Citizen-News* because they belonged to the Printing Trades Union, Inc., a TNT-sponsored independent labor organization. ITU officials told the Regional Labor Board that it was a company-controlled union. Upon investigation, the board found that the complaint was correct; its decision was upheld by the NLRB in Washington, D.C., and Harlan Palmer was ordered to disband the union.[96]

In contrast with the printing trades unions, the retail clerks had never been a strong group in Los Angeles. But they began to come into their own in the late 1930's. In 1934–1935 the Ladies' Wearing Apparel Salesmen's Union, chartered directly by the Executive Council of the AFL, was affiliated with the Central Labor Council. In 1936 the Retail Clerks International Protective Association, AFL, established Pharmacists Local No. 840 and gave it jurisdiction over drug clerks. A year later locals of retail clerks were organized among department, grocery, hardware, and furniture store personnel, as well as men's clothing and shoe salesmen. A union of credit and collection clerks was also formed late in 1937, but it did not then affiliate with the Retail Clerks International.[97]

Another clerks' union, Department Store Employees Local No. 1210, AFL, did not gain many new members among the workers in large retail stores. Retail Shoe Clerks Local No. 406, however, obtained union- or closed-shop contracts in 1937 with C. H. Baker, Leeds, Chandler, Burt, Berland, Bentley, Meyer, Karl, Kirby, Kay, Gallenkamp, and Greater shoe stores as well as the shoe departments of Swelldom and Gorton's Baby Shop. Most of the contracts provided for wages of $30 a week, an eight-hour day, a forty-eight-hour week, time and a half for overtime, a commission on all or a part of gross sales, a one-week vacation with pay for all employees with a year's service, several annual holidays with pay, and the designation of Local No. 406 as the sole bargaining agent for the workers. Most of these contracts were renewed in 1938 and were extended to cover a few additional firms, including Brand, S.C.M.A., Reeves, and National Dollar stores. Stoner's signed a contract, but it did not provide for a closed shop.[98]

Retail Clothing Salesmen and Haberdashers Local No. 1054, AFL, signed contracts with a number of clothing firms in Los Angeles, including Royalbilt, Furmbilt, and Brooks, several shirt shops, and some army and navy stores. By June, 1937, the managements of more than twenty-six concerns, employing 200 workers, had signed union contracts. Most of the agreements provided for weekly wages of $40 for clothing salesmen, $30 for haberdashers, a forty-eight-hour week, time and a half for overtime, a week's vacation with pay each year, and sole collective bargaining rights for the union. Western Auto Supply Company and eight hardware firms signed agreements with representatives of Hardware and Automobile Parts Clerks Local No. 1215, AFL.[99]

Retail Food Clerks Local No. 770, AFL, negotiated an agreement in 1937 with Safeway Stores, Inc., for southern California, and signed a contract covering the clerical personnel in fifteen supermarkets of the E. F. Smith Company. Not all organizational efforts were peaceful, however, as No. 770 called a number of strikes jointly with Local No. 421 of meatcutters and butchers. The C. S. Smith Company and several other firms fought these strikes by securing injunctions. Aided by Allied Food Industries, they sought to weaken the unions' case by adopting minimum wages which were satisfactory to their employees. What could have developed into the most serious strike of the period occurred in December, 1937, when it was claimed that almost 15,000 retail food clerks employed in more than 1,000 stores of the Retail Grocers' Association in southern California were going to walk out. The unionists demanded a fifty-hour week and a weekly minimum wage of $20. The actual numerical strength of the union was not sufficient, however, to enable them to enforce the threat.[100]

In February, 1938, Local No. 770 joined with teamsters, culinary workers, actors, and musicians in forming the AFL Food Alliance. Through this coördinating body the unionists hoped to organize the workers in all retail and wholesale markets, restaurants, and cabarets, and to obtain closed-shop contracts. Hardly had the alliance been established when Local No. 770 called a strike against all the units of Safeway Stores, Inc., after contract renewal negotiations broke down. The strike actually began on April 16 against all Safeway stores in Los Angeles County. Safeway officials granted the wage demands, but refused to consider a request for a fifty-hour week with time and a half for all overtime beyond fifty-four hours. They wanted to maintain a fifty-eight-hour workweek. After two days the 800 strikers agreed to return to work during negotiations and signed a new contract which became effective on June 9. It provided for a fifty-four-hour week, a vacation of one week with pay after a year of employment, six legal holidays a year, a weekly minimum wage of $20 with automatic increases up to a maximum of $25.50, and prohibition of discriminatory discharges for union activity. At its inception the agreement covered the clerks in 270 stores; eventually it applied to the clerical employees in 490 Safeway units in southern California. Local No. 770 also participated in a national contract negotiated by the Retail Clerks International with the Great Atlantic and Pacific Tea Company. In 1938 the E. F. Smith Company and a number of other firms renewed their contracts. By May, 1938, Local No. 770 had placed fifty-six concerns on its fair list, several of which had many branch outlets.[101]

The organized retail clerks also were active in produce markets and in the credit and collection field. In the produce markets Local No. 770 ran into independent unionism in the form of the Southern California Retail Produce Workers Union, Inc., supported by The Neutral Thousands. The members of this union were employed mainly in Japanese vegetable and fruit stands in large food stores. One of the biggest jurisdictional disputes between the two unions occurred in 1938 at the stands operated in thirty-five markets by the 3-Star Produce Company.

In January, 1938, the clerks chartered a new local called the Credit and Collection Employees Union, AFL. Its officials were able to organize the credit and collection clerks in several credit clothing stores in the city, including those at Brooks, one of the largest retailers of men's clothing.[102]

Independent unionism was a serious problem for locals of the United Rubber Workers, CIO; it did more to retard their organizing campaign than their expulsion from the Central Labor Council in 1937. Although Local No. 44 was recognized by the United States Rubber Company in Los Angeles late in 1936, Locals No. 43, 100, 117, and 131 were forced to compete with independent unions at the other tire-manufacturing plants in the city. In 1937 the Regional Labor Board conducted elections to determine the collective bargaining agents for the workers at the Goodyear, Goodrich, and Firestone plants. In each instance the employees voted for the United Rubber Workers, which was subsequently certified as bargaining agent at all three plants, thus gaining a clear victory over the independents. The latter dropped out of the picture except at the Firestone plant, where in 1938 URW Local No. 100 charged the management with supporting a company union and releasing workers affiliated with the CIO organization. The accusation was presented before the Regional Labor Board, which ordered Firestone to reinstate five of its employees with back pay, permit its workers to join any labor organization, and disestablish the company union.[103]

The Steel Workers Organizing Committee, like the rubber workers, was affiliated with the CIO. It began to organize steelworkers in Los Angeles and vicinity in March, 1937, establishing a local of about 1,000 members at the Columbia Steel Company in Torrance. There had been no industrial union of steelworkers in the Los Angeles area after Torrance Lodge No. 7 of the Amalgamated Iron, Steel and Tin Workers of North America was disbanded in May, 1934. Later in 1937 workers were organized in the plants of the Continental Can, American Can, and International Harvester companies, a number of small welding concerns, several steel fabrication mills, and some manufacturing firms. Some of the managements negotiated contracts with SWOC officials. One of the firms that did not sign a contract was the American Can Company, and in subsequent months the SWOC tried unsuccessfully to negotiate an agreement. Finally, Local No. 1549 called a work stoppage on June 22, 1938, in coöperation with unionists working at four other branches of the firm in California. Demands included a uniform wage of 67½ cents an hour for the workers in all the plants, preferential hiring of unionists, and vacations with pay. A few days later the 1,500 SWOC members in the five plants struck, declaring that they would not work until the company granted their demands. William Dalrymple, regional director of the CIO at this time, ordered the strikers to return to work, but his orders were repudiated. Local SWOC officials protested against his dictatorial attitude and requested the national officers of the CIO to remove him from his position.[104]

John Doherty, an international representative of the SWOC, came to California to investigate the charges made against Dalrymple. Dalrymple stood his ground, asserting that he had been correct in ordering the men back to work because they had violated national policy by striking during negotiations. He pointed out that both 1937 and early 1938 were mainly organizing periods and that strikes for recognition were not yet encouraged by the SWOC. The steelworkers were in no mood for compromise, however, and soon resorted to violence. This included assaults, beatings, the throwing of bricks through the windows of workers' homes, damage to automobiles, and the placing of sand in the wheel bearings of railroad freight cars. The strikers closed down the Los Angeles plant, but the management obtained an injunction that permitted only one picket for each twenty-five feet of frontage and two pickets on each side of the entrances to the factory. The injunction was granted because the mass picketing of as many as 500 strikers was believed responsible for some of the violence. The company then resumed operations, hiring guards from the Bodell Detective Agency for the duration of the dispute.[105]

On July 13, 100 of the striking steelworkers participated in a sit-down strike at the offices of the State Relief Administration in an attempt to obtain assistance. They were unsuccessful because the American Can Company was operating and their jobs were technically available. A few days later Doherty vindicated Dalrymple. Negotiations were then begun to return the strikers to their jobs. Officials of Local No. 1549 agreed to terminate the dispute and accepted management's offer to rehire the strikers at the end of July. Before the end of the year a contract was signed, but repercussions from the strike echoed in two court cases arising from incidents that had occurred during the dispute. In one case, fourteen strikers were fined for violating the injunction against mass picketing. In a longer case, Mike Yavendetti, president of Local No. 1549, and fourteen other persons were arrested on felony charges of conspiracy to commit assault on nonunionists and other planned acts of violence. The charges were presented to the grand jury by representatives of the district attorney. CIO officials countered that District Attorney Fitts often converted simple assault charges into felony counts in order to force unions to deplete their treasuries to pay trial costs. Labor leaders believed that Fitts was in league with open-shop supporters who, in turn, were behind the antipicketing ordinance campaign in Los Angeles in 1938. At the conclusion of the trial six of the defendants were convicted of simple assault, including Yavendetti. Appeals were made for new trials, but Superior Court Judge Arthur Crum granted these petitions only with respect to four of the five counts in the conviction of Yavendetti. The other defendants were sentenced on January 11, 1939, to thirty days in the county jail.[106]

By the end of 1938, in addition to the contract with American Can, the SWOC had agreements with Continental Can, Columbia Steel, Emsco Derrick and Equipment Company, American Manganese Casting Company, and International Harvester. It claimed that the membership of the lodges in Los Angeles and vicinity totaled 7,000. In the latter part of 1938 the smaller locals were amalgamated with the larger ones in order to build up a stronger organization to combat the open-shop movement and AFL organizational activity among steelworkers. The AFL efforts, which were of minor significance, were conducted mainly by the International Association of Bridge, Structural and Ornamental Iron Workers. Local No. 433 of this union called a strike against the Pacific Steel Building Company in Vernon late in 1937, demanding wage increases for seventy men, but its real purpose was to organize the workers in the plant. After three judges had disqualified themselves from hearing the case on various grounds, the company finally secured a permanent injunction prohibiting the unionists from further picketing because a lawful strike did not exist. Only six employees engaged in the outside construction of steel service stations had struck. These were replaced by other workers shortly after the dispute began.[107]

Like the SWOC, the United Automobile Workers of America, CIO, dealt mainly with local branches of national firms. In 1937 UAW locals, after joining the Los Angeles Industrial Union Council, launched an organizing campaign which met its most severe test at the Long Beach plant of the Ford Motor Company. Local No. 406, the union involved, participated in the nationwide drive to organize Ford workers by distributing windshield stickers reading: "Americanism, Not Fordism" and "My Last Ford." The management of the Long Beach plant, in accordance with Ford policy, refused to recognize the union, although it was certified as the collective bargaining agent in December, 1937. Members of Local No. 406 thereupon voted to join the national strike against Ford which was beginning in the Eastern and Midwestern plants of the corporation, if and when such action became necessary.[108]

Early in March, 1938, officials of Local No. 406 filed charges with the Regional Labor Board accusing the Ford Motor Company of fostering a company union at its Long Beach plant, indulging in unfair labor practices, refusing to negotiate with union representatives, and showing discrimination in the discharge of twenty-seven UAW members. They also threatened a strike if the company did not discontinue such practices. The strike did not actually begin, however, until April 15, when it was precipitated by a fight between a member of Local No. 406 and a representative of the company union. Picket lines were established at once, and by April 18, 300 men were marching around the plant while martial music was played on phonographs placed in sound trucks. Factory operations were continued, though on a reduced scale. I. B. Groves, plant manager, admitted that about half of the 437 production workers were on strike, but union officials claimed that 402 men had walked out. Similar conflicting reports were issued throughout the first few weeks of the dispute.[109]

Some members of Local No. 406 returned to their jobs within a week, but the strike was not without violence. By April 22 the police in Los Angeles and Long Beach had recorded twenty-five cases involving overt acts. Towne Nylander of the Regional Labor Board failed in an attempt to mediate the dispute; management argued that recognition of the union would be contrary to Ford's national labor policy, that the company had decided to curtail production before the strike, and that it would therefore rehire without discrimination only 77 men so that no more than 350 employees would be working on the assembly line. As the company was adamant, between 600 and 800 pickets continued to march around the factory area whenever employees entered or left the plant, and 60 manned the lines at other times. When additional efforts of the Regional Labor Board to induce the plant's management to compromise were unsuccessful, the board indicted the local Ford executives and ordered a hearing on the dispute.[110]

The strike continued into May. Picketing operations were maintained with support from other CIO unions, and a mass meeting to shape public opinion was held at Trinity Auditorium in Los Angeles. Upton Sinclair, the featured speaker, stated that the "Ford empire is the nearest thing to fascism that has yet appeared in America." In June the Regional Labor Board held its hearings. Spokesmen for Local No. 406 charged that a company union had been fostered in the plant, and that the management had refused to bargain collectively, discouraged membership in labor unions, opposed the holding of an election to determine the proper employee representative, and hired guards and spies to prevent any discussion of the UAW. They also testified that the plant used lead-grinding machines that were detrimental to the health of the employees. Company representatives entered a general denial, but board examiner R. N. Denham issued an intermediate decision in favor of the unionists. It provided for the reinstatement of approximately 450 members of Local No. 406, with back pay from the date they struck, and disestablishment of the company union.[111]

Although the case was referred to the NLRB in Washington, the management still refused to negotiate with the union. Strikers remained on the picket lines in greatly reduced numbers throughout the remainder of the year, but most of them sought employment elsewhere because adequate funds were not received for their subsistence. The national CIO convention inaugurated a nationwide boycott of Ford products, and revived the campaign to place stickers reading "Don't Buy Ford" on the windshields of automobiles driven by unionists. But the firm still refused to abandon its open-shop policy. By the end of

1938 most of the strikers who were still without work were in serious straits, and the ladies' auxiliary of the Los Angeles Industrial Union Council was collecting old clothes for the strikers' families. Local No. 406 had become so weak that it could no longer hamper operations at the factory. On December 8, 1939, the NLRB, ruling that the Ford management was responsible for the dispute, ordered the company to reinstate 275 strikers with back pay and establish collective bargaining negotiations with Local No. 406. It did announce, however, that the independent union at the plant was not dominated by the company. The plant's management took no immediate steps to conform to the NLRB order, and so the company was not unionized until World War II had more impact on the national economy.[112]

A number of other unions were energetic enough in 1937–1938 to catch the public eye. Barbers Local No. 295, AFL, put on an organizing drive in the early months of 1937, concentrating on the rapidly growing southeast section of the city, where it placed union-shop cards in ninety-six establishments. Later in the year, Soap and Cosmetics Workers Local No. 21361, AFL, launched a campaign to unionize the thousands of cosmetics workers in Hollywood. In 1938 the barbers realized there were too many shops and too many barbers. Price cutting became the practice in an effort to gain business from rival shops, but it only reduced the dollar sales volume for everyone. In attempts to stabilize prices, stench bombs were thrown and windows of shops that refused to comply with stated union prices were broken. Of the five unionists arrested and accused of these actions, three were officers of Local No. 295: Rea Last, secretary; Alexander Alexander, business agent; and S. R. Turner, recording secretary. After a trial, attorneys for the defense made a motion for dismissal. Superior Court Judge Ingall W. Bull granted the motion on the ground of lack of evidence, except for Turner and another defendant, Abe Solinski, who were each fined $200 and placed on probation for two years.[113]

The same kind of destructive tactics marred the organizing campaign of the International Building Service Employees Union, AFL, in 1937 and early 1938. The acts of violence included not only throwing stench bombs, but also spraying windows with acid, assaulting employees, and, in one instance, cutting the ropes of the scaffold used by a building worker. The union, however, seemed not to lose in repute because of these incidents, as charters were installed for several new locals, including Theater Janitors Local No. 72, Window Washers Local No. 101, and Elevator Operators Local No. 62.[114]

The AFL laundry workers and musicians also were active. As in years past, the former found that open-shop laundry owners and unskilled female employees constituted an almost insuperable obstacle to effective unionization. Local No. 52 of the laundry workers was formed and a number of contracts were signed, but the unionists encountered strong opposition. The employers obtained injunctions restraining picketing, and several union members received heavy fines for violating court orders. The musicians, with the help of the Hollywood studios, continued to be relatively strong. Local No. 47 was the largest union in the city, with a membership of 5,600. It was presided over by Jack Tenney, a state assemblyman and composer of *Mexicali Rose.* Tenney later won notoriety for his alleged "book-burning" proclivities and attempts to root out Communist propaganda in the state's public education system.[115]

In 1937 and 1938 both the AFL and the CIO started campaigns to organize employees of Los Angeles city and county. The Los Angeles County Board of Supervisors, though ruling that county employees might join any labor union they wished, would not permit them to strike. Nor would exclusive bargaining rights be granted to any single union so long as it did not represent all the workers. Eventually AFL representatives set up two locals of the American Federation of State, County and Municipal Employees in the city. One consisted of Board of Education employees; the other, of Los Angeles County General Hospital employees. In addition, the memberships of the Miscellaneous Foremen and Superintendents, the Municipal Laborers, the Municipal Drivers, Electrical Workers Local No. 18, and the American Federation of Teachers were composed largely of city employees. The CIO was successful in chartering State, County and Municipal Workers of America, Local No. 84. In December, 1937, this union demanded wage increases which, if granted, would have totaled $1,640,000 annually for 6,031 employees of the county charities; but the requests were tabled by the Board of Supervisors. Local No. 84 was not the exclusive bargaining agent for county employees, for it had to compete with the independent Los Angeles County Employees Association. A jurisdictional dispute with the CIO destroyed the AFL union at the Los Angeles General Hospital in 1938, but the Board of Education AFL local survived the year. The CIO also entered the public utility field when Local No. 132, Utility Workers Organizing Committee, organized the workers at the Southern California Gas Company in 1938. But a contract was not negotiated. Local No. 155 of the same international was recognized by the Los Angeles Department of Water and Power as the collective bargaining agent for those employees who were members of the union.[116]

Another new area of organizing activity in 1937–1938 was in banking. Evidence of this came to light when officials of the Bank of America became defendants in a hearing conducted by the Regional Labor Board. E. C. Washer, a former investment specialist for the bank, claimed that he was discharged because, in propagandizing for the United Office and Professional Workers of America, CIO, he had mailed a leaflet concerning the union to bank employees. At the hearing, defense attorneys refused to produce the records of the institution, arguing that the Bank of America, as a national bank, was an arm of the United States government and hence not subject to the NLRA. Washer had been discharged, not for encouraging employees to join a union, but for padding his expense account. Trial examiner R. N. Denham ruled against the bank, however, and ordered the reinstatement of Washer with back pay, directing that there be no interference with the rights of employees to organize for the purpose of bargaining collectively.[117]

The activities of unions in 1937 and 1938 reveal that there was more life in the Los Angeles labor movement than ever before. Although unions were far from being fully accepted, they were definitely on their way up; moreover, they seemed to have leaped the barrier that had held them back since 1890, when the campaign to maintain the open shop was launched under the leadership of the *Times* and the M and M. Union aggressiveness was shown not only by widespread activity and frequent success in organizing drives, but also by the size of unfair lists. In December, 1938, for example, the *Citizen* published the largest unfair list in the history of the Central Labor Council. It contained the names of ninety-six firms or products against which active boycotts were in progress. The increase in union membership also testified to the resurgence of the labor movement. Useful figures are not available on CIO strength in Los Angeles, but the AFL published estimates listing a per capita tax membership in the Central Labor Council of 44,063 on May 31, 1938, as compared with 34,478 a year earlier. Secretary Buzzell believed there were between 100,000 and 115,000 AFL members in Los Angeles, though a large number of them belonged to locals not affiliated with the council. Of the 157 locals that did belong, however, thirteen were new additions.[118]

It is particularly noteworthy that this growth of the Los Angeles labor movement was accomplished despite internal disputes over

Communism and over industrial versus craft organization. The fear of Los Angeles open-shop employers that unions might be here to stay was seen in their last-ditch efforts to stem the organizing tide through such groups as Southern Californians, Incorporated. The only point of agreement between organized labor and the open-shop forces was that the continued influx of indigents into the state must be prevented. To Southern Californians, Incorporated, however, unemployed vagrants meant lower job standards and higher relief burdens and tax loads, whereas unionists saw in them a labor reserve that constantly threatened the jobs of those who were employed. On all other points, at every opportunity, the battle between the open-shop front and the unionists was joined.

XIV. THE BEGINNING OF THE END
OF THE OPEN SHOP

1. OUT OF DEPRESSION—INTO WAR

THE IMPROVEMENT in business conditions late in 1938 continued into 1939, a trend accentuated by the beginning of World War II. The nation began to feel the economic impact of becoming the "arsenal for democracy," even though the so-called "phony war" did not flare into a more serious conflict until 1940. The improvement in economic conditions did not mean that the depression was over, however, as above-normal unemployment plagued the nation's economy.

Public relief was necessary throughout 1939. Federal funds were added to monies from state and local governments in order to finance emergency relief programs. The Works Progress Administration was reorganized, assuming the new name of Work Projects Administration on July 1. Its officials were assigned the dual function of supervising nonfederal, locally sponsored work projects and of coördinating the relief programs of different governmental agencies.[1]

The conflict between the AFL and the CIO continued, as the unification terms proposed by AFL officials were unacceptable to CIO leaders. They feared that the industrial union structure would disappear unless the craft-dominated AFL Executive Council, in a genuine change of viewpoint, would give enough autonomy to the new internationals to permit their survival. AFL leaders continued to criticize the NLRA and members of the NLRB. CIO leaders stood fast on the law, fearing its possible emasculation by changes proposed by Senator David I. Walsh of Massachusetts, with the advice and assistance of the AFL. CIO President John L. Lewis was particularly outspoken against what he called the NLRB policy of deciding bargaining unit cases in favor of the AFL. NLRB General Counsel Charles Fahy denied Lewis' charges that the board was biased. He pointed out that the two rivals had won about the same number of cases for representation, recognition, the establishment of contracts, and the reinstatement of discharged unionists. The AFL voted in 1939 to continue a special per capita assessment of one cent a month in order to provide funds to oppose the CIO. When the International Typographical Union refused to pay this tax, it was suspended by the AFL Executive Council.[2]

The AFL-CIO conflict was a source of embarrassment to California Governor Culbert L. Olson, who completed his first year in office in

1939. It was almost impossible to please both sides simultaneously. State Federation of Labor officials condemned him for using officers of the California Highway Patrol to maintain order during a lumber strike in northern California. Further, they claimed he was inclined to favor the CIO, which, in turn, accused him of appeasing employers and large farm operators. The CIO feared that he would cease to be a liberal in state politics.

Meanwhile, Labor's Non-Partisan League remained in the center of the state AFL-CIO controversy. Delegates to the 1939 convention of the California State Federation of Labor passed a resolution against supporting the league. Nevertheless, a number of Los Angeles AFL unions maintained their affiliation with it. The Los Angeles Board of Education renewed the ban on the use of public school buildings for league meetings, mainly because of the belief that Communists were active among its members.[3]

Through the intervention of Governor Olson, the California labor movement gained a long-time goal in the pardon of Thomas J. Mooney. Mooney and Warren K. Billings, AFL unionists, had been imprisoned for their complicity in a bombing incident which killed several persons in San Francisco on Preparedness Day, 1916. Over the years California AFL unionists had given moral and financial support to Mooney and Billings in their legal and political efforts to secure freedom. The two men became symbols of martyrdom for the cause of justice in California—a cause whose adherents placed open-shop employers among the unjust. Labor leaders maintained that the men had been convicted by antiunion forces by means of perjured evidence. The Los Angeles Central Labor Council had joined in general support of the plea of innocence made by the two prisoners. While a member of the California Legislature, Governor Olson had upheld Mooney whenever his request for a pardon had been under consideration. When campaigning for the governorship, Olson had promised that, if elected, he would attempt to free him. True to this promise, he pardoned Mooney early in January, 1939.[4]

Thirty-five thousand persons gathered to greet Mooney at a mass meeting held at the Los Angeles Coliseum on January 15. The meeting was sponsored by the Los Angeles Industrial Union Council without prior consultation with the Central Labor Council. Ironically, because of this rebuff, the AFL council refused an invitation for its members to attend the rally, although it had long sought to gain Mooney's release. Mooney's fellow prisoner, Warren K. Billings, had his sentence commuted by Governor Olson to time served by October

17, 1939. Under the laws of the state, he could not receive a full pardon because he had previously been convicted of a misdemeanor.[5]

The most important state-wide political issue of interest to organized labor in 1939 was the Retirement Life Payments Act, or "Ham and Eggs," which was revived after its 1938 defeat. Its advocates found enough support for this old-age pension plan to place it again on the ballot. They wanted to hold a special election in August, when many voters who might be against it would possibly be out of the state and public interest would be at a minimum. Olson delayed the election, however, and issued strong statements against the initiative when it was announced that the balloting would occur in November. Leading supporters of the plan, who had thought Olson favored the cause, considered his action traitorous. Lieutenant Governor Ellis Patterson supported the proposition and curried the political favor of its advocates. Many reputable economists as well as political leaders in both state and nation, including President Roosevelt, opposed "Ham and Eggs." Lengthy articles and editorials appearing in Los Angeles newspapers, particularly the *Times,* condemned it without qualification. Also against it were supporters of the rival pension plan formulated by Dr. Francis E. Townsend. The mere threat that the Retirement Life Payments Act would pass caused interest rates for new issues of state bonds to rise rapidly, as the market shrank because of the possible harm to California's credit rating.[6]

The Los Angeles Industrial Union Council and most of the organizations affiliated with the CIO supported "Ham and Eggs." Members of the Communist Party actively campaigned for the measure. The Los Angeles Central Labor Council did not endorse it, partly because subsection 3 of Section 2 of the initiative declared that it was unlawful to curtail or limit and make unproductive the flow of goods or services. AFL officials believed that this provision could be used to limit strikes or boycotts. The Los Angeles Building and Construction Trades Council and the officials of the California State Federation of Labor likewise refused to make any statements on the issue. In the election on November 7, the plan was decisively defeated. Its sponsors placed primary responsibility for its defeat on Governor Olson, and tried to start a movement to have him recalled. Opposition to their plan was so severe that the governor's tenure was not seriously threatened.[7]

Organized labor in California, particularly in the southern part of the state where there was a concentration of the unemployed, was much interested in Governor Olson's relief measures. In his first year in office, in an effort to improve relief administration, he established the California Commission on Reemployment to analyze the problems. Very little of the governor's program became effective, however, as the members of the legislature did not approve of his production-for-use plan of state-owned producers' and consumers' coöperatives. In a sixteen-page report, the legislative committee that investigated the State Relief Administration charged that espionage was common, employee morale was low, and politics was rife in the organization. The governor denied the charges and claimed that the report was a political scheme to promote the return of relief administration to the counties, where Republican supervisors were predominant.[8]

At the 1939 AFL state convention Olson received another blow, for the state federation showed that its support of the governor was not unqualified. At this time the CSFL was assertedly in the strongest economic position in its history, although during 1938 its total membership had decreased by 24,335 to a reported 267,401. Delegates to the convention became very exercised over reports that the CIO was unfairly proselyting members of AFL unions. The engendered ill feeling carried over into the election of a secretary-treasurer for the ensuing year. Edward D. Vandeleur was reëlected after a bitter verbal exchange with Alexander Watchman, president of the San Francisco Central Labor Council, a supporter of Governor Olson, and an advocate of coöperation with the CIO and Labor's Non-Partisan League. The defeat of Watchman was interpreted by many labor and political leaders as a loss for Olson and a portent of his decline in favor with labor voters.[9]

The state-wide California CIO Council became stronger in 1939. It strengthened the coöperation between central bodies and CIO unions through numerous conferences of state officers and local CIO leaders as well as a general expansion of the industrial union movement throughout California. The Los Angeles Industrial Union Council exemplified this effort to consolidate gains and strengthen the industrial union structure. In August, 1939, under the presidency of Robert Wilson of ILWU Local No. 1-13, it comprised sixty unions with a total membership of about 50,000 workers. The majority of these unions were in the automobile, steel, utility, warehouse, rubber, and maritime industries.[10]

2. LABOR, LOCAL POLITICS, AND THE OPEN SHOP

The Los Angeles Industrial Union Council actively supported WPA workers who participated in work stoppages in the city in 1939. One of the most important of these in terms of numbers occurred in July, when several thousand workers conducted a peaceful demonstration against proposed changes in the national administration of the WPA which would have resulted in the dismissal of 30,000 recipients of work relief in California. As in previous years, the demonstrators were led by the Workers Alliance, with the local stoppage only a part of a nationwide protest. Although this and other stoppages were embarrassing to city officials, they were usually peaceful in nature and served to strengthen Mayor Bowron's desire to form a council of labor leaders and employers to mediate industrial disputes. The mayor invited prominent AFL and CIO officials, as well as employer group representatives, to participate in the formation of such a council, but the plan bogged down when local AFL leaders refused to serve on a committee with CIO members. And some business leaders believed that the establishment of a permanent mediation body was tantamount to admitting that Los Angeles was a city of unionized workers.[11]

Towne J. Nylander, head of the Los Angeles Regional Labor Board, was suspended from his position in February, 1939. Officially, his suspension was a result of charges that, in a public address printed in the *Inglewood Daily News,* he had stated that employers did not "have a chance" when they participated in an NLRB hearing. Nylander claimed that he was misquoted in the newspaper. Both CIO and AFL leaders defended him, indicating that they considered him quite impartial. Central Labor Council officials, however, claimed that CIO officers were responsible for his suspension. After an investigation Nylander was exonerated and reinstated, but he resigned the following July. Walter P. Spreckels, formerly in charge of labor relations under the WPA in New York City, took his place.[12]

Central Labor Council officials said that Nylander's suspension and subsequent resignation were caused by attempts of CIO members and the Communist Party to control the Regional Labor Board. This was denied by Nylander. Although not stated in so many words, the real reason for his resignation seems to have been a strained relationship between him and the NLRB after his suspension. A hearing held later in Washington revealed that a number of field investigators appointed to the Los Angeles Regional Labor Board were supporters of left-wing unions affiliated with the CIO. These men had been opposed by Nylander, but it is not certain that their retention was an element in his resignation. It is worth noting that by December, 1939, Spreckels had replaced six field investigators who had worked under Nylander.[13]

Regardless of the true facts in the Regional Labor Board controversy, with its overtones of AFL-CIO disharmony, the Central Labor Council accusations were made from a position of strength. In January, 1939, the council was composed of the largest number of locals in its history. As the year went along, however, some unions dropped out, so that by June, on net balance, there was a total of 145 affiliated organizations, or ten fewer than in June, 1938. On the other hand, the number of workers represented was slightly larger. Estimates indicated that total AFL unionists in Los Angeles County increased during this period to about 120,000. Simultaneously, there was a substantial decrease in the number of delegates at the weekly council meetings in the first eight months of 1939, attributable to widespread adoption of the five-day workweek. This change caused many locals to hold their meetings on Friday nights, and thus their delegates could not regularly attend council sessions on the same evening. To obviate the difficulty, the council changed its official meetings to Monday night, after having met on Friday evenings for thirty-seven years. The subsequent increase in attendance for the remainder of the year justified the change.[14]

The Central Labor Council hired Steve O'Donnell as a publicity agent to assist in the organizing campaigns of 1939. CIO officials called O'Donnell an employers' agent, pointing out that he had been in charge of public relations for some of the large retail stores during the May Company strike in 1937, had handled the state-wide radio broadcasts in favor of Proposition No. 1 in 1938, and had directed the publicity for former Mayor Frank L. Shaw in the 1938 recall campaign. Buzzell countered by accusing the CIO of being pro-Communist and the successor to the Trade Union Unity League. His hatred of communism was likewise evident in his identification of the American League for Peace and Democracy as a Communist organization, and in his refusal to contribute news to the *People's World,* the newspaper of the Communist Party. With O'Donnell's help, the council actively pushed the organizing campaigns of constituent unions. Results of this effort were seen in December, 1939, when a new peak was reached in the number of names on the council's unfair list. Approximately 137 firms, products, and persons were listed, excluding the local branch establishments of nationally boycotted concerns.[15]

The Los Angeles Industrial Union Council also carried on an intensive organizing campaign in 1939, but without much assistance from its newspaper, the *Industrial Unionist,* which did not prove to be a financial success and was discontinued late in the year. Some of the resultant publicity gap during part of 1939 was covered by a radio broadcast on station KRKD, called "Our Daily Bread." And the

"Dawn Patrol" used in the 1938 campaign was revived. The CIO's purpose was to initiate a new offensive against the open shop, to oppose the AFL in Los Angeles, and to organize the workers in the city's larger industries.[16]

In 1939, as in the past, both CIO and AFL factions were active in local politics. Generally speaking, Mayor Bowron was considered fair to unionists. Candidates for the City Council endorsed by the mayor in the May 2 election were, in most instances, supported by organized labor. Union representatives asked Bowron to remove William F. Hynes, former head of the Intelligence Bureau, from the Police Department, but the matter was only taken under advisement. Labor's record in other areas of city politics was spotty. Unionists supported a proposition requiring two men to operate a streetcar. This proposition, long a bone of contention between labor and the Los Angeles Railway, was approved at the May 2 election. Labor viewed the one-man car as a threat to employment, though union leaders officially argued the matter on a safety basis. Another proposition supported by the Central Labor Council, but opposed by the open-shop Los Angeles Railway, advocated a municipal bus system. The proposition failed, however, at a special city election held on December 12.[17]

The struggle to repeal the city ordinance regulating picketing, which had been passed in September, 1938, was continued in 1939. The AFL and the CIO buried the hatchet long enough to coöperate with a number of political organizations in support of a series of cases to test the constitutionality of the ordinance. They also planned to circulate petitions for repeal of the law at a special election, and perhaps to establish another political alliance with the supporters of the California Retirement Life Payments Act to the same end. President Green of the AFL tentatively approved the appointment of Paul Scharrenberg to head the anticipated campaign. But in July three principal provisions of the ordinance were held to be invalid by the Appellate Department of the Los Angeles County Superior Court.[18] The court declared that those parts of the law which "forbid picketing (1) by other than employees of the plant picketed, (2) by persons who have been employed less than 30 days, (3) in a case of a strike, unless it was voted by a majority of employees," were arbitrary and discriminatory.[19] Immediately after this decision was rendered, Los Angeles unions resumed mass picketing and dropped all plans to repeal the law through initiative procedure.

Southern Californians, Incorporated, which had led the opposition to labor's legal attempts to destroy the effectiveness of the law, was disappointed in the outcome of the test cases. Its officials pointed out that, according to police records, the number of strikes in the first seven months after the law went into effect was 65.9 per cent smaller than in the same period of the preceding year. They also pointed to a reduction of 97.3 per cent in the number of arrests for assault, and of 97.1 per cent in the number of arrests for sabotage originating from labor disputes. These figures did not deter CIO officials from undertaking to test the remaining provisions of the ordinance through a stipulation with the city attorney's office. Subsequently, in December, 1939, the Appellate Department of the Superior Court invalidated most of the significant sections of the law which were still effective. This decision was appealed, but it was later upheld by the California Supreme Court.[20]

The invalidation of the ordinance against picketing did not mean that the open shop was no longer of importance. Although apparently losing ground, the open shop was still supported by its main advocate, the M and M. The association did not oppose the right of a worker to join a union of his own choosing, but it usually refused to endorse any agreement that would make membership in a labor organization a condition of continued employment. Other like-minded groups maintained close coöperation with the M and M in its open-shop position. In 1939 the Central Labor Council published a list of eighteen such organizations in the state, including Southern Californians, Incorporated; The Neutral Thousands; Associated Farmers; Women of the Pacific; Farmers' Transportation Association; and the Waterfront Employers' Association. Labor leaders asked the Senate Civil Liberties Committee, better known as the La Follette Committee, to investigate all these organizations. The committee began hearings late in 1939. Its revelations were an indictment of the techniques used by open-shop supporters to maintain their system of industrial relations in the city, techniques that included the use of spies, strikebreakers, detective agencies, company-controlled unions, front groups such as The Neutral Thousands, black-listing, and antiunion propaganda. The evidence was damning and difficult to deny.[21]

Meanwhile, the activities of Southern Californians, Incorporated, assumed a state-wide aspect in 1939, when the organization established a legislative agent in Sacramento to serve during meetings of the state legislature. Its representatives also acted as *amicus curiae* in trials of unionists in Los Angeles, particularly in those cases testing the constitutionality of the picketing ordinance. SCI advocated strict enforcement of the law, requested remedial legislation to change statutes it considered unfair to employers, conducted a publicity campaign on good business practices, and upheld the payment of fair wages and the maintenance of reasonable working hours and conditions. Thus, although SCI was still fighting to maintain the open shop, its tactics became increasingly indirect.[22]

In 1939 SCI tried, with varying degrees of success, to organize additional groups in other southern California cities in support of the open shop. But its demise as an autonomous body was not far off. Evidence was mounting that unions were gaining in strength and organizational achievement, particularly in Los Angeles. The La Follette Committee hearings were exposing the *sub rosa* activities of SCI and the M and M against organized labor. Further, there was considerable duplication in the objectives and the operations of the two associations. With these circumstances in mind, M and M leaders proposed that Southern Californians, Incorporated, merge with the parent body. After months of negotiations in 1939 and early 1940, an integration plan was approved. It led to the establishment of a revamped body called the Merchants' and Manufacturers' Association of Southern California. At first the old open-shop objectives were upheld, but the outbreak of World War II, with the growing industrialization of Los Angeles and the increase in union power, was soon to sound their death knell. The impact of these forces could already be seen in 1939 in the growing tendency of managements to confer with union representatives and to agree to secret as well as open contracts providing for union shops.[23]

Just before the amalgamation with the M and M, the leaders of Southern Californians, Incorporated, conducted an investigation of its stepchild, The Neutral Thousands. Because SCI provided the chief financial support for TNT, it wanted to know how funds were being spent and what was being accomplished. In April, 1939, after completion of the investigation, TNT was disbanded, basically because of SCI's objection to the establishment of independent unions, many of which were not subject to employer control. SCI, however, hired TNT's chairman, Mrs. Bessie Ochs, to address women's clubs on the subject of labor relations, and retained the unofficial TNT employment service operated by G. L. Huff and Clay C. Rittenhouse. These two men were placed in charge of a new organization called the Employees Advisory Service, financed by SCI. The service organization conducted a placement bureau for nonunionists throughout the remainder of 1939 and also counseled employees regarding their individual rights in union campaigns to secure collective bargaining representation for workers within particular firms. Huff and Ritten-house changed many of the independent unions established by TNT into secret societies, clubs, and social organizations. As these groups were not company-controlled unions, they were not subject to the NLRA.[24]

After the disbandment of TNT, Women of the Pacific was the lead-ing women's organization dedicated to maintenance of the open shop in Los Angeles. These two groups had been quite similar in that they charged no dues or assessments; they accepted voluntary contributions; they disclaimed outside dictation of policy in the disbursement of funds; they did not publish the names of contributors or records of disbursement; they announced officers rather than elected them; and they allegedly represented spontaneous rebellions against labor tyr-anny. Women of the Pacific placed stronger emphasis on the role of the closed or union shop in raising the prices of consumer goods and had a more definite program of action for its members, whereas TNT stressed the establishment of independent unions. After the death of TNT, Women of the Pacific became less aggressive and more indirect in its opposition to closed and union shops. In September, 1939, Mrs. Edwin Selvin, its head, instituted a new eight-page biweekly called the *American Worker-Consumer*. Edited by her husband, the news-paper was dedicated to the support of the open shop and to the pro-tection of employees from coercion by either employers or unions. This project actually marked the end of Women of the Pacific as an effective force against the growing strength of unionism.[25]

3. Los Angeles Unions at the End of the 1930's

Through reorganization, disbandment, and changed tactics, the open-shop organizations seemingly admitted that all was not going well with their efforts to resist organized labor's growth, but unions still did not find the road to success unobstructed. The seventy-one strikes called in Los Angeles in 1939, involving 11,765 employees who lost 145,023 man-days of work, attested to the instability of labor's posi-tion. M and M records indicated that seventeen cases of assault and twenty-three instances of sabotage occurred as a result of these con-flicts. But these figures actually showed a decline in the number of labor disputes as compared with similar data for 1937 and 1938, peak years of conflict with the open shop. M and M spokesmen believed that the decline was due primarily to convictions of unionists on charges of violence, extortion, sabotage, and assault, and that the ordinance regulating picketing was also of importance; but the evidence was not conclusive. Unionists, in turn, used the same data to substantiate their claims that the open-shop front was weakening and that organized labor was gaining increased acceptance in Los Angeles.[26]

Jurisdictional conflict between individual AFL and CIO unions in the city continued in 1939. Possibly the most outstanding illustration of this interunion warfare appeared in the aircraft industry. Representatives of the United Automobile Workers of America, CIO, established an aircraft division at their second annual convention in April, 1939. Shortly thereafter, Wyndham Mortimer was sent by the UAW General Executive Board to direct the Los Angeles campaign to organize aircraft workers, a few of whom already belonged to the International Association of Machinists, AFL. Both the CIO and AFL organizations were opposed by several existing independent unions.

Mortimer and other UAW officials soon discovered that their opposition was not confined to rival unions. Employers were found to be hiring workers directly from training schools at wages of 40 cents an hour, while thousands of experienced, unemployed mechanics searched vainly for jobs because they insisted on 65 to 70 cents. UAW leaders also asserted that, after paying for their training, the new workers were employed only until their hourly wages reached 65 cents; then they were discharged and replaced by more recent graduates of the training schools. Employers were further attacked for operating a black list. The AFL opposition came largely from the IAM, which, according to the UAW, was interested only in skilled craftsmen and had informal agreements with employers directed toward the elimination of CIO unions. Apparently the IAM enjoyed some success, for it signed a contract with Lockheed covering a few hundred skilled workers out of the thousands of employees in the firm. An example of independent-union opposition was seen in November, 1939, when the United Aircraft Welders of America was recognized by the Douglas management as the collective bargaining agent for the welders in its Santa Monica and El Segundo plants, although the union had only a few more than 100 members. Most aircraft employees did not belong to any union, but stood on the side lines while the CIO and AFL fought for the privilege of organizing them. Effective labor organizations were not to gain footholds in the aircraft industry until after the bombing of Pearl Harbor and the entry of the United States into World War II.[27]

There was some CIO-AFL rivalry in the building trades in Los Angeles. Representatives of the ILWU, CIO, petitioned the Regional

Labor Board for designation of their union as the collective bargaining agent for the workers at the Blue Diamond Corporation, a building materials firm. There was also inconclusive evidence that members of a CIO building trades union were working in San Pedro and Wilmington. AFL building trades officials expressed concern that former members of the Workers Alliance might seek to convert some AFL construction unions into CIO locals. Their fears were based on the knowledge that Workers Alliance groups had often supported CIO unions and central bodies on economic issues. Generally speaking, however, these fears were unfounded, for the CIO made little headway in Los Angeles or elsewhere in the country in overcoming the entrenched position of AFL craft organizations in the construction field.[28]

To a greater degree, jurisdictional warfare continued to plague the city's furniture industry. Several coöperative attempts by AFL and CIO leaders to designate certain plants as wholly under the jurisdiction of either Furniture Workers Local No. 1561, AFL, or United Furniture Workers Local No. 576, CIO, had little success. The mutual distrust between officials of the two unions could not be overcome. It was compounded by the addition of William Busick, a former organizer for the International Ladies' Garment Workers Union, to the staff of Local No. 1561. Los Angeles CIO leaders believed that Busick could not be trusted and would sell his services to the highest bidder. Whatever the truth of this contention, Local No. 1561 won the right to represent workers at several plants, and established new agreements with a number of other furniture-manufacturing concerns. It renewed contracts drawn up in 1938 and, in several instances, obtained wage increases. By the end of 1939 the local was laying plans with Central Labor Council officials to inaugurate a 1940 membership campaign to defeat CIO Local No. 576 and organize more than a minority of the furniture workers in Los Angeles. But Local No. 576 was not idle during this time. Its officials also believed that a majority of the thousands of furniture workers in the city were ripe for organization. After celebrating its first anniversary in January, 1939, No. 576 conducted a drive that resulted in new agreements with several plants. It received assistance in this effort from the Dawn Patrol sponsored by the Los Angeles Industrial Union Council. Members of the patrol gathered at the gates of furniture factories early in the morning and urged the workers to join the union.[29]

A somewhat different facet of the CIO-AFL conflict appeared in a strike of the Los Angeles Newspaper Guild, CIO, against the *Hunt-*

ington Park Signal. Members of Credit and Collection Employees Union, Local No. 20363, AFL, under the leadership of Mrs. Florence Simmons, supported the Guild and aroused the ire of the Central Labor Council. Some members of the council, particularly Buzzell, frowned upon supporting any CIO union in any dispute. Mrs. Simmons, therefore, was adjudged guilty of aiding a dual union and was expelled as a delegate to the council. As an aftermath of her censure, a majority of the members of Local No. 20363 left the organization in December, 1939, and formed a new union affiliated with the Los Angeles Industrial Union Council. Earlier in the year the Retail Clothing Salesmen and Haberdashers Union, Local No. 1054, AFL, had coöperated with unionists in nearby cities in an effort to establish a new agreement with the Brooks clothing stores. Negotiations had failed, however, and the firm had remained on the unfair list of the Central Labor Council. When the credit and collection employees formed a new CIO union, most of the membership of Local No. 1054 joined it. The Labor Council continued to support Local No. 20363, but failed in its attempts to have employers discharge former members of this union who had joined the CIO.[30]

The teamsters furnished several noteworthy exceptions in 1939 to the almost universal rule that contacts between CIO and AFL unions ended in disputes. These exceptions occurred, as in the past, in relationships with the longshoremen. The first instance developed out of teamster efforts to organize nonunion drivers hauling farm produce under the auspices of the Associated Farmers. Longshoremen refused to handle a load of oranges delivered at the dock of the Pan-Pacific Steamship Company by a nonunion driver from the Knudsen Trucking Company of Redlands, an open-shop firm. The Associated Farmers supported Knudsen, but they could not force the longshoremen to load the oranges on vessels. The fruit was subsequently removed by the Knudsen company. A second instance of coöperation occurred when longshoremen refused to load the furniture of several naval officers who were bound for overseas assignments, because the furniture was delivered at Los Angeles Harbor by nonunion drivers for the Ace Van and Storage Company.[31]

With this kind of support, the teamsters gained strength in 1939. At the end of the year it was estimated that there were approximately 25,000 union teamsters in the Los Angeles trade area. During the year the locals renewed contracts with members of the Motor Truck Association of Southern California, which also signed agreements with sixteen lodges of auto mechanics affiliated with the IAM. In September the teamsters conducted a successful twenty-four-hour strike against some thirty interstate truck lines in Los Angeles. One union, Local No. 93, renewed its contract with dairy products distributors associated with Milk Products Industries, Inc. The agreement, becoming effective on November 15, covered 3,800 members of the local. Shortly afterward, Milk Products Industries was discontinued as an active organization, thus paving the way for acceptance of the teamsters by Los Angeles dairies.

The teamsters actively aided the warehousemen in organizing workers at a number of warehouses in Los Angeles in 1939. Flour, Feed and Cereal Workers Local No. 21830, AFL, was chartered in January, replacing old Local No. 757. The new local negotiated contracts with several firms, including the Albers, Taylor, and Sperry grain mills. ILWU Local No. 1-26, CIO, challenged the jurisdiction of Local No. 21830 at the Taylor Milling Company, but the AFL union won. The Regional Labor Board cited the Taylor management for discriminating against unionists and ordered the reinstatement of eight employees.[32]

The longshoremen, besides aiding the teamsters at the harbor, made some progress on their own. Local No. 1-26 of the ILWU renewed contracts with nine Los Angeles drug warehouses covering approximately 800 employees. They encountered opposition only from the Los Angeles Drug Company, which had sanctioned an independent union. In December, 1938, more than forty members of Local No. 1-26 struck, and then were locked out by this company. Their major grievances included charges of discrimination against members of the union, especially Jews; intimidation of unionists by nonunion employees; and the hiring of new workers through The Neutral Thousands employment office. According to company spokesmen, the men were discharged for conducting a sit-down strike aimed at forcing the management to insist that certain employees join Local No. 1-26.[33]

The longshoremen initiated a boycott against the Los Angeles Drug Company by sending a circular letter to its customers as well as to civic and political groups in the city. In February, 1939, after the strike had lasted six weeks, four pickets had been arrested, and the firm had been cited by the NLRB for unfair labor practices, the dispute was compromised. Union officials dropped the charges filed with the NLRB, in return for which the management attempted to secure the release of the four pickets arrested for violating the city's anti-picketing ordinance. The outcome was the establishment of grievance and arbitration procedures, as well as a hiring hall, and a promise by company officials that they would discharge superintendents and foremen who discriminated against unionists.[34]

Four months later the contract between Local No. 1-26 and the California Milling Company was terminated. Earlier in the year the unionists had encountered difficulties in enforcing a clause in the contract providing for the union shop. Management objected to the inclusion of such a provision in any new agreement. The union, wanting to ensure continuance of the union shop, called a strike. The dispute had some colorful aspects, especially when the strikers' "wives" took part. On June 2, for example, a group of women who claimed to be the wives of some of the strikers marched alongside the pickets carrying signs with such statements as "My Husband Is One of These Damn Fools," "Walking Won't Feed Our Children," and "How About Our Car Payment?" Police took the placards from the women and persuaded them to disperse. CIO representatives claimed that the "housewives" were led by Mrs. Ochs, former head of The Neutral Thousands, and that only one was the wife of a picket, the rest being hired impersonators. The union ended the strike in July and filed a charge with the Regional Labor Board against the company, asking for reinstatement of all the strikers. Shortly thereafter the Los Angeles County Grand Jury indicted seventeen members of the union for conspiracy and felonious assaults on nonunionists. After a trial in Superior Court before Judge A. A. Scott, nine of the union members pleaded guilty to misdemeanor charges and were fined. The charges against the eight other defendants were dismissed.[35]

Local No. 1-26 conducted another strike in June against the California Mill Supply Company and the Berg Metals Corporation, dealers in scrap iron. The principal union demands were for wage increases, which the firms said they were unable to grant. The walkout was followed by mass picketing. Police soon arrested six men at California Mill Supply, charging them with violating the city's antipicketing ordinance. After the strike had been under way for two weeks, new contracts were negotiated. They provided for hourly pay increases of 5 to 10 cents for the 223 workers in both plants, a straight eight-hour day, and recognition of Local No. 1-26 as the sole collective bargaining agent for the firms' employees.[36]

As Local No. 1-26 discovered in organizing Los Angeles scrap-iron yards, the metal trades industries of California were ripe for unionization. Employment opportunities for metal trades workers in 1939 were better than they had been in the preceding decade, partly because of the revival of the shipbuilding industry. Moore Dry Dock

Company in Oakland launched a vessel on September 15, 1939, the first ship in seventeen years to slide down the ways in California. The Los Angeles Metal Trades Council, AFL, coöperated during the year with the Chamber of Commerce and several shipbuilding firms in an attempt to secure government contracts to build vessels in the Los Angeles Harbor area. Whether or not these efforts were directly responsible, Consolidated Steel Corporation received contracts early in August for the construction of four 11,500-ton, 413-foot, C-1 type, steel cargo ships. By December, the increased amount of shipbuilding at the port permitted unionists to institute an organizing campaign which increased the strength of the Los Angeles Metal Trades Council. It was but a prelude to the growth experienced by metal trades unions as the industrialization of Los Angeles grew apace under the impetus of American participation in World War II. On October 5, 1939, the Metal Trades Council signed the first blanket agreement in its history with the Plomb Tool Company, one of the largest manufacturers of hand tools in the country. This firm had been an open shop, but in an NLRB election a majority of the workers voted to be represented in collective bargaining by AFL unions, including Machinists Local No. 311, Blacksmiths Local No. 212, and Metal Polishers Local No. 67. The contract covered 135 men and provided for a forty-hour week; an eight-hour day; double pay for all overtime or work on Saturdays, Sundays, and established holidays; wage increases; and a union shop. Officials of the unions or of the Metal Trades Council were to serve as hiring agents.[37]

The Steel Workers Organizing Committee, CIO, also gave impetus to union growth in the metal trades by securing a number of new agreements, one of them with the Boyle Manufacturing Company. SWOC representatives also renewed most of the contracts negotiated in 1938, including those with American Can Company, Western Pipe and Steel, and International Harvester. The contract with Western Pipe and Steel Company evolved from a victory over three AFL craft unions in a collective bargaining election. Although the SWOC stronghold in southern California was Columbia Steel Lodge No. 1414 at Torrance, other lodges existed at Bethlehem Steel, American Manganese Steel, and the Emsco Derrick and Equipment Company. In this organizing period Bethlehem Steel and the Johnson Pump Company were charged by the NLRB with operating company unions. The board issued disestablishment orders, thus giving the SWOC a freer hand in organizing the workers in these firms.[38]

The 1939 pickup in employment in the metal trades was also reflected in the building industry; by June, both the membership of the Los Angeles Building and Construction Trades Council and the number of agreements providing for union shops were the largest in the council's history. Much of the increase in construction trades employment developed from a Los Angeles slum clearance project begun under the auspices of the Federal Housing Authority. Late in 1939 council officials launched a new organizing campaign, reëstablishing the old flying squads under the name "contact squads." The squads sought to curtail construction work on Saturdays and encourage building tradesmen to join unions. By November the total membership of the council's constituent unions was estimated at 12,000, and the council had to employ three full-time officers, in addition to secretarial help, to conduct its business.[39]

Several of the building trades unions were highly pleased when the Weber Showcase and Fixture Company, which for more than three years had opposed all attempts to organize its workers, finally capitulated. In 1939 Weber signed an agreement which was approved by the Los Angeles County District Council of Carpenters. It covered wages and hours for millmen, cabinetmakers, painters, sheet metal workers, and teamsters.

At Graves Lumber Company, however, union millmen were not so successful. Lumber and Sawmill Workers Local No. 2788, which had signed a contract with the firm in 1937, struck in February, 1939, because the management refused to assist in the collection of union dues. Graves battled the union throughout the year. Members of Local No. 2788 as well as teamsters in Locals No. 420 and 692 accused the firm of unfair labor practices. Strike pressure forced Graves to use an assumed name while attempting to place lumber orders with other concerns which employed unionists. Some building contractors ceased using Graves products at the request of union officials. The millmen were encouraged when the NLRB formally indicted the company for unfair labor practices, but the conflict dragged on into 1940. It ended then, without union satisfaction.[40]

The Graves dispute was not the only one in the lumber and milling industry in 1939. When the agreement signed in 1938 with forty-one members of the Lumber and Allied Products Institute, Inc., expired on June 2, 1939, labor leaders demanded an increase in pay and a reduction in the workweek from forty-four to forty hours. The employers, however, requested a 10 per cent cut in the wages paid for cabinet, sash, and door work; a clause that would prevent the establishment of a union shop; no reduction in the total hours worked each week except as provided by the Fair Labor Standards Act; and deductions from earnings for any decreases in the workweek. Failure to negotiate an agreement satisfactory to both sides led to a summer strike against the largest lumber yards in Los Angeles and San Pedro.[41]

Mayor Fletcher Bowron and conciliators from the U.S. Department of Labor immediately attempted to settle the dispute. Few acts of violence occurred because the largest firms were closed down, unionized longshoremen and teamsters respected picket lines around ships and lumber yards, and the strike was not called against a number of smaller, independent companies. The estimates of employers and union leaders as to the number of strikers in the San Pedro–Los Angeles area varied from a minimum of 1,500 to a maximum of 5,000. Both sides submitted proposals and counterproposals to the negotiators. Building operations in the city slackened and, in some instances, ceased as lumber became scarce. A few firms unaffiliated with the Lumber and Allied Products Institute signed contracts, but the first break did not come until several weeks after the walkout began. At that time a satisfactory agreement was reached between the unions and five of seventeen struck firms in the harbor area, thus returning about 300 strikers to their jobs.

The dispute ended on July 27, after James Wallace, a mediator appointed by Mayor Bowron, negotiated an agreement between the unions and the rest of the struck firms. The one-year contract provided for an immediate 4 per cent wage increase, plus a 1 per cent raise on October 24. On that date the forty-four-hour week was to be reduced to forty hours. Time and a half was to be paid for overtime, and union members were to be given preference in employment. A closed shop, however, was not granted. Locals No. 2788 and 2607, AFL, of the lumber and sawmill workers signed the contract along with Local No. 235, AFL, of the operating engineers. According to the *Citizen,* more than 140 independent concerns as well as members of the Lumber and Allied Products Institute accepted the new agreement. One of its outgrowths was the formation of the Independent Lumber Dealers' Association by firms not affiliated with the Lumber Institute.[42]

As in the lumber and milling industry, small, independent firms continued to predominate in cleaning and dyeing. In 1939, because of price wars and jurisdictional conflicts, this industry failed to maintain hours and working conditions acceptable to Local No. 268 of the Amalgamated Clothing Workers, CIO. The unionists countered with an organizing campaign, and threatened to strike if the managers of wholesale plants resisted efforts to unionize their employees. Mayor Bowron appointed a three-man commission to mediate the controversy, but it failed to prevent the walkout on June 19. Approximately 600 employees struck thirty wholesale plants, curtailing the operations of a large number of retail stores and affecting almost 3,000 additional workers. Local No. 268 demanded the 1937 wage scale, a forty-hour week, and union recognition by the operators of wholesale plants. Twelve firms agreed to most of the union demands at the outset of the walkout. Shortly thereafter, five other plants followed suit and operations were quickly resumed. The volume of output in these seventeen plants was such that a large amount of the city's cleaning and dyeing was again accomplished without delay—an indication of overcapacity in the industry. The rest of the firms held out against the union despite an organizing effort during which Local No. 268 also urged the drivers of cleaning trucks and owners of retail tailoring shops to join the union.[43]

The culinary unions also conducted an intensive organizing campaign in 1939. They experienced many setbacks; several night clubs in which unionists were employed were closed, and open-shop supporters gave active opposition. Nearly every issue of the *Citizen* contained a list of unfair restaurants and cafés. Among the many strikes that occurred were those called against the Ambassador Hotel, the White Spot cafés, the Florentine Gardens, and the Coco Tree Café. Women of the Pacific entered the White Spot dispute by requesting housewives to patronize the struck cafés and thus help them to maintain an open-shop policy. Culinary workers continued to picket the branches of Globe Dairy Lunch throughout 1939, but did not win their demands. Globe, like most of the employers, belonged to the Southern California Restaurant Association, which maintained a strong open-shop position.[44]

Open-shop employers continued to frustrate the efforts of Bakery and Confectionery Workers Local No. 37 and Bakery Drivers Local No. 276. These locals attempted, without success, to organize the workers in the Helms, Cal-Ray, Davis-Perfection, and Olson bakeries. Women of the Pacific aided these firms in their resistance. However, not all the unionists' efforts were ineffectual. In June, 1939, Local No. 37 renewed its 1937 agreement with fifteen wholesale bakeries in Los Angeles, Orange, Santa Barbara, San Bernardino, and Riverside counties. The new two-year contract was to be in effect until May 1, 1941. In essence, it provided an average weekly wage of $35 for bakers, with an additional $1 per week after December 31, 1939.

The activities of Women of the Pacific and The Neutral Thousands were most evident in the Cal-Ray and Helms struggles. Cal-Ray had recognized a TNT-established independent union. Early in January, 1939, Cracker Bakers Local No. 418, assisted by Bakery Drivers Local No. 276, called a walkout at Cal-Ray in an effort to refute the claims of the independent union to collective bargaining rights and to organize the workers under the AFL banner. The Cal-Ray management fought back by obtaining a temporary restraining order which limited the number of pickets, while TNT and Women of the Pacific issued letters to their "members" and others, advocating the purchase of Cal-Ray products. They sought to increase purchases by housewives in order to offset the effect of a secondary boycott established by the unionists. The dispute dragged on through the year, however, without a clear-cut victory for either side.

A similar yet slightly different situation prevailed in the Helms dispute. Locals No. 37 and 276 included a boycott against Helms products in their organizing campaign, and the *Citizen* made accusations of substandard hours and wages. These were denied by Paul H. Helms and subsequently retracted by union officials. Women of the Pacific again attempted to offset the boycott by issuing letters requesting consumers to patronize Helms. *Times* editorials commented on the unfair tactics of the unionists. This open-shop opposition proved too strong for the bakers; Helms was able to prevent effective organization of his employees and to ward off a strike.[45]

The clothing workers had similarly failed to establish a union or closed shop throughout the city's silk and wool dress–manufacturing industry, although the ILGWU had directed a number of strikes toward this end. Manufacturers who had signed a three-year agreement in 1936 therefore refused to renew it in July, 1939, on the ground that ILGWU officials had failed to keep their promise to organize the entire industry. Nonunion manufacturers, with cheaper labor costs, could undersell unionized firms. ILGWU leaders called a strike for July 1, the expiration date of the contract, against the employers under the agreement, but postponed it for thirty days. Further negotiations resulted in a new contract. Thus the walkout was avoided even though only a part of the silk and wool dress industry was unionized at the time. The union attempted, without success, to organize additional firms during the remainder of the year in order to stabilize competition. In December the ILGWU General Executive Board replaced the general manager of the Los Angeles Joint Executive Board and International Vice-President Israel Feinberg with George Wishnak and

Louis Levy, respectively. These new leaders immediately laid plans to win a closed shop in 1940.[46]

The ILGWU became involved in a scandal in connection with an agreement negotiated by William Busick in September, 1937, between Local No. 266 and the Hollywood Maxwell Company, a manufacturer of women's undergarments. The firm refused to renew the contract when it expired in September, 1938, supporting, instead, a company union. Officials of Local No. 266 appealed to the Regional Labor Board, which conducted hearings in 1939 and indicted the company on charges of unfair labor practices. The hearings revealed that Busick had received payments from Hollywood Maxwell for discouraging the growth of the ILGWU in the plant and for encouraging the company union. It was further disclosed that he was paid to influence Nylander to hold an NLRB election to determine the collective bargaining agent for the firm's workers at a time when the company union would win a majority of the votes. Meanwhile, Busick had left the ILGWU to become an organizer for Furniture Workers Local No. 1561. When the Hollywood Maxwell activities were exposed, he was suspended by the furniture workers even though he denied the charges. Soon thereafter he left the city.[47]

The tailors affiliated with the Amalgamated Clothing Workers also sponsored an organizing campaign in 1939. They conducted a two-day demonstration strike in March against approximately forty firms employing 400 workers, because some of the manufacturers had allegedly failed to consider grievances arising from violations of a closed-shop contract. In April the tailors' cause was handicapped when the district attorney arrested two ACW organizers and a representative of an association of clothing manufacturers, charging them with attempted extortion and conspiracy to commit same. They had allegedly tried to get funds from employers under the pretense of acting for the union. One of the arrested men, Ben Peppercorn, was an officer of the Amalgamated in Cleveland, Ohio. He was accused of ordering more than a dozen manufacturers, under threat of a strike, to post cash bonds of $150 in order to guarantee the performance of contracts with the union.[48]

The three men were indicted by the Los Angeles County Grand Jury. Jack Menzo, the manufacturers' representative, pleaded not guilty. Ben Peppercorn and Ed Hammer, ACW officials, filed demurrers, but were indicted again. Speaking in his own defense, Peppercorn testified that the three groups of manufacturers—ready-made, contract, and cut, trim, and make shops—had been engaging in price-cutting tactics to the point where chaotic competitive conditions had developed. To stabilize prices in the industry, employers in the contract and cut, trim, and make shops had formed associations. The cut, trim, and make association had then asked each member to post a bond of $150 with the organization as a guarantee of his participation in the plan to stabilize prices. Peppercorn claimed that one employer in the new association who was dissatisfied with the price agreement was attempting to implicate the unionists in its price policy. It was this proprietor who had complained to District Attorney Fitts and initiated the action that had resulted in the indictments. The grand jury issued three indictments against the three men over a period of several months. Each was rejected by Superior Court Judge Clarence L. Kincaid on the ground that a public offense had not been proved. In the fall of 1939, however, the Appellate Department of the Superior Court reviewed the cases and reinstated the charges. The defendants were ordered to trial in 1940, and on January 17 of that year the charges were again dismissed.[49]

In August, 1939, another clothing union, Local No. 87 of the International Fur and Leather Workers, CIO, won a dispute with Maurice Ball, Inc., an old opponent. The strike was called to gain Ball's adherence to a preferential-hiring clause in an agreement. There were other disputes, including one with a fur shop on Western Avenue, but, in the judgment of union officials, the Ball walkout was the most important because of the hard core of management opposition.

A similar employer viewpoint was encountered by the United Electrical, Radio and Machine Workers, CIO. This union sponsored an organizing campaign in 1939, negotiating agreements with the American Record Company, the Star Lighting Company, and the Dura Steel Company. The agreement with Star Lighting was obtained only after overcoming a lockout.[50]

Local No. 52, Laundry Workers International Union, AFL, achieved a significant victory against the open shop in early 1939 when it established agreements with the Torrance Laundry and the Los Angeles, Johnson, and California overall-cleaning companies. The significance lay not in the number of workers affected, but in the headway made in an industry long characterized by low wages, long hours, and the employment of marginal female workers not easily unionized. During the year, union laundry workers also secured agreements with Chefs Laundry Service and the Welch Overall Laundry. The contract with Welch was signed after Local No. 52 had won a jurisdictional dispute with Local No. 357 of the Amalgamated Clothing Workers.

Local No. 357 had greater success in a strike it called against the Wardrobe Laundry Company over the discharge of ten employees for union activity. The CIO local obtained a contract in March after the walkout had lasted for seven weeks. It provided for preferential union hiring; recognition of Local No. 357 as the sole bargaining agent for the firm's employees; wage increases of 10 to 25 per cent in all departments of the laundry; an eight-hour day; time and a half for overtime, Sundays, and holidays; an annual one-week vacation with pay; grievance adjustment; seniority rights; no discharge without a cause satisfactory to union representatives; reinstatement with back pay of any unionists who had been discharged without cause; and an equitable distribution of the available work during slack seasons. One result of the strike was the disclosure, substantiated by M and M records, that the Wardrobe Laundry Company was paying subnormal wages. Officials of Local No. 357 subsequently filed a suit against several of the firm's executives alleging that the California Labor Code had been violated. They asserted that female employees in the establishment worked before 6 A.M. and more than eight hours a day for less than the minimum wage, and that time records were not kept. Three company officials pleaded guilty to the charges, and each received a suspended sentence of thirty days in jail or a fine of $150. In addition, the court awarded $2,000 in back pay to the employees concerned.[51]

Wage scale problems afflicted Musicians Local No. 47 in 1939. Because of the high wages requested by local orchestras, the Biltmore Hotel threatened to close its large ballroom unless rates were reduced. But the controversy was resolved, and the musicians maintained their status as one of the largest labor organizations in southern California. Because of the musicians' numerical strength, Labor's Non-Partisan League lost one of its most important supporters when Local No. 47 decided to withdraw its affiliation. It was one of the last AFL unions to leave the league. In all probability, a change of officers in Local No. 47 affected the decision. In a contest for the presidency, J. K. Wallace had defeated Jack B. Tenney, a supporter of the Los Angeles Newspaper Guild, CIO, in its fight with the *Hollywood Citizen-News*, thus removing a CIO sympathizer from union leadership.[52]

Tenney's active coöperation had been a factor aiding the Los Angeles Newspaper Guild in its 1938 struggle with the *Citizen-News*. If the AFL had coöperated as fully, the *Citizen-News* strike might have brought a more substantial union victory. But the left-wing leadership of the Guild under Philip M. Connelly, later editor of the Communist-oriented *Daily People's World*, precluded strong AFL support.

Connelly was displaced by Tom O'Connor as president in 1939. Under O'Connor's direction, the Guild's internal structure and organization became more solid, and wages were stabilized, with established scales as shown in table 8.

TABLE 8

WAGES UNDER AMERICAN NEWSPAPER GUILD
CONTRACTS, LOS ANGELES, 1939

Employee classification and years of experience	Minimum weekly wages
Reporters	
1	$25.00
2	32.50
3	37.50
4	45.00
5	50.00
6	55.00
Outside classified salesmen	
1	25.00
2	35.00
Display salesmen (major accounts)	
1	35.00
2	40.00
3	45.00
4	50.00
5	55.00
6	60.00
Display salesmen (minor accounts)	
1	25.00
2	30.00
3	35.00
4	42.50
5	47.50
6	50.00

SOURCE: "Collective Bargaining by the American Newspaper Guild," *Monthly Labor Review*, L (April, 1940), 839.

A new agreement between the Guild and the *Evening Herald and Express* became effective on April 10, 1939. Negotiations for this contract had been clouded by months of wrangling, so severe that at one point the unionists threatened to call a strike. The agreement covered 465 employees and provided for a total yearly pay increase of $115,000, assertedly the highest wage boost ever obtained by the Guild. It was also the first contract in which the Los Angeles Guild won jurisdiction over the employees in all departments of a newspaper except the mechanical divisions manned by AFL craftsmen. The outstanding provisions included salary increases of as much as $25 a week; the establishment of weekly minimum wages of $55 and $60 in the editorial and advertising departments, respectively; two weeks of paid vacation each year; sick leave with pay; and severance indemnity payments for as many as twenty-eight weeks after fourteen years of service.[53]

The Guild also signed a contract with the *Illustrated Daily News* and the *Evening News,* both of which were owned by Manchester Boddy. It provided for a union shop; a five-day, forty-hour week in nearly all departments; overtime payments; sick leave with pay; two weeks of paid vacation each year; reimbursement at 7 cents a mile whenever it was necessary for an employee to use a private automobile on business; severance payments for a maximum of twenty-eight weeks based on one week's salary for each six months of employment; and minimum wages. This contract replaced an earlier agreement which had covered only editorial workers. It was the first one with southern California metropolitan newspapers in which a closed Guild shop was established in all departments except those employing printing craftsmen.[54]

On September 11, 1939, the Newspaper Guild called a strike against the *Huntington Park Bulletin,* a newspaper in the southeastern part of Los Angeles. The dispute began when Max Ward, the publisher, would not negotiate over the discharge of several employees for union activities, and refused to stop encouraging the AFL to form what Guild officials called a company union. The walkout was not entirely peaceful. Several Guild members were arrested for operating sound trucks in violation of a city ordinance requiring a license for such activity. Strikers also picketed the shops and stores of about a hundred *Bulletin* advertisers, and this caused the issuance of a permanent injunction against the picketing of third parties. Twelve members of the union were fined $50 each in a contempt action which arose from violation of the preliminary restraining order. The contempt charge was dismissed and the fines were suspended, however, because of a legal technicality in filing papers in the case. Central Labor Council officials opposed the strike because it was conducted by CIO unionists and jeopardized the jobs of printing trades union members employed in the *Bulletin*'s mechanical departments. Further, a large number of the merchants who were picketed for advertising in the newspaper employed AFL unionists. Hence, AFL members were asked to patronize picketed establishments, and printing trades unionists employed at the *Bulletin* refused to respect plant picket lines.

On November 13 the Central Labor Council passed a resolution condemning Guild members for intimating that the strike had been sanctioned by AFL representatives and for publishing a newspaper called the *Bulletin Striker*. Pictures in the *Striker* had been printed from photoengraving cuts made in an open shop. A few AFL unionists supported the strikers, however, and even participated in the picketing. Despite Guild efforts to discourage circulation, utilize primary and secondary picketing, conduct public demonstrations, and secure petitions favorable to its cause from well-known personalities and groups, the strike dragged on until April 15, 1940. The settlement at that time provided for the return of discharged employees with one week's back pay and the establishment of a standard Guild contract.[55]

The Los Angeles Newspaper Guild also conducted a strike in 1939 against *Southwest Topics,* another local newspaper with a limited neighborhood circulation. After a seven-day walkout the union signed a contract that provided for a Guild shop and most of the benefits obtained in previous agreements with larger Los Angeles newspapers. Meanwhile, the Guild was fighting a court case that had developed out of the 1938 *Hollywood Citizen-News* walkout. The point at issue was the distribution of handbills during the strike in violation of a city ordinance. In June, 1939, Federal Judge Leon R. Yankwich issued an injunction restraining members of the Los Angeles Police Department from enforcing the law, which he considered unconstitutional. Two months later the City Council repealed it, and in October passed another ordinance permitting the public distribution of argumentative literature in pamphlet form. The old ordinance received the final blow on November 22, 1939, when the United States Supreme Court declared it unconstitutional by deciding in favor of Kim Young, who had been arrested in Los Angeles for distributing handbills about the civil war in Spain.[56]

Other court cases developed from conflicts between nonunion and union workers at the local plant of the Chrysler Motor Corporation. On December 11, 1938, Paul L. Brooks, a Chrysler employee, obtained a preliminary injunction forbidding the members of UAW Local No. 230 to interfere with his right to remain independent. But the union ignored the injunction and announced that all eligible employees in the plant must join by January 3, 1939. Later efforts to enforce compliance with this edict caused the Los Angeles County Grand Jury to indict fifteen officers and members of Local No. 230. Prior to Brooks's action, Chrysler had recognized Local No. 230 as the collective bargaining agent for UAW members employed in the factory, but continued to operate an open shop. After the grand jury indictments, plant officials reported to District Attorney Fitts that members of the local had initiated reprisals against nonunion men who had testified during the investigation. One man, for example, had been injured by a heavy bolt thrown at him; another worker had received threats of physical violence; and an attorney for the company had been told to fear for his life.[57]

The district attorney's office arraigned the fifteen men on thirteen counts each of conspiracy, extortion, and attempted extortion with a total of fifty-five overt acts charged against them. The charges of extortion were based on the asserted use of coercive methods in the collection of a $5 initiation fee and dues from certain Chrysler employees, who had testified before the grand jury that they had been intimidated into joining the union. Unusual significance attached to the case, as it marked the first time in the state's history that laws concerning extortion were used against union organizing activities. CIO spokesmen declared that the indictments were well-timed efforts by District Attorney Fitts to defeat projected attempts to repeal the city's picketing ordinance. They claimed that the case had been planned late in 1938 by Southern Californians, Incorporated, and The Neutral Thousands in support of the open shop. It had a sufficient impact on labor as a whole to cause Central Labor Council officials temporarily to coöperate with the CIO and instruct their attorneys to sit in with the defendants as friends of the court. The council believed that the indictments were a threat to the freedom of unions to collect dues and encourage workers to join labor organizations. Subsequent legal attempts to gain the release of the indicted men were dismissed. The trial of fourteen of the defendants began in May; the fifteenth, who had been injured in an automobile accident, was not able to stand trial until a later date.[58]

Defense attorneys asserted during the trial that only twenty-two of the approximately 900 employees in the Chrysler plant did not belong to the union at the time of the alleged commission of the acts of extortion and violence. They further claimed that The Neutral Thousands and Southern Californians, Incorporated, had conspired to drive Local No. 230 from the plant and substitute a company union. To expedite its formation, The Neutral Thousands allegedly had subsidized Brooks, a former member of Local No. 230, paying his expenses when he obtained the December, 1938, preliminary injunction against CIO efforts to organize the plant. On the other side, witnesses for the prosecution testified that they had been forced to pay membership fees of $5 each to Local No. 230 representatives or face physical violence and loss of their jobs. The prosecution also cited instances of the ejection of nonunionists from the plant by UAW members.

After seven weeks of testimony the case went to the jury, which reached a deadlock after deliberating for ten days. Superior Court Judge Frank G. Swain then dismissed the panel, declaring a mistrial, denied a defense motion to dismiss the indictments, and ordered a new trial, which began in August, 1939, with all the defendants present. After five weeks of testimony before Superior Court Judge Arthur Crum, the case again went to the jury. On September 30 the jurors acquitted the men on eleven counts of attempted extortion or conspiracy, two of the counts having been dismissed earlier. Los Angeles labor leaders deemed the acquittals a victory over the open shop and District Attorney Fitts. There was further rejoicing when, on November 16, the NLRB certified the UAW as the sole collective bargaining agent for the workers at eleven Chrysler plants, including the factory at Los Angeles.[59]

Difficulties in establishing representation rights were similarly experienced by meatcutters and packinghouse workers in 1939. In January, Packing House Butchers Local No. 563 had 1,200 members and agreements with twenty-six meat-packing establishments. Swift and Company, however, continued to resist Local No. 563 and Meat Cutters Local No. 421, despite strike conditions and a boycott that had been maintained by the unions for more than two years. The Packing House Workers of California, an independent union, also opposed the two AFL organizations in their efforts to win representation rights at Swift. In 1939 the strike at Swift's Los Angeles plant spread to other branches in California, Oregon, Washington, and Nevada. The unions won settlements at the plants outside Los Angeles, but failed to organize the local branch. Several injunctions were granted against the efforts of Locals No. 421 and 563 to organize in various retail meat establishments. One of these was obtained by the Great Atlantic and Pacific Tea Company, though it finally renewed its agreement with Local No. 421. The contract contained standard clauses providing for a fifty-four-hour week, payment of time and a half for overtime, a graduated wage scale based on years of service, and an annual one-week paid vacation for workers who had been employed continuously for at least a year.[60]

Although the printing trades unions were much more secure in 1939 than the meatcutters and the packinghouse butchers, they too faced a determined open-shop employer—the *Downtown Shopping News*. They conducted a boycott during most of the year against this throw-away publication, which was distributed throughout the city and served as an advertising medium for department stores. Its open-shop character was evident in its editorials in support of Proposition No. 1 in 1938, as well as in the fact that it was printed by a nonunion firm. Local labor leaders urged unionists to leave signs on their porches requesting that the *Shopping News* not be left at their homes. The boycott gradually diminished in intensity as the year rolled along, and was finally abandoned. This lack of success did not seriously handicap the printing trades unions, which gained members in 1939. The Allied Printing Trades Council reached a membership of twelve locals, the largest in its history. By November, 128 firms were entitled to use the union labels of the council or of its affiliates. The rise in the use of the labels was partly due to the establishment of an organizing committee for this purpose by the council.[61]

Whereas the printing trades unions had little difficulty in maintaining their contracts, their fellow unionists among the unskilled and semiskilled retail clerks experienced rough sledding at times during the year. Retail shoe clerks of Local No. 406, for example, had to call strikes to get their contracts renewed at the Chandler, Berland, Burt, Leeds, and Gallenkamp shoe stores. Retail Food Clerks Local No. 770 negotiated a number of new contracts with the larger markets. Most of them provided for a union shop, a forty-eight-hour week, a weekly minimum wage of $22.50 for new clerks and as much as $40 for managers, seniority rights, six holidays with pay, and a one-week paid vacation after a year of employment. The union was hampered in its efforts to organize the workers in Japanese markets because an employers' organization discriminated against union employees. The existence of the Southern California Retail Produce Workers Union, an independent labor organization, likewise discouraged membership in the AFL local.[62]

The rubber workers, plagued by independent unions in the earlier years of the decade, were much stronger by 1939. The only publicized dispute began on January 30 when Local No. 43 called a strike at the B. F. Goodrich plant. Union spokesmen alleged that the firm had refused to negotiate the proper number of work hours in a proposed new contract. The management replied that the workers had been employed on four six-hour shifts each day, and that the firm wanted to establish three eight-hour shifts with no change in pay. Five hundred and fifty men maintained a picket line at the plant for two and a half weeks, without acts of violence. The agreement that finally settled the dispute provided that six-hour shifts would be retained in those departments where they had previously existed. Provision was made for the introduction of eight-hour shifts if and when general employment conditions improved.[63]

Other unions also made gains in 1939. The rear-guard action fought by retreating open-shop groups was effective in many instances, but the security and the progress of organized labor seemed to be assured by the end of the year. In his 1939 annual report, Secretary Buzzell of the Central Labor Council stated:

Los Angeles cannot help but be recognized as one of the most difficult places in which the Trade Union movement can operate, facing problems that are met nowhere else in the United States. These problems, however, are not new to the Trade Unionists here, but are not easily understood by those from afar. In spite of all its handicaps, however, it continues to go forward, and except in one year, 1932, there has never been an annual report to this Council which showed a lesser membership or a less amount of progress, over a preceding year.[64]

At the end of 1939 Los Angeles unions were on the threshold of a period of rapid expansion which was possible primarily because of the foundations laid during the preceding seven years under the impetus of favorable national labor legislation as well as the slowly increasing industrialization of the area. Though the open shop had long been the outstanding characteristic of the city's industrial relations, it was now becoming an institution of waning significance to both labor and management. The change was ably summarized by Mayor Fletcher Bowron in an address before the second annual southern California CIO conference on July 16, 1939, when he said: "Even the most conservative manufacturers have come to realize that workers must organize, that bargaining cannot be with individuals, and that the effort to maintain the open shop is a lost cause."[65]

XV. TIME RUNS OUT
FOR THE OPEN SHOP

THE CITY's industrial leaders were by no means agreed in 1939 that the open shop was on the decline. Many would not accept Mayor Bowron's statement that "the most conservative manufacturers have come to realize that workers must organize . . . and that the effort to maintain the open shop is a lost cause."[1] But, added the mayor, Los Angeles was now the seventh city in industrial importance in the United States and led all others in the motion picture and aircraft industries. In his opinion, its future growth would depend upon the development of closer understanding between capital and labor. He believed that such understanding would come about if free, unhampered collective bargaining relationships were established.

Whether or not Mayor Bowron's opinion was accepted by local industrial leaders depended partly on their historical perspective. It was indeed difficult to deny that organized labor was becoming a potent force in the city's industrial relations. This was in sharp contrast with its position in the years around the turn of the century. The strike of the printers against the city's four newspapers in August, 1890, had sparked a campaign against organized labor, led by General Harrison Gray Otis of the *Times,* which affected labor adversely for many years. Further, the establishment of the Merchants' and Manufacturers' Association provided Los Angeles industrial leaders with a medium of effective action against the labor movement, with the *Times* functioning as the mouthpiece for the open shop. By 1906–1907 unionists scarcely dared to be known as such, and often met only in secret. But the metal trades strike of 1910 and the bombing of the *Times* building in October of that year brought the conflict more into the open, with favorable results for the unions in the next several years. Even though the metal trades strike was generally conceded to be a failure and the trial of the McNamara brothers for the *Times* bombing a reflection on organized labor, the years immediately preceding World War I marked a leveling off of sentiment against unions. Progress was painfully slow—at times even negligible—but the unions held their own and were not forced out of the city.[2]

The impact of World War I and the death of General Otis improved growth expectations for the Los Angeles labor movement, but not for long. The city was too far removed from the European conflict for the unions to reap much benefit in employment and wages, except in shipbuilding and related industries. Even here, the open-shop movement retarded the best of the organizers' efforts, as the shipbuilding firms were led by local men steeped in the tradition of "industrial freedom" upheld by the *Times*. The noticeable upsurge of unionism which did occur during World War I quickly subsided thereafter, as it did in the nation as a whole. But a hard core of unionism remained, though the subsequent prosperity of the 1920's proved of no great help to the unions locally. Like their national parent organizations, they found little to encourage them except in the brash, young motion picture industry. The establishment of the so-called Basic Agreement for the crafts in motion picture production provided at least a foothold in the late 1920's—an island of strength in a sea of weakness.

Beginning in 1929, the local and national labor movements entered a phase of discouragement caused by loss of membership growing out of rising unemployment. This phase ended in 1933 when the National Industrial Recovery Act gave impetus to organizing activity. Further momentum developed as a result of the Railway Labor Act Amendments of 1934, the National Labor Relations Act of 1935, and the election in the late 1930's of state and local government officials who were more favorable toward organized labor. By 1939 unionization was increasing throughout the state in nearly every industry. Los Angeles was no exception. Although the relatively small local was the basic organizational unit, the Los Angeles labor movement was reasonably well knit, despite the AFL-CIO conflict, and able to meet employer opposition. But the open shop made the city's workers difficult to organize, a fact not readily understood by labor leaders from other areas, many of whom were not conversant with the character of the struggle that had gone on in Los Angeles since 1890.[3]

To say that the open shop was the sole reason for the difficulties experienced by Los Angeles labor leaders in organizing the city's workers would gloss over some of the fundamental characteristics of the area's economy. These worked against organizers' efforts until the beginning of World War II. Historically speaking, the extractive industries, including agriculture, and those manufacturing activities dependent thereon had formed the economic base of the state and, with the service industries, that of the city. As late as 1937 the major manufacturing activities in California were petroleum refining and the canning and processing of fruits and vegetables. Organized labor had little to say and less to do in these industries, primarily because of the difficult problem of organizing workers in oil fields and on farms.[4]

The over-all trend in the development of manufacturing in Los Angeles was another characteristic that aided the long tenure of the open shop. Although from 1899 to 1939 the value added by manufacture in Los Angeles increased seventy fold, it was so insignificant in the base year that its spectacular growth was not impressive in absolute terms. The depression after 1929 slowed this growth, and not until the beginning of the war in Europe did it aggressively resume. Detroit was often compared with Los Angeles because it, too, was strongly open shop. Yet in total manufacturing Detroit was considerably different from Los Angeles. Almost half of the total employment in the automobile city during 1930–1940 was in manufacturing, compared to only a fifth in Los Angeles. The problem of maintaining the open shop was much simpler in Los Angeles, with its service and extractive industry base. Relatively more of the city's workers were in these largely unorganized industries than was true of the major Midwestern or Eastern cities. Thus, Los Angeles was still a young industrial area up to the 1940's.[5]

Another characteristic of the Los Angeles economy which favored the open shop was the regional nature of the market served by its young industrial complex. Until World War II it was heavily dependent on manufactured imports from the East. As expected, the largely unorganized trade and service industries were predominant in the economy. As late as 1940 they provided as much as 68.3 per cent of the total employment opportunities. Moreover, except for citrus production, the Los Angeles area's agricultural products were largely perishable. The petroleum, airframe, rubber, and motion picture industries of course had a wider market, but in general the area's industry supplied regional and local needs. Los Angeles was a large city, thanks to its extraordinarily high rate of population growth, but it still was isolated from other large metropolitan centers and served a vast undeveloped surrounding area.

Because Los Angeles industry was regional in character and served a local market, it developed a pattern of diversification. As late as 1940 no one industry had 25 per cent of all employed persons. Organized labor thus had to function in many industries in order to unionize a significant number of the city's workers. The emphasis on the service industries reflected not only regionalism but also the high rate of population growth, which provided a large consumer market. Furthermore, the regional market and industrial diversification made Los Angeles characteristically a small-plant town with respect to nearly every industry except airframe manufacturing and rubber. Los

Angeles had fewer workers per plant than San Francisco, Detroit, Chicago, Cleveland, or Pittsburgh. But in output per worker in these six cities in 1939, Los Angeles was surpassed only by San Francisco. The economic characteristic of small plants coupled with relatively few workers per plant made for close contact between employer and employee, which retarded effective unionization.[6]

Thus, the basic reasons for the nearly fifty years of open-shop supremacy in Los Angeles stem from the characteristics of the city's economic development. On the other hand, the success of the open shop probably had little to do with the area's outstanding economic growth. In each decade from 1860 to 1940 the population increased in Los Angeles County by the striking figure of more than 24 per cent. As a factor behind this growth, the area's climate cannot be overemphasized in its appeal to potential members of the labor force —the person tired of shoveling snow, the aged, the health seeker, and the man who wanted a few acres with some chickens and a garden. Further, Los Angeles had other advantages related to climate and geography which began to attract industry in the decades after the turn of the century. Power became available at a cost lower than the national average. Building costs were less than in Midwestern or Eastern cities, partly because the climate permitted less expensive cover and enclosure. There was likewise little need for heat in southern California industrial plants. Climate was also an important determinant in industrial location, particularly for airframe manufacturing and moving picture production. Nor should natural resources be overlooked in accounting for the city's industrial development, especially petroleum and agricultural production. Finally, as is characteristic of a rapidly developing region, the per capita income was relatively high in California and Los Angeles in comparison with the older areas of the country. This, in turn, had a feed-back effect in attracting more people to the "City of the Angels."[7]

As noted above, some characteristics of the Los Angeles economy favored particular industries over others. Although employment tended to be heavier in these industries, except for motion picture production they were not among the first to feel the impact of unions. In addition to the airframe-manufacturing, petroleum, motion picture, and certain agricultural industries, climate and resources favored the growth of the tourist trade and a corollary rise of recreation and amusement activities. The city's position as a regional market center contributed to the extensive development of wholesale trade and allied retail service industries. Relatively high per capita income and the heavy tourist influx promoted all kinds of restaurants and allied activities, as well as business repair services. The growth and rapid turnover of the population stimulated industries such as real estate, finance, insurance, cleaning, dyeing, and laundering. Tied in with the extractive and service industries were the city's manufacturing enterprises, the most important of which in terms of employment were in the nondurable goods category. In 1939 the leading classifications were food and textiles, each of which provided a higher proportion of total employment than the largest durable goods industry, iron and steel and their products. Thus the manufacturing segment of the economy had a closer tie with the consumption needs of an increasing population than with its capital requirements. The rapid rise of manufacturing, relative to total industrial activity in Los Angeles, in the last five years of the 1930's seemed to be most closely related to the growth of the aircraft industry. It was in this period that southern California became known as the nation's major aircraft production center.[8]

Employment figures for the period 1899–1940 clearly reflect the industrial growth of the Los Angeles area. These figures show that manufacturing, though only a minor industrial category, was the most rapidly growing source of jobs throughout the forty years. Employment in manufacturing expanded at a higher rate in Los Angeles than in any other area in the United States. From 1899 to 1914 the number of manufacturing wage earners in Los Angeles increased at an average annual rate of 11 per cent. The average yearly rate of increase from 1921 to 1931 (to exclude the abnormal periods of World War I and most of the depression) dropped to 4.5 per cent, but this was still substantial as compared with the rate in other cities in the nation. By 1940, eight Los Angeles manufacturing industries employed about 75 per cent of all employees in this classification. In order of importance these were: transportation equipment except automobiles; food and kindred products; machinery; iron and steel and their products; petroleum products; printing and publishing; furniture and wood products; and apparel.[9]

Total employment figures in Los Angeles for 1920 and 1940 reflect the rapid growth of industry between these two years. In 1920 Los Angeles had 17.5 per cent of the employed working force of the state and .6 per cent of the nation's. Twenty years later the figures were 41 and 2.3 per cent, respectively, or 1,036,984 employed workers. Employment in 1940 was most heavily concentrated in wholesale and retail trade (24 per cent of total employment), manufacturing (19.8

per cent), personal services (10.6 per cent), and amusement and recreation (4.2 per cent). During the period 1920–1940, the percentage of total employment found in the service industries increased, whereas that in manufacturing and extractive activities decreased, although all industrial groups rose in the aggregate. Total employment in Los Angeles and California had been rising rapidly since the days of the gold rush of 1849. In the following century the nation's population increased more than sixfold, but that of California was multiplied by sixty-four, with the rates of employment expansion tending to keep pace, though not always in direct proportion. During the 1930's, for example, because of the business cycle, manufacturing employment declined in the early years of the decade and rose by 40 per cent from February, 1933, to June, 1937. Between the latter month and January, 1939, it declined by 22 per cent. Yet the population increased steadily throughout the decade.

As might be expected because of the rapid population growth, construction employment figured very prominently as a source of jobs in the Los Angeles economy. A significant amount of urban total employment is always evident in construction; rapidly growing Los Angeles was no exception. In 1920, 4 per cent of the city's total employment was to be found in the construction trades; by 1940 the figure had risen to 6.3 per cent. It is understandable that building trades unions were eager to organize construction craftsmen. The fact that employment in the extractive industries declined, even though only slightly, as a percentage of total employment, from 3.8 per cent in 1920 to 3.4 per cent in 1940, further demonstrates the changing character of the city's economy. This decline becomes more significant when compared with the rise in service industry employment relative to that in manufacturing, although all categories increased in absolute terms. Extractive industry employment would have fallen more drastically relative to total employment if the petroleum segment had not expanded so rapidly in these two decades.[10]

The manufacturing employment figures, especially for the late 1930's, give some clue to the growing strength of unions in Los Angeles and point to the eventual decline of open-shop influence. As noted earlier, the service industries rose in relative employment strength between 1920 and 1940. This in itself would not account for any rise in influence of organized labor, as the AFL and, later, the CIO were not strong in these fields. Nor, as implied earlier, were unions important in the extractive industries. But the absolute increase in manufacturing employment, especially during the recovery phases of the depression, accounts to some degree for the rise in union activity. Further, the increase was marked in the durable goods segment, where both craft and industrial unions were most evident. Some light is shed on this matter by the employment figures in table 9, comparing Los Angeles, San Francisco, and the state as a whole for the period 1935–1940.[11]

TABLE 9

Estimated Number[a] of Wage Earners[b] in Manufacturing in
California, Los Angeles, and San Francisco, 1935–1940
(In thousands)

Year	California			Los Angeles[d]			San Francisco[e]		
	Total[c]	Non-durable goods	Durable goods	Total	Non-durable goods	Durable goods	Total[c]	Non-durable goods	Durable goods
1935	239.1	146.2	92.9	94.0	55.1	38.9	77.0	48.4	28.5
1936	266.2	152.6	113.6	110.4	61.1	49.3	82.3	48.7	33.6
1937	302.2	167.0	135.2	128.6	66.4	62.2	88.4	51.0	37.3
1938	260.8	147.0	113.8	116.4	61.6	54.8	74.0	44.7	29.3
1939	276.2	151.3	125.0	127.9	64.1	63.8	76.4	45.3	31.0
1940	320.1	154.1	166.0	152.8	65.3	87.5	83.9	47.8	36.1

[a] Average for the year.
[b] Includes production and related workers in production and other departments, such as shipping, maintenance, and warehousing. Does not include administrative, supervisory, sales, technical, and office personnel, nor force-account construction workers and employees in government establishments.
[c] Detail may not add to total because of rounding.
[d] Los Angeles Industrial Area equals Los Angeles County.
[e] San Francisco Industrial Area includes Alameda, Contra Costa, Marin, San Francisco, and San Mateo counties.
Source: California Department of Industrial Relations, *Labor in California, 1943–1944* (San Francisco, 1945), p. 28.

The expansion of manufacturing in Los Angeles during these years, in contrast with San Francisco, is clearly seen in table 9. Open-shop advocates were prone to point to the more rapid industrial growth of the southern city as positive proof of the restrictive power of Bay area unions. Firms were said to prefer the industrial climate of Los Angeles for this reason, and also because it attracted an employee group that lacked interest in unionization. The fact that the rapid rise in manufacturing employment in Los Angeles occurred at a time when unions were increasing in power in the city seems to have been overlooked in this argument. But statistics on strikes and idle man-hours vividly illustrate that industrial peace was more characteristic of Los Angeles than of San Francisco (see table 10). After the 1920's Los Angeles had

TABLE 10

WORKERS INVOLVED AND MAN-DAYS IDLE IN STRIKES, LOS ANGELES
CITY AND SAN FRANCISCO BAY AREA, 1927-1939

Year	Number of strikes[a]		Workers involved[b]		Man-days idle[b]	
	Los Angeles	Bay area	Los Angeles	Bay area	Los Angeles	Bay area
1927	6	7	200	174	8,521	4,446
1928	8	3	624	90	5,812	1,270
1929	9	8	1,648	3,651	27,864	22,103
1930	3	3	906	66	25,391	282
1931	5	10	228	846	2,519	18,324
1932	2	7	20	478	200	4,290
1933	20	8	13,029	1,001	211,297	18,468
1934	18	42	4,738	97,665	60,994	328,826
1935	42	60	3,790	11,549	70,938	142,291
1936	50	76	10,502	18,882	239,497	422,737
1937	78	65	20,544	26,872	264,778	719,867
1938	40	55	8,627	17,877	170,656	462,770
1939	71	58	11,765	26,178	145,023	348,918

a Enumerated on basis of strikes beginning in year.
b Excludes intercity strikes except in 1938 and 1939.
SOURCE: California Department of Industrial Relations, *Biennial Statistical Report to the Legislature, 1939-1940*
(San Francisco, 1941), p. 55.

more manufacturing workers than San Francisco, yet had fewer on
strike and lost fewer man-days in most of the years concerned. This
favorable record was used by open-shop supporters as constructive
evidence of what happened when unions were not permitted to get an
economic stranglehold on a city, and when its industries attracted
workers who were uninterested in unionization—or, at least, in going
on strike!

Robert D. Sangster, manager of the Industrial Department of the
Los Angeles Chamber of Commerce, testified on this subject before
the La Follette Committee in January, 1940. He pointed out that the
population of Los Angeles County had increased from 101,454 to
2,208,492, or 2,076 per cent, from 1890 to 1930, while that of the five
counties surrounding San Francisco Bay had risen from 429,535 to
1,306,938, or only 204 per cent. The Chamber of Commerce, seeing
this tremendous population growth as a potential source of labor, had
begun a great drive for new industry in 1919, when the value of manufactured output had been $418 million, exclusive of motion pictures.
By 1937 the figure had increased to $1,205 million. In contrast, the
value of manufactures in the San Francisco Bay area during the same

period rose from $971 million to only $1,052 million. The progress made by Los Angeles was, in Sangster's opinion, a reflection of the difference between "the open-shop labor relations for which Los Angeles industry is noted and the closed-union-shop relations in the strike-torn San Francisco Bay area." [12]

The question of how strong an impact unions had had on the northern city, as compared with Los Angeles, was not so easily resolved. Open-shop supporters seemed to be correct in attributing the higher labor costs in San Francisco to greater unionization, but the effect of cheaper labor in accounting for the contrasting growth of the southern city cannot be exactly determined. Table 11 illustrates the wage differ-

TABLE 11

AVERAGE WEEKLY AND HOURLY EARNINGS AND AVERAGE HOURS
WORKED PER WEEK IN MANUFACTURING INDUSTRIES,
LOS ANGELES AND SAN FRANCISCO COUNTIES,
AUGUST, 1938, TO JUNE, 1939[a]

Year and month	Average weekly earnings		Average hourly earnings		Average hours worked per week	
	Los Angeles	San Francisco	Los Angeles	San Francisco	Los Angeles	San Francisco
1938						
August	$27.05	$30.13	$.708	$.784	38.2	38.4
September	27.07	29.05	.706	.777	38.3	37.4
October	27.66	29.01	.708	.793	39.1	36.6
November	27.33	28.66	.719	.801	38.0	35.8
December	28.69	29.70	.732	.806	39.2	36.9
1939						
January	28.22	29.51	.742	.817	38.0	36.1
February	28.19	29.80	.722	.815	39.0	36.6
March	28.32	30.20	.719	.807	39.4	37.4
April	27.56	29.71	.716	.811	38.5	36.6
May	27.93	30.14	.716	.806	39.0	37.4
June	28.18	30.09	.716	.797	39.3	37.7

[a] Excludes crude petroleum producing; motion pictures; laundering, cleaning, and dyeing; and steam railroad repair shops.
SOURCE: California Department of Industrial Relations, *California Labor Market Bulletin*, August 21, 1939.

ential between the two cities. A differential in manufacturing industries existed as late as 1939, and workers were employed for longer hours each week in Los Angeles. Similar data for industries other than manufacturing show that, in general, a higher hourly pay rate characterized San Francisco as late as 1940. Rates were 20 cents an hour higher for building trades helpers and laborers. Street railway wages were above those paid in Los Angeles. Similar benefits prevailed for workers in wholesale and retail trade, hotels, and laundering, cleaning, and dyeing. Summary data for 1940 indicate that hourly money earnings in the Bay city averaged 82 cents, as against 74 cents in Los Angeles. Wages in San Francisco were higher in durable goods manufacture (by 12 cents) and in the production of nondurables (by 6 cents). In nonmanufacturing areas the differential in favor of Bay city workers was smallest in wholesale and retail trade (9 cents) and largest in laundering, cleaning, and dyeing (15 cents).[13]

In 1940 it seemed that Los Angeles had higher pay scales than the nation as a whole, but the average for the country was held down by the low wage structures in Southern states. Whereas in Los Angeles the average hourly rate in manufacturing industries was 74 cents, it was only 66 cents over the country. In only two industries of statistical significance were wages higher in Los Angeles than in San Francisco: the rubber industry, where workers in the southern city had the advantage by 16.5 cents an hour, and structural and ornamental iron work. Although sometimes the differential in favor of San Francisco was unrelated to unions, for the most part the higher average wages in the Bay area seemed to stem from more extensive unionization in comparison with Los Angeles.[14]

Although hourly wages were higher on the average in San Francisco than in Los Angeles, workers in the southern city would not be worse off economically if their cost of living was lower. Open-shop supporters often claimed that employees were actually better off in Los Angeles because of their higher real income and their freedom from union "tyranny." The evidence that Los Angeles living costs were lower in the years before World War I, however, is not conclusive. By the 1930's the cost-of-living argument used to justify lower wage scales was becoming a bit specious. A case could still be made from some data, as shown in table 12, but table 13 demonstrates that the argument was not supported by state statistics for 1939, 1940, and 1941.

Although increasing industrialization and the accompanying unionization of Los Angeles seemed to be factors in raising wages in the city, it may also be argued that the rapidity of industrial growth and a developing manpower shortage were primary and inevitable elements in pushing up pay scales. If this was true in the late 1930's, the attempts of groups like the M and M and Southern Californians, Incorporated, to oppose the unions could have had little, if any, effect in holding down wage rates. At most, their efforts may have kept the rates some-

TABLE 12

ESTIMATED COST OF LIVING FOR A FOUR-PERSON MANUAL WORKER'S
FAMILY AT MAINTENANCE LEVEL[a] IN LOS ANGELES AND
SAN FRANCISCO, AS OF MARCH 15 AND
SEPTEMBER 15, 1939

Category	Los Angeles		San Francisco		Percentage difference	
	3/15/39	9/15/39	3/15/39	9/15/39	3/15/39	9/15/39
	$1,341.54	$1,331.52	$1,460.41	$1,462.25	8.1	8.9
Food	452.19	446.58	486.79	494.68	7.1	9.7
Clothing	167.42	167.73	170.97	170.99	2.1	1.9
Housing	246.75	245.58	284.62	285.28	13.3	13.9
Fuel and light	74.83	72.05	86.67	84.94	13.7	15.2
Furniture, furnishings, household equipment	34.94	34.94	37.30	37.20	6.3	6.1
Miscellaneous	365.41	364.64	394.06	389.16	7.3	6.3

[a] As defined by the Works Progress Administration.
SOURCE: *Violations of Free Speech and Rights of Labor*, Hearings before a Subcommittee of the Senate Committee on Education and Labor, 74th Cong., 3d sess., S. Res. 266 (Washington, 1940), Part 52, p. 19275.

what lower than they would otherwise have been. Because average hourly wages in Los Angeles were above those of the nation in 1940, however, it is doubtful that the attempt to maintain the open shop even retarded a rise in wage scales. Although the antiunion battle may have been fought to keep unions from taking advantage of a manpower shortage in the revival phase of the depression, the forces leading to wage increases seem to have been almost inexorable, unrelated to unionization, and deeply seated in the traditional factors of supply and demand.[15]

The M and M's encouragement of the payment of "reasonable" wages in the late 1930's may well have been a recognition that rising rates in Los Angeles were more the result of rapid growth and industrialization than of union pressure. Whatever the reason, the open-shop struggle came to center more on the issue of job control than on wages. Employers were concerned about their prerogatives, especially their control over hiring and firing, hours, working conditions, and other aspects of employment. This is not to say that they were uninterested in wage scales, but only that the open- versus union-shop issue raised more important questions than pay rates in the years immediately preceding World War II.

TABLE 13

ESTIMATED COST OF LIVING, LOS ANGELES, 1939–1941, BY QUARTERS, AS
COMPARED WITH SAN FRANCISCO AND THE UNITED STATES
(1939 = 100)

Year and month	Los Angeles	San Francisco	United States
1939			
March	100.2	100.1	99.6
June	99.4	99.1	99.1
September	100.9	100.8	101.2
December	99.5	100.0	100.1
1940			
March	99.8	99.6	100.3
June	99.9	99.9	101.0
September	100.2	100.6	100.9
December	101.2	101.4	101.2
1941			
March	101.6	102.2	101.7
June	104.7	105.2	105.1
September	107.1	107.6	108.6

SOURCE: California Department of Industrial Relations, *The Cost of Living in California, 1914–22 and 1930–41* (Sacramento, 1941), p. 7.

Even though Los Angeles wages were higher than the national average by 1940, the city's employers were not paying top scales. Available figures show that Los Angeles rates were well below those prevailing in a number of other cities. In a study of twenty major cities as of January, 1941, Los Angeles and Chicago tied for eleventh place, though Chicago was a much more heavily unionized city. The index for Los Angeles was 96 compared with an average of 100 for the entire group.[16]

In 1940, therefore, in labor costs as well as in climate, Los Angeles, in contrast with many major cities, continued to offer advantages to manufacturing industries. But materials costs in relation to value of product tended to be higher in Los Angeles than in Midwestern and Eastern areas because of the city's distance from raw material supplies, excepting crude petroleum and a few other indigenous items. Moreover, the labor-cost advantage was tapering off and was destined to become even less important. The removal of the wage issue from the open-shop struggle, increasing industrialization, and the developing World War II manpower shortage made the future rise of pay scales a certainty, regardless of unionization. By December, 1946, hourly wage scales in Los Angeles manufacturing industries were only 2 cents below those of San Francisco, and in the nondurable goods sector Los Angeles scales were actually 2 cents higher.[17]

A further factor in reducing the wage differential between Los Angeles and San Francisco, and in bringing the pay structure in the southern city more in line with that of Eastern industrial centers, was the establishment of branch plants of national concerns in the Los Angeles area. The wage scales and policies of many of these firms were set in their Eastern headquarters by men who were used to dealing with unions and not so imbued with the open-shop philosophy. This created an environment more favorable to the development of unions than was likely to be provided by locally owned and operated firms. From 1931 through 1935, a period of severe depression, more than twenty-three national concerns established Los Angeles branches, including such well-known firms as General Motors, Armour, Chrysler, Dow Chemical, Studebaker, Sherwin-Williams, General Cable, Canada Dry, Firestone, and General Foods. The total initial investment was estimated at $10.4 million. Many of these firms were subsequently among the first to make peace with the CIO. This action affected the wage levels in their Los Angeles plants.

These branches tended to be larger than locally owned plants, thus eliminating the relatively close tie between employer and employee which had been typical in Los Angeles. Although open-shop supporters claimed that some of the national concerns moved into the area partly because of lower labor costs and the weakness of unions, the basic reason seems to have been a desire to serve the rapidly growing Los Angeles regional market. They were thus less likely to quibble over unionization and its possible wage impact in the face of expanding sales opportunities in southern California.[18]

Some Los Angeles employers feared that increasing industrialization, coupled with the growth of local branches of national firms, would contribute to instability in the local economy. Many open-shop leaders had long contended that the Los Angeles economy was insulated from that of the nation; that workers did not need to fear periodic unemployment as perhaps they did in Eastern and Midwestern industrial centers. Further, they claimed, in California's benign climate a man could always have a little garden which would tide him over a difficult period. Hence unions were not needed as protective devices against employment insecurity. Such statements, however, were only partly true. Even though Los Angeles was less affected by business cycles than some older, more industrialized areas of the country, it shared in the nationwide panics and depressions. Its tendency to recover from contractions more rapidly than the nation as a whole was more the result of strong economic growth than of any other factor. Nor did the relative diversity of the economy or its concentration on nonmanufacturing enterprises insulate it from business cycle changes. Thus there seemed to be no evidence to substantiate arguments against unionization which were based on the relatively isolated, diversified nature of the economy. Certainly it was no longer insulated by 1941, when the impact of World War II began to be felt by industries in the area.[19]

In 1939 and 1940 Los Angeles was on the verge of becoming one of the great industrial centers of the nation. No longer was it likely to be known as "the white spot of America"; though open-shop advocates were not quite ready to admit this, the trend was unmistakable. There was also some evidence that the general public was tiring of the struggle between organized labor and employer groups. Compulsory arbitration was suggested as a possible solution. One group, Labor Peace for California, Inc., drafted a proposed constitutional amendment to create a state mediation board of five members to be appointed by the CIO, the AFL, the California Chamber of Commerce, the California Farm Bureau Federation, and the governor. Its job would be to mediate all labor disputes. If this failed, the board would have the power to prescribe settlements, with orders enforced by the courts. In a sense, this and similar organizations expressed the bitterness of some sections of the public toward a decade of strikes and labor unrest. Labor Peace for California, Inc., was opposed, however, by both organized labor and employers, open-shop or otherwise. Unions and employers showed an increasing desire to get together on their own initiative to resolve their differences without recourse to the public press. Along these lines, several employer groups suggested the establishment of a comprehensive labor relations forum, an idea that was beginning to take hold in other cities, including San Francisco. Regular discussions in Los Angeles were held in 1939 under the name of "Town Hall," but there were few constructive results applicable to labor relations. Nevertheless, that such a forum was suggested and held indicated that at least some employers were willing to accept unions as permanent institutions in Los Angeles.[20]

The reorganization of the M and M and Southern Californians, Incorporated, and their consolidation into one body were symptomatic of this growing acceptance of unions. By 1939 the M and M was definitely trying to bring wages and working conditions into competitive alignment in the region's industries in an effort to minimize opportunities for unionization and, at the same time, to soft-pedal its antiunion reputation. Its leadership began not only to realize the favorable implications for unions of advancing industrialization, but also to believe that a union-baiting line was actually a greater challenge to organize than silence about the advantages of the open shop. The new M and M program, after the elimination in 1940 of Southern Californians, Incorporated, as a separate organization, was to accept collective bargaining as an established fact, even though its published policy favored the open shop. It took steps to provide employers engaged in collective bargaining with experienced negotiators backed by a research staff which furnished comparative information on wages and working conditions and other necessary data.[21]

What, then, was the position of Los Angeles organized labor in 1940 as it stood on the threshold of a new and accepted status in an increasingly industrialized city? Although no local industries were entirely covered by union agreements, building construction, trucking, motion pictures, longshoring, and printing were largely under union job control. Organized labor also had important nuclei in mass-production industries and in nearly all light manufacturing industries, as well as in many branches of retail and wholesale trade and the related consumer service fields. But in almost every industry there were still many employers who operated on a nonunion or an open-shop basis. This situation was characteristic of the restaurant, furniture, clothing, machinery, and metal trades industries, but it was also to some extent true of the more heavily unionized construction, trucking, and printing activities. Where there was organization, the relatively small local predominated rather than the large union which was more typical of mass-production industrial centers in the East. Most of the members of these locals were covered by agreements, a majority of which were written rather than oral.[22]

The consensus of those active in the Los Angeles labor movement was that the lean years were past. Southern Californians, Incorporated, The Neutral Thousands, and other open-shop groups that came into existence in the closing years of the decade represented, in labor's opinion, the city's last stand in the fifty-year war for the open shop. Whether the "open shop" was interpreted by employers as a nonunion shop or a true open shop, unions were being increasingly accepted by many industrial leaders who had formerly been part of the hard core of opposition. After the activities of the open-shop groups were aired by the La Follette Committee in 1939 and 1940, union leaders launched new organizational drives, particularly among the teamsters and the workers in the burgeoning aircraft industry. By the time the United States came to the brink of war in 1941, organized labor was making exceedingly good progress in membership drives and in obtaining contracts with employers. Unions at this time claimed 50 per cent of the city's workers as members, but employers stated that the figure was closer to 40 per cent. In either event, the "white spot" designation of Los Angeles as an open-shop town was no longer valid. Not that the city was thoroughly unionized; but the militant antiunion period was a thing of the past. At the end of 1940 labor leaders claimed that there were 120,000 AFL members in Los Angeles, not counting the CIO, the railroad brotherhoods, and bona fide independent locals.[23]

The entrance of the United States into World War II unleashed forces that completed the transition of Los Angeles from an open-shop center to just another large city in which unions were active and accepted. A labor reserve, small-sized plants, the lack of industrial concentration, and other factors that had restricted unions in earlier years but were unrelated to the open shop itself, rapidly declined in importance. The placement of ten billion dollars in war contracts for aircraft, ships, and ordnance helped to change a manufacturing pattern not previously characterized by emphasis on durable goods output. The labor force in Los Angeles County rose from 1,198,726 workers in April, 1940, to approximately 1,600,000 by August, 1944. About 315,-750 of this number were employed in the manufacture of durable goods. This was almost twice the number in manufacturing of all types in 1940. With both labor and management concerned over war and mutual survival, the unions made gains that placed them in a solid position to continue their progress during the postwar industrial expansion.[24] The Los Angeles business community began to realize the implications of the statement that "labor's actions, as well as its aspirations, are neither new-born, nor menacing, nor obscure. They express the dynamics of a continuous drive toward that better life implicit in democratic government and in unionism which in this country began at about the same time."[25]

NOTES

PREFACE

[1] Grace Heilman Stimson, *Rise of the Labor Movement in Los Angeles* (Berkeley and Los Angeles: University of California Press, 1955).

[2] Frank C. Pierson, *Community Wage Patterns* (Berkeley and Los Angeles: University of California Press, 1953), p. 138. The quotation represents Pierson's conclusion after studying the industrial development of Los Angeles and the unfolding wage patterns in the area.

[3] Leo Wolman, *Ebb and Flow in Trade Unionism* (New York: National Bureau of Economic Research, 1936).

I. THE PAST SHAPES THE FUTURE

[1] John R. Commons and Associates, *History of Labor in the United States, 1896–1932* (New York: Macmillan, 1921–1935), III, 293–295.

[2] *Record* (Los Angeles), July 1, 1911.

[3] U.S. Commission on Industrial Relations, *Final Report* (Washington, 1915), p. 28; Howard R. Smith, *Economic History of the United States* (New York: Ronald Press, 1955), pp. 486–490.

[4] Margaret S. Gordon, *Employment Expansion and Population Growth: The California Experience, 1900–1950* (Berkeley and Los Angeles: University of California Press, 1954), p. 92; Los Angeles *Times* (hereinafter referred to as the *Times*), Jan. 1, 1913; California Bureau of Labor Statistics, *Twentieth Biennial Report, 1921–1922*, p. 84.

[5] *Los Angeles, "The Magic City and County"* (Los Angeles: County Board of Supervisors, 1951), p. 3.

[6] George E. Mowry, *The California Progressives* (Berkeley and Los Angeles: University of California Press, 1951), pp. 7–8; *Los Angeles, "The Magic City and County,"* p. 6.

[7] *Times*, Jan. 1, 1913; Jan. 1, 1926.

[8] Harrison Gray Otis, "Los Angeles—A Sketch," *Sunset*, XXIV (Jan., 1910), 14.

[9] Frank C. Pierson, *Community Wage Patterns* (Berkeley and Los Angeles: University of California Press, 1953), pp. 23–24; *Times*, Aug. 15, 1911.

[10] *Times*, Sept. 10, 1911.

[11] *Ibid.*, Jan. 1, 1913.

[12] Commons and Associates, *op. cit.*, III, 60–61.

[13] See chapters xxi and xxii of Grace Heilman Stimson, *Rise of the Labor Movement in Los Angeles* (Berkeley and Los Angeles: University of California Press, 1955), for an excellent treatment of this event and its repercussions.

[14] *Ibid.*, p. 422.

[15] *Times*, Jan. 5, 1913.

[16] *Los Angeles, "The Magic City and County,"* p. 14.

[17] *Citizen*, Aug. 7, 1913; *Record*, Dec. 17, 18, 1913; Los Angeles Central Labor Council, *Minutes*, Dec. 19, 1913; *Times*, Dec. 27, 1913.

[18] Los Angeles Central Labor Council, *Minutes*, Jan. 5, 1914; *Citizen*, Jan. 9, 1914.

[19] *Record*, Oct. 14, 1913; see also Oct. 15–18, 1913.

[20] Los Angeles Central Labor Council, *Minutes*, Oct. 24, 1913; *Citizen*, Jan. 2, 1914.

[21] *Record*, Dec. 1, 1913.

[22] *Final Report and Testimony Submitted to Congress by the Commission on Industrial Relations*, 64th Cong., 1st sess., S. Doc. 415 (Washington, 1916), VI, 5563–5564, 5841.

[23] *Ibid.*, p. 5720.

²⁴ *Times*, March 30, 1912; *Citizen*, May 2, 1913; May 29, 1914; *Record*, Nov. 16, Dec. 1, 4, 1914; *Proceedings of the American Federation of Labor, 1914*, p. 282.
²⁵ Commons and Associates, *op. cit.*, III, 171; *Citizen*, April 9, 1915.
²⁶ *Record*, Dec. 19, 1913; Jan. 13, 1914; *Times*, Dec. 31, 1913; Jan. 15, 1914.
²⁷ *Final Report and Testimony* . . . , VI, 5840.
²⁸ *Citizen*, Jan. 16, 1914; Los Angeles Central Labor Council, *Minutes*, Jan. 23, 1914; *Proceedings of the California State Federation of Labor, 1914*, p. 55; *Record*, March 9, 20, 21, 23–30, 1914.
²⁹ *Record*, March 27, 28, April 2, 1914; *Times*, Jan. 24, 1916; *Citizen*, March 5, 1915.
³⁰ Stimson, *op. cit.*, p. 420.
³¹ *Times*, Sept. 8, 1914; see also U.S. Commission on Industrial Relations, *Final Report*, p. ii.
³² U.S. Commission on Industrial Relations, *Final Report*, p. 87.
³³ *Ibid.*, pp. 23, 90–91.
³⁴ *Times*, Aug. 25, 1915.
³⁵ Frederick Palmer, "Otistown of the Open Shop," *Hampton's Magazine*, XXVI (Jan., 1911), 35.
³⁶ Mowry, *op. cit.*, p. 48.
³⁷ *Final Report and Testimony* . . . , VI, 5568, 5570.
³⁸ *Ibid.*, p. 5501; *Times*, Sept. 9, 1914.
³⁹ Palmer, *op. cit.*, pp. 38–39.
⁴⁰ *Final Report and Testimony* . . . , VI, 5521–5522, 5607, 5650–5651, 5654–5655.
⁴¹ *Ibid.*, pp. 5857–5859.
⁴² *Ibid.*, pp. 5858–5861.
⁴³ *Ibid.*, pp. 5564–5565, 5718; *Times*, Sept. 12, 1914.
⁴⁴ John A. Fitch, "Los Angeles, A Militant Anti-Union Citadel," *Survey*, XXXIII (Oct. 3, 1914), 4.
⁴⁵ *Times*, Sept. 9, 1914.
⁴⁶ Stimson, *op. cit.*, p. 360.

II. LABOR SMOLDERS, 1911–1914

¹ Grace Heilman Stimson, *Rise of the Labor Movement in Los Angeles* (Berkeley and Los Angeles: University of California Press, 1955), pp. 421–422.
² J. W. Buzzell, "An Open Shop Citadel Falls," *American Federationist*, XLVIII (April, 1941), 6.
³ *Citizen*, Feb. 2, March 15, 29, Aug. 2, 1912; Feb. 14, 1913.
⁴ *Final Report and Testimony Submitted to Congress by the Commission on Industrial Relations*, 64th Cong., 1st sess., S. Doc. 415 (Washington, 1916), VI, 5553–5555, 5587.
⁵ *Ibid.*, pp. 5935–5952.
⁶ *Ibid.*, p. 5864.
⁷ *Ibid.*, pp. 5553–5555, 5583, 5585; *Times*, Sept. 10, 1914.
⁸ *Final Report and Testimony* . . . , VI, 5842–5843.
⁹ *Ibid.*, pp. 5625–5626.
¹⁰ Frederick Palmer, "Otistown of the Open Shop," *Hampton's Magazine*, XXVI (Jan., 1911), 41; *Times*, Sept. 10, 1914.
¹¹ Los Angeles Central Labor Council, *Minutes*, May 24, 1913; *Citizen*, Feb. 7, 14, 1913; May 29, June 5, July 31, Aug. 21, 1914; April 9, 1915; *Record*, June 27, 1914; *Times*, March 9, 1912; *The Forty-Year War for a Free City; A History of the Open Shop in Los Angeles* (Los Angeles: Times-Mirror Publishing Co., 1929), p. 18.
¹² Los Angeles Central Labor Council, *Minutes*, Aug. 30, 1912; *Citizen*, Feb. 21, March 14, 1913.

[13] Los Angeles Central Labor Council, *Minutes,* Aug. 4, Nov. 24, 1911; March 28, 1913; *Proceedings of the California State Federation of Labor, 1914,* pp. 27-28.

[14] William Haber, *Industrial Relations in the Building Industry* (Cambridge: Harvard University Press, 1930), pp. 157-158; Robert A. Christie, *Empire in Wood* (Ithaca: New York State School of Industrial and Labor Relations, 1956), pp. 109, 197; Los Angeles Central Labor Council, *Minutes,* Nov. 12, 1913.

[15] *Los Angeles, "The Magic City and County"* (Los Angeles: County Board of Supervisors, 1951), pp. 14, 18; *Times,* Sept. 24, 1911; June 23, 1912; Jan. 1, 1913.

[16] *Citizen,* Feb. 28, Aug. 8, 1913; Los Angeles Central Labor Council, *Minutes,* June 13, 1913; *Final Report and Testimony . . . ,* VI, 5998-5999.

[17] Ira B. Cross, *A History of the Labor Movement in California* (Berkeley: University of California Press, 1935), p. 284.

[18] *Times,* March 9, May 9, June 12, Aug. 11, 1912; *Record,* June 12-14, 29, 1912; Los Angeles Central Labor Council, *Minutes,* June 21, 1912; Cross, *op. cit.,* p. 284.

[19] Los Angeles Central Labor Council, *Minutes,* Aug. 19, 1912; March 18, 1913; *Times,* Aug. 22, 25, 1912; Jan. 26, 1913; *Record,* Feb. 20, 1913.

[20] Christie, *op. cit.,* p. 2; *Final Report and Testimony . . . ,* VI, 5631-5632; *Record,* July 3, 1911; *Citizen,* Aug. 4, 1911; May 9, 1913.

[21] *Final Report and Testimony . . . ,* VI, 5591, 5595-5602, 5617-5618, 5636-5637, 5643, 5863-5864; *Times,* Sept. 10, 11, 1914; *Citizen,* Feb. 14, April 4, 1913; Los Angeles Central Labor Council, *Minutes,* July 20, 1914.

[22] *Proceedings of the American Federation of Labor, 1914,* p. 480; *Citizen,* March 7, 1913; *Final Report and Testimony . . . ,* VI, 5504-5505, 5649; *Times,* June 17, 1912.

[23] Los Angeles Central Labor Council, *Minutes,* Sept. 22, 1911; Feb. 16, 1912; Oct. 3, 1913; June 4, Nov. 19, 1915; *Times,* May 19, 1912; Jan. 31, May 28, 1913; *Record,* Aug. 30, 1913; *Citizen,* Jan. 7, 1912; Feb. 14, 1913; April 3, 1914.

[24] *Citizen,* Feb. 21, April 17, May 9, Oct. 17, 1913; Los Angeles Central Labor Council, *Minutes,* June 14, 1912; Oct. 10, 1913; April 10, 1914; *Times,* Dec. 30, 1913.

[25] *Final Report and Testimony . . . ,* VI, 5657-5660, 5662-5664; Los Angeles Central Labor Council, *Minutes,* Jan. 19, 1912.

[26] Los Angeles Central Labor Council, *Minutes,* Dec. 6, 1912; *Citizen,* Feb. 14, March 14, 1913; *Record,* Feb. 17, 20, March 18, 1913.

[27] Los Angeles Central Labor Council, *Minutes,* June 28, 1912; March 18, 1913; *Citizen,* April 4, 11, 25, 1913.

[28] *Citizen,* May 9, 1913; *Record,* May 23, 24, Nov. 22, 1913; *Proceedings of the American Federation of Labor, 1914,* pp. 135-137.

[29] Los Angeles Central Labor Council, *Minutes,* Aug. 1, 1913; Feb. 13, April 3, Oct. 16, 1914; *Citizen,* Aug. 8, Oct. 17, Dec. 12, 1913; March 27, April 10, June 5, Nov. 6, Dec. 4, 1914; *Times,* Nov. 17, 1913; *Proceedings of the California State Federation of Labor, 1914,* p. 54.

[30] Stimson, *op. cit.,* pp. 361, 394; Los Angeles Central Labor Council, *Minutes,* July 7, Sept. 22, 29, Oct. 20, Dec. 29, 1911; Feb. 3, 5, 27, Sept. 20, 30, 1912; *Record,* Sept. 5, 1911; Jan. 15, 20, 1912; *Times,* March 11, 12, 1912; *The Forty-Year War for a Free City,* p. 24.

[31] *Proceedings of the California State Federation of Labor, 1914,* p. 54; Los Angeles Central Labor Council, *Minutes,* Oct. 6, 1911; Dec. 5, 1912; *Citizen,* Feb. 7, March 7, 1913.

[32] Stimson, *op. cit.,* pp. 337-339, 355; *Citizen,* Feb. 2, 1912.

[33] *Proceedings of the California State Federation of Labor, 1914,* p. 54; *1925,* pp. 51-52; *Citizen,* Aug. 4, 1911; Feb. 2, 1912; Feb. 7, 28, 1913; July 10, 17, 31, Aug. 14, 21, 1914; Los Angeles Central Labor Council, *Minutes,* Nov. 3, 17, Dec. 17, 1911; July 3, 1914.

[34] Los Angeles Central Labor Council, *Minutes,* July 14, Sept. 22, 29, Oct. 6, 1911; Nov. 1, 15, Dec. 6, 1912; April 3, 1914; *Citizen,* July 2, 1911; Feb. 2, 1912; Feb. 14, 21,

March 7, April 4, May 16, July 25, Oct. 31, 1913; Jan. 2, April 10, Nov. 20, 1914; "What Our Organizers Are Doing," *American Federationist*, XX (March, 1913), 228.

[35] *Citizen*, July 28, 1911; March 7, 21, 1913; Sept. 4, 1914; *Record*, March 4, 21, 1913; July 18, 1914; *Times*, March 12, 1913; *Proceedings of the California State Federation of Labor, 1914*, pp. 54–55; *Final Report and Testimony* . . . , VI, 5684–5685.

[36] *Final Report and Testimony* . . . , VI, 5902–5930.

[37] *Ibid.*, pp. 5969–5970.

[38] *Citizen*, July 7, 1911; March 28, April 18, May 16, 1913; Los Angeles Central Labor Council, *Minutes*, Sept. 20, 1912.

[39] Los Angeles Central Labor Council, *Minutes*, Aug. 4, Nov. 10, 1911; Nov. 20, 1914; *Citizen*, Feb. 21, April 11, 1913; Sept. 11, 1914; March 12, 1915; *Proceedings of the California State Federation of Labor, 1914*, p. 54; *Times*, May 2, 1914.

[40] Stimson, *op. cit.*, p. 104.

[41] *Final Report and Testimony* . . . , VI, 5489–5491, 5536, 5538, 5542, 5545, 5899; *Times*, Sept. 9, 10, 13, 1914.

[42] *Final Report and Testimony* . . . , VI, 5536, 5538, 5540, 5899; *Citizen*, Aug. 14, 1914.

[43] *Final Report and Testimony* . . . , VI, 5758, 5760–5769

[44] *Ibid.*, pp. 5770–5772.

[45] *Ibid.*, pp. 5778–5779.

[46] *Citizen*, July 7, 21, Aug. 4, 1911; Feb. 2, 1912; Los Angeles Central Labor Council, *Minutes*, July 7, 14, 21, 1911; Jan. 5, 19, Feb. 26, 1912; Aug. 29, 1913; March 6, 1914; Earl C. Crockett, "The History of California Labor Legislation, 1910–1930" (unpublished Ph.D. dissertation, University of California, Berkeley, 1931), p. 31; Stimson, *op. cit.*, p. 359.

[47] Los Angeles Central Labor Council, *Minutes*, May 1, 1914; *Record*, June 12, 20, 1914; *Proceedings of the California State Federation of Labor, 1914*, pp. 28, 54; *Times*, May 1, 2, 1914; *Citizen*, May 8, June 19, July 3, 1914.

[48] *Citizen*, Oct. 23, 1914; *Record*, June 13, 1914; *Final Report and Testimony* . . . , VI, 5673–5675, 5683–5684.

[49] *Final Report and Testimony* . . . , pp. 5685, 5695–5696; *Times*, April 16, 1912; *Record*, Feb. 14, 1914; Stimson, *op. cit.*, pp. 424–425.

[50] *Final Report and Testimony* . . . , VI, 5698–5711. The quotation is from page 5703.

[51] Stimson, *op. cit.*, pp. 312–313; interview with L. W. Butler, Sept. 10, 1958.

[52] *Times*, Jan. 26, 1913; Los Angeles Central Labor Council, *Minutes*, June 19, 1914; *Citizen*, July 3, Aug. 14, 1914; *Proceedings of the California State Federation of Labor, 1914*, pp. 54–55; *Final Report and Testimony* . . . , VI, 5666–5669.

[53] Los Angeles Central Labor Council, *Minutes*, July 11, 1911; Nov. 13, 1913; *Citizen*, July 21, 1911.

[54] *Times*, Jan. 22, 1915.

[55] *Citizen*, Feb. 2, 28, Aug. 8, 1913; June 26, July 3, Sept. 4, 25, 1914; Los Angeles Central Labor Council, *Minutes*, July 21, 1913.

[56] *The Forty-Year War for a Free City*, p. 18; *Citizen*, Oct. 17, 24, Dec. 5, 1913; April 3, Nov. 6, 1914; Los Angeles Central Labor Council, *Minutes*, Nov. 7, Dec. 26, 1913; May 15, 1914; *Record*, Nov. 8, 29, Dec. 27, 1913; March 28, 1914; Los Angeles Central Labor Council, *Report of the Organizing Committee*, Feb. 27–March 4, 1914; *Proceedings of the California State Federation of Labor, 1914*, p. 54.

[57] *Proceedings of the California State Federation of Labor, 1914*, p. 56; *Record*, April 14, May 2, 9, 16, 1914; Los Angeles Central Labor Council, *Minutes*, June 5, 1914; *The Forty-Year War for a Free City*, p. 18; *Final Report and Testimony* . . . , VI, 5624.

III. THE OPEN RAILS

[1] John R. Commons and Associates, *History of Labor in the United States, 1896–1932* (New York: Macmillan, 1921–1935), IV, 368–369; Grace Heilman Stimson, *Rise of the Labor Movement in Los Angeles* (Berkeley and Los Angeles: University of California Press, 1955), p. 303.

[2] Commons and Associates, *op. cit.*, IV, 369, 371–372; *Final Report and Testimony Submitted to Congress by the Commission on Industrial Relations*, 64th Cong., 1st sess., S. Doc. 415 (Washington, 1916), X, 9866.

[3] Howard R. Smith, *Economic History of the United States* (New York: Ronald Press, 1955), p. 483; *Times*, March 14, Aug. 28, Sept. 9, 30, 1911; *Record*, Aug. 26, 29, 1911.

[4] *Final Report and Testimony* . . . , X, 9738, 9870–9871, 9880–9883, 9915–9916; *Times*, Aug. 6, 1911.

[5] *Record*, Aug. 8, 1911; *Times*, Aug. 9, 1911; *Final Report and Testimony* . . . , X, 9870–9871, 9880–9883.

[6] *Times*, Aug. 5, 11, 23, 25–28, 1911; *Record*, Aug. 12, 1911; *Final Report and Testimony* . . . , X, 9970–9971, 9980–9981.

[7] *Times*, Sept. 1, 3, 7, 8, 11, 27, 29, 30, 1911.

[8] *Final Report and Testimony* . . . , X, 9699, 9710, 9728, 9744, 9764, 9782, 9865.

[9] Los Angeles Central Labor Council, *Minutes*, Oct. 27, Nov. 24, 1911; *Times*, Oct. 1, 1911.

[10] *Times*, Oct. 1, 1911.

[11] *Ibid.*

[12] *Ibid.*, Oct. 2, 1911.

[13] *Record*, Oct. 3, 6, 9, 17, 1911; *Times*, Oct. 7, 27, 1911; Los Angeles Central Labor Council, *Minutes*, Oct. 15, 1911; *Citizen*, Dec. 1, 1911; *The Forty-Year War for a Free City; A History of the Open Shop in Los Angeles* (Los Angeles: Times-Mirror Publishing Co., 1929), p. 18.

[14] *Final Report and Testimony* . . . , X, 9953, 10065; *Times*, Nov. 7, 18, 1911; *Record*, Nov. 17, 1911.

[15] *Times*, Oct. 3, 5, 7, 8, Nov. 2, 27, Dec. 17, 1911; Commons and Associates, *op. cit.*, IV, 370; *Final Report and Testimony* . . . , X, 9943.

[16] Commons and Associates, *op. cit.*, IV, 371–373; *Times*, Oct. 10, Nov. 12, 1911.

[17] *Record*, Oct. 5, 7, 23, 1911; *Times*, Oct. 24, 1911.

[18] *Times*, Oct. 29, 1911.

[19] *Record*, Nov. 20, 1911; *Times*, Jan. 6, 1912; *Citizen*, May 17, 1912; *Labor Clarion*, Feb. 2, 1912.

[20] Los Angeles Central Labor Council, *Minutes*, June 14, 1912.

[21] Commons and Associates, *op. cit.*, IV, 371–373; *Final Report and Testimony* . . . , X, 10065.

[22] *Times*, Aug. 26, 28, 1911.

[23] *Final Report and Testimony* . . . , X, 9904, 9962, 10049, 10065; *Record*, Jan. 9, June 27, 1914.

[24] *Times*, Sept. 30, Oct. 6, 1911.

[25] Quoted in the *Times*, Oct. 9, 1911.

[26] *Proceedings of the American Federation of Labor, 1915*, p. 179.

[27] Smith, *op. cit.*, pp. 483, 509–510; *Final Report and Testimony* . . . , X, 9923.

[28] Sidney L. Miller, *Inland Transportation* (New York: McGraw-Hill, 1933), p. 149; Emory R. Johnson and Thurman W. Van Metre, *Principles of Railroad Transportation* (New York and London: Appleton, 1922), pp. 485–486.

[29] *Times*, Aug. 2, 1914; *The Forty-Year War for a Free City*, p. 18.

[30] *The Forty-Year War for a Free City*, p. 18.

[31] *Record*, May 11, 1915; Sept. 26, 1916.

[32] *Ibid.*, Feb. 21, Aug. 3, Nov. 17, 1916; March 15, 1917; Johnson and Van Metre, *op. cit.*, pp. 493–494.

[33] *Record*, Nov. 18, 21, 1916; March 15, 19, 1917.

[34] Smith, *op. cit.*, pp. 493–494.

[35] Edwin L. Lewis, "Historical Data Concerning Street Railway Transportation in Los Angeles Since First Franchise Applied for July 2, 1883" (a collection of unpaged, dated, but largely unidentified newspaper clippings), Huntington Library, San Marino; Los Angeles *Herald*, Feb. 11, April 25, 26, 30, May 1, 1903.

[36] *Record*, July 14, 1911; April 28, 29, 1913; *Final Report and Testimony . . .*, VI, 5836.

[37] *Record*, July 14, 26, 29, 1913.

[38] *Final Report and Testimony . . .*, VI, 5747–5748.

[39] *Ibid.*, pp. 5337–5338, 5747–5751, 5757.

[40] *Ibid.*, pp. 5739–5740, 5836–5837.

[41] *Ibid.*, pp. 5746–5748, 5750, 5755, 5835–5836, 5838.

[42] *Ibid.*, pp. 5736–5737, 5743–5744, 5838; *Record*, June 13, 1914; *Citizen*, Feb. 14, 1913.

[43] *Final Report and Testimony . . .*, VI, 5740.

[44] *The Forty-Year War for a Free City*, p. 19.

[45] *Citizen*, Aug. 16, 1918; *Record*, Aug. 14, Dec. 10, 1918; *Times*, July 2, Aug. 11, 1918.

[46] *Times*, July 2, 1918.

[47] *Ibid.*, April 12, 1919; *Citizen*, Sept. 13, 20, 27, Oct. 4, Dec. 13, 1918; Feb. 14, April 18, 1919; *Record*, Aug. 10, Dec. 10, 1918; "Conciliation Work of the Department of Labor," *Monthly Labor Review*, VII (Nov., 1918), 306.

[48] *Citizen*, June 13, 1919; *Record*, April 30, June 7, July 2, 5, 1919; *Times*, June 12, 30, 1919; "Unionism in Los Angeles," *Survey*, XLII (July 26, 1919), 633.

[49] *Citizen*, July 4, 18, 1919; *Times*, July 4, Aug. 15, 16, 1919; *Record*, July 17, 23, 1919.

[50] *Times*, June 20, 1915; *Citizen*, March 30, 1917; *Record*, Aug. 31, 1915; Sept. 26, Oct. 10, 1916.

[51] *Times*, May 4, 1917; *Record*, Oct. 24, 1917.

[52] *Record*, Jan. 29, 1917; May 21, 31, June 1, 1918; *Times*, June 5, 1918. The quotation is from the *Times*.

[53] *Record*, July 1, 1918.

[54] *Ibid.*, July 1, 2, 1918; Jan. 1, 1919; *Times*, July 1, 3, 1918; "Conciliation Work of the Department of Labor," *Monthly Labor Review*, VII (July, 1918), 202.

[55] *Times*, July 3, 1918; *The Forty-Year War for a Free City*, p. 20.

[56] *Times*, July 3, 1918.

[57] *Ibid.*, July 3, 4, 1918; *Record*, July 3, 1918.

[58] *Citizen*, July 5, 1918; *Record*, July 6, 10, 11, 1918; *Times*, July 6, 11, 1918; *Hitchman Coal & Coke Co. v. Mitchell*, 245 U.S. 229 (1917). The quotation is from the *Times*, July 11.

[59] *Times*, July 3, 4, 11, 1918; *Record*, July 4, 11, 1918. The quotation is from the *Times*, July 3.

[60] *Record*, July 16, 29, Oct. 10, 1918; *Times*, July 12, 16, 1918; *Citizen*, Aug. 16, 1918.

[61] *Times*, Aug. 7, 12, 14, 16, 1919; *Record*, Dec. 31, 1918; Jan. 11, 13, Feb. 4, July 23, Aug. 7, 15, 1919.

[62] Ira B. Cross, *A History of the Labor Movement in California* (Berkeley: University of California Press, 1935), p. 286; *Times*, Aug. 16, 1919.

[63] *Record*, Aug. 16, 1919; *Times*, Aug. 16, 17, 1919.

⁶⁴ *Citizen*, Nov. 28, 1919; *Times*, Aug. 16, 18–20, 1919; *Record*, Aug. 18, 19, 1919; *The Forty-Year War for a Free City*, p. 21.

⁶⁵ *Times*, Aug. 17, 20, 1919; *Record*, Aug. 16, 18, 20, 1919; *Citizen*, Aug. 22, 1919.

⁶⁶ *Times*, Aug. 17, 21–23, 1919; *The Forty-Year War for a Free City*, p. 21; Cross, *op. cit.*, pp. 285–286.

⁶⁷ *Citizen*, Aug. 22, 1919; *Record*, Aug. 22, 26, 1919; *Times*, Aug. 16, 20–22, 1919.

⁶⁸ *Record*, Aug. 20–22, 1919; *Times*, Aug. 23, 1919.

⁶⁹ *Record*, Aug. 22, 23, 1919; *Times*, Aug. 22–25, 29, 1919.

⁷⁰ *Record*, Aug. 25–28, 30, Sept. 1, 1919; *Times*, Aug. 26, 27, 29–31, 1919.

⁷¹ *Citizen*, Sept. 5, 12, 19, 1919; *Record*, Sept. 4, 8, 13, 23, 1919; *Proceedings of the California State Federation of Labor, 1919*, pp. 78, 86; *Times*, Aug. 27, 30, Sept. 3–6, 23, 1919.

⁷² *Record*, Oct. 28, 1919; *Times*, Oct. 31, Nov. 19, Dec. 22, 1919; *Citizen*, Dec. 5, 1919.

⁷³ John W. Love, "The Wreck of the B. of R.T.," *Survey*, XLIV (April 24, 1920), 135–136; "The Railroad Men's Revolt," *Nation*, CX (April 17, 1920), 502; Commons and Associates, *op. cit.*, IV, 453–454.

⁷⁴ "The Outlaw Strike Collapses," *Independent*, CII (May 1, 1920), 171; Commons and Associates, *op. cit.*, IV, 452–454; Miller, *op. cit.*, p. 173; *Times*, April 9, 1920.

⁷⁵ *Times*, April 9, 12, 13, 1920.

⁷⁶ *Ibid.*, April 14, 1920.

⁷⁷ *Ibid.*, April 14–17, 20, 21, 23, 1920.

⁷⁸ *Ibid.*, April 15, 1920; Commons and Associates, *op. cit.*, IV, 455–456.

⁷⁹ *Times*, May 11, 13, June 3, Aug. 15, Oct. 15, 27, 1920; Oct. 4, 1921.

⁸⁰ Commons and Associates, *op. cit.*, IV, 455–456; *Examiner*, June 22, 1920; *Times*, July 21, Sept. 15, 1920.

⁸¹ *Citizen*, Feb. 15, 22, 1918; Feb. 14, 1919; *Record*, May 31, July 25, 1918; *Times*, June 12, 1918.

⁸² *Citizen*, Feb. 28, 1919; *Record*, March 31, Dec. 26, 1919; *Times*, Aug. 26, 28, 1919; Commons and Associates, *op. cit.*, IV, 515–516.

⁸³ Commons and Associates, *op. cit.*, IV, 515–520; Smith, *op. cit.*, pp. 524–525.

⁸⁴ *Times*, Nov. 30, 1920; *Citizen*, Dec. 31, 1920; Oct. 21, 1921; interview with Abraham Plotkin, Feb. 7, 1957.

⁸⁵ *Times*, July 2, 13, 1922; *Citizen*, July 7, 1922; interview with Abraham Plotkin, Feb. 7, 1957.

⁸⁶ *Times*, July 4, 5, 7, 1922; *Citizen*, July 7, 1922; Smith, *op. cit.*, pp. 524–525.

⁸⁷ *Times*, July 11, 14, 1922; *Citizen*, July 21, 28, Aug. 11, 1922; "First Weeks of the Railroad Strike," *Literary Digest*, LXXIV (July 29, 1922), 11–12.

⁸⁸ *Times*, July 30, Aug. 18, 1922; *Citizen*, Aug. 4, 11, 25, 1922; Commons and Associates, *op. cit.*, IV, 520–521; *Proceedings of the California State Federation of Labor, 1922*, p. 58; Los Angeles Central Labor Council, *Minutes*, Aug. 8, 1922.

⁸⁹ Commons and Associates, *op. cit.*, IV, 521–523; *Citizen*, Sept. 8, 15, 22, 1922; "The Railway Strike," *Outlook*, CXXXI (Aug. 16, 1922), 627–628; Smith, *op. cit.*, pp. 524–525.

⁹⁰ *Citizen*, Sept. 22, 29, Oct. 27, 1922; March 9, 1923; *Times*, Sept. 26, 1922; Jan. 3, 1923; *Proceedings of the California State Federation of Labor, 1922*, pp. 42–43; Commons and Associates, *op. cit.*, IV, 520; "The 'Desert Strikers' Convicted," *Literary Digest*, LXXVI (Jan. 13, 1923), 12–13; *Machinists Monthly Journal*, souvenir issue of May, 1950, p. 142.

IV. LABOR AND THE WAR, 1915–1919

¹ Leo Wolman, *Ebb and Flow in Trade Unionism* (New York: National Bureau of Economic Research, 1936), pp. 21–22; *Citizen*, Feb. 21, 1936.

[3] Howard R. Smith, *Economic History of the United States* (New York: Ronald Press, 1955), p. 505.

[3] *Ibid.; The Forty-Year War for a Free City; A History of the Open Shop in Los Angeles* (Los Angeles: Times-Mirror Publishing Co., 1929), p. 19; John R. Commons and Associates, *History of Labor in the United States, 1896–1932* (New York: Macmillan, 1921–1935), III, 71; IV, 403, 408.

[4] Wolman, *op. cit.*, pp. 21, 26, 27; *Proceedings of the American Federation of Labor, 1919*, p. 62; *Proceedings of the California State Federation of Labor, 1915*, pp. 36–37; *Citizen*, June 23, 1916; Marion Dixon, "The History of the Los Angeles Central Labor Council" (unpublished M.A. thesis, University of California, Berkeley, 1929), p. 12.

[5] *Proceedings of the California State Federation of Labor, 1917*, pp. 54–55.

[6] *Citizen*, Feb. 1, 1918; Feb. 14, Sept. 5, Oct. 10, 1919; *Record*, Oct. 1, 1918; *Proceedings of the California State Federation of Labor, 1918*, p. 62; *1919*, p. 77; *Times*, Sept. 2, 1919.

[7] *Record*, Feb. 15, 25, March 16, June 16, Oct. 1, 5, Nov. 16, 18, Dec. 31, 1915; Jan. 12, March 10, April 5, Oct. 31, Dec. 15, 1916; *Proceedings of the California State Federation of Labor, 1915*, p. 17.

[8] Margaret S. Gordon, *Employment Expansion and Population Growth: The California Experience, 1900–1950* (Berkeley and Los Angeles: University of California Press, 1954), pp. 100–102; *Record*, April 26, 1915; Feb. 28, Nov. 13, 1916; Jan. 17, Oct. 16, 1917; *Times*, Jan. 1, Feb. 7, June 11, 1916; Jan. 1, June 27, 1917; Jan. 1, Feb. 21, July 2, 1918; *Citizen*, May 5, June 9, 1916; *Proceedings of the California State Federation of Labor, 1915*, p. 53; *Los Angeles, "The Magic City and County"* (Los Angeles: County Board of Supervisors, 1951), pp. 18, 24; *The Forty-Year War for a Free City*, p. 26.

[9] *Citizen*, Aug. 13, 1915; *Record*, Nov. 26, 1915; *Times*, Oct. 5, 1915; *Proceedings of the California State Federation of Labor, 1915*, pp. 36–37; *Proceedings of the American Federation of Labor, 1915*, p. 470.

[10] *Times*, Nov. 24, 1915.

[11] *Ibid.*, Nov. 29, 1915.

[12] *Ibid.*, Dec. 10, 30, 1915; *Record*, Dec. 30, 1915; June 23, 1916; *Citizen*, June 9, 23, 1916; *The Forty-Year War for a Free City*, p. 19; Dixon, *op. cit.*, p. 12.

[13] *Citizen*, June 9, Oct. 6, 1916; *Proceedings of the California State Federation of Labor, 1917*, pp. 64–66.

[14] *Citizen*, March 26, June 4, Oct. 29, 1915; May 12, June 9, 1916; *Record*, May 23, 1916; *Times*, April 28, May 5, 29, 1916; Los Angeles Central Labor Council, *Minutes*, July 9, 1915; *Proceedings of the California State Federation of Labor, 1915*, pp. 19–20.

[15] Quoted in the *Times*, May 29, 1916.

[16] *Citizen*, Oct. 6, Nov. 3, 1916; Feb. 23, 1917.

[17] *Times*, Oct. 22, 1915; March 3, May 28, 1916; Dixon, *op. cit.*, p. 163; *Citizen*, Aug. 27, Dec. 17, 1915.

[18] *The Forty-Year War for a Free City*, p. 19; *Citizen*, Dec. 10, 1915; Jan. 21, 28, Feb. 18, 1916; *Record*, Jan. 21, 1916; *Times*, Jan. 13, March 3, April 19, 1916.

[19] *Citizen*, May 29, 1914; Jan. 14, May 12, June 23, 30, Aug. 4, 11, 18, Nov. 3, 10, 1916; Jan. 15, 1917.

[20] *Ibid.*, March 31, April 7, 14, June 16, July 21, 1916; *Times*, April 19, 1916.

[21] Ira B. Cross, *A History of the Labor Movement in California* (Berkeley: University of California Press, 1935), p. 287; Los Angeles Central Labor Council, *Minutes*, April 28, 1916; Dixon, *op. cit.*, pp. 162–163; *Times*, May 5, 1916; *Record*, April 22, 1916; *Citizen*, April 28, May 5, June 9, 1916.

[22] Dixon, *op. cit.*, pp. 164–166; *Citizen*, Aug. 31, Sept. 7, 14, Oct. 5, 1917; Feb. 1, Dec. 13, 1918; Jan. 3, 1919; *Proceedings of the California State Federation of Labor, 1917*, pp. 21, 55.

[23] *Citizen*, Feb. 1, March 29, Aug. 2, Dec. 13, 1918; Jan. 31, April 25, May 16, 1919; Dec. 24, 1920; *Record*, Aug. 29, 1919.

[24] Grace Heilman Stimson, *Rise of the Labor Movement in Los Angeles* (Berkeley and Los Angeles: University of California Press, 1955), pp. 236, 398–407; Cross, *op. cit.*, p. 287; George E. Mowry, *The California Progressives* (Berkeley and Los Angeles: University of California Press, 1951), pp. 8, 9; *Citizen*, Feb. 12, 1912; *Record*, Oct. 21, Dec. 11, 1911.

[25] Los Angeles Central Labor Council, *Minutes*, July 8, 1912; *Times*, Dec. 6, 1912; March 25, May 25, 1913; *Record*, March 7, May 8, June 4, 1913; Dixon, *op. cit.*, p. 139.

[26] *Record*, Feb. 7, 11, 18, March 4, June 14, 24, 1913.

[27] *Ibid.*, Dec. 13, 1913; Jan. 19, 23, May 15, June 22, 1914; *Times*, Sept. 16, 1913; Sept. 8, 1914; Los Angeles Central Labor Council, *Minutes*, Oct. 16, 1914; *Proceedings of the California State Federation of Labor, 1915*, p. 54.

[28] Los Angeles Central Labor Council, *Minutes*, March 27, June 26, 1914; *Citizen*, July 3, 1914.

[29] Dixon, *op. cit.*, p. 139; *Record*, May 29, 1915; *Citizen*, Sept. 17, 1915; *Times*, Dec. 11, 1915; Jan. 4, 1916.

[30] *Times*, Oct. 5, 1915; Dixon, *op. cit.*, p. 140; Los Angeles Central Labor Council, *Minutes*, June 9, 1916; *Record*, Jan. 22, 1916; *Citizen*, June 2, Aug. 18, Oct. 6, 13, Nov. 3, 10, Dec. 29, 1916.

[31] Dixon, *op. cit.*, p. 140; *Citizen*, Jan. 26, June 1, 8, 1917; *Record*, April 26, May 8, June 6, 1917.

[32] Dixon, *op. cit.*, p. 140; *Times*, June 4, Aug. 14, 1919; *Record*, Sept. 3, 7, 10, 17, 19, 20, Oct. 29, 1918; Aug. 14, 1919; *Citizen*, Nov. 1, 8, 1918; April 4, 11, May 9, June 6, 13, July 4, 1919.

[33] *Times*, Oct. 30, 31, 1919; *Record*, Oct. 29, 31, 1919; *Citizen*, Oct. 31, 1919.

[34] *Times*, Jan. 1, 1917; "Average Retail Food Price and Percent of Increase in 39 Cities, 1918 Compared with 1913," *Monthly Labor Review*, VIII (March, 1919), 103–110; William F. Ogburn, "A Study of Food Costs in Various Cities," *Monthly Labor Review*, IX (Aug., 1919), 1–25; "Rents in the United States," *Monthly Labor Review*, IX (Sept., 1919), 9–30.

[35] California Department of Industrial Relations, *The Cost of Living in California, 1914–22 and 1939–41* (Sacramento, 1941), p. 4; *Times*, Aug. 26, 1920; California Bureau of Labor Statistics, *Twenty-third Biennial Report, 1927–1928*, pp. 26–27.

[36] Robert DeWitt Morgans, "A History of Organized Labor in Long Beach, California" (unpublished M.A. thesis, University of California, Berkeley, 1940), pp. 23–26; *Final Report and Testimony Submitted to Congress by the Commission on Industrial Relations*, 64th Cong., 1st sess., S. Doc. 415 (Washington, 1916), VI, 5603–5605, 5607; *Times*, Sept. 11, 1914; Robert A. Christie, *Empire in Wood* (Ithaca: New York State School of Industrial and Labor Relations, 1956), pp. 223–225; Maxwell C. Raddock, *Portrait of an American Labor Leader: William L. Hutcheson* (New York: American Institute of Social Science, 1955), p. 95; Commons and Associates, *op. cit.*, IV, 404; *Proceedings of the California State Federation of Labor, 1918*, pp. 24–25.

[37] Morgans, *op. cit.*, pp. 39–41; *The Forty-Year War for a Free City*, pp. 18–19; *Proceedings of the California State Federation of Labor, 1916*, pp. 77–78; *Record*, Jan. 12, Feb. 28, March 18, May 1, 1916; *Times*, Jan. 1, Feb. 7, May 2, 1916; Cross, *op. cit.*, p. 285.

[38] Morgans, *op. cit.*, p. 40; *The Forty-Year War for a Free City*, p. 19; *Times*, July 29, 1916; *Record*, May 1, 12, July 28, 1916; Aug. 31, 1917; *Citizen*, May 19, 26, June 2, 9, 16, 30, July 7, Aug. 11, 18, 25, Sept. 8, 29, Oct. 27, Dec. 1, 15, 1916; Jan. 12, Feb. 9, 1917; Cross, *op. cit.*, p. 285.

[39] James Clifford Findley, "The Economic Boom of the 'Twenties in Los Angeles" (unpublished Ph.D. dissertation, Claremont College, Claremont, Calif., 1958), pp.

123–124; Dixon, *op. cit.*, pp. 90–91; Christie, *op. cit.*, p. 223; Raddock, *op. cit.*, pp. 96–99; Commons and Associates, *op. cit.*, IV, 404; *Times,* March 28, 1917; *Record,* Sept. 17, 18, 25, 28, Oct. 1, 27, 1917.

⁴⁰ Raddock, *op. cit.,* p. 99; Dixon, *op. cit.,* p. 91; *Citizen,* Nov. 9, Dec. 28, 1917; Feb. 1, 1918; *Record,* Dec. 24, 26, 1917; Jan. 9, 30, March 6, July 5, 6, 8, Sept. 18–20, 26, 30, Oct. 11, 1918.

⁴¹ Dixon, *op. cit.,* pp. 91–94; *Proceedings of the California State Federation of Labor, 1918,* p. 60; *Citizen,* Nov. 8, 15, 1918; *Record,* Oct. 28, Nov. 13, 1918; Feb. 4, 1919; *Times,* Feb. 3, 4, 1919.

⁴² Dixon, *op. cit.,* p. 94; Cross, *op. cit.,* pp. 285–286; William A. Spalding, comp., *History and Reminiscences, Los Angeles City and County, California* (Los Angeles: J. R. Finnell & Sons Publishing Co., [1931]), I, 390; *The Forty-Year War for a Free City,* p. 21; *Times,* Feb. 5, 9, March 14, May 3–5, 21, 1919; *Record,* Feb. 3, 5, 8, 14, April 4, 11, May 3, 5, 20, 21, 1919; *Citizen,* April 18, May 23, 1919.

⁴³ Dixon, *op. cit.,* pp. 95–96; *The Forty-Year War for a Free City,* p. 21; *Citizen,* June 6, 1919; *Record,* May 24, 27–29, June 5, 6, 9, 13, 19, 21, 23–28, July 9, 1919; *Times,* May 22, 23, 25, 27, 30, June 1, 2, 6, 7, 10, 13, 20, 21, July 4, 1919.

⁴⁴ Dixon, *op. cit.,* p. 99; *The Forty-Year War for a Free City,* p. 21; *Times,* July 11, 15, 28, Sept. 24, Nov. 10, 18, 1919; *Record,* July 9, 10, 17, 1919; *Citizen,* Nov. 21, 1919.

⁴⁵ *Proceedings of the California State Federation of Labor, 1919,* pp. 76–77; "Unionism in Los Angeles," *Survey,* XLII (July 26, 1919), 633; *Citizen,* Oct. 3, 31, 1919; *Record,* Oct. 1, 2, 8, 10, 30, 1919; *Times,* Sept. 24, 29, 30, Oct. 1, 2, 7, 10, 24, 27, 1919; Dixon, *op. cit.,* pp. 97–100.

⁴⁶ *Proceedings of the California State Federation of Labor, 1920,* p. 68; Los Angeles Central Labor Council, *Minutes,* Jan. 14, June 30, 1920; "What Our Organizers Are Doing," *American Federationist,* XXIX (March, 1922), 226; *Citizen,* Dec. 19, 1919; Jan. 23, Feb. 13, 27, April 9, July 9, Sept. 24, 1920; *Times,* Nov. 1, 6, 9–11, 18, 20, 1919; Dixon, *op. cit.,* p. 98.

⁴⁷ *Citizen,* March 3, Oct. 13, Nov. 17, Dec. 8, 16, 1916; Jan. 19, April 6, 1917; *Record,* Jan. 5, 1917; Los Angeles Central Labor Council, *Minutes,* Nov. 10, 1916; *The Forty-Year War for a Free City,* p. 8.

⁴⁸ Dixon, *op. cit.,* p. 10; *Proceedings of the California State Federation of Labor, 1917,* pp. 64–65; *Citizen,* Jan. 19, April 27, Aug. 24, Sept. 28, 1917; *Times,* Jan. 19, Feb. 27, 1918; *Record,* Feb. 27, 1918.

⁴⁹ *The Forty-Year War for a Free City,* p. 20; *Citizen,* March 1, 15, Aug. 23, Nov. 1, Dec. 13, 1918; *Record,* Jan. 30, Feb. 6, 9, March 5, 1918; *Times,* Jan. 10, 19, 20, Feb. 5, 9, 27, March 15, 1918.

⁵⁰ *Times,* June 11, 12, 16, 18, 1918; *Record,* June 10, 14, 1918; *Citizen,* June 14, 1918.

⁵¹ *Times,* June 11, 12, 16, 19, 1918; *Record,* June 14, 1918; *Citizen,* June 21, 1918.

⁵² *Times,* Dec. 24, 25, 1918; *Record,* Dec. 25, 1918; *Citizen,* Nov. 15, Dec. 20, 1918; Aug. 8, Dec. 19, 1919; *Proceedings of the California State Federation of Labor, 1918,* pp. 25–26, 62.

⁵³ *Citizen,* Feb. 1, April 5, 1918; Jan. 17, Feb. 7, May 2, 1919; "Conciliation Work of the Department of Labor," *Monthly Labor Review,* VII (Sept., 1918), 339.

⁵⁴ *Citizen,* May 19, 1916; Aug. 16, 1918; Feb. 14, April 11, May 30, Dec. 12, 26, 1919; *Proceedings of the California State Federation of Labor, 1915,* p. 53.

⁵⁵ *Times,* Jan. 15, June 12, 1918; July 4, 1919; *Citizen,* Nov. 17, 1916; Jan. 19, Sept. 21, 1917; Sept. 20, 1918; Feb. 14, Sept. 5, 1919; Jan. 16, Feb. 6, May 14, 1920; *The Forty-Year War for a Free City,* p. 20.

⁵⁶ *Citizen,* Feb. 26, April 23, 1915; *Times,* May 28, 1916; *The Forty-Year War for a Free City,* p. 19.

[57] *Citizen,* Feb. 25, May 5, Aug. 4, 11, Nov. 10, 24, Dec. 8, 1916; April 22, May 4, June 15, July 6, 20, 27, 1917; *Times,* Aug. 30, 31, 1917; *Proceedings of the California State Federation of Labor, 1915,* p. 53; *1917,* pp. 64–65.

[58] *Times,* Aug. 31, Sept. 1, 8, 10, 11, Oct. 12, 1917; *Record,* Sept. 7, 10, Oct. 26, 1917; *Citizen,* Sept. 21, Oct. 5, 26, Nov. 23, 1917; *The Forty-Year War for a Free City,* p. 20.

[59] *Times,* Sept. 11, 1918; Jan. 5, Sept. 3, 1919; *Citizen,* April 4, Aug. 15, 29, Sept. 12, 1919; *Record,* June 17, 1919.

[60] *Times,* June 20, 1917; *Citizen,* Aug. 20, 1915; Sept. 8, 22, Oct. 13, 20, 27, Nov. 17, Dec. 1, 1916; Feb. 9, Aug. 24, 1917.

[61] *Times,* Feb. 22–24, 1918; *Citizen,* Feb. 15, March 15, 22, Sept. 27, 1918; *Record,* Feb. 22, 27, March 7, 1918.

[62] *Citizen,* Dec. 8, 1916; Jan. 19, June 8, Sept. 21, 1917; April 11, 1919; *Record,* Feb. 15, March 7, April 18, May 19, June 5, 13, 14, 1919.

[63] *Record,* June 16, 17, 1919; *Times,* June 17, 18, 1919.

[64] *Times,* June 17, 18, 20, 21, 1919; *Record,* June 18–20, 1919.

[65] *Citizen,* June 27, July 4, 1919; *Times,* June 23, 24, 29, July 1, 1919; *Record,* June 24–26, 30, July 1–3, 10, 15, 1919.

[66] *Citizen,* July 18, 1919; *Times,* July 12, 13, 21–23, 1919; *Record,* July 17, 19, 21, 22, Aug. 1, 1919.

[67] *Citizen,* Sept. 12, 1919; *Record,* Aug. 22, 25, Oct. 30, Nov. 25, 1919; *Times,* Dec. 22, 1919; Dixon, *op. cit.,* p. 133; *Proceedings of the California State Federation of Labor, 1919,* p. 86; *The Forty-Year War for a Free City,* p. 21.

[68] *Citizen,* May 5, 26, June 2, 23, 30, Aug. 4, 25, Oct. 6, 27, Nov. 3, 24, Dec. 12, 1916; Jan. 5, 19, Feb. 9, 1917; *Times,* May 3, 4, 28, 1916; July 4, 1919; *Record,* July 5, 1919.

[69] *Citizen,* March 5, April 9, 1915; Oct. 20, Nov. 17, 24, 1916; Jan. 5, Oct. 19, Dec. 21, 1917; Aug. 23, Dec. 20, 1918; Jan. 31, 1919; *Record,* Dec. 20, 1916; Sept. 19, 21, 1917; *Times,* Dec. 20, 1917; Feb. 17, 1918; April 2, 4, Sept. 3, 1919; *The Forty-Year War for a Free City,* p. 21; "Conciliation Work of the Department of Labor," *Monthly Labor Review,* VIII (May, 1919), 288–291.

[70] *Citizen,* March 12, 1915; Jan. 21, Feb. 17, June 30, Aug. 4, Sept. 22, Nov. 3, Dec. 29, 1916; Feb. 2, Oct. 5, 14, 1917; Jan. 13, June 20, Sept. 6, 1918; Jan. 24, Sept. 5, 26, Dec. 12, 1919; *Times,* Jan. 4, 5, 1919; *Record,* July 5, Oct. 19, 1917.

[71] *Times,* Sept. 23, 1915; Dixon, *op. cit.,* pp. 102–103; Commons and Associates, *op. cit.,* IV, 497; *The Forty-Year War for a Free City,* p. 9.

[72] *Citizen,* March 2, June 29, Sept. 14, 21, Oct. 5, Dec. 7, 1917; Dec. 13, 20, 1918; Jan. 17, March 28, April 18, Sept. 5, Nov. 7, 1919; *Record,* Aug. 9, 1915.

[73] *Times,* Aug. 25, 28, 29, 1917; *Citizen,* Oct. 15, 1915; Feb. 4, 1916; Aug. 24, 31, Sept. 7, 1917; Feb. 1, 1918; *Record,* May 14, Aug. 21, Sept. 14, 1915; Aug. 7, 9, 16, 17, 29, 1917; *The Forty-Year War for a Free City,* p. 18; *Proceedings of the California State Federation of Labor, 1916,* p. 61.

[74] *Times,* July 13, 1918; June 25, July 16, Aug. 2, 26, Oct. 20, 28, 1919; *Record,* July 13, 1918; June 24, July 9, 1919; *Citizen,* Sept. 13, 1918; Aug. 1, 8, Sept. 5, 1919; "Conciliation Work of the Department of Labor," *Monthly Labor Review,* VII, 335–341; *Proceedings of the California State Federation of Labor, 1918,* p. 62.

[75] Los Angeles Central Labor Council, *Minutes,* June 4, 1915; Nov. 10, 1916; *Record,* June 23, 24, 1919; *Citizen,* Dec. 1, 1916; May 31, 1918; Feb. 14, April 11, 18, 1919; *Times,* April 13, May 29, June 12, 25, Nov. 10, 1919.

[76] *Record,* Sept. 30, Oct. 16, Nov. 25, 1919; *Times,* Aug. 31, Sept. 1, Oct. 16, Nov. 10, 11, 1919; *Citizen,* Aug. 31, Sept. 5, Nov. 28, 1919; Jan. 23, March 12, 1920; *The Forty-Year War for a Free City,* p. 21.

[77] *Citizen,* Jan. 1, 22, June 4, 1915; Feb. 4, July 7, 1916; Feb. 15, 1918; Aug. 8,

Nov. 28, 1919; Los Angeles Central Labor Council, *Minutes*, May 28, Aug. 6, 1915; June 30, 1916; *The Forty-Year War for a Free City*, p. 20; *Proceedings of the California State Federation of Labor, 1915*, p. 53; *1917*, pp. 64–65.

⁷⁸ *Citizen*, Aug. 11, 18, 1916; June 15, July 20, 1917; Feb. 1, 2, June 21, 1918; Feb. 4, Aug. 29, Sept. 12, 1919; *Times*, June 11, Dec. 1, 1918; Los Angeles Central Labor Council, *Minutes*, Aug. 4, 1916.

⁷⁹ *Record*, June 5, 1919; *Times*, Dec. 28, 1917; Jan. 5, 1919; Feb. 16, 1920; *Citizen*, Feb. 4, June 23, Dec. 22, 1916; Jan. 26, March 9, April 20, 1917; Feb. 1, 1918; Jan. 10, Feb. 14, Aug. 29, Nov. 7, 21, 1919; Jan. 14, 1921; *Proceedings of the California State Federation of Labor, 1915*, p. 53; *1919*, pp. 30, 61.

⁸⁰ *Record*, July 1, 1916; *Times*, June 9, 10, 29, 30, 1916; *Citizen*, Feb. 12, 19, 26, March 9, 1915; June 2, 16, 23, July 7, 14, 21, 28, Aug. 4, 25, Oct. 13, Nov. 3, 24, 1916; *The Forty-Year War for a Free City*, p. 19; Cross, *op. cit.*, p. 285; *Proceedings of the California State Federation of Labor, 1916*, p. 61.

⁸¹ *Times*, Sept. 25, 1918; June 12, 1919; *Citizen*, Sept. 8, 26, Dec. 29, 1916; Aug. 23, Sept. 27, 1918; May 9, Dec. 12, 1919; *Record*, Sept. 26, 1918; May 6, 7, 1919.

⁸² *Citizen*, Oct. 5, Dec. 28, 1917; Jan. 25, June 14, 1918; *Times*, Aug. 15, 1918; Jan. 5, 1919; *Record*, Dec. 21, 1917; Jan. 15, 28, 1918; March 8, 1919; "Conciliation Work of the Department of Labor," *Monthly Labor Review*, VI (Feb., 1918), 216–218.

⁸³ *Times*, March 28, 1916; *Citizen*, May 26, 1916; Aug. 8, 1919; *Record*, Sept. 5, Dec. 10, 1916; Nov. 7, 23, 1917; Jan. 8, April 27, 1918; *Proceedings of the California State Federation of Labor, 1916*, p. 62; "Employment and Living Conditions of Women in California," *Monthly Labor Review*, VI (Jan., 1918), 114–118.

⁸⁴ *Citizen*, Jan. 25, Feb. 1, Aug. 16, Oct. 4, 1918; Feb. 14, July 4, Aug. 1, 8, 29, 1919; Jan. 30, 1920; *Times*, June 11, 26, 1918; Jan. 24, Sept. 13, Dec. 16, 1919; *Record*, July 15, Sept. 22, 1919; *Proceedings of the California State Federation of Labor, 1915*, p. 36.

⁸⁵ *Times*, Sept. 10, 11, 1918; *Record*, June 21, Aug. 17, Sept. 2, 5, 7, 9, 10, 1918; *Citizen*, Sept. 6, 20, 1918; *Proceedings of the California State Federation of Labor, 1916*, p. 61.

⁸⁶ *Citizen*, June 13, 1919; *Times*, June 12, 14–16, 20, 24, 27, 1919; *Record*, April 28, June 7, 9, 11, 14, 17, July 2, 3, 1919; *Proceedings of the California State Federation of Labor, 1919*, p. 86.

⁸⁷ Los Angeles Central Labor Council, *Minutes*, June 2, 1916; *Proceedings of the California State Federation of Labor, 1916*, p. 61; *1919*, p. 23; *Record*, June 15, Sept. 1, 11, 1915; Nov. 5, 6, 1917; *Times*, Oct. 18, 1917; *Citizen*, Feb. 14, June 9, 23, 30, 1916; March 30, May 17, July 20, Oct. 19, Nov. 9, Dec. 4, 1917; Jan. 4, Feb. 1, March 8, 1918; Feb. 28, March 7, 28, June 20, July 4, 18, Aug. 8, 1919.

⁸⁸ *Citizen*, May 26, Oct. 6, Dec. 15, 1916; April 27, Sept. 21, 1917; June 28, Aug. 16, 23, Sept. 27, Oct. 4, Dec. 31, 1918; Feb. 14, March 14, May 9, 30, Aug. 29, Oct. 10, Dec. 5, 1919; *Record*, July 15, Sept. 28, 1915; May 17, July 20, Sept. 26, 1917; Feb. 1, 1918; Los Angeles Central Labor Council, *Minutes*, July 16, 1915; *Proceedings of the California State Federation of Labor, 1915*, p. 53; *1918*, p. 61; *Report of the Executive Council of the American Federation of Labor, 1919*, p. 26.

⁸⁹ *Record*, May 31, 1916; May 23, 25, June 6, July 6, 1918; May 16, Oct. 9, Dec. 9, 1919; *Times*, Oct. 5, 1915; Sept. 11, 12, 16, Dec. 9, 1919; "Unionism in Los Angeles," *Survey*, XLII (July 26, 1919), 633.

⁹⁰ *Record*, March 19, May 20, Sept. 30, 1918; Oct. 15, 21, Nov. 5, 1919; *Times*, Oct. 3, 1918; Oct. 10–12, 16, 23, 25, 30, 1919; *Citizen*, Aug. 8, Oct. 17, 24, 31, 1919; *The Forty-Year War for a Free City*, p. 1.

⁹¹ *Record*, March 13, 19, 1918; Aug. 22, 25, 1919; *Times*, Aug. 25, Sept. 16, Oct. 12, 16, Nov. 4, 5, 7, 1919; "Rates of Pay of Policemen in 24 Cities," *Monthly Labor Review*, IX (Oct., 1919), 147.

⁹² *Times*, Sept. 2, 1919.

⁹³ *Times*, Sept. 16, Oct. 12, 16, Nov. 4, 5, 7, 11, 1919; Jan. 4, 1920; *The Forty-Year War for a Free City*, p. 21.

⁹⁴ Florence Peterson, *Survey of Labor Economics* (New York: Harper, 1947), pp. 481–486.

V. THE CHANGING TIDES—MARITIME WORKERS, 1911–1933

¹ Jeff Wilson, *The Hard Realities of Shipping* (San Francisco: Daily Commercial News, [1946]), p. 29.

² Grace Heilman Stimson, *Rise of the Labor Movement in Los Angeles* (Berkeley and Los Angeles: University of California Press, 1955), pp. 81–82; Howard R. Smith, *Economic History of the United States* (New York: Ronald Press, 1955), p. 493; Paul S. Taylor, *The Sailors' Union of the Pacific* (New York: Ronald Press, 1923), pp. 112, 115–118; John R. Commons and Associates, *History of Labor in the United States, 1896–1932* (New York: Macmillan, 1921–1935), IV, 160, 162; Hyman Weintraub, *Andrew Furuseth, Emancipator of the Seamen* (Berkeley and Los Angeles: University of California Press, 1959), p. 130.

³ Taylor, *op. cit.*, pp. 117–118, 134–135.

⁴ Stimson, *op. cit.*, pp. 85, 133; *Citizen*, July 7, 1911; *Times*, July 20, 22, 23, 25, 1912; *Record*, Oct. 4, 1913; Los Angeles Central Labor Council, *Minutes*, Nov. 21, 1913; March 15, 1915; *Proceedings of the California State Federation of Labor, 1915*, p. 51; Betty V. H. Schneider and Abraham Siegel, *Industrial Relations in the Pacific Coast Longshore Industry* (Berkeley: Institute of Industrial Relations, University of California, 1956), pp. 4–6.

⁵ Taylor, *op. cit.*, pp. 134–136; Commons and Associates, *op. cit.*, IV, 404–405.

⁶ Taylor, *op. cit.*, p. 138; *Times*, Aug. 15, 1919; *Seamen's Journal*, XXXII (Aug., 1919), 6.

⁷ Taylor, *op. cit.*, pp. 138–139; Commons and Associates, *op. cit.*, IV, 494–495.

⁸ Taylor, *op. cit.*, pp. 139–140; Commons and Associates, *op. cit.*, IV, 494–495; *Times*, May 9, 1921; *The Forty-Year War for a Free City; A History of the Open Shop in Los Angeles* (Los Angeles: Times-Mirror Publishing Co., 1929), p. 22.

⁹ Taylor, *op. cit.*, pp. 139–141; *The Forty-Year War for a Free City*, p. 22; *Times*, May 13, 20, June 22, 1921.

¹⁰ *The Forty-Year War for a Free City*, p. 22; *Times*, May 9, 10, 19, June 14, 26, 1921; Taylor, *op. cit.*, p. 140.

¹¹ *The Forty-Year War for a Free City*, p. 22; Taylor, *op. cit.*, pp. 140–141.

¹² *The Forty-Year War for a Free City*, p. 22; Taylor, *op. cit.*, pp. 140–141; Commons and Associates, *op. cit.*, IV, 495–496; *Times*, July 20, 28, 31, Aug. 6, 1921.

¹³ Taylor, *op. cit.*, pp. 141, 143; Commons and Associates, *op. cit.*, IV, 496.

¹⁴ Taylor, *op. cit.*, pp. 140–143; *Times*, June 14, July 31, 1921; Hyman Weintraub, "The I.W.W. in California, 1905–1931" (unpublished M.A. thesis, University of California, Los Angeles, 1947), pp. 220–222.

¹⁵ *Citizen*, Nov. 4, 1921; Weintraub, "The I.W.W. in California," pp. 223, 225; Taylor, *op. cit.*, pp. 144–145; Commons and Associates, *op. cit.*, IV, 495–497.

¹⁶ *Citizen*, Aug. 1, 19, 1921; Taylor, *op. cit.*, p. 144; *Times*, Aug. 3, Dec. 3, 1922; Weintraub, "The I.W.W. in California," pp. 223–225.

¹⁷ Taylor, *op. cit.*, p. 142; *Times*, Aug. 3, Dec. 3, 1922; Feb. 10, 1924; Weintraub, "The I.W.W. in California," pp. 226–227.

¹⁸ Edward Levinson, *Labor on the March* (New York: Harper, 1938), p. 259.

¹⁹ *Record*, April 28, June 1, 2, 1916; *Citizen*, June 2, 1916; Ira B. Cross, *A History of the Labor Movement in California* (Berkeley: University of California Press, 1935), p. 285; *The Forty-Year War for a Free City*, p. 19; *Proceedings of the*

California State Federation of Labor, 1916, p. 78; *Coast Seamen's Journal,* June 7, 1916.

²⁰ *Times,* June 13, 1916; *Citizen,* June 2, 9, 1916; *Record,* June 1, 8, 10, 12, 1916; *The Forty-Year War for a Free City,* p. 19; Cross, *op. cit.,* p. 285; *Coast Seamen's Journal,* June 7, 1916.

²¹ *Record,* June 21, 22, 1916; *Citizen,* June 16, 1916; *Times,* June 13, 14, 1916; *The Forty-Year War for a Free City,* p. 19.

²² *Times,* June 28, 1916; *Citizen,* June 23, 1916; *Record,* June 22, 23, 1916.

²³ *The Forty-Year War for a Free City,* p. 19; *Record,* June 26, July 5, 1916; *Citizen,* June 30, July 7, 1916; *Times,* July 8, 1916.

²⁴ *The Forty-Year War for a Free City,* p. 19; *Record,* July 12, 14, 1916; *Times,* July 12, 13, 15, 1916; *Citizen,* July 14, 1916.

²⁵ *Coast Seamen's Journal,* July 26, 1916; *The Forty-Year War for a Free City,* p. 19; *Citizen,* July 14, 21, 28, 1916; *Record,* July 17–19, 22, 1916.

²⁶ *Citizen,* July 28, 1916; *Times,* July 1, 4, 1916; *The Forty-Year War for a Free City,* p. 19; *Record,* July 28, 29, Aug. 1, 1916.

²⁷ *The Forty-Year War for a Free City,* p. 19; *Times,* Aug. 9, 1916; *Coast Seamen's Journal,* Aug. 16, 1916; *Citizen,* Sept. 22, 29, 1916; June 18, 1917; *Record,* Sept. 19, 26, 1916; *Proceedings of the California State Federation of Labor, 1916,* pp. 29, 62; *1917,* p. 55.

²⁸ *Citizen,* Nov. 2, 9, Dec. 7, 21, 1917; *Record,* Nov. 1, 1917; *Proceedings of the California State Federation of Labor, 1917,* p. 55; "Conciliation Work of the Department of Labor," *Monthly Labor Review,* V (Dec., 1917), 240; "What Our Organizers Are Doing," *American Federationist,* XXV (Jan. 1, 1918), 64.

²⁹ *Times,* Oct. 25, 26, Nov. 4, 1919; *Record,* Oct. 22, 1919; *Citizen,* Nov. 14, 1919.

³⁰ Schneider and Siegel, *op. cit.,* pp. 9–11; Weintraub, "The I.W.W. in California," pp. 219, 220, 225; *The Forty-Year War for a Free City,* p. 22; "Conciliation and Arbitration," *Monthly Labor Review,* XV (July, 1922), 181.

³¹ Weintraub, "The I.W.W. in California," p. 226; *Citizen,* May 11, 18, 1923.

³² Weintraub, "The I.W.W. in California," p. 227; Taylor, *op. cit.,* p. 146; *The Forty-Year War for a Free City,* p. 22; Commons and Associates, *op. cit.,* IV, 430; George P. West, "After Liberalism Had Failed," *Nation,* CXVI (May 30, 1923), 629; *Times,* April 21, 26, 29, 1923.

³³ "Conciliation and Arbitration," *Monthly Labor Review,* XVII (July, 1923), 226; *The Forty-Year War for a Free City,* p. 22; *Record,* May 2, 1923; *Times,* April 29, May 2, 1923.

³⁴ *Times,* May 2, 3, 5, 1923.

³⁵ *Ibid.,* May 6, 7, 11, 12, 14, 19, 1923; *Citizen,* May 11, 18, 1923; *Record,* May 5, 1923.

³⁶ "Upton Sinclair Defends the Law," *Nation,* CXVI (June 6, 1923), 647; *Record,* May 15, 17, 18, 1923; *Times,* May 14, 19, 1923; *Citizen,* May 18, 1923.

³⁷ "Conciliation and Arbitration," *Monthly Labor Review,* XVII (July, 1923), 226; Weintraub, "The I.W.W. in California," p. 233; *Record,* May 24, 1923; *Times,* May 21, 22, 24, 29, 1923.

³⁸ West, *op. cit.,* p. 629; *Times,* June 1, 5, 1923; *Record,* June 2, 1923.

³⁹ *Times,* June 28, 1923.

⁴⁰ Weintraub, "The I.W.W. in California," p. 233; *The Forty-Year War for a Free City,* p. 22; *Times,* July 12, 13, 1923.

⁴¹ *Times,* July 12–14, 1923; Weintraub, "The I.W.W. in California," p. 233.

⁴² *Proceedings of the California State Federation of Labor, 1923,* p. 49; *The Forty-Year War for a Free City,* p. 23; *Times,* July 16, 18, 20, 1923.

⁴³ *Proceedings of the California State Federation of Labor, 1923,* p. 49; *Times,* Sept. 8, 1923.

[44] "What Our Organizers Are Doing," *American Federationist*, XXXI (Feb., 1924), 180; *Times*, Aug. 31, Sept. 8, 1923; Feb. 10, 1924.
[45] *Times*, Feb. 10, 1924.
[46] Weintraub, "The I.W.W. in California," pp. 236–238; *Times*, March 17, 19, June 16, 24, 30, 1924; Mary Reed, "San Pedro," *Nation*, CXIX (July 9, 1924), 45–46; *Record*, June 23, 1924.
[47] Weintraub, "The I.W.W. in California," p. 244; *Times*, June 24, 30, July 7, Aug. 16, Oct. 20, 1924; Jan. 15, 1926.
[48] *Los Angeles, "The Magic City and County"* (Los Angeles: County Board of Supervisors, 1951), p. 24; James C. Findley, "The Economic Boom of the 'Twenties in Los Angeles" (unpublished Ph.D. dissertation, Claremont College, 1958), pp. 107, 111; *The Forty-Year War for a Free City*, p. 23.
[49] Schneider and Siegel, *op. cit.*, pp. 9–11; Wilson, *op. cit.*, pp. 30–31; *Southern California Labor Press*, Sept. 25, 1925; "Conciliation and Arbitration," *Monthly Labor Review*, XX (Feb., 1925), 211; *Citizen*, Dec. 16, 1932.

VI. LABOR'S DARKEST YEARS

[1] John R. Commons and Associates, *History of Labor in the United States, 1896–1932* (New York: Macmillan, 1921–1935), IV, 409–411, 580–582; Howard R. Smith, *Economic History of the United States* (New York: Ronald Press, 1955), pp. 513, 516–517, 520–521, 541, 542–545; Edward Levinson, *Labor on the March* (New York: Harper, 1938), p. 43; Leo Wolman, *Ebb and Flow in Trade Unionism* (New York: National Bureau of Economic Research, 1936), pp. 21, 26–27.
[2] Robert A. Christie, *Empire in Wood* (Ithaca: New York State School of Industrial and Labor Relations, 1956), pp. 236–243; Marion Dixon, "The History of the Los Angeles Central Labor Council" (unpublished M.A. thesis, University of California, Berkeley, 1929), p. 8; *Citizen*, Dec. 14, 1923; Feb. 8, 1924; *Times*, March 23, 1924; *Southern California Labor Press*, March 7, 1924.
[3] Commons and Associates, *op. cit.*, IV, 539, 543–546, 558; John Spargo, "Why the I.W.W. Flourishes," *World's Work*, XXXIX (Jan., 1920), 243–247; Anthony Bimba, *The History of the American Working Class* (New York: International Publishers, 1927), pp. 287–288; *Citizen*, Sept. 2–Oct. 14, 1921; June 30, 1922; *Proceedings of the American Federation of Labor, 1923*, p. 333.
[4] Commons and Associates, *op. cit.*, IV, 497–498; Dixon, *op. cit.*, pp. 102, 104, 107–110; *Citizen*, July 8, 1927.
[5] *Times*, July 14, 1920; Oct. 26, Nov. 25, 1926; *Citizen*, Nov. 26, 1928; Feb. 15, Sept. 6, 1929; April 11, 18, 25, Dec. 19, 1930; Nov. 21, 1931; Jan. 8, March 4, 1932; "Double Union Membership Campaign," *American Federationist*, XXXVI (Oct., 1929), 1234–1245; "Extent of 5-Day Week in Building Trades," *Monthly Labor Review*, XXX (March, 1930), 137.
[6] *Times*, June 4, 1920; April 25, 1926; Aug. 16, Sept. 5, 1927; Wolman, *op. cit.*, pp. 35–39; Temporary National Economic Committee, *Investigation of Concentration of Economic Power*, 76th Cong., 3d sess., Monograph 37 (Washington, 1941), pp. 104–106.
[7] *Times*, Oct. 25, 1929; Smith, *op. cit.*, p. 545; Commons and Associates, *op. cit.*, IV, 614.
[8] Smith, *op. cit.*, pp. 562–563, 565; Commons and Associates, *op. cit.*, III, 155, 223–224.
[9] Commons and Associates, *op. cit.*, III, 158–160, 178, 180; Smith, *op. cit.*, pp. 567, 569; *Times*, March 8, Aug. 21, Oct. 8, Nov. 5, 1931; July 23, Aug. 27, 1932.
[10] *Times*, May 8, June 30, Aug. 15, Sept. 12, Oct. 19, Dec. 16, 1920; Jan. 1, June 6,

1921; *Citizen*, April 2, 9, 16, June 4, Dec. 31, 1920; *Proceedings of the California State Federation of Labor, 1920*, p. 60.

[11] *The Forty-Year War for a Free City; A History of the Open Shop in Los Angeles* (Los Angeles: Times-Mirror Publishing Co., 1929), p. 21; *Proceedings of the California State Federation of Labor, 1920*, p. 60; *Record*, Jan. 15, 1920; *Citizen*, Feb. 20, June 18, 1920; *Times*, Feb. 10, 14, 1920.

[12] *The Forty-Year War for a Free City*, p. 22; *Citizen*, Feb. 29, April 18, 1920.

[13] *The Forty-Year War for a Free City*, p. 22; Commons and Associates, *op. cit.*, IV, 497–498; *Times*, Aug. 18, Sept. 9, Nov. 2, 1920.

[14] *Times*, Nov. 5, Dec. 28, 1920; *Record*, Feb. 24, 1920.

[15] Dixon, *op. cit.*, pp. 140, 141, 143; Commons and Associates, *op. cit.*, IV, 5–8; *Citizen*, Jan. 15, 23, Dec. 31, 1920; *Times*, June 7, Aug. 21, Sept. 6, Dec. 11, 1920; *Record*, March 29, April 27, June 16, 1920.

[16] *Times*, May 12, June 11, Dec. 24, 1921; Dec. 30, 1922; Jan. 7, July 8, 1923; Jan. 29, 1924; *Citizen*, Nov. 17, 1920; April 20, Sept. 30, 1921; Philip Neff and Annette Weifenbach, *Business Cycles in Los Angeles* (Los Angeles: Haynes Foundation, 1949), pp. 7-15; Dixon, *op. cit.*, p. 191; James C. Findley, "The Economic Boom of the 'Twenties in Los Angeles" (unpublished Ph.D. dissertation, Claremont College, 1958), pp. 142–143; Margaret S. Gordon, *Employment Expansion and Population Growth: The California Experience, 1900–1950* (Berkeley and Los Angeles: University of California Press, 1954), p. 103; *Los Angeles, "The Magic City and County"* (Los Angeles: County Board of Supervisors, 1951), pp. 8, 32.

[17] *Los Angeles, "The Magic City and County,"* p. 8; Findley, *op. cit.*, pp. 142–143, 237–238; Dixon, *op. cit.*, p. 199; *Proceedings of the Californa State Federation of Labor, 1928*, pp. 16–17; *Record*, Dec. 31, 1924; *Times*, Oct. 9, 1924.

[18] *Record*, May 24, 1920; *Times*, Jan. 28, Oct. 8, 18, 1920; June 3, 1921; *The Forty-Year War for a Free City*, p. 8; Findley, *op. cit.*, p. 245.

[19] *Record*, May 24, 1920; *Times*, March 4, Nov. 9, 1921; *Citizen*, July 5, 1921; George P. West, "Good News from California," *Nation*, CXII (June 22, 1921), 867–869; *Proceedings of the California State Federation of Labor, 1920*, p. 59; *1921*, p. 9; *1922*, p. 54; *The Forty-Year War for a Free City*, p. 23; *Pay Policies for Public Personnel*, Report of the Municipal and County Government Section of Town Hall (Los Angeles: Town Hall, 1961), pp. 17–20.

[20] Dixon, *op. cit.*, pp. 169–183; *Citizen*, Feb. 2, 1922; "Recent Minimum Wage Levels," *Monthly Labor Review*, XVII (July, 1923), 118–119; "Organization," *American Federationist*, XXXIV (Feb., 1927), 235.

[21] *Citizen*, June 29, 1923; Jan. 30, Feb. 12, May 1, May 29, 1925; June 1, 1928; *Southern California Labor Press*, April 8, May 1, 1925; Dixon, *op. cit.*, pp. 169–183; *Proceedings of the California State Federation of Labor, 1928*, p. 17; interview with Abraham Plotkin, Feb. 7, 1957.

[22] Christie, *op. cit.*, pp. 240–243; Dixon, *op. cit.*, p. 8; *Times*, July 4, Aug. 30, 1923.

[23] *Times*, July 4, 18, 1923; March 23, 1924; *Citizen*, Dec. 14, 1923; Feb. 15, 22, March 28, 1924; Dixon, *op. cit.*, p. 166.

[24] *Times*, March 23, 1924.

[25] *Citizen*, Feb. 8, 15, 22, March 28, 1924; March 27, 1925; *Times*, March 23, 1924; *Southern California Labor Press*, March 7, May 23, 1924; July 3, 1925; Jan. 27, 1928.

[26] *Citizen*, Feb. 22, March 28, 1924; Oct. 16, 1925; June 25, 1926; Dec. 9, 1927; Jan. 27, July 27, 1928; July 10, 1931; June 17, 1932; *Southern California Labor Press*, March 5, 1926; Oct. 7, 1927; Jan. 27, 1928.

[27] *The Forty-Year War for a Free City*, p. 22; *Citizen*, Dec. 22, 1922; Feb. 10, 24, 1924; *Times*, Oct. 27, 1924.

[28] *The Forty-Year War for a Free City*, p. 22; *Golden Anniversary 1901–1951* (Los Angeles: Central Labor Council, 1951), unpaged; *Citizen*, Feb. 3, Dec. 22, 1922;

Jan. 12, 26, March 23, April 20, Oct. 12, 1923; *Times,* Dec. 28, 1920; Dec. 15, 16, 20, 1922; Jan. 23, Oct. 16, 1923.

[29] *Times,* April 2, 1921; June 6, 1924; *Citizen,* March 7, May 23, July 4, 1924; *The Forty-Year War for a Free City,* p. 23.

[30] *Citizen,* Oct. 28, Nov. 4, 1921; Feb. 3, Nov. 10, 24, 1922; July 27, 1923; July 4, 1924; *Times,* Oct. 8, 1920; Oct. 24, 29, Nov. 1, 1921; *The Forty-Year War for a Free City,* p. 24; *Proceedings of the California State Federation of Labor, 1922,* p. 57.

[31] *Citizen,* Jan. 10, 21, July 29, 1921; Feb. 3, 1922; April 27, 1923; Feb. 10, July 4, 1924; *Times,* Jan. 6, 8, 13, 1921.

[32] "Conciliation and Arbitration," *Monthly Labor Review,* XIV (March, 1922), 166–167; *Times,* Dec. 17, 1921; Jan. 19, 1922; May 2, Oct. 12, 22, 1923; Jan. 29, Feb. 10, 1924; interview with Abraham Plotkin, Feb. 2, 1957.

[33] *Citizen,* Feb. 11, 1921; Aug. 18, 1922; May 18, Oct. 12, 1923; "Conciliation and Arbitration," *Monthly Labor Review,* XVII (Aug., 1923), 214–216; *The Forty-Year War for a Free City,* p. 8.

[34] *Citizen,* June 17, 1921; Feb. 3, May 12, 1922; *Southern California Labor Press,* April 18, 1924; "What Our Organizers Are Doing," *American Federationist,* XXXI (June, 1924), 512; XXXI (July, 1924), 589; *Proceedings of the California State Federation of Labor, 1924,* pp. 70–71.

[35] *Southern California Labor Press,* Dec. 25, 1925; March 5, April 30, July 16, 1926; *Citizen,* July 10, Nov. 6, Dec. 25, 1925; July 16, 1926; July 8, Aug. 5, Sept. 16, 1927; July 13, Dec. 28, 1928; Aug. 2, 1929; *Times,* April 1, 8, Oct. 20, 1921; Dixon, *op. cit.,* pp. 104, 108–110; "Conventions of International Unions," *American Federationist,* XXXI (Jan., 1924), 94.

[36] Walter Wentz, "History of the Los Angeles Newspaper Guild" (unpublished M.A. thesis, Claremont College, 1958), pp. 18–19, 36–37.

[37] *Citizen,* Jan. 28, Feb. 11, 18, 25, May 13, June 17, Dec. 16, 23, 1921; Feb. 3, March 24, June 16, 1922; Jan. 19, June 22, Aug. 31, Oct. 19, Nov. 9, 1923; Feb. 10, May 9, Sept. 19, Nov. 14, 1924; *Times,* Jan. 12, 1921; Aug. 23, Oct. 16, 1923; *The Forty-Year War for a Free City,* p. 23; Commons and Associates, *op. cit.,* IV, 499–500; *Proceedings of the California State Federation of Labor, 1924,* pp. 46–47.

[38] Wolman, *op. cit.,* pp. 33–34; *Proceedings of the California State Federation of Labor, 1932,* p. 31; *The Forty-Year War for a Free City,* p. 23; "Organization," *American Federationist,* XXXIII (Sept., 1926), 1124–1130; *Times,* July 1, Oct. 16, 24, Dec. 31, 1926; *Citizen,* March 5, 12, 1926; July 1, 1927; June 28, 1929; *Southern California Labor Press,* May 15, 1925.

[39] *Times,* Oct. 24, 1926; *Citizen,* March 12, 1926; July 1, 1927; Dixon, *op. cit.,* pp. 10–11; *Violations of Free Speech and Rights of Labor,* Hearings before a Subcommittee of the Senate Committee on Education and Labor, 76th Cong., 3d sess., S. Res. 266 (Washington, 1940), Part 52, p. 19376.

[40] Dixon, *op. cit.,* pp. 196–197; *Proceedings of the California State Federation of Labor, 1927,* pp. 15, 76; *1928,* p. 17; "Organization," *American Federationist,* XXXIII (Sept., 1926), 1125–1126; Frank L. Johnston, "California," *American Federationist,* XXXV (Sept., 1928), 1128; "Los Angeles Initiates a Master Plan," *American Federationist,* XXXVI (April, 1929), 493–494; *Citizen,* March 12, June 25, 1926; June 24, July 1, Sept. 2, 1927; June 22, 1928; *Times,* March 6, 14, July 1–Dec. 31, 1926; *Southern California Labor Press,* Sept. 24, 1926; Sept. 2, 1927.

[41] "Los Angeles Plans Action," *American Federationist,* XXXVI (March, 1929), 364; "Los Angeles Initiates a Master Plan," pp. 493–494.

[42] "The Los Angeles Plan at Work," *American Federationist,* XXXVI (May, 1929), 614; "Double Union Membership Campaign," *American Federationist,* XXXVI (Oct., 1929), 1236; Louis Adamic, "The Collapse of Organized Labor: Is the A. F. of L. on Its Deathbed?" *Harper's,* CLXIV (Jan., 1932), 167–168; *Record,*

Oct. 10, 1919; Jan. 9, 15, 1920; Sept. 2, 1929; *Citizen*, Dec. 16, 1921; Nov. 27, 1925; Dec. 11, 1926; Feb. 16, 1927; June 28, 1929; June 23, 1933; *Times*, June 13, Sept. 12, Dec. 24, 1920; Dec. 27, 1922; Dec. 25, 1924; March 15, 1925; Feb. 16, Oct. 27, Nov. 30, Dec. 25, 1926; Jan. 7, 19, Feb. 20, March 14, July 11, 1927; *Proceedings of the California State Federation of Labor, 1930*, pp. 15–16.

   43 *Citizen*, Jan. 18, 1929.

   44 Dixon, *op. cit.*, p. 1; *Citizen*, Feb. 6, June 5, July 17, Sept. 18, 1925; *Times*, July 1, 1925.

   45 Dixon, *op. cit.*, pp. 155–156; *Citizen*, March 12, June 25, 1926; Jan. 21, 1927; *Times*, March 14, 18, 1926; Jan. 12, Feb. 15, 19, 1927.

   46 Dixon, *op. cit.*, p. 157; *Times*, April 29, May 4, 10, June 9, 18, 28, 30, July 4, 15, Aug. 10, Dec. 31, 1927; *Record*, May 4, 1927.

   47 *The Forty-Year War for a Free City*, p. 23; *Record*, June 1, 1928; July 24, 1929; *Citizen*, June 15, 22, July 19, 26, 1928; *Times*, March 14, 26, 1929; *Proceedings of the California State Federation of Labor, 1929*, pp. 14–16, 81.

   48 *Times*, Sept. 2, Oct. 10, 1925.

   49 *Ibid.*, Oct. 9, Nov. 8, 1925; Aug. 5, 1926; *Citizen*, Oct. 23, 1925; *The Forty-Year War for a Free City*, p. 24.

   50 *Times*, Aug. 5, Sept. 6, 1926; April 20–22, 27, 28, 1927; May 29, 30, July 3, 28, 1928; Aug. 3, 4, Oct. 28, 1929; *Record*, Sept. 3, 6, 1926; Sept. 10, 1927; *Citizen*, April 2, 1926; Sept. 2, 16, 1927; Aug. 3, 1928; Aug. 2, 9, 1929; *Southern California Labor Press*, Sept. 16, 1927; *The Forty-Year War for a Free City*, pp. 24–25.

   51 *Citizen*, June 12, 19, 1925; June 17, 24, 1927.

   52 *Times*, Feb. 27, 1927; *Citizen*, July 17, 1925; March 18, 1927; June 22, 1928; *Proceedings of the California State Federation of Labor, 1925*, p. 69.

   53 *Citizen*, May 15, Sept. 4, Nov. 6, 1925; *Times*, Oct. 14, 30, Nov. 4, 6, 22, Dec. 24, 1925; Jan. 13, 20, 22, 23, 30, Feb. 9, 14, March 5, 6, 1926; Nov. 27, Dec. 1, 1927; *The Forty-Year War for a Free City*, p. 23; "Organization," *American Federationist*, XXXII (Nov., 1925), 1042; "Conciliation and Arbitration," *Monthly Labor Review*, XXI (Dec., 1925), 199–201; XXII (March, 1926), 182; XXII (April, 1926), 169; *Southern California Labor Press*, Jan. 8, 1926.

   54 *Southern California Labor Press*, Aug. 7, 18, 1925; June 18, Sept. 10, 1926; *Times*, May 10, 18, 1926; Nov. 22, 23, 1927; *Citizen*, May 7, 1926; Dec. 6, 1929; *Record*, May 17, 1926; Sept. 30, 1927; "Conciliation and Arbitration," *Monthly Labor Review*, XXIII (July, 1926), 172–175; XXVII (Sept., 1928), 113; "The 1927 Convention," *American Federationist*, XXXIV (Nov., 1927), 1297.

   55 *Proceedings of the American Federation of Labor, 1928*, pp. 69–70; *Times*, May 10, 1926; Feb. 28, 1929; *Citizen*, Oct. 16, 1925; March 18, 1927; June 22, 1928; June 28, 1929; *The Forty-Year War for a Free City*, p. 24; "California," *American Federationist*, XXXVI (Feb., 1929), 240.

   56 *Citizen*, April 10, May 15, July 17, Nov. 27, 1925; June 24, Aug. 5, 12, Oct. 28, 1927; May 11, June 22, Aug. 4, Sept. 21, 1928; Aug. 23, Oct. 4, 11, 1929; *Times*, Feb. 25, April 21, 1926; Jan. 26, May 3, 1927; "Conciliation and Arbitration," *Monthly Labor Review*, XXIV (April, 1927), 71; XXIX (Oct., 1929), 116; XXIX (Dec., 1929), 106.

   57 "Conciliation and Arbitration," *Monthly Labor Review*, XXI (July, 1925), 199; XXVII (Sept., 1928), 113; *Citizen*, Aug. 7, Sept. 18, 1925; March 5, April 30, May 14, Oct. 15, 29, 1926; Feb. 4, July 15, 1927; Jan. 20, March 2, Nov. 30, Dec. 21, 1928; Jan. 18, Oct. 4, 1929; *Times*, May 10, Oct. 6, 1926; Feb. 23, 1929; *The Forty-Year War for a Free City*, p. 23; interview with Abraham Plotkin, Feb. 7, 1957; "The Cloakmakers' War on Communism," *Literary Digest*, XCI (Dec. 25, 1926), 10.

   58 *The Forty-Year War for a Free City*, pp. 23–24; "What Our Organizers Are Doing," *American Federationist*, XXXII (March, 1925), 196; "Conciliation and Arbitration," *Monthly Labor Review*, XXIX (July, 1929), 147–151; William A.

Spalding, comp., *History and Reminiscences, Los Angeles City and County, California* (Los Angeles: J. R. Finnell & Sons, [1931]), I, 488; *Times,* May 25, 26, 1925; June 17, July 21, 27, Dec. 7, 1926; July 1, 24, 1927; May 9, 1929; *Citizen,* Dec. 17, 1926; Aug. 12, 1927; *Record,* July 21, 23, 27, 1926; July 1, 1927.

[59] *Southern California Labor Press,* Dec. 26, 1924; Sept. 24, 1926; *Citizen,* Jan. 9, July 17, 1925; Oct. 1, 1926; July 13, Aug. 17, 1928; Aug. 9, 23, Sept. 13, Nov. 29, 1929; *Times,* April 30, 1926; Aug. 3, 1929; "Conciliation and Aribitration," *Monthly Labor Review,* XX (March, 1925), 247; "What Our Organizers Are Doing," *American Federationist,* XXXII (March, 1925), 196.

[60] *Citizen,* July 17, 1925; June 25, Nov. 5, 1926; March 18, April 1, 1927; May 11, 1928; March 29, June 28, Sept. 20, Nov. 22, 1929; *Southern California Labor Press,* Sept. 16, 1927; *Proceedings of the California State Federation of Labor, 1926,* p. 26.

[61] *Record,* Oct. 6, 1925; *Citizen,* July 17, Nov. 6, 1925; May 7, 14, Aug. 13, 20, 1926; June 24, Aug. 26, 1927; Dec. 28, 1928; June 28, 1929; *Times,* April 21, May 2, 3, 5, 1926; *Proceedings of the California State Federation of Labor, 1927,* pp. 48–51.

[62] *Citizen,* Aug. 28, Nov. 20, 1925; March 26, Oct. 8, 1926; Feb. 18, March 25, Aug. 20, Nov. 14, 1927; June 22, Nov. 16, 1928; June 14, 28, 1929.

[63] "Conciliation and Arbitration," *Monthly Labor Review,* XXIX (Oct., 1929), 113–116; *Times,* March 2, 1926; *Citizen,* March 2, June 25, Aug. 6, 1926; Jan. 21, June 24, Oct. 28, 1927; Aug. 2, 1929.

[64] *Record,* Oct. 13, 1924; July 16, 1925; May 23, 1927; *Times,* Jan. 11, 1927; *Citizen* June 27, 1930; *Proceedings of the California State Federation of Labor, 1929,* p. 48.

[65] *Golden Anniversary 1901–1951* (Los Angeles: Central Labor Council, 1951), unpaged.

[66] Commons and Associates, *op. cit.,* III, 223–230; IV, 614, 617, 618; Levinson, *op. cit.,* pp. 49–50; Smith, *op. cit.,* pp. 562–563, 565–566, 569; *Times,* July 23, 1932.

[67] "Labor and Social Conditions of Mexicans in California," *Monthly Labor Review,* XXXII (Jan., 1931), 83–89; "California Unemployment Commission," *Monthly Labor Review,* XXXII (March, 1931), 73; "Unemployment Relief in California," *American Federationist,* XXXVIII (March, 1931), 344–346; *Times,* Aug. 31, Nov. 20, 24, 28, 29, 1931; Jan. 17, March 15, April 4, 14, July 22, 1932.

[68] *Times,* Nov. 4, 26–28, Dec. 3, 1930; Jan. 3, 7, 30, Feb. 24, April 14, June 16, 19, Dec. 12, 1931; *Citizen,* Dec. 5, 12, 26, 1930; Jan. 23, Feb. 6, June 19, Aug. 10, 14, 1931; July 29, 1932; "Unemployment Relief in California," *American Federationist,* XXXVIII (Feb., 1931), 206; H. C. Fremming, "Los Angeles Meets Unemployment," *American Federationist,* XXXVIII (July, 1931), 855–856; Guy W. Finney, *Angel City in Turmoil* (Los Angeles: American Press, 1945), p. 110.

[69] *Record,* Dec. 11, 1931; *Times,* Jan. 22, Feb. 6, March 8, April 15, June 5, Dec. 1, 8, 11, 1931; Jan. 5, 15, 21, 24, 25, Feb. 22, March 14, May 25, 1932.

[70] *Record,* May 26, July 17, 1931; *Citizen,* Jan. 16, Feb. 3, 27, 1931; *Times,* Nov. 10, Dec. 8, 10, 14, 1930; Feb. 23, 27, March 5, 30, April 8, Aug. 22, 26, Sept. 11, 1931; May 11, June 17, 25, Aug. 29, Sept. 11, 14, 1932; *Proceedings of the California State Federation of Labor, 1932,* p. 16; *Report and Recommendations of the California State Unemployment Commission* (Sacramento, 1933), p. 51.

[71] *Record,* Feb. 5, 11, 1931; *Citizen,* Feb. 6, 1930; Jan. 30, 1931; *Times,* June 7, 10, July 10, 1932; Bimba, *op. cit.,* p. 363.

[72] *Citizen,* March 6, July 10, Aug. 7, 1931; Jan. 15, June 24, 1932.

[73] *Ibid.,* Dec. 2, 1932; *Record,* July 24, 1929; Aug. 8, 1932.

[74] *Citizen,* June 27, 1930; July 10, 1931; May 10, June 10, 1932.

[75] *Ibid.,* June 6, 27, Sept. 12, Dec. 30, 1930; July 10, 24, Oct. 16, 1931; April 8, 1932; William Haber, *Industrial Relations in the Building Industry* (Cambridge: Harvard University Press, 1930), pp. 288–289; *Proceedings of the California State Federation of Labor, 1932,* p. 16.

[76] *Citizen*, June 27, 1930; July 10, 1931; June 17, Dec. 2, 1932; *Report and Recommendations of the California State Unemployment Commission*, p. 45.

[77] *Times*, May 29, 30, 1928; July 4, 1931; March 18, 23, June 22, 1932; *The Forty-Year War for a Free City*, p. 23; *Citizen*, Jan. 20, Dec. 12, 1930; Jan. 2, 23, March 13, July 10, 1931; Aug. 26, 1932.

[78] "Conciliation and Arbitration," *Monthly Labor Review*, XXXI (Nov., 1930), 135; Wolman, *op. cit.*, pp. 100, 103; *Record*, July 15, Oct. 17, 18, 1930; *Times*, July 23, Sept. 4, 6, 7, 1930; July 28, Aug. 5, 1931; *Citizen*, Aug. 29, Sept. 5, 12, 19, Oct. 3, 10, 24, 31, 1930.

[79] *Times*, April 18, July 7, Oct. 4, 1931; Oct. 4, 1932; *Citizen*, April 24, July 10, Sept. 11, Oct. 2, 1931; June 17, 1932; interview with Abraham Plotkin, Feb. 7, 1957.

[80] *Citizen*, June 27, 1930; July 10, 1931; June 17, July 29, Aug. 12, 1932; "Longshore Labor Conditions in the United States," *Monthly Labor Review*, XXXI (Oct., 1930), 813; *Times*, June 27, 1930; June 12, 20, July 10, 16, Nov. 24, Dec. 16, 1931; Jan. 16, Sept. 9, 1932.

[81] *Citizen*, Jan. 31, June 27, 1930; March 27, Nov. 6, 1931; June 17, Aug. 5, Sept. 9, Oct. 7, 1932.

[82] *Times*, Jan. 8, 1930; Jan. 6, May 30, Sept. 26, Nov. 14, 19, 23, 25, Dec. 8, 16, 22, 30, 1931; Jan. 5, 30, 1932.

[83] *Citizen*, Jan. 10, Feb. 7, March 21, May 30, June 27, Dec. 12, 1930; March 20, May 8, July 10, Oct. 2, 12, 1931.

[84] *Ibid.*, April 25, May 16, June 27, Aug. 22, Sept. 19, 1930; May 29, July 10, Oct. 30, 1931; Jan. 15, May 27, June 3, Aug. 5, 26, 1932; *Times*, Jan. 24, 1930; June 17, Oct. 29, Nov. 26, 29, Dec. 19, 1931; Feb. 10, 12, 1932.

[85] Gordon S. Watkins and Paul A. Dodd, *Labor Problems* (3d ed.; New York: Crowell, 1940), p. 550.

[86] *Proceedings of the California State Federation of Labor, 1932*, p. 17.

VII. RENEWAL OF THE STRUGGLE

[1] Edward Levinson, *Labor on the March* (New York: Harper, 1938), p. 48; Gordon S. Watkins and Paul A. Dodd, *Labor Problems* (3d ed.; New York: Crowell, 1940), p. 884.

[2] *Economic Trends in California, 1929–1934* (Sacramento: California Emergency Relief Administration, Division of Research and Surveys, 1935), p. 1.

[3] *Ibid.*; *Times*, July 6, 1933; *Transients in California* (Sacramento: State Relief Administration, 1936), pp. 3, 7.

[4] *Citizen*, June 23, 1933; *Times*, Feb. 24, 1931.

[5] *Times*, May 3, 18, 1933.

[6] *Handbook of Sources of Economic Data Pertaining to California* (San Francisco: California State Chamber of Commerce, 1941), Part I, p. 64.

[7] *Times*, Aug. 18, 22, 1933; *Citizen*, Aug. 25, 1933.

[8] *Citizen*, Aug. 25, 1933.

[9] *Times*, Dec. 14, 1933; Philip Taft, *Economics and Problems of Labor* (2d ed.; Harrisburg, Pa.: Stackpole and Heck, 1948), p. 113.

[10] *Times*, April 22, 1933; George H. Cecil, "Ten Years Forest Work in One Summer," *Southern California Business*, XII (Aug., 1933), 10.

[11] "Self-Help Activities of the Unemployed in Los Angeles," *Monthly Labor Review*, XXXVI (April, 1933), 717.

[12] Guy W. Finney, *Angel City in Turmoil* (Los Angeles: American Press, 1945), pp. 108–109; *Citizen*, Jan. 6, March 10, 1933.

[13] D. J. Saposs, "The American Labor Movement since the War," *Quarterly Journal of Economics*, XLIX (Feb., 1935), 246; *Times*, April 28, 1933.

[14] Levinson, *op. cit.*, p. 50; *Citizen*, June 30, 1933; "Labor Laws," *Monthly Labor Review*, XXXVII (July, 1933), 74; "Collective Bargaining in the N.I.R.A.," *New Republic*, LXXVII (Jan. 3, 1934), 210; "Review of Strikes in the United States," *Monthly Labor Review*, XLVI (May, 1938), 1059.

[15] *Proceedings of the California State Federation of Labor, 1933*, p. 74; "Labor Legislation during 1933," *Monthly Labor Review*, XXXVIII (March, 1934), 561; *Citizen*, Sept. 22, 1933.

[16] *Citizen*, June 23, 1933; interview with Charles B. Hamner, Oct. 26, 1948.

[17] *Citizen*, June 23, 1933; June 15, 1934.

[18] *Ibid.*, July 7, 1933.

[19] *Violations of Free Speech and Rights of Labor*, Hearings before a Subcommittee of the Senate Committee on Education and Labor, 76th Cong., 3d sess., S. Res. 266 (1940), Part 52, pp. 19027–19028, 19325; *Citizen*, July 14, 21, 1933.

[20] *Citizen*, July 28, 1933; James H. Collins, "Recovery—A Sight Draft on Buying Power," *Southern California Business*, XII (Aug., 1933), 12; *Violations of Free Speech and Rights of Labor*, Part 52, pp. 19026–19027, 19029.

[21] *Citizen*, July 28, 1933; *Times*, July 24, 1933.

[22] *Times*, June 18, 1933.

[23] *Citizen*, Sept. 15, Oct. 13, 1933.

[24] *Ibid.*, July 28, 1933; Oliver Carlson, "Los Angeles Grows Up," *Nation*, CXLVI (Jan. 8, 1938), 43; interview with Charles B. Hamner, Oct. 26, 1948.

[25] *Citizen*, July 14, 21, Sept. 1, 8, 1933. Hyans' estimates seem to err on the high side. The actual membership increase was probably substantially less than this figure.

[26] *Times*, Aug. 30, 1933.

[27] *Citizen*, Sept. 1, 1933.

[28] Rose Pesotta, *Bread upon the Waters* (New York: Dodd, Mead, 1944), pp. 21, 351.

[29] *Ibid.*, pp. 1, 21, 24; *Citizen*, Sept. 15, 1933.

[30] *Citizen*, Oct. 6, 1933; Pesotta, *op. cit.*, p. 30.

[31] *Citizen*, Jan. 19, 1934; Pesotta, *op. cit.*, p. 37.

[32] Pesotta, *op. cit.*, p. 52; *Times*, Oct. 13, 1933.

[33] *Times*, Oct. 14, 16, 1933.

[34] *Ibid.*, Oct. 18–20, 22, 24, 26, 31, 1933.

[35] *Ibid.*, Nov. 3, 1933; *Citizen*, Nov. 10, 1933.

[36] *Times*, Nov. 8, 1933; Pesotta, *op. cit.*, p. 58; *Citizen*, Nov. 10, 1933.

[37] Pesotta, *op. cit.*, p. 60; *Citizen*, Dec. 8, 15, 1933; Feb. 16, 1934; *Times*, Dec. 7, 1933; Jan. 2, 1934.

[38] Interview with Hyman Schneid, international organizer and one of the founders of the Amalgamated Clothing Workers of America, Dec. 19, 1947; Benjamin Stolberg, *The Story of the C.I.O.* (New York: Viking Press, 1938), p. 53; *Violations of Free Speech and Rights of Labor*, Part 64, pp. 23581–23582.

[39] "Conciliation Work of the Department of Labor in December, 1933," *Monthly Labor Review*, XXXVIII (Feb., 1934), 335; *Citizen*, Dec. 8, 1933; March 9, 30, 1934.

[40] *Citizen*, Feb. 24, Sept. 1, 1933.

[41] *Ibid.*, May 26, 1933; *Times*, May 26, 1933; *Proceedings of the American Federation of Labor, 1934*, pp. 678–680.

[42] *Official Year Book of the Organized Labor Movement of Los Angeles and Vicinity, 1933* (Los Angeles: The Citizen, 1933), pp. 32–33; "Wage Rates and Hours of Labor Set by Agreement in the Woodworking Industry," *Monthly Labor Review*, XXXVII (Sept., 1933), 675; *Citizen*, June 23, 1933.

[43] *Citizen*, Sept. 8, Oct. 13, 1933.

[44] *Ibid.*, July 14, 1933.

[45] *Ibid.*; *Times*, Oct. 29, Nov. 11, 21, 1933; *Violations of Free Speech and Rights of Labor*, Part 52, p. 19378.

[46] *Times,* Nov. 22, 23, Dec. 1, 1933; *Violations of Free Speech and Rights of Labor,* Part 15-D, p. 7113; *Citizen,* Dec. 1, 1933.

[47] *Times,* June 14, 1933; *Citizen,* June 23, Oct. 27, 1933; *Violations of Free Speech and Rights of Labor,* Part 64, pp. 23573, 23578–23579. The last reference details some of the activities of the Furniture Workers Industrial Union, Local No. 1561. Also see "Conciliation Work of the Department of Labor in October, 1933," *Monthly Labor Review,* XXXVII (Dec., 1933), 1430.

[48] *Citizen,* Aug. 18, 1933.

[49] *Ibid.,* Sept. 8, Oct. 6, 1933; *Violations of Free Speech and Rights of Labor,* Part 64, pp. 23535–23537.

[50] *Citizen,* Dec. 1, 15, 1933; *Times,* Dec. 19, 1933.

[51] *Citizen,* Feb. 9, Dec. 21, 1934.

[52] "Conciliation Work of the Department of Labor in September, 1933," *Monthly Labor Review,* XXXVII (Nov., 1933), 1144; *Proceedings of the California State Federation of Labor, 1933,* p. 12; *Official Year Book,* pp. 34–35; *Citizen,* Aug. 18, Oct. 20, Dec. 29, 1933.

VIII. THE BLUE EAGLE, 1933–1935

[1] Gordon S. Watkins and Paul A. Dodd, *Labor Problems* (3d ed.; New York: Crowell, 1940), p. 886.

[2] "What Are the Principal Features of the Work-Relief Bill Recently Passed by Congress?" *Labor Information Bulletin,* II (April, 1935), 21; "Federal Government Employment and Relief in January, 1935," *Labor Information Bulletin,* II (Feb., 1935), 16; "Old Age Provisions of the Social Security Act," *Labor Information Bulletin,* II (Aug., 1935), 19–21; "Federal Social Security Act," *Monthly Labor Review,* XLI (Sept., 1935), 581.

[3] "Upton Sinclair's Victory," *Nation,* CXXXIX (Sept. 12, 1934), 285.

[4] "Better News from California," *New Republic,* LXXXIII (May 22, 1935), 41; George P. West, "California Sees Red," *Current History,* XL (Aug., 1934), 658.

[5] Upton Sinclair, "Correspondence: EPIC Plan," *Nation,* CXLI (Nov. 6, 1935), 535; *Citizen,* Sept. 21, 28, Oct. 19, 26, Nov. 2, 9, 1934; also see "Upton Sinclair's Victory," p. 285.

[6] *Citizen,* Jan. 12, Feb. 16, Nov. 9, 1934.

[7] Constantine Panunzio, *Self-Help Cooperatives in Los Angeles* (Berkeley: University of California Press, 1939), pp. 1, 10–11; Paul S. Taylor and Clark Kerr, "Whither Self-Help?" *Survey Graphic,* XXIII (July, 1934), 329.

[8] *Violations of Free Speech and Rights of Labor,* Hearings before a Subcommittee of the Senate Committee on Education and Labor, 76th Cong., 3d sess., S. Res. 266 (1940), Part 64, pp. 23631–23632. Also see pages 23507–23694 for an extended report on radical activities; *Times,* Jan. 18, 1934.

[9] *Citizen,* Feb. 16, 17, 1934; *Times,* Feb. 23, 1934.

[10] *Citizen,* Feb. 23, March 2, 9, 1934.

[11] *Ibid.,* June 15, Aug. 31, Sept. 21, Oct. 5, 1934.

[12] *Ibid.,* March 15, May 17, Nov. 29, 1935.

[13] *Ibid.,* Aug. 2, 1935.

[14] *Ibid.,* July 12, 1935.

[15] *Ibid.,* Dec. 22, 1933; Feb. 9, 1934; *Times,* Sept. 12, 21, 1933; Jan. 10, 12, Feb. 6, 1934; *Violations of Free Speech and Rights of Labor,* Part 58, pp. 21321–21322.

[16] *Citizen,* Nov. 24, Dec. 8, 1933.

[17] *Ibid.,* Dec. 15, 1933.

[18] *Ibid.,* Dec. 22, 1933.

[19] *Ibid.,* March 9, 1934.

[20] *Ibid.*, June 15, 1934; George Creel, "Closed during Altercations," *Saturday Evening Post*, CCX (May 14, 1938), 105; *Official Year Book of the Organized Labor Movement of Los Angeles and Vicinity, 1934* (Los Angeles: The Citizen, 1934), pp. 36–37, 52–65; *Union Bulletin*, Sept. 15, 1936.

[21] *Citizen*, June 15, 1934.

[22] *Ibid.*, Oct. 18, Nov. 1, 8, 1935.

[23] *Ibid.*, Dec. 20, 1935.

[24] *Ibid.*, Jan. 11, March 29, 1935; *Proceedings of the American Federation of Labor, 1935*, p. 447.

[25] *Citizen*, April 12, 19, June 7, Oct. 11, 1935; *Times*, Oct. 22, 1935.

[26] *Citizen*, Oct. 11, 1935; Feb. 14, 1936; *Times*, Oct. 22, 1935.

[27] *Citizen*, Feb. 28, March 27, June 26, Nov. 20, 1936.

[28] *Ibid.*, June 11, July 20, 24, 1934; *Times*, July 11, 1934.

[29] *Citizen*, Aug. 17, 1934.

[30] *Ibid.*, April 12, 1935; Rose Pesotta, *Bread upon the Waters* (New York: Dodd, Mead, 1944), p. 335; Herbert Harris, *American Labor* (New Haven: Yale University Press, 1938), p. 216.

[31] *Citizen*, Jan. 18, May 31, Sept. 20, Dec. 20, 1935; also see "Collective Agreements in the Ladies' Garment Industry," *Monthly Labor Review*, XLI (Nov., 1935), 1301.

[32] *Citizen*, March 8, June 14, Dec. 20, 1935.

[33] *Ibid.*, Nov. 9, 1934; *Times*, Oct. 13, 1934.

[34] *Citizen*, March 8, Nov. 22, 1935; *Times*, Nov. 15, 17, 1935.

[35] *Citizen*, April 6, 1934.

[36] *Ibid.*, May 11, July 11, 1934.

[37] *Ibid.*, Aug. 3, Sept. 14, 1934; *Times*, Sept. 11, 1934.

[38] *Times*, March 21, 1934; *Citizen*, March 20, 1935.

[39] *Citizen*, March 22, 29, April 2, 1935; *Times*, March 25, 1935.

[40] *Times*, April 12, 18, 1935; *Citizen*, April 26, May 17, Aug. 2, 1935.

[41] *Times*, April 7, May 5, 1934.

[42] *Citizen*, March 2, 1934.

[43] *Ibid.*, June 8, 1934.

[44] *Ibid.*, July 20, 1934; *Violations of Free Speech and Rights of Labor*, Part 64, pp. 23396–23410, gives full details on the emergency fund, including contributions to and disbursements from it, and on the employment bureau.

[45] *Citizen*, July 20, Aug. 10, 31, Sept. 7, 1934; June 28, 1935; *Times*, July 22, Aug. 18, 1934; *Violations of Free Speech and Rights of Labor*, Part 64, p. 23407.

[46] *Times*, July 22, 1934; *Citizen*, July 27, Aug. 17, 24, Sept. 28, 1934; Nov. 29, 1935.

[47] *Citizen*, April 26, May 3, 10, Nov. 29, 1935; *Times*, April 17, 24, 26, 28, 30, May 9, 1935.

[48] *Citizen*, May 10, July 7, 26, Aug. 16, 1935; *Violations of Free Speech and Rights of Labor*, Part 52, p. 19039; Part 64, p. 23579.

[49] *Citizen*, Sept. 20, Oct. 4, Nov. 8, 29, 1935; Jan. 24, 1936.

[50] *Violations of Free Speech and Rights of Labor*, Part 64, pp. 23573–23575, indicates how police operatives described the pending strike and the composition and activities of the union; *Times*, Oct. 26, 1934; *Citizen*, Oct. 12, 26, 1934; Jan. 18, 1935.

[51] *Citizen*, Jan. 12, Oct. 26, Nov. 16, 1934; July 5, Aug. 16, 1935.

[52] *Times*, April 30, May 9, June 5, 1935.

[53] *Ibid.*, June 6, 11, 1935; *Citizen*, June 7, Aug. 16, 1935; *Violations of Free Speech and Rights of Labor*, Part 52, p. 19098; "Conciliation Work of the Department of Labor in August, 1935," *Monthly Labor Review*, XLI (Oct., 1935), 1006.

[54] *Citizen*, Jan. 5, Feb. 16, Sept. 21, 1934; April 12, 1935.

[55] *Times*, June 2, 1934; *Violations of Free Speech and Rights of Labor*, Part 53, pp. 19401, 19404; Part 64, p. 23545.

[56] *Citizen*, Feb. 9, April 30, June 18, 1934; Oct. 11, Dec. 13, 1935.

[57] *Ibid.*, March 30, 1934; *Times*, March 28, May 25, June 13, 1934. Also see "Wage Changes Reported by Trade Unions since March 1934," *Monthly Labor Review*, XXXIX (July, 1934), 124–126.

[58] *Citizen*, May 25, June 8, 1934; *Times*, April 11, 1935.

[59] *Citizen*, Feb. 23, 1934; *Violations of Free Speech and Rights of Labor*, Part 64, pp. 23605–23606.

[60] *Violations of Free Speech and Rights of Labor*, Part 53, p. 19404; Part 64, p. 23545; *Citizen*, July 27, Oct. 5, 1934; Jan. 11, 1935; *Times*, May 24, 1935.

[61] *Times*, April 11, 1935; *Citizen*, April 12, May 3, June 7, 1935; *Violations of Free Speech and Rights of Labor*, Part 64, p. 23618.

[62] U.S. Bureau of Labor Statistics, *Southern California Aircraft Workers in Wartime*, Work and Wage Experience Studies, Report no. 6 (Washington, 1946), p. 6; *Citizen*, Aug. 24, 1934.

[63] *Times*, Aug. 14, 1933.

[64] *Citizen*, Nov. 24, 1933; June 15, 1934.

[65] *Ibid.*, Nov. 23, 1934; *Times*, Nov. 22, 1934

[66] *Times*, Nov. 23, 24, 1934.

[67] *Ibid.*, Dec. 3, 4, 16, 20, 21, 1934; *Citizen*, Dec. 21, 28, 1934

[68] *Times*, March 10, 1935.

[69] *Ibid.*, Jan. 7, 1934; *Citizen*, Feb. 3, Dec. 8, 15, 1934; "Labor Awards and Decisions," *Monthly Labor Review*, XL (Feb., 1935), 373.

[70] *Citizen*, April 6, June 22, Aug. 24, Oct. 12, 1934.

[71] *Ibid.*, Nov. 9, 1934; *Times*, Nov. 2, 16, 1934.

[72] *Times*, Nov. 22, 1934; *Citizen*, Nov. 23, 30, 1934.

[73] *Violations of Free Speech and Rights of Labor*, Part 15-D, pp. 6953, 6993, 6995–6996; *Citizen*, Dec. 14, 1934; *Times*, Nov. 23, 25, 1934.

[74] *Times*, Nov. 24, 25, 1934; *Citizen*, Nov. 30, 1934.

[75] *Citizen*, Dec. 21, 1934.

[76] *Ibid.*, Dec. 28, 1934; "Strikes and Lockouts in December, 1934," *Monthly Labor Review*, XL (Feb., 1935), 360; *Times*, Nov. 25, 1934.

[77] *Times*, Nov. 25, 26, 1934.

[78] *Ibid.*, Nov. 27, 28, 1934; *Citizen*, Nov. 30, 1934.

[79] *Times*, Nov. 27, 28, Dec. 5, 1934; *Citizen*, Nov. 30, Dec. 5, 1934.

[80] *Citizen*, Dec. 14, 21, 1934.

[81] *Ibid.*, Dec. 21, 1934.

[82] *Ibid.*, Dec. 28, 1934; *Times*, Dec. 29, 1934; "Labor Awards and Decisions," p. 374; "Strikes and Lockouts in December, 1934," p. 360; *Violations of Free Speech and Rights of Labor*, Part 64, pp. 23569–23570.

[83] *Citizen*, Feb. 8, Sept. 6, Nov. 8, 1935; *Times*, Jan. 8, Feb. 2, 1935; *Violations of Free Speech and Rights of Labor*, Part 64, p. 23572; *Proceedings of the California State Federation of Labor, 1935*, p. 72.

[84] *Violations of Free Speech and Rights of Labor*, Part 64, pp. 23570–23571; *Citizen*, Feb. 1, 1935.

[85] *Citizen*, Feb. 1, June 7, 14, 21, 1935; *Evening Herald and Express*, March 25, 1935.

[86] "Labor Agreements, Awards and Decisions," *Monthly Labor Review*, XL (April, 1935), 971.

[87] *Evening Herald and Express*, March 14, 1935; *Daily News*, March 16, 1935; *Times*, March 19, 1935; *Citizen*, March 29, 1935.

[88] *Citizen*, Aug. 9, Sept. 13, Oct. 25, 1935.

[89] *Ibid.*, Nov. 15, 1935; June 26, 1936.

[90] "Wage Agreement in the Borax Industry on the Pacific Coast," *Monthly Labor Review*, XLI (Sept., 1935), 676–677; *Times*, Nov. 11, 1933; *Citizen*, Nov. 16, 1934; Feb. 1, 15, March 29, May 3, July 5, 1935.

[91] D. A. McCabe, "The Effects of the Recovery Act upon Labor Organization," *Quarterly Journal of Economics*, XLIX (Nov., 1934), 56; "Selection of Employees' Representatives," *Monthly Labor Review*, XL (Jan., 1935), 1; *Citizen*, Dec. 1, 1933.

[92] "Characteristics of Company Unions," *Monthly Labor Review*, XLVI (April, 1938), 821–830; *Violations of Free Speech and Rights of Labor*, Part 52, p. 19312; Part 58, pp. 21321–21322; *Times*, Sept. 12, 21, 1933; Jan. 10, 12, Feb. 6, 1934; *Citizen*, Dec. 22, 1933; Feb. 9, June 15, 1934.

[93] *Citizen*, June 15, 1934.

[94] *Proceedings of the California State Federation of Labor, 1934*, p. 12.

[95] *Ibid.*, p. 69.

[96] *Times*, May 28, Sept. 25, 1934; *Citizen*, March 2, Sept. 28, Nov. 9, 1934.

[97] *Citizen*, May 3, 1935; "National Recovery Program," *Monthly Labor Review*, XL (June, 1935), 1466–1488; XLII (Feb., 1936), 334; Leo Wolman, *Ebb and Flow in Trade Unionism* (New York: National Bureau of Economic Research, 1936), p. 54; *Schechter Poultry Corp. v. United States*, 295 U.S. 495 (1935).

[98] Paul H. Douglas, "American Labor Relations Acts," *American Economic Review*, XXVII (Dec., 1937), 744; "National Labor Relations Act," *Monthly Labor Review*, XLII (Aug., 1935), 369. Among the significant cases that validated the constitutionality of the NLRA were *NLRB v. Jones & Laughlin Steel Corp.*, 301 U.S. 1; *Associated Press v. NLRB*, 301 U.S. 103; *NLRB v. Friedman-Marks Clothing Co.*, 301 U.S. 58; *NLRB v. Fruehauf Trailer Co.*, 301 U.S. 49; *Washington, V. & M. Coach Co. v. NLRB*, 301 U.S. 142, all decided in 1937.

[99] Interview with Charles B. Hamner, Oct. 26, 1948.

[100] *Citizen*, June 7, July 12, 1935.

[101] *Ibid.*, July 5, 1935; Jan. 24, June 26, 1936; *Official Year Book of the Organized Labor Movement of Los Angeles and Vicinity, 1935* (Los Angeles: The Citizen, 1935), pp. 53–62. The figures that Secretary Buzzell submitted to the Federal Communications Commission in connection with the request for the KCLC radio station permit in 1935 showed 130 unions in the Central Labor Council with a total membership of 42,000. Twenty thousand more union members were affiliated with central labor councils in Long Beach, Pasadena, Santa Monica, San Pedro, Wilmington, and Orange County. These figures do not agree with the total of 97 locals he listed as belonging to the Central Labor Council in his annual report of July 5, 1935. See the *Citizen*, May 10, July 5, 1935.

IX. UNION SUCCESS IN THE MOVIE INDUSTRY

[1] Hugh Lovell and Tasile Carter, *Collective Bargaining in the Motion Picture Industry* (Berkeley: Institute of Industrial Relations, University of California, 1955), pp. 1–3, 33, 52–53; Murray Ross, *Stars and Strikes* (New York: Columbia University Press, 1941), pp. 3, 5, 203–204, 213; *The Forty-Year War for a Free City; A History of the Open Shop in Los Angeles* (Los Angeles: Times-Mirror Publishing Co., 1929), p. 25; *Times*, Oct. 31, 1929.

[2] Ross, *op. cit.*, pp. 5, 6, 203–204; *The Forty-Year War for a Free City*, p. 14; *Record*, April 26, 1915.

[3] Ross, *op. cit.*, pp. 27, 213–214; *The Forty-Year War for a Free City*, pp. 14, 25; *Times*, Oct. 31, 1929.

[4] Lovell and Carter, *op. cit.*, p. 3; Ross, *op. cit.*, p. 27.

[5] Ross, *op. cit.*, p. 213.

[6] *Ibid.*, pp. viii, ix.

[7] *Ibid.*, p. 8; Lovell and Carter, *op. cit.*, pp. 3, 15.

[8] Ross, *op. cit.*, pp. 8, 218; Lovell and Carter, *op. cit.*, p. 3.

[9] Lovell and Carter, *op. cit.*, p. 15; *Citizen*, Jan. 7, June 23, 1916; *Times*, Aug. 20,

1916; Aug. 30, 1917; Murray Ross, "Labor Relations in Hollywood," *Annals of the American Academy of Political and Social Science,* CCLIV (Nov., 1947), 58; *The Forty-Year War for a Free City,* p. 25.

¹⁰ *The Forty-Year War for a Free City,* p. 25; *Proceedings of the American Federation of Labor, 1918,* pp. 261–262; *Citizen,* Feb. 8, 15, 22, March 8, 10, 1918; *Times,* Jan. 24, 1918.

¹¹ *The Forty-Year War for a Free City,* p. 25; *Record,* Aug. 28, 29, 1918; *Times,* Aug. 29, 31, Sept. 1, 11, 1918; *Citizen,* Aug. 2, Sept. 13, Oct. 4, 1918; Ross, *Stars and Strikes,* p. 7.

¹² Lovell and Carter, *op. cit.,* p. 16; *Proceedings of the California State Federation of Labor, 1919,* p. 232; *Proceedings of the American Federation of Labor, 1921,* pp. 137–140, 467–468; *Times,* Jan. 29, Sept. 16, 18, 1919; July 24, Sept. 8, 12, 15, 1920; *Citizen,* Jan. 31, Feb. 14, July 14, Sept. 19, 1919; *Record,* Sept. 15, 17, 1919.

¹³ Marion Dixon, "The History of the Los Angeles Central Labor Council" (unpublished M.A. thesis, University of California, Berkeley, 1929), p. 112; Ross, *Stars and Strikes,* p. 7; *Times,* July 15, 18, 19, 26–28, 1921; *Citizen,* July 22, 29, 1921.

¹⁴ Ross, *Stars and Strikes,* p. 7; Dixon, *op. cit.,* pp. 113, 115; *Times,* July 31, Aug. 3, 11, Sept. 19, 20, Oct. 29, Dec. 26, 1921; *Citizen,* Aug. 5, 19, 26, Sept. 23, Nov. 4, 11, 25, Dec. 16, 23, 1921; Feb. 3, 1922.

¹⁵ Ross, *Stars and Strikes,* pp. 11–15; *The Forty-Year War for a Free City,* p. 25; Ross, "Labor Relations in Hollywood," pp. 58–59; Dixon, *op. cit.,* p. 116; Lovell and Carter, *op. cit.,* pp. 16–17; California Bureau of Labor Statistics, *Twenty-second Biennial Report, 1925–1926,* pp. 131, 134–135, 140; *Jurisdictional Disputes in the Motion-Picture Industry,* 80th Cong., 1st sess., H. Res. 111 (Washington, 1948), II, 1262–1263; *Los Angeles, "The Magic City and County"* (Los Angeles: County Board of Supervisors, 1951), p. 18; *Citizen,* June 25, Sept. 17, Oct. 22, Nov. 12, 19, 26, Dec. 3, 31, 1926; *Times,* Feb. 10, 1923; Oct. 20, Nov. 9, 10, 26, 1926; *Record,* Dec. 31, 1926.

¹⁶ Lovell and Carter, *loc. cit.;* Ross, *Stars and Strikes,* pp. 141–143, 204–206; *Jurisdictional Disputes in the Motion-Picture Industry,* I, 31, 69; Dixon, *op. cit.,* pp. 118–119; *Citizen,* Nov. 16, 1928; Jan. 7, 1931; *Times,* Jan. 11, 1927; July 14, 1930; *Southern California Labor Press,* Jan. 21, March 4, 11, 1927.

¹⁷ Dixon, *op. cit.,* pp. 118–119; *Southern California Labor Press,* Jan. 21, March 4, 1927; *Citizen,* Nov. 16, 1928; May 4, 1929; May 9, June 27, 1930; Feb. 12, July 10, 17, 1931; June 17, July 29, Aug. 12, 1932; *Times,* July 20–24, Aug. 6, 1932.

¹⁸ Ross, *Stars and Strikes,* pp. 44, 89–90, 132–133; Ross, "Labor Relations in Hollywood," pp. 60–61; *Times,* June 23, Oct. 23, 1931; April 18, Nov. 3, 29, 1932; March 9, 10, 14, 15, 1933; *Citizen,* July 10, Oct. 30, 1931; April 29, Nov. 4, Dec. 2, 1932.

¹⁹ Ross, *Stars and Strikes,* pp. 140–141, 216–217; Ross, "Labor Relations in Hollywood," p. 61; Lovell and Carter, *op. cit.,* p. 3.

²⁰ Ross, "Labor Relations in Hollywood," p. 62; Ross, *Stars and Strikes,* pp. 142–146; "Labor and the N.R.A.," *New Republic,* LXXVI (Aug. 30, 1933), 75; Lovell and Carter, *op. cit.,* p. 17; "The New Deal in Hollywood," *Nation,* CXXXVII (Sept. 20, 1933), 325; *Jurisdictional Disputes in the Motion-Picture Industry,* I, 31, 55, 69, 70, 148; *Times,* July 2–4, 23–25, 29, 30, Aug. 12–14, 22, 24, 25, 1933; *Citizen,* July 14, 18, 28, Aug. 25, 1933; Feb. 2, 1934; New York *Times,* Aug. 24, 1933.

²¹ "The New Deal in Hollywood," p. 326; Benjamin Stolberg, *The Story of the C.I.O.* (New York: Viking Press, 1938), p. 17; *Citizen,* June 2, Sept. 1, 15, 1933; March 16, April 6, 1934; *Times,* Aug. 27, 29, Sept. 13, Nov. 25, 1933.

²² Ross, *Stars and Strikes,* pp. 191–192; *Citizen,* Oct. 5, 1934; Dec. 13, 1935; Jan. 3, 17, April 24, May 1, 1936; *Times,* Jan. 17, 1936; Ross, "Labor Relations in Hollywood," p. 62; Lovell and Carter, *op. cit.,* p. 18.

²³ *Citizen,* June 17, Aug. 12, 1932; June 2, 1933; April 16, 23, 30, May 7, 14, 21, 28, June 11, 18, Aug. 6, Oct. 1, 1937; New York *Times,* May 3, 1937; Ross, *Stars and Strikes,* p. 193; Lovell and Carter, *op. cit.,* p. 19.

[24]Ross, *Stars and Strikes*, p. 196; *Citizen*, Dec. 3, 31, 1937; Jan. 7, 1938; Murray Ross, "C.I.O. Loses Hollywood," *Nation*, CXLIX (Oct. 7, 1939), 374–377; Lovell and Carter, *op. cit.*, pp. 18–20; *Herald and Express*, Dec. 30, 1937; Jan. 3, 1938; *Daily News*, Jan. 4, 1938.

[25] *Citizen*, March 4, April 29, May 20, July 8, Dec. 2, 23, 1938; Feb. 3, 17, March 3, 17, April 14, May 19, 26, Aug. 18, 25, Sept. 8, 29, Oct. 6, 1939; Ross, "C.I.O. Loses Hollywood," pp. 374–377; Ross, *Stars and Strikes*, pp. 197–199; *Herald and Express*, March 30, 1938; *Hollywood Citizen-News*, March 30, 1938; *News*, April 5, 1938; *Daily News*, June 20, 1938; "Actors' Row Ends," *Business Week*, Sept. 9, 1939, p. 52; George Creel, "Closed during Altercations," *Saturday Evening Post*, CCX (May 14, 1938), 106.

[26] Ross, "C.I.O. Loses Hollywood," pp. 374–377; *Citizen*, Oct. 13, 20, 27, Nov. 3, 10, 24, Dec. 8, 15, 22, 1939.

[27] Ross, *Stars and Strikes*, p. 202; Lovell and Carter, *op. cit.*, p. 20; *Citizen*, Dec. 15, 29, 1939; Dec. 14, 1940.

[28] Ross, "C.I.O. Loses Hollywood," pp. 374–377; Ross, *Stars and Strikes*, pp. 199–200.

[29] *Ibid.*; "Actors' Union Drama," *Business Week*, July 29, 1939, pp. 28–29; "Actors' Row Ends," p. 52.

[30] Lovell and Carter, *op. cit.*, pp. 21–22.

[31] *Ibid.*, p. 22.

[32] *Ibid.*, pp. 33–34.

[33] John R. Commons and Associates, *History of Labor in the United States, 1896–1932* (New York: Macmillan, 1921–1935), IV, 445–446; *Record*, June 25, 1929; Ross, *Stars and Strikes*, p. 23; Heywood Broun, "Insurgency in Equity," *Nation*, CXL (May 15, 1935), 574; Alfred Harding, "The Motion Pictures Need a Strong Actors' Union," *American Federationist*, XXXVI (March, 1929), 282–283.

[34] Harding, *op. cit.*, pp. 282–286; Ross, *Stars and Strikes*, pp. 23–24; *Proceedings of the American Federation of Labor, 1919*, pp. 291, 429; *Citizen*, Sept. 20, Dec. 27, 1918; April 4, Nov. 21, 1919; March 5, 1920; Oct. 9, 1925; *The Forty-Year War for a Free City*, p. 25; Ross, "Labor Relations in Hollywood," p. 59; Lovell and Carter, *op. cit.*, pp. 34–35; *Times*, July 1–Dec. 31, 1926; June 23, 25–27, 29, July 1, 3–5, 7, 13–15, 19, 21, 25, 29, 1927; *Record*, June 27, July 1, 7, 20, 1927.

[35] *Times*, July 29, Nov. 22, 1927; Jan. 17, Sept. 6, 7, 9, 1928; *Record*, July 24, 1927; Ross, *Stars and Strikes*, p. 29; Lovell and Carter, *op. cit.*, p. 35; "From the Atlantic to the Pacific," *American Federationist*, XXXIV (Oct., 1927), 1251.

[36] Ross, *Stars and Strikes*, pp. 30, 38; Ross, "Labor Relations in Hollywood," p. 59; *The Forty-Year War for a Free City*, pp. 25–26; "Guild: Movie Actors Win Long Fight and Unite with Equity," *Newsweek*, V (Jan. 26, 1935), 26; Harding, *op. cit.*, pp. 282–286.

[37] "The Other Side of the Talking Picture 'Shield,'" *Literary Digest*, CII (Aug. 10, 1929), 24–25; Somerset Logan, "Revolt in Hollywood," *Nation*, CXXIX (July 17, 1929), 61–62; Somerset Logan, "The Battle of Hollywood," *New Republic*, LIX (Aug. 7, 1929), 309; *The Forty-Year War for a Free City*, p. 26; *Record*, June 6, 29, July 1–6, 8, 15, 1929.

[38] Ross, *Stars and Strikes*, p. 39; *Record*, July 9–12, 15, 16, 19, 22, 25, 27, Aug. 2, 7, 12, 1929; *Times*, June 10, 11, 21, Aug. 4, 7, 11–13, 1929; *Citizen*, June 21, 28, July 5, 12, 19, 26, Aug. 2, 16, 23, 1929.

[39] Ross, *Stars and Strikes*, pp. 31–36; *The Forty-Year War for a Free City*, p. 25; *Proceedings of the State Federation of Labor, 1929*, p. 16.

[40] *Times*, Feb. 20, 1930; Ross, *Stars and Strikes*, pp. 40–42, 160; Lovell and Carter, *op. cit.*, pp. 36–37.

[41] *Record*, Oct. 22, Dec. 11, 1925; *Southern California Labor Press*, Dec. 24, 1926; *Times*, Dec. 14, 15, Nov. 25, 1925; Jan. 11, July 12, Aug. 28, 1926; Lovell and Carter,

op. cit., pp. 34–35; Ross, *Stars and Strikes*, pp. 64–67, 70–72; California Bureau of Labor Statistics, *Twenty-second Biennial Report*, p. 149.

[42] Ross, *Stars and Strikes*, pp. 70–72, 74–76, 86, 120–123.

[43] *Ibid.*, pp. 127–132; Ross, "Labor Relations in Hollywood," p. 61.

[44] Ross, *Stars and Strikes*, pp. 85, 164; Lovell and Carter, *op. cit.*, p. 37; *Citizen*, June 19, 1936.

[45] "Strikes of the Week," *Time*, XXIX (May 17, 1937), 17; *Hollywood Citizen-News*, Feb. 28, 1938; *Evening Herald and Express*, Dec. 3, 18, 1937; *Citizen*, Dec. 10, 1937; Ross, *Stars and Strikes*, p. 164.

[46] *Citizen*, Feb. 24, 1939; Ross, *Stars and Strikes*, pp. 169–171.

[47] *Evening Herald and Express*, Jan. 19, 1941; Ross, *Stars and Strikes*, pp. 167–171.

[48] Ross, *Stars and Strikes*, pp. 144, 149, 173; Morton Thompson, "Hollywood Is a Union Town," *Nation*, CXLVI (April 2, 1938), 381–383; "Guild: Movie Actors Win Long Fight and Unite with Equity," pp. 26–27.

[49] Ross, *Stars and Strikes*, pp. 89–99, 150–152; Lovell and Carter, *op. cit.*, pp. 7–8, 36; Thompson, *op. cit.*, p. 382; Ross, "Labor Relations in Hollywood," p. 61; *Times*, July 26, Oct. 13, 14, 18, Nov. 2, 1933.

[50] *Times*, Nov. 2, 1933; May 24, June 20, 1934; *Citizen*, March 16, 30, 1934; Ross, *Stars and Strikes*, pp. 99–107, 152.

[51] Ross, *Stars and Strikes*, pp. 107–112.

[52] *Ibid.*, pp. 112, 152–159; *Times*, Nov. 24, 1934.

[53] Ross, *Stars and Strikes*, pp. 115–118, 160; Ross, "Labor Relations in Hollywood," p. 61; Lovell and Carter, *op. cit.*, pp. 36–37; "Union Control of Actors Salary Reductions," *Monthly Labor Review*, XXXIX (Nov., 1934), 1137; *Citizen*, Nov. 9, Dec. 20, 1934; April 18, 1935; *Times*, Oct. 22–24, Nov. 3, 14, 1934.

[54] John R. Chaplin, "Hollywood Goes Closed Shop," *Nation*, CXLII (Feb. 19, 1936), 225; "Frantic Stars: To Strike or Not To Strike," *Literary Digest*, CXXIII (May 15, 1937), 12; Ross, *Stars and Strikes*, pp. 160–162, 193, 217–218; Lovell and Carter, *op. cit.*, pp. 37–38; Ross, "Labor Relations in Hollywood," pp. 61–62; *Citizen*, Sept. 4, 25, Oct. 15, 16, 1936; April 23, May 14, 1937; Morrie Ryskind, "It Happened One Night," *Nation*, CXLIV (May 15, 1937), 563.

[55] *Screen Actor*, Dec., 1940; June, 1941; Ross, *Stars and Strikes*, pp. 172, 383; Thompson, *op. cit.*, p. 383; "Actors' Union Merger," *Business Week*, Sept. 23, 1939, p. 40; *Citizen*, July 16, Sept. 10, 1937; Feb. 18, Sept. 30, 1938; July 7, Aug. 11, 18, Sept. 1, 8, 15, Dec. 22, 1939; *Examiner*, Jan. 19, Feb. 14, 1938; *Evening Herald and Express*, Dec. 13, 1937; *Daily News*, Nov. 22, 1937; Jan. 23, 1939.

[56] Lovell and Carter, *op. cit.*, pp. 38, 44.

[57] *Ibid.*, pp. 33, 41–42; Ross, *Stars and Strikes*, pp. 48–49, 52.

[58] Ross, *Stars and Strikes*, pp. 48–49, 51–54, 56–57, 60–61; Ross, "Labor Relations in Hollywood," p. 60.

[59] Ross, *Stars and Strikes*, pp. 57–62, 175; Lovell and Carter, *op. cit.*, pp. 34–38; William P. Mangold, "Hollywood Fights Its Writers," *New Republic*, LXXXVII (May 27, 1936), 70–71.

[60] Lovell and Carter, *op. cit.*, pp. 34–35, 36–38; Ross, *Stars and Strikes*, pp. 177–182; Mangold, *op. cit.*, pp. 70–71; "Rupert Hughes," *Nation*, CXLII (May 27, 1936), 662.

[61] Lovell and Carter, *op. cit.*, pp. 38, 41; Ross, *Stars and Strikes*, pp. 183–189; Ross, "Labor Relations in Hollywood," p. 62; *Times*, Dec. 2, 1937; June 7, 1938; March 10, 1940; *Citizen*, Oct. 1, 1937; Feb. 25, March 25, June 10, July 1, 29, Sept. 30, Dec. 23, 1938; March 10, Aug. 18, 1939; *Examiner*, Feb. 22, April 27, June 7, 1938; *Hollywood Citizen-News*, June 8, 28, 1938; *Evening Herald and Express*, Dec. 2, 1937; Feb. 21, June 23, July 2, 12, 1938; *Evening News*, Dec. 2, 1937.

[62] Chaplin, *op. cit.*, pp. 225–226; Ross, *Stars and Strikes*, pp. 208–209; *Proceedings of the American Federation of Labor, 1931*, pp. 267–268; *Times*, July 23, 1927.

[63] Ross, *Stars and Strikes*, pp. 209–210; *Citizen*, Feb. 25, 1938; Feb. 24, 1939; *Hollywood Citizen-News*, Aug. 20, 1938; *Evening Herald and Express*, Oct. 5, 1938.

[64] Ross, *Stars and Strikes*, pp. 134–135, 211.

[65] Anthony Bower, "Films," *Nation*, CLII (March 1, 1941), 249–250; Ross, *Stars and Strikes*, pp. 211–212.

[66] Frank L. Kidner and Philip Neff, *Los Angeles: The Economic Outlook* (Los Angeles: Haynes Foundation, 1946), p. 23; Ross, *Stars and Strikes*, p. 215.

[67] Kidner and Neff, *op. cit.*, p. 23; Ross, *Stars and Strikes*, p. 219; Conference of Studio Unions, *The Hollywood Story* (Los Angeles, 1946), unpaged.

[68] Ross, *Stars and Strikes*, p. 218.

[69] Lovell and Carter, *op. cit.*, pp. 1, 53–54; Ross, "Labor Relations in Hollywood," pp. 58–59, 63–64; Irving Bernstein, *Hollywood at the Crossroads* (Los Angeles: Hollywood A. F. of L. Film Council, 1957).

X. REVIVAL AT THE HARBOR

[1] Frank M. Kleiler, "Maritime Labor Grows Up," *Survey Graphic*, XXVIII (Jan., 1939), 19; Bruce Minton and John Stuart, *Men Who Lead Labor* (New York: Modern Age Books, 1937), p. 181; Jeff Wilson, *The Hard Realities of Shipping* (San Francisco: Daily Commercial News, [1946]), p. 30; Oliver Carlson, "The San Francisco Waterfront," *Nation*, CXLII (Jan. 22, 1936), 105; Betty V. H. Schneider and Abraham Siegel, *Industrial Relations in the Pacific Coast Longshore Industry* (Berkeley: Institute of Industrial Relations, University of California, 1956), pp. 3, 28–36, 42, 45.

[2] Paul S. Taylor and Norman L. Gold, "San Francisco and the General Strike," *Survey Graphic*, XXIII (Sept., 1934), 405–411; Ira B. Cross, *A History of the Labor Movement in California* (Berkeley: University of California Press, 1935), p. 256.

[3] Paul Eliel, *The Waterfront and General Strikes, San Francisco, 1934* (San Francisco: Hooper Printing Co., 1934), p. 5; *Citizen*, Dec. 29, 1933; Jan. 5, 12, 26, 1934.

[4] Eliel, *op. cit.*, pp. 5, 6; *Citizen*, March 23, 1934; *Violations of Free Speech and Rights of Labor*, Hearings before a Subcommittee of the Senate Committee on Education and Labor, 76th Cong., 3d sess., S. Res. 266 (1940), Part 8, p. 3084; Part 64, pp. 23549–23550; Schneider and Siegel, *op. cit.*, p. 11.

[5] *Times*, March 23, 31, May 8, 1934; Eliel, *op. cit.*, pp. 8, 10; Minton and Stuart, *op. cit.*, p. 182; Chester S. Williams, "Buchmanism 'Settles' the Coast Strike," *Christian Century*, LI (July 25, 1934), 969; *Citizen*, May 11, 1934; "Settling the Long-shoremen's Strike on the Pacific Coast," *Labor Information Bulletin*, I (Nov., 1934), 5–8.

[6] "Labor Standards in Domestic Water Transportation," *Labor Information Bulletin*, III (Nov., 1936), 7.

[7] *Times*, May 9, 1934; *Citizen*, May 11, 1934; *Violations of Free Speech and Rights of Labor*, Part 52, p. 19143; Part 63, p. 23030.

[8] *Violations of Free Speech and Rights of Labor*, Part 15-D, p. 6998; Part 52, p. 19072; *Times*, May 16, 1934; *Citizen*, May 18, 1934.

[9] *Times*, May 10, 16, 18, 28, 1934; *Citizen*, May 25, 1934; Eliel, *op. cit.*, pp. 20, 24; Lew Levenson, "California Casualty List," *Nation*, CXXXIX (Aug. 29, 1934), 245; *Voice of the Federation*, June 28, 1935; Schneider and Siegel, *op. cit.*, p. 13.

[10] Eliel, *op. cit.*, pp. 33, 206; *Times*, May 27, 1934; *Citizen*, June 8, 15, 1934; *Violations of Free Speech and Rights of Labor*, Part 58, pp. 21328–21329.

[11] *Times*, May 23, June 2, 3, 7, 13, 1934; *Citizen*, June 8, 1934; *Violations of Free Speech and Rights of Labor*, Part 63, p. 22940; Eliel, *op. cit.*, pp. 26–27.

[12] *Times*, June 6, 9, 19, 1934; *Citizen*, June 1, July 13, Oct. 5, 1934.

¹³ Eliel, *op. cit.*, pp. 69, 218; *Times*, June 18, 1934; *Citizen*, June 15, 22, 1934; Schneider and Siegel, *op. cit.*, pp. 12–13.

¹⁴ "National Recovery Program," *Monthly Labor Review*, XXXIX (Aug., 1934), 317; Eliel, *op. cit.*, pp. 175, 224, 226; *Maritime Strikes on the Pacific Coast* (San Francisco: Waterfront Employers' Association, 1936), p. 3; *Times*, July 26, 1934; Schneider and Siegel, *op. cit.*, pp. 14–15.

¹⁵ *Times*, July 20, 23, 27, 28, 30, 1934; Eliel, *op. cit.*, p. 32.

¹⁶ Wilson, *op. cit.*, p. 41; *Times*, Aug. 4, 1934.

¹⁷ *Times*, Aug. 15, 1934.

¹⁸ *Citizen*, Sept. 21, 1934; "Settling the Longshoremen's Strike on the Pacific Coast," p. 6; Eliel, *op. cit.*, p. 240; *Maritime Strikes on the Pacific Coast*, p. 4; Wilson, *op. cit.*, pp. 31–32; Schneider and Siegel, *op. cit.*, pp. 14–15.

¹⁹ Schneider and Siegel, *op. cit.*, pp. 14–15; *Citizen*, Oct. 19, 1934; *Times*, Oct. 15, 1934; "Settling the Longshoremen's Strike on the Pacific Coast," p. 8; "Settlement of Grievances under Union Agreement," *Monthly Labor Review*, L (Feb., 1940), 310; Betty V. H. Schneider, "The Maritime Industry," *Monthly Labor Review*, LXXXII (May, 1959), 554.

²⁰ "Agreement and Arbitration Award in Shipping Industry on Pacific Coast," *Monthly Labor Review*, XLI (July, 1935), 107–109; *Maritime Strikes on the Pacific Coast*, pp. 5–7; "Agreement of Radio Telegraphists on Pacific Coast," *Monthly Labor Review*, XLI (July, 1935), 106.

²¹ "From the Atlantic to the Pacific," *American Federationist*, XLII (June, 1935), 648; Schneider and Siegel, *op. cit.*, pp. 14–16; Wilson, *op. cit.*, pp. 7, 29, 33–34, 41–42, 45–46; *Maritime Strikes on the Pacific Coast*, pp. 9–15, 21, 23, 26–27, 29.

²² *Maritime Strikes on the Pacific Coast*, pp. 16–17, 30; Wilson, op. cit., pp. 32, 35; Schneider and Siegel, *op. cit.*, pp. 28–36.

²³ *Violations of Free Speech and Rights of Labor*, Part 61, pp. 22407–22408.

²⁴ "Strikes and Lockouts in June, 1935," *Monthly Labor Review*, XLI (Aug., 1935), 381; *Citizen*, March 15, 1935.

²⁵ *Voice of the Federation*, June 14, 21, Aug. 23, 30, 1935; "From the Atlantic to the Pacific," *American Federationist*, XLII (Nov., 1935), 1247; *Violations of Free Speech and Rights of Labor*, Part 15-D, p. 7162; Part 64, pp. 23551–23554; *Times*, June 18, Dec. 8, 1935.

²⁶ *Citizen*, Jan. 24, Feb. 14, May 1, 1936; *Times*, March 3–6, April 22, 1936; Edward Levinson, *Labor on the March* (New York: Harper, 1938), p. 257; "Organized Labor Movement, 1929 to 1937," *Monthly Labor Review*, XLIV (Feb., 1937), 303; "Conciliation Work of the Department of Labor in January, 1936," *Monthly Labor Review*, XLII (March, 1936), 680.

²⁷ Richard L. Neuberger, "Bad-Man Bridges," *Forum and Century*, CI (April, 1939), 195; *Citizen*, May 10, 1935; Jan. 17, July 24, 1936.

²⁸ *Citizen*, Jan. 31, 1936; "The Maritime Strikes of 1936–37," *Monthly Labor Review*, XLIV (April, 1937), 814; Carlson, *op. cit.*, pp. 105–106.

²⁹ "The Case of Harry Bridges," *Business Week*, Jan. 18, 1936, p. 22; "Labor Right vs Left," *Business Week*, Feb. 1, 1936, p. 31; "The Maritime Strikes of 1936–37," p. 814; *Maritime Strikes on the Pacific Coast*, p. 29.

³⁰ *The Pacific Maritime Labor Crisis* (San Francisco: Coast Committee for the Shipowners, 1936), p. 2; Kleiler, *op. cit.*, p. 18; *Times*, Nov. 15, 1936; "Hard Problems in Ship Fight," *Business Week*, Nov. 14, 1936, p. 19; "Seamen: Marine Workers Fight Each Other and the Shipowners," *Newsweek*, VIII (Oct. 10, 1936), 13.

³¹ *Citizen*, Aug. 28, Nov. 20, 1936; "Uncovering the Waterfront," *Business Week*, Sept. 19, 1936, p. 18; "The Maritime Strikes of 1936–37," p. 815; "The Maritime Strike," *New Republic*, LXXXIX (Nov. 18, 1936), 61.

³² *Times*, Sept. 20, Oct. 27, Nov. 15, 1936; *Citizen*, Oct. 2, 1936; "The Maritime Strikes of 1936–37," p. 816; Miriam A. De Ford, "The Waterfront Showdown,"

New Republic, LXXXIX (Nov. 18, 1936), 72; "Seamen: Commission Ultimatum and Union Feuds Delay Strike," *Newsweek,* VIII (Oct. 24, 1936), 18; "Strike: Rebel Mariners Discard Peace Talk for Walkouts, and 'The Public Takes the Beating.'" *Newsweek,* VIII (Nov. 7, 1936), 11–12.

[33] "West Coast Anchors Lifted," *Business Week,* Feb. 6, 1937, p. 24; "No Easy Out in Ship Strike," *Business Week,* Nov. 7, 1936, p. 15; *Times,* Oct. 3, 31, 1936; *Citizen,* Oct. 30, 1936; *Violations of Free Speech and Rights of Labor,* Part 64, p. 23561.

[34] "Review of Strikes in the United States," *Monthly Labor Review,* XLVI (May, 1938), 1061; *Citizen,* Nov. 13, 27, 1936; Jan. 8, 1937; *Times,* Jan. 9, 1937.

[35] *Times,* Nov. 28, 1936.

[36] *Ibid.,* Nov. 4, 1936.

[37] *Ibid.,* Jan. 13, 1937; *Citizen,* Nov. 20, 1936; Jan. 1, 15, Feb. 26, 1937.

[38] "Pacific Coast Strike Menaces All Business," *Business Week,* Nov. 28, 1936, p. 16; "Shipping Strike Costly," *Business Week,* Dec. 12, 1936, pp. 30–31; *Times,* Dec. 27, 1936; Jan. 25, Feb. 5, 1937.

[39] *Citizen,* Jan. 1, 1937; Wilson, *op. cit.,* p. 34

[40] "Maritime Strike Ended on Pacific Coast," *Commercial and Financial Chronicle,* CXLIV (Feb. 6, 1937), 871; "West Coast Anchors Lifted," p. 24; Kleiler, *op cit.,* p. 20.

[41] "West Coast Anchors Lifted," p. 24; "Maritime Strike Ended on Pacific Coast," p. 871; *Times,* Feb. 14, 1937; Schneider and Siegel, *op. cit.,* pp. 18–19.

[42] "Waterfront Employers Cooperate on a Coastwide Basis for Benefit of Both Management and Shoreside Labor," *Pacific Coast Maritime Report,* I (March 6, 1947), 2; "Win Marine Peace," *Business Week,* Sept. 24, 1938, p. 32; *Times,* March 26, 1937; Schneider and Siegel, *op. cit.,* p. 19.

[43] *Times,* April 15, May 30, June 29, Sept. 24, Oct. 5, 1937; Los Angeles Industrial Union Council, *Minutes,* Aug. 2, 1937.

[44] *Times,* Sept. 20, 21, 28, 1937; *Citizen,* Oct. 8, 1937; *Proceedings of the American Federation of Labor, 1937,* p. 515.

[45] *Labor Herald,* Oct. 13, 1937; *Evening Herald and Express,* Dec. 3, 9, 25, 1937; *Times,* Oct. 9, Nov. 2, Dec. 16, 1937; *Citizen,* Oct. 22, Nov. 5, 1937.

[46] *Times,* Sept. 28, 1937; Jan. 7, 1938; *Citizen,* Nov. 19, 1937; *Evening Herald and Express,* Dec. 13, 1937; Jan. 31, 1938.

[47] *Labor Herald,* Jan. 27, 1938; *Daily News,* Jan. 25, 1938; *Examiner,* Jan. 11, 25, 1938; *Times,* Jan. 22, 29, 1938; *The Carpenter,* LVII (Nov., 1937), 16.

[48] *Times,* Feb. 5, March 19, July 1, 1938; *Industrial Unionist,* July 1, 1938; *Evening News,* April 26, 1938; *Labor Herald,* April 28, 1938; "CIO Union Victor over A.F. of L., in NLRB Decision," *Commercial and Financial Chronicle,* CXLVI (June 25, 1938), 4050; Levinson, *op. cit.,* p. 262; Schneider and Siegel, *op. cit.,* pp. 19–20; "From the Atlantic to the Pacific," *American Federationist,* XLIV (Nov., 1937), 1366; XLIV (Dec., 1937), 1251.

[49] *Evening News,* March 2, 1938; *Times,* March 19, 22, Sept. 14, 1938; *Industrial Unionist,* March 17, 1939; *Citizen,* Oct. 20, 1939.

[50] Schneider and Siegel, *op. cit.,* pp. vii–ix, 59–60; "United Only in Front," *Business Week,* Jan. 16, 1937, pp. 44–45; Edward Levinson, "Waterfront East and West," *New Republic,* XCVI (Sept. 14, 1938), 151–152; Levinson, *Labor on the March,* pp. 259–260.

[51] Schneider and Siegel, *op. cit.,* pp. 19, 59–60, 63; Levinson, "Waterfront East and West," pp. 151–152; "Coast Schism Grows," *Business Week,* June 18, 1938, p. 25; *Citizen,* June 17, 1938; *Proceedings of the American Federation of Labor, 1939,* p. 47.

[52] "Men of the Sea and Their Unions," *Newsweek,* XI (June 13, 1938), 34; "As Bridges Slips, Curran Gains," *Business Week,* May 7, 1938, p. 23; *Evening Herald and Express,* April 22, 23, 1938; *Times,* April 24, 1938.

[53] *Evening Herald and Express*, April 27, 1938; *Times*, Sept. 22, 1938; Levinson, "Waterfront East and West," pp. 151–152; Schneider and Siegel, *op. cit.*, p. 60.

[54] "Analysis of Strikes in March, 1938," *Monthly Labor Review*, XLVII (July, 1938), 91; *Times*, March 10, 11, 1938; *Evening Herald and Express*, March 10, 1938.

[55] *Hollywood Citizen-News*, March 10, 1938.

[56] *Times*, March 12, 1938.

[57] *Evening Herald and Express*, March 14, 1938; *Daily News*, March 16, 1938; *Evening News*, March 15, 21, 1938; *Times*, March 15, 21, 1938.

[58] *Examiner*, March 22, 1938; *Times*, March 24, 25, 1938; *Daily News*, March 28, 1938; *Citizen*, April 22, 1938.

[59] *Industrial Unionist*, June 6, Sept. 30, 1938; *Evening News*, Aug. 17, 1938; *Times*, Sept. 2, 27, 1938.

[60] *Times*, Dec. 10, 1938; Jan. 5, Feb. 3, 1939; *Industrial Unionist*, Dec. 16, 30, 1938; Jan. 6, 1939; *Citizen*, Dec. 16, 1938; Feb. 10, 1939; *Examiner*, Jan. 4, 1939; San Francisco *Chronicle*, Jan. 5, 1939.

[61] *Industrial Unionist*, May 19, Aug. 4, 1939; *Times*, Sept. 27, 29, Oct. 2, 1939; "Fear Coast Marine Tie-up," *Business Week*, Aug. 5, 1939, p. 30; "War Eases Ship Labor Crisis," *Business Week*, Sept. 9, 1939, pp. 50–51; Schneider and Siegel, *op. cit.*, p. 21.

[62] *Times*, Oct. 2, Nov. 11, 18, 1939; *Citizen*, Oct. 27, Nov. 24, 1939; "Unquiet Waterfront," *Business Week*, Oct. 14, 1939, p. 51.

[63] *Times*, July 24, 30, Aug. 24, 27, 29, 30, Dec. 7, 1939; *Evening Herald and Express*, Dec. 6, 1939; *Industrial Unionist*, May 19, July 28, Aug. 4, 18, Sept. 1, 1939; *Citizen*, Sept. 22, 1939; "Stevedore Penalties," *Business Week*, July 22, 1939, pp. 36–37; "War Eases Ship Labor Crisis," pp. 50–51.

[64] Schneider, *op. cit.*, p. 555.

XI. 1936—YEAR OF TRANSITION

[1] "Works Projects under the Works Program, 1935–36," *Monthly Labor Review*, XLIV (Feb., 1937), 363.

[2] Edward Levinson, *Labor on the March* (New York: Harper, 1938), p. 125; *Labor's Non-Partisan League, Its Origin and Growth* (Washington, D.C.: Labor's Non-Partisan League, n.d.), p. 3; Gordon S. Watkins and Paul A. Dodd, *Labor Problems* (3d ed.; New York: Crowell, 1940), p. 644.

[3] "Drought Refugee and Labor Migration to California in 1936," *Monthly Labor Review*, XLIII (Dec., 1936), 1360; *Transients in California* (San Francisco: California State Relief Administration, 1936), pp. 42, 245.

[4] *Citizen*, March 27, Sept. 25, 1936; *Proceedings of the California State Federation of Labor, 1936*, pp. 49–50.

[5] Interview with Charles B. Hamner, Labor Relations Department, Los Angeles Central Labor Council, Oct. 26, 1948; interview with George B. Roberts, district representative, District No. 5, United Rubber, Cork, Linoleum and Plastic Workers of America, Dec. 13, 1948; *Union News Service*, Sept. 7, 1936.

[6] *Times*, March 9, May 19, July 19, Oct. 24, 1936.

[7] *Citizen*, July 3, Aug. 7, 28, Oct. 30, 1936.

[8] *Ibid.*, June 26, Sept. 11, 1936; *Times*, Sept. 8, 1936.

[9] *Citizen*, Nov. 22, 1935; *Violations of Free Speech and Rights of Labor*, Hearings before a Subcommittee of the Senate Committee on Education and Labor, 76th Cong., 3d sess., S. Res. 266 (1940), Part 52, pp. 19043–19044, 19052, 19057, 19141, 19154, 19335.

[10] *Violations of Free Speech and Rights of Labor*, Part 52, p. 19053.

[11] *Ibid.*, Part 52, pp. 19050, 19054, 19126, 19331, 19339, 19342, 19370–19373; Part

63, p. 23206; Part 65, p. 23721; *Times*, June 14, 21, 22, 23, 24, 1936. Pages 19126, 19342, and 19371–19372 in *Violations of Free Speech and Rights of Labor* list the trade associations to which the M and M offered its services. Those assisted did not need to be members of the M and M, as it was interested in stopping outside union inroads into all industries. A dated list of actual meetings held with employer groups in September and October is found in Part 63, page 23058, and is followed by further testimony on this subject.

[12] *Violations of Free Speech and Rights of Labor*, Part 52, pp. 19014, 19324, 19331.

[13] *Union Bulletin* (official organ of the Optical Technicians and Workers Union, Local No. 18521), Sept. 15, 1936; *Times*, June 22, 23, 1936.

[14] *Times*, June 21, 1936.

[15] *Ibid.*, June 14, 24, 26, 1936; *Citizen*, June 5, 1936.

[16] *Citizen*, Oct. 23, Dec. 11, 1936; *Union Bulletin*, Sept. 15, 1936.

[17] *Proceedings of the California State Federation of Labor, 1936*, pp. 10–11.

[18] *Citizen*, Dec. 18, 1936.

[19] *Ibid.*, June 26, 1936.

[20] "Review of Strikes in 1936," *Monthly Labor Review*, XLIV (May, 1937), 1221–1235; *Violations of Free Speech and Rights of Labor*, Part 64, p. 23450; *Organizer* (issued bimonthly by the Western Mechanics Industrial Union, Local No. 188, UAW-CIO), Oct. 21, Dec. 3, 1936; *Plane Facts* (issued by the Northrop Committee of the Western Mechanics Industrial Union), Nov. 10, 1936; Arthur P. Allen and Betty V. H. Schneider, *Industrial Relations in the California Aircraft Industry* (Berkeley: Institute of Industrial Relations, University of California, 1956), pp. 10–11.

[21] *Citizen*, April 10, July 17, 24, 1936; *Times*, July 14–16, 1936.

[22] *Citizen*, Jan. 10, May 15, Aug. 14, Oct. 23, 30, 1936; *Violations of Free Speech and Rights of Labor*, Part 64, p. 23605.

[23] *Citizen*, March 20, April 3, 1936.

[24] *Ibid.*, April 17, 1936; "Conciliation Work of the Department of Labor in April, 1936," *Monthly Labor Review*, XLII (June, 1936), 1578.

[25] "Conciliation Work of the Department of Labor in April, 1936," p. 1578; *Times*, April 27, 1936; *Citizen*, May 29, 1936; *Violations of Free Speech and Rights of Labor*, Part 52, p. 19357.

[26] *Violations of Free Speech and Rights of Labor*, Part 52, pp. 19357–19360; Part 64, pp. 23339–23340, 23345–23346; *Times*, June 16, 1936. The articles of incorporation of the Cabinet and Store Fixture Association of California are in *Violations of Free Speech . . .*, Part 64, pp. 23333–23334.

[27] *Violations of Free Speech and Rights of Labor*, Part 52, pp. 19091–19096, 19100–19116, 19362–19365; Part 64, pp. 23335–23346; *Citizen*, Oct. 16, 1936.

[28] *Citizen*, June 19, 1936.

[29] *Ibid.*, Feb. 14, 28, May 8, 15, 22, June 5, Dec. 11, 1936; *Times*, Dec. 4, 1936; *Violations of Free Speech and Rights of Labor*, Part 63, pp. 23185–23186.

[30] *Citizen*, July 24, 1936.

[31] Among the strikes conducted by unionized culinary workers in 1936 were those at Dinty Moore's Buffet, King's Diner, Brewer's Café, Oakes Coffee Shop, La Salle Café, Mike's Grill, Katie Kohn's Café, Fradelis Restaurants, Our Gang Café, Three Little Pigs Night Club, Bradley's Coffee Shop, Sam's Sandwich Shop, and Jack's Grill. In most instances the union members demanded wage increases and shorter hours, though occasionally they requested the discharge of Oriental and alien employees. The majority of these strikes were settled satisfactorily, except for the dispute at Katie Kohn's Café.

[32] *Citizen*, Aug. 14, 1936; *Violations of Free Speech and Rights of Labor*, Part 58, p. 21440.

[33] *Times*, April 21–23, Nov. 19, 22, 26, 27, Dec. 1, 10, 1936; *Citizen*, Dec. 4, 11,

1936; *Violations of Free Speech and Rights of Labor*, Part 53, pp. 19406–19409, 19601–19602. The last reference mentions total contributions of $18,056.25 to the special truck fund. Pages 19603–19606 itemize receipts and disbursements of the special fund, including expenditures for guard service furnished by the Glen E. Bodell Detective Agency under contract as per statement on pages 19617–19618. Also see Part 64, pp. 23382, 23540.

[34] *Violations of Free Speech and Rights of Labor*, Part 64, pp. 23351–23354. These pages print the articles of incorporation and bylaws of Allied Food Industries, Inc. The membership list is on pages 23355–23356. Exhibit 10020, page 23362, shows that the organization had an emergency fund to be used in labor disputes. Exhibit 10053, page 23381, describes a black list that was to be used in discharging "disloyal" employees.

[35] *Ibid.*, Part 58, p. 21342, indicates that officials of the M and M assisted in incorporating Dairy Industries, Inc. The bylaws and the constitution were adopted on October 2, 1936, and are printed on pages 21529–21531. Also see pages 21542 ff. for data on other employer groups, dues, assessments, etc. Further information on groups outside the dairy industry is in Part 53, pages 19406 and 19601, and Part 64, pages 23537–23538.

[36] *Citizen*, Aug. 7, 1936; *Times*, July 30, 1936.

[37] *Citizen*, Sept. 18, Dec. 25, 1936.

[38] *Ibid.*, Aug. 28, Sept. 5, Oct. 23, Dec. 18, 1936; Jan. 22, Feb. 19, 1937.

[39] *Ibid.*, Feb. 7, 1937.

[40] *Ibid.*, Feb. 7, May 22, 1936.

[41] *Ibid.*, May 15, 29, Aug. 7, 1936; *Times*, Aug. 6, 1936.

[42] *Violations of Free Speech and Rights of Labor*, Part 52, pp. 19075–19076. Also see Part 64, pages 23347–23353, for the articles of incorporation of the Southern California Garment Manufacturers' Association. Further data on the organization are found in Part 52, pages 19059–19068, 19077–19082, 19353–19354.

[43] *Citizen*, Aug. 14, 1936.

[44] *Ibid.*, Dec. 18, 1936; March 5, Oct. 1, 1937.

[45] *Ibid.*, April 24, May 15, June 26, 1936; Jan. 1, July 2, 1937.

[46] *Ibid.*, Aug. 28, 1936; *Violations of Free Speech and Rights of Labor*, Part 64, pp. 23607–23608.

[47] *Citizen*, June 12, Nov. 27, 1936.

XII. A NEW OFFENSIVE FOR THE OPEN SHOP, 1937–1938

[1] "Federal Work Relief Act of 1937," *Monthly Labor Review*, XLV (Sept., 1937), 640; "Work Relief Act of 1938," *Monthly Labor Review*, XLVII (Aug., 1938), 345.

[2] "Status of Social Security at End of June, 1937," *Monthly Labor Review*, XLV (Sept., 1937), 584; "The First Three Years," *Survey*, LXXIV (Aug., 1938), 265.

[3] "National Labor Relations Act Declared Constitutional," *Monthly Labor Review*, XLIV (May, 1937), 1192; *Times*, Dec. 9, 10, 16, 1937. Los Angeles labor leaders also were pleased with this decision. See *Citizen*, April 16, 1937.

[4] *Citizen*, June 3, 1938; *People's World*, Feb. 5, 1938; San Francisco *Chronicle*, Sept. 3, 1938; *Times*, July 5, 1938; New York *Times*, Dec. 1, 1938; Lois MacDonald, "The National Labor Relations Act," *American Economic Review*, XXVI (Sept., 1936), 412–427.

[5] "The Fair Labor Standards Act of 1938," *Labor Information Bulletin*, V (July, 1938), 1; "Federal Wages and Hours Law of 1938," *Monthly Labor Review*, XLVII (July, 1938), 107; "Industrial Relations in 1938," *Monthly Labor Review*, XLVIII (March, 1939), 499; *Daily News*, Oct. 25, 1938.

[6] Howard R. Smith, *Economic History of the United States* (New York: Ronald Press, 1955), pp. 607, 610–614; Florence Peterson, *Strikes in the United States, 1880–*

1936, U. S. Bureau of Labor Statistics, Bull. no. 651 (1937), p. 21; Edward Levinson, *Labor on the March* (New York: Harper, 1938), pp. 133, 236; "C.I.O. Becomes Congress of Industrial Organizations," *Monthly Labor Review*, XLVII (Dec., 1938), 1326.

[7] *Citizen*, July 16, Sept. 17, 1937.

[8] *Ibid.*, Sept. 17, 1937; Levinson, *op. cit.*, p. 134.

[9] *Evening News*, July 11, 1938; *Industrial Unionist*, Aug. 20, 1938; *Labor Herald*, Aug. 25, 1938; *Examiner*, Aug. 21, 1938; *Proceedings of the California State Federation of Labor, 1938*, pp. 57, 98, 139.

[10] *Times*, Feb. 21, 1938; *Evening Herald and Express*, Feb. 15, 1938; *Citizen*, April 8, 1938; *Industrial Unionist*, June 24, 1938.

[11] *Times*, March 21, July 11, 1938; *People's World*, July 12, Aug. 25, 1938; *Citizen*, April 1, Aug. 19, 1938.

[12] *Citizen*, Oct. 21, 28, Nov. 11, 1938; *Times*, Oct. 18, 22, 1938; *Labor Herald*, Oct. 20, 1938; *Industrial Unionist*, Oct. 21, 1938; "How Will Olson Handle Labor," *Business Week*, Nov. 26, 1938, p. 25.

[13] "Wildcat Pensions," *Nation*, CXLVII (Oct. 22, 1938), 397.

[14] Philip Neff and Annette Weifenbach, *Business Cycles in Los Angeles* (Los Angeles: Haynes Foundation, 1949), pp. 17–18; Smith, *op. cit.*, pp. 622–623.

[15] *Citizen*, May 21, 1937.

[16] *Ibid.*, April 2, 1937; *Labor Herald*, June 8, 1937; *Union News Service*, May 10, 1937; *Industrial Unionist*, May 2, 1938; *A Statement to All Locals from the Executive Board and Delegates of the Los Angeles CIO Council* (Los Angeles: Los Angeles Industrial Union Council, March 16, 1945); interview with George B. Roberts, district representative, District No. 5, United Rubber, Cork, Linoleum and Plastic Workers of America, Dec. 13, 1948.

[17] *Citizen*, Jan. 29, 1937; *Union News Service*, June 14, 1937; *Evening News*, Dec. 21, 1937; *Times*, Feb. 22, 1938; *Violations of Free Speech and Rights of Labor*, Hearings before a Subcommittee of the Senate Committee on Education and Labor, 76th Cong., 3d sess., S. Res. 266 (1940), Part 64, pp. 23613–23614; Los Angeles Industrial Union Council, *Minutes*, Nov. 1, 1937.

[18] *Citizen*, Jan. 15, Feb. 19, March 5, 12, April 30, May 28, 1937.

[19] *Ibid.*, June 4, July 23, Oct. 15, 1937; George Creel, "Closed during Altercations," *Saturday Evening Post*, CCX (May 14, 1938), 106.

[20] *Evening Herald and Express*, Feb. 11, May 18, 1938; *Citizen*, Feb. 11, May 20, 1938.

[21] *Violations of Free Speech and Rights of Labor*, Part 65, p. 23894.

[22] *Ibid.*, Part 63, pp. 22791–22792, 23057–23059, 23076, 23083. Part 52, p. 19393, gives a long list of firms which were paying wages considered to be too low and therefore conducive to unionization. Part 63, p. 23160, refers to the extent of the problem faced by the M and M and the need for higher wage scales in Los Angeles. Also see Part 52, pp. 19148–19154, 19381–19384, for lists of bureau placements in 1937, 1938, and 1939 by name of firm, number of men sent, and date, and for information concerning placement under strike conditions. Testimony presented on page 19142 indicates that a high percentage of placements were made under strike conditions. "Big Labor Drive in Los Angeles," *Business Week*, April 10, 1937, pp. 39, 40, 42, gives percentages of unionized workers in various industries at the end of March, 1937: truck drivers, 51 per cent at the harbor, 20 per cent elsewhere; rubber, 10 per cent (chiefly CIO); automobile assembly, 10 per cent; steel, 10 per cent (CIO); oil-field and refinery workers, 25 per cent; service stations, 10 per cent; men's clothing, 90 per cent (in the larger shops); women's clothing, 90 per cent; millinery, 50 per cent; printing and publishing, 10 per cent; musicians, 100 per cent; cooks and waiters, 50 per cent; structural steel workers, 90 per cent; electrical workers, 90 per cent; plasterers, 50 per cent; lumber trades, 50 per cent. Further information is found in the *Citizen*, March 5, 1937, and in the Los Angeles Industrial Union Council *Minutes*, Oct. 11, 1937.

[23] *Violations of Free Speech and Rights of Labor,* Part 65, p. 24037; Part 66, pp. 24002–24004, 24006–24007, 24010. See Part 56, pp. 20697–20701, for the articles of incorporation and the bylaws, and Part 66, pp. 24177–24178, for a sketch of Mrs. Ochs's background. Also see Part 56, pp. 20429–20433, 20686–20688; Part 66, pp. 24002–24010.

[24] *Ibid.,* Part 56, pp. 20707–20708; Part 57, pp. 20903–20906; Part 66, pp. 24039, 24046–24047, 24097–24106. Also see "Business Goes After the Consumer Movement," *Consumers Union Reports,* Dec., 1939, p. 16C.

[25] *Violations of Free Speech and Rights of Labor,* Part 56, pp. 20695, 20707; Part 57, pp. 20888–20889; Part 66, p. 24010. Also see "Open Shop under Fire," *Business Week,* Jan. 27, 1940, p. 27.

[26] *Violations of Free Speech and Rights of Labor,* Part 56, pp. 20476–20477, 20715–20716, 20722–20729. These pages also detail the articles of incorporation and the bylaws. Part 57, p. 20992, and Part 65, pp. 23864, 23885–23890, summarize the conditions leading to the formation of Southern Californians, Incorporated. The "Declaration of Principles" of the organization is presented in Part 65, p. 23787, and the membership list and the board of directors are given on pages 23777–23780. Also see *Times,* Dec. 22, 1937, for the basic creed of the organization.

[27] *Violations of Free Speech and Rights of Labor,* Part 61, pp. 22390–22395, gives a full report of the luncheon under the auspices of Southern Californians, Incorporated. Also see Part 56, pp. 20480 ff.; *Times,* Dec. 14, 24, 1937; *Daily News,* Dec. 24, 1937; *Citizen,* Dec. 24, 31, 1937; Jan. 14, 1938; "Los Angeles Union Drive Weaker," *Business Week,* Sept. 25, 1937, p. 38.

[28] *Times,* Feb. 21, 1938.

[29] *Violations of Free Speech and Rights of Labor,* Part 56, pp. 20579–20580, indicates the type of research data used. The program of the organization is outlined on pages 20763–20766. Part 57, pp. 21315–21318, describes the activities of officials of Southern Californians, Incorporated. Also see Part 56, pp. 20433–20435.

[30] *Ibid.,* Part 56, pp. 20494–20496, 20498–20499, 20752–20759. Part 56, pp. 20737–20748, lists 433 institutional members, 171 individual members, and 390 contributors, and gives the amount of their contributions. Pages 20749–20751 list contributions of $500 or more for two years beginning with November, 1937. Part 65, pp. 23792–23794, indicates the open-shop creed of Southern Californians, Incorporated. Also see Part 57, p. 21305; Part 65, pp. 23776–23777, 23810, 23880; *Citizen,* May 13, 1938.

[31] *Violations of Free Speech and Rights of Labor,* Part 58, pp. 21400–21404, 21596–21597.

[32] *Ibid.,* Part 66, pp. 24447–24457, gives a full transcript of the meeting. See *Citizen,* Feb. 25, March 4, 11, 1938, for the Central Labor Council viewpoint.

[33] *Times,* April 15, June 16, July 1, 3, 22, 1938; *Evening Herald and Express,* June 3, 1938; *Citizen,* June 17, July 29, 1938; *Violations of Free Speech and Rights of Labor,* Part 65, pp. 23830, 24445–24447; Part 66, p. 24014; "Urge Anti-Union Law," *Business Week,* Aug. 6, 1933, p. 33.

[34] *Citizen,* July 23, 1937.

[35] Los Angeles Industrial Union Council, *Minutes,* Oct. 25, Nov. 8, 1937; *Daily News,* Nov. 30, 1937; *Times,* Jan. 1, 1938.

[36] *Citizen,* Sept. 23, 1938; *Evening News,* July 15, 1938; *Daily News,* June 4, 1938.

[37] *Violations of Free Speech and Rights of Labor,* Part 53, pp. 19470–19473, 19475; *Hollywood Citizen-News,* July 1, 1938; *Times,* July 26, 1938.

[38] *Violations of Free Speech and Rights of Labor,* Part 56, pp. 20443–20454, 20461, 20709; Part 57, pp. 20895, 20970–20975; Part 66, pp. 24012 ff., 24056, 24083. See also Part 66, pp. 24011, 24179, 24441–24442. The TNT method of establishing independent unions is described in detail in Part 57, pp. 20870–20880. Employer domination of these organizations is shown in Part 56, pp. 20454–20455, 20707–20709. Part 66, p. 24166, indicates the duties of Huff and Rittenhouse as organizers for TNT.

Also see Part 56, pp. 20584–20599; Part 57, pp. 20882–20883; Part 66, pp. 24075–24076, 24106–24149; *Examiner*, Jan. 15, 1938; *Citizen*, Jan. 21, 1938.

[39] *Violations of Free Speech and Rights of Labor*, Part 66, p. 24047, proves the establishment of at least 150 independent unions. The names of the labor organizations and those of the firms concerned are given on pages 24168–24169, 24172–24173, 24184–24188. Also see Part 56, pp. 20423–20425, 20489–20490; Part 57, pp. 20896, 20976, 20980; Part 66, pp. 24170–24171, 24201–24202, 24422; *Examiner*, Nov. 30, 1937; Jan. 4, 1938. Part 66, pp. 24154–24159, indicates that league officials disavowed any direct connection with the M and M and TNT, and were determined to establish an effective third party in the labor politics of the state. See *Examiner*, Feb. 11–13, 1938; *Times*, Feb. 13, 1938.

[40] *Municipal Code of the City of Los Angeles* (Los Angeles: Parker, Stone and Baird Co., 1936), p. 192.

[41] *Violations of Free Speech and Rights of Labor*, Part 57, p. 20855; Part 65, p. 23786; *Hollywood Citizen-News*, Dec. 6, 1937; *Evening Herald and Express*, Dec. 29, 1937.

[42] *Examiner*, Dec. 30, 1937.

[43] *Times*, Jan. 5, 1938; *Evening Herald and Express*, Jan. 7, 10, Feb. 4, 1938; *Daily News*, Jan. 8, 1938; *Examiner*, Jan. 8, Feb. 13, 1938; *Citizen*, Jan. 14, 1938.

[44] *Violations of Free Speech and Rights of Labor*, Part 65, pp. 23792, 23797, 23806, 23811, 23816; *Times*, March 2, 1938; *Citizen*, April 22, 1938; *Evening Herald and Express*, April 23, 1938.

[45] *Times*, June 1, 27, 1938; *Citizen*, June 17, Aug. 12, Sept. 2, 1938; *Examiner*, Sept. 3, 1938; *Evening Herald and Express*, Sept. 17, 1938.

[46] *Evening Herald and Express*, Sept. 17, 1938; *Violations of Free Speech and Rights of Labor*, Part 57, pp. 20860, 20943. Pages 20862–20869 indicate that Southern Californians, Incorporated, established a law enforcement committee which, as *amicus curiae*, participated in hearings of violations of the new ordinance. This committee also lobbied for enforcement of the law by public officials. A list of court cases in which attorneys for Southern Californians, Incorporated, sat as consultants or advised the prosecution is given on pages 20944–20948. All these cases were tried between September 30, 1938, and August 11, 1939. Also see pages 20948–20949. Part 65, pp. 23957–23958, indicates a certain amount of coöperation between representatives of Southern Californians, Incorporated, and the police in the enforcement of the law. The *Citizen* for Oct. 21, 1938, itemizes the $33,064.12 spent in 1938 by AFL leaders in opposing the ordinance to regulate picketing. Part 57, p. 21307, gives figures on the decrease in monthly wage losses after passage of the ordinance.

[47] *Industrial Unionist*, Sept. 23, 1938; "Farmers," *California Citrograph*, XXIII (Sept., 1938), 495; *Violations of Free Speech and Rights of Labor*, Part 75, pp. 27717–27721, presents some of the preliminary correspondence before initiation of the campaign. Southern Californians, Incorporated, and the Associated Farmers were most prominent in endeavoring to secure passage of the proposal. Pages 27722–27724 list the sponsors of the committee. Also see Part 75, pp. 27725–27734; "Urge Anti-Union Law," p. 33.

[48] *Violations of Free Speech and Rights of Labor*, Part 75, pp. 27742–27746, describes the county organization established to support the campaign for Proposition No. 1. Pages 27757–27793 present a number of examples of the publicity and propaganda activities of the California Committee for Peace in Employment Relations and indicate the extent of the campaign. In Los Angeles County the effort to secure the passage of Proposition No. 1 really began after September 16. Also see Part 66, pp. 24057–24063, 24421–24422; *Industrial Unionist*, Sept. 16, Nov. 4, 1938; "L.A.'s Last Stand," *Business Week*, Jan. 18, 1941, p. 48.

[49] "California, Here We Fight," *Business Week*, Sept. 17, 1938, p. 24; *Industrial Unionist*, Nov. 4, 1938; *Citizen*, Oct. 7, Sept. 30, Nov. 4, 1938.

[50] *Citizen*, Nov. 4, 1938; *People's World*, Oct. 10, 1938; *Industrial Unionist*, Oct. 14, 1938; "How Will Olson Handle Labor," *Business Week*, Nov. 26, 1938, p. 25.

[51] *Industrial Unionist*, Nov. 11, 18, 1938; *Citizen*, Nov. 11, Dec. 3, 9, 23, 1938. *Violations of Free Speech and Rights of Labor*, Part 57, p. 21312, indicates that Southern Californians, Incorporated, disbursed $119,235.21 in the campaign. Part 61, pp. 22436–22440, lists contributions received and sums disbursed by the organization. The California Committee for Peace in Employment Relations also collected funds for the state-wide as well as the southern California campaign for Proposition No. 1. See Part 61, pp. 22427–22436. A total of nearly $300,000 was spent by the members of all groups advocating passage of the initiative.

[52] *Report on Labor Legislation and Labor Record of Senators and Members of Assembly, Fifty-Second Session of the California Legislature* (San Francisco: California State Federation of Labor, 1937), p. 9; *Citizen*, Feb. 19, 26, 1937.

[53] D. W. Pontius, "Municipal Busses or Not?" *Pacific Electric Magazine*, XVII (April 10, 1937), 2–3.

[54] *Violations of Free Speech and Rights of Labor*, Part 65, pp. 23953–23956; *Times*, Dec. 5, 1937; Oct. 7, 1939; *Examiner*, Dec. 7, 1937; *Hollywood Citizen-News*, Dec. 6, 1937; *Citizen*, Dec. 10, 1937; *Evening News*, Dec. 22, 1937. Also see *People's World*, Feb. 15, 1938, for a statement on what seemed to be the political ramifications of Fitts's drive. He was declared to be "the strong arm for open-shop interests in Los Angeles."

[55] *Citizen*, March 25, Sept. 9, 1938; *Industrial Unionist*, Sept. 16, Nov. 25, 1938.

[56] *Daily News*, Oct. 20, 1938.

XIII. SKIRMISHES ON THE LOCAL UNION FRONT, 1937–1938

[1] Los Angeles Industrial Union Council, *Minutes*, Aug. 9, 1937.

[2] *Citizen*, Sept. 10, 1937.

[3] *Ibid.*, Dec. 10, 1937.

[4] Los Angeles Industrial Union Council, *Minutes*, Dec. 13, 1937.

[5] *Times*, Feb. 13, 1938; *Evening News*, April 1, 1938; *Industrial Unionist*, April 18, 1938; *Examiner*, April 22, 1938.

[6] Oliver Carlson, "Los Angeles Grows Up," *Nation*, CXLVI (Jan. 8, 1938), 44; *Citizen*, June 17, 1938; *Industrial Unionist*, April 18, 1938.

[7] *Industrial Unionist*, April 11, June 17, July 29, Sept. 16, 1938; *Citizen*, Feb. 4, 1938.

[8] Interview with George B. Roberts, district representative, District No. 5, United Rubber, Cork, Linoleum and Plastic Workers of America, Dec. 13, 1948; Benjamin Stolberg, *The Story of the C.I.O.* (New York: Viking Press, 1938), p. 152.

[9] "Leaders of Four Los Angeles Unions of CIO Vote To Withdraw from Harry Bridges Council," *Commercial and Financial Chronicle*, CXLVII (Aug. 13, 1938), 976–977; *Industrial Unionist*, Aug. 12, Oct. 28, Nov. 4, 1938; *Citizen*, Nov. 4, 1938; *CIO News*, Aug. 27, 1938.

[10] *Times*, Sept. 17, 1937; Sept. 6, 1938; *Examiner*, Dec. 1, 1937.

[11] *Violations of Free Speech and Rights of Labor*, Hearings before a Subcommittee of the Senate Committee on Education and Labor, 76th Cong., 3d sess., S. Res. 266 (1940), Part 57, pp. 20989–20992; Part 64, pp. 23513–23514; *Times*, Oct. 7, 1937.

[12] "Paul Shoup Named President of 'Southern Californians,'" *Pacific Electric Magazine*, XVIII (June 10, 1938), 4; *Violations of Free Speech and Rights of Labor*, Part 57, pp. 20913, 21306; Part 65, pp. 23813, 23830; *Citizen*, Jan. 14, June 17, July 29, 1938; *Daily News*, March 1, 1938; *Evening Herald and Express*, March 25, 1938; *Hollywood Citizen-News*, July 23, 1938; *Times*, July 2, 1938.

[13] *Times*, Feb. 27, March 16, 1939.

[14] *Examiner*, Feb. 22, 1938; *Industrial Unionist*, Oct. 7, 1938.

[15] "Los Angeles Stays Open Shop," *Business Week*, March 6, 1937, p. 16.

[16] *Times*, Feb. 23, 24, 1937; *Citizen*, Feb. 26, March 5, 1937; Edward Levinson, *Labor on the March* (New York: Harper, 1938), p. 173.

[17] *Citizen*, March 5, 12, 1937; *Industrial Unionist*, July 7, 1939.

[18] *Times*, Feb. 28, March 3, 9, 12, 1937; *Citizen*, April 16, 1937.

[19] *Times*, Aug. 31, 1937.

[20] Los Angeles Industrial Union Council, *Minutes*, Oct. 18, 1937; *Citizen*, Dec. 31, 1937; *Examiner*, Dec. 21, 1937.

[21] *Times*, June 2, 1937; *Examiner*, April 21, 1938; *Daily News*, April 22, 1938.

[22] *Times*, April 24, May 3, 5, 11, 12, 1938. *Violations of Free Speech and Rights of Labor*, Part 66, pp. 24190–24191, points out that The Neutral Thousands actively assisted the Aircraft Workers Union in maintaining its existence.

[23] *Daily News*, May 11, 1938.

[24] *Evening Herald and Express*, Dec. 8, 1938; *Citizen*, Sept. 22, 1939; *Times*, Sept. 18, Dec. 5, 1939.

[25] "Los Angeles Stays Open Shop," p. 16; *Times*, March 7, 1937; *Citizen*, March 12, 1937.

[26] *Times*, Feb. 27, March 5, 6, 1937; *Citizen*, March 5, 1937.

[27] *Times*, Aug. 20, Sept. 8, 11, Oct. 18, 22, 1937; *Citizen*, Dec. 10, 1937; *Violations of Free Speech and Rights of Labor*, Part 57, p. 20973; Los Angeles Industrial Union Council, *Minutes*, Oct. 4, 1937.

[28] *Daily News*, Dec. 8, 1937; *Evening Herald and Express*, Feb. 10, 1938; *Evening News*, Feb. 24, 1938; *Industrial Unionist*, April 11, 1938.

[29] *Violations of Free Speech and Rights of Labor*, Part 52, pp. 19082–19084; Part 63, pp. 23176–23177; *Citizen*, Sept. 1, 1939.

[30] *Citizen*, Feb. 26, June 4, 1937; Jan. 7, Feb. 25, June 3, 1938; *Times*, July 21, 1938.

[31] *Citizen*, Jan. 29, 1937.

[32] *Ibid.*, Feb. 26, March 12, 1937; J. W. Buzzell, "An Open Shop Citadel Falls," *American Federationist*, XLVIII (April, 1941), 7.

[33] *Times*, Sept. 26, 1937; *Citizen*, May 21, July 23, 1937.

[34] *Times*, Sept. 25, 1937; May 15, 1938; *Citizen*, May 21, July 23, Oct. 15, Nov. 19, Dec. 10, 24, 1937; Jan. 7, April 1, May 13, 20, 1938. *Violations of Free Speech and Rights of Labor*, Part 63, pp. 23178–23185, describes the formation of the Contractors' Council of Southern California and the effort to influence the managements of firms in other cities to build their Los Angeles branches under open-shop working conditions.

[35] *Citizen*, March 26, June 25, 1937.

[36] *Times*, June 8, July 6, 23, 26, 1938; *People's World*, July 25, 1938.

[37] *Citizen*, Oct. 1, Dec. 17, 31, 1937; May 6, 1938; July 28, 1939; *Violations of Free Speech and Rights of Labor*, Part 52, pp. 19116–19119, 19368–19369; Part 57, p. 20996.

[38] *Citizen*, July 2, Nov. 5, 26, 1937; Jan. 21, 1938.

[39] *Times*, April 18, 1937; *Daily News*, Nov. 22, Dec. 1, 1937; *Examiner*, Dec. 16, 1937; Feb. 17, 1938; *Evening Herald and Express*, March 26, 1938.

[40] *Hollywood Citizen-News*, April 26, June 8, 1938; *Citizen*, April 15, 1938; *Times*, May 10, 11, 1938.

[41] *Hollywood Citizen-News*, June 8, 1938.

[42] *Times*, Sept. 29, Oct. 5, 1938; Jan. 11, April 11, 1939; *Evening News*, Oct. 5, 1938; *Examiner*, Dec. 6, 1938; *Evening Herald and Express*, Feb. 15, 1939.

[43] *Violations of Free Speech and Rights of Labor*, Part 56, pp. 20514–20519, describes the formation of Group A, its secret nature, officers, and purposes. Page 20774 discusses the growth of the organization, and pages 20778–20779 list the

names of the concerns that were parties to the agreement. Also see Part 56, pp. 20535–20541; Part 64, pp. 23411–23415.

[44] *Ibid.*, Part 56, pp. 20525–20527, 20791–20800; Part 63, pp. 23295–23302; *Times,* Sept. 8, Oct. 27, Dec. 3, 1937; *Citizen,* Aug. 13, Sept. 10, 1937.

[45] *Violations of Free Speech and Rights of Labor,* Part 56, pp. 20544–20575; Part 57, p. 20961; Part 58, p. 21456; Part 63, pp. 23190–23191; Part 64, pp. 23426–23430; Part 66, pp. 24194, 24297–24311; *Citizen,* March 4, April 15, 22, Aug. 26, 1938.

[46] *Times,* Sept. 24, 1936; Aug. 18, 20, 1937; *Citizen,* Jan. 22, July 23, Oct. 29, Nov. 19, 1937; *Violations of Free Speech and Rights of Labor,* Part 64, p. 23581.

[47] *Citizen,* April 8, 1938; *Evening Herald and Express,* Jan. 27, 1938.

[48] *Citizen,* April 8, 1938; *Times,* Feb. 12, 16, 1938; *Examiner,* Feb. 16, 26, 1938.

[49] *Industrial Unionist,* April 18, June 13, July 2, Sept. 30, Oct. 21, 1938; *Examiner,* July 28, 1938; *Citizen,* July 22, Oct. 7, 21, Dec. 2, 1938; *Times,* July 28, 1938.

[50] Los Angeles Industrial Union Council, *Minutes,* July 25, 1937; *Citizen,* May 28, 1937; *Industrial Unionist,* May 2, 1938.

[51] *Citizen,* Jan. 29, April 2, 9, 16, 1937.

[52] *Ibid.,* July 9, Oct. 8, 1937; *Times,* Dec. 15, 1937; *Evening Herald and Express,* Jan. 11, 1938; *Violations of Free Speech and Rights of Labor,* Part 57, pp. 20942, 20962, 20993, 21300–21305; Part 66, pp. 24197, 24325–24328.

[53] *Industrial Unionist,* Aug. 20, 1938; *Citizen,* Sept. 10, 1937.

[54] *Industrial Unionist,* April 27, 1938; *Labor Herald,* May 5, 1938; *Citizen,* Nov. 26, 1937.

[55] *Citizen,* Sept. 18, 1936; May 21, 1937; *Examiner,* May 14, 15, 1937; *Times,* Oct. 28, 1937; *Violations of Free Speech and Rights of Labor,* Part 66, pp. 24159–24165.

[56] *Evening Herald and Express,* July 26, 1937; *Times,* Aug. 26, 28, 31, 1937; *Citizen,* Nov. 5, 26, 1937; *Examiner,* Dec. 1, 1937; *Evening News,* Dec. 22, 1937.

[57] *Violations of Free Speech and Rights of Labor,* Part 53, pp. 19608–19609, describes the establishment of the hiring hall, and testimony on pages 19409–19412 shows why the members of the M and M decided on such action. Also see pages 19610–19612; *Times,* March 8, 1937; *Citizen,* March 12, 1937.

[58] *Times,* April 1, 1937; *Violations of Free Speech and Rights of Labor,* Part 53, pp. 19421–19423, 19613–19617. Pages 19662–19664 outline the circumstances of the strike and describe the union "beef squads" which followed the trucks of the Pacific Freight Lines and intimidated and beat nonunion employees. See pages 19426–19429 for the use of guards and undercover agents by the management, and pages 19656–19657 for the activities of the guards. Part of the financial support given to the trucking firm during the dispute apparently came from the M and M special truck fund (see p. 19418). Also see Part 63, pp. 23226–23243; Part 65, p. 23909.

[59] *Violations of Free Speech and Rights of Labor,* Part 58, pp. 21349, 21535, 21538–21542; *Citizen,* Aug. 27, 1937.

[60] *Times,* Jan. 27, 1938.

[61] *Ibid.,* Feb. 20, 1938; *Violations of Free Speech and Rights of Labor,* Part 58, pp. 21377–21378, 21395, 21397, 21408, 21548–21549, 21586–21589, 21610–21611; *Citizen,* Feb. 25, 1938.

[62] *Times,* Feb. 12, 19, 22, 1938.

[63] *Ibid.,* Aug. 20, 23, Sept. 8, 1938; *Violations of Free Speech and Rights of Labor,* Part 58, pp. 21405–21406, 21608–21609.

[64] *Times,* July 29, 1938; *Citizen,* Aug. 5, 1938; *Violations of Free Speech and Rights of Labor,* Part 58, pp. 21613–21622.

[65] *Violations of Free Speech and Rights of Labor,* Part 58, pp. 21370–21371, 21439, 21555–21557, 21565. Pages 21634–21635 present the articles of incorporation of the Farmers' Transportation Association, and page 21644 outlines the purposes of the new organization. Also see "Fight Trucking Situation," *Business Week,* Jan. 8, 1938, pp. 35–36; *Times,* Jan. 21, March 1, Dec. 31, 1938.

⁶⁶ *Citizen,* April 9, July 2, Sept. 3, 1937; Feb. 25, Nov. 25, Dec. 16, 1938.

⁶⁷ *Violations of Free Speech and Rights of Labor,* Part 63, pp. 23036–23037; *Proceedings of the American Federation of Labor, 1937,* p. 519.

⁶⁸ *Times,* Oct. 3, 1937; *Evening Herald and Express,* April 13, 1938.

⁶⁹ *Citizen,* Nov. 25, Dec. 16, 1938.

⁷⁰ *Examiner,* Dec. 18, 1937; *Labor Herald,* Feb. 10, 1938; *Citizen,* Feb. 25, 1938.

⁷¹ *Hollywood Citizen-News,* March 31, 1938; *Evening News,* April 6, 1938; *Industrial Unionist,* April 11, May 9, Aug. 26, Nov. 25, 1938; *Citizen,* Feb. 18, April 1, 1938; *Times,* Feb. 17, 1938.

⁷² *Examiner,* Dec. 16, 1937.

⁷³ *Citizen,* July 23, Oct. 22, 1937; *Times,* Nov. 28, 30, Dec. 5, 1937. Editorials and articles on Seattle under Dave Beck's rule regularly appeared in the *Times* in October, November, and December, 1937.

⁷⁴ *Evening Herald and Express,* Dec. 1, 1937.

⁷⁵ *Daily News,* Dec. 9, 1937.

⁷⁶ *Ibid.,* Dec. 7, 1937; *Examiner,* Dec. 14, 1937.

⁷⁷ *Evening News,* Dec. 3, 4, 1937; *Times,* Dec. 5, 9, 13, 14, 1937; Jan. 7, 1938; *Evening Herald and Express,* Dec. 11, 1937; "Union Climax in L.A.," *Business Week,* Jan. 29, 1938, p. 35.

⁷⁸ *Hollywood Citizen-News,* April 23, 1938; *Times,* Dec. 5, 1937; *Examiner,* Dec. 9, 16, 1937; *Citizen,* Dec. 24, 1937; *Daily News,* Dec. 9, 1937; *Evening Herald and Express,* Dec. 14, 1937; *Violations of Free Speech and Rights of Labor,* Part 65, p. 23722.

⁷⁹ *Examiner,* Dec. 5, 1937; *Times,* Dec. 14, 29, 1937; April 15, 1938; *Evening News,* Dec. 29, 1937; *San Francisco News,* March 15, 1938; *Evening Herald and Express,* July 30, 1938; *Violations of Free Speech and Rights of Labor,* Part 52, p. 19155.

⁸⁰ *Evening Herald and Express,* Jan. 4, 1938; *Examiner,* April 19, 1938; *Hollywood Citizen-News,* April 21, 1938; *Violations of Free Speech and Rights of Labor,* Part 58, pp. 21650–21654; *Times,* May 3, 5, 1938.

⁸¹ *Citizen,* April 29, 1938; *People's World,* April 20, May 2, 1938.

⁸² *Citizen,* July 15, 1938; *Evening Herald and Express,* Oct. 12, 1938; *Evening News,* Oct. 14, 1938; *Times,* Nov. 29, 1938; *Violations of Free Speech and Rights of Labor,* Part 58, pp. 21446–21447, 21451–21452, 21655–21660.

⁸³ *Examiner,* Aug. 11, 1938; *Times,* March 26, 1938.

⁸⁴ *Citizen,* April 1, June 17, 1938.

⁸⁵ "Collective Bargaining by the American Newspaper Guild," *Monthly Labor Review,* L (April, 1940), 825–826; *Citizen,* May 18, 1934; Dec. 18, 1936; Sept. 3, Oct. 8, 1937; *Labor Herald,* Sept. 1, Oct. 6, 1937; Los Angeles Industrial Union Council, *Minutes,* Sept. 27, Nov. 8, 29, 1937.

⁸⁶ *Hollywood Citizen-News,* May 17, 1938.

⁸⁷ *Ibid.; Citizen,* May 27, June 17, 1938.

⁸⁸ *Citizen,* June 10, 1938; *Industrial Unionist,* May 30, June 6, 1938; *People's World,* June 6, 1938.

⁸⁹ *Times,* June 8, July 2, 1938; *Evening News,* June 30, July 30, 1938; *Industrial Unionist,* July 1, 15, Sept. 30, 1938; *Hollywood Citizen-News Striker,* July 23, 1938; *Citizen,* July 29, 1938.

⁹⁰ *Times,* July 12, 1938; *Industrial Unionist,* July 15, Oct. 7, 1938; *Violations of Free Speech and Rights of Labor,* Part 57, pp. 21154–21156; Part 66, pp. 23214–23215.

⁹¹ *Examiner,* July 31, 1938; *Times,* July 31, 1938; *Industrial Unionist,* Aug. 20, 1938.

⁹² *Citizen,* June 18, July 9, 23, Nov. 19, 1937; *Times,* Aug. 19, Nov. 16, 1937.

⁹³ *Evening Herald and Express,* March 3, 1938; *Citizen,* Dec. 9, 1938.

⁹⁴ *Citizen,* Oct. 28, 1938; *Examiner,* May 8, 1938; *Times,* Aug. 31, 1938.

⁹⁵ *Citizen,* Feb. 5, 12, March 26, July 23, Nov. 5, 1937.

⁹⁶ *Ibid.*, Sept. 2, Dec. 23, 1938; *Violations of Free Speech and Rights of Labor,* Part 66, pp. 24442–24444.

⁹⁷ *Citizen,* July 23, 1937.

⁹⁸ *Ibid.*, April 2, 9, 30, May 7, 16, June 25, 1937.

⁹⁹ *Ibid.*, June 4, Sept. 24, Oct. 29, 1937.

¹⁰⁰ *Ibid.*, Sept. 3, Oct. 1, 1937; *Times,* Dec. 6, 1937; *Violations of Free Speech and Rights of Labor,* Part 64, pp. 23383–23384.

¹⁰¹ *Examiner,* Feb. 4, April 17, 1938; *Hollywood Citizen-News,* April 16, 18, 1938; *Citizen,* May 20, June 17, 1938.

¹⁰² *Violations of Free Speech and Rights of Labor,* Part 57, pp. 21234, 21240, 21244; Part 66, pp. 24354–24360; *Times,* Sept. 3, 1938; *Citizen,* Dec. 16, 1938.

¹⁰³ *Violations of Free Speech and Rights of Labor,* Part 56, pp. 20421–20423; *Labor Herald,* Sept. 15, 1937; *Times,* March 14, Sept. 11, 1937; *Industrial Unionist,* April 25, June 6, 1938.

¹⁰⁴ *Times,* May 27, 1934; June 27, 1938; *Industrial Unionist,* June 24, 1938; *Citizen,* March 19, 26, 1937.

¹⁰⁵ *Violations of Free Speech and Rights of Labor,* Part 57, pp. 21000–21008, describes the acts of violence in detail. See also Part 65, p. 23723; *Citizen,* Aug. 5, 1938.

¹⁰⁶ *Evening Herald and Express,* July 14, Nov. 23, 1938; *Citizen,* Aug. 5, 1938; *Industrial Unionist,* July 22, Oct. 14, 1938; Jan. 13, 1939; *Violations of Free Speech and Rights of Labor,* Part 57, pp. 21009–21016; Part 58, p. 21495.

¹⁰⁷ *Times,* Jan. 4, 1938; *Evening Herald and Express,* Jan. 7, 1938; *Industrial Unionist,* Aug. 5, Dec. 23, 1938.

¹⁰⁸ *Industrial Unionist,* May 23, 1936; Dec. 3, 1937.

¹⁰⁹ *Ibid.*, April 18, 1938; *Times,* March 8, 1938; *Evening Herald and Express,* April 18, 1938.

¹¹⁰ *Times,* April 22, 1938; *Hollywood Citizen-News,* April 22, 1938.

¹¹¹ *Industrial Unionist,* May 23, June 13, 1938; *Evening News,* June 7, 1938; *Times,* Aug. 23, 1938; *Citizen,* Aug. 26, 1938.

¹¹² *Industrial Unionist,* Dec. 9, 23, 1938; *Times,* Dec. 9, 1939; *Labor Herald,* Dec. 14, 1939.

¹¹³ *Evening News,* April 7, 1938; *Times,* April 30, 1938; *Citizen,* March 19, 1937.

¹¹⁴ *Citizen,* June 25, 1937.

¹¹⁵ *Ibid.*, Dec. 24, 1937; *Times,* Dec. 10, 1937.

¹¹⁶ *Citizen,* June 17, 1938; *Industrial Unionist,* July 15, 1938.

¹¹⁷ *Examiner,* June 14, 28, Aug. 31, 1938; *Times,* June 29, 1938.

¹¹⁸ *Citizen,* May 6, June 17, Dec. 16, 1938.

XIV. THE BEGINNING OF THE END
OF THE OPEN SHOP

¹ Gordon S. Watkins and Paul A. Dodd, *Labor Problems* (3d ed.; New York: Crowell, 1940), p. 887; "Government Reorganization Act," *Monthly Labor Review,* XLIX (Aug., 1939), 378; "Four Hundred Thousand Back at Work," *American Federationist,* XLVI (July, 1939), 752–753; "Industrial Employment Rises Further," *American Federationist,* XLVI (Jan., 1939), 82–85.

² *Industrial Unionist,* Feb. 3, 1939; *Times,* Oct. 5, 10, Dec. 25, 1939.

³ *Times,* June 10, Nov. 21, 1939; *Citizen,* Feb. 3, March 17, 24, July 14, Nov. 24, 1939; *Industrial Unionist,* April 7, May 19, 1939.

⁴ See, for example, the resolution passed at the Labor Council meeting of May 15, 1936, as published in the *Citizen* on May 22. Also see *Industrial Unionist,* Jan. 13, 1939; *Citizen,* Jan. 20, 1939.

⁵ *Industrial Unionist,* Jan. 20, 1939; *Citizen,* Jan. 20, 1939; *Times,* Oct. 17, 1939.

[6] "$30 Thursday Fight," *Business Week*, July 15, 1939, p. 18; " '$30 Thursday' Vim," *Business Week*, Aug. 19, 1939, pp. 21–22.

[7] "Ham and Eggs Sizzling," *Business Week*, Sept. 16, 1939, p. 36; Carey McWilliams, "Ham and Eggs," *New Republic*, C (Oct. 25, 1939), 332; *Industrial Unionist*, July 7, 1939; *Citizen*, Sept. 15, 22, Nov. 10, 1939; *Times*, Sept. 20, Dec. 28, 1939; *Labor Herald*, Nov. 16, 1939.

[8] "Recommendations of California Commission on Reemployment," *Monthly Labor Review*, L (Feb., 1940), 329; *Times*, Dec. 28, 1939.

[9] *Citizen*, June 23, 1939; *Times*, Sept. 26, 30, 1939.

[10] *Labor Herald*, Oct. 5, 1939; *Industrial Unionist*, Feb. 10, May 12, Aug. 25, 1939; *Times*, Feb. 4, 1939; *Third Annual Yearbook* (Los Angeles: Los Angeles Industrial Union Council, 1939), p. 5.

[11] *Times*, Jan. 24, July 21, 1939; *Industrial Unionist*, July 21, 1939; *Hollywood Citizen-News*, Jan. 23, 1939.

[12] *Times*, Feb. 28, July 15, Sept. 13, 1939; *Industrial Unionist*, March 3, 1939; *Citizen*, March 3, 10, 1939.

[13] *Times*, July 16, 1939; New York *Times*, Dec. 13, 1939.

[14] *Violations of Free Speech and Rights of Labor*, Hearings before a Subcommittee of the Senate Committee on Education and Labor, 76th Cong., 3d sess., S. Res. 266 (1940), Part 64, p. 23441; *Citizen*, July 14, Aug. 4, 1939.

[15] *Industrial Unionist*, June 30, 1939; *Citizen*, March 3, 17, July 14, Aug. 1, Dec. 1, 29, 1939.

[16] *Industrial Unionist*, June 23, July 28, Sept. 1, 1939; *Third Annual Yearbook*, p. 5.

[17] *Violations of Free Speech and Rights of Labor*, Part 64, p. 23508; *Industrial Unionist*, May 5, 1939; *Citizen*, May 5, Dec. 15, 1939; "Proposition No. 1 on the December 12th Ballot," *Pacific Electric Magazine*, XX (Nov. 10, 1939), 18–19.

[18] *Industrial Unionist*, Feb. 24, March 17, May 5, 1939; *Citizen*, April 28, May 5, 26, June 9, 23, 30, July 7, 14, 21, 1939; "Los Angeles Open Shop Fight," *Business Week*, June 24, 1939, p. 28; *Violations of Free Speech and Rights of Labor*, Part 65, p. 23940.

[19] "Clip Anti-Picket Law," *Business Week*, July 29, 1939, p. 13; *Industrial Unionist*, July 21, 1939; *Times*, July 19, 1939; *Citizen*, July 21, 1939.

[20] *Times*, July 20, 1939; *Citizen*, July 28, Aug. 11, 1939; *Violations of Free Speech and Rights of Labor*, Part 56, pp. 20761–20762; Part 57, pp. 20869, 10943–20944; J. W. Buzzell, "An Open Shop Citadel Falls," *American Federationist*, XLVIII (April, 1941), 30.

[21] *Citizen*, Jan. 6, March 17, July 28, 1936; *Our Declaration of Principles in Action* (Los Angeles: Merchants' and Manufacturers' Association, 1947), pp. 2, 3, 5, 6; *The Carpenter*, L (Feb., 1940), 7–8.

[22] *Violations of Free Speech and Rights of Labor*, Part 57, pp. 21309–21311, 21315–21317; Part 65, pp. 23848–23849; *Citizen*, Jan. 13, 1939.

[23] *Violations of Free Speech and Rights of Labor*, Part 57, pp. 20918, 21319–21320; Part 63, pp. 23084, 23086–23091, 23291–23292; Part 65, pp. 23854–23875; "New Open Shop Front," *Business Week*, June 1, 1940, pp. 38–39.

[24] *Violations of Free Speech and Rights of Labor*, Part 56, pp. 20428, 20709; Part 57, pp. 20978–20980; Part 65, pp. 23855, 23866; Part 66, pp. 24428–24429. In Part 66, pp. 24429–24440, the activities of the Employees Advisory Service are described. A full account of the system used to replace independent organizations by secret societies, clubs, and social associations is presented on pages 24403–24410. Also see *Times*, Nov. 10, 1939; *Citizen*, Nov. 3, 1939.

[25] "Business Goes After the Consumer Movement," *Consumers Union Reports*, Dec., 1939, pp. 16C–16D; "Women's Bombshell," *Business Week*, Oct. 7, 1939, p. 36; *Citizen*, Sept. 29, 1939.

[26] "Strikes in 1939," *Monthly Labor Review*, L (May, 1940), 1094; *Violations of*

Free Speech and Rights of Labor, Part 58, pp. 21693, 21699–21700; *Times,* June 4, 1939.

[27] *Industrial Unionist,* April 7, May 5, 12, 26, July 14, 21, 28, Aug. 16, 18, Sept. 8, 1939; *Times,* Nov. 25, 1939; Arthur P. Allen and Betty V. H. Schneider, *Industrial Relations in the California Aircraft Industry* (Berkeley: Institute of Industrial Relations, University of California, 1956), p. 16.

[28] "C.I.O. After Building," *Business Week,* July 29, 1939, p. 28; *Citizen,* July 14, 1939; *Times,* Dec. 29, 1939.

[29] *Industrial Unionist,* March 31, Aug. 18, 1939; *Citizen,* July 28, Sept. 29, 1939.

[30] *Citizen,* April 7, Nov. 17, 24, Dec. 1, 22, 1939; *Labor Herald,* Dec. 14, 1939. A more fundamental reason for the expulsion of Mrs. Simmons from the council lay in personal differences between her and Secretary Buzzell regarding his policies in supervising the council's work.

[31] *Times,* Jan. 1, 7, April 22, 1939; *Industrial Unionist,* Jan. 6, April 28, 1939.

[32] *Violations of Free Speech and Rights of Labor,* Part 58, pp. 21440, 21623–21631; *Citizen,* July 28, Nov. 17, 1939; *Times,* Sept. 20, Nov. 15, 1939; "From the Atlantic to the Pacific," *American Federationist,* XLVI (March, 1939), 309.

[33] *Industrial Unionist,* Dec. 23, 1938; Aug. 4, 1939; *Times,* Dec. 27, 1938.

[34] *Industrial Unionist,* Feb. 10, 1939.

[35] *Ibid.,* June 30, July 14, 1939; *Times,* June 23, July 11, 12, Oct. 9, 10, 1939; *Examiner,* June 23, 1939; *Violations of Free Speech and Rights of Labor,* Part 57, pp. 21020–21053.

[36] *Industrial Unionist,* June 2, 16, 1939.

[37] *Times,* Nov. 12, 1939; *Citizen,* Aug. 11, Oct. 13, 1939.

[38] *Times,* April 28, Oct. 8, 1939; *Steel Labor,* Sept. 29, 1939; Jan. 26, 1940.

[39] *Citizen,* March 24, May 26, July 14, Aug. 11, 18, Sept. 1, 8, 22, 29, Oct. 6, 27, Nov. 10, 24, Dec. 22, 1939; "Labor Highlights," *American Federationist,* XLVII (Aug., 1940), unpaged.

[40] *Violations of Free Speech and Rights of Labor,* Part 52, pp. 19368–19369; Part 57, pp. 20996, 21133–21136, 21138–21147; Part 65, pp. 23921–23922; *Citizen,* March 3, 31, July 28, Aug. 25, Oct. 13, 1939; *Times,* April 8, May 13, 1939.

[41] *Violations of Free Speech and Rights of Labor,* Part 65, p. 23920; Part 57, pp. 21137–21138; *Citizen,* June 9, 16, 1939; *Examiner,* June 17, 1939; *Times,* June 21, 1939.

[42] *Times,* June 22, 24, July 15, 18, 26–28, 1939; *Industrial Unionist,* June 23, 1939; *Violations of Free Speech and Rights of Labor,* Part 57, p. 21137; Part 63, pp. 23197–23201; *Citizen,* July 28, Aug. 4, 1939; "From the Atlantic to the Pacific," *American Federationist,* XLVI (Nov., 1939), 1247.

[43] *Industrial Unionist,* Jan. 20, March 24, May 12, 19, June 16, 23, 30, July 28, Aug. 4, 11, 1939; *Times,* June 17, 20, 1939; *Daily News,* June 19, 1939; *Examiner,* June 20, 1939.

[44] *Violations of Free Speech and Rights of Labor,* Part 58, p. 21402; Part 64, pp. 23389–23394, 23442.

[45] *Ibid.,* Part 57, pp. 20995, 21149–21152; Part 58, pp. 21598–21600; Part 66, p. 24067; *Times,* Jan. 20, June 8, Sept. 30, Oct. 3, Dec. 20, 1939; *Citizen,* Feb. 3, July 14, Sept. 1, 22, Oct. 20, Nov. 17, 1939; *Examiner,* Jan. 12, 1939; *Industrial Unionist,* April 14, 1939.

[46] *Citizen,* June 16, Dec. 22, 1939; *Times,* June 9, 13, Aug. 1, Dec. 30, 1939.

[47] Rose Pesotta, *Bread upon the Waters* (New York: Dodd, Mead, 1944), pp. 348–349; *People's World,* June 23, 1939; *Industrial Unionist,* June 30, July 28, 1939; *Times,* July 6, 1939.

[48] *Times,* March 31, April 7, 1939; *Daily News,* April 7, 1939.

[49] *Times,* April 12, 13, 22, 26, Sept. 30, Nov. 7, 1939; *Industrial Unionist,* April 14,

May 26, 1939. The office of the Clerk of the Superior Court, Criminal Division, supplied information on the final disposition of the case, no. 76249.

[50] Walter Galenson, *Rival Unionism in the United States* (New York: American Council on Public Affairs, 1940), p. 15; *Industrial Unionist*, July 7, 14, 21, 28, Aug. 11, 18, 25, Dec. 29, 1939.

[51] *Industrial Unionist*, Feb. 17, 24, March 3, 17, 24, 31, June 30, July 7, 21, 1939; *Citizen*, Jan. 20, Sept. 1, Oct. 6, 1939; *Evening News*, March 28, 1939; *Times*, March 15, 22, April 11, 1939; *Violations of Free Speech and Rights of Labor*, Part 52, pp. 19145–19147.

[52] *Evening Herald and Express*, March 8, 1939; San Francisco *News*, March 9, 1939; *Citizen*, July 28, Dec. 22, 1939.

[53] *Industrial Unionist*, April 14, 1939; *People's World*, June 5, 1939; Walter Wentz, "History of the Los Angeles Newspaper Guild" (unpublished M.A. thesis, Claremont College, Claremont, Calif., 1958), pp. 83–86, 106.

[54] *Industrial Unionist*, Aug. 4, 1939.

[55] Wentz, *op. cit.*, pp. 115–117; *Times*, Sept. 12, Oct. 26, 1939; New York *Times*, Oct. 26, 27, 1939; *Citizen*, Oct. 6, 27, Nov. 17, 24, Dec. 8, 15, 1939.

[56] *Industrial Unionist*, June 23, Aug. 25, 1939; *Citizen*, Aug. 25, Oct. 6, Dec. 1, 1939; *Times*, Oct. 3, Nov. 23, 1939.

[57] *Industrial Unionist*, Jan. 6, Feb. 10, 1939; *Evening Herald and Express*, March 24, 1939; *Times*, Dec. 10, 1938; Feb. 16, 1939; *Examiner*, Feb. 17, 1939.

[58] *Violations of Free Speech and Rights of Labor*, Part 57, pp. 21053–21101; *Industrial Unionist*, Feb. 17, 1939; *Labor Herald*, Feb. 23, 1939; *Citizen*, March 10, May 12, 1939.

[59] *Citizen*, June 16, 1939; *Times*, May 19, 25, July 1, Aug. 21, 30, Oct. 1, Nov. 17, 1939; *Industrial Unionist*, May 19, 26, June 9, 1939; *Labor Herald*, May 25, Oct. 5, 1939; *Violations of Free Speech and Rights of Labor*, Part 57, pp. 21055–21065.

[60] *Citizen*, Jan. 20, May 26, Nov. 24, 1939; "From the Atlantic to the Pacific," *American Federationist*, XLVI (May, 1939), 534; XLVI (July, 1939), 759.

[61] *Citizen*, Dec. 2, 1938; Jan. 20, Feb. 3, April 21, Nov. 17, 1939.

[62] *Ibid.*, March 3, 31, July 21, Oct. 27, 1939; *Violations of Free Speech and Rights of Labor*, Part 66, p. 24361.

[63] *Evening Herald and Express*, Jan. 30, 1939; *Times*, Jan. 31, Feb. 19, 1939; *CIO News*, Feb. 20, 1939; *Evening News*, Feb. 20, 1939.

[64] *Citizen*, July 14, 1939.

[65] *Industrial Unionist*, July 21, 1939.

XV. TIME RUNS OUT FOR THE OPEN SHOP

[1] *Industrial Unionist*, July 21, 1939.

[2] Grace Heilman Stimson, *Rise of the Labor Movement in Los Angeles* (Berkeley and Los Angeles: University of California Press, 1955), pp. 104 ff.; J. W. Buzzell, "An Open Shop Citadel Falls," *American Federationist*, XLVIII (April, 1941), 6, 7, 30, 31.

[3] "Organized Labor Movement, 1929 to 1937," *Monthly Labor Review*, XLIV (Jan., 1937), 1; Paul H. Douglas, "American Labor Relations Acts," *American Economic Review*, XXVII (Dec., 1937), 736; California Department of Industrial Relations, *Digest of "Union Labor in California, June 1939,"* p. 1; *Citizen*, March 12, 1937; July 14, 1939.

[4] California Department of Industrial Relations, *Labor in California, Biennial Statistical Report to the Legislature, 1939–1940*, p. 15; Carey McWilliams, *Factories in the Field* (Boston: Little, Brown, 1939), p. 267.

[5] Philip Neff, Lisette C. Baum, and Grace E. Heilman, *Favored Industries in Los Angeles* (Los Angeles: Haynes Foundation, 1948), pp. 4, 6; Philip Neff and Annette Weifenbach, *Business Cycles in Los Angeles* (Los Angeles: Haynes Foundation, 1949), p. 4.

[6] Frank L. Kidner and Philip Neff, *Los Angeles: The Economic Outlook* (Los Angeles: Haynes Foundation, 1946), pp. 2, 3; Neff, Baum, and Heilman, *op. cit.*, p. 7; Neff and Weifenbach, *op. cit.*, pp. 4, 6.

[7] Kidner and Neff, *op. cit.*, pp. 2, 3, 4.

[8] *Ibid.;* Neff and Weifenbach, *op. cit.*, p. 6; Margaret S. Gordon, *Employment Expansion and Population Growth: The California Experience, 1900–1950* (Berkeley and Los Angeles: University of California Press, 1954), pp. 105–106.

[9] Kidner and Neff, *op. cit.*, p. 9.

[10] *Ibid.*, pp. 3, 7, 8; Neff and Weifenbach, *op. cit.*, pp. 8, 9; Gordon, *op. cit.*, p. 1.

[11] California Department of Industrial Relations, *Labor in California, 1941–1942,* p. 2.

[12] *Violations of Free Speech and Rights of Labor,* Hearings before a Subcommittee of the Senate Committee on Education and Labor, 74th Cong., 3d sess., S. Res. 266 (1940), Part 58, p. 21571.

[13] Frank C. Pierson, *Community Wage Patterns* (Berkeley and Los Angeles: University of California Press, 1953), pp. 25, 26; Nedra Bartlett Belloc, *Wages in California* (Berkeley and Los Angeles: University of California Press, 1948), pp. 20, 21, 77.

[14] Pierson, *op. cit.*, pp. 25, 26; Belloc, *op. cit.*, pp. 20, 77.

[15] This is Pierson's contention, and it seems to have considerable validity.

[16] Pierson, *op. cit.*, pp. 19, 25, 26.

[17] Kidner and Neff, *op. cit.*, pp. 10, 11; Neff, Baum, and Heilman, *op. cit.*, pp. 7, 25; Belloc, *op. cit.*, pp. 3, 4.

[18] "Industry Takes a Tip from Greeley," *Business Week,* May 23, 1936, pp. 26–29; "Big Labor Drive in Los Angeles," *Business Week,* April 10, 1937, pp. 39–42.

[19] Kidner and Neff, *op. cit.*, p. 6; Neff and Weifenbach, *op. cit.*, pp. 18–19, 23, 24; Buzzell, *op. cit.*, pp. 6, 7.

[20] "Arbitration by Law," *Newsweek,* XV (Feb. 19, 1940), 50–52; "Los Angeles Open Shop Fight," *Business Week,* June 24, 1939, pp. 28–29.

[21] "L.A.'s Last Stand," *Business Week,* Jan. 18, 1941, pp. 48, 49; "Coast Farmers Map War on Unions," *Business Week,* Dec. 2, 1939, pp. 29–30.

[22] Pierson, *op. cit.*, pp. 136–138; Kidner and Neff, *op. cit.*, p. 5; California Department of Industrial Relations, *Union Labor in California, 1941,* pp. 8–9; *Digest of "Union Labor in California, June 1939,"* p. 2.

[23] Interview with Charles B. Hamner, Labor Relations Department, Los Angeles Central Labor Council, Oct. 26, 1948; interview with George B. Roberts, district representative, United Rubber, Cork, Linoleum and Plastic Workers of America, Oct. 16, 1948; "L.A.'s Last Stand," pp. 48, 50, 51; Buzzell, *op. cit.*, pp. 6, 31.

[24] Kidner and Neff, *op. cit.*, pp. 4, 5.

[25] Herbert Harris, *American Labor* (New Haven: Yale University Press, 1938), p. v.

BIBLIOGRAPHY

BIBLIOGRAPHY

MANUSCRIPTS

Lewis, Edwin L. *Historical Data Concerning Street Railway Transportation in Los Angeles Since First Franchise Applied for July 2, 1883.* Huntington Library, San Marino, California.

Los Angeles Central Labor Council. *Minutes.* July 7, 1911–December 22, 1941.

———. *Report of the Organizing Committee.* Correspondence file, February 27–March 4, 1914.

Los Angeles Industrial Union Council. *Minutes.* July 19–December 27, 1937.

Railroad Union Labor, 1937. Huntington Library, San Marino, California.

Sheppard, James C. *Collection of Newspaper Clippings from California Newspapers on Ham and Eggs Old Age Pension, Labor Union Activities, Etc.* 12 vols. Huntington Library, San Marino, California.

LABOR AND REFORM NEWSPAPERS AND PERIODICALS

American Federationist, 1912–1940. Published by the American Federation of Labor.

The Carpenter, 1936–1941. Published by the Brotherhood of Carpenters and Joiners.

The CIO News, January 29, 1938–February 20, 1939. Incomplete file. Published by the Congress of Industrial Organizations.

The Citizen, January 20, 1911–December 26, 1941. Published by the Los Angeles Central Labor Council.

Coast Seamen's Journal, San Francisco, December, 1910; June, 1916; *Seamen's Journal,* April, 1918–December, 1937.

Hollywood Citizen-News Striker, June 22, July 28, 1938. Published by the Los Angeles Newspaper Guild.

Industrial Unionist, May 23, 1936–December 30, 1939. Incomplete file. Published by the Los Angeles Industrial Union Council.

Labor Clarion, San Francisco, February 2, 1912.

Labor Herald, Oakland, June 8, 1937–December 21, 1939. Incomplete file.

Labor's Non-Partisan League National Bulletin, February 2, May 2, 1940.

Organizer, Los Angeles, October 21, December 3, 1936. Published by Local 188 of the Western Mechanics Industrial Union.

People's World, January 24, 1938–December 29, 1939. Incomplete file.

Plane Facts, Los Angeles, February 2, November 10, December 4, 1936. Published by the Northrop Committee of the Western Mechanics Industrial Union.

Screen Actor, Los Angeles, January, 1938–May, 1940. Incomplete file. Published by the Screen Actors Guild.

Southern California Labor Press, Los Angeles, February 29, 1924–January 27, 1928.

Steel Labor, Indianapolis, September 29, 1939. Published by the Steel Workers Organizing Committee.

Union Bulletin, Los Angeles, September 15, 1936. Published by the Optical Technicians and Workers Union No. 18521.

Union News Service, September 7, 1936–August 12, 1938. Incomplete file.
Published by the Committee for Industrial Organization.
Voice of the Federation, San Francisco, June 14, 1935–August 2, 1941. Pub-
lished by the Maritime Federation of the Pacific.
Western Worker, Los Angeles, September 20, December 9, 20, 1937.

OTHER NEWSPAPERS AND PERIODICALS

American Labor Legislation Review, December, 1915; September, 1921;
December, 1927; December, 1929; December, 1931; December, 1933.
Business Week, August 6, 1933–February 1, 1941.
California Citrograph, September, 1938.
Claremont *Courier,* October 28, 1938.
Commercial and Financial Chronicle, February 6, 1937; June 25, August 13,
1938.
Hollywood Citizen-News, December 6, 1937; March 1–December 21, 1938;
January 23, 1939.
Hynes Journal, October 27, 1938.
Illustrated Daily News, March 16, 1935; November 22, 1937–December 7, 1939.
Indio *News,* October 28, 1938.
Literary Digest, June 1, 1912; March 1, 1919; November 27, 1920; July 29,
1922; January 13, June 2, 1923; October 24, 1925; December 25, 1926;
August 3, 10, 1929; January 11, February 15, 1936; May 15, 1937.
Los Angeles *Downtown Shopping News,* December 4, 8, 1937; September 14,
1938.
Los Angeles *Evening Herald,* September 6, 1919.
Los Angeles *Evening Herald and Express,* January 27, 1932; March 14, 22, 25,
1935; July 26, October 29, November 13, December 1–18, 21–29, 31, 1937;
January 3–October 12, November 3, 10, 23, December 7–9, 1938; January
30–February 2, 8, 10, 11, 15, 16, March 8, 24, November 18, December 6,
1939.
Los Angeles *Evening News,* February 2, 1936–March 31, 1940.
Los Angeles *Examiner,* June 8, 1919; June 22, 1920; May 14, 1937–December
22, 1938; January 4, 12, 24, 26, 31, February 1, 21, March 2, April 8, June
18, 20, 27–29, July 25, October 18, 1939.
Los Angeles *Herald,* February 11, April 10, 25, 26, 30, May 1, 1903.
Los Angeles *Morning Tribune,* June 1, 1918.
Los Angeles *News,* December 1, 1937–December 23, 1938; January 11, 13,
February 20, March 28, 1939.
Los Angeles *Record,* October 20, 1907–November 1, 1933; *Post-Record,* No-
vember 2, 1933–April 2, 1934; *Evening Post-Record,* May 1, 1934–February
1, 1936.
Los Angeles *Times,* June 1, 1911–December 31, 1941.
Newsweek, July 14, 1934; January 26, 1935; October 10, 24, November 7, 28,
1936; June 13, July 4, 1938; February 19, 1940.
New York *Times,* January 16, November 17, December 1, 1938; October 26,
27, December 13, 1939.
Oakland *Post-Enquirer,* September 2, 1938.
Pacific Coast Maritime Report, March 6, 21, 1947.

Pacific Electric Magazine, April 10, 1937; June 10, 1938; October 10, November 10, 1939.

Riverside *Daily Press,* April 28, 1938.

Sacramento *Bee,* April 7, 18, 1939.

San Bernardino *Daily Sun,* October 30, 1938.

San Clemente *Sun,* November 4, 1938.

San Diego *Union,* October 31, 1938.

San Francisco *Chronicle,* March 16, August 25, September 3, 28, November 14, 1938; January 5, 1939.

San Francisco *News,* March 15, July 8, September 5, 20, October 5, 1938; March 9, 1939.

Santa Ana *Register,* October 31, 1938.

Santa Monica *Evening Outlook,* October 31, 1938.

Southern California Business, "Employment," April–December, 1933; January–March, 1934.

Time, May 17, September 20, 1937.

Two Bells (publication of Los Angeles Railway employees' group), November, 1936; April, 1937.

OFFICIAL PUBLICATIONS OF THE STATE OF CALIFORNIA

Bureau of Labor Statistics. *Fifteenth Biennial Report, 1911–1912* through *Twenty-third Biennial Report, 1927–1928.* Sacramento, 1912–1929.

Department of Industrial Relations.

First Biennial Report, 1927–1930. Sacramento, 1931.

Second Biennial Report, 1930–1932. Sacramento, 1933.

Report, 1933–1937. Sacramento, 1938.

Annual Report, June 30, 1938–July 1, 1939. Sacramento, 1939.

Biennial Report, 1939–1940. Sacramento, 1940.

The California Labor Market Bulletin, August 21, 1939.

The Cost of Living in California, 1914–22 and 1939–41. Sacramento, 1941.

Digest of "Union Labor in California, June 1939." Sacramento, 1940.

Labor in California, Biennial Statistical Report to the Legislature, 1939–1940. San Francisco, 1941.

Labor in California, 1941–1942. San Francisco, 1943.

Labor in California, 1943–1944. San Francisco, 1945.

Union Labor in California, 1941. San Francisco, 1942.

Union Scales of Wages and Hours of Labor, 1929 and 1930. Sacramento, 1931.

Emergency Relief Administration. *Economic Trends in California, 1929–1934.* Sacramento, 1935.

Governor's Commission on Reemployment. *Reemployment.* Sacramento, 1939.

State Relief Administration. *Handbook of Consumers Cooperatives in California.* San Francisco, 1935.

———. *Transients in California.* Sacramento, 1936.

State Unemployment Commission. *Report and Recommendations of the California State Unemployment Commission . . . November, 1932.* Sacramento, 1933.

OFFICIAL PUBLICATIONS OF THE UNITED STATES GOVERNMENT

Bureau of Labor Statistics.
Labor Information Bulletin, September, 1934–November, 1938.
Monthly Labor Review, July, 1915–December, 1959.
Southern California Aircraft Workers in Wartime. Washington, 1946. 17 pp.
Strikes in the United States, 1880–1936, by Florence Peterson. Bull. no. 651.
   Washington, 1937.
Commission on Industrial Relations.
Final Report. Washington, 1915. 448 pp.
*The National Erectors' Association and the International Association of
   Bridge and Structural Ironworkers,* by Luke Grant. Washington, 1915.
   192 pp.
Report on the Colorado Strike, by George P. West. Washington, 1915.
   189 pp.
Congress.
House. *Jurisdictional Disputes in the Motion-Picture Industry.* 80th Cong.,
   1st sess., H. Res. 111. 3 vols. Washington, 1948. 2,446 pp.
Senate. *Final Report and Testimony Submitted to Congress by the Commis-
   sion on Industrial Relations.* 64th Cong., 1st sess., S. Doc. 415. Washing-
   ton, 1916. Vol. VI, pp. 5087–5999. Vol. X, pp. 9057–10066.
———. *Investigation of Concentration of Economic Power.* Temporary
   National Economic Committee. 76th Cong. 3d sess. Washington, 1941.
   Monograph 37, 135 pp. Monograph 43, 92 pp.
———. *Violations of Free Speech and Rights of Labor.* Hearings before a
   Subcommittee of the Senate Committee on Education and Labor. 76th
   Cong., 3d sess., S. Res. 266. Parts 8, 15–D, 52, 53, 55–58, 61, 63, 64–66,
   68, 70, 75. Washington, 1940.
Department of Commerce.
Fourteenth Census of the United States, 1920. Vol. IX. *Manufactures.*
Fifteenth Census of the United States, 1930. Vol. III. *Manufactures.*
Sixteenth Census of the United States, 1940. Vol. I. *Population.* Vol. III.
   Manufactures.

PUBLICATIONS OF LABOR ORGANIZATIONS

American Federation of Labor. *Report of the Executive Council of the American Federation of Labor.* . . . 1919; 1929.
———. *Report of Proceedings of the . . . Annual Convention of the American Federation of Labor.* . . . 1911–1940.
———. *Report of Proceedings of the . . . Annual Convention of the Building Trades Department, American Federation of Labor.* . . . 1934–1935;
   1938.
California CIO Council. *CIO Councils—What They Do.* 1945. Unpaged.
California State Federation of Labor. *Proceedings of the . . . Annual Convention of the California State Federation of Labor.* . . . 1914–1940.
———. *Report on Labor Legislation and Labor Record of Senators and Members of Assembly . . . of the California Legislature.* 1937; 1939.

———. *Yearbook.* 1937. 148 pp.

Conference of Studio Unions. *The Hollywood Story.* Los Angeles, 1946. Unpaged.

Congress of Industrial Organizations. *The Truth about CIO.* Washington, 1946. 11 pp.

International Association of Machinists. *Machinists Monthly Journal.* Washington, May, 1950.

Labor's Non-Partisan League. *Labor's Non-Partisan League, Its Origin and Growth.* Washington, [1939]. 26 pp.

Los Angeles Central Labor Council. *Golden Anniversary 1901–1951.* Los Angeles, October 1, 1951. 71 unnumbered pages.

———. *Year Book.* . . . 1924; 1929; 1931; 1933–1935.

Los Angeles CIO Council. *Constitution of the Los Angeles CIO Council.* Los Angeles, March 16, 1945. Unpaged.

———. *A Statement to All Locals from the Executive Board and Delegates of the Los Angeles CIO Council.* Los Angeles, March 16, 1945. Unpaged.

Los Angeles Industrial Union Council. *Joint Meeting of the Advisory Board to the Regional Office and Executive Board of the Industrial Union Council.* Los Angeles, November 3, 1937. Unpaged.

———. *Third Annual Yearbook.* Los Angeles, 1939. Unpaged.

Los Angeles Joint Board, Amalgamated Clothing Workers of America. *Souvenir Journal.* Los Angeles, 1943. Unpaged.

Robinson, Aileen W. *A Critical Evaluation of the American Federation of Teachers.* Chicago: American Federation of Teachers, [1934]. 60 pp.

Transit Employees of Los Angeles. *Bulletin.* Los Angeles, February 12, 1937. 1 p.

PAMPHLETS AND MONOGRAPHS

Allen, Arthur P., and Betty V. H. Schneider. *Industrial Relations in the California Aircraft Industry.* Berkeley: Institute of Industrial Relations, University of California, 1956. 59 pp.

Bernstein, Irving. *Hollywood at the Crossroads.* Los Angeles: Hollywood A.F. of L. Film Council, 1957. 78 pp.

California State Chamber of Commerce. *Handbook of Sources of Economic Data Pertaining to California.* San Francisco, 1941. Part I, 77 pp. Part II, 95 pp.

Citizens' Industrial Fact Finding Committee. *Tentative Report on the Furniture Industry of Los Angeles.* Los Angeles, [1936?]. 7 pp.

Coast Committee for the Shipowners. *The Pacific Maritime Labor Crisis.* San Francisco, 1936. 12 unnumbered pages.

Daugherty, Carroll R. *Labor under the N.R.A.* Boston: Houghton Mifflin Co., 1934. 38 pp.

Gillingham, J. B. *The Teamsters Union on the West Coast.* Berkeley: Institute of Industrial Relations, University of California, 1956. 90 pp.

Kidner, Frank L., and Philip Neff. *Los Angeles: The Economic Outlook.* Los Angeles: Haynes Foundation, 1946. 24 pp.

Los Angeles County Chamber of Commerce. *Los Angeles: "The Magic City and County."* Los Angeles: County Board of Supervisors, 1951. 48 pp.

Los Angeles *Times. The Forty-Year War for a Free City; A History of the Open Shop in Los Angeles.* Los Angeles: Times-Mirror Publishing Company, 1929. 28 pp.

Lovell, Hugh, and Tasile Carter. *Collective Bargaining in the Motion Picture Industry.* Berkeley: Institute of Industrial Relations, University of California, 1955. 54 pp.

McEntire, Davis. *The Labor Force in California.* Berkeley: Institute of Industrial Relations, University of California, 1952. 101 pp.

Merchants' and Manufacturers' Association of Los Angeles. *Los Angeles and the Open Shop.* No. III. Los Angeles, June, 1922. 4 pp.

———. *Our Declaration of Principles in Action.* Los Angeles, 1947. 9 unnumbered pages.

Neff, Philip, Lisette C. Baum, and Grace E. Heilman. *Favored Industries in Los Angeles.* Los Angeles: Haynes Foundation, 1948. 25 pp.

Neff, Philip, and Annette Weifenbach. *Business Cycles in Los Angeles.* Los Angeles: Haynes Foundation, 1949. 25 pp.

Schneider, Betty V. H., and Abraham Siegel. *Industrial Relations in the Pacific Coast Longshore Industry.* Berkeley: Institute of Industrial Relations, University of California, 1956. 89 pp.

Sinclair, Upton. *The Epic Plan for California.* Pamphlet no. 2. [Los Angeles], 1934. 31 pp.

Town Hall. *Pay Policies for Public Personnel.* A Report of the Municipal and County Government Section of Town Hall. Los Angeles, May, 1961. 96 pp.

Waterfront Employers' Association. *Maritime Strikes on the Pacific Coast.* San Francisco, November 26, 1936. 30 pp.

———. *Pacific Coast Longshore Dispute Machinery—Explanation with Chart.* Educational Pamphlet Series no. 1. San Francisco, 1947. 3 pp.

Wilson, Jeff. *The Hard Realities of Shipping.* San Francisco: Daily Commercial News, [1946]. 46 pp.

THESES

Crockett, Earl C. "The History of California Labor Legislation, 1910–1930." Unpublished Ph.D. dissertation. University of California, Berkeley, 1931.

Dixon, Marion. "The History of the Los Angeles Central Labor Council." Unpublished M.A. thesis. University of California, Berkeley, 1929.

Findley, James Clifford. "The Economic Boom of the 'Twenties in Los Angeles." Unpublished Ph.D. dissertation. Claremont College, Claremont, California, 1958.

Lopez, Espiridion B. "The History of the California State Federation of Labor." Unpublished M.A. thesis. University of California, Berkeley, 1932.

Morgans, Robert DeWitt. "A History of Organized Labor in Long Beach, California." Unpublished M.A. thesis. University of California, Berkeley, 1940.

Perry, Louis B. "A Survey of the Labor Movement in Los Angeles, 1933–1939." Unpublished Ph.D. dissertation. University of California, Los Angeles, 1950.

Weintraub, Hyman. "The I.W.W. in California, 1905–1931." Unpublished M.A. thesis. University of California, Los Angeles, 1947.

Wentz, Walter. "History of the Los Angeles Newspaper Guild." Unpublished
M.A. thesis. Claremont College, Claremont, California, 1958.

ARTICLES

Adamic, Louis. "The Collapse of Organized Labor: Is the A.F. of L. on Its
Deathbed?" *Harper's Monthly Magazine,* CLXIV (Jan., 1932), 167–178.
———. "Harry Bridges Comes East," *Nation,* CXLIII (Dec. 26, 1936), 753.
———. "Los Angeles! There She Blows!" *Outlook,* CLV (Aug. 13, 1930),
563–565, 594–597.
Alexander, Gross W. "California, Here Come Some More," *Christian Century,*
LI (March 28, 1934), 427.
Altmeyer, Arthur J. "One Year's Work of the Social Security Board," U.S.
Bureau of Labor Statistics, *Labor Information Bulletin,* III (Dec. 1936), 1–6.
Amidon, Beulah. "Section 7–A," *Survey Graphic,* XXIII (May, 1934), 213–217.
Avé-Hallement, Theodore M. "The Open-Shop Issue," *Outlook,* CXXV
(April 11, 1920), 637–642.
"The Battle of Sacramento," *New Republic,* LXXXII (Feb. 20, 1935), 37–39.
Beckner, Earl R. "The Trade Union Educational League and the American
Labor Movement," *Journal of Political Economy,* XXXIII (Aug., 1925),
410–431.
"The Beginning of the End of the Railroad Strike," *New Republic,* XXXII
(Sept. 27, 1922), 111–112.
"Better News from California," *New Republic,* LXXXIII (May 22, 1935),
41–42.
Bliven, Bruce. "Hey, Rube," *New Republic,* XCVIII (Feb. 8, 1939), 10–12.
———. "Roses in January: Morons in June," *New Republic,* LXXXV (Dec.
18, 1935), 166–168.
Bohn, William E. "The Industrial Workers of the World," *Survey,* XXVIII
(May 4, 1912), 220–225.
Bookhout, Russell. "Why We Struck," *Atlantic Monthly,* CLX (Aug., 1937),
243–248.
Bower, Anthony. "Films," *Nation,* CLII (March 1, 1941), 249–250.
Brooks, John Graham. "The Shadow of Anarchy: The Industrial Workers of
the World," *Survey,* XXVIII (April 6, 1912), 80–82.
Broun, Heywood. "Insurgency in Equity," *Nation,* CXL (May 15, 1935), 574.
"Business Goes After the Consumer Movement," *Consumers Union Reports,*
Dec., 1939, pp. 16A–16D.
Buzzell, J. W. "An Open Shop Citadel Falls," *American Federationist,*
XLVIII (April, 1941), 6, 7, 30, 31.
"California's Wanderers," *Survey,* LXIII (Dec. 15, 1929), 349.
Calverton, V. F. "Decline of Organized Labor in America," *Current History,*
XXXV (Nov., 1931), 220–223.
Canterbury, J. B. " 'Ham and Eggs' in California," *Nation,* CXLVII (Oct. 22,
1938), 408–410.
Carlson, Oliver. "Los Angeles Grows Up," *Nation,* CXLVI (Jan. 8, 1938),
43–44.
———. "The San Francisco Waterfront," *Nation,* CXLII (Jan. 22, 1936), 105–
106.

Cecil, George H. "Ten Years Forest Work in One Summer," *Southern California Business,* XII (Aug., 1933), 10–11.

Chaplin, John R. "Hollywood Goes Closed Shop," *Nation,* CXLII (Feb. 19, 1936), 225–226.

Clark, Evans. "The Public Loses the Shop Strike," *Nation,* CXVI (Jan. 3, 1923), 14.

Clement, Travers. "Red-Baiters' Holiday in Sacramento: The Criminal Syndicalism Trial," *Nation,* CXL (March 13, 1935), 306–308.

Coe, George A. "End Poverty in California," *World Tomorrow,* XVII (March 29, 1934), 159–160.

Colcord, Joanna C. "General Cargo from California," *Survey,* LXXI (Sept., 1935), 267–269.

"Collective Bargaining in the N.I.R.A.," *New Republic,* LXXVII (Jan. 3, 1934), 210.

Collins, James H. "Concealed Weapons," *Southern California Business,* XII (Aug., 1933), 5.

———. "Recovery—A Sight Draft on Buying Power," *Southern California Business,* XII (Aug., 1933), 12–13.

"Communism in American Labor Unions," *Independent,* CXV (Aug. 1, 1925), 116.

"Constitutionality of California's Criminal Syndicalism Act Upheld," *Congressional Digest,* VI (June–July, 1927), 210–212.

Creel, George. "Closed during Altercations," *Saturday Evening Post,* CCX (May 14, 1938), 25, 104–108.

Dawson, Anthony. "Patterns of Production and Employment in Hollywood," *Hollywood Quarterly,* IV (Summer, 1950), 338–353.

De Ford, Miriam Allen. "An Injury to All," *Overland Monthly and Out West Magazine,* LXXXII (Dec., 1924), 536–537.

———. "The Waterfront Showdown," *New Republic,* LXXXIX (Nov. 18, 1936), 72.

Dondo, Anna. "Trade Unions or Open Shop?" *Overland Monthly and Out West Magazine,* LXXXII (March, 1924), 112–113, 143; LXXXII (April, 1924), 170, 181.

Douglas, Paul H. "American Labor Relations Acts," *American Economic Review,* XXVII (Dec., 1937), 735–761.

"The Epic of Upton Sinclair," *Nation,* CXXXIX (Oct. 31, 1934), 495–496.

"The Fight To Break the Unions," *Nation,* CXI (Dec. 1, 1920), 609.

Fine, Nathan. "Left and Right in the Needle-Trades Unions," *Nation,* CXVIII (June 4, 1924), 639–640.

"The First Three Years," *Survey,* LXXIV (Aug., 1938), 265.

Fitch, John A. "Los Angeles, A Militant Anti-Union Citadel," *Survey,* XXXIII (Oct. 3, 1914), 4–6.

———. "Old and New Labor Problems in California," *Survey,* XXXII (Sept. 19, 1914), 609–610.

———. "The Way of the Transgressor in a Closed-Shop City," *Survey,* XXXII (Sept. 26, 1914), 632–633.

Foster, Charles H. "Despised and Rejected of Men: Hoboes of the Pacific Coast," *Survey,* XXXIII (March 20, 1915), 671–672.

Fremming, H. C. "Los Angeles Meets Unemployment," *American Federationist*, XXXVIII (July, 1931), 855–856.

"Gains in Security," *Survey*, LXXI (Aug., 1935), 243.

Green, William. "Recent Trend in the Organized Labor Movement," *Annals of the American Academy of Political and Social Science*, CXLIX (May, 1930), 183–191.

Harding, Alfred. "The Motion Pictures Need a Strong Actors' Union," *American Federationist*, XXXVI (March, 1929), 282–283.

Hill, Mary Anderson. "The Free Speech Fight at San Diego," *Survey*, XXVIII (May 4, 1912), 192–194.

Hoagland, H. E. "Closed Shop versus Open Shop," *American Economic Review*, VIII (Dec., 1918), 752–762.

"Housing and Labor Camps in California," *Survey*, XXXIV (June 19, 1915), 265.

"It's Up to Labor," *New Republic*, LXXVII (Jan. 3, 1934), 211–212.

Johnston, Frank L. "California," *American Federationist*, XXXV (Sept., 1928), 1128.

Kerr, Clark. "West Coast Labor: Its Past and Prospects," *Monthly Labor Review*, LXXXII (May, 1959), 489–491.

Kleiler, Frank M. "Maritime Labor Grows Up," *Survey Graphic*, XXVIII (Jan., 1939), 18–22.

Klein, Hebert, and Carey McWilliams. "Cold Terror in California," *Nation*, CXLI (July 24, 1935), 97–98.

Krysto, Christine. "California's Labor Camps," *Survey*, XLIII (Nov. 8, 1919), 70–78.

"Labor and the N.R.A.," *New Republic*, LXXVI (Aug. 30, 1933), 75–76; LXXVII (Nov. 22, 1933), 48–49; LXXVII (Jan. 31, 1934), 335–336.

"Labor and the Open Shop," *Survey*, XLV (March 5, 1921), 830–832.

"Labor in 1918," *New Republic*, XVI (Sept. 7, 1918), 156–157.

"Labor Wars in the West," *Sunset*, XXXIII (Oct., 1914), 651–652.

"The Lessons of an 'Outlaw' Strike," *New Republic*, XXII (May 12, 1920), 330–332.

Levenson, Lew. "California Casualty List," *Nation*, CXXXIX (Aug. 29, 1934), 243–245.

———. "The Case of Thomas Sharpe," *Nation*, CXXXIX (Sept. 5, 1934), 272.

Levine, Louis. "The Development of Syndicalism in America," *Political Science Quarterly*, XXVIII (Sept., 1913), 451–479.

Levinson, Edward. "Waterfront East and West," *New Republic*, XCVI (Sept. 14, 1938), 151–153.

Logan, Somerset. "The Battle of Hollywood," *New Republic*, LIX (Aug. 7, 1929), 308–310.

———. "Revolt in Hollywood," *Nation*, CXXIX (July 17, 1929), 61–62.

Lorwin, Lewis. "Labor under the NIRA," *Survey Graphic*, XXII (Sept., 1933), 467–470.

"Los Angeles Studying Her Labor Conditions," *Survey*, XXVIII (Aug. 31, 1912), 680–681.

Love, John W. "The Wreck of the B. of R.T.," *Survey*, XLIV (April 24, 1920), 135–136.

McCabe, D. A. "The Effects of the Recovery Act upon Labor Organization," *Quarterly Journal of Economics*, XLIX (Nov., 1934), 52–78.

McCleary, James T. "Big Business and Labor," *Annals of the American Academy of Political and Social Science*, XLII (July, 1912), 25–37.

MacDonald, Lois. "The National Labor Relations Act," *American Economic Review*, XXVI (Sept., 1936), 412–427.

McWilliams, Carey. "Ham and Eggs," *New Republic*, C (Oct. 25, 1939), 331–333.

————. "La Follette Hearings: Final Sessions," *New Republic*, CII (March 25, 1940), 400–403.

Mangold, William P. "Civil War in the A.F. of L.," *New Republic*, LXXXIV (Oct. 30, 1935), 326–328.

————. "Hollywood Fights Its Writers," *New Republic*, LXXXVII (May 27, 1936), 70–71.

"The Maritime Strike," *New Republic*, LXXXIX (Nov. 18, 1936), 61–62.

"Memories of Men and Business in California, 1887–1931: The Reminiscences of Shannon Crandall," *Claremont Quarterly*, V (Spring, 1958), 41–58.

Merritt, Walter Gordon. "The Closed Shop," *North American Review*, CXCV (Jan., 1912), 66–74.

"More Trouble on the Waterfront," *New Republic*, LXXXIX (Nov. 11, 1936), 35.

Morrow, Felix. " 'Red Unions' and the A.F. of L.," *Nation*, CXXXIII (Dec. 30, 1931), 722–724.

"The Movies Swing an Election," *Reader's Digest*, XXIX (Aug., 1936), 4.

"Municipal Control of Charity in Los Angeles," *Survey*, XXXI (Oct. 4, 1913), 1–2.

Mussey, Henry Raymond. "Trade Unions and Public Policy: Democracy or Dynamite," *Atlantic Monthly*, CIX (April, 1912), 441–446.

Neal, Elbridge H. "The 'Open' Shop," *North American Review*, CXCV (May, 1912), 618–629.

Neuberger, Richard L. "Bad-Man Bridges," *Forum and Century*, CI (April, 1939), 195–199.

————. "C.I.O.: Far Western Front," *Nation*, CXLIV (June 26, 1937), 725–726.

"New Charter for Los Angeles," *Survey*, XXVIII (Sept. 28, 1912), 796.

"The New Deal in Hollywood," *Nation*, CXXXVII (Sept. 20, 1933), 325–326.

Norton, Edmund. "Politics in Los Angeles," *The Public*, XIV (Nov. 24, 1911), 1190–1192.

"The Open-Shop Crusade," *New Republic*, XXV (Dec. 8, 1920), 28–30.

Otis, Harrison Gray. "Los Angeles—A Sketch," *Sunset*, XXIV (Jan., 1910), 12–16.

"The Outlaw Strike Collapses," *Independent*, CII (May 1, 1920), 171.

Oxnam, G. Bromley. "The Mexican in Los Angeles from the Standpoint of the Religious Forces in the City," *Annals of the American Academy of Political and Social Science*, XCIII (Jan., 1921), 130–133.

Packard, Rose Marie. "The Los Angeles Border Patrol," *Nation*, CXLII (April 4, 1936), 295.

Palmer, Frederick. "Otistown of the Open Shop," *Hampton's Magazine*, XXVI (Jan., 1911), 29–44.

Pontius, D. W. "Municipal Busses or Not?" *Pacific Electric Magazine,* XVII (April 10, 1937), 2–3.

"The Present Plight of 'Labor': The Effect of the McNamara Cases on Union Management—What the Federation of Labor Is," *World's Work,* XXIII (Feb., 1912), 409–415.

"President Roosevelt and the Trade Unions," *New Republic,* LXXVI (Aug. 16, 1933), 4–6.

"The Railroad Men's Revolt," *Nation,* CX (April 17, 1920), 502.

"The Railway Strike," *Outlook,* CXXXI (Aug. 16, 1922), 627–628.

Ratcliffe, S. K. "Roosevelt and the Trade Unions," *Fortnightly Review,* CXXXV (May, 1934), 47–58.

Reed, Mary. "San Pedro," *Nation,* CXIX (July 9, 1924), 45–46.

"Renewing the Open-Shop Fight," *Sunset,* XXXIII (Oct., 1914), 652.

"Retreat from Hollwood," *Outlook,* CLIII (Sept. 4, 1929), 13–14.

Ross, Arthur M. "Major Trends in Labor Relations," *Monthly Labor Review,* LXXXII (May, 1959), 536–538.

Ross, Murray. "The C.I.O. Loses Hollywood," *Nation,* CXLIX (Oct. 7, 1939), 374–377.

———. "Labor Relations in Hollywood," *Annals of the American Academy of Political and Social Science,* CCLIV (Nov., 1947), 58–64.

"Rupert Hughes," *Nation,* CXLII (May 27, 1936), 662.

Ryder, David Warren. "California: Ashamed and Repentant," *New Republic,* LI (June 1, 1927), 41–44.

———. "San Francisco's Fight for Industrial Freedom," *American Review of Reviews,* LXXV (Jan., 1927), 82–85.

———. "The Unions Lose San Francisco," *American Mercury,* VII (April, 1926), 412–417.

Ryskind, Morrie. "It Happened One Night," *Nation,* CXLIV (May 15, 1937), 563.

"San Francisco: Act One," *New Republic,* LXXIX (July 25, 1934), 280–282.

Saposs, D. J. "The American Labor Movement since the War," *Quarterly Journal of Economics,* XLIX (Feb., 1935), 236–254.

Scharrenberg, Paul. "The Attitude of Organized Labor towards the Japanese," *Annals of the American Academy of Political and Social Science,* XCIII (Jan., 1921), 34–38.

Scherer, James A. B. "What Kind of a Pittsburgh Is Los Angeles," *World's Work,* XLI (Feb., 1921), 382–392.

Schleicher, A. "The Unemployment Problem," *Southern California Business,* XI (July, 1932), 7.

Schneider, Betty V. H. "The Maritime Industry," *Monthly Labor Review,* LXXXII (May, 1959), 552–557.

Seiler, Conrad. "Cantaloupes and Communists," *Nation,* CXXXI (Sept. 3. 1930), 243–244.

Sinclair, Upton. "Correspondence: EPIC Plan," *Nation,* CXLI (Nov. 6, 1935), 535–536.

———. "End Poverty in Civilization," *Nation,* CXXXIX (Sept. 26, 1934), 351.

Smith, Roy L. "Ministers 'Meddle' in Union Strikes," *Christian Century,* L (Nov. 8, 1933), 1417.

Spargo, John. "Why the I.W.W. Flourishes," *World's Work,* XXXIX (Jan., 1920), 243–247.

Stewart, Kenneth. "The Free Press in California," *American Mercury,* XXXIV (Jan., 1935), 112–117.

Swing, Raymond G. "EPIC and the Ohio Plan," *Nation,* CXXXIX (Oct. 3, 1934), 379–381.

Symes, Lillian. "After EPIC in California," *Nation,* CXLII (April 22, 1936), 509–511.

———. "California, There She Stands," *Harper's Monthly Magazine,* CLXX (Feb., 1935), 360–368.

Taft, Philip. "Labor's Changing Political Line," *Journal of Political Economy,* XLV (Oct., 1937), 634–650.

———. "Strife in the Maritime Industry," *Political Science Quarterly,* LIV (June, 1939), 216–236.

Talbott, E. Guy. "The Armies of the Unemployed in California," *Survey,* XXXII (Aug. 22, 1914), 523–524.

Taylor, Paul S., and Norman L. Gold. "San Francisco and the General Strike," *Survey Graphic,* XXIII (Sept., 1934), 405–411.

Taylor, Paul S., and Clark Kerr. "Whither Self-Help," *Survey Graphic,* XXIII (July, 1934), 328–331.

"Terrorism in California," *New Republic,* LXXIX (Aug. 1, 1934), 305–306.

Thompson, Morton. "Hollywood Is a Union Town," *Nation,* CXLVI (April 2, 1938), 381–383.

"Unionism in Filmland," *Nation,* CXXIX (Aug. 28, 1929), 211.

"Unionism in Los Angeles," *Survey,* XLII (July 26, 1919), 633.

"Upton Sinclair Defends the Law," *Nation,* CXVI (June 6, 1923), 647.

"Upton Sinclair's Victory," *Nation,* CXXXIX (Sept. 12, 1934), 285–286.

Villard, Oswald G. "Upton Sinclair Startles California," *Nation,* CXXXIX (July 11, 1934), 35.

Wagenet, Elizabeth M. "Amos, the Prophet, in California," *Survey,* XXXVI (June 24, 1916), 335–336.

"Washington Notes," *New Republic,* LXXIX (Aug. 1, 1934), 317–318.

West, George P. "After Liberalism Had Failed," *Nation,* CXVI (May 30, 1923), 629.

———. "California Sees Red," *Current History,* XL (Aug., 1934), 658–662.

———. "Good News from California," *Nation,* CXII (June 22, 1921), 867–869.

"The West Goes Red Hunting," *Nation,* CXXXIX (Aug. 1, 1934), 116.

"What the Seamen Want," *Nation,* CXLIII (Nov. 21, 1936), 593.

"Wildcat Pensions," *Nation,* CXLVII (Oct. 22, 1938), 397.

Williams, Chester S. "Buchmanism 'Settles' the Coast Strike," *Christian Century,* LI (July 25, 1934), 969–970.

Woehlke, Walter V. "Terrorism in America," *Outlook,* C (Feb. 17, 1912), 359–367.

"The World's Greatest City in Prospect," *World's Work,* XLVII (Dec., 1923), 140–142.

"Worse Than an Earthquake," *Nation,* CXXXIX (July 25, 1934), 89.

BOOKS

Adamic, Louis. *Dynamite.* New York: Viking Press, 1934. 495, x pp.

Belloc, Nedra Bartlett. *Wages in California.* Berkeley and Los Angeles: University of California Press, 1948. 98, vi pp.

Bimba, Anthony. *The History of the American Working Class.* New York: International Publishers, 1927. 385, viii pp.

Brissenden, Paul F. *The I.W.W.* 2d ed. New York: Columbia University Press, 1920. 438 pp.

Chesebro, Ray L., comp. *Municipal Code of the City of Los Angeles.* Los Angeles: Parker, Stone and Baird Co., 1936. 970 pp.

———. *Municipal Code of the City of Los Angeles.* Los Angeles: Parker and Co., 1946. 978 pp.

Christie, Robert A. *Empire in Wood.* Cornell Studies in Industrial and Labor Relations, Vol. VII. Ithaca: New York State School of Industrial and Labor Relations, 1956. 356, xvii pp.

Commons, John R., and Associates. *History of Labor in the United States, 1896–1932.* New York: Macmillan Co., 1921–1935. 4 vols.

Cross, Ira B. *A History of the Labor Movement in California.* Berkeley: University of California Press, 1935. 354 pp.

Cummins, E. E., and Frank T. de Vyver. *The Labor Problem in the United States.* 3d ed. New York: D. Van Nostrand Co., 1947. 587 pp.

Dunne, George H. *Hollywood Labor Dispute: A Study in Immorality.* Los Angeles: Conference Publishing Co., [1950]. Unpaged.

Eliel, Paul. *The Waterfront and General Strikes, San Francisco, 1934.* San Francisco: Hooper Printing Co., 1934. 256 pp.

Finney, Guy W. *Angel City in Turmoil.* Los Angeles: American Press, 1945. 211 pp.

Foster, William Z. *American Trade Unionism.* New York: International Publishers, 1947. 383 pp.

Galenson, Walter. *Rival Unionism in the United States.* New York: American Council on Public Affairs, 1940. 317 pp.

Gordon, Margaret S. *Employment Expansion and Population Growth: The California Experience, 1900–1950.* Berkeley and Los Angeles: University of California Press, 1954. 192, xii pp.

Green, Charles H. *The Headwear Workers.* New York: United Hatters, Cap and Millinery Workers International Union, 1944. 254 pp.

Haber, William. *Industrial Relations in the Building Industry.* Cambridge: Harvard University Press, 1930. 593, xviii pp.

Haber, William, and Harold M. Levinson. *Labor Relations and Productivity in the Building Trades.* Ann Arbor: Bureau of Industrial Relations, University of Michigan, 1956. 266, xi pp.

Harris, Herbert. *American Labor.* New Haven: Yale University Press, 1938. 459, vi pp.

Huberman, Leo. *The Truth about Unions.* New York: Pamphlet Press, 1946. 87 pp.

Johnsen, J. E., comp. *The Reference Shelf*. Vol. 11, no. 3. New York: H. W. Wilson Co., 1937. 320 pp.

Johnson, Emory R., and Thurman W. Van Metre. *Principles of Railroad Transportation*. New York and London: D. Appleton and Co., 1922. 617 pp.

Levinson, Edward. *Labor on the March*. New York: Harper and Bros., 1938. 325 pp.

Lyon, Leverett S., Paul T. Homan, Lewis L. Lorwin, George Terborgh, Charles L. Dearing, and Leon C. Marshall. *The National Recovery Administration*. Washington, D.C.: The Brookings Institution, 1935. 947 pp.

McWilliams, Carey. *Factories in the Field*. Boston: Little, Brown and Co., 1939. 334 pp.

———. *Southern California Country*. New York: Duell, Sloan and Pearce, 1946. 387 pp.

Miller, Sidney L. *Inland Transportation*. New York: McGraw-Hill Book Co., 1933. 822 pp.

Millis, Harry A., and Royal E. Montgomery. *Organized Labor*. Vol. III. New York: McGraw-Hill Book Co., 1945. 930 pp.

Minton, Bruce, and John Stuart. *Men Who Lead Labor*. New York: Modern Age Books, Inc., 1937. 270 pp.

Mowry, George E. *The California Progressives*. Berkeley and Los Angeles: University of California Press, 1951. 349, xi pp.

Panunzio, Constantine. *Self-Help Cooperatives in Los Angeles*. Publications of the University of California at Los Angeles in Social Sciences, Vol. 8, no. 1. Berkeley: University of California Press, 1939. 148 pp.

Pesotta, Rose. *Bread upon the Waters*. New York: Dodd, Mead and Co., 1944. 435 pp.

Peterson, Florence. *Survey of Labor Economics*. New York: Harper and Bros., 1947. 843 pp.

Pierson, Frank C. *Community Wage Patterns*. Berkeley and Los Angeles: University of California Press, 1953. 213, xvii pp.

Raddock, Maxwell C. *Portrait of an American Labor Leader: William L. Hutcheson*. New York: American Institute of Social Science, Inc., 1955. 430, xvi pp.

Ross, Murray. *Stars and Strikes*. New York: Columbia University Press, 1941. 224, x pp.

Smith, Howard R. *Economic History of the United States*. New York: Ronald Press Co., 1955. 763, x pp.

Spalding, William A., comp. *History and Reminiscences, Los Angeles City and County, California*. Los Angeles: J. R. Finnell & Sons Publishing Co., [1931]. 3 vols.

Stein, Emanuel, and Jerome Davis. *Labor Problems in America*. New York: Farrar and Rinehart, Inc., 1940. 909 pp.

Stimson, Grace Heilman. *Rise of the Labor Movement in Los Angeles*. Berkeley and Los Angeles: University of California Press, 1955. 529, xvi pp.

Stolberg, Benjamin. *The Story of the C.I.O.* New York: Viking Press, 1938. 294 pp.

Taft, Philip. *Economics and Problems of Labor*. 2d ed. Harrisburg: Stackpole and Heck, Inc., 1948. 822 pp.

Taylor, Paul S. *The Sailors' Union of the Pacific.* New York: Ronald Press Co., 1923. 188 pp.

Viau, Joseph M. *Hours and Wages in American Organized Labor.* New York: G. P. Putnam's Sons, 1939. 301 pp.

Vorse, Mary H. *Labor's New Millions.* New York: Modern Age Books, Inc., 1938. 312 pp.

Watkins, Gordon S., and Paul A. Dodd. *Labor Problems.* 3d ed. New York: Thomas Y. Crowell, 1940. 1,128, xiii pp.

Weintraub, Hyman. *Andrew Furuseth, Emancipator of the Seamen.* Berkeley and Los Angeles: University of California Press, 1959. 267 pp.

Wolman, Leo. *Ebb and Flow in Trade Unionism.* New York: National Bureau of Economic Research, Inc., 1936. 251 pp.

Wright, Chester M. *Here Comes Labor.* New York: Macmillan Co., 1939. 122 pp.

INDEX

INDEX

Academy of Motion Picture Arts and Sciences, 330, 359; organization, 319–320; and NRA code, 327, 345, 348–349; vs. Actors Equity, 338–342; standard contract, 339, 342; and extras, 344–345; vs. SAG, 347–351; and writers, 354–355

Actors, 35, 331; AAAA vs. IATSE, 334–335; Actors Equity, 337–342, 351; wages and/or hours, 342, 352, 353; and AMPAS, 342–343; SAG, 346–353. *See also* Extras, motion picture

Adamson Act, 2, 70

Aircraft workers, 235; organizing drives, 297–298, 405–406, 424, 447–452; wages, 447, 450; AFL-CIO conflict, 451, 502

Alexander, Alexander, 488

Alexander, George, 116

Alfs, B. F., 156

All-Year Club, 213

Amar, E. J., 371

Ambrose, Thomas L., 449

American Can Co., 484, 485, 507

American Civil Liberties Union, 185–186, 191, 431

American Federation of Labor, 63, 195, 226, 277; jurisdictional disputes, 27, 33–34, 193–194, 323, 329, 330, 335, 360; membership figures, 107, 236, 237, 243; national organizing efforts in Los Angeles, 110, 212, 322; and Communists, 194, 259–260; on federal relief, 242; on NRA, 313; and CIO, 386, 398–399, 400, 419–422, 492; on NLRA, 418–419, 492. For local activities, *see* Central Labor Council; Labor movement, Los Angeles; and specific trades

American Plan, 162, 193, 201, 211, 213–214

Apparel Manufacturers of Los Angeles, Associated, 253, 254, 279

Arbitration of labor disputes: butchers, 295; cleaners and dyers, 406; culinary workers, 460; garment workers, 255–257, 464; maritime workers, 370, 371–373, 392–394, 396; millmen, 291–292; motion picture crafts, 323; railroad workers, 68–69, 99; shipbuilding workers, 126, 127; teamsters, 156; upholsterers, 289; warehousemen, 505

Arnold, R. H., 30

Arnoll, A. G., 247

Asbestos workers, 235, 291

Associated Farmers, 429, 432, 436, 468–469, 499, 504

Associated General Contractors, 197, 200, 269, 270–271

Atlantic Agreement (seamen), 166

Atlantic and Pacific Tea Co., 409, 483, 519

Atwill, Lionel, 351

Automobile workers, 444, 477; organizing drives, 420, 424, 486–488

Badham, W. E., 216

Bagley, C. L., 35

Baker, Fred L., 126, 225; and open shop, 18, 25, 124; on wages, 24; and labor disputes, 128–130, 134–135

Baker, Newton D., 126

Baker Iron Works, 18, 24, 25, 134–136

Bakers, 9, 114, 161, 235; wages and/or hours, 44, 264, 406, 453, 510; organizing drives, 44–45, 153–154, 210, 223–224, 249, 264–265, 293, 406, 452–453, 510–511

Bakers' Assn., Southern California, 153

Bakers' League, Hebrew, 224

Ball, Inc., 413, 465, 513

Banning, Joseph, 368

Bar Association, Los Angeles, 389, 431

Barbers, 9, 113, 114, 157, 235; wages and hours, 45; on Sunday closing, 120; organizing drives, 224, 249, 311, 488

Barker, Tom, 115, 137

Barker, W. A., 88

Barrymore, John, 338, 351

Barrymore, Lionel, 338, 351

Bartenders, 39–40, 114, 151–152, 285, 410. *See also* Beverage dispensers

Beach, Seneca C., 148

Beaudry, William E., 271

Beauty operators, 224

Beck, Dave, 411, 434, 439, 468, 469–470, 472, 474

Beirne, Edward, 32

Belcher, Frank, 51

Benton, O. M., 386

Bergen, Edgar, 352

Better America Federation, 200–201, 213, 215

Bevan, George E., 110

Beverage dispensers, 158, 221, 259

Bibby, J. W., 28

Biddle, Lemuel D., 71, 114